Cahokia
and the
Hinterlands

Cahokia
and the
Hinterlands

---

*Middle Mississippian Cultures
of the Midwest*

Edited by
Thomas E. Emerson
and
R. Barry Lewis

*Published in cooperation with
the Illinois Historic Preservation Agency*

University of Illinois Press
Urbana and Chicago

© 1991 by the Board of Trustees of the University of Illinois
Manufactured in the United States of America
C   5   4   3   2   1

This book is printed on acid-free paper.

Library of Congress Cataloging-in-Publication Data

Cahokia and the hinterlands : middle Mississippian cultures of the
  Midwest / edited by Thomas E. Emerson and R. Barry Lewis.
      p.   cm.
    Includes bibliographical references.
    ISBN 0-252-01705-6 (alk. paper)
    1. Cahokia Site (East Saint Louis, Ill.)   2. Mississippian
culture—Illinois—American Bottom.   3. Mississippian culture—
Middle West.   4. American Bottom (Ill.)—Antiquities.   5. Illinois—
Antiquities.   6. Middle West—Antiquities.   I. Emerson, Thomas E.,
1945–   II. Lewis, R. Barry.   III. Illinois HistoricPreservation
Agency
E99.M6815C34   1991
977.3'89—dc20
                                                    90–10759
                                                    CIP

Contents

PART THREE

The Southern Hinterlands

PART FOUR

Observations

Preface

THOMAS E. EMERSON

R. BARRY LEWIS

The volume editors come to this book with very different perspectives. Thomas E. Emerson has a great deal of field experience in the northern Midwest and in the American Bottom. He has been a member of the American Bottom FAI-270 Archaeological Mitigation Project, and during his tenure with that project, he worked as a supervisor on the Julien site excavation and later directed excavations at the Mississippian village and cemetery sites of Sandy Ridge Farm, Marcus, Florence, and BBB Motor. R. Barry Lewis, on the other hand, has worked mostly in the southern Midwest and the Lower Mississippi Valley. He has been involved in numerous Mississippi-period research projects in the Ohio and Mississippi rivers' confluence region and has developed a continuing research program aimed principally at Mississippian towns. In stark contrast to Emerson, the extent of Lewis's firsthand familiarity with the American Bottom is one short trip to the Cahokia site to guide a visiting archaeologist from Siberia.

We have been drawn together by Emerson's concern with the regional implications of the new Mississippian data from the FAI-270 Project and by the strengths of our research experiences, which tend to complement one another. Emerson, however, is the catalyst that made it all happen (this sentence written by Lewis). As Emerson has attempted to work with the wealth of new data emerging from the FAI-270 Project, it has become clear that regional and interregional analyses are difficult to do in a nontrivial manner because much of the data from both the American Bottom and the Mississippian centers in other regions is poorly documented.

We are not the first to tackle this tough problem. There have been two previous attempts to synthesize and disseminate information about American Bottom prehistory for a wide audience. In 1972 Melvin Fowler chaired a Society for American Archaeology (SAA) symposium on the prehistory of Cahokia and the surrounding American Bottom. This was followed in early 1973 by a symposium organized by Robert L. Hall at the Central States Anthropological Society in which the participants emphasized the regional influences of Cahokia. Unfortunately, most of the papers delivered at these symposia remain unpublished.

Emerson decided in early 1982 to make yet another attempt to draw together regional syntheses that were framed in reference to the late prehistory of the American Bottom. The first step was a symposium entitled "Mississippian Cultural Development and Variation in the Central and Upper Mississippi River Drainage," which was presented at the 1983 annual meeting of the SAA in Pittsburgh. Nineteen papers were read, many of which were the first drafts of chapters published in this book.

The second step was yet another conference, but one that emphasized active interactions between researchers, an environment that we felt simply could not be created in the context of a large national meeting. This conference was the Mississippian Roundtable, which was held on the University of Iowa campus in October 1983, just prior to the Midwest Archaeological Conference in Iowa City. The first day was set aside for the presentation of nine additional papers solicited after the SAA symposium. The second day was given over to topical discussions and "sherd-shuffling" of the representative materials participants had been encouraged to bring. As had been our experience in other similar conferences, the informal artifact handling session generated some of the most intensive and fruitful discussions of the conference.

In organizing both of the conferences, we placed few restrictions on the participants outside of broad chronological and geographical parameters that were suggested to focus the discussions. With regard to chronology, participants were asked to concentrate on Mississippian groups present between the tenth and fifteenth centuries A.D. (i.e., during the centuries for which there is the greatest archaeological evidence at Cahokia). The geographical limits were roughly the Upper Mississippi River Valley and its tributaries to the north and the Missouri Bootheel to the south.

This book represents the third and final step in our plan to synthesize and disseminate important regional Mississippian data. The book's organizational structure reflects the research biases of the participants as well as the distinct perspectives of the two editors.

The major themes that emerged from our symposia and discussion groups and defined the focus of this book are: the delineation of regional sequences for the late prehistory; the examination of the uniformity and diversity between regional Mississippian groups; and an assessment of the role of Cahokia in these processes. To some extent these are the same major research problems that interested archaeologists in the 1972 and 1973 symposia. They tend to focus on understanding the role of Cahokia in late prehistoric cultural developments in the prehistoric eastern United States and explicating its interregional relationships. What distinguishes this book, however, is the relative emphasis placed on understanding the internal development of regional Mississippian cultures and, consequently, the somewhat lessened emphasis on studies of the interaction between such cultures.

Cahokia has served as the focal point for all Mississippi-period research in the Upper Mississippi River Valley for several generations of regional archaeologists, yet it is one of the least-known archaeological manifestations in the area. The first part of this volume presents four articles that summarize current interpretations of a number of topical questions concerning Cahokia and the American Bottom.

Robert L. Hall's overview chapter, the result of many years of study, provides the reader with a succinct history of research at Cahokia, the current culture history, and an in-depth discussion of modeling both Cahokian development and regional interaction. As Hall notes, "there is remarkably little in the literature that attempts to explain why Cahokia came to be and why it ceased to be." It is an unfortunate commentary on much of the past archaeological research at Cahokia that this significant site has played such an insignificant role in the archaeological discipline's understanding of complex societies. Hall has been one of the few to deal in a broad perspective with the factors that may have been critical in the formation and dissolution of Cahokian society. In this presentation he weaves an intriguing picture of environmental and subsistence changes, shifts in trade networks, political influences, and ritual relationships to form a holistic perspective of this complex prehistoric society.

The next two chapters in this section concentrate on a specific topic and each examines the importance of that factor in understanding some aspect of Cahokian development. Some of the most significant research produced in the American Bottom during the past decade has dealt with subsistence (Johannessen 1984a; Kelly and Cross 1984). David Rindos and Sissel Johannessen's study of the ethnobotanical evidence supports a Late Woodland–Mississippian floral exploitation continuum, but they go on to stress the importance of human-plant interactions. They argue that maize was a major factor not only in the rise of Cahokia but also in its decline.

William I. Woods and George R. Holley offer a perspective on the upland Mississippian utilization and occupation around the American Bottom. This research has shown the complexity of the Mississippian expansion into the uplands, which involved the formation of small farmsteads, hamlets, and multimound town sites in such locations. This upland-oriented research has provided major insights into the stages of Cahokian culture history and the Mississippian dispersion.

The final chapter on Cahokia returns us from a concentration on the specific to the broader sweep of interregional exchanges. John E. Kelly argues that the gateway model of geographers provides insights into understanding the formation of Cahokia as a boundary-related phenomenon. The key to this development was founded in a broad regional economic exchange system. This paper presents a comprehensive review of Cahokian contacts with the hinterlands and sets the stage for the regional studies in the following two parts.

There has always been at least de facto acknowledgment by Cahokia scholars that this culture's influences have been diametrically opposite to the north and to the south. The chapters in this volume clearly substantiate this assumption, and consequently, we have separated the discussion of the northern Cahokia hinterlands from the discussion of those to the south.

Kenneth B. Farnsworth, Emerson, and Rebecca Miller Glenn provide critical insights into the northern spread of Mississippian culture from the American Bottom in their summary of new research in the Lower Illinois River Valley. An understanding of American Bottom–Central Illinois River Valley Mississippian relationships has long been hampered by the lack of information about this intervening area. This summary confirms the differing nature of the early Mississippian utilization of this area and provides new data on the presence of late Mississippian occupations. Most intriguing, however, is the evidence suggesting the continued occupation of the Lower Illinois Valley by Late Woodland Jersey Bluff populations well into the A.D. 1100s, creating a buffer zone between the Mississippians of the American Bottom and the Central Illinois Valley. For the first time we are in a position to explore the complex political, social, and religious interactions of such contemporaneous groups.

The Spoon River Mississippian culture of the Central Illinois River Valley has been known for years. It was investigated during some of the earliest scientific archaeological research conducted in the state (Cole and Deuel 1937) and was thought to be one of the most clearly delineated Mississippian sequences (Bennett 1952; Conrad and Harn 1972). However, as Lawrence A. Conrad's major new synthesis indicates, this previous view was only a simplified outline of what is an extremely complex cultural situation. Not only does he clarify the Spoon River sequence, but he also chronicles the presence of a new La Moine River Mississippian culture and the intrusion of significant Oneota populations during late Mississippian times.

At the opposite end of the scale, building on his previous detailed work with the Larson phase settlement pattern, Alan D. Harn addresses the nature of farmstead occupations. A critical problem in understanding the Spoon River settlement system has been the relationship of the central temple towns to the outlying hamlets and farmsteads. One important aspect of this research can be seen in Harn's reaffirmation of the Middle Mississippian nature of the Larson phase peoples.

Outside of the American Bottom and the Illinois River Valley, the only known concentration of northern Mississippian peoples is in the northwestern corner of Illinois in the Apple River Valley. After a lull of almost half a century, archaeological investigations have again been undertaken in this area. These new excavations and a review of the previous collections allow Emerson to establish a basic cultural chronology for the newly defined Apple River Mississippian culture, to discard the old Apple River Focus, and to postulate regional relationships.

To the west, Joseph A. Tiffany demonstrates that Middle Mississippian cultural traits in Iowa are the results of diffusion and contact, likely as part of local groups' participation in an extensive trade system, rather than as part of an intrusion of Mississippian peoples. Guy E. Gibbon, who looks at the data from southeastern Minnesota, argues that there too similarities are the result of the participation of local groups in a Cahokia-centered exchange network rather than the result of any population influx. Aztalan is revisited by Lynne G. Goldstein and John D. Richards, who provide the first thorough discussion of the site's ecological context, making it clear that the site's location is not as anomalous as some archaeologists previously believed.

The final chapter in this section is an attempt by Emerson to synthesize the current information on Cahokia and American Bottom Mississippian cultural history and to relate it to the processes that led to the northern Mississippian expansion.

Cahokian population movements, influences, and trade networks are central to understanding the cultural history of the Mississippi River Valley north of the American Bottom. A different picture emerges to the south. Cahokian influences on the Lower Mississippi and Ohio valleys and their tributaries appear to have been relatively minor. This interpretation emerges from Charles R. Moffat's detailed delineation of the Mississippian culture in the Upper Kaskaskia Valley, Robert J. Barth's examination of the Wabash Valley data, Brian M. Butler's reassessment of the Kincaid sequence, and Lewis's examination of Early Mississippi-period developments in the Ohio and Mississippi rivers' confluence region. The major Mississippian influences in the latter regions appear to be derived from the Mid-South and grafted onto what were essentially in situ cultural developments. Thus Cahokia's influence to the south was apparently of minor consequence.

The concluding section of this volume contains observations by Jon Muller and Jeanette E. Stephens on the adaptive nature of the Mississippian phenomenon in a broader perspective. They argue for a definition of Mississippian that places the emphasis on the economic aspects of the cultural manifestations when seeking to delineate the phenomenon. In their view, many of the papers included in this volume do not discuss true Mississippian societies. To some extent they continue the arguments of numerous previous researchers (such as Griffin 1985) in stressing the need to view Mississippian as a system rather than as a material culture assemblage.

Readers should be familiar with several regional issues and themes that crosscut many of the chapters in this book; these regard chronology, cultural taxonomy, and the movement of cultural traits.

A critical aspect of midwestern Middle Mississippian studies is the nature of the chronological base. Characteristically, most Mississippian researchers in the Midwest present their radiocarbon determinations uncorrected and correlate them accordingly with the Cahokia chronology (Fowler and Hall 1972, 1975). We have followed that tradition in this volume. However, as Hall discusses in chapter 1, this Cahokia sequence was constructed as an arbitrary radiocarbon year timescale but has been rather uncritically used as if it were a calendrical timescale. It is essential that researchers outside the region be aware of this important distinction when making chronological comparisons.

The most important chronological and cultural change that has taken place in the Upper Mississippi Valley has been the recognition of the complex cultural development that preceded the Mississippian florescence in the Cahokia area. Extensive excavations by the FAI-270 Project (Bareis and Porter 1984) revealed in some detail the presence of societies in the process of becoming Mississippian. Emergent Mississippian-period cultures are now recognized as occupying the American Bottom between about A.D. 800 and 1000 (Kelly, Ozuk et al. 1984). The identification of these groups has allowed archaeologists throughout the Midwest to identify possible American Bottom interaction in their area at least a century earlier than previously believed possible.

Emergent Mississippian cultures in the American Bottom possess two distinct geographical variants, each with its own phase sequence between A.D. 800 and 1000. In the southern American Bottom, these phases are Dohack (A.D. 800–850), Range (A.D. 850–900), George Reeves (A.D. 900–950), and Lindeman (A.D. 950–1000). In the northern section, there are the Loyd (A.D. 800–900), Merrell (A.D. 900–950), and Edelhardt (A.D. 950–1000) phases.

As we now understand this Emergent Mississippian phenomenon (Emerson and Jackson 1987a; Kelly 1982, 1987; Kelly, Ozuk et al. 1984), it involves the coalescence of a number of diverse traits, foreign influences, and social, political, and religious transformations that bridge a cultural threshold to create a new operational system—Middle Mississippian. It is clear, however, that these transformations occur primarily within the context of the indigenous Late Woodland populations.

Increased information on this transitional development has allowed researchers to pinpoint the beginnings of developed Middle Mississippian society and has led to the definition of the Lohmann phase (A.D. 1000–1050). In the previous sequence created by the 1971 Cahokia Ceramic Conference (Fowler and Hall 1972), the Fairmount phase (A.D. 900–1050) represented that transitional period from Late Woodland to Mississippian culture. Kelly (1982) recognized the usefulness of dividing this phase into an early and late portion. This later portion formed the basis for the identification of the initial Middle Mississippian Lohmann phase by the FAI-270 Project (Milner et al. 1984). The subsequent Mississippian Stirling (A.D. 1050–1150), Moorehead (A.D. 1150–1250), and Sand Prairie (A.D. 1250–1400) phases remain essentially the same as in the Cahokia sequence, with the exception that the Sand Prairie phase has been shortened by a century.

The assumption of the introduction of Mississippian material culture throughout the Upper Mississippi River Valley is widespread in the regional archaeological literature. Yet the study of the mechanisms of such "intrusion or diffusion" has been minimal. To some extent, theories of Mississippian expansion in the Midwest have followed the broader patterns delineated by Bruce D. Smith (1984b) for explanations of Mississippian expansion in the Eastern Woodlands. Such theories have included large-scale migrations, cultural colonization, site-unit intrusions, and cultural diffusion (see Emerson's conclusions in chapter 12). As in the broader scene (Smith 1984b:29–30), archaeologists have tended to swing away from migrations toward diffusion and local development to account for Mississippian groups to the north of Cahokia.

Yet as the chapters in this book demonstrate, the issue is far from settled. Despite this, little substantive research has been conducted on the movement of people or goods in the Upper Mississippi Valley. Studies such as John A. Walthall's (1981) of galena sources and trade or Blakely's (1973) and Droessler's (1981) examinations of Late Woodland–Mississippian population relationships stand as excellent examples of the results possible if such research is conducted. It is clear that much more directed research is required to answer the question of diffusion or intrusion and that the answers will be both complex and multicausal.

ACKNOWLEDGMENTS

As with all such projects, time projections are usually extremely optimistic at the outset. When we first conceived of this project, we hoped to have a volume in press by late 1985. Both the scope of the volume and unforeseen delays postponed our efforts until late 1987. Because of the delay between the initial preparation of some papers and the final publication, all articles were returned to the authors in the spring and summer of 1988 for final revisions. The result of this effort is the compilation, in this one place, of a comprehensive volume containing the culture histories, the latest research, and various perspectives, theories, and models in order to present a thorough portrayal of the Middle Mississippian peoples of the Midwest.

The assistance of several institutions has been extremely helpful in bringing this volume to fruition. Emerson has received support from the Illinois Historic Preservation Agency (IHPA) and the State Historic Preservation Office (SHPO). This support was first enthusiastically provided by William G. Farrar, Deputy SHPO, when the SHPO was located within the Illinois Department of Conservation. It was later continued by Theodore Hild, Deputy SHPO, and Dr. Michael Devine, Director, IHPA. This support has been programmatic, logistical, and monetary. One of the primary goals of this study has been to summarize our existing knowledge of Illinois Mississippian cultures within the regional context. This synthetic regional approach, first utilized in a book on the Early Woodland period (Farnsworth and Emerson 1986), has now become an integral part of the Illinois SHPO's program on comprehensive planning for archaeological resources. This book is part of our continuing efforts in that direction.

In addition, the Preservation Services Division of IHPA has generously provided the important duplicating and mailing services so essential to the logistics of editing such a work. Perhaps most important, IHPA provided the monetary subvention that allowed us to include the maximum amount of data in this volume. Monetary support was also provided by the Iowa Office of the State Archaeologist through the efforts of Dr. Joseph A. Tiffany. This publication was financed in part with federal funds provided by the U.S. Department of the Interior and administered by the Illinois Historic Preservation Agency. However, the contents and opinions do not necessarily reflect the views or policies of the U.S. Department of the Interior or the Illinois Historic Preservation Agency.

The contributors would like to thank all these agencies and offices for their assistance in this work. Paul P. Kreisa performed the arduous task of compiling the combined bibliography. Numerous colleagues read and commented on the various chapters, but we especially thank James B. Griffin, Christopher Pebbles, R. Berle Clay, and Judith Knight for helpful suggestions. A special debt of gratitude is owed to Elizabeth Dulany, her intrepid staff, Barbara E. Cohen, and the University of Illinois Press for undertaking the task of editing and producing this massive volume.

PART ONE

Cahokia

1

Cahokia Identity and Interaction Models of Cahokia Mississippian

ROBERT L. HALL

The first useful description of the Cahokia archaeological site does not come from the pen of Jacques Marquette or any other of the early French or British chroniclers in the Illinois country but is the brief account entered in a field notebook by a deputy surveyor named Messinger in 1808. His account was incidental to a survey executed to adjust a town boundary line that today serves as the Madison–St. Clair county line.

Working east from the "caving banks" of the Mississippi River opposite St. Louis, Missouri, Messinger noted "two large Mounds Bearing N.E. in the Edge of a large Prairie." One of these can only be the enormous Powell Mound that once stood at the western limit of the Cahokia site. Archaeological excavations at this location in 1931 produced the first evidence of a cultural sequence for prehistoric Cahokia. At this location the culture of a premound "Old Village" component was distinguished from a subsequent "Bean Pot" culture (Griffin 1949; Kelly 1932:489; Kelly 1933; Kelly and Cole 1932).

Survey parties in 1808 were required to supply commentaries on features of the landscape relevant to the purpose of the land survey—locating township, section, and quartersection corners and appraising the agricultural potential of the land. This day, however, Messinger added the following: "Twenty four or more of those mounds in Sight at one View—one whose Base is nearly 6 acres by Estimation—& 100 Feet in Height—Others of Various sizes from 6, to forty feet in height, & Various forms —some round, some oblong or Rect. angled Parallelograms and others irregular—All covered with Simtoms of ancient Ruins—Soil first Rate" (1808).

The line Messinger was surveying by pure chance happened almost to coincide with the main or east-west axis of the Cahokia site (modern U.S. Highway 40 follows this line). The mound Messinger estimated to be 100 feet high could only have been Monks Mound, but the area of this mound was closer to sixteen acres than to the six acres he attributed to it at a distance of almost two miles.

About a year after Messinger's field book entry, a tract of land including Monks Mound was donated to a group of Trappist monks from Kentucky who maintained a monastery there until 1813 (Fowler 1969a:7–8). It is from this association that the "Great Cahokia Mound" came to be known as Monks Mound. The historical Trappist association with prehistoric Cahokia also provided a convenient name for archaeologists to use in replacing Bean Pot culture, which became the Trappist Focus of the Monks Mound Aspect of the Middle Phase of the Mississippi Pattern in the terminology of the Midwestern Taxonomic System.

Prehistoric Cahokia, the Cahokia site of midwestern archaeology, might be called the type site for the Cahokia Mississippian tradition. That would be somewhat misleading, however. Cahokia is presumably the seat of the Cahokia variant of the Mississippian cultural tradition, but it is hardly a typical Mississippian site or even a site typical of the many sites of the Cahokian tradition any more than Chicago is a typical Illinois settlement. Cahokia has tested the imagination of every scientist who has ever had anything to do with it. One of the first tasks of Cahokia investigators was to establish the credibility of the concept of a prehistoric Indian settlement occupying five square miles of the American Bottom of the Mississippi River and containing a greater number of artificial earthen mounds than some Illinois villages had Indians.

The Origin of the Cahokia Mounds

The purchase of the site of Cahokia for state park use was first recommended by a commission created by the Forty-sixth Illinois General Assembly in 1909 to investigate and report on the preservation of certain lands for public parks (Anon. 1923:492–93). For various reasons little action was taken on this recommendation until June 1, 1925, when the "Great Cahokia Mound" and some surrounding mounds were purchased after condemnation proceedings for what eventually became Cahokia Mounds State Historic Site. No additions were made until 1963, but the area in state ownership has increased steadily since then. One of the reasons for the failure of the state to take action was the unwillingness of several geologists in positions of authority to support strongly the acquisition. A. H. Worthen, as director of the Illinois Geological Survey, had been a witness to one phase of the destruction of the great mound of the St. Louis group west of the Mississippi River from Cahokia. From his interpretation of the stratigraphy of this mound, Worthen went on to infer that

> [the] many elevations scattered over the surface of the [American] Bottom, locally known as "mounds," the formation of which have very generally been referred to human agencies [were not in fact] artifical elevations, raised by the aboriginal inhabitants of the country, as has been assumed by antiquaries generally, but on the contrary, they are simply outliers of loess and drift, that have remained as originally deposited, while the surrounding contemporaneous strata were swept away by denuding forces (1866:314–15).

Worthen's opinion died hard. In 1911 the geologist N. M. Fenneman restated Worthen's view of the basically natural origin of the Cahokia mounds but allowed that the higher mounds with steeper sides appeared to have a composite origin, having been reworked by humans (1911: 12). Dr. A. R. Crook, a geologist and chief of the Illinois State Museum, basically agreed with Worthen and Fenneman (1916:84). State officials seeking advice on the need for preserving the Great Cahokia mounds sometimes received quite adverse opinions from geologists (see, for example, Wheeler letter to Crook, 1921).

Although we must thank Crook for arranging for the first effective use of air photography on an archaeological site in the New World (figs. 1.1 and 1.2; Crook 1922; Hall 1968), Crook did not yield much ground when he eventually acknowledged that some of the Cahokia mounds must be constructed by humans, after seeing the results of Moorehead's first season in the field (Crook 1922). Crook felt that the rectangular plan of the mounds was the result of years of plowing in a north-south and east-west direction that had given the mounds "an artificial appearance . . . well shown in the aerial photographs" (1922:4).

He noted also that "many [mounds] show upstream faces which are rather steep" and "downstream edges which trail out into long tongues." Presumably he included in this category Monks Mound itself, whose extensive first terrace faces downstream (fig. 1.1).

Fortunately, not all geologists agreed with Worthen, Fenneman, and Crook. Professor M. M. Leighton of the University of Illinois was a witness to Warren K. Moorehead's excavations at Cahokia and from his observations held for the human construction of the Cahokia mounds (Crook 1922:5; Leighton 1923, 1928).

It is Moorehead, the first archaeologist to conduct a sustained program of excavation at Cahokia, beginning in 1921, who must be credited with generating the official recognition of the monumental character of Cahokia as the work of prehistoric Indians (e.g., Moorehead 1929). In the face of what must have seemed an unreasonable obstancy from one of the sponsors of his expedition, Moorehead made a great effort to sample quickly as much of the Cahokia site as possible, often using eight-inch auger holes to do so, and he sought also to make the "big find" that might dispel any public apathy toward the project. It is easy today to criticize Moorehead for his field methods and his interest in seeking cemeteries with abundant grave goods or other spectacular finds that would generate interest in his work and, in the end, help to preserve them. One after another unprotected mound has been sold for "fill" or leveled to the ground for agricultural purposes. One of these, Mound 51, is shown in figure 1.2 as it looked in 1922 before being sold by the truckload as dirt, as it was in the 1960s.

It has also been easy to criticize Crook, Fenneman, Worthen, or others who did not have the familiarity of Moorehead and other archaeologists with prehistoric Indian mounds. The geologists were really arguing from quite reasonable grounds. It would not have been unusual for Indians to make use of part of an existing natural formation as a base for a platform or temple mound otherwise of artificial construction, as Fenneman suggested for Cahokia (1911:12). This actually turns out to have been the case at Aztalan in Wisconsin (Maher 1958:83). Worthen himself had observed a major cut through the large St. Louis mound and found it "to consist of about fifteen feet of common chocolate-brown drift clay at the base, which was overlaid by thirty feet or more of the ash colored marly sands of the loess, the line of separation between the two deposits remaining as distinct and well defined as they usually are in good artificial sections in the railroad cuts through these deposits" (1866:314).

Crook (1922:6) noted that some of the yellowish brown layers identified as "burnt floors" by Moorehead actually

Figure 1.1. Aerial view of the Cahokia site looking west, Monks Mound at center right, taken in April of 1922 by Lt. G. W. Goddard at an altitude of 3000 feet from a plane piloted by Lt. H. K. Ramey. Official photograph, U.S. Army Air Service Photographic Section, from a copy in the Illinois State Museum, Springfield.

Figure 1.2. Aerial view of Mound 51 at the Cahokia site, looking northwest, taken in April of 1922 by Lt. G. W. Goddard at an altitude of 200 feet from a plane piloted by Lt. H. K. Ramey. Official photograph, U.S. Army Air Service Photographic Section, from a copy in the Illinois State Museum, Springfield.

sloped at angles as steep as forty-five degrees. We know now that Crook was right in being skeptical about the identification of some of these yellowish brown layers as "burnt." In 1964 James W. Porter identified some similar layers in Monks Mound as bands of limonite, a hydrated iron oxide formed through slow oxidation on an exposed surface or through deposition from solution along the interfaces of mound strata. Such layers outlined some post molds and filled pits and could sometimes be seen at angles of forty-five degrees or steeper in soil profiles (Reed, Bennett, and Porter 1968:141–43, fig. 5). Some stained areas in the Cahokia mounds are in fact the products of burning, but others are not, as Crook correctly questioned.

As recently as 1965 the discovery of a thick layer of black, highly organic clay at a depth of about forty feet in a soil core penetrating Monks Mound from its summit gave momentary pause to archaeologists conducting a solid-core soil test of this 100-foot-high Cahokia mound (James W. Porter, personal communication, 1965; see Stage F in Reed, Bennett, and Porter 1968). The fleeting thought crossed the minds of the investigators that Monks Mound might after all be largely a natural erosional remnant as Crook and others had thought, perhaps a clay end-plug within an old sediment-filled oxbow lake in a once higher river terrace now elsewhere eroded away. The continuation of the same coring operation completely removed all such doubts and proved once and for all that Monks Mound was of human construction in its entirety, but not before newspapers in several states had headlined the erroneous story that prehistoric Cahokians had used "pre-fab" mounds (e.g., Orthwein 1965). Monks Mound is now known to have been built in a number of stages over a period from about A.D. 900 to 1150 (Skele 1988).

The Cahokia Site and Cahokia Community

In investigating prehistoric Cahokia it is easy to make comparisons or to use models that are possible, even reasonable, but that have no more actual empirical basis than the argument for the totally artificial character of Monks Mound in the days of Worthen, Fenneman, and Crook. One can in good faith infer that Cahokia was "urban," or the seat of a "state," and one can infer that Cahokia "controlled" resources and "dominated" trade routes in areas of the Midwest for the benefit of a population numbering up to 38,000 for the Cahokia site alone, wherein one could find "markets," but these statements rely heavily on inference. With only a fraction of a percent of prehistoric Cahokia excavated and only a few of 120 mounds known with any degree of thoroughness, it is not possible to make definitive interpretive statements.

Admitting that one has to look to Mexico to find anything like Cahokia in magnitude, one need not, however, look to Mexico for many of the models needed for the interpretation of Cahokia as a functioning community or for historical contacts or migrations necessary to account for Cahokian development. As Melvin L. Fowler suggests, researchers can legitimately use Cahokia to explore the processes by which urban settlements come into being without feeling the compulsion to call Cahokia a city in fact (Fowler 1974:14 passim; cf. O'Brien 1972b). Similarly, we may seek the processes at work in the American Bottom that led to state formation, but this need not now force the issue of whether Cahokia was actually the capital of a proper state rather than the seat of a chiefdom in the sense of Service (1962; cf. Conrad and Harn 1972; Gibbon 1974). Given the level of evidence available, it should be adequate to describe prehistoric Cahokia as the capital of a state in formation or as a site urban in proportions, and the Mississippian tradition as a civilization that died aborning, recognizing that any stronger position now presumes much of the evidence we are seeking.

The problem of the definition of the Cahokia site and community has in recent years been attacked intensively by Melvin L. Fowler of the University of Wisconsin-Milwaukee; in doing so he has usefully summarized in print and in an atlas both the present state of knowledge of Cahokia and a history of past efforts to describe Cahokia (Fowler 1969a, 1974, 1975, 1978, 1979, 1989; Fowler, ed. 1969). Notable earlier descriptive summaries were made by William McAdams (1881, 1882, 1887, 1895), John Francis Snyder (1913, 1914, 1917), David I. Bushnell, Jr. (1904, 1922), Crook (1922), Warren K. Moorehead (1922, 1923, 1929), Paul F. Titterington (1938), and R. E. Grimm (1950). The broader local setting of the Cahokia site is described in the American Bottom surveys of Patrick J. Munson (1971) and Alan D. Harn (1971a) and more recently in the reports and summary volume of the FAI-270 Project (e.g., Bareis and Porter 1984). The chronology and phasing of the Cahokia development, ceramics in particular, have been given special attention by James B. Griffin (1949), Melvin L. Fowler (1962, 1963), Joseph O. Vogel (1964, 1975), Robert L. Hall (1966, 1967b, 1967d, 1972, 1975a), Fowler and Hall (1972, 1975, 1978), Patricia J. O'Brien (1972a), and Kelly (1982).

Doctoral dissertations written on special aspects of Cahokia or Cahokia area archaeology include that of Patricia J. O'Brien on the western or Powell Tract area of Cahokia (University of Illinois at Urbana-Champaign,

1969) published by the Illinois Archaeological Survey
(O'Brien 1972a); that of William W. Chmurny on sub-
Mound 51 stratigraphy and Mississippian ecology (Uni-
versity of Illinois at Urbana-Champaign, 1973); one by
James W. Porter on the excavation of the Mitchell site, a
major Mississippian temple town north of Cahokia (University of Wisconsin at Madison, 1974); that of Elizabeth
Benchley on the first terrace of Monks Mound and certain functional aspects of mound architecture at Cahokia
(University of Wisconsin-Milwaukee, 1974); and one by
Michael L. Gregg on settlement morphology and production specialization (University of Wisconsin-Milwaukee,
1975b). Ceramic and house sequences in the Merrell Tract
area of Cahokia are treated in a dissertation by John E.
Kelly (University of Wisconsin at Madison, 1980; published in 1982); and controlled surface collections east
of Monks Mound are analyzed and interpreted in a dissertation by Barbara J. Vander Leest (1980). Shorter
articles are presented or conveniently referenced in *Explorations into Cahokia Archaeology* (Fowler, ed. 1969),
Perspectives in Cahokia Archaeology (J. A. Brown 1975),
Cahokia Archaeology: Field Reports (Fowler, ed. 1975),
and in the three annual reports of the American Bottom
archaeological project of 1961–64 (Fowler, ed. 1962,
1963, 1964). Data sources for Cahokia studies are summarized in tabular form by Fowler and Hall (1972:10–
14). Published works and technical reports written on
the Cahokia site are listed in the summaries for Madison and St. Clair counties of *A Bibliography of Illinois
Archaeology* (Bennett 1984).

Site definition, simple enough in concept, remains a
major problem at Cahokia. At fault is the problem of
recognizing the areas that were occupied simultaneously
when (1) only a fraction of a single percent of the site
has been excavated; (2) many years of collecting have
removed much valuable surface evidence in the cultivated areas; (3) it is difficult to identify areas reserved for
plazas, post circles, enclosures, and other purposes that
leave little or no surface indications or material remains
by which they can be recognized or dated (see Wittry

1969); and (4) it remains a problem to distinguish temporal and functional differences at a site in which one
anticipates the presence of social segments of different
cultural backgrounds.

In current usage the term *Cahokia site* refers to a large
but restricted area of the metropolitan East St. Louis area
including Monks Mound and 120 smaller surrounding
mounds, comprising a diamond-shaped archaeological
zone with an east-west axis of 4.58 kilometers and a
north-south axis of 3.67 kilometers (Fowler 1974, 1975).
It is located entirely within a broad expanse of the floodplain of the Mississippi River on the opposite side of
the river from St. Louis, Missouri, between East St.
Louis and Collinsville, Illinois. This floodplain came to
be known as the American Bottom, presumably because
the Mississippi River once divided the western territories
of the infant United States from Spanish (later, French)
landholdings west of the Mississippi, St. Louis included.

Outside of the Cahokia site proper there are certain
outlying mound groups that represent contemporary, or
at least coeval, towns of major importance. Together
with the Cahokia site these may have constituted something of a greater Cahokia community or prehistoric
metropolitan Cahokia area, comparable to a modern city
with its suburban surroundings. These secondary mound
groups are known in the literature as the St. Louis,
East St. Louis, Mitchell, and Lunsford-Pulcher groups.
Unfortunately, this impression of metropolitan organization is largely just that, an impression, because so
little is known of any of the outlying groups other than
Mitchell (Porter 1974). Within a hierarchical classification of Cahokia area settlement types proposed by Fowler
(1974:26–32), Cahokia is unique as a first-line community—a mound center of the first order; Mitchell, East
St. Louis, St. Louis, and Lunsford-Pulcher as smaller,
multiple-mound centers are second-line communities; a
number of single-mound towns are third-line communities; and the numerous moundless "hamlets, villages,
and farmsteads" that cluster around the larger towns are
fourth-line communities.

Cultural Phases at Cahokia

Within the time frame for Cahokia established at the 1971
Cahokia Ceramic Conference (Fowler and Hall 1972), the
periods of Cahokia Mississippian occupation fell between
A.D. 800 and 1500, including an unnamed initial phase
between A.D. 800 and 900, a Fairmount phase between
A.D. 900 and 1050, a Stirling phase between A.D. 1050
and 1150, a Moorehead phase between A.D. 1150 and
1250, and a Sand Prairie phase between A.D. 1250 and
1500. More properly, the various phases were *assigned* to

the mentioned time periods. In 1971 there were still relatively few radiocarbon dates available from Cahokia, considering the length of occupation and complexity of the
site, especially after the necessity of discounting whole
series of questionable dates from particular laboratories.
There was also considerable disagreement in radiochemi-
cal circles on the validity of the tree-ring calibrated "correction curves" of the type of Stuiver and Suess (1968)
that allowed for pronounced, short-term fluctuations of

atmospheric radiocarbon. As a result, the timescale of the 1971 conference was a best approximation for its day of what a more accurately based chronology might someday look like.

The existence of "kinks" in the correction curves has now been confirmed and quite generally accepted, and the relevance of such short-term fluctuations to archaeological data is now appreciated (see Blakeslee 1983). The University of Michigan, which originally produced most of the carbon dates for Cahokia and Cahokia area sites, has discontinued its radiocarbon dating facility, but its place has been ably taken by the University of Wisconsin and Illinois State Geological Survey radiocarbon laboratories. These laboratories have now each produced long series of precision dates relevant to Cahokia prehistory. Excavations by the University of Illinois FAI-270 Project have resulted in a broad, regional, deep-time perspective on the culture history of the American Bottom with a revised chronology for both the Cahokia area and the more southern parts of the American Bottom (Bareis and Porter 1984). This newer chronology is based too uncritically upon the suggested absolute timescale of the 1971 Cahokia Ceramic Conference, which unfortunately continues to be treated as an accurately corrected calendar timescale.

Elsewhere (Hall 1984d, 1985a) I have shown that it is not possible to derive either the 1971 or the more recent FAI-270 American Bottom timescale satisfactorily from the mass of radiocarbon information now available. For this reason I refer in the present paper to dates "assigned" to the various periods and phases. In my own evaluation of the radiocarbon information, the 1971 Cahokia timescale is seen to become more consistent with calibrated dates if the time assignments are moved forward variously by fifty to a hundred years or more years, beginning with the Patrick phase (originally A.D. 600–800) and ending with the Moorehead phase, which would then be more like A.D. 1200–1275 rather than A.D. 1150–1250 and would occupy part of the thirteenth century previously assigned to the Sand Prairie phase (fig. 1.3). This dating matter is introduced to make readers aware that valid interregional comparisons cannot be made if the assigned dates continue to be treated as though expressed in calendar years rather than in radiocarbon years.

Fairmount corresponded to what in the past I have called Pre-Ramey, Pre–Old Village, Pulcher phase (following Howard D. Winters), and also Early Cahokia, the last following Gordon R. Willey (Hall 1966, 1967a; Willey 1966:194, 251). Willey's Early Cahokia phase was based partly upon Donald E. Wray's comment that "Cahokia was apparently a cultural center before Old Village with a temple mound complex of southern origin which is pre-Middle Mississippian . . . combined

with a utilitarian complex of Jersey Bluff Late Woodland type" (1952:159). Wray attributed his own information to James B. Griffin (citing personal communication), who was impressed by the pervasiveness of typologically Woodland pottery at a site regarded as Mississippian (e.g., Griffin and Spaulding 1951:79). All work since has confirmed the extensive Woodland occupation at Cahokia, calling into question the real value of a term like *Woodland* in this context.

In trying to characterize the early but typologically Mississippian materials at Cahokia, I have found it useful to use as a beginning point a suggestion of Howard D. Winters (personal communication, 1962) that there had been an early Mississippian horizon in southern Illinois that lacked such a diagnostic Old Village Focus trait as Ramey Incised pottery. In material excavated at Cahokia by Warren L. Wittry for the Illinois State Museum in 1960 and 1961, I have identified an "emergent Mississippian" ceramic complex that lacked Ramey Incised pottery and for which I subsequently obtained radiocarbon dates that showed it to be earlier at the time than all but one date for Ramey Incised at Cahokia (Hall 1964, 1966, 1967c).

The dates also supported the observation that the Pre-Ramey (alias Pre–Old Village, alias Pulcher) phase was one in which southeastern rather than Caddoan area contacts were important (Hall 1966:5). This observation has been confirmed by the results of excavations that show "that the tempo of proposed local trade, and of trade from the central, or lower, Mississippi River Valley increases during the Emergent Mississippian occupations of the FAI-270 Project area . . . [without] indications of trade with the Caddoan area during this period" (Griffin 1984: 260). Evidence of contacts with the Caddo area does appear in the form of arrowpoints of the Scallorn and Alba types found abundantly in Cahokia Mound 72 (Fowler and Hall 1975:4–5) and perhaps in the fact itself of grave objects of bundled arrows. It was a Caddo funeral practice for mourners to present offerings of arrows to the bereaved wife or mother "in whatever number their affection for the deceased suggested" and then to place them with the dead (Griffith 1954:96). Mound 72 has been assigned to the Lohmann phase (Melvin L. Fowler, personal communication, 1987).

I have used the term *emergent Mississippian* both in the sense of a Late Woodland culture antecedent and transitional to Early Mississippian (Hall 1975a:22) and in the sense of the Early Mississippian culture recently emerged from this Late Woodland background (Hall 1964:12; Hall 1966:6). Kelly (1982) has subsequently formalized and standardized a concept of Emergent Mississippian for Cahokia, limiting it to the transitional material once called Late Bluff and formerly regarded as Late Woodland.

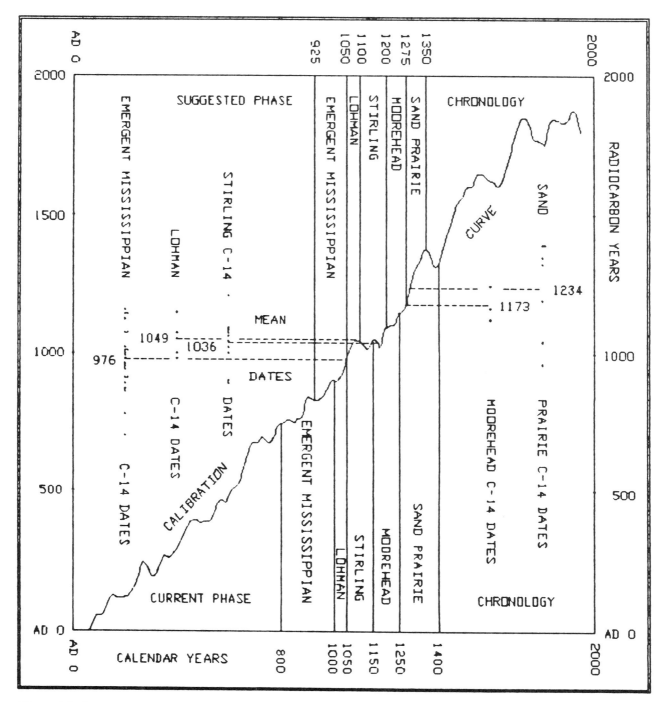

Figure 1.3. Currently assigned and suggested new phase chronologies for the Mississippian period in the American Bottom, Illinois, showing their relationship to radiocarbon dates reported in Bareis and Porter (1984:266–69) and to a bidecadal radiocarbon calibration curve (Stuiver and Reimer 1986). This radiocarbon calibration curve was created by the author from the bidecadal radiocarbon calibration dataset given as file ATM20.C14 accompanying the microcomputer program CALIB, Rev. 2.0, of Stuiver and Reimer (1986) and the Quaternary Research Center of the University of Washington, Seattle, plotted and smoothed using the microcomputer program GENERIC CADD (Version 2.0), of Generic Software, Redmond, Washington.

In interpreting the Pre-Ramey or Pre–Old Village material excavated by Wittry, I drew special attention to points of resemblance of this complex to the earliest Mississippian complexes elsewhere. Absent was Ramey Incised pottery, whose trailed scroll motif, so typical at Cahokia, is not a mode found on pottery at Macon Plateau in Georgia or in other Early Mississippian sites in the Tennessee Valley, for instance. On the other hand, this early Pre-Ramey complex at Cahokia included some material that seemed to tie into the area of Mississippian development south of Cahokia—a globular funnel or "juice press" form, the water bottle form, the fabric-impressed pan, as well as red-filming as surface finish in the type Merrell Red Filmed, a type compared to Larto Red Filmed in the Lower Mississippi Valley (Hall 1966:7). This appeared to me to reflect interaction between certain Late Woodland, actually emergent Cahokia Mississippian, peoples and carriers of another emergent regional Mississippian culture located not very far to the south. Kelly (1982:65–66) sees the red-filmed and grog-tempered ware from the Merrell Tract at Cahokia as possible examples of the lower valley type Larto Red Filmed and adds his identification of other pottery as equivalent to Varney Red Filmed, a shell-tempered Early Mississippian type typical of Early Mississippian contexts in southeastern Missouri and northeastern Arkansas, as at the Zebree (Sebree) site in Arkansas (Morse 1975; cf. Kelly, Ozuk et al. 1984:147). The product of this interaction over time was a northern Mississippian tradition—Cahokia Mississippian—that was different from lower Mississippi River alluvial valley Mississippian to the south, yet that owed much to it.

At Cahokia the local Mississippian emergence probably began with organizational changes within a society that was Woodland in most of those details that archaeologists use to classify cultures, but as the emergence intensified the physical identity of the Cahokia tradition changed also with the interaction of Cahokia peoples through the area north and northwest of Cahokia. This area of interaction gave Cahokia Mississippian much of its identity as a regional Mississippian tradition.

The Cahokia site was a gateway on the northwestern frontier of the Mississippian heartland (Hall 1967a:175–76; Kelly 1982:207–9). Finds of Cahokia-related ceramics are distributed in a pattern something like the tails of a comet (fig. 1.4). The head is in the greater East St. Louis area, but the influences are flared outward, largely to the north into areas occupied by Late Woodland peoples, and not into areas like the Tennessee-Cumberland or Cairo Lowland archaeological provinces. Cahokia had strong contacts to the south, but its role in these contacts was more passive (as a recipient of influences) than active.

The Fairmount phase as such does not exist within the phase chronology of the FAI-270 Project reports. What had been late Fairmount, assigned dates between A.D. 1000 and 1050, has been redesignated the Lohmann phase (Bareis and Porter 1984: fig. 3). Earlier Fairmount, once assigned to A.D. 900–1000, now constitutes part of the Emergent Mississippian period in the FAI-270 chronology and is comprised of a series of phases specific to the northern and southern American Bottom. During the Fairmount phase Cahokia developed into the seat of authority for a chiefdom that appears to have dramatized its power in very material ways. This includes the construction of early stages of Monks Mound.

The power and authority of the Cahokia leadership is dramatized powerfully by discoveries in Mound 72. This is a single mound small enough to have been overlooked during one mapping of Cahokia. Nevertheless in Mound 72 Fowler discovered burials accompanied by a trove of exotic manufactures, some indicating far-flung contacts reaching south into the Caddo area. Within Mound 72 an individual of high status was laid to rest in death on a blanket of thousands of shell beads. A deposit of grave furnishings left nearby included 400 arrows in bundles or quivers, nineteen polished "chunky stones" or "discoidals," about two bushels of uncut mica in sheets, a quantity of sheet copper, and the bodies of three men and three women, which have been interpreted as retainers in life of the individual laid to rest on the beads. Elsewhere in the same mound other evidence of sacrifice was found, including one mass grave of over fifty young women and a nearby burial of four "beheaded and behanded" males (Fowler 1969a, 1974). Only a person of central importance would have been buried with such an expenditure of life and effort: "These data suggest that the individual interred on the bead platform held a status in Cahokia society of the Fairmount Phase which controlled the redistribution of exotic goods. I feel that this individual functioned as the pinnacle of the sociopolitical system, with goods flowing to him as tribute rather than as trade items" (Fowler 1974:22).

The Stirling phase (assigned to A.D. 1050–1150) corresponds closely to the Old Village Focus of the older literature and to the Mississippian complex at the Aztalan site in Wisconsin. The name of the Stirling phase acknowledges the work of Gene Stirling in excavating the sequence in the Powell Mound area of Cahokia where older Mississippian village materials underlay a later Mississippian complex. Much is now known of Old Village at Cahokia but as a phase in the continuum of Cahokia development rather than as the earliest of two supposedly discrete occupations. Aztalan, by contrast, is hardly the colony of Cahokia it was once thought to be (see Goldstein and Richards, chap. 10).

Aztalan may be an illustration of the "domino effect"

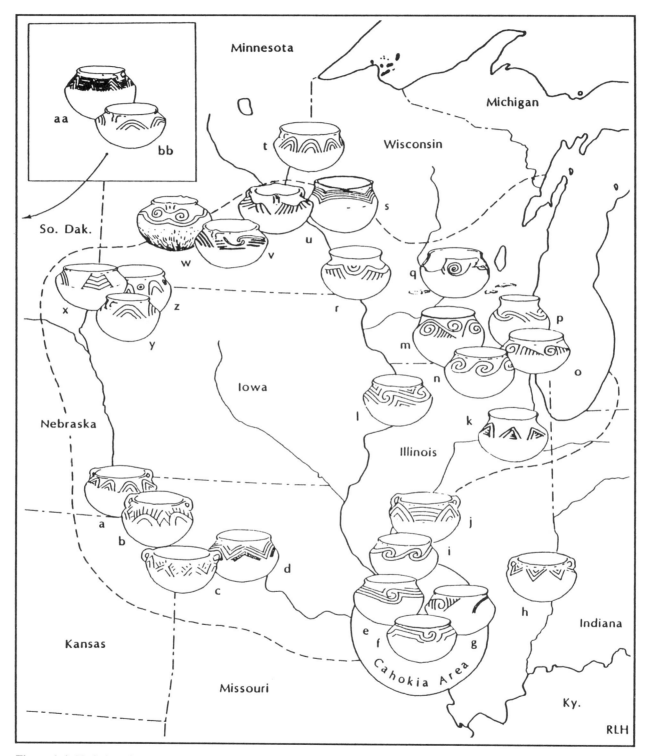

Figure 1.4. Varieties of Ramey Incised Pottery and Influenced Types (*see full caption on facing page*)

in the process of Mississippianization. It has been known now for forty years that about three-quarters of Aztalan pottery is Woodland, not Mississippian (Moreau Maxwell, personal communication, 1950; Bleed 1970; Hall 1973:1). I regard Aztalan as one of the better-known of many examples of a Woodland culture heavily acculturated toward the Mississippian pattern and more likely derived most directly from northern or east-central Illinois rather than from anywhere in the Cahokia area. The Aztalan Woodland ceramics are distinctive from those at Cahokia but are very similar to those of some Late Woodland complexes in northern and eastern Illinois that were interacting with Cahokia during the Lohmann and/or Stirling phases—the Collins site near Danville, Illinois, for example. Collins site Late Woodland in the Wabash Valley (Douglas 1976) was only one of several regional Late Woodland traditions distinct from American Bottom "Bluff Culture" that were modified in the Mississippian direction through interaction with Cahokia.

The Moorehead phase (assigned to A.D. 1150–1250) includes ceramics carried over from Stirling (Ramey Incised, Powell Plain) and others as well that are typical also of the succeeding Sand Prairie phase (cordmarked, shell-tempered jars and shell-tempered plates). Moorehead corresponds most closely to the episode at Cahokia that James B. Griffin (personal communication, 1966) once informally designated "Cahokia Climax," a phase bridging Old Village and Trappist. During this "climax," interaction with the Caddo area and lower alluvial valley of the Mississippi was possibly at a maximum. In the perspective of recent investigations the term *climax* may be better applied to the Stirling phase.

The Trappist Focus corresponds closely to today's Sand Prairie phase except that Oneota materials which occasionally show up at Cahokia and in the Cahokia area could belong in a later part of Sand Prairie or in still later prehistoric or protohistoric times. This is reflected in the two different time scales given for the Sand Prairie phase. Fowler and Hall (1972) assigned Sand Prairie to the period A.D. 1250–1500. Bareis and Porter (1984: fig. 3) place Sand Prairie in the period A.D. 1250–1400 and add a Vulcan (Oneota) phase at A.D. 1400–1600. There is therefore a century of overlap between late Sand Prairie in one scheme and early Oneota in the other.

The Old Village and Trappist foci of the Midwestern Taxonomic System fell respectively within the Early and Late Mississippi periods of Griffin (1946:76) and the Temple Mound I and Temple Mound II periods of Ford and Willey (1941) and Willey (1966:251). Within the Midwestern Taxonomic System, Old Village and Trappist were subsumed as foci within the Monks Mound Aspect of Middle Mississippi (see Bennett 1945:152–53; Bennett 1952:119–21; Cole and Deuel 1937:204–9; Griffin 1946:87–88). Because of the stratigraphy in the Powell Mound area of Cahokia, which involved a "nonconformity" as W. C. McKern has described it, between Old Village and Trappist, these entities enjoyed the kind of taxonomic distinction that the Midwestern Taxonomic System could provide. The evidence of Aztalan seemed to support it. Not everyone saw this dichotomy as an accurate representation of the situation at Cahokia: "I've been trying to tell you for some time that there is evidence that there is this gradual change [from Old Village to Trappist]. The amateurs believe that we're crazy in believing that there's any separation between Old Village and the Trappist material. In burials they find Old Village

Figure 1.4. Varieties of Ramey Incised Pottery and Influenced Types (vessel size variable): (a) Kansas City Mississippian, Shepherd Mound, Missouri, after Wedel (1943:141 and pl. 39c); (b) Kansas City Mississippian, Gresham site, Missouri, after Shippee (1972: fig. 18a); (c) Kansas City Mississippian, Vandiver Mounds, Missouri, after Shippee (1972: fig. 5f); (d) Kansas City Mississippian, Steed-Kisker site, Missouri, after Shippee (1972: fig. 14a); (e) Ramey Incised, Cahokia site, Illinois, after Hall (1962: pl. 55c); (f) Ramey Incised, Cahokia site, after Hall (1962: pl. 55b); (g) Ramey Incised, Cahokia site, based on a rimsherd from the University of Michigan Museum of Anthropology; (h) Ramey Incised, from the Late Woodland Albee Complex, Catlin site, Indiana, after Winters (1967: fig. 17a); (i) Ramey Incised, Schild site, Illinois, after Perino (1971b: fig. 47a); (j) Spoon River Mississippian vessel, Dickson Mound, Illinois, after Harn (1971b: fig. 22; (k) Langford Trailed, Gentleman Farm mound, Illinois, after Brown et al. (1967: fig. 10a); (l) Ramey Incised, John Chapman site, Illinois, after Bennett (1945: pl. 24c); (m) Ramey Incised, Aztalan site, Wisconsin, after Hall (1962: pl. 50b); (n) Ramey Incised, Aztalan site, after Hall (1962: pl. 46c); (o) Carcajou Curvilinear vessel, Carcajou site, Wisconsin, after Hall (1962: pl. 21a); (p) Grand River Trailed, Milwaukee, Wisconsin, after Hall (1962: pl. 63a); (q) grit-tempered vessel resembling the Cambria C type, after Hall (1962: pl. 51a), from the Schultz site, Wisconsin; (r) Diamond Bluff Trailed, Diamond Bluff site, Wisconsin, after Hall (1962: pl. 56a); (s) grit-tempered, red-filmed vessel from an intrusive pit in a Late Woodland burial mound of the Wakanda group, Wisconsin, after Wittry (1959: fig. 6); (t) unclassified vessel from Burnett County, Wisconsin, Hall (1962: pl. 57c); (u) shell-tempered vessel from the Bryan site, Minnesota, after Blessing (1967: figs. 10–11); (v) shell-tempered vessel from the Cambria site, Minnesota, resembling the grit-tempered Cambria C type, based on rimsherd from the Minnesota Historical Society; (w) vessel of the Cambria C type from the Cambria site, after Wilford (1945b: fig. 3e); (x) Ramey Incised, Broken Kettle site, Iowa, after Ives (1962: fig. 17a); (y) Cambria C vessel from an unidentified Mill Creek phase site in northwestern Iowa, after Ives (1962: fig. 14a); (z) Cambria C vessel from an unidentified Mill Creek phase site in northwestern Iowa, after Ives (1962: fig. 15b); (aa) vessel of the grit-tempered type Mitchell Broad-Trailed, Over Focus, South Dakota, after Hurt (1954: fig. 6e); (bb) Mitchell Broad-Trailed vessel, Over Focus, South Dakota, after Hurt (1954: fig. 6f). The dashed line indicates the approximate area of the subsequent Oneota Interaction.

Table 1.1. Row Number Trends in Illinois, Wisconsin, and Missouri Archaeological Corn

Archaeological Site	Cultural Phase or Period	Mean Number of Rows	Number of Cobs	% of Total Cobs Rows				
				8	10	12	14	16+
Rock Island, IL	Historic Sauk A.D. 1790–1810	8.3	1300	86	12	2	–	–
Zimmerman, IL	Historic Kaskaskia-Illini A.D. 1683–1691	8.5	13	77	23	–	–	–
Little Osage, MO	Historic Osage A.D. 1790–1815	8.9	328	63	30	6	1	–
Cahokia (First Terrace, Monks Mound), IL	Historic Cahokia-Illini A.D. 1700s (?)	8.9	40	65	28	7	–	–
Utz, MO	Protohistoric Missouri, Oneota Trad.	9.4	22	46	41	13	–	–
Cahokia (Merrell Tract), IL	Sand Prairie	9.5	91	42	43	15	–	–
Plum Island, IL	Langford Tradition	9.7	17	38	41	20	1	–
Walker-Hooper, WI	Grand River, Oneota Trad.	9.9	19	53	21	10	16	–
Cahokia (top of Monks Mound), IL	Moorehead(?)	10.4	10	20	40	40	–	–
Cahokia (Tract 15B), IL	Sand Prairie(?)	10.7	64	13	48	31	6	2
Turner-Snodgrass, MO	Powers	10.8	51	6	49	35	8	2
Loyd, IL	Stirling/Moorehead	11.1	63	10	38	43	8	1
Hoecake, MO	Baytown	11.3	3	–	33	67	–	–
Cahokia (beneath Mound 51), IL	(Late) Fairmount	11.6	99	10	25	44	15	6
Cahokia (beneath Mound 34), IL	"Mississippian"	11.9	27	7	19	48	22	4
Cahokia (beneath Mound 31), IL	"Mississippian"	12.0	1	–	–	100	–	–
Aztalan, WI	Rock River	12.0	1	–	–	100	–	–
Dietz, WI	Late Woodland	12.0	1	–	–	100	–	–
Kane, IL	Loyd	12.2	80	6	20	46	13	15
Cahokia (under Kunneman Mound), IL	Early Mississippian	12.3	46	–	20	56	15	9
Cahokia (Mound 72), IL	Fairmount	?	4	"12- to 14-rowed"				

Source: Cutler and Blake 1969, 1973:17–25, 39–41, 71–73.

pots and Trappist pots" (James B. Griffin quoted in Orr 1950:37).

The phase chronology proposed at the 1971 Cahokia Ceramic Conference attempted to correct the situation by recognizing a multiple-phase Cahokia tradition with continuities throughout (Fowler and Hall 1972). Through four of these phases (proposed originally with suggested dates between A.D. 900 and 1500), the organizational structure at Cahokia was considered to be Mississippian in level, although already waning with the beginning of Sand Prairie at A.D. 1250 (i.e., about A.D. 1300 in calendar years). There is a radiocarbon date of 1110 ± 100 R.C.Y.A.D. (M-1636) for a hearth in the next-to-last occupational surface of the fourth (summit) terrace of Monks Mound (Reed, Bennett, and Porter 1968:144). A late prehistoric level of the broad first terrace of Monks Mound is located in time by the dates 1110 ± 55, 1125 ± 60, 1145 ± 60, 1260 ± 50, and 1280 ± 50 R.C.Y.A.D (Wis-

365, 547, 546, 362, and 443; Benchley 1974). These dates average 1184 R.C.Y.A.D, a mean consistent with a date of 1210 ± 55 R.C.Y.A.D for a structure on the small earthen platform on the southwest corner of the first terrace. The final prehistoric construction activity on the principal mound at Cahokia would thus appear to have been sometime around 1200 R.C.Y.A.D (i.e., around calendar A.D. 1275, adapting to this situation the radiocarbon calibration data of Stuiver 1982; compare Hall 1984d, 1985a). A sample of forty corn cobs found by Charles J. Bareis in excavations of the first terrace of Monks Mound has a mean row number of 8.9, indicating a probable historic origin with a date in the 1700s (table 1.1; see Cutler and Blake 1969, 1973). Evidence of an eighteenth-century French and Indian presence on the first terrace has been reported by Walthall and Benchley (1986).

Interaction Models

The criteria for distinguishing the developmental phases at Cahokia reflect the great dependence of the archaeologist on pottery, as one might expect for a phase chronology originally developed at a ceramic conference. Such a situation forces attention also on the question of the nature and cause of the changes recognized by the archaeologist in the shift from one phase to another, whether from Fairmount or Lohmann to Stirling and on through Moorehead to Sand Prairie or from Old Village to Trappist in the older scheme. What is happening and what do the changes represent? In 1961 Joseph R. Caldwell presented colleagues with a thought on the problem of Cahokia's identity:

> I now view with suspicion the propriety of regarding Old Village, Eveland, or even Aztalan as Middle Mississippian. . . . One advantage of distinguishing the Old Village-Aztalan-Eveland materials as not Middle Mississippi is that it enables us to postulate different areas of Mississippian interaction at different times. Griffin could quite properly write in 1949 that Powell Plain and Ramey Incised, Old Village types, do not appear in the central Mississippi Valley to the southward, and that the specific connections of pottery from the Cahokia center were to the north and northwest. This is not, however, clearly the case with the later Trappist materials. Nearly all ceramic forms characteristic of Trappist and Spoon River, but not of Old Village and Eveland, can be duplicated, or they find very close analogies in the St. Francis, Tennessee-Cumberland, and Arkansas area to the south. . . . If we regard these southward pointing features as representing Middle Mississippian per se we are enabled to do two things. First we can look at this Middle Mississippian as in process of development, i.e. as a development achieved mostly after Old Village times. Secondly, we can suggest that the proposed development was in part due to a heightened interaction among the various societies which shared these specific features (1961).

Caldwell was writing before there was an awareness of the existence of a pre–Old Village Mississippian phase at Cahokia influenced by Early Mississippian cultures to the south, but he was aware of the magnitude of the Woodland-like (now Emergent Mississippian occupation) at Cahokia. He was also aware of the strength of the interaction between central Illinois Valley Late Woodland on the Eveland site at Dickson Mounds and what would now be called Stirling phase Mississippian. The Eveland complex included houses of wall-trench construction, typically Mississippian, together with ceramics including some of Cahokia Mississippian form and decoration in local Late Woodland pastes and others more at home in the Glenwood and Mill Creek foci of western Iowa (Caldwell, personal communications, 1961–67; Harn 1975b; Conrad, chap. 6; and personal observations).

At the beginning of the Sand Prairie phase with Cahokia already going into decline, Cahokia looks stylistically very much like its southern Mississippian neighbors. Thinking in a similar vein one of our colleagues has added the observation, "By the time Cahokia really has a southern Mississippian flavor, it's all done!" By the close of the Sand Prairie phase there is little at Cahokia to

speak of except an elusive Oneota presence (Hall 1963: 27; Hall 1974; Milner et al. 1984:181–82; O'Brien 1972a: 88; Perino 1959:132).

What Caldwell was getting at was the idea of a classification based on the nature and directions of interaction of Cahokians at various phases of Cahokia development. He later formalized a similar model in his concept of the interaction sphere applied to the interpretation of the Hopewellian complex (Caldwell 1964). Caldwell's interaction perspective was possibly influenced by a view of the origins of Mississippian culture previously expressed by Philip Phillips, James A. Ford, and James B. Griffin. Griffin in particular had questioned the idea of a single point of origin for Mississippian for most of his professional life (Smith 1984b:19–20). "[W]e are becoming increasingly doubtful that a single center for the Mississippian development exists anywhere. We envisage rather a number of centers in which this culture was developing more or less simultaneously along parallel lines with continuing interaction between them" (Phillips, Ford, and Griffin 1951:451).

Let there be no mistake. Caldwell did not himself apply an interaction model to Mississippian origins in the spring of 1961 or believe in convergent Mississippian development then any more than he did in 1958 (see Caldwell 1958:28–29). He did formalize an interaction model for Hopewell and present it at the annual meeting of the American Anthropological Association in Philadelphia in December of 1961. This was his familiar paper "Interaction Spheres in Prehistory" published in 1964. He then encouraged the application of an interaction model to Mississippian culture history in interpreting the results of the Illinois State Museum's Cahokia salvage excavations, begun by Caldwell with operations on Mound 31, continued by Warren L. Wittry with excavations on the archaeological locations dubbed Merrell Tract 15A and Tract 15B, in 1961 and 1960 respectively, and continued under my direction in 1963 at Tract 15A after Wittry's departure from the museum in 1962 to take a new position. One product of this stimulation was the interaction and integration model incorporated by Joseph O. Vogel in his report on the domestic ceramics from Tracts 15A and 15B (Vogel 1964, 1975).

> That there was a steady rain of influence onto the American Bottoms [sic] out of the south is evident. That these new traits are absorbed into the existent pattern is equally evident. The changes to the Cahokia ceramic complexes are seen as having been wrought in a fashion consistent with traditional practices, thus obviating the necessity for [hypotheses requiring] mass migrations and a complete repeopling of the American Bottoms [sic] near the close of the first millenium A.D.
>
> It must therefore be postulated that Mississippian cul-

ture entered the American Bottom in an incipient form as part of an interaction situation no later than the 900's. The Mississippian phenomena at the Cahokia site were the product of the successful integration of many modes from a variety of sources, spread over as much as two centuries of Late Woodland–Mississippian interaction as well as the interaction to be expected between early Mississippian centers. The fathers of the "Old Village" were many and many of them local (Vogel 1964:26).

Another product was the interaction model that I began to develop in subsequent papers (e.g., Hall 1966, 1967a, 1973, 1975c; Fowler and Hall 1978:565–66) and my more recent pursuit of the ideologies of midwestern great traditions, both Hopewellian (Hall 1979) and Mississippian (Hall 1984a).

> [A]fter A.D. 800 Woodland peoples in the Plains and in the Mississippi Valley were starting to develop toward a Mississippian way of life along parallel lines, partly in response to climatic changes that had a beneficial effect for many people over a broad area of the Eastern United States at approximately the same time. . . . In the Central Mississippi Valley [Middle Mississippi] may have developed out of Baytown. I will suggest that in the Cahokia area another local tradition, one which in Illinois we would call Late Woodland, probably served as a host for culturing certain ideas and practices in circulation after A.D. 800 which came to have an identity as Mississippian. . . . Our image of what Mississippi meant then was determined in part by the inventory of traits that various cultures *happened to have* at a point in time when they lifted themselves by their own bootstraps [i.e., evolved], or were assisted in lifting themselves [i.e., acculturated], to a new level of socioeconomic organization. Interaction between these peoples served to erase some of the differences that existed, and migrations extended the area of interaction even further (Hall 1967a:180–81, emphasis added).

A third product was the interaction model of Spoon River Mississippian origins developed by Alan D. Harn, who had worked closely with Caldwell at Dickson Mounds and who also had extensive field experience in the American Bottom.

> Although current knowledge of the local Late Woodland population does not allow a comprehensive discussion of these people, available evidence suggests that the rapid displacement of Woodland traditions by Mississippian culture [in the central Illinois Valley] did not result from submersion of the indigenous population by a superior number of Cahokians. Indications are that the occupants of the region, already beginning to develop toward a Mississippian lifeway through external contacts with both Cahokia and Woodland peoples in the Western Prairie and Eastern Plains (Hall 1967a:180–81), simply adopted a more advanced version of a lifestyle in which they had already begun to participate. Out of this hybridization

came the Spoon River variant, which we have suggested was essentially composed of a Late Woodland population whose cultural traditions became closely affiliated with the Cahokia-Mississippian movement (Harn 1973) [Harn 1975b].

A fourth product was the interaction model utilized by James A. Brown to examine the Prairie Peninsula as an interaction area in prehistory. Brown acknowledges an academic debt to Joseph Caldwell for stimulating his interest in "problems of the cultural interaction between regional and local traditions" (1965:ii): "The Prairie Peninsula is, above all, a regional interaction area. It is one that is not always coincident with areas of common cultural-ecological adaptations. And for this reason it stands as an example of a regional area with certain cultural unity that does not completely have its base in subsistence adaptation" (1965:213).

Recently Charles R. Moffat (1983; chap. 13) has endorsed an interaction model of Mississippian development as it relates to the Kaskaskia Valley in Illinois well east of Cahokia:

> The new data from the Kaskaskia Valley seem to be more consistent with the second [multiple centers] model than the first [single center]. It is becoming clear that the lower Wabash Valley was the site of a regional Mississippian tradition which exerted strong influence over much of eastern Illinois and may have limited Cahokia's influence in this direction. . . .
>
> Recognizable Cahokia influences on ceramics [in the upper Kaskaskia Valley] appear only after the evolution of Mississippian culture in the Upper Kaskaskia Valley was well under way. The original impetus for this development does not seem to have come from Cahokia (1983: 28, 23–24).

Moffat's earliest Mississippian occupation of the upper Kaskaskia Valley (Shelbyville I) equates in time with the Stirling phase at Cahokia but is said to be difficult to compare culturally with Stirling. Moffat notes that plates and cordmarked jars are present in Shelbyville I but absent in Stirling, while "a number of characteristic Stirling Phase ceramic types, particularly Ramey Incised and the various red or black-filmed jar forms, are poorly represented in the Upper Kaskaskia Valley" (1983:20–23). Since shell-tempered plates and shell-tempered cordmarked jars definitively appear at Cahokia during the Moorehead phase, *following* Stirling, it is thus possible to see in the shift from Stirling to Moorehead at Cahokia a reintensification of contacts between Cahokia and the southeastern Mississippian heartland, although perhaps only indirectly through the agency of Kaskaskia Valley Mississippians themselves perhaps only recently emerged from the Late Woodland closet (see Hall 1966:7; Hall 1967a:180).

Moffat calls attention to the fact that the lithic complex of the upper Kaskaskia Valley Mississippians lacked certain diagnostic Cahokia chipped stone artifacts, such as notched triangular projectile points (less than two percent of triangular points), Ramey knives, chipped stone hoes, and microdrills, while it included end scrapers, triangular knives, and "hump-backed knives"—artifacts rare in the Cahokia area (Moffat 1983; Moffat 1985:293, 366). Hump-backed triangles, sometimes called scrapers and sometimes knives, are not found or are not typical of either Cahokia Mississippian sites or of Oneota tradition sites (except for Huber and related sites) but occur distributed among late prehistoric sites from northeastern and east-central Illinois and northwestern Indiana as far east as southwestern Pennsylvania through an area once occupied largely by Algonquian peoples (Munson and Munson 1972). In northeastern Illinois humpbacks are found in the Langford and Fisher traditions and in Huber Focus Oneota, which I see as derived from Fisher and which I accept as probably ethnically Miami, that is Algonquian (Hall 1973:4–5). In Wisconsin hump-backed triangles have recently been found in the lithic complex of a site believed to have been the seventeenth century "lost Mascouten village" at which Kickapoo, Miami, and other Central Algonquian tribes were occasional residents (Rusch 1985: fig. 2f, m).

Kelly (1982:163–88) has conveniently summarized several models of Mississippian development at Cahokia, beginning with two approaches identified by Porter (1974: 6–8). These approaches include an "evolutionary model" and a "migration-contact model," to which Kelly has added his own "integration model." The first of these Kelly illustrates with the work of Fowler (1974), Benchley (1974), and Gregg (1975b) and characterizes as having an emphasis on in situ evolutionary development within a local cultural base. The migration-contact model emphasizes the role of outside influences and the acculturation of Cahokia area Late Woodland peoples. Kelly illustrates this model by the works of Vogel, which I have already discussed, Glen A. Freimuth, and Porter. Kelly's integration model is a middle road said largely to follow the migration-contact perspectives of Porter and Vogel. To the extent that Kelly's model was influenced by Vogel, it is thus also a secondary product of the influence of Caldwell in stimulating interest in Mississippian interaction. "It is referred to as an integration model because it is an attempt to integrate the evolutionary trends of increased complexity with patterns of increased interaction that were evident over a larger geographic area, i.e. the Mississippi River Valley. . . . [C]ahokia's emergence is attributed to socio-economic developments occurring throughout the central and lower Mississippi River Valley" (Kelly 1982:170–71).

In considering migration-contact models one must also include that of Donald W. Lathrap, which called for the derivation ultimately from Mexico of the organizing principles of Cahokia Mississippian and the intrusion into the American Bottom of peoples with a developed Mississippian culture through or from the Caddoan area. Lathrap saw more than coincidence in the sudden florescence of culture in the Caddo area and the availability of Mexican prototypes for the projectile points and engraved, polished ceramics of the Gibson Aspect (Lathrap, personal communication, 1971).

Lathrap's hypothesis was never formalized, although its influence may be reflected in the work of students. One senses its presence in the importance given to contacts with the Caddo area by Freimuth (1974) and to aspects of the seriation study by O'Brien (1972a). In her seriation of ceramics from the Powell Tract at Cahokia, O'Brien originally proposed that an initial Late Woodland ("Period I") occupation of the tract was followed without intermediate stages by a fully developed Mississippian culture including Ramey Incised pottery. An occupation that O'Brien later placed in the period of the Fairmount phase (about A.D. 900–1050) she had originally assigned to a much later "Period V" with a terminal date around A.D. 1400 (see Hall 1974; Fowler and Hall 1972:5). Bruce Smith (1984b) has recently summarized the history of the model for migration and contact for the spread of Mississippian culture generally.

Fowler sees the basis of Cahokia formation in technological innovations involving a successful adaptation of maize to the area combined with the use of the hoe to permit intensive cultivation, the combination leading soon to population growth and the appearance of village farming communities (Fowler 1974). He argues that even if one accepts a diffusionist model one would still have to address the problem of why the Cahokia site came to be where it was and what the processes of integration and development were within the American Bottom. While continuing to see the emergence of Mississippian in the neighborhood of Cahokia, Fowler does allow for outside influences, migration, and contact:

> Centering around the central Mississippi Valley area a cultural development took place . . . first in the St. Louis, Missouri, area in a pocket of land known as the American Bottoms [*sic*]. From here its influences and migrations of people spread up and down the Mississippi Valley, up the Ohio and into the southeastern United States. . . .
>
> This culture known as the Mississippian is truly Mesoamerican in inspiration being characterized by temple mounds built around plazas, rather large fortified towns, and various art styles reminiscent of Mesoamerican motifs. . . . No one seriously proposes it as a result of migrations from Mesoamerica. . . .

The beginnings of Mississippian in the area of St. Louis seems to have been involved with the Late Woodland inhabitants of the area. . . . Personally it looks to me more as if the early Mississippian is an intrusion into the area where it lives side by side with the Late Woodland peoples already resident there. This leaves the question still open as to the point or time of origin of Mississippian (1971: 399).

Kelly and Porter are explicit in seeing economic motives for the appearance of Mississippians in the American Bottom and markets and frontier outposts as integral features of Cahokia Mississippian development and expansion. Porter speaks of "a merchant class from elsewhere" exploiting the aboriginal part-time farmers of the American Bottom and attributes to others endorsement of the roles in Cahokia development of in-place evolution and population pressure resulting from improved farming techniques (1974:28, 186). He is also somewhat disparaging of the role of religion in Cahokia development: "These town squares are the market places in my view and could have served for religious functions as well. There is no question that religious support of the exchange system is necessary. I find archaeological dependence upon ceremonialism as an explanation of phenomena highly unrealistic. We are wearing out the hinges on the 'back door' of ceremonialism" (1969:160–61).

Porter is also known for his delineation of a settlement model for the American Bottom involving an initial "chain settlement" followed by a shift toward a "hexagonal pattern" (Porter 1974). Fowler, with his students, is

recognized for his work on the definition and organization of the Cahokia site proper and on a settlement model for the greater Cahokia area that divides settlements into first-line, second-line, third-line, and fourth-line communities (Benchley 1974; Fowler 1978; Gregg 1975b; Vander Leest 1980). Kelly provides a succinctly stated outline for the course of events leading to the emergence of Cahokia as the principal town in a climax area of prehistoric Mississippi Valley culture:

The growth in population, with corn as an important subsistence item, ultimately provided the conditions necessary to social stratification. These conditions are posited here to include a circumscribed, sufficiently dense population in need of raw materials and commodities. It was the control of the distribution of a variety of resources (e.g., chert, salt) that led to social stratification in the *central* Mississippi Valley rather than competition for scarce agricultural land. . . .

In essence, Cahokia was a response to economic conditions that had been taking place in the Mississippi Valley for at least 400 years. The site's relationship to the local Late Woodland antecedents is fortuitous and not simply an *in situ* evolutionary sequence. . . .

Basically, it is postulated that these [mound] centers, distributed the length of the Mississippi River Valley, functioned as 1) central places either as incipient market places and/or for the redistribution of materials by the elite and 2) where traders could easily meet for the exchange of finished products and raw materials from other areas of the Mississippi Valley. . . . Cahokia emerged subsequent to the above model (1982:220, 221, 231).

The Cahokia and Oneota Interactions

The interaction concept can be quite useful for investigating Cahokia development. As the Mississippian level of culture faded in Illinois after A.D. 1400, ceramic evidence indicates that midwestern Indians were engaging increasingly across the prairie in an interaction that may conveniently be called Oneota, the Oneota Interaction. Not only the Winnebago, Chiwere Sioux (Oto, Ioway, and Missouri), and some Dhegiha Sioux (Kansa and probably Osage) were involved to some extent, but perhaps also the Algonquian Miami and Illinois (see Gibbon 1972: 173; Henning 1970:140–48). Brown (1965) has statistically demonstrated the existence of interactions through the Prairie Peninsula in Middle Woodland, Early Mississippian, and Late Mississippian times.

The spread of Oneota ceramic modes does not define the interaction but does provide clues to the arena of interaction. In concert with the increasing importance and spread of Oneota cultures, the more complex Mississippian (Middle Mississippi) level of social organization

with its intensive agricultural adaptation was finally replaced in Illinois by the simpler tribal level of social organization and the mixed hunting and horticultural adaptation of the prairie-dwelling tribes of our ethnographies. Community life simplified, temple towns disappeared, and society devolved.

The Mississippian devolution in Illinois began too early to be attributable to the Spanish entrada in the Southeast and to introduced disease, much less to the arrival of the French or English. Porter sees the Mississippian decline in the North mainly in terms of exchange relationships. Speaking especially of the Mitchell site, he sees the persons in control of trade and markets as having "grown as wealthy as possible" and the "market exchange system . . . beginning to decay," after which there was a *return* from a market system to the redistribution system (1969:162, emphasis added). Speaking more specifically of Cahokia, Porter says: "Cahokia, as a major market center (in its simplest form), is all that is needed to explain a great deal of the 'Mississippian problem.' When the center 'died' so went changes at the edges of the sphere" (1969:160–61).

Fowler correlated the Cahokia decline with the "gradual destruction of the resource niches in the American Bottoms [*sic*] area, as a result of intense population pressures," which "brought about the decline of the immediate area to support the central control community," resulting in a reintegration consisting of "the formation of a large number of Mississippian towns . . . scattered throughout the alluvial valleys of the Mississippi and its tributaries," after which Cahokia remained "but not as the control and redistribution center that it had been" (1974:34).

Griffin (1937) suggested that the archaeological culture of the prehistoric Chiwere Sioux and Winnebago was that known as Oneota and in a later paper went on to relate the Dhegiha Sioux and Chiwere Sioux-Winnebago to an original homeland "along the west side of the Mississippi River from northeastern Arkansas to the mouth of the Illinois at approximately A.D. 1000 where they were participating in the development of Middle Mississippi culture" (1960b:861). He went on to suggest that the proto-Oneota people moved outward and northward to eventually appear as the Ioway, Oto, Missouri, and Winnebago.

In a later paper Griffin proposed that Oneota culture appeared within the period A.D. 1300–1650 during a time of worsening climate and a shift away from a "marked dependence on agriculture to a heavier emphasis on hunting" accompanied by a "marked drop in cultural level" (1961:710–11). Gibbon related the collapse of "the Ramey State and its symbiotic extractive exchange network" itself to a "flaw in internal social organization" exacerbated by climate change (1974:136). Griffin's migration hypothesis has since been modified by others in the direction of limited migration from Cahokia and/ or acculturation and interactive Mississippianization of proto-Chiwere and Winnebago peoples in situ (see Gibbon 1974, 1982, 1983; Hurley 1970).

Vander Leest (1980:266–68) suggests that the decline of Cahokia could have been a consequence of the shifting of the channel of the Mississippi River westward from a former location in what is now Horseshoe Lake. Bareis (1964) called attention to the favorable circumstances that allowed a site of the size and duration of Cahokia to have formed at all. Except for the stability of the channel of the Mississippi in Late Woodland and Mississippian times in the Cahokia area, the Cahokia environs would have been literally swept away by channel migration on the American Bottom, located as Cahokia was on the outside of the Horseshoe Lake meander. Bareis saw Horseshoe Lake as the location of the main channel of the Missis-

sippi during the period of Cahokia development, which would place the large Powell Mound at the west end of the Cahokia site on the left or east bank of the Mississippi in its day. Munson (1974) dates the cutoff of Horseshoe Lake to "pre-900 B.P.," hence before 1050 radiocarbon years A.D. If we accept this date, then Cahokia would necessarily have begun to *rise* after the cutoff rather than *decline*. Vander Leest acknowledges that her suggestion presumes a slightly later date for the Horseshoe Lake cutoff than that estimated by Munson, a date "closer to A.D. 1200," but adds:

> Even without Munson's proposed river cut-off, a cultural shift west toward the main river channel may still have led to the decline of Cahokia. The location of Cahokia was probably due to the availability of agricultural land and exploitable bio-zones, and the ease of intra-American Bottom communication considerations. The westward shift may indicate a change in cultural emphasis toward the importance of commercial and ideological communication with Mississippian centers far outside the American Bottom" (1980:266–67).

The Oneota tradition appears to have begun in the Upper Mississippi Valley around 950 R.C.Y.B.P., say calendar A.D. 1100, possibly with an original adaptation to the alluvial Upper Mississippi River Valley environment in adjacent parts of Minnesota, Iowa, Illinois, and Wisconsin, and to have moved toward a prairie adaptation, spreading across Iowa and Missouri as far as South Dakota, Nebraska, and Kansas (Gibbon 1972: 176–78; Gibbon 1983; Henning 1970:140–62; W. Wedel 1959:131–72). Mississippians of Cahokia tradition were adapted to the alluvial valleys of the larger rivers in central and southern Illinois. This adaptation seems to have either failed or lost its advantage under changing circumstances and with this adaptation went much of the archaeologically visible identity of the Mississippians.

No sites have been located or excavated that can provide the positive links necessary to demonstrate whether the Illinois Mississippians just ceased to be, moved southward and survived among or as some Muskogean or Siouan group lower in the Mississippi Valley, or remained within the Midwest and survived among or as some historically known Siouan or Algonquian resident of the Prairie Peninsula.

An interaction model is useful because understanding the emergence of the Cahokia Mississippian tradition involves problems of identity and definition. At what point can we say that inhabitants of the American Bottom have achieved a Mississippian level of adaptation and organization? Two problems are actually involved: recognizing the appearance of the level of adaptation characteristic of the Mississippian tradition and recognizing the appearance of the stylistic content peculiar to the Mississippian tradition among all traditions sharing the same kind of adaptation. Griffin once defined Mississippian as "a wide variety of adaptations made by societies which developed a dependence on agriculture for their basic, storable food supply" (1967:189). This definition was meaningful for the broader evolutionary picture but seemed to ignore the uniqueness of particular regional and local traditions particularly in the South. He has elsewhere explained that cultures such as those of the Caddoan area, while distinctive in many ways, were nevertheless linked to the Southeast ideologically and in a manner not always visible archaeologically. Compared to other neighboring culture areas with which it might be compared, the Caddoan area "is closely linked in a great many art styles, in the ceremonial behavior, and the myths and the beliefs and the fundamental practices of the culture—all are part of what can be called the Mississippian pattern. This is not to take anything away from the unique genius of these local traditions; it's simply to indicate that these people did not live in local parochial vacuums and that the way in which societies progress is by interaction and by stimulation" (Griffin quoted in Davis, Wyckoff, and Holmes 1971:49).

The use of the term *Mississippian* for a particular cultural tradition and also for the structural parallels of various regional traditions has been confusing. Participants of the 1974 Santa Fe advanced seminar Reviewing Mississippian Development, sponsored by the School of American Research and chaired by Stephen Williams, sought to resolve the matter by recommending the term *Pan-Southern* for reference to the broad pattern of aboriginal ranked society throughout the southeastern United States. The term was meant to replace the use of "Mississippian" for cultures that in economic level and sociopolitical organization were like the late cultures of the middle Mississippi, Cumberland, and Tennessee river valleys but not like them in specific details of ceramics, stonework, and other artifacts. *Mississippi* remained as a period designation, but as a tradition Mississippian was seen to be limited to the particular historical development earlier known as *Middle Mississippi*.

An interaction model of Mississippian development sketched in broad strokes would presumably involve several regional whole cultural traditions with deep pre-Mississippian roots, such as Baytown in the lower alluvial Mississippi Valley and the Late Woodland "Bluff" cultures of southern Illinois and adjacent Missouri, to mention only two. The particular cultural identity of Cahokia Mississippian between, say, calendar A.D. 1100 and 1300 owes much to Cahokia's regional Late Woodland roots and to its prairie interactions. For instance, the so-called Cahokia point, the side-notched triangular

point, is important for the archaeological identity of the Cahokian Mississippian tradition, but points of this type are not characteristic of Tennessee-Cumberland or other more southerly varieties of Mississippian. They are characteristic of Cahokia and Cahokia-related sites, including Aztalan, as Griffin indicated over forty years ago (1946: 89). Such points hardly originated at Cahokia. They have a broad distribution west and northwest of the Mississippian heartland from the American Southwest and trans-Mississippi South through the Great Plains and into the northern Mississippi Valley, through the Prairie Peninsula and its northern woodland margins.

Where in the 1930s it was common to attribute the presence of a side-notched triangle at a Late Woodland site in Illinois or Wisconsin to "contact" with Cahokia or Aztalan, there has since been good reason to look upon the side-notched triangle as an artifact type that was becoming popular at many locations in the upper Midwest at the time of the Mississippian emergence, Cahokia among them. Cahokia had to be a very important regional center of diffusion, or rediffusion, and the side-notched triangular "gem" points of Cahokia are fabled, but the side-notched triangle as an artifact category could be better thought of as part of a regional cultural identity that Cahokia shared as a reflection of its sphere of interaction (Hall 1967a:177–78; Hall 1975c). Griffin has more recently observed that "the increasing number of notched triangular arrowpoints in the Stirling to Moorehead phases forms a good contrast with their absence in late Emergent Mississippian contexts" (1984:260). The notched triangles were a product of a different interaction through a different area at a different time period than that which initially stimulated the development of the Cahokia Mississippian tradition.

Ramey Incised pottery, typical of Cahokia in the Stirling and Moorehead phases, turns up as "trade" pottery or in imitated form from South Dakota to the Wabash and northward into Wisconsin, Minnesota, and Michigan at sites that are either Late Woodland or Mississippian only in the older generic sense of "Upper Mississippi" and "Plains Mississippi." This distribution helps to circumscribe the area of Cahokia interaction in which this pottery played a role (fig. 1.4). This should not exclude the probability of other kinds or areas of interaction in which other Cahokia material goods could have played a role, such as marine shell beads or gorgets processed at Cahokia and exchanged southward into Caddo country (Griffin cited in Davis, Wyckoff, and Holmes 1971: 54). Cahokia was a cultural pump that seems to have mediated various kinds of interareal contacts and exchanges in ways at which we can only guess.

The spherical jar form common to Monks Mound Red as a type, one of several forms, seems to be a late local expression of the so-called mesoamerican *tecomate* form with a history extending several thousand years into the past in nuclear America (Ford 1969:92–95). This does not imply mesoamerican derivation of the pottery type, since the pottery form is an imitation of a gourd bowl and the cultivation of gourds in the United States long predated the appearance of the tecomate-form bowl. The use of limestone temper associated at Cahokia with Monks Mound Red is part of a ceramic tradition rooted in the pre-Mississippian horizons of the Ozark Highland and spilling over into the American Bottom south of Cahokia. The red-filmed surface finish is presumed to have a southern origin as it has a considerably deeper history in that area (Phillips, Ford, and Griffin 1951:104–5). In Monks Mound Red, then, there are a number of different ceramic modes with southern affiliations of various time depths that combine in the Cahokia area in a distinctive manner and are diffused broadly into a vast area where the modes appear quite exotic.

The concern of archaeologists for pottery types such as Monks Mound Red, Powell Plain, or Ramey Incised should not be confused with a trait list attitude toward prehistory. The special nature of this pottery and the pattern of its occurrence outside Cahokia suggest that its diffusion was an incidental event in some form of intertribal activity. The historic example of the Pawnee Calumet Ceremony (called the Hako by Alice C. Fletcher) shows one way in which pottery vessels might be diffused over great distances. Food and jars or bowls for carrying ritual water and for use as mirrors (when water-filled) were carried between villages or tribes and left behind (Fletcher and Murie 1904:213, 259–60).

The smooth polished surface of the Ramey-Powell series, the sharp shoulder, and the scroll motifs so characteristic of Ramey Incised were not part of the early Mississippian tradition in the Southeast in the particular combination we know at Cahokia. Ramey Incised and Powell Plain, as types involving unique combinations of ceramic modes, were distinctive products of the Cahokia area. Ramey Incised in particular can be looked upon as reflecting in its origin a set of interareal contacts not shared by the peoples to the south and southeast of Cahokia who were participating in the elaboration of the Mississippian tradition. In this sense the Cahokia Mississippian tradition was a single eddy in the vortex of Mississippian development just as Mississippian itself was a single eddy in the vortex of development of Pan-Southern Ranked Society.

Cultural Processes at Cahokia

To account for Cahokia one must explain the rise of Cahokia from a barely occupied location to the largest population center with probably the most complex social organization and most expansive political influence ever seen in the United States, and then the return of the same location after several centuries to essentially the insignificance from which it had arisen. Considering how long Cahokia has been a subject for investigation, there is remarkably little in the literature that attempts to explain why Cahokia came to be and why it ceased to be. Many investigators in their thinking emphasize the strategic location of Cahokia with respect to resource areas and river transportation routes and the probable importance of a horticultural base made more efficient by hoe cultivation and northern-adapted corn varieties, combined probably with climatic amelioration (e.g., Fowler 1974). Many consider also the probability of some strategic trade position for Cahokia (e.g., Porter 1969:160–62; Porter 1974:176).

With the power that must have been wielded by the central leadership of Cahokia, a situation may have evolved in which that leadership assured the safety of anyone passing through the Cahokia area for exchange or other peaceful purposes. Exactly such a situation obtained when Col. Robert Dickson of the British Army, using the power and authority of his office, established a rule that Indians should not engage in war with each other within twenty-five leagues of Prairie du Chien, Wisconsin, providing a wide belt of territory that was strictly neutral ground (Shaw 1888:213).

One of the commonest materials from which peace pipes were made was the red pipestone known as catlinite, which was widely traded in the northern Mississippi Valley from about the time of the beginning of the Oneota Interaction. It is well known that in historic times the quarries of this pipe material were neutral ground, places of asylum and sanctuary, not only the better-known western Minnesota quarry but also the less well known northern Wisconsin quarry, and in the absence of strong central authority the neutrality of the grounds was assured by their sanctity (Beaubien 1957:3; De La Ronde 1876:348–49). At Cahokia the sanctity of holy places may have ensured safety for traders rendezvousing in the shadow of Monks Mound.

From archaeological evidence we assume that the chert trade between Cahokia and quarries in Union County, Illinois, and others near St. Charles, Missouri, was voluminous. Many basic substances—salt, venison, hides, fibers, lodge poles, pottery, limestone, firewood—were also undoubtedly heavily exchanged. There is evidence both direct and inferential for exchange, and it is hard to imagine Cahokia existing without it, but the greater the distance from Cahokia the less likely it is that exchange served only domestic needs or that it served only an economic function. Exchange relations between Cahokia and such far-flung locales as western Missouri and adjacent Kansas, western Iowa, southern Minnesota, southern Wisconsin, eastern Illinois, and adjacent Indiana may have been only partly economic and more importantly ritual as part of a system of exchange to foster peaceful intertribal relations beyond the limit of easily enforceable Cahokia authority. To the extent that this was the case, one cannot say that a particular Cahokia presence outside of the American Bottom represented an outpost to control access to this or that commodity.

When the historic period opened in the Mississippi and Missouri valleys, one of the most important mechanisms for maintaining peaceful intertribal relationships was the Calumet Ceremony. The mechanism was not fear of the absolute authority of a divine leader or the police power of a state but mutual recognition of the value of peace and mutual acceptance of the mystery and sanctity of the calumet. Blakeslee has emphasized the basically noneconomic aspect of calumet ceremonialism by pointing to the redundancy of exchange in connection with calumet ceremonialism. One striking feature of the trade was the redundancy in the goods exchanged:

> People traded for items of the sort that they could readily acquire for themselves. Products of the hunt, such as meat and hides, were regularly exchanged for other meat and hides. Another important feature of the trade system is its reticular structure. Instead of having one or two major trading centers, the trade network was composed of a multitude of approximately equivalent trade centers scattered across the plains. These included the villages of the horticulturalists and rendezvous of the nomads (1975: abstract).

Blakeslee (1975, 1981) dates the beginning of a Plains Interband Trading System, within which calumet ceremonialism as historically known sooner or later came to function, to the onset of the Pacific climatic episode after A.D. 1200 apparent in the decreasing reliability of rainfall for maize agriculture. The Calumet Ceremony as classically described (e.g., Fletcher and Murie 1904) did not necessarily begin at that time, but there is evidence of a complex history for calumets and for aspects of the Calumet Ceremony with roots extending back possibly even into the mortuary ceremonialism of the Middle Woodland Period (Hall 1976, 1977, 1982, 1983a, 1983c, 1984b; Hall 1985b:187–88; Hall 1987).

> The major features of the trade system, its location on the plains, the importance of food, the redundancy in goods

exchanged, and the reticular structure of the system, are understandable if the trade system is viewed as an adaptation to the localized food shortages which periodically occurred on the plains. . . . [E]xchanges of food during times of plenty maintained the acceptability of food as an item of exchange so that it could be obtained when a shortage occurred. Items available for trade in exchange for food were primarily goods available to all plains societies through their own efforts. Redundant exchanges maintained the acceptability of receiving goods of this sort when hungry people came to trade for food, and redundant exchanges during times of plenty maintained the social ties necessary for the functioning of the system. The reticular rather than centralized structure can also be seen as an adaptation to the droughts. A local band or village affected by a localized drought could fission into smaller groups and visit several trade centers. Furthermore, a single central place would eventually be affected by drought itself, making it dysfunctional (Blakeslee 1975: abstract).

One cannot understand Cahokia without understanding the implications of its geographical setting. It is well favored for its latitude with a frost-free growing season of about 190 days, but it is uniquely disfavored among Mississippian locations with unpredictable summer rainfall. The extension of the Prairie Peninsula into Illinois, the Prairie State, is a consequence partly of high evaporation rates and summer rainfall that fluctuate greatly with variations in the velocity of westerly winds across the Great Plains, the combination contributing to a pattern of recurrent moisture stress. Shifts from weak to strong westerly winds can result in a drop of expected summer rainfall for the greater Cahokia area somewhere between twenty-five and fifty percent (Bryson and Baerreis cited in Henning 1968: fig. 1.5; Bryson, Baerreis, and Wendland 1970: 64).

The Mississippi River floodplain location of Cahokia provided an enormous expanse of easily cultivated bottomland with associated lakes in abandoned river channels. The adjacent bluffs with their loess soils provided vast areas amenable to hoe cultivation, more susceptible to drought than the alluvium of the floodplain but more protected from water damage in wet years and in years of severe flooding. The Cahokia area lies just south of the junction of the Missouri, Mississippi, and Illinois rivers. The benefits that the American Bottom with a long mean annual frost-free growing season may have for dry farming must be matched against the liabilities of its susceptibility to submergence in the spring, delays in planting, or to the washing out of entire seedings.

William W. Chmurny (1973) has surveyed the practices of a group of farmers who had both successful and unsuccessful farming careers in the 1930s or earlier in the Cahokia area. He was able to distinguish patterns for success and failure that have relevance for prehistory. The unsuccessful farmers attempted to gamble upon their ability to predict the pattern of moisture stress for the year, investing their limited resources in plantings on well-drained soils or well-watered soils within the limits of their particular farm. The intention was to maximize their yields by planting only on those soils they expected to be productive in any given year.

The successful farmers divided their risks between well-drained and well-watered locations on their particular farm and also planted in other parts of the bottom or upland to which they had access through family relations. The farmers who gambled on maximum profits frequently lost their gamble. The farmers who divided their risks never became rich in a single season but survived to become well off in the long run. Chmurny sees a direct relevance to factors for the success of twentieth-century farmers in the Cahokia area and for the success of Mississippian cultivators in the same location in prehistory:

> In a effort to overcome the highly variable and unpredictable, but highly localized hydrology, Mississippian communities and homesteads were dispersed into other parts of the Bottom and adjacent uplands to reduce the risk of crop failure by bringing many different soil types and climatic localities under cultivation. In order to effectively support a large population, this tactic must include some formalized means of redistribution of gains and losses. Social controls and leadership are necessary to levy the surplus in the more successful areas and ration it out to those communities which would necessarily have less productive harvest. In contrast, extended kinship ties were sufficient to insure success for the much smaller social units of American farmers by providing access to scattered farm plots and the principle for the distribution of the economic proceeds among the members of the ramage. The Mississippian system may have originated in this fashion, with formal redistribution replacing kinship as the functioning principle as population increased. . . . Once established on this basis, redistribution can be expanded and social control enhanced by exchanges of exotic goods among geological and/or ecological zones (1973: 253–54).

If there was beauty in an equation it is here in the isomorphism of Mississippian and modern Cahokia area farming strategies for buffering the vagaries of nature. Cahokians did not have the technology to counter directly the moisture stress resulting from unpredictable summer rainfall or waterlogging resulting from seasonal flooding. They could have met the problem indirectly by organizing a social system that permitted them to take advantage of the abundant natural benefits of their location while minimizing risks to the individual through collective risk taking. One is reminded of the conspicuous success of highly cooperative religious groups like the Mormons and Hutterites in adapting to arid and semiarid parts of North America through collective activity.

The rise of Cahokia to power correlates with the Neo-Atlantic climatic episode between A.D. 900 and 1200, during which a global warming trend was correlated with an influx of moist tropical air bringing sufficient summer rainfall into the Plains to permit the expansion of farming westward into the Plains beyond the limits of some earlier and later centuries. The Cahokia adaptation was apparently one that could successfully balance the advantages of possibly longer growing season and increased summer rainfall in the Cahokia area against the increased danger of flooding. By A.D. 1200 the pattern of the Pacific climatic episode of A.D. 1200–1550 was established. Stronger winds of Pacific origin descending dry from the Rockies and blowing eastward across the Plains are believed to have brought more frequent swings toward drought conditions in their wake (Baerreis and Bryson 1965, 1968).

The descent of Cahokia from climax appears to have proceeded rapidly through the Sand Prairie phase. This correlates with several events. For one thing, more frequent extremes of moisture stress of the Pacific climatic episode may have been greater than the Cahokia system could accommodate through organization alone, although Chmurny thinks not. The important point is that agricultural success as well as crop failure could have had equally distastrous results for the Cahokia system: "A self-sufficient Cahokia not only could have brought ruin to the specialized outlying communities but destroyed the economic basis (redistribution) of the society" (Chmurny 1973:138).

The Mississippian adaptation at Cahokia is one that presumably involved not only an improved agricultural technology but also, more importantly, organizational solutions to subsistence problems. The fall of Cahokia is possibly due in part to the success of a newer adaptive strategy in the Midwest involving an improved technology requiring less elaborate social overhead to sustain it. The Mississippian population did not disappear in the greater Cahokia area during the period of the Sand Prairie phase as it was doing at Cahokia; there was actually a population increase in such areas as the Silver Creek valley paralleling the American Bottom several miles to the east (Pauketat and Koldehoff 1983).

The decline of Cahokia after calendar A.D. 1300 is coeval with the maximum expansion of Oneota peoples and the intensification of the Oneota Interaction through the same area in which for centuries Cahokia influences had been dominant (figs. 1.4–1.5). The decline of the Cahokia center also correlated with the appearance or increasing archaeological visibility of eight-rowed Northern Flint corn and beans through the northern Mississippi

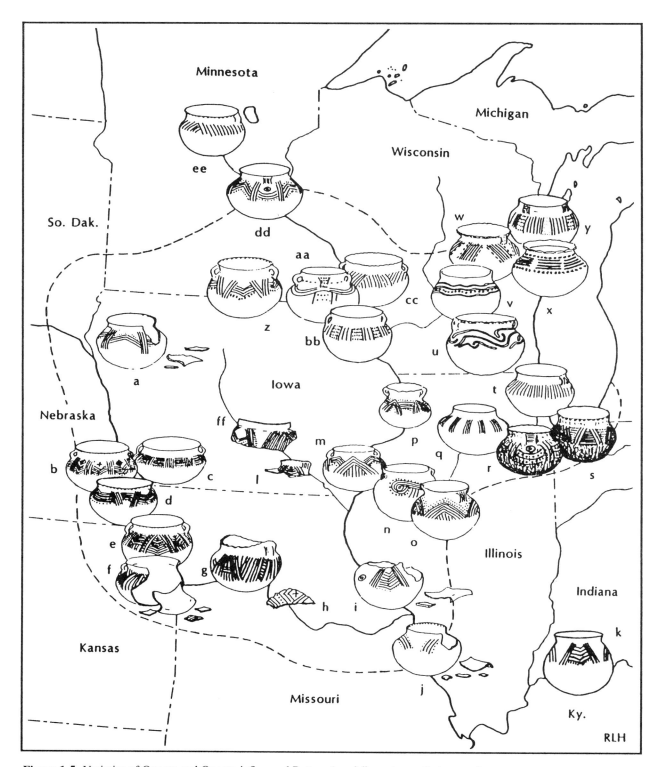

Figure 1.5. Varieties of Oneota and Oneota-influenced Pottery (*see full caption on facing page*)

Valley (see table 1.1; Cutler and Blake 1969:134–35; Cutler and Blake 1973 passim; Munson 1973:111, 119, 130). Not only do beans complement corn by providing amino acids in which corn is deficient and harbor nitrogen-fixing bacteria important for maintaining soil fertility, but beans are a rich protein food that can be stored for deferred use and can substitute for animal protein.

Northern Flint is a corn whose seed is resistant to rotting during wet springs, a corn adapted to the lengths of day of any latitude at which corn was historically grown, and to frost-free growing seasons as short as those of Canada. Equally important, Northern Flint is a corn that is also drought-resistant and capable of producing a crop under conditions of severe moisture stress. Following Cutler and Blake (1969:134), Chmurny (1973:134) suggested that Cahokia remained very conservative in the corn varieties it cultivated and possibly conservative also in not taking full advantage of beans as a cultigen and as a staple, whereas its neighbors were beginning to cultivate beans and the better-adapted corns. Wild beans do show up commonly at American Bottom sites, but domesticated beans have not been reported for sites in the FAI-270 Project area excavated by FAI-270 crews.

The oldest corn in the central Mississippi Valley is found in twelve- and fourteen-rowed varieties. As eight-rowed Northern Flint spread into the area and became dominant by Late Mississippi times, the mean row number of corn cobs found archaeologically begins to diminish (Blake and Dean 1963:92; Cutler 1958:4; Cutler and Blake 1973:6). The effect of the intrusion of Northern

Flints on row number is shown in table 1.1. The eight-rowed varieties of corn, which were the agricultural base of the economies of all farming tribes in the Midwest during the late precontact and historic periods, become common in the Cahokia area only as the Cahokia Mississippian tradition rapidly descended from climax during the period of the Sand Prairie phase. Sissel Johannessen indicates that at the Julien site south of Cahokia "some maize cupules from the Sand Prairie phase features only exhibited the wide, shallow, crescent shape characteristic of the eight-row Northern Flint race of maize" (1984b: 264).

Also correlated with the Oneota expansion may be the increasing availability of bison. This is hard to evaluate. Just as Waldo R. Wedel (1959:667–68) had noted that bison remains increased in frequency over other animal remains between Woodland and later farming cultures in the Plains, so also have others more recently noted the increasing proportion of bison remains over those of other fauna within collections from Mill Creek sites in northwestern Iowa (Bryson, Baerreis, and Wendland 1970:66; Frankforter 1969). It is far from certain whether this is because of increases in the buffalo populations, shifts in the locations of buffalo ranges, or changing hunting patterns. Tom D. Dillehay (1974) has summarized the literature to show that for the southern Plains there were "temporal and spatial contours for long-term changes in bison populations" with periods of absence from about 6000 or 5000 b.c. until 2500 b.c. and a.d. 500 to a.d. 1200–1300. These changes are hard to relate directly to the Prairie Peninsula because of the alternation of rainfall

---

Figure 1.5. Varieties of Oneota and Oneota-influenced Pottery (vessel size variable): (a) Dixon site, Iowa, after Henning (1961: pl. 4g); (b) Leary site, Nebraska, based on shoulder decoration illustrated by Hill and Wedel (1936: fig. 4a); (c) Leary site, after Hill and Wedel (1936: pl. III-1); (d) Leary site, after Hill and Wedel (1936: pl. III-2); (e) Fanning Trailed from the Fanning site, Kansas, after W. Wedel (1959: pl. 9b); (f) Fanning Trailed vessel from the Fanning site, after W. Wedel (1959: fig. 19a); (g) Utz site, Missouri. after Chapman and Chapman (1964: 83); (h) Guthrey site, Missouri, after Henning (1970: fig. 8d); (i) Pere Marquette State Park, Illinois, based on a sherd in the University of Michigan Museum of Anthropology; (j) Oneota vessel from the Cahokia site, Illinois, after O'Brien (1972a: fig. 75e); (k) Oneota-influenced vessel of the Caborn-Welborn phase of southwestern Indian, after Green and Munson (1978: fig. 11.2-a); (l) Kingston site, Iowa, after Straffin (1971: pl. 17a); (m) Kingston site, after Straffin (1971: pl. 14); (n) Oneota-like late Spoon River Mississippian vessel from the Crable site, Illinois, based on a rimsherd in the Department of Anthropology, University of Illinois at Chicago; (o) Oneota-like late Spoon River Mississippian vessel from the Crable site, based on a rimsherd in the Department of Anthropology, University of Illinois at Chicago; (p) Oneota funerary vessel from a cemetery in Jo Daviess County, Illinois, after Bennett (1945: pl. 21); (q) vessel of the grit-tempered type Langford Trailed from the Heally complex at the Zimmerman site, Illinois, after Brown (1961: fig. 9a);

(r) funerary vessel of the shell-tempered type Fisher Trailed at the Fisher site, Illinois, after J. W. Griffin (1946: pl. I-21); (s) vessel of the shell-tempered type Fifield Trailed from the Griesmer site, Indiana, after Faulkner (1972: pl. XIIa); (t) Huber Trailed from the Huber site near Blue Island, Illinois, after Griffin (1943: pl. CXL-1; cf. Faulkner 1972: fig. 9); (u) Carcajou Curvilinear from the Carcajou site, Wisconsin, after Hall (1962: pl. 23c); (v) Grand River Trailed from a mound in Green Lake County, Wisconsin, after Hall (1962: pl. 70e); (w) Lake Winnebago Trailed from the Karow cemetery, Wisconsin, after McKern (1945: pl. 62, no. 2); (x) Oneota vessel of the type Lake Winnebago Trailed from the Karow cemetery, after McKern (1945: pl. 62, no. 1) and Hall (1962: pl. 74b); (y) Allamakee Trailed from the Point Sable site, Wisconsin, after Hall (1962: pl. 77a); (z) Oneota vessel of the Blue Earth type from Minnesota, after Johnson (1969:24; cf. Wilford 1945b: fig. 3b); (aa) Allamakee Trailed from the O'Regan site, Iowa, after M. Wedel (1959: fig. 33f; cf. Johnson 1969:24); (bb) Allamakee Trailed from the Hogback site, Iowa, after M. Wedel (1959: fig. 30b; cf. figs. 27a and 28a); (cc) Midway site, Wisconsin, after Hall (1962: pl. 77d); (dd) Lee Mill Cave, Minnesota, after Johnson and Taylor (1956: pl. C); (ee) Oneota vessel from a mound in Mille Lacs-Kathio State Park, Minnesota, after Johnson (1969:24); (ff) Red Rock Reservoir, Iowa, after Osborn (1982: fig. 6). The dashed line indicates the approximate area of the Oneota Interaction.

patterns between parts of the central and southern Plains (Bryson, Baerreis, and Wendland 1970:67–68).

Bison do not appear to have been at all important east of the Mississippi in Illinois until very late, possibly until sometime just before the period of European contact (Brown 1961:68–69; Griffin and Wray 1946; Wray 1952: 162). Bison bone has not been found in archaeological contexts within the American Bottom and occurrences elsewhere in prehistoric Mississippian contexts in Illinois are almost exclusively limited to easily traded artifacts, such as bison rib bracelets and bison scapula hoes (Harn 1975b:425). The increasing availability of bison west of the Mississippi would in time have been a force for fission of the Cahokia center. If Cahokians themselves were not actually drawn away from their center, the circumscribing effect of surrounding populations would have been weakened as these peoples were attracted elsewhere.

Actually, any combination of increased availability or use of beans, bison, or better-adapted corn could easily have spelled disaster for the Mississippian adaptation in Illinois. Participation in the Cahokia sphere of relations would have had ever decreasing advantages through the period of the Moorehead and Sand Prairie phases. The so-called Upper Mississippi pattern of many historic northern Mississippi Valley tribes came to replace the Middle Mississippi pattern of Cahokia and that of the Spoon River tradition in the central Illinois Valley. Crable, the last Spoon River town of the tradition, exhibited evidence in its ceramic decoration of an Oneota presence around calendar A.D. 1350–1400 contemporaneously with the appearance of Oneota site intrusions in the same county, and then Spoon River Mississippian disappears from the archaeological record (Lawrence A. Conrad, Alan D. Harn, Duane Esarey, and Robert L. Hall, unpublished field data). Whether the Cahokia and Spoon River Mississippian peoples participated in the shift toward a more balanced hunting and horticultural adaptation, or succumbed to others who did, cannot be said with present evidence.

I attribute the decline of Cahokia, in sum, to the operation of what I call the Shmoo Effect, a frontier effect bringing about the devolution or breaking down of social organization in the face of abundance and diminished need for interdependence (Hall 1980:431–32; see also Fiedel 1987:255). The Shmoo Effect operates in reverse of the principle of circumscription that Robert L. Carneiro (1970) offers in explanation of the origin of the state. An example of a frontier effect selected from the literature of anthropology would be that provided by Elman R. Service for the Maori of New Zealand:

> The Maori originally came from the central region of Polynesia where chiefdoms were highly developed, but when they colonized the huge, open environment of New Zealand they subdivided and scattered. In so doing they reverted to a less centralized and less organized form of society, eventually coming to resemble tribal society more than their original chiefdom form. . . .
>
> [T]he Polynesians who settled New Zealand found a wide-open environment to expand into, so that frontier-like pioneering was possible and a leader of low hereditary position could nevertheless by charismatic force gain a following and raise his status by achievement in carving out a new domain. Thus the Maori of New Zealand have been described as more "democratic" than most of the other Polynesian chiefdoms (1962:147, 161).

A frontier, of course, can be opened by migration and discovery, sometimes assisted by force of arms, or by technological innovation that creates a new resource area or improves an old one. If this frontier model is correct, it makes the process of Mississippian decline in the Cahokia area essentially isomorphic with the process of Hopewellian decline in Illinois a thousand years earlier, as that decline has been interpreted by several investigators (Cleland 1966:95; Farnsworth 1973:29; Fowler 1973:51; Fowler 1974:33; Hall 1980).

Mississippians and Middle Woodland Indians utilized basically similar riverine habitats. The decline of the Hopewellian Interaction in Illinois seems to correlate with a decreasing advantage to preferred access to floodplain zones, which could be correlated with a new or increasing dependence upon corn as a staple food and/or the availability of the bow and arrow for hunting game animals. The latter of these options would now seem to be the better explanation in the absence of evidence of efficient maize utilization before the Emergent Mississippian period in Illinois (see Kelly, Ozuk et al. 1984:132, 154). With Hopewellians (presumably as with Mississippians) and historic Indians, exchange would have been linked intimately with status systems, with intertribal relations, and with the organization of society. "The [Hopewellian] interaction sphere organization provided a mechanism for the distribution and equalization of cyclical differences in resources" (Fowler 1973:50). "To insure that exchange networks remain open and available, some mechanism of preserving social contacts between groups would have great value" (Diener 1968, quoted in Fowler 1973:50).

The Hopewellian decline in Illinois may have been one effect of a new adaptation that obviated the special advantage of interdependence and lessened the importance of social mechanisms to maintain it while opening a broader frontier for human occupation. If this is a correct perspective on the close of the Middle Woodland and the beginning of Late Woodland, we might expect demographic expansion to have resulted in increasing competition for resources, ultimately in the return of favored river bottom locations to positions of central importance in the economy and the return of groups with preferred access to those bottoms to positions also of central importance. A cycle would have been completed, but the system would have stabilized at a new and higher level. I have no doubt that the process would have been repeated with a third culture climax at a still higher level had not the advent of European diseases forestalled this progression (see Hall 1980:446–47).

We can profitably view the elaboration of the formative stage of development in the Mississippi Valley from the perspective of Carneiro's "Reappraisal of the Roles of Technology and Organization in the Origin of Civilization." He rejects the view that "technological advance was the prime cause of early civilizations": "Beyond the invention of agriculture and of stone cutting-tools, no particular technical advance was essential to the origins of civilization. Instead, civilization was the climax of a series of *organizational solutions* to problems posed by a limited food supply, population pressure, and warfare, to name the most important" (1974:184, emphasis added).

The Illinois Hopewell and Cahokia Mississippian situations could have been basically organizational solutions to recurring environmental problems in the Prairie Peninsula. The falls from these climaxes appear to me to have been responses to the inability of Hopewellian and Mississippian systems to cope with the potential abundance created by certain technological advances and/or natural events. The far-flung networks of exchange of Hopewellians and Mississippians might similarly be looked upon in part as responses to the need for stabilizing intertribal relations, minimizing the threat of warfare, formalizing the etiquette and protocol of intertribal relations, assuring the friendship of allies in times of need, and validating or legitimating these relationships with ritual, religious sanctions, and gifts.

The rise of intensive maize agriculture undoubtedly also produced genuine economic as opposed to ceremonial and social needs, which were satisfied by trade between Mississippian centers. The trade in salt was one of these, serving a physiological need aggravated by increasing dependence upon maize. The trade in Mill Creek (Illinois) chert for hoes was probably another. Slash-and-burn cultivation can be conducted with only a digging stick and an ax to girdle the shading trees of the forest, but a field cannot be cultivated for many years before a sharp hoe is needed to keep down the weeds and woody plants that begin to invade the fields. When demographic pressure and increasing sedentism force one to plant the same field year after year because moving is not an option, hoes become necessary.

Chmurny (1973) and I agree with David Rindos and Sissel Johannessen (chap. 2) that the centralization of Cahokia society could have been in great part a social means of buffering the unpredictable character of maize agriculture in a part of the Prairie Peninsula through redistribution. Yet redistribution would have been only one function that a chiefdom might efficiently accomplish for the community benefit. A second and certainly equally important function would have been social control.

Kelly makes the point that Mississippian communities emerged in the Cahokia area within an "intense competitive atmosphere," that complex sociopolitical institutions arose under "competitive conditions," and that "societal hierarchies presumably emerged for purposes of maintaining internal order, combating external strife, and controlling the allocation of local resources" (1982:231). It is hard to imagine dense populations within a circumscribed (see Hall 1980:448) bottomland environment without, as Kelly phrases it, "social mechanisms to mitigate competition." The kind of elite social order by which Cahokia must have been governed is hard to imagine without the social pressures that must have led to it. Carneiro (1970) saw competition, population circumscription, and geographic circumscription as factors leading to the origin of the state, quite independent of considerations of redistribution. It would follow that with a release from the competition that prevailed in the American Bottom, the reason-for-being of the sanctity and absolute authority of the elite of Cahokia would also dissipate, and with it the distinctive pyramidal social order that must have existed.

The Mechanism of the Cahokia Interaction

If one plots the distribution of finds of Ramey Incised jars and of Oneota jars, one will quickly see that the distributions coincide almost exactly (figs. 1.4–1.5). The areas of the Cahokia Interaction and the following Oneota Interaction are one and the same! The coincidence takes on added significance when it is realized that some of the most distinctive decorative elements of early Oneota ceramic decoration rarely but occasionally appear on Ramey Incised pottery.

One motif acknowledged to be typical of Oneota is that of nested chevrons, commonly bracketed by multiple parallel lines and bordered by punctates. This combination is rare but does occur on Ramey Incised at Cahokia and outside of Cahokia (fig. 1.4x, 1.6i–k; see also Hall 1975b). It is sufficiently rare that one may question whether this particular combination on Ramey Incised actually could have influenced the development of the Oneota nested chevron style. It is more logical to think that before

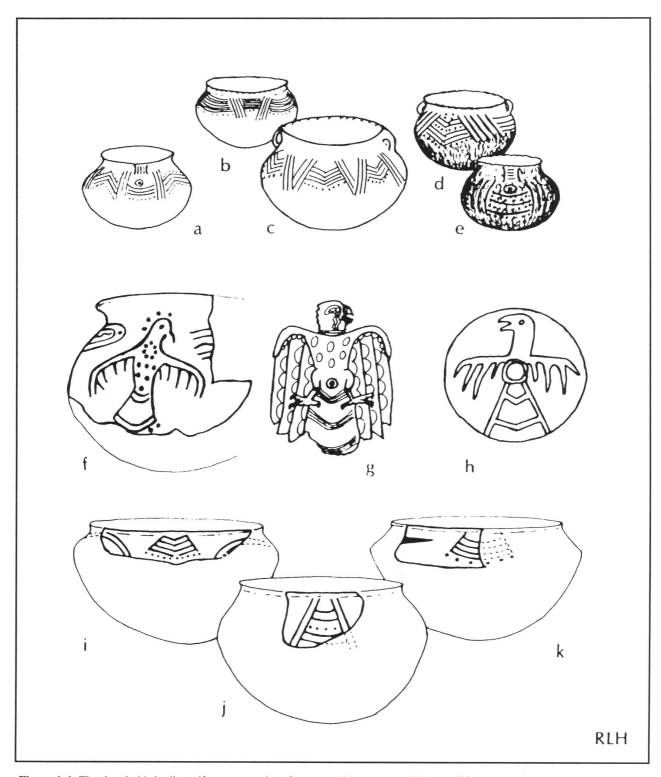

Figure 1.6. The thunderbird tail motif as expressed on Oneota tradition pottery, Fisher tradition pottery, and Mississippian pottery (*see full caption on facing page*)

Ramey Incised disappeared at Cahokia it was itself being influenced in the direction of the contemporaneously developing Oneota ceramics. Possibly Ramey Incised and Oneota were both being influenced from a third source not yet recognized. If the latter, what might that third source have been?

In 1972 Adolph W. Link discovered an Oneota jar with a trailed, only somewhat stylized bird design during salvage excavations at the Bryan site near Red Wing, Minnesota (1982: fig. 1). Bryan is a site grouped with several others in a Silvernale phase associated with a flat-topped pyramidal mound and a ceramic complex that includes both everted rimmed jars of Oneota form and jars of the rolled-rim type characteristic of Ramey Incised and its companion type Powell Plain at Cahokia (Anfinson 1979:183–90; Gibbon 1973, 1983). The higher or straight-rimmed jars relate to the Blue Earth phase of Oneota.

A trailed bird motif is almost unique on northern Mississippi Valley ceramics after Middle Woodland times, but its importance lies not in its rarity but in the relationship of the bird to both Mississippian and Oneota symbolism. The tail of the bird, apparently a thunderbird of falcon form, is clearly the prototype for the punctate bordered, nested chevron motif of Oneota that appears also on some Ramey Incised pottery. I have noted elsewhere that the distinctive chevron motif of much Oneota pottery appears to be derived from a stylization of the tail of a thunderbird and that the occurrence of the thunderbird on the Bryan site jar was logically an unabbreviated expression of the same symbolism (Hall 1981).

Accepting this interpretation of the nature of the chevron design, it becomes easy to explain the nucleated circle that sometimes appears over the chevron. This element patently corresponds to the nucleated circle in the "umbilical" region of a Missisippian sheet copper falcon found near Peoria, Illinois (fig. 1.6g) or the circular element in the "heart" region of the Bryan site bird (fig. 1.6f). Not being mammals, birds do not, of course, have an actual umbilicus.

The V-shaped, so-called weeping eye element found occasionally on Ramey Incised pottery is thought to represent the pattern of feather coloration around the eye of a falcon, and the falcon was widely associated with warrior status in the eastern United States. The thunderbird was a mythical creature but took as its models such predatory, diurnal, carnivorous birds as the hawk, falcon, and eagle. Representations of warriors in falcon costume are a well-known item of Mississippian symbolism. The eagle was commonly associated with the sun or an empyrean power. The tail of a falcon or thunderbird could have been used simply as a symbol representing the whole bird, much as the falconid eye pattern represented the whole falcon or warrior. In figurative expression this would be called a *synecdoche* (Hall 1977), an instance of a part standing for the whole. Or the chevron motif may have been meant to stand only for the tail itself because of some special association of the tail.

The complete design on Adolph Link's remarkable vessel was a combination of thunderbirds alternated with comet-shaped objects that Link (personal communication, 1985) interprets as lightning bolts flashing from the thunderbirds' eyes. This interpretation has to be absolutely correct, because a Ramey Incised motif from Cahokia contains very much this same combination—the tail of a thunderbird bordered by circular punctates, alternating with the comet-shaped or forked eye pattern of the falcon (Griffin 1960b: pl. II-h). The Ramey design is simply the abstracted version of what appears in a more natural form on the Bryan site jar.

The round-stemmed calumet used in the Calumet Ceremony was typically hung with a fan of eagle feathers, specifically tail feathers. The calumet was a highly decorated, symbolic arrow with a sky association (the eagle feathers representing sun rays), often but not always combined with a pipe bowl to make a calumet-pipe (Hall 1977, 1983a). The Calumet Ceremony is said to have originated with the Pawnee, a Caddoan tribe of the central Plains, and to have spread to other tribes.

Fans of turkey feathers were used by the Creek and Yuchi Indians of the Southeast, among whom such fans were a sign of leadership (Swanton 1946:456). Fans specifically made of turkey tail feathers were used by the Yuchi (Speck 1909:52, cited in Swanton 1946:456). Fans of eagle wings were common in the Plains, and bird wing fans were used by Mississippians of Spoon River tradition in Illinois, where their presence is recognized as a trait shared with the Plains (Harn 1975b:425). The well-known Sauk leader Black Hawk was painted by the artist George Catlin holding in his hand a fan of hawk tail

Figure 1.6. The thunderbird tail motif as expressed on Oneota tradition pottery (a-c), Fisher tradition pottery (d-e), and Mississippian pottery of the type Ramey Incised (i-k), and the thunderbird and/or falcon motifs as expressed on an Oneota jar (f), a repousse copper plaque (g), and an earspool (h): (a) from Lee Mill Cave, Minnesota, artist's reconstruction after Johnson and Taylor (1956: pl. C); (b) from the Leary site, after Hill and Wedel (1936: pl. III-2); (c) from Minnesota after Johnson (1969:24); (d-e) from the Fisher site, Illinois, after J. W. Griffin (1946: pl. I, vessels 26 and 21); (f) from the Bryan site, Minnesota, after Link (1982: fig. 1); (g) from Peoria, Illinois, after Howard (1968: fig. 8d); (h) from the Spiro site, Oklahoma, after Hamilton (1952: pl. 81); (i) from the Broken Kettle site, Iowa, after Ives (1962: 17a); (j-k) from the Cahokia site, Illinois, after sketches in the possession of the author.

feathers. "When I painted this chief, he was dressed in a plain suit of buckskin, with strings of wampum in his ears and on his neck, and held in his hand, his medicine-bag, which was the skin of a black hawk, from which he had taken his name, and the tail of which made him a fan, which he was almost constantly using" (Catlin 1973, 2: pl. 283 and p. 211).

Among the Winnebago the chieftainship of the tribe was hereditary within the Thunderbird Clan of a sky moiety, known as Those Who Are Above. War and peace functions (i.e., external tribal relations) were centered within this sky moiety, which also included the Buffalo and the Hawk or Warrior Clan (Radin 1970:135–38, 272). The Thunderbird Clan was associated with peace as well as with war because the Winnebago saw the thunderbird generally as a *deity granting long life* (Radin 1970:138, emphasis added).

It would appear that the tail fan of the thunderbird, as well as the whole thunderbird, was capable of carrying the symbolism of leadership. The thunderbird was also associated with the gift of long life, which was one of the stated purposes of the Calumet Ceremony and one of the reasons the person honored was commonly a small child, usually the son or daughter of the elder receiving the calumet from a neighboring tribe.

In the Pawnee Calumet Ceremony the child was made the recipient of a gesture with the calumets hung with eagle tail feather fans. The child had previously had an arch painted on his/her forehead representing the dome of the sky and abode of Tira'wa atius, "the giver of life and power to all things" (Fletcher and Murie 1904:233). From the center of this arch a vertical line was drawn down the center of the forehead and along the ridge of the nose. This line represents the breath of Tira'wa atius. "It descends from the zenith, passing down the nose to the heart, *giving life to the child*" (Fletcher and Murie 1904: 233, emphasis added).

The decorative motifs on Ramey Incised jars were commonly spiral forms, sometimes combined in series, apparently representing the whorl of a large marine univalve and, by metonymic association, water. Water, in turn, was associated with life and continuity of life. Omaha *ni*, for instance, meant both "water" and "to exist, live." The symbolism of the Ramey Incised jars was thus tied closely to water and by extension to *continuity of life* (Hall 1973:2), much as the symbolism on Oneota jars was tied to the thunderbird, and the thunderbird in its turn tied to the gift of life. One of the symbolic objects used by the Pawnee in their Four-Pole Ceremony was a wooden bowl filled with water to represent the primordial sea. "In the water was a shell to represent running water and the continuity of life" (Weltfish 1977:261).

The basic function of the Calumet Ceremony was to create fictions of kinship uniting otherwise unrelated individuals in other villages, bands, or tribes. It was an adoption ceremony. This was a function that was important for intergroup stability, which in turn permitted intergroup exchange. The stated purpose, however, was to honor a beloved child. In the following description of a part of the Pawnee Calumet Ceremony it can be seen how this or a similar ceremony could have provided a mechanism for the movement of pottery vessels from one village to another:

> On the preceding evening, before the Children [recipient group] had gathered within the lodge, the Ku'rahus had sent a young man to fill a vessel from a running stream. . . . The child is now told to look into the bowl of water and behold its face. The running water symbolizes the passing on of generations, one following another. The little child looks on the water and sees its own likeness, as it will see that likeness in its children and children's children. The face of Tira'wa atius is there also, giving promise that the life of the child shall go on, as the waters flow over the land. . . .
>
> [A] bundle, containing the bowl which held the water into which the child looked and other things that have been used, and all the mats on which the people have been sitting, are brought to the Son and presented to him. . . . The Son, to whom the Hako [calumet] has been presented . . . must keep for himself the sacred objects of the ceremony. They have brought to him the promise of long life and children, and have established peace and security through a tie as that of kinship (Fletcher and Murie 1904: 213, 241, 259–60).

The fact that the areas of the Cahokia Interaction and the subsequent Oneota Interaction were almost coextensive provokes many questions, among them that of the mechanism of the interactions. The Oneota Interaction was late enough to consider the Calumet Ceremony or some prototype or variant as the means by which Oneota peoples extended their influence over the area they did. Certainly, in historic times the Chiwere Sioux and their neighbors were still using the Calumet Ceremony in consolidating group and individual friendships and alliances. But what of the Cahokia Interaction? What clues are there to the ceremonialism of that period, aside from the parallels in the symbolism of the decorative motifs on Ramey Incised and Oneota trailed jars? Such symbolism suggests themes perhaps to be found in the mechanism, but not the way in which the themes were incorporated.

A clue that jumps from the literature is the distribution and temporal placement of the so-called Long Nose God masquettes, examples of which have been found in copper and marine shell through the area of the Cahokia

Interaction (fig. 1.7) as well as through the area of distribution of the Southeastern Ceremonial Complex, all in Early Mississippi times (Williams and Goggin 1956). Curiously, no examples of these small masquettes have been found at Cahokia itself, although they have been found as close as the great mound of the St. Louis group west of Cahokia (Williams and Goggin 1956: fig. 2) and at the Booker T. Washington (Greene) site eight miles south of Cahokia near the former Pittsburgh Lake (Perino 1959:131–32; Perino 1966). The St. Louis and Aztalan examples are in copper; others found in the northern Mississippi Valley are in shell. Although often referred to as masquettes, these Long Nose God representations are known to have been used by males as earrings from specimens shown on shell engravings and on a carved stone pipe at Spiro, Oklahoma (Hamilton 1952: cover and pl. 10; Phillips and Brown 1975, 1: fig. 247; 2: pl. 17), and from the finding of the small shell masks in place at the ears of a male in a prehistoric burial at the Booker T. Washington site (Perino 1959:132).

I have elsewhere (Hall 1983b, 1984a) shown the relationship of the Long Nose God masquettes/earrings to the Winnebago and Ioway mythological hero or demigod best known as Red Horn or He Who Wears Human Heads as Earrings (Radin 1948; Skinner 1925:456–58). This correspondence conveniently ties a pre-Oneota symbol into the mythology of two tribes believed at the time of historical contact to have been carriers of the Oneota archaeological culture. It provides valuable continuity. The absence of copper or shell masquettes at Cahokia is a puzzle, but may be qualified by information produced by Robert J. Salzer of Beloit College. Salzer has found a human form portrayed in a southern Wisconsin rock painting (1987: figs. 20, 21, 23) with what appears to me to be Long Nose God masquetttes tatooed on his chest in the area of each nipple. One of Red Horn's sons had little human heads on each breast; the other had human head earrings like his father.

The Calumet Ceremony was principally an adoption rite to create fictions of blood relationship, useful in cementing intertribal relations, and adoption was conceived as rebirth. To the extent that the deeper roots of the Calumet Ceremony were in mourning ritual such rebirth amounted to the reincarnation of the person mourned. Red Horn died, but was returned to life by his sons. His bones were reincarnated.

In consideration of the above, it appears logical to consider that in Early Mississippi times Long Nose God masquettes and tatoos were used to identify participants in a ritual drama involving persons representing the character we know as Red Horn/He Who Wears Human Heads as Earrings and his sons, that this drama was part of an adoption ceremony used to provide a ceremonial relationship between the participants through a fiction of kinship, and that the ceremony was specifically used to establish friendly relations between otherwise unrelated groups. In other words, the proposed ceremony would have functioned almost exactly like the historic Calumet Ceremony, which, after all, had its roots in a drama of captivity, death, and rebirth with adoption as a metaphor of rebirth. In both ceremonies one also finds the theme of continuity of life, a theme represented in the symbolism of both Ramey Incised and Oneota pottery.

The principal difference of the ceremonies proposed as mechanisms of the Cahokia and Oneota interactions is that the former would presumably have been performed upon the initiative of the leader (Sun? Thunder Chief?) of the Cahokia chiefdom to establish formal relationships with regional leaders, and the latter was probably performed, as in historic times, upon the personal initiative of local leaders to relate themselves to other local leaders at a more egalitarian level, not within a regional hierachy.

Interpreting the Long Nose God masquette in the way presented above does not conflict in any important way with the possibility that these objects could have been associated somehow with traders (see Griffin 1967:190; Kelly 1982:210–12). The Calumet Ceremony was used extensively in historic times to establish trade relationships, as is well known. The Long Nose God ritual suggested above would undoubtedly also have tied into some exchange relationship as the very ceremony that may have legitimated that exchange. The possibility of any close relationship of the Mississippian Long Nose God to Yacatecuhtli, the long-nosed god of the Aztec *pochteca* or long-distance traders (see Porter 1969:139, 157–58) is much more remote. There were several long-nosed gods in Mesoamerica, related in complicated ways, as well as several long-nosed supernaturals in North America, related in equally complicated ways, one of them Hopewellian (Hall 1984a:34–41).

The Mexican god Xolotl can be related indirectly to the Mississippian Long Nose God complex in particular. In the *Codex Borgia* Xolotl is shown with a human hand painted over his lower face with his mouth occupying the palm area (see Caso 1958:20). This is the same pattern of face painting found on the falcon warrior represented in repousse copper on one of the Wulfing plates found at Malden, Missouri (Howard 1968: fig. 6; Watson 1950: fig. 3; see also Hall 1984c). This particular falcon warrior has in his hair a long-nosed god face. For purposes of understanding the workings of the Cahokia Interaction it is not necessary to unsort the intricate genealogies of the various long-nosed gods. Generically speaking, however, the distribution and suggested associations of Long

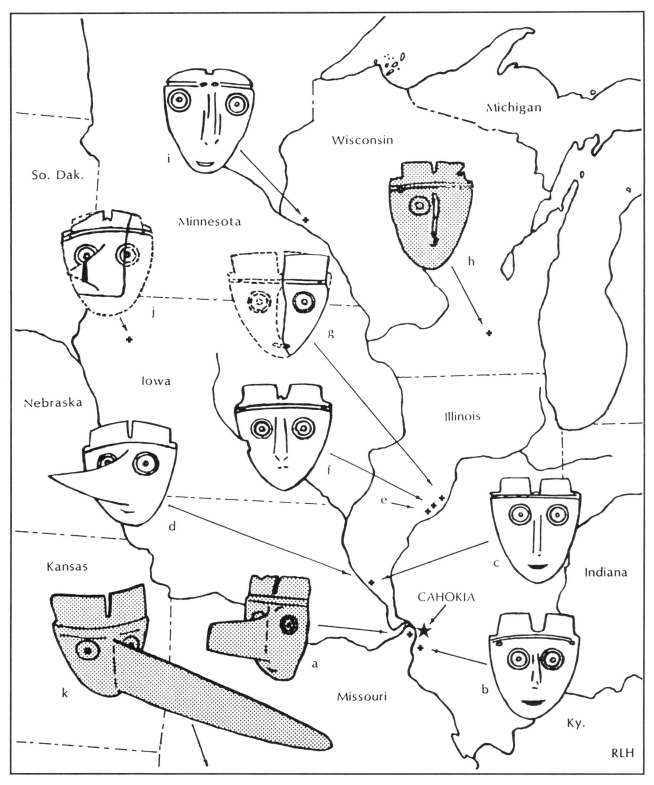

Figure 1.7. Long-nosed and Short-nosed God Masquette Earrings in Copper and Shell (*see full caption on facing page*)

Nose God masquettes do conform to a model proposed by Gibbon:

> Perhaps the "Southeastern Ceremonial Complex" insignia played the same role between Midwest and Upper Plains peoples and more prestigious trading partners in the Caddoan area as that Parsons (1971:236) assigns to the Olmec insignia during the Early and Middle Formative periods in the Valley of Mexico. . . .
>   The Early and Middle Formative periods in the Valley

of Mexico were marked by external influences and marginal but growing participation by some communities in exchange relationships with demographically and organizationally superior populations located in more humid, frost-free regions. Parsons (1971:236) noted that "In this manner, a few groups . . . acquired the material insignia of Olmec type and style as they formulated alliances with prestigious trading partners to the south and attempted to enhance their own standing in an area where such outside contacts were otherwise lacking" (1974:133, 131).

Summary

Formal research at Cahokia began with problems as obvious as that of demonstrating that the Cahokia mounds were in fact of human origin. Professional disagreement over the origin of the mounds led to the excavations at Cahokia by Moorehead and to the aerial photographic studies of the mounds arranged by Crook and then to the preservation of a part of the site by state purchase.

As excavations continued and dating methods improved, the prehistory represented in the Cahokia archaeological zone was found to be ever more complex, with episodes of occupation extending from around A.D. 600 or shortly thereafter through to the period of historic Indian and European occupation. The period of most extensive mound construction and use appears to have been from sometime after A.D. 900 until around 1300, during which time prehistoric Cahokia was the seat of the largest political chiefdom and probably the most complex socially ranked society in North America, a city-state in process of formation.

The origin of the Cahokia chiefdom has been attributed in varying degrees to evolution from roots in local cultures or to the influence of a foreign elite, with and without migration. The currently best-supported interpretation of Cahokia origins calls for Cahokia to have been one of a number of centers of regional cultural development based upon maize agriculture, each interacting in complex ways with the others to produce a hierarchically organized society in which problems of social control, population expansion, and agricultural production were solved within the structure of a Pan-Southern Ranked Society, one participating tradition of which is known as Mississippian.

Cahokia is seen as having had several changing faces, each reflecting an episode of interaction with other cultures. The first of those that can be called Mississippian saw interaction to the south and in particular to the lower alluvial Mississippi Valley. This was followed by the period of the Cahokia Interaction, which saw the development of the distinctive Cahokia Mississippian tradition and the spread of its influence through a broad area to the north and west of Cahokia. Following the period of the Cahokia Interaction, southern Mississippian influences reasserted themselves in the Cahokia area briefly until the collapse or devolution of Cahokia as a population center and center of political and cultural influence. This episode was partly contemporaneous with the developing Oneota Interaction, which succeeded the Cahokia Interaction within the same area and soon manifested itelf in the Cahokia area in late prehistoric times.

The decline of Cahokia is attributed to improved techno-environmental adaptations that reduced the advantages of large Mississippian population centers in major river bottoms and permitted smaller scattered populations to live in a greater variety of locations at a tribal level of organization. These new adaptations probably included the use of eight-row Northern Flint corn. Bison hunting may have contributed by attracting Illinois and eastern Missouri populations westward and reducing the population circumscription of the greater Cahokia area.

The mechanisms of the Cahokia and Oneota inter-

Figure 1.7. Long-nosed and Short-nosed God Masquette Earrings in Copper (a, h, k) and Shell (all others): (a) St. Louis mound center, after Williams and Goggin (1956: fig. 2; copper, long-nosed); (b) Booker T. Washington site, Illinois, after Perino (1966: fig. 2; 1 of 2 found; short-nosed); (c) Yokem site, Illinois, after Perino (1971c: fig. 73c; short-nosed); (d) Yokem site, Illinois, after Bareis and Gardner (1968: fig. 2a; 1 of 3 long-nosed); (e) Crable site, location of finds of two masquettes of shell (see Harn 1975a:6); (f) near the Emmons site, Illinois, after Griffin and Morse (1961: fig. 2; short-nosed); (g) Dickson Mound, Illinois, after Harn (1975a: fig. 1; removable long nose missing); (h) Aztalan site, Wisconsin, after Williams and Goggin (1956: fig. 13b; copper, 1 of 2 with noses lost); (i) Mero site near Diamond Bluff, Wisconsin, after Lawshe (1947:82; short-nosed); (j) Site 12CK1, Iowa, after Anderson (1980: fig. a; long-nosed); (k) Gahagan Mound, Louisiana, after Williams and Goggin (1956: fig. 12a; copper, long-nosed).

actions were probably based upon rituals featuring the creation of fictions of relationship between otherwise unrelated individuals. The model of the Calumet Ceremony is available for the mechanism of the Oneota Interaction. The historic Calumet Ceremony is related to prehistoric Oneota contexts by examination of the symbolism of Oneota pottery, which is seen to include the motif of the tail fan of the thunderbird and the symbolic referent of long life and life continuity. A related ritual is proposed for the Cahokia Interaction in which Long Nose God masquettes and the motifs on Ramey Incised pottery have survived as the principal material evidence and the Ioway and Winnebago myth cycle of Red Horn (He Who Wears Human Heads as Earrings) as the only evidence in oral tradition. The symbolic referents of Ramey Incised and Oneota pottery are seen to coincide in important ways.

NOTE

This chapter is based in part upon a paper (Hall 1975c) originally prepared as a contribution to the proceedings of the advanced seminar "Reviewing Mississippian Development: A Study in the Dynamics of Cultural Growth in the Eastern United States" organized by Stephen Williams and James B. Griffin, sponsored by the School of American Research and held in Santa Fe, New Mexico, November 11–15, 1974.

2

Human-Plant Interactions and Cultural Change in the American Bottom

DAVID RINDOS

SISSEL JOHANNESSEN

The Mississippian people of the American Bottom lived in a complex cultural landscape of towns, villages, farmsteads, gardens, and fields scattered among the many floodplain lakes and marshes. Small farming hamlets were dispersed across the landscape, and occasional larger towns had administrative, economic, or ceremonial functions. The center was at Cahokia, the largest known site complex from prehistoric America north of Mexico. This center was made up of 120 temple and burial mounds and covered eight square kilometers (Fowler 1974, 1977, 1978; Fowler and Hall 1972). The complex society of the people who made and lived in this cultural landscape did not spring into existence fully formed; it was, instead, only one segment of a continuum of human habitation that has spanned at least five thousand years in this region.

In considering the origin, development, and subsequent decline of Mississippian culture, the mode of subsistence of the people is of major importance. This chapter focuses on the role of plant sources of food in the development and decline of American Bottom Mississippian culture. We place major emphasis upon changes that occurred in the system of human-plant interaction and on the selective pressures that directed these changes. Evidence pertaining to these questions is drawn from the physical remains of the human-plant interaction—the plant debris from archaeological sites.

Methods

Prior to the late 1960s, flotation recovery was not commonly practiced in American Bottom archaeological excavations. Analyses were biased toward large, easily visible plant remains such as maize cobs (e.g., Cutler and Blake 1977). Thus maize was held to have provided the basis for prehistoric agricultural economies. The present paper is largely possible due to the vastly different picture of plant use that emerged after the widespread adoption of flotation recovery by archaeologists in this region. The data upon which our analyses are based were systematically recovered and analyzed to preclude fragment size bias and to allow comparisons between and among sites. Thus the enhanced data base greatly expands the picture of Mississippian agricultural human-plant interactions and provides insight into the evolutionary forces that affected cultural change in the American Bottom.

Our data are drawn from the analysis of plant remains from nine Mississippian components at seven sites (fig. 2.1; table 2.1). Three components have been assigned to the Lohmann phase (A.D. 1000–1050); four components are assignable to the Stirling phase (A.D. 1050–1150); and one component each was analyzed from the Moorehead (A.D. 1150–1250) and Sand Prairie (A.D. 1250–1400) phases. The sites studied span the Mississippian period. With the exception of one upland Lohmann phase site (George Reeves), the sites are situated in the floodplain.

Flotation-recovered plant remains were examined from a total of 5,500 liters of fill from 171 Mississippian features at these sites. The methods used during sampling, recovery, and analysis were held constant to minimize bias and to promote comparability among components (see discussion in Johannessen 1988).

During excavation, standard soil samples of ten liters of fill were collected from every cultural stratum of each excavated feature. These samples were water-floated ac-

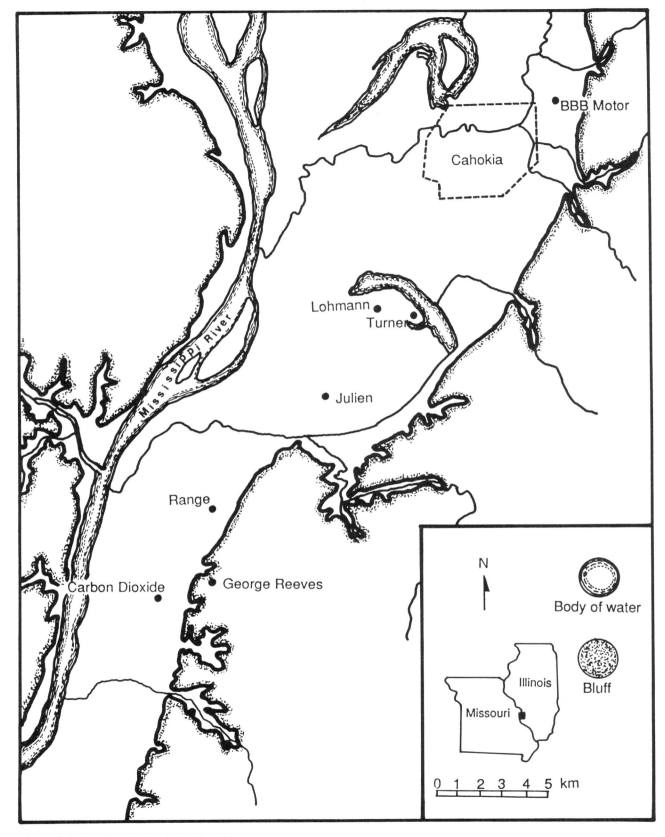

Figure 2.1. Location of Sites in the Study Area

Table 2.1. Mississippian Sites from which Plant Remains Were Analyzed

Site Name	Site Number	References
A.D. 1000–1050, Lohmann phase		
George Reeves	11-S-650	McElrath and Finney 1987; Johannessen 1987
Carbon Dioxide	11-Mo-594	Finney 1985; Johannessen 1985
Lohmann	11-S-49	Esarey with Good 1981; Johannessen 1981a
A.D. 1050–1150, Stirling phase		
Range	11-S-47	Mehrer 1982; Whalley 1983a
BBB Motor	11-Ms-595	Emerson and Jackson 1984; Whalley 1984
Julien	11-S-63	Milner and Williams 1984; Johannessen 1984b
Turner	11-S-50	Milner and Williams 1983; Whalley 1983b
A.D. 1150–1250, Moorehead phase		
Julien	11-S-63	Milner and Williams 1984; Johannessen 1984b
A.D. 1250–1400, Sand Prairie phase		
Julien	11-S-63	Milner and Williams 1984; Johannessen 1984b

cording to the Illinois Department of Transportation system (Wagner 1976, 1982), which is a method of tub-flotation using #40 mesh (0.4 mm^2) screen.

The subset of samples for analysis came from features selected randomly from each class of feature types (e.g., structures, pits within features, deep bell-shaped pits, shallow basin pits) present at each component. A minimum of one ten-liter sample was chosen from each stratum of the selected features. By randomly selecting a number of features from different feature classes, we hoped to recover an assemblage of plant remains characteristic of the site or component as a whole, rather than only from features of a single type or those with especially dense plant debris.

The heavy fractions of selected samples were refloated if necessary in a chemical solution (Struever 1968) to separate the charred plant remains from the residue of soil, bone, lithics, and other materials remaining after water flotation. The resultant clean samples of plant debris were then divided into two size fractions by sieving through a two-millimeter screen. Both size fractions were sorted under magnification. All plant material greater than two millimeters was sorted into categories (e.g., wood, nutshell, maize), weighed, and counted. The less-than-two millimeter fraction was scanned and all seeds, broken seeds, and remains of domesticated plants such as maize or squash rind fragments were retrieved. The carbonized material was identified with the aid of standard manuals (Martin and Barkley 1961; Montgomery 1977; Panshin and de Zeeuw 1970), and ultimately by comparison to specimens in a modern reference collection.

Data

Plant remains from the nine Mississippian components are summarized in table 2.2. The table lists the major taxa in each of the categories, such as nuts, wood, and seeds, and the percentage of each taxon within that category. Many other plant taxa than those in the table were identified in the assemblages, but only in very small quantities. For example, a minimum of forty-two seed taxa were present in the samples, but the eleven listed made up the vast majority. Similarly, at least twenty-three taxa of wood were identified although only seven were common.

Several quantitative measures are provided in table 2.2. The number of features and fill volumes that were analyzed are listed under the site number of each component. The percentages by count of the taxa in each category for all nine components combined are also given in the column "overall percentage." Because a number of authors (e.g., Dennell 1976) object to the use of counts and percentages as a measure of the relative abundance of plant types, a presence/absence column (marked "overall ubiquity") is also included in the table, indicating in what percentage of all the features analyzed the taxon occurred. The overall percentage and the presence/absence statistics each contain useful information, and we have attempted to take both measures into account in a summary measure in the last column of table 2.2. This index of relative abundance was calculated by adding the overall percentage of each taxon and its relative frequency in features. The taxa listed within each of the categories have been ranked by this index.

Table 2.2. Major Taxa of Nut, Wood, and Seeds and Their Percentages from Nine Mississippian Components

Phase	Lohmann			Stirling				Moore-head	Sand Prairie	Overall[1] Per-centage	Overall[2] Ubiquity (n=171)	Relative Abun-dance[3]
Site (11-)	S-650	Mo-594	S-49	S-47	Ms-595	S-63	S-50	S-63	S-63			
Features analyzed (n)	11	8	29	21	24	15	35	14	14			
Liters analyzed (n)	252	607	367	736	726	474	1115	415	641			
Nuts												
Total fragments (n)	232	550	681	3565	250	82	492	5481	6251	(n=17, 483)**		
Carya spp. (true hickories)	77%	37%	64%	45%	32%	52%	51%	51%	60%	54%	56%	110
Juglandaceae (hickory and walnut)	21	57	30	33	33	38	15	39	38	37	54	91
Carya illinoensis/cordiformis (pecan)	–	–	3	20	<1	9	12	8	2	8	20	28
Quercus spp. (acorns)	1	2	7	2	30	1	15	1	<1	2	24	26
Total	99%	96%	94%	100%	96%	100%	93%	99%	96%	101%		
Wood												
Total fragments (n)	1134	2738	1082	4771	4097	953	2499	506	6410	(n=3424)**		
Quercus, red group (red oak)	17%	5%	29%	31%	11%	48%	15%	5%	34%	22%	50%	72
Carya spp. (true hickories)	41	20	18	31	5	14	15	–	23	19	44	63
Quercus spp. (oaks)	16	17	18	6	2	9	5	2	5	7	31	38
Salicaceae (cottonwood/willow)	–	1	9	6	19	1	17	8	8	10	20	30
Unknown Type Q	–	–	–	–	14	9	7	32	1	6	16	22
Carya illinoensis/cordiformis (pecan)	–	10	–	3	4	1	11	–	2	3	18	21
Quercus, white group (white oak)	6	1	1	9	3	4	1	–	4	5	13	18
Total	80%	54%	75%	86%	58%	86%	71%	47%	77%	72%		
Native Seeds and Fruits												
Total (n)	134	538	5724	3819	2776	965	2499	580	1468	(n=9921)**		
Phalaris caroliniana (maygrass)	66%	59%	38%	43%	50%	70%	54%	6%	39%	44%	70%	114
Chenopodium sp. (goosefoot)	9	12	38	27	27	18	21	3	24	28	61	89
Polygonum erectum (erect knotweed)	7	12	15	10	9	4	3	48	<1	11	36	47
Strophostyles helvola (wild bean)	1	–	3	1	3	1	2	3	3	2	30	32
Panicum sp. (panic grass)	3	–	1	2	4	1	6	<1	8	3	23	26
Solanum americanum (black nightshade)	–	<1	2	1	1	1	3	1	2	1	23	24
Helianthus annuus (sunflower)	–	–	<1	7	2	–	2	<1	9	2	21	23
Gramineae (grasses)	11	3	<1	2	1	<1	1	<1	1	1	18	19
Polygonum spp. (knotweeds)	–	1	1	<1	<1	<1	4	2	1	2	14	16
Hordeum pusillum (little barley)	–	–	<1	–	<1	<1	2	–	<1	<1	10	11
Iva annua (marsh elder)	–	–	–<1	–	–	–	27	1	1	4	5	
Total	97%	87%	99%	94%	98%	97%	98%	83%	89%	96%		
Tropical Cultigens												
Zea mays (maize) (gram weight)	0.5	1.7	7.4	15.9*	18.9	5.2*	21.7*	4.7	6.5	–	86%	–
Cucurbita sp. (squash, no. rind frags.)	–	–	2	13	8	–	2	–	–	–	6	–
Lagenaria siceraria (gourd, no. rind frags.)	–	–	–	–	2	–	–	–	–	–	1	–
Nicotiana sp. (tobacco, no. seeds)	–	–	–	–	7	–	1	–	–	–	3	–

*Not included in these weights are 553 grams of maize from four "smudge pits" at these components
**Number of *identifiable* fragments or seeds (*not* total number recovered)

[1] Percentage of identifiable fragments or seeds
[2] Percentage of total features (171) in which the taxon occurred
[3] Sum of the two percentages

Mississippian Plant Usage Patterns

Table 2.2 illustrates that certain plant taxa occur in large quantities at each component, often in surprisingly similar percentages. This core utilization pattern is composed of the few taxa that occur most abundantly in terms of both quantity and presence. Within each category a large number of additional taxa occur sporadically and contribute little to the overall quantity of preserved remains.

NUT REMAINS

The true hickories (*Carya* spp.), a group that includes shagbark, pignut, and mockernut, are the dominant nut remains in each component. The Juglandaceae percentages can largely be subsumed under *Carya*. Fragments were assigned to Juglandaceae when they were too small to identify with certainty as either *Carya* or *Juglans*. However, since *Juglans* is represented very sparsely throughout the record, most of the fragments attributed to Juglandaceae are probably *Carya*. The percentages of true hickory nutshell, therefore, actually range from 65% to 96% by count, with a mean value of about 90%. The dominant thick-shelled hickories are followed in abundance by the pecan hickories (*Carya illinoensis* or *C. cordiformis*). Acorn shell (*Quercus* spp.) was identified at all components and, although generally sparse, is well represented in two assemblages.

WOOD CHARCOAL

Although a minimum of twenty-three wood taxa were recovered, three taxa—the oaks (*Quercus* spp.), hickories (*Carya* spp.), and the cottonwood/willow group (Salicaceae) make up about three-quarters of the wood fragments at each component. Oaks and hickories are the dominants of the climax forest in this area (Shelford 1963; Telford 1927), whereas cottonwood and willow are typical of wet soils on the floodplain.

SEEDS AND FRUITS

Native seeds and fruits show a similar pattern of domination by a few taxa. Three species of starchy-seeded annuals combined make up about 90% of the seeds at most components: maygrass (*Phalaris caroliniana*), a goosefoot (*Chenopodium* sp., probably *C. berlandieri* spp. *jonesianum*; see Asch and Asch 1985; Smith 1984a, 1985a, 1985c, 1987b; Wilson 1981), and a knotweed (*Polygonum erectum*). Several other taxa are common but occur in smaller quantities. These include a wild bean (*Strophostyles helvola*), two grasses (*Panicum* sp. and *Hordeum pusillum*), black nightshade (*Solanum americanum*), sunflower (*Helianthus annuus*), and marsh elder

(*Iva annua*). In addition to these consistently abundant seed/fruit types, a large variety of other remains (not listed in table 2.2) were of taxa that occur sporadically and in small numbers. Many of these are seeds of dry or fleshy fruits of probable economic value, for example grape (*Vitis* spp.), persimmon (*Diospyros virginiana*), pokeweed (*Phytolacca americana*), sumac (*Rhus* sp.), American lotus (*Nelumbo lutea*), and cherry (*Prunus* sp.).

Sunflower and marsh elder are widely held to have been domesticated by the native Americans of the Eastern Woodlands (Asch and Asch 1978; Ford 1981; Heiser 1985; Yarnell 1972, 1978). The evidence of domestication includes distributional patterns indicating range extension and increasing achene/seed size in archaeological contexts through time with ultimate sizes greater than the sizes of the wild individuals of the species. It is also clear that the small starchy-seeded taxa were widely used crops. By Middle Woodland times, many groups of the Eastern Woodlands grew maygrass far outside its natural range, harvested knotweed in far greater quantities than could be produced by natural stands, and grew a domesticated variety of goosefoot (Arzigian 1987; Asch and Asch 1977, 1985; Asch, Farnsworth, and Asch 1979; Cowan 1978; Fritz 1984, 1986; Smith 1984a, 1985a, 1985c, 1987a, 1987b; Wilson 1981). The beans, nightshades, fruits, and grasses were either harvested from truly wild (self-sustaining) populations, or were cultivated or encouraged in regions of human habitation. As discussed in greater detail below, we reject a simple dichotomization of domestication and nondomestication and hold that many of the species encountered in the paleoethnobotanical record from the American Bottom are best understood as representing plants having differing types of relationships with humans (see Harlan 1975).

NON-NATIVE CULTIGENS

In addition to the evidence for native plant use, the remains of four non-native domesticated plants were recovered: maize (*Zea mays*), squash (*Cucurbita* sp.), bottle gourd (*Lagenaria siceraria*), and tobacco (*Nicotiana* sp.). Maize is very common in the Mississippian context, occurring in practically every feature analyzed, although seldom in large quantities. Squash and bottle gourd rind fragments, as well as tobacco seeds, occur infrequently.

SUMMARY

The Mississippian paleoethnobotanical data are characterized by a core complex of plants that occur abundantly in all of the examined components. This complex is defined as the typical Mississippian pattern of plant use. The basic pattern includes the choice of oaks, hickories, and cottonwood/willow for fuel in combination with a highly diagnostic pattern of food-plant remains. Native plants of importance include hickory nuts and the starchy and oily seeds such as maygrass, goosefoot, knotweed, sunflower, and marsh elder. Tropical cultigens are maize, squash, bottle gourd, and tobacco. Finally, numerous other seed and fruit species occur so regularly throughout the record that some patterning in consumption and the likely existence of a symbiotic relationship between humans and these plants must be presumed.

Discussion

The complex of plants just described represents the minimum components of a culturally regulated system of human-plant interaction that existed during Mississippian times. Important foods such as tubers and green vegetables are not represented in this record due to preservation bias. Similarly, dietary contributions from fruits and other unprocessed items are probably underestimated. Nevertheless, we have recovered at least some of the plant types important in the system. The regularity of their occurrence at each component throughout the Mississippian period indicates that the people had well-defined notions of the "proper" plants to use and how to use them; in other words, the regularity reflects shared ideas about food and fuel.

Now we turn to more detailed consideration of this system of human-plant interaction. We describe the system and its evolution and consider how it related to the earlier subsistence systems in the American Bottom. Major emphasis is placed upon the effect of changes in the system (plausibly created by the widespread adoption of storable forms of maize) on the demography and the social and cultural institutions within the region.

As Sauer notes, "An environment can only be described in terms of the knowledge and preferences of the occupying persons; 'natural resources' are in fact cultural appraisals" (1969b:2). This culturally directed body of "knowledge and preference," which is discernible in the regularity of the pattern of plant remains, shows a certain continuity not only throughout the Mississippian period, but also back as much as a thousand years. When a single major item, maize, is removed from table 2.2, the remaining data are similar to data from the analysis of sites in this area at any time in the preceding millennium. A pattern of plant use that has strong qualitative and quantitative similarities (with the exception of maize) to that of the Mississippian occurred in the area at least since Middle Woodland times (150 B.C.–A.D. 300) (Asch, Farnsworth, and Asch 1979; Johannessen 1984a: Parker 1989). The Mississippian pattern of plant use, like Mississippian culture itself, did not spring full-blown out of a void, but rather represented the development of a tradition that was established in much earlier times.

Let us first consider the links that bind the Mississippian subsistence system to earlier times. Here we will consider the systemic interactions between cultural behavior and two major sources of food, nuts and the starchy seed complex that includes maygrass, goosefoot, and knotweed.

Reliance on nuts has an ancient history in the American Bottom, one that stretches back to the earliest sites that have been investigated (e.g., the McLean site dated 3000–2300 B.C.; McElrath 1986). To understand the significance of nuts in the diet, and ultimately the role they play in cultural evolution in this region, requires an understanding of the effects of human consumption of this resource on the local flora.

Humans are not simply passive consumers taking food from resources such as nut trees; instead they are members of a symbiotic relationship that links them to the plants and animals on which they feed (Rindos 1984: chap. 3). When a group of humans feed consistently and regularly upon a resource such as nuts, they will, in fact, increase the number of nut trees in the region by dispersing the plant. The occasional loss of nuts following harvest is well-nigh inevitable, and since the tree is reproduced by the nuts, these losses offer the tree species an opportunity for dispersal. Such dispersals occur in various locations in the local environment as a function of the probability that humans use those areas. Hence, over time, useful resources accumulate in those very regions most often occupied by humans. Furthermore, because the tree species provides a valued food resource it is also protected by humans; the nut trees are preserved when encountered and other species of trees are used instead (for example, for construction or firewood). Indeed, we find that tree types other than hickory (generally elm, hackberry, ash, locust, and mulberry) were used for firewood during those periods (Archaic and Early Woodland) when nuts were most important in the diet (Johannessen 1984a).

This type of dispersal and protection symbiosis has been described by one of us as "incidental domestication" (Rindos 1984:153). It is a common phenomenon and over millennia can have major effects upon the total number of individuals of a tree species growing in an area, and hence upon the potential crop available to humans (see the discussion of the human-increased hickory population in Munson 1986). As in any symbiotic relationship, the interaction between the two species raises the carrying capacity of the environment for both. Hence, increased populations of the resource that provide a greater total yield can bring about increased human populations living in the area.

In contrast to the early importance of nuts, the starchy seed complex does not occur in substantial quantities in the paleoethnobotanical record of the American Bottom until the Middle Woodland period (Johannessen 1984a). At this time this complex became dominant in a diagnostic pattern of plant use that survived through the Mississippian period.

Human use of this complex was by no means uniquely a local development. Use of the starchy seed complex was widespread throughout the eastern United States. Many details of the evolution of the complex are still unknown, but evidence from Kentucky and Tennessee (Chapman and Shea 1981; Cowan et al. 1981; Crawford 1982; Crites 1978; Jones 1936; Yarnell 1969, 1974) indicates that it was used to the south and east for many centuries before its appearance in Illinois and was not, therefore, a completely in situ development.

The precise nature of the relationship between humans and the plants in this complex is the subject of a continuing debate. We believe that the question of whether these plants were "true" domesticates is, in the final analysis, of little interest. Domestication is a process, not an event. Within the context of the American Bottom, we know that the contribution of these plants to the diet increased over time. This indicates a developing symbiosis between humans and the plants of the complex. We have no direct evidence that the plants were consciously sown in agricultural fields, nor should we expect that such evidence will ever be forthcoming.

Nevertheless, investigations have shown that the remains of many of these plants are morphologically differentiated from those now occurring in the wild. It is now clear that sunflower, marsh elder, goosefoot, and probably knotweed show morphological markers that can be read as compatible with the hypothesis that the plants were grown by the humans who were consuming them (Asch and Asch 1977, 1978, 1985; Fritz 1984, 1986; Smith 1984a, 1985a, 1985c, 1987a, 1987b; Yarnell 1972, 1978). On the basis of these markers, we infer that the cultivated varieties are genetic variants of the species as they occur in the wild. This is significant since it indicates that particular human behaviors such as sowing, weeding, and saving seed went into making and maintaining these genetic variants. One of the most significant markers of specialized domestication is isolation of the consumed plants from wild relatives. It is only by means

of such isolation that the phenotypic differences distinguishing the utilized and wild populations can arise and be maintained.

However we interpret the morphology of the archaeological remains of the indigenous seed complex, an important fact remains: these plants made a substantial and increasingly important contribution to human subsistence. Therefore, it is essential to consider the relationships that existed between humans and these plants. It appears likely that this relationship of humans to the plants in this starchy seed complex represents an example of specialized domestication, a specific type of symbiotic relationship in which human behaviors isolate utilized plants from their wild relatives. Such isolation, and the morphological change accompanying it, allows evolutionary change that both benefits the humans as consumers and reduces the ability of the plant to survive outside of the symbiosis (Rindos 1984:158–64). Ultimately, specialized domestication provides the selective forces for the evolution of the agroecology, or the community of cultivated plants, into what is generally recognized as full-blown agricultural subsistence (Rindos 1984:164–78).

It is important to recognize that relationships between humans and plants were not necessarily constant through the centuries. During the earliest periods, people might have been merely dispersing the plants into regions of human settlements. Over fairly long periods of time such dispersals created increasingly larger local populations of the plants and hence a greater potential harvest (incidental domestication). Yet as the plants became specialized to grow in the anthropogenic habitat, and as humans began to encourage them, the new behaviors toward plants became part of the cultural norm, and a new type of ecology, the agroecology, in which new selective pressures changed or intensified the evolutionary trends of the plant-people interaction, evolved. Plants became adapted to the conditions existing under cultivation because the selective pressures of the anthropogenic habitat differed from those existing in the wild (e.g., constant disturbance, harvesting, higher fertility levels, and human selection of some morphologies over others). These processes brought about genetic change in plants involved in relationships with humans. Given a continuous evolutionary process such as this, it is impossible to speak of a "moment" when either humans became "agricultural" or when plants became "domesticated." Consequently, it seems wiser to concentrate on the process itself rather than on such artificial distinctions.

Data from the American Bottom indicate that the starchy seed complex first began to grow in importance during the Middle Woodland period. The contribution of this complex to the paleoethnobotanical record, in both absolute and relative terms, increased throughout the Late Woodland period and maintained these levels throughout the Mississippian until the very latest phases. The plant data contain other reflections of the increased importance of these cultivated seed plants in the subsistence system; for example, the increase in the seed complex was accompanied by a decline in the frequency of nuts, a previously important source of food (Johannessen 1984a, 1988). Also at this time (beginning in the Middle Woodland), the wood charcoal from American Bottom sites began to be dominated by oak and hickory, which replaced the earlier elm-ash-oak dominance (Johannessen 1984a). This change in fuel use may reflect a reduction in the perceived importance of these trees (i.e., oaks and hickories) as nut bearers, and thus that they were no longer protected as food plants, but rather used for fuel.

Further inferences about the importance of the relationship between humans and the members of this complex may be drawn from what occurred when maize came into sudden widespread use, a phenomenon that may have been a consequence of the introduction of high-yielding storable forms of maize into the area. At about A.D. 750, maize begins to appear throughout the American Bottom plant record. Kernels and cob fragments have been recovered from 30% to 90% of the features analyzed at Emergent Mississippian period (A.D. 750–1000) sites (Johannessen 1984a; Parker 1988). In sites dated to the earlier Patrick (A.D. 600–750) and Mund (A.D. 450–600) phases, maize is virtually unknown, having been recovered in minute quantities from only 2% of the features analyzed. This evidence indicates a widespread and remarkably abrupt adoption of maize throughout the entire region at around A.D. 750. The fact that the starchy seed complex remains abundant in the paleoethnobotanical record despite the new importance of maize (see table 2.2) indicates that maize was not grown instead of the existing plant complex, but rather was grown in addition to plants that had been part of a system in operation for as much as one thousand years.

The fact that maize was merely added to an already existing system may be used to draw implications concerning the nature of the subsistence system at the time when maize was introduced. Maize is an "agricultural domesticate" (Rindos 1984:153) completely dependent upon humans at all stages of its life cycle. Growth and maturation of the crop requires not only the presence of a highly specialized environment, but also specific human behaviors, which minimally include tilling, planting, weeding, harvesting, and the preservation of seed for the next year's planting. Evidence indicates that such behaviors have considerable antiquity in North America, well before the spread of maize use. These agricultural behaviors may have been practiced first with the cultivation of domesticated squash perhaps as early as 5000 B.C. (Conard et al. 1984; but see also Smith 1987b). Clearly, agricultural behaviors were common in some parts of the Eastern Woodlands by 1000 B.C.; they would have been necessary to maintain the domesticates (squash, sunflower, marsh elder) that appear in sites of this period (Asch and Asch 1985; Cowan et al. 1981; Chapman and Shea 1981; Crawford 1982; Jones 1936; King 1980, 1985; Yarnell 1969, 1974).

Finally, it should be recognized that the introduction of a crop is not necessarily synonymous with the introduction of agriculture itself. The diffusion of maize into this region could not have been as successful as it was unless humans were already practicing the necessary agricultural behaviors. Given the speed with which maize appears throughout the region following its introduction, we must assume that an indigenous agricultural system in which the starchy seed complex was important was already in place and that maize was merely "plugged into it."

From this discussion it should be apparent that the introduction of maize into the American Bottom did not mark the beginning of agriculture in the region. A subsistence system that incorporated agricultural behaviors and a substantial dependence on the products of plant husbandry had clearly evolved long before this event. Yet to admit all of this is not to claim that the introduction of maize was unimportant. The introduction of storable maize was, without a doubt, one of the most important events in the prehistory of the American Bottom region. Not only was it associated with the social and cultural transformations that followed, but what at first glance might appear to have been a great gain from a new food source was also, we believe, a factor in the decline of this Mississippian system and its great center at Cahokia.

INSTABILITY AND CULTURAL CHANGE

Thus far we have seen that the substantial use of maize was introduced into a cultural and agricultural system that had been operating for at least one thousand years. Following its adoption, major changes occurred. Settlements shifted to a more nucleated pattern (i.e., towns emerged). Population increased, or at least the nucleated distribution may have resulted in population "pseudo-density" caused by locational factors (e.g., Bronson 1977). Increased social complexity and centralization of authority were plausibly associated with these shifts. By the Stirling phase (A.D. 1050–1150) a hierarchy of settlements with Cahokia at its head provided economic and ritual integration (Fowler 1974, 1977, 1978; Fowler and Hall

1972). A hundred years later, in the Moorehead phase (A.D. 1150–1250), a reduction of the American Bottom population is evident (Milner 1986b), and an apparent movement to the uplands occurred (Pauketat and Koldehoff 1983; Woods and Holley, chap. 3). By the end of the Mississippian period, the region was largely depopulated. What connection is there between these events and the new crop, maize?

Let us step back into the Late Woodland and review the plant component of the subsistence system dominant at that time. The existing agricultural complex (with crops of maygrass, knotweed, goosefoot, sunflower, marsh elder, and squash) provided staple starches and oils. Nuts provided an important protein and fat supplement to the diet. The animal component of the diet included fish, deer, small mammals, and waterfowl, and no major changes in use are evident between the Late Woodland, Emergent Mississippian, and Mississippian periods (Kelly and Cross 1984).

It has already been noted that maize became important in the paleoethnobotanical record during the Emergent Mississippian period (A.D. 750–1000). In addition to the evidence from the plant remains, carbon isotope studies of human bone confirm that maize did not contribute significantly to the diet before this time (Bender, Baerreis, and Steventon 1981; Lynott et al. 1986). With the widespread adoption of maize, several major changes occurred in the interactive system linking human and plant populations.

Maize is a high-yielding crop and population levels probably increased in response to the heightened carrying capacity of the land. Yet these heightened yields were likely associated with a large variability in yield. Hence, at the same time that the population was increasing, the variance in yield of the maize crop may also have been increasing. At the same time, as carbon isotope studies show, maize was growing in importance in the people's diet. In essence, then, more people were receiving an increasing proportion of their food from a less stable resource.

Let us explore the interaction of increased yield and instability in yield in more depth. What is meant by increased variability in yield? An increase of variability in yield may be understood as a greater sensitivity of the agricultural system to the inevitable variation that exists in the environment. Put in other terms, any change in growing conditions would have had a greater impact on the Mississippian maize-based agricultural system than it would have had on earlier subsistence systems.

The pre-maize crop complex included a number of species that show differing responses to climatic variation; a bad year for goosefoot may be a good year for knotweed or maygrass. The members of this complex also show, at least in their modern forms, a greater tolerance to variations in soil and moisture conditions than maize does. They grow in a variety of soil types and are relatively indifferent to both wet and dry soils (Gleason and Cronquist 1963). A subsistence pattern based upon this complex will likely show a lower yearly variation in yield than will a subsistence pattern in which maize was dominant.

It is important to note that the change in absolute yield is different from changes in the variability of that yield. It is also true that any increase in absolute yield will be "progress" only at the moment of its first occurrence; over relatively brief periods, yield increases will literally be eaten up by the increased population they generate.

It has been noted that population redistribution and probable increase were among the major correlates with maize cultivation in the American Bottom. These demographic shifts had important effects upon the local agroecologies and on the reliability of the subsistence system as a whole. As population density increased, either absolutely throughout the entire region or relatively in areas of settlement concentration, so did the need for farm land. People were probably clearing land for fields as early as Middle Woodland times, since it was in this period that seed remains grew in importance, the quantity of nutshell decreased, and the wood of nut-bearing trees (oak and hickory) became dominant in the record. We may reasonably presume that the clearing was for agricultural purposes. Later, coincident with the appearance of maize in the Emergent Mississippian, a further decline in the absolute and relative frequency of nut remains occurred (Johannessen 1984a). If pressure was placed upon land as a resource, we expect that existing nut groves would have been cleared to make room for the higher-yielding maize crop. In essence, nuts became a less-valued resource because of the presence of maize in the agrosystem. Hence, the high productivity of maize permitted the population growth that demanded more land to grow still more maize.

Decline in nut consumption may have represented more than just the diminution of a single food source. Nuts provide important nutrients; for example, hickory nuts are composed of 13% protein and also contain a remarkable 69% fat (Watt and Merrill 1963). Furthermore, during pre-Mississippian times, the consumption of nuts could have acted as a buffer to existing instabilities in agricultural production. But as populations rose and nucleated, not only would per-capita production from existing stands inevitably decrease, but locational constraints would also limit access to the source. The opportunities for increased yields of nuts evolving via incidental domestication would be minimal for several reasons. First, gathering of nut masts would be sporadic rather than regular and would be tied to periods of crisis. Second, and of greater importance, protection of the nut trees would be prohibited by the need for agricultural land.

Milner (1986b) estimates that by the end of the Stirling phase, the American Bottom populations had reached their peak, and for the next 350 years they declined, until by A.D. 1500 the region was largely depopulated. Milner calculates that Moorehead phase population levels were less than half those of the preceding Stirling phase, and that Sand Prairie levels were further decreased drastically, perhaps to as little as one-thirtieth of Moorehead levels.

Is it plausible to attribute a population decline of this magnitude, along with its associated changes in settlement and cultural structuring, to the outcome of a new interaction with plants? The increased instability in yield of the maize-based agriculture was a function of reduced resilience of the system to previously insignificant environmental perturbations. Is there evidence of such a perturbation?

One possible disturbance that may have affected the subsistence systems of the Stirling phase has been proposed by Emerson and Milner (1982) in a study of changing settlement patterns in the American Bottom. By the Stirling phase, the settlement clusters that had been characteristic of earlier communities had disappeared and were replaced by a pattern in which households were strung linearly along the higher and better-drained sand ridges of the floodplain. Also, the mean elevation of the house floors rose through time. At many sites, occupation did not continue past the Stirling phase, and Moorehead and Sand Prairie communities were located on the highest available ridges. Furthermore, although the population of the floodplain itself declined radically during the Moorehead and Sand Prairie phases, the relative number of occupations in the uplands began to rise at this same time. A number of Moorehead and Sand Prairie mound centers exist in the uplands, but upland settlement during the previous Stirling phase appears to have been sparse (Pauketat and Koldehoff 1983; Woods and Holley, chap. 3).

Emerson and Milner (1982) suggest that a rising water table may have been the cause of the Mississippian shift to higher ground. Greater flooding and a higher water table would have had major effects upon a maize-based subsistence system by decreasing the arable land available. Yet since populations were already high because of the previously high yields of maize, people would have needed to move to regions suitable for the continued cultivation of maize. Changes in the settlement system were a consequence of the environmental sensitivity of a recently altered subsistence pattern interacting with heightened population levels.

We have already mentioned that the native small-grain complex might have been more resilient to changes in climate or in the water table. A change such as that which apparently occurred after the Stirling phase may represent the extreme of long-term fluctuations in the climate of the region, or may be the result of changing local geomorphological conditions (White 1984) or of changed hydrology from reduction of the forest cover (Lopinot and Woods 1988). Had changes of a similar nature occurred before the local beginnings of maize agriculture, they would not have had major effects on the subsistence system and hence upon the settlement pattern. The close interdependency of the maize-human relationship that developed after A.D. 750 was such that even slight changes in the environment produced severe perturbations in the subsistence economy. Never before the Mississippian period had so many people been so closely tied to each other, to a single crop, and to the floodplain. The interaction of increasing population, increasing dependence on a single crop with high but variable yield (in comparison to the starchy seed complex), and the environmental consequences of the developing agricultural system brought about a situation in which a previously adaptive subsistence system induced its own decline.

In closing, let us try to reconstruct the subsistence system of the smaller human population living on the floodplain at the end of the Mississippian period. The paleoethnobotanical data from the Moorehead and Sand Prairie phases are not conclusive, but there are some indications of a shift in the subsistence economy at this time. A shift is also evident in recent analysis of plant remains from the Moorehead/Sand Prairie component at the Radic site (Parker 1987) and from the late occupations at the Cahokia site (Lopinot and Woods 1988). Table 2.2 shows that our sample from these late phases is small compared to earlier phases; this is probably a reflection of the tremendous population decline that had taken place. Nevertheless, the picture painted by the plant remains from these late phases is an interesting one in several ways. The quantity of nutshell is much higher than in previous phases; in fact, the frequency is higher than in almost any phase recorded since the Late Archaic (Johannessen 1984a). Also, the percentage of the starchy seed complex relative to other indigenous seeds and fruits is lower than in previous phases (in the Lohmann phase sites the starchy seeds made up 90% of the seed assemblage, in the Stirling phase 82%, and for the combined Moorehead and Sand Prairie material the percentage is only 61%). Given these observations it seems possible that a shift to a more diversified diet occurred during the terminal Mississippian. Yet in spite of the increased importance of nuts and wild plants in the diet, maize apparently was still maintaining itself as the primary carbohydrate source. Maize, after several centuries of prominence in the system, was now entrenched in the cultural body of "knowledge and preference."

The picture drawn of subsistence and settlement in the late Mississippian period is one of a decimated population returning to an old pattern of considerable use of naturally occurring plant foods. Nevertheless, this new diversification of the diet also occurred within the context of a recently evolved but now highly standardized diet based on maize. The now-traditional maize diet was augmented by wild resources. However, we should note that this shift was permitted by the decline in population that occurred after the height of the Mississippian period. Ironically, this decline in population itself was consequent to the previous high reliance upon a particular resource, maize, which brought with it far-reaching ecological and economic consequences.

The phenomenon that occurred in the American Bottom gives us insights into the general demographic consequences of a maize diet in the region as a whole. The interaction of denser populations with an unstable subsistence base brought about increasingly common episodes of local food shortage. Humans, like other animals, respond to these times of stress simply by emigrating. Cahokia didn't collapse, it evaporated.

3

Upland Mississippian Settlement in the American Bottom Region

WILLIAM I. WOODS

GEORGE R. HOLLEY

The impressiveness of the Cahokia site and the wealth of Mississippian-period archaeological resources have frequently drawn archaeologists to the American Bottom. The extensive work begun in the 1960s by Melvin L. Fowler, James W. Porter, Charles J. Bareis, Patrick J. Munson, Alan D. Harn, and others has focused on the relationship of surrounding areas to Cahokia (Bareis and Porter 1984; Benchley 1976; Fowler 1974, 1975, 1978; Fowler and Hall 1975, 1978; Gregg 1975b; Harn 1971a, 1980a; Kelly, Linder, and Cartmell 1979; Linder, Cartmell, and Kelly 1978; Munson 1971; Porter 1974). All of these efforts have focused on the American Bottom proper and the adjacent bluff edge with little attention to Mississippian developments in upland settings.

However, this wealth of American Bottom research does have benefits for upland archaeology. Refinements in the ceramic sequence of Cahokia and the American Bottom permit a greater control over chronology for upland sites. Settlement data have led to inferences regarding the dynamics of this Mississippian settlement system. It is becoming increasingly clear that Mississippian societies in general were not static through time, but were perhaps inherently unstable, exhibiting episodes of growth, decline, and reformulation (see Emerson, chap. 12). In order to examine fully these dynamics, the entire settlement system must be addressed.

It is our contention that although the upland occupation was not as intensive or continuous as that of the bottomlands, it was not culturally distinct. Because our interpretations of the Mississippian occupation of the interior upland hinge greatly on developments in the American Bottom, we will briefly sketch an interpretation of the Emergent Mississippian and Mississippian period for that area (see also Emerson, chap. 12; Hall, chap. 1; Kelly, chap. 4).

It is not possible to discuss Mississippian developments without a consideration of the Emergent Mississippian period. This period, lasting from A.D. 800 to 1000, was marked by a number of trends that were elaborated upon in the succeeding Mississippian period (Kelly 1987; Kelly, Ozuk et al. 1984). Prominent among these trends was the adoption of maize agriculture.

The Late Bluff ceramic vessel assemblage, characteristic of most of the Emergent Mississippian period, consisted of jars with plain necks and cordmarked lower bodies, cordmarked bowls, and the enigmatic stumpware boot. Spatial variability along with the timing of changes anticipating a Mississippian ceramic assemblage combine to create a diverse ceramic record. Differences are noted between the Prairie Lake locality of the south-central American Bottom and the northern American Bottom in terms of temper, relative proportions of stylistic traits, and rates of change (Kelly, Ozuk et al. 1984). It is because of this diversity that it is necessary in some areas to retain the Fairmount phase designation for occupations that span the terminal Emergent Mississippian and early Mississippian periods.

Most Emergent Mississippian settlements in the American Bottom are small, although it appears there existed a chainlike series of single and multimound centers along the bottomlands (Porter 1974). Cahokia, and perhaps the Lunsford-Pulcher site, may have dwarfed other settlements during this time, but not to the degree that was attained later in the Mississippian period.

Beginning with the earliest identified Mississippian phase, Lohmann (A.D. 1000–1050), Cahokia began to dominate the Mississippian landscape and the site witnessed a remarkable explosion in site plan and function. Major constructions were undertaken, including a massive burial program (Mound 72). The occupation of Cahokia expanded from a compact village to encompass most of the presently understood site boundaries. Occupation away from the mound centers appears, on the basis of present evidence, to have been minimal, perhaps attributable to the centripetal forces that gave rise to the maximal chiefdom developing at the Cahokia site. Ceramic assemblages, particularly at the Cahokia site, display pure Mississippian characteristics, with only traces of the Emergent Mississippian period. It is likely that sites in the Prairie Lake locality and perhaps in the northern upland were slower to adopt these characteristics.

By Stirling times (A.D. 1050–1150), the Mississippian occupation at Cahokia and in the surrounding bottomlands appears to have reached a peak. New mound centers probably emerged at sites such as Mitchell (Porter 1974); however, the picture is murky regarding the East St. Louis and the St. Louis mound centers. The Stirling phase ushered in widespread stylistic homogeneity in the American Bottom, and Cahokian styles were broadcast great distances outside the region. Late during the Stirling phase, however, changes are evident that suggest conflict

and the beginnings of the breakdown of the Cahokian polity. The central palisade was erected sometime within the Stirling phase and was rebuilt several times into the succeeding Moorehead phase. It is also possible that a greater number of smaller settlements dotted the American Bottom landscape during Stirling times, suggestive of centrifugal forces, pulling away from the centralizing process initiated during the Lohmann phase (Harn 1980a; Milner et al. 1984).

The succeeding Moorehead phase (A.D. 1150–1250) is marked by a dramatic decline in population density both at Cahokia and in the surrounding bottomlands. Whether Cahokia was transformed into a primarily ceremonial center or reduced to a smaller power confined within the central palisade is unknown at present. The final Mississippian phase, Sand Prairie (A.D. 1250–1400), is best characterized as "rump" Mississippian, which is distinguished by minimal mound construction and occupation of the central precincts of most mound centers in the region. Populations continued to decline in the area and less organizational complexity indicates a devolving society (Milner 1986b). The Oneota Vulcan phase occupation is poorly known and may have overlapped in time with the Sand Prairie occupation.

Environmental Setting

We have defined our domain as the Illinois Upland, which refers particularly to those drainages that were most directly affected by Mississippian developments within the American Bottom. As defined, these uplands encompass over 430,000 hectares, roughly four times the size of the American Bottom. Included within this area are large portions of Madison, St. Clair, and Monroe counties, as well as smaller segments of Jersey, Macoupin, Montgomery, Bond, and Randolph counties (fig. 3.1). Major drainages within the region include Wood River and Cahokia, Silver, and Richland creeks, as well as a number of small streams flowing into the American Bottom and the lower Kaskaskia River (fig. 3.2).

In general, the upland topography consists of moderately to deeply incised stream courses separated by rolling hills and gently sloping interfluves that increase in width toward the east. Moderately wide expanses of floodplain and terrace are found only in portions of the Wood River, Cahokia Creek, and Silver Creek valleys. Except in isolated outcrops along some of the dissected stream valleys, the underlying Mississippian and Pennsylvanian bedrock is covered with a thick Pleistocene mantel of Illinoian glacial till and Wisconsinan loess. There is also an extensive area of sinkhole topography found in extreme southwest-

ern St. Clair County and western Monroe and Randolph counties.

Prior to historic clearing, a number of vegetation communities were present in the uplands (Lopinot and Woods 1988). Within the northern portion, an approximately three- to six-kilometer-wide fringe of oak-hickory forest existed along the moderately to heavily dissected terrain of the American Bottom bluff edge. Further to the interior, a series of interfluvial prairies and prairie isolates of varying size were surrounded by open woodlands. To the east, a narrow band of oak-hickory forest was associated with Silver Creek and its tributaries, beyond which were large expanses of prairie and savanna. In the southern part of the uplands, closed canopy forests would have been present only along stream courses, with hill prairies along the American Bottom bluff line and prairie isolates and open woodlands in the interior.

The uplands would have provided a variety of natural resources for prehistoric Mississippian populations. A number of materials contained within glacial till exposures, including chert, igneous rock, and metamorphic erratics, were widely utilized, as were some of the cherts associated with Mississippian-system limestone outcrops. These lithic sources would have been especially signifi-

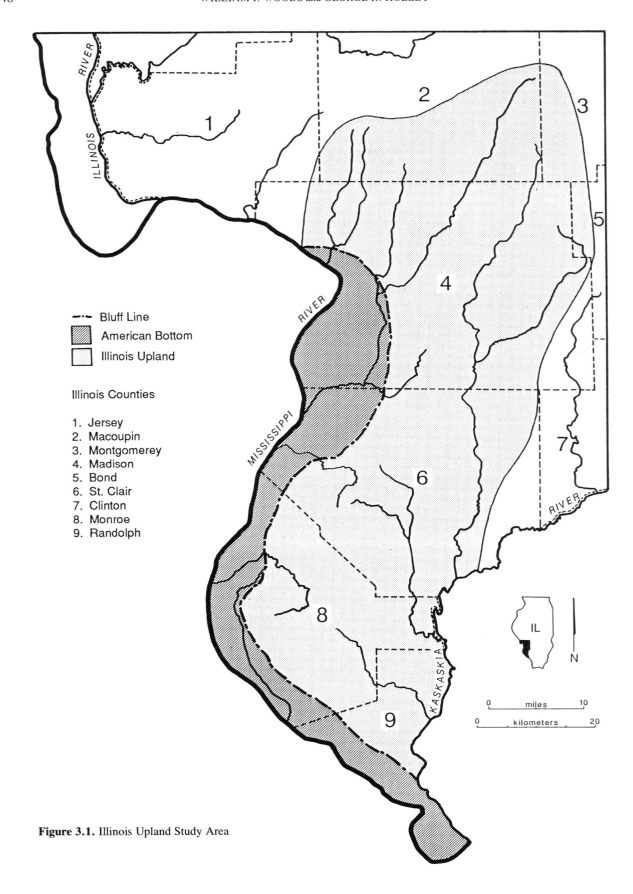

Figure 3.1. Illinois Upland Study Area

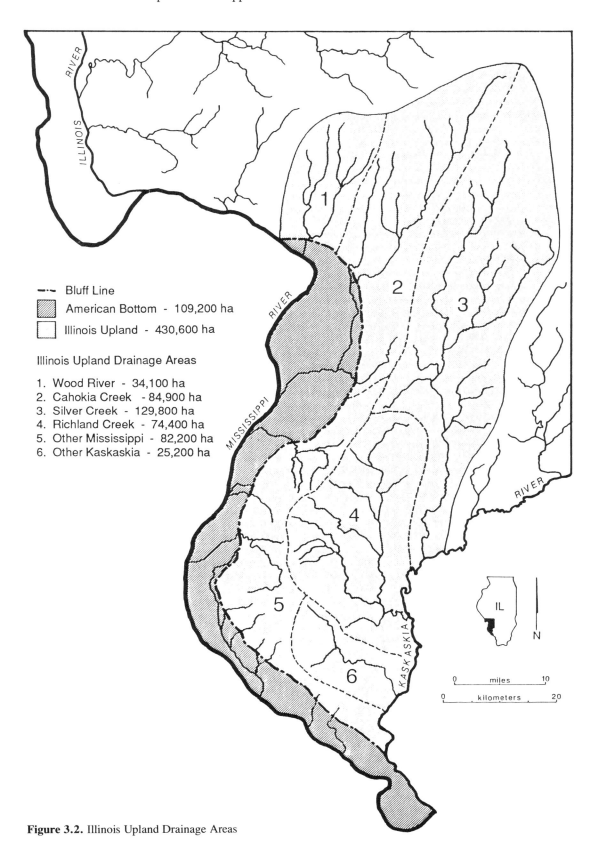

Bluff Line

American Bottom - 109,200 ha

Illinois Upland - 430,600 ha

Illinois Upland Drainage Areas

1. Wood River - 34,100 ha
2. Cahokia Creek - 84,900 ha
3. Silver Creek - 129,800 ha
4. Richland Creek - 74,400 ha
5. Other Mississippi - 82,200 ha
6. Other Kaskaskia - 25,200 ha

Figure 3.2. Illinois Upland Drainage Areas

cant, as they were the closest available to American Bottom populations. Because stands of timber were limited in the American Bottom, the oak-hickory forests of the adjacent uplands would have been extensively exploited for fuel and building materials. For subsistence, the plentiful deer and small mammal populations and rich nut masts of these forests would also have provided important resources. However, for a society relying to a great extent upon food production, fertile, friable soils would have been a primary resource consideration. In this regard, a more detailed discussion of the pedology of the uplands and its cultural implications is warranted.

In the uplands, soil development took place in loessal or alluvial sediments under the various vegetation communities indicated above. With modern agricultural management, the loessal soils are quite productive, and their prehistoric agricultural utilization in upland prairie and forested bluff-edge settings has been suggested by Perino (quoted in Williams 1971:15–16) and Fowler and Hall (1978:561). However, strong objections can be raised against the aboriginal use of these soils. In prairie settings, high acidity, extremely poor drainage, and the dense root network would have reduced productivity and greatly hindered tillage. Fires would also have presented a clear danger to the maturing crops in late summer and early fall. Problems associated with cultivation of the bluff top soils include low organic matter content, high rates of erosion, and poor sustained levels of productivity without fertilization. Rather, it is in upland alluvial settings that aboriginal fields are expected to have been located.

Various investigators have noted the close association of Mississippian sites and fertile, friable bottomland soils (for a summary, see Woods 1987), and ethnohistorical accounts of aboriginal farming practices in the eastern United States and the Missouri River drainage almost without exception refer to field areas in alluvial settings. From the perspective of the Mississippian maize-oriented agricultural strategy, a nonacid silt loam with initially high and periodically renewed nutrient levels and good hydrologic characteristics (including drainage and frequency and periodicity of flooding) would be the optimum matrix. Of the over 150 soil series and subseries present within the Illinois Upland, only soils of the Wakeland silt loam series exhibit all of these properties (Goddard and Sabata 1986; Higgins 1987; Wallace 1978). With the exception of portions of the Silver and Richland creek drainages, where they are more concentrated, Wakeland soils have a noncontinuous distribution in most of the upland alluvial settings and encompass about five percent of the area. Further discussion of the significance of the Wakeland soils will follow.

Previous Archaeological Research

Although we have defined the Illinois Upland to include the bluff edge in areal computations, the following review of archaeological research in the area excludes a one kilometer swath of the uplands adjacent to the bottomlands. It is very likely that these settlements were exploiting both upland and bottomland environments. Furthermore, this area has received extensive discussion in Munson's (1971) and Harn's (1971a) surveys of the American Bottom and adjacent bluff edge. Also, the FAI-270 program has conducted a number of excavations and surveys associated with borrow pit areas along the bluff edge (e.g., McElrath and Finney 1987).

The history of archaeological research in the interior uplands has been limited primarily to surveys. Although some of the more prominent Emergent Mississippian- and Mississippian-period sites were identified early (e.g., Griffin and Spaulding 1951) before extensive survey coverage, they are unfortunately still poorly known.

Large-scale site survey in the uplands has been done primarily under the aegis of the Illinois State Historic Preservation Office (SHPO) Historic Sites Survey (HSS) Program and through various projects sponsored by the Illinois Department of Transportation (IDOT). The HSS Program included two projects that were conducted between 1971 and 1974 within the Illinois Upland.

The second major source of survey coverage is the group of projects initiated in the mid-1960s and funded by the Illinois Department of Transportation. Within the study area, these IDOT projects resulted in a series of reports of work on FAI-64, FAP-409, FAP-410, and FAP-413. A number of more limited investigations augment the larger surveys and have included survey and excavation in borrow pit areas, state highway expansions, and bridge relocations by the University of Illinois Resource Investigation Program and other cultural resource management (CRM) studies. In addition, small-scale CRM projects, too numerous to mention here, have contributed to our understanding of the upland.

At present, fewer than a dozen sites dating from the Emergent Mississippian through Mississippian periods have been tested or extensively excavated. An examination of the Illinois Archaeological Survey (IAS) site files, coupled with the research reviewed in this study, indicate that known Mississippian sites in the upland study area number roughly 100.

An analysis of all extant collections relevant to the

study area was not attempted, although ceramic collections from the Richland Creek and Cahokia Creek drainages were examined. Our temporal assignments for known sites have thus relied on the limited materials examined, published data, and information contained within the IAS site files.

Discussions of previous archaeological research will be presented by drainage area. The six drainages have been divided strictly on a geomorphologic basis (fig. 3.2). The only exception is Drainage Area 5, which encompasses both Pennsylvanian and Mississippian surficial bedrock formations and was not subdivided because of the lack of relevant archaeological research to warrant a division.

WOOD RIVER DRAINAGE

Encompassing 34,100 hectares, the Wood River drainage (fig. 3.2, drainage area 1) flows into the Mississippi River and in its upper reaches joins the divide with Macoupin Creek. The drainage has been subjected to two extensive survey programs; however, only one site has been excavated.

Survey of FAP-413 alignments in the interior upland of the Wood River drainage revealed more Emergent Mississippian than Mississippian sites (Linder, Cartmell, and Kelly 1978:29; Hawks 1985). Evidence was recovered for only three interior upland Mississippian sites, one of which dates to the Moorehead/Sand Prairie time span (Linder, Cartmell, and Kelly 1978:31; Hawks 1985).

The Wood River Survey program, funded by IDOT, involved the pedestrian survey of the upland sections of the Wood River drainage within Madison County, concentrating on the floodplain and adjacent bluffs (Jackson 1979). The survey located 119 newly defined sites and twelve previously recorded sites, overlapping a portion surveyed during the FAP-413 project. Of the upland sites, seventy-five could be assigned temporal affiliations. Twenty-six sites (34.7%), including two with mounds, were identified as Late Bluff (Emergent Mississippian). The Emergent Mississippian ceramic assemblage was dominated by grit-tempered, Late Bluff jars (plain neck and cord-marked body), with a few examples of limestone- and shell-tempered ceramics that may have been imported from the American Bottom. Mississippian sites and shell-tempered ceramics were notably scant. Five Mississippian sites were identified (6.7%), including the Olin site (11-Ms-133). With the exception of the Olin site, these Mississippian sites cannot be assigned a more precise temporal affiliation.

Numerous additional surveys on a smaller scale have failed to identify Mississippian-period habitations. On the basis of these surveys and earlier and ongoing research, Mississippian-period usage of the Wood River drainage appears to be concentrated on the bluff edge proper.

The only Mississippian-period site excavated in this upland drainage is the Olin site (11-Ms-133) located on the bluffs overlooking the East Fork of Wood River, approximately two kilometers inland from the American Bottom (fig. 3.3). This multicomponent site was originally surveyed in 1963 by Patrick J. Munson (1971:9, 14) and subsequently excavated by Sidney G. Denny between 1971 and 1975 (Denny 1974; Denny, Woods, and Koldehoff 1983). The first intensive occupation of the site consisted of numerous pit features dating from the Emergent Mississippian period. After an occupational hiatus, the site was intensively occupied late in the Mississippian period.

The Mississippian occupation has been divided into two components. The first component, dating from late Stirling through early Moorehead phase, is represented by a village surrounded by a palisade of single-post construction (Denny, Woods, and Koldehoff 1983). The second component, from the late Moorehead through early Sand Prairie phase, is also enclosed within a palisade, measuring twenty-three meters on each side, with three rounded bastions. Evidence of nearly fifty wall-trench structures was recovered for the Mississippian occupation. Structure shapes included typical rectangular and square forms, as well as possible multiroom and circular buildings. In-place rebuilding was quite common.

Extensive survey coverage of the Wood River drainage has produced abundant evidence of Emergent Mississippian-period occupation. Ceramic data are indicative of "classic" Late Bluff assemblages. It is possible that a number of these sites date to the later time span of the Emergent Mississippian period, as judged by the number of ceramic diagnostics recovered by Jackson (1979). The small number of shell-tempered ceramics, especially those recovered from Emergent Mississippian sites, may not represent a separate Mississippian-period occupation, but rather the importation of vessels manufactured in the bottomlands. Except for the Olin site, there is little evidence of a Stirling occupation for the upland portions of this drainage. Later Mississippian utilization is poorly understood, again with the exception of the Olin site.

CAHOKIA CREEK DRAINAGE

The Cahokia Creek drainage (fig. 3.2, drainage area 2), encompassing 84,900 hectares, begins in Macoupin and Montgomery counties to the north and includes all of the drainages south to Little Canteen Creek. This is the only drainage directly associated with the Cahokia site. Although there have been a number of small-scale surveys, with the most extensive coverage resulting from the HSS work in 1973–74 (Denny and Anderson 1974,

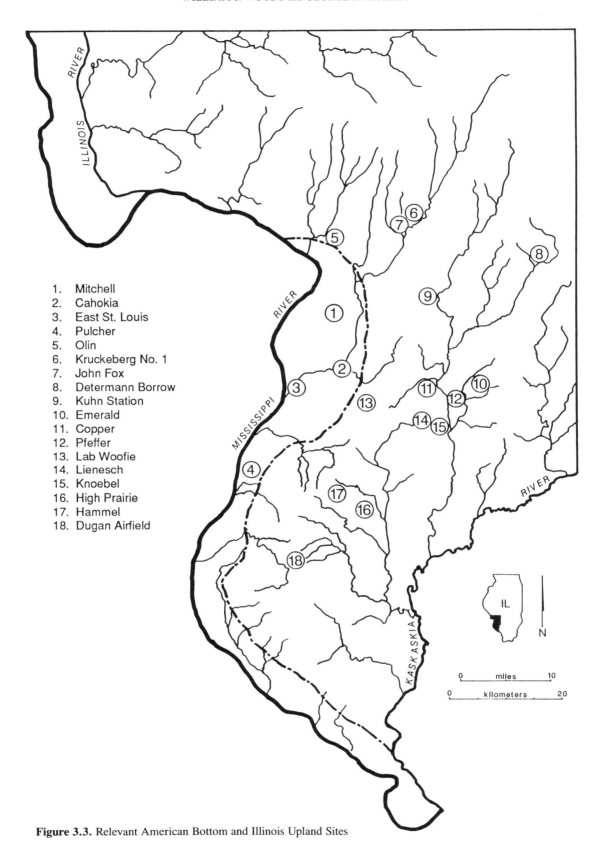

1. Mitchell
2. Cahokia
3. East St. Louis
4. Pulcher
5. Olin
6. Kruckeberg No. 1
7. John Fox
8. Determann Borrow
9. Kuhn Station
10. Emerald
11. Copper
12. Pfeffer
13. Lab Woofie
14. Lienesch
15. Knoebel
16. High Prairie
17. Hammel
18. Dugan Airfield

Figure 3.3. Relevant American Bottom and Illinois Upland Sites

1975), these have yielded little data relevant to this study. No sites have been excavated.

A survey program, unique for the upland, was implemented in 1982 by William I. Woods. This survey was designed to test the hypothesis that Mississippian agricultural settlements were most likely to be found in areas proximal to soils of the Wakeland silt loam series (Woods 1986, 1987, 1988; Woods and Denny 1982). The study area included the 25,500-hectare portion of the main stem Cahokia Creek drainage within the uplands of Madison County. Because of the size of the study area, sampling was necessary. It was determined that simple random sampling would be the most efficient for this situation. Furthermore, the rectangular grid of the General Land Office system provided an in-place basis for division. A 5% random sample of seventy-seven forty-acre (16.2 hectare) units was surveyed during 1982.

As a result of the survey, 108 prehistoric sites were identified, and of these, forty-five components could be assigned to temporal positions. Four components were assigned to the Mississippian period on the basis of recovered ceramics. Although Emergent Mississippian ceramics were not recovered in the survey, an examination of local collections indicated that this period was represented in the drainage.

The Mississippian settlement pattern within the study area was observed to be the most restricted. Mississippian sites were found only in positions exhibiting multiple prior occupations and a close proximity to large areas of Wakeland soils and the main stem of Cahokia Creek. Within a one-kilometer radius of the center of each Mississippian site, a mean total of 25% of the soils are Wakeland. Given that Wakeland soils cover only 5% of the study area and exhibit a sporadic distribution, their selection by Mississippians is clear. Although areally more extensive, other bottomland soils exhibited much lower correlations with Mississippian sites and in many cases appear to have been consciously avoided. This suggests that, although hunting and gathering continued as subsistence activities, horticultural and agricultural pursuits were of paramount importance in choice of site location. Indeed, the distribution of chert hoes and resharpening flakes recovered by the project and reported by local collecters conforms to Mississippian sites or areas of Wakeland soils.

Three of the Mississippian sites appear to have been farmsteads or hamlets, whereas the fourth, Kruckeberg No. 1 (11-Ms-341), represents a more intensive village occupation. At the latter site Mississippian ceramics were confined to a rectangular zone bounded on three sides by steep slopes. Later examination of a large-scale aerial photograph of the site revealed that this zone was bordered by dark lines, possibly indicating a stockade. If

so, Ms-341 may have functioned as a nodal community to which the local dispersed population fled in times of danger.

On the basis of ceramics recovered during the Cahokia Creek survey, the major portion of the Mississippian occupation can be placed within the Moorehead phase. Kruckeberg No. 1 produced the largest sample of ceramics, in excess of 100 sherds and seventeen rims. Cahokia Cordmarked sherds and angled-rim jars predominate (fig. 3.4). Other shapes present include bowls (fig. 3.4g), basins with modified rims (fig. 3.4h-i), along with possible examples of a plate (fig. 3.4f), a bottle, and a funnel.

The majority of the ceramics are tempered with shell, and only a few Cahokia Cordmarked sherds are tempered with both shell and grog. Red slips and smudged-black surfaces are equally represented, but the majority are plain or weathered. Another angled-rim jar was recovered from the D. Hitchens site (11-Ms-1124) (fig. 3.4b). The only departure from this Moorehead pattern is a single rim (fig. 3.4a) recovered from the John Fox site (11-Ms-1108). This rim, with an overhanging rolled/everted treatment, may date to the Lohmann/Stirling time span.

In addition to the random sample survey, we have reviewed the previously reported sites in the drainage and are in the process of accumulating distributional data from local collectors. Currently, this continuing effort has identified additional Mississippian sites in the project area, all of which are closely associated with Wakeland soils. Outside the sampled survey area, one site in the drainage has been reported to contain a mound (11-Ms-25), and other mound sites are known. The temporal affiliation for these mounds cannot be determined from the existing data.

In summary, there is little evidence for extensive Emergent Mississippian- and early Mississippian-period occupations in the drainage. In contrast, later Mississippian occupations are well represented and appear to be confined to the Moorehead phase. A variety of settlement types has been identified for this phase.

SILVER CREEK DRAINAGE

The Silver Creek drainage (fig. 3.2, drainage area 3), encompassing 129,800 hectares, is the largest drainage in the Illinois Upland. The creek trends north to south and feeds into the Kaskaskia River. The drainage has witnessed the longest history of archaeological investigation in the uplands, including early work at major sites, extensive survey, and comparatively more excavation than other upland drainages.

The earliest recorded investigations in Silver Creek were initiated by John Francis Synder (1877:434, and

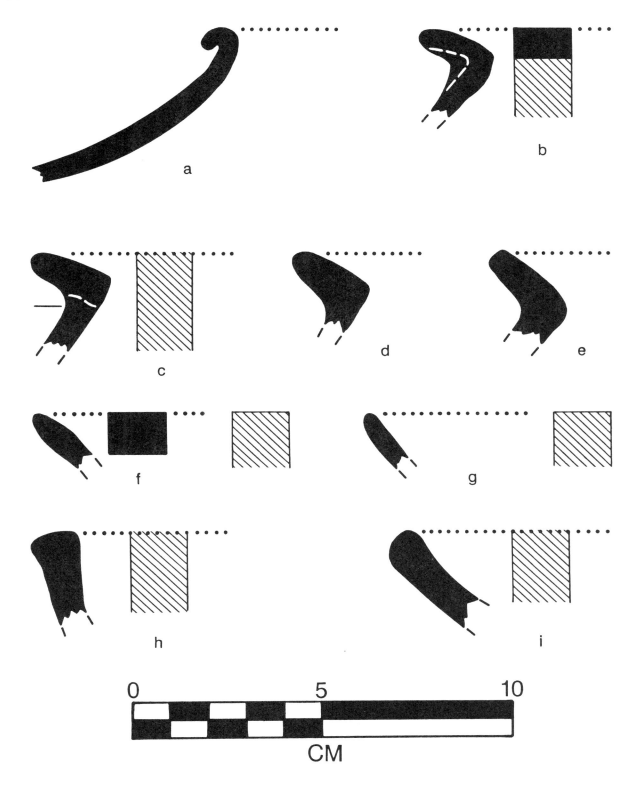

Figure 3.4. Mississippian Shell-tempered Vessels from the Cahokia Creek Survey: (a) John Fox (11-Ms-1108); (b) D. Hitchens (11-Ms-1124); (c-i) Kruckeberg No. 1 (11-Ms-341). Bars depict the location and color of slipped surfaces; diagonal lines depict red slips and solid areas depict smudged-black surfaces.

1909:74–77), who in 1876 visited and described the Emerald site (11-S-1) as including five mounds and a village area (fig. 3.3). He noted the mound dimensions and mentioned the trace remains of a trail that led from Emerald to the Cahokia site. Warren K. Moorehead (1929: 64–65) tested unspecified mounds at the site but was disillusioned by his lack of spectacular finds.

James B. Griffin visited a number of prominent sites in the area in 1947 as part of the Central Mississippi Valley Archaeological Survey. In addition to reporting on the Emerald site, he was the first to report the Copper site (11-S-3) (fig. 3.3), dating this multimound site to late in the Mississippian period (Griffin and Spaulding 1951: pl. 4, fig. 1). Stone-box graves and exotic artifacts were reported as deriving from the site. Analysis of artifacts from the Copper site by Pauketat and Koldehoff (1983) supports a Sand Prairie phase date.

The Emerald site continued to be a focal point for research in the area. Winters and Struever (1962) tested the apron of the principal mound and a smaller mound (Mound 2) and collected materials from the village area. Based on their results, the site was occupied first during the Late Woodland period and was extensively occupied during the Emergent Mississippian period, particularly the Fairmount phase. It is likely that the mounds were constructed during the Fairmount phase; however, ceramics dating to the Sand Prairie phase were recovered from a pit in Mound 2. Further salvage work at the Emerald site was undertaken by Robert L. Hall in 1964 (Hall 1965; see also Benchley 1974:242). Hall apparently excavated a secondary mound on the summit of the principal mound (Benchley 1974:243). Analysis of Hall's collection by Pauketat and Koldehoff (1983) indicates that the excavated material dates to the Sand Prairie phase. A radiocarbon date of A.D. 1500 for this summit occupation of the principal mound has been reported (Benchley 1974:239).

Subsequent excavations during 1967–69, related to the construction of FAI-64, resulted in the excavation of an Emergent Mississippian community at the Knoebel site (Munson 1968; Bareis 1969, 1976). The site (11-S-71) is located on a terrace overlooking Silver Creek to the east, approximately nine kilometers southwest of the Emerald site (fig. 3.3). Knoebel represents a village settlement and displays a transition from the terminal Emergent Mississippian period to the Lohmann phase of the Mississippian period. The occupational sequence includes a shift from the single-post Emergent Mississippian style structure to the Mississippian wall-trench structure, with features clustering around a plaza demarcated by a central "marker" post.

Ceramics from Knoebel (Bareis 1976) display stylistic features that can be readily encompassed within the Cahokia and northern American Bottom ceramic sequence. Judging by the presence of grit-and-grog-tempered jars with modified and notched rims, stumpware boots, and Merrell Red bowls, a relatively late placement within the Emergent Mississippian period seems indicated. The presence of Monks Mound Red and shell-tempered, red-slipped jars with extruded rims are also Lohmann phase diagnostics (Holley 1989). An even later (Moorehead phase?) occupation may be represented (but not reported) at the site, based on the presence of a shell-tempered jar with an angled rim (Bareis 1976: fig. 3j). The apparent rarity of black-smudged surfaces may indicate either an early placement during the Lohmann phase for the Mississippian component or a lag in the appearance of Cahokia-derived traits in this drainage. When assessed in conjunction with the presence of Yankeetown-related material, which was also recovered from the Emerald site (Winters and Struever 1962), the Knoebel ceramic assemblage is clearly on a par with developments and influences witnessed in the Cahokia environs.

Between 1971 and 1974, an HSS project directed by Charles Bareis extensively covered the Silver Creek drainage (Rauh 1971, 1975; Rauh and Wilson 1972, 1974). A total of 391 new sites was reported, 307 with identified temporal affiliation. Although only nine sites were reported as dating to the Mississippian period, six additional sites contained both Late Woodland and Mississippian components. In addition, the larger sample of 106 Late Woodland sites probably includes a number of Emergent Mississippian-period occupations. Sufficient data to place these sites into the established Mississippian sequence are not provided in the published information. All of these sites are positioned along the main stem of Silver Creek and its major tributaries.

Also as part of the HSS Program, an additional Mississippian site (11-Ms-549) was identified and tested by Denny and Anderson (1975:139–41). This site is located on the drainage divide between Cahokia and Silver creeks, near the town of Maryville, in Madison County. Only one shell-tempered sherd, a Madison point, and a possible wall trench relating to the Mississippian occupation were recovered from this multicomponent site.

Another IDOT project in the area was a survey of the FAP-409 R.O.W. (Hendrickson, Cartmell, and Kelly 1977), a proposed east-west alignment located one kilometer south of Lebanon, Illinois. No evidence of Mississippian occupation was recovered within this alignment.

Numerous Mississippian sites were previously reported to the IAS by a number of sources. Among these was another multimound site, the William Pfeffer #2 and #3 site complex (11-S-204, 205) (fig. 3.3). This site was reported as having two mounds and an associated village. The mounds are presently on a golf course. Emergent Mississippian and possibly Mississippian occupations were identified. Recent excavations at the southern limits of the site (Gums and Brown 1986) revealed the remains of pit features dating to the Late Woodland period. In addition, examination of materials recovered from recent construction activities near the mounds has identified a Lohmann component (John E. Kelly, personal communication, 1988).

Additional sites with information pertaining to the Mississippian period within the Silver Creek drainage are the Kuhn Station (11-Ms-29) and Determann Borrow (11-Ms-1060) sites (fig. 3.3). Originally reported in 1954, the Kuhn Station site is a single mound village located about twenty kilometers upstream from the Emerald site. The site is a compact, planned village (about 0.3 hectares in size) surrounded by an earthen embankment (Van Hartesveldt 1980). Within the enclosure are fifty depressions, interpreted as structure basins, and a low pyramidal mound surrounding a possible plaza. Shell-tempered ceramics reported from the site include Cahokia Cordmarked sherds and a broad-rim plate, which date to the Moorehead/Sand Prairie time span.

The Determann Borrow site (Jackson 1984) is located in the northeastern section of the Silver Creek drainage (fig. 3.3). This multicomponent site yielded only a single, rectangular wall-trench structure and associated internal pit feature. Based on the scant material remains recovered, the site appears to represent a short-term Mississippian occupation of unknown temporal affiliation.

The sequence of occupation for Silver Creek appears uninterrupted from early during the Emergent Mississippian period through early in the Mississippian period. Although we are unsure of the nature of early aspects of the Emergent Mississippian period, a pattern develops later that can be clearly identified as the Fairmount phase. During this phase a settlement hierarchy is present. The multimound Emerald site dominates the settlement system. Unlike other sites, it is situated some distance from higher-order stream courses. The Pfeffer site, with two mounds, constitutes the second level. Villages, such as the Knoebel site, are more numerous, as are hamlets and farmsteads. Ceramics recovered from these sites are stylistically related to the Cahokia site, as opposed to the southern American Bottom.

An occupational hiatus follows this Fairmount florescence, and the area does not appear to be inhabited with any intensity during the Stirling and Moorehead phases. However, the Sand Prairie phase is well represented. There is Sand Prairie reoccupation at the Emerald site and a degree of mound modification occurred. Mound construction at the Copper site during this phase is unique for the uplands.

RICHLAND CREEK DRAINAGE

The Richland Creek drainage (fig. 3.2, drainage area 4) encompasses 74,400 hectares. The predominant direction of flow is toward the south into the Kaskaskia River. This is the closest drainage to the south-central portion of the American Bottom.

Two related surveys in this drainage were conducted by Sidney G. Denny (1976) and Brad Koldehoff (1982b). The Denny survey, funded by IDOT, was concentrated on the main channel of Richland Creek and adjacent bluffs and extensively utilized Koldehoff's collections from Douglas Creek as representative of the area. Denny recorded the discovery of 125 sites in addition to twenty-three previously reported sites. Forty-two were of unknown temporal affiliation. Of the sites for which components could be identified, nineteen (17.9%) can be dated within the Mississippian period. Unlike the Silver Creek survey data, in which sites recorded as Late Woodland may date to the Emergent Mississippian period, available data do not appear to indicate the same case for Richland Creek.

Fifteen of the Mississipppian sites are located in the Douglas Creek drainage. Douglas Creek is a second-order tributary of Richland Creek, situated in southwestern St. Clair County about twenty-five kilometers southeast of the Cahokia site. The principal soil type within the alluvial valley of Douglas Creek is Wakeland silt loam. Survey data were generated over a seven-year period by Brad Koldehoff (1982b), and although the survey was unsystematic and some portions of the drainage were surveyed more thoroughly than others, these problems are largely offset by the fact that extensive areas have been intensively covered and all sites have been revisited five or more times (Denny, Woods, and Koldehoff 1983). Therefore, considerably more is known about each site than would normally be the case. Five additional sites were added to the roster of Denny's original survey on the basis of Koldehoff's efforts, bringing the total to twenty-four Mississippian sites in the Richland Creek drainage. Four of these sites were added to the Mississippian roster on the basis of the presence of Mill Creek hoe debitage and triangular projectile points. An additional site, the St. Clair County Farm and Nature Preserve (11-Ms-442), yielded a significant collection of ceramic artifacts. An extension of this site, designated the High Prairie site, had limited salvage excavations, but no subsurface features were exposed (Brad Koldehoff, personal communication, 1988). Finally, one site, Hammel (11-S-554), was partially excavated in a salvage operation.

Based on detailed records of collections provided by local informants, Koldehoff's (1982b) descriptions, and an analysis of ceramics collected from the surface, the Mississippian occupation can be divided into at least three broadly defined phases. The early component can be placed within the Fairmount phase, which includes terminal Emergent Mississippian and early Mississippian (Lohmann) phases. Examples of the Late Bluff jar, representative of earlier Emergent Mississippian styles, are conspicuously absent. A qualification of the ceramic sequence, however, is in order. Based on research in the south-central American Bottom, it appears that Emergent Mississippian ceramic styles, involving limestone tempering and red slipping, continued well into the Stirling phase in this region (Kelly, Ozuk et al. 1984; Mehrer 1982). Thus typical Lohmann and Stirling phase diagnostics may be rarely recovered from this drainage.

Ceramics assumed to date from the Fairmount phase are characterized by a variety of temper types. As expected, limestone tempering is dominant, followed by shell and to a lesser extent grog. Red slipping is prevalent. Vessel shapes include extruded-rim jars, bowls, and seed jars. A unique imported vessel was recovered from the High Prairie site (Koldehoff 1982a) that can be classified as relating to a variety of the French Fork Incised type of the Lower Mississippi Valley. Seven sites, including one multicomponent site, are securely dated to the Fairmount phase.

The High Prairie site occupies a prominent interfluvial area located immediately to the north of the drainage divide between Douglas Creek and the West Fork of Richland Creek (fig. 3.3) and represents an exception to the Mississippian settlement pattern in Richland Creek. All other reported sites are located proximal to the main stem of either Richland or Douglas creeks. Outside the Douglas Creek area, a number of other large Fairmount settlements appear to be the analogues of the High Prairie site (Koldehoff 1982a, 1982b). These sites are located on prominent points along local drainage divides and include the Dugan Airfield site (11-Mo-718) on the Mississippi-Kaskaskia divide (Woods and Mitchell 1978) and the Holliday (Griffin and Spaulding 1951) and Miller Farm (Koldehoff 1982b) sites on the interfluves between Richland and Silver creeks.

One site, Bonnie (11-S-562), is dated by Koldehoff (1982b) to a Stirling/Moorehead time frame. This is based on the recovery of Powell Plain jars, including a rolled rim, and a Ramey Incised jar. A Cahokia Cordmarked sherd was also recovered and a Fairmount component may also be present.

The last occupation of the area dates to the Moorehead/Sand Prairie span and is represented by five sites. Ceramic diagnostics include the predominance of shell tempering; Cahokia Cordmarked sherds and angled-rim

jars; jars with direct rims and high, flaring necks; funnels; basins; bowls; and bottles. Red slipping appears commonly. Fabric-impressed sherds are also present. On the basis of rim morphology, the majority of the ceramics for this component date from the Sand Prairie phase. Six sites are dated to this time span. The partially excavated Hammel site (11-S-554) yielded a burned square to rectangular wall-trench structure enclosing an area 5.8 by 4.8 meters, with an interior pit and hearth (fig. 3.3). To the north of the structure was an extended burial, partially cremated, with two associated effigy bowls (Koldehoff 1982b).

Small samples of ceramics from an additional six sites included shell-tempered sherds with red slips. Due to the popularity of red slips early and late in the sequence, it is not possible to place these samples into either component. Finally, five sites were dated as Mississippian on the basis of projectile points or hoe-related debitage.

Three sites have received additional attention in the confines of the Richland Creek drainage. The Holliday site (11-S-26) is located 0.25 kilometers north of the Lienesch site (fig. 3.3), at the headwaters of Richland Creek, near the drainage divide. This site has a long history of exploration, most of which was not systematic. Based on Griffin's (Griffin and Spaulding 1951:80, pl. 4, fig. 2) reporting of material recovered by Robert E. Grimm, it appears to date from the Fairmount phase.

The Lienesch site (11-S-67), excavated as part of the FAI-64 project (Bareis 1972), is situated at the headwaters of Richland Creek, to the west of Knoebel, and exhibited an Emergent Mississippian/Fairmount component. This occupation appears to have consisted of a farmstead containing two single-post structures erected in shallow basins and a number of associated pits. Ceramics from both sites indicate close affinity to the Silver Creek drainage sites, such as Knoebel, as opposed to the ceramic assemblages recovered further downstream.

The Roos site (11-S-692) is located on the main stem of the West Fork of Richland Creek, the drainage immediately to the south of Douglas Creek. Little remained of the site that was exposed during excavation (Bender and Webb 1983). Ceramics indicate a Fairmount occupation, with affinities to the south-central American Bottom.

Unlike the previously described drainages, Richland Creek exhibits two distinct ceramic traditions for the Emergent Mississippian to early Mississippian time span. The headwaters of Richland Creek appear associated with shell and grit-grog tempers typical of the adjacent central Silver Creek drainage and northern American Bottom, whereas downstream the ceramics are affiliated with a limestone-tempered ceramic tradition that is rooted in the southern American Bottom.

A new pattern of settlement placement emerges in the southern drainages during the Fairmount phase in which a number of fairly intensively occupied settlements were placed on drainage divides. This is not expected given the predilection of these agriculturally based peoples for rich alluvial soils. These prominent locations seem more important in relation to the control of overland transportation. The lower-order settlements conform to the expected pattern and are found on the main stems of the major creeks and their tributaries.

The Stirling phase is weakly represented in the drainage; however, as with other areas of the upland, resettlement is evident late during the Mississippian period. This late occupation consists only of lower-order settlements (hamlets and farmsteads).

OTHER UPLAND DRAINAGES

We have combined the last two upland drainage areas (fig. 3.2, drainage areas 5 and 6). This area is characterized by many small drainages flowing into the American Bottom and the Kaskaskia River. None of the drainages has received sufficient archaeological attention, nor are they large enough to warrant separate consideration.

A number of small-scale surveys (e.g., Ahler 1984; Koldehoff, Wells, and Woods 1983) produced no evidence of Emergent Mississippian and Mississippian occupations. Only two large-scale surveys have been conducted in the southern sections of our study area.

In 1976 and 1977 a series of proposed alternate highway alignments designated FAP-410 were surveyed by Southern Illinois University at Edwardsville (Williams and Woods 1977). A portion of these alignments was located within the upland study area in Monroe and Randolph counties, between the Richland Creek drainage and drainages flowing into the Mississippi River to the west and into the Kaskaskia to the south (fig. 3.2). Of the forty-three sites identified in the study area, sixteen were assigned temporal affiliation, although a large number of the other sites may date to the Archaic period. Ceramic remains were uncommon and only two sites dated to the Fairmount phase, based on the presence of Monks Mound Red sherds. Only one Mississippian site was represented by a black-smudged sherd, which may date to the Stirling/Moorehead time span. No Mississippian sites were identified within the drainages flowing into the Kaskaskia River.

Another IDOT-funded survey in the Dupo-Waterloo Anticline area identified fifty-four sites, eleven of known temporal affiliation (Woods and Mitchell 1978). Only one Mississippian site (11-Mo-683), probably dating to the Fairmount phase on the basis of a variety of temper recipes (limestone, shell, grit, and grog) and red slipping, was recorded. The site is significant in that it is situated in an area of sinkhole topography. An additional four sites were reported by Koldehoff immediately to the south of project area at the headwaters of Fountain Creek. Three of the sites date to the Emergent Mississippian period and one of these, the Dugan Airfield site (11-Mo-718), also dates to the Mississippian period (Woods and Mitchell 1978). A minor Moorehead/Sand Prairie phase affiliation appears to be indicated for the Mississippian occupation.

Only two sites within this portion of the uplands have been excavated (fig. 3.3). In the spring of 1977 as part of an IDOT relocation project, the Lab Woofie site (11-S-346) was identified. It is located 1.6 kilometers east of the bluff edge along Schoenberger Creek, a small tributary feeding into the American Bottom. The site is a late Stirling phase farmstead consisting of two wall-trench structures and associated pit features (Prentice and Mehrer 1981). The two structures may have been functionally or seasonally distinct and were most likely occupied by a single family with a variety of site activities, including horticulture, evident (Prentice and Mehrer 1981:39).

Approximately four hundred meters to the north of the Lab Woofie site, the Holdener (11-MS-685) site was examined in 1979-80 due to the excavation of an FAI-270 borrow pit (Wittry, Arnold, and Witty 1982). Excavations revealed a unique set of truss trenches interpreted as platforms for defleshing human remains. Based on the presence of a few shell-tempered sherds in two pits and a radiocarbon date of A.D. 1100 for one of the truss features, a specialized Mississippian mortuary complex has been projected at the site.

These drainages have had the least archaeological coverage within the study area. Therefore, characterization of the occupation is problematic. There are a number of minor, narrow drainages leading into the American Bottom and we might expect that interior upland occupation would be directly tied to this area. This does appear to be the case at least for the southern portion, which on the basis of the recovery of limestone-tempered ceramics is related to the more intensive developments in the southern American Bottom.

Synthesis

With the beginning of the Emergent Mississippian period and the development of an agriculturally dependent, sedentary life-style, occupations in the American Bottom and Illinois Upland underwent marked changes. Coming out of a fairly homogeneous Late Woodland base, the entire region began to diversify during the Emergent Mississippian period. This trend accelerated toward the end of the Emergent Mississippian period and into the early Mississippian period (i.e., the Fairmount phase). Diversification is evident in population, settlement patterns, and ceramic styles.

In the American Bottom, a series of mound sites (single and multiple) developed in a chainlike fashion (Porter 1974) parallel to the Mississippi River and proximal to the outlets of upland drainages. These centers developed only in areas of more agriculturally productive, extensive bottomland situations. In the uplands, only the central portion of Silver Creek possessed similar conditions; it is here that two multiple-mound centers appeared.

Assessing upland topography and its relationship to the American Bottom, Wood River and Cahokia Creek lead directly into the bottom, whereas similar access to the bottom from the Silver and Richland creeks is possible only through overland routes. Evidence for the importance of overland transportation is found in the placement of intensively occupied settlements on drainage divides (e.g., Dugan Airfield, High Prairie, and Holliday). This was not expected given the documented association for these peoples with rich alluvial soils. Throughout the upland, lower-order settlements conform to the expected pattern and are found in close association with Wakeland soils on the main stems of the major creeks and their tributaries.

Ceramic data for the Fairmount phase throughout the uplands closely parallel the patterns in the American Bottom. The postulated ceramic stylistic and chronological division between a southern zone, dominated by limestone tempering, and a northern zone, characterized by a diversity of temper recipes, appears to be mirrored in the uplands. The division between the zones occurs in the American Bottom in the vicinity of Prairie Du Pont Creek, and based on our limited data, it would appear to follow the same latitude into the uplands across the headwaters of Richland Creek into the Silver Creek drainage.

At all mound centers to the south and east of Cahokia, developments were apparently interrupted by the end of the Fairmount phase and lack evidence for more than minimal Stirling phase occupations. Cahokia continued to increase in size and became the ruling polity in the region. The growth of Cahokia produced centrifugal forces, which moved people from the uplands to the bottomlands. These forces are evident early during the Mississippian period within the Wood River and Cahokia Creek drainages, where evidence for resident populations during the Lohmann/early Stirling time span is scarce. A similar depopulation of the Silver Creek and southern drainages was delayed until the Stirling phase.

Centripetal forces were in operation by the end of the Stirling phase and contribute to what might be

called a Cahokia diaspora. Settlements began to reappear in the uplands, although probably not in the form of planned colonization. Explanations for the breakdown of the Cahokia polity and the resultant repopulation of the uplands are complicated and involve both social and environmental disruptions. Social disruptions are linked to changes in the site plan of Cahokia and to its presumed population decline. The erection and successive modification of the central palisade at the Cahokia site attest to social disharmony. Outside the Cahokia site, at least one new mound center emerged at the Mitchell site, perhaps indicating a breakdown in the maintenance of a hierarchical polity. Coincident with the construction of the Cahokia palisade are a series of known and hypothesized palisaded villages in the northern uplands—Olin, Kuhn Station, and Kruckeberg No. 1. These villages may have been placed to afford protection for local populations from northern incursions.

Hypotheses of environmental degradation are linked to extraregional climatic and local anthropogenic changes. Griffin (1960a, 1960b, 1961) postulates a link between climatic changes and Mississippian developments in the Midwest. He hypothesizes that warmer climatic conditions fueled the growth and expansion of Mississippian culture. With the onset of cooler conditions, which adversely affected agricultural practices, Mississippian culture contracted in the Midwest.

Supportive evidence (e.g., Baerreis and Bryson 1965; Baerreis, Bryson, and Kutzbach 1976; Bryson and Wendland 1967; Penman 1988) for Griffin's model has documented the climatic effects in the Upper Mississippi Valley. These changes would not have substantially affected the long growing season of the American Bottom region. However, extraregional climatic change associated with the Middle and Upper Missouri drainage, characterized by droughty summer conditions during the Pacific episode (post A.D. 1100) (e.g., Anderson 1987; Bryson, Baerreis, and Wendland 1970; Wendland 1978), may have had implications for the Cahokia area. Increased erosion in the Missouri drainage, associated with drier conditions, would have led to increased sedimentation in the Mississippi trench, producing a shallower, wider channel more subject to flooding and possibly also heightened water tables in the local region.

Coupled with these pan-regional changes are hypothesized anthropogenic changes to local hydrology. Overexploitation of wood resources as well as agricultural field clearing in the watersheds bordering the American Bottom (Lopinot and Woods 1988) would have resulted in increased rates of erosion and runoff, filling in of stream channels, and extensive flooding during heavy summer rainstorms. Evidence for these changes derives from shifts in habitation to higher ground for late Mississippian occupations in the southern bottomlands (Emerson and Milner 1982; Milner 1984; Milner and Williams 1983, 1984) and at the Cahokia site (Brown et al. 1986), and abandonment of occupation at the Goshen site in the northern American Bottom during the Mississippian period (Brown et al. 1988; Holley and Brown 1988). Similar conditions of flooding associated with deforestation were noted historically in the American Bottom before emplacement of levees (Bowman 1907). The results of the hypothesized summer flooding would have been catastrophic for bottomland maize fields associated with Cahokia (Woods and Meyer 1988). These conditions probably contributed to a reoccupation of the interior upland during the Moorehead phase, coupled with the decline in population in the American Bottom (Milner 1986b).

Although a ceramic division existed in the American Bottom and interior upland in the Fairmount phase, stylistic homogeneity characterized the region for the Stirling and Moorehead phases. Based on ceramic data, Moorehead occupation of the uplands seems most evident in the Cahokia Creek and Wood River drainages. However, in the southern drainages, due to the inadequate size of ceramic samples and the apparent diversity within Sand Prairie phase assemblages (Milner 1984), it is difficult to differentiate the two phases clearly. Settlements in all drainages were located proximal to main stems and Wakeland soils, with the exception of the Emerald site. Mound construction, on a limited scale, may also have occurred during Sand Prairie times in the Silver Creek drainage (e.g., Emerald, Copper, and Kuhn Station). In none of the upland drainages do population densities appear to have been high and the articulation between Cahokia and the upland communities is unclear. During Sand Prairie times, the evidence for developments, at least in the Silver Creek drainage, appears to be on a par with the greatly diminished occupations in the American Bottom. Unlike the main bottom, no evidence for Oneota-affiliated occupations has been identified in the interior uplands.

Conclusions

We have shown that interior upland Mississippian developments were complementary to the American Bottom sequence. However, each drainage does display a slightly different sequence of occupation. The only pan-upland pattern is the interregnum during the Stirling phase.

Mississippian settlements in the Illinois Upland were never as numerous as in the American Bottom, at least until Sand Prairie times. For the most part, settlements appear strongly correlated with Wakeland soils. Settlement hierarchy is problematic and the only conclusive examples of multiple-mound centers are limited to the central Silver Creek drainage and these bracket the interregnum.

The Fairmount phase in the uplands reflects the heterogeneity of the American Bottom. In the Wood River drainage the Emergent Mississippian occupations may overlap in time with the Fairmount occupations of the southern upland drainages. Fairmount ceramic assemblages in the south are closely tied to developments in the Prairie Creek locality of the American Bottom. Only in the central Silver Creek drainage is there a recognized transition from the Emergent Mississippian period to the Mississippian period.

The timing of the post-Stirling reoccupation and the duration of occupation for the upland late in the Mississippian period appear to be staggered. Moorehead phase ceramics are assuredly present in the Wood River and Cahokia Creek drainages. In the south, however, Sand Prairie ceramics are more diagnostic.

ACKNOWLEDGMENTS

We wish to thank a number of people for helping us to finish this project. Christy L. Wells provided the timely and necessary editing chores. Mike Skele, Maura Carriel, and Bonnie L. Gums provided the illustrations. John E. Kelly and Brad Koldehoff offered insights into the largely unpublished world of upland archaeology.

4

Cahokia and Its Role as a Gateway Center in Interregional Exchange

JOHN E. KELLY

Cahokia has drawn attention as a unique archaeological site since the early 1800s (Fowler 1969a:5–11). In addition to its overwhelming size and complexity, it is a relatively early center on the northern edge of Mississippian developments. For the northern American Bottom, Cahokia is the focal point of a Mississippian settlement system consisting of at least eight other mound centers (fig. 4.1; Fowler 1974:94–96) along with numerous other Mississippian settlements (Benchley 1976; Harn 1971a; Kelly, Linder, and Cartmell 1979; Milner et al. 1984; Munson 1971). Archaeologists have viewed Cahokia in a number of different ways (see Hall, chap. 1). These interpretations include the presence of a large resident population (Gregg 1975a), an urban center (O'Brien 1972b), a state (Gibbon 1974), and a market center (Porter 1969). Others (Ford 1974; Emerson, chap. 12), however, view Cahokia in simpler terms.

Investigations at Cahokia have resulted in the delineation of a sequence covering at least eight hundred years of occupation (Fowler and Hall 1975). Recent work elsewhere in the American Bottom has modified this sequence (Kelly, Finney et al. 1984; Kelly, Ozuk et al. 1984; Milner et al. 1984). These data emphasize that the site and its settlement system have a long developmental history. Although Cahokia may have been established as a Mississippian mound center prior to A.D. 1000, the clearest evidence indicates that Cahokia's climax took place between A.D. 1000 and 1200.

Cahokia can be viewed as the result of developments termed *Emergent Mississippian* (Kelly 1982) that occurred throughout the central and lower Mississippi River Valley between A.D. 800 and 1000. These events included increases in population, the appearance of a ranked social organization, the establishment of maize as a major component in the diet, and intra- and extraregional trade. These developments set the stage for Cahokia's expansion to the north. In order to understand Cahokia's role in a much larger context, this discussion is restricted to the site's climax at ca. A.D. 1000–1200, which covers the Lohmann, Stirling, and the initial part of the Moorehead phases.

Considerable debate has been generated as to the role of Cahokia in developments to the north and west. Ties between Cahokia and northern sites such as Aztalan in southeastern Wisconsin were recognized by S. Barrett and others in the 1930s. Although no attempt will be made to review the history of this research (because it is dealt with by other authors in this book), it is important to note significant contributions by Duane C. Anderson (1969), Guy E. Gibbon (1974), James B. Griffin (1960b), Robert L. Hall (1967a, 1975a), Alan D. Harn (1975b), Dale R. Henning (1967), and Patricia J. O'Brien (1978a, 1978b). This chapter summarizes that data and interprets the nature of Cahokia's role with regions to the north and west.

Gateway Model

The presence of trade or exchange products represents one way in which interaction between various cultural entities can be verified. The methods used in documenting trade have recently evolved with a number of studies that attempt to delineate the networks and possible agents involved. In some cases, for example, the

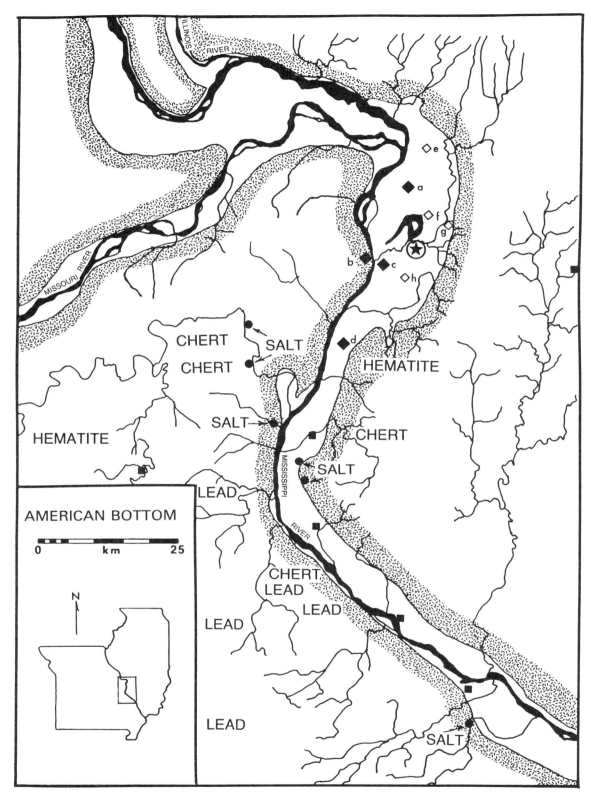

Figure 4.1. Distribution of Mississippian Mound Centers and Resources in the American Bottom Region: first-line center ✪; second-line centers ◆ (*a* Mitchell, *b* St. Louis, *c* East St.Louis, *d* Pulcher); third-line centers ◇ (*e* Smith Farm, *f* Horseshoe Lake, *g* McDonough Lake, *h* Lohmann); other mound centers ■.

integration of the spatial patterning of artifacts and raw materials and settlement types involved have been examined (Renfrew 1977). In the Midwest such studies have included Howard D. Winters's (1968) study of Late Archaic exchange; Stuart Struever and Gail L. Houart's (1972) model of Middle Woodland transaction centers; and James W. Porter's (1969, 1974) discussion of exchange systems at Cahokia, including the applicability of central place theory.

In 1967 Hall made reference to Cahokia as "one gateway on the northern frontier of the Mississippi heartland" (1967a:176). Although his discussion focused primarily on Cahokia and its relationship to the Plains area, it still represents one of the major syntheses on Cahokia's relationship to its frontier. In many respects, the gateway concept is a viable way to view Cahokia's relationship with its frontier to the north as well as its cultural cognates to the south. The gateway concept is one also used by geographers (e.g., Burghardt 1971) and has recently been applied to several other archaeological situations, including Mesoamerica (Hirth 1978) and medieval Europe (Hodges 1982). Although Hall initially used the term *gateway* to characterize Cahokia, A. F. Burghardt's discussion of this concept provides a more complete means of assessing its utility.

Burghardt (1971) has attempted to establish a concept that explains the development of centers in boundary zones as contrasted with central places. By definition, a gateway city is located eccentrically toward the edge of its tributary area. It is an entrance to producing regions with a fan-shaped tributary area. As noted in Burghardt's study, a gateway city's activities are centered on transportation and wholesaling; thus such sites are located along major transportation routes. Basically, they "develop dynamically along a moving frontier of settlement, or statically, on or close to the boundary (or the zone) between areas of differing intensities or types of production (e.g., ports, humid/arid, fertile/infertile, lowland/upland, industrial/non-industrial contrasts)" (1971:272). Burghardt has also examined the development of gateway cities. The initial stage is one "in which the gateway grows rapidly as it profits from the sudden influx of wealth and effort into an extended tributary region" (1971:272). This also includes the presence of relatively large populations and the potential development of a hierarchy of gateway cities with secondary and tertiary rankings. The next stage of development is dependent in part on the size of the tributary area. A large tributary area results in the emergence of "large competitive central places," whereas a smaller area lacks such developments. With the development of large competitive central places, the role of the gateway is reduced to that of a "central place with a service area not much larger than that of its newer competitors" (1971:272), although it "retain[s] its transportation nodality" and "remain[s] one level above its competitors in the central place hierarchy." In conjunction with the development of competing centers, Burghardt (1971:284) has also emphasized that many of these are gateway cities that develop along the frontier as its position shifts over time. Finally Burghardt (1971:285) has also described the presence of twin cities in which one location functions as a central place and the other as a gateway city.

While the concepts of gateway and central place exhibit different spatial configurations, they really reflect different functions within the economic system. That is, the gateway is tied to long-distance trade, whereas a central place focuses on more localized trade and is thus generally located in the center of its tributary area. Burghardt (1971:270) seems to indicate in his discussion that these concepts are mutually exclusive with regard to any single center; he clearly indicates that central places engage in long-distance trade but their focus is on local transactions; likewise, local trade does occur in the case of the gateway city but its principal role is in long-distance trade. Thus in one sense a settlement can serve as both a central place for local economic transactions and as a gateway to a much larger area of economic activity.

Both of the concepts "gateway cities" and "central places" have been developed in the context of modern economic systems. The extent to which they can be used to explain the economic role of prehistoric settlements is certainly open to question, especially in light of the controversy within economic anthropology regarding the application of modern economic principles to prehistoric contexts (see Dowling 1983; Hodder 1982). The applicability of this model to the Cahokia example is examined in the discussion below.

The Evidence

The evidence used in identifying trade in this study generally consists of raw materials and commodities derived from distant sources. Verification of nonlocal items has depended primarily on megascopic examination, and most of the materials referenced herein are based on their identification in the existing literature. In a few instances, more detailed methods have been used (e.g., Bareis and Porter 1965; Walthall 1981).

The emphasis here is generally on nonperishable materials, but it is important not to forget that perishable

Table 4.1. Trade Materials in the American Bottom from Southern Sources, Including the Ozarks

Sites	N	Marine Shell	Lower Valley Ceramics	Mica	Mill Creek Chert	Quartz Crystals	Fireclay	Lead[e]	Barite
Cahokia	1[a]	1	1	1	1	1	–	1	–
Second-line centers	4[b]	3	3	–	3	1	–	–	–
Third-line centers	2[c]	1	2	–	2	–	–	–	–
Fourth-line settlements	5[d]	2	5	2	5	3	2	2	1

Note: The numbers represent the number of known sites with these materials.

[a] O'Brien 1972a; Fowler 1974; Chmurny 1973; Perino 1971b
[b] Mitchell (Porter 1974; Walthall 1981; Winters 1981); St. Louis (Williams and Goggin 1956); Pulcher (Griffin and Jones 1977); East St. Louis (Rau 1867, 1869)

[c] Horseshoe Lake (Gregg 1975b); Lohmann (Esarey with Good 1981)
[d] Lily Lake (Norris 1978); BBB Motor (Emerson and Jackson 1984); Turner and DeMange (Milner and Williams 1983); Julien (Milner and Williams 1984; Walthall 1981); Lab Woofie (Prentice and Mehrer 1981; Walthall 1981)
[e] Based on Walthall's (1981) analysis

Table 4.2. Trade Materials in the American Bottom from Northern Sources

Sites	N	Copper	Pipestone/Catlinite	Steatite	Lead[f]	Hixton Silicified Sediment	Plains Ceramics	Cambered Rims[e]	Bison
Cahokia	1[a]	1	1	1	1	1	1	1	–
Second-line centers	4[b]	4	1	–	–	–	1	2	1
Third-line centers	2[c]	1	–	–	–	–	–	1	–
Fourth-line settlements	5[d]	2	–	–	2+	–	–	2	–

Note: The numbers represent the number of known sites with these materials.

[a] Titterington 1938; Hall 1967a; O'Brien 1972a; Fowler 1974; Walthall 1981
[b] Mitchell (Porter 1974; Winters 1974; Howland 1877; McAdams 1881); St. Louis (Williams and Goggin 1956); East St. Louis (Howland 1877; Rau 1867)

[c] Horseshoe Lake (Woolverton 1974); Lohmann (Esarey with Good 1981)
[d] see table 4.1[d] for references
[e] shell-tempered Mississippian vessels with cambered rims similar to Plains mode
[f] Based on Walthall's (1981) analysis

goods were an integral part of long-distance trade prehistorically. The ethnohistoric literature contains references to an analogous trade in such items around the Great Lakes (Wright 1967), on the Plains (Blakeslee 1978), and in the Southeast (Swanton 1946:736).

The evidence for trade with Cahokia consists of the presence at the site of items made from raw materials whose source is extraregional and the recovery of American Bottom materials at sites outside the region. In addition to trade, two other types of evidence serve to document Cahokia's interaction with its neighbors, especially to the north. The first consists of intrusive Mississippian settlements, while the second is the indirect influence on artifact styles and decorative motifs.

Various items were imported into the American Bottom (tables 4.1, 4.2, and 4.3). An examination of tables 4.1-4.3 indicates that a majority of the traded items were derived from southern sources, including sources in the nearby Ozarks. Ceramic vessels, marine shell, lead, and Mill Creek chert hoes are the most commonly recognized

traded artifacts. The few trade items derived from northern sources include ceramic vessels from the Plains, and copper, catlinite, steatite, lead, and Hixton silicified sediment. With the exception of lead, hardly any of these materials from northern sources have been recovered from contexts in the American Bottom other than the mound centers such as Cahokia and Mitchell (table 4.2). On the other hand, raw materials and commodities from southern sources are generally present at many of the outlying Mississippian settlements in the American Bottom. Outside the American Bottom, the evidence for Cahokia interaction consists of trade goods derived from or through Cahokia and intrusive Mississippian settlements.

To the north, three sites have generally been recognized as Mississippian mound centers based on the unique configuration of elements present (fig. 4.2). Excavations at the Aztalan site in southeast Wisconsin, the Collins site in northeast Illinois, and the Mills site in northwest Illinois have clearly documented the presence of platform mounds, along with wall-trench structures in the case of

Table 4.3. Distribution of Marine Shell within the American Bottom

Taxa	Cahokia	2d-line centers	3d-line centers	4th-line settlements
	5[a]	3[b]	1[c]	2[d]
Gastropods:				
Conch/Whelk	–	–	–	n
Busycon sp.	2-n	m	–	–
Busycon perversum	4-n	–	–	–
B. carica	1	–	–	–
B. canali culatum	1	–	–	–
B. spiratum	2	–	–	–
Strombus pugilis	1	–	–	–
S. alatus	1	–	–	–
Pleuroploca gigantea	2	–	–	–
Littorina irrorata	1	–	–	–
Phalium granulatum	1	–	–	–
Thais haemastona floridiana	1	–	–	–
Fasciolaria hunteria	1	–	–	–
F. tulipa	1	–	–	–
Marginella	–	–	n	n
Prunum apicinum	5	m,n	–	–
Oliva sayana	2	–	–	–
Cancellaria reticulata	1	–	–	–
Bivalves:				
Pectinidea	1-n	–	–	–
Rangia cuneata	2	–	–	–
Dinocarium robustum	1	–	–	–
Macrocallista nimbosa	1	–	–	–

Note: The numbers represent the number of known contexts for these materials.

[m] mortuary contexts;

[n] nonmortuary contexts

[a] Chmurny 1973; "n" refers to nonmortuary contexts from beneath Mound 51, otherwise from Mound 34, James Ramey Mound, and Powell Mounds 1 and 2.

[b] Mitchell (Porter 1974); St. Louis (Williams and Goggin 1956); East St. Louis (Rau 1869)

[c] Lohmann (Esarey with Good 1981)

[d] Julien (Milner and Williams 1984); Lab Woofie (Prentice and Mehrer 1981)

Aztalan. Aztalan (Goldstein and Richards, chap. 10) and Collins appear to be the only Mississippian sites in their respective localities. However, in the Apple River locality a number of other Mississippian settlements have been identified (Emerson, chap. 8). Most of the ceramics at the Aztalan (Bleed 1970) and Collins (Douglas 1976; Riley and Apfelstadt 1978) sites are Late Woodland, in marked contrast to the virtual lack of Late Woodland ceramics at the Mills site.

These sites represent a geographic extension of the Cahokia settlement system during the period A.D. 1000–1200. As such their particular locations are critical in interpreting their role in the trade networks of the Upper Midwest. The Collins site is situated along the Middle-fork of the Vermillion River, a tributary of the Wabash River. Within fifty kilometers are the headwaters of the Kaskaskia and Sangamon rivers and tributaries that empty into the upper Illinois River. From the latter, access to Lake Michigan can be obtained. Also near Collins is a salt source that was important during the historic period (Gates 1966), and it may have been one of the reasons for the site's location prehistorically.

Aztalan was established in a similar setting along the tributary of a major river system (Goldstein and Richards, chap. 10). From this location the Wisconsin River, Lake Michigan, and Green Bay by Lake Winnebago could be readily accessed. Most of the resources such as copper, Hixton silicified sediment, and possibly steatite were located at some distance but could have been obtained through the river systems. While Aztalan represents the northern limits at which Mississippian agriculture could be safely pursued, such concerns may not have been, as originally suggested by Griffin (1960a, 1960b), the basis for this northern expansion.

The Mills site and its satellite settlements were situated along Apple River, which provides access to the upper Mississippi River. Nearby was a major source of lead ore (galena) exploited by the Mississippians (Walthall 1981).

Five other sites (Gibbon 1979; Griffin 1960a; Hall 1962) have been referred to in the discussion of the Mississippian occupation because of the presence of platform mounds. First, there is some old evidence from the Trempealeau site (Squier 1905), recently brought to light (Stevenson, Green, and Speth 1983), that indicates there might be an Early Mississippian or even earlier component (tied to Coles Creek developments in the Lower Mississippi Valley) present. Several shell-tempered Mississippian sherds have been recovered, corroborating an Early Mississippian Lohmann phase affiliation. William Green (personal communication, 1988) says that this center may have initiated the Mississippian contacts in the Red Wing area to the north. The platform mound at the Bryan and Silvernale sites is actually located between the two sites and has produced little evidence to substantiate its Mississippian affiliation (Gibbon, chap. 11). The remaining sites with possible rectangular platform mounds include one site along the Ontonagen River of Michigan's upper peninsula (Hall 1962:123) and two sites in Yellow Medicine County in southwestern Minnesota (Gibbon 1979; see also chapter 11). There is little additional information to indicate their affiliation.

The Central Illinois River Valley between Meredosia

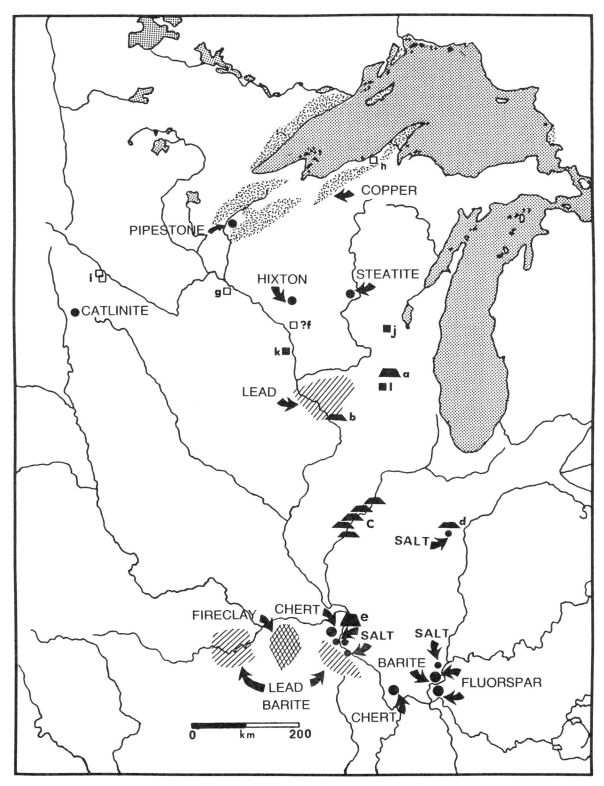

Figure 4.2. Distribution of Resources and Sites or Localities with Evidence of Rectangular Platform Mounds or Fortifications ca. A.D. 1000–1200: sites with platform mounds and Mississippian materials ▲ (*a* Aztalan, *b* Mills, *c* Spoon River region, *d* Collins, *e* Cahokia); sites with rectangular platform mounds and no evidence of Mississippian materials □ (*f* Trempealeau, *g* Bryan/Silvernale, *h* Ontonagen, *i* Yellow Medicine County); fortified sites with Mississippian material ■ (*j* Hamilton-Brooks, *k* Hartley Fort, *l* Carcajou Point).

and Peoria has produced further evidence for Mississippian settlements (Conrad, chap. 6). The unique architectural and ceramic assemblage from the Eveland site has been used to suggest that Cahokia was directly involved in the emergence of Spoon River Mississippian culture in the Central Illinois River Valley (Conrad 1972; Harn 1975b). Although over twenty sites with Eveland phase occupations have been identified, none appears to be associated with mound centers (Harn 1975b). Platform mounds, however, do appear in the subsequent Larson phase of the Spoon River sequence.

Three other sites (Hamilton-Brooks, Hartley Fort, and Carcajou Point) are particularly intriguing (fig. 4.2). Hamilton-Brooks (Hall 1962, 1967a) in central Wisconsin and Hartley Fort (McKusick 1973; Tiffany, chap. 9) in northeast Iowa are fortified settlements that contain Cahokia ceramics (Ramey Incised or Powell Plain) in association with Late Woodland ceramics. A fourth site, Fred Edwards (Finney and Stoltman 1986), in southwest Wisconsin represents a village with possible fortifications and a ceramic assemblage composed of Late Woodland ceramics along with Ramey Incised and Powell Plain.

Excavations by Robert L. Hall (1962) and G. Richard Peske (1973) at the Carcajou Point in southern Wisconsin revealed one possible Ramey Incised sherd (Hall 1962: 59) along with other Mississippian ceramics in association with wall-trench structures and a wall-trench fortification. Some of the ceramics look like those from the Apple River sites (Hall 1962:59) and may postdate the Aztalan assemblage. The structures appear to be the size of those found in the Moorehead phase in the American Bottom (Milner and Williams 1984). Generally these three sites are not considered Mississippian, although they may represent an as-yet-to-be-defined form of Mississippian settlement.

The most compelling evidence of contact with the Cahokia locality is the presence of Ramey Incised or Powell Plain ceramics. Other Mississippian ceramic vessels such as red-filmed seed jars, bowls, and beakers have occasionally been recovered from sites north of Cahokia and may have been derived from the American Bottom. Although Hall (1967a:177) has indicated that the multiple-notched triangular Cahokia points are common to Cahokia, it is difficult to differentiate these from local copies. Other Mississippian artifacts such as earspools and biconcave discoidals are also occasionally present. Burlington chert and lead, which was available from the Ozark region, have been identified from sites outside both regions. Bauxite, marine shell and Mill Creek chert hoes, and Ramey knives represent additional traded products that have been recovered from sites north of the Cahokia area (table 4.4).

Ramey Incised and Powell Plain jars (Griffin 1949) are quite distinctive, and they were important in the definition of the Stirling phase (Fowler and Hall 1975). Ironically, their combination of technological elements (shell tempering and polished surfaces) and design elements is not entirely indigenous to the American Bottom (Hall 1967a:179; Hall 1975c:27, 29). Although these vessels have occasionally been recovered from mortuary contexts in the American Bottom (e.g., Emerson and Jackson 1984), in the neighboring Lower Illinois Valley (Goldstein 1980b; Perino 1971b), and from the central Kaskaskia Valley (Binford et al. 1970), they are an integral part of the assemblage at habitation sites throughout the American Bottom. Their ownership does not appear to have been restricted to any one segment, such as elite personages, of Cahokia Mississippian society.

These ceramics have been identified from over sixty sites outside the American Bottom (table 4.5, fig. 4.3). This distribution covers a large area that extends from the upper Great Lakes south to Mississippi and from southwest Ohio west to northwest Iowa and eastern Oklahoma (table 4.2, fig. 4.3). The majority (over three-fourths) of these sites are north of Cahokia. The contextual pattern observed for Ramey Incised and Powell Plain vessels in the American Bottom appears to be the same for those sites outside the American Bottom. That is, they are generally recovered from habitation areas.

Although other Mississippian ceramics such as bowls, seed jars, beakers, bottles, and jars are present in the area to the north of Cahokia, they are not as ubiqitous as Ramey Incised and Powell Plain are. In general, most of these other ceramics are restricted to the Spoon River area and to the sites of Aztalan, Collins, and Mills, where such ceramic diversity is expected with the presence of Mississippian populations there. These vessels have also been reported from a number of Mill Creek and Steed-Kisker culture sites. However, the majority of those from Steed-Kisker sites are from mortuary contexts (Shippee 1972), whereas those recovered from Mill Creek sites are from habitation areas. Mississippian ceramics have also been reported from the Ozark area (Chapman 1980), but only a few may be associated with the Cahokia area. The remainder, such as those from along the Current, Black, and St. Francis rivers, are probably related to Emergent Mississippian developments (Morse and Morse 1983; Price and Price 1984) further south, whereas those in southwest Missouri are related to cultural developments in the Caddoan area.

A number of indigenous ceramic copies occur in addition to the Ramey Incised and Powell Plain ceramics. These copies exhibit, to varying degrees, attributes that characterize Ramey Incised and Powell Plain, including temper, vessel form, surface treatment, and decoration. Their distribution basically coincides with the Cahokia

Table 4.4. Distribution of Marine Shell and Other Resources at Localities Outside the American Bottom

	Lower Illinois and Adjacent Mississippi	Spoon River	Apple River	Aztalan	Red Wing	Cambria	Mill Creek	Steed-Kisker
Marine shell	m	–	n	–	?	?	–	–
Conch/whelk	m	–	–	m	?	–	–	m
Busycon sp.	–	m	–	?	–	–	m,n	–
Busycon perversum	–	m	n	–	–	–	n	–
B. caria	–	–	–	?	–	–	–	–
Fasciolaria hunteria	m	–	–	–	–	–	–	–
Marginella	m	m	–	–	–	–	–	–
Prunum apicinum	–	m	–	?	–	–	n	–
Oliva sayana	m	m	–	?	–	–	n	–
Olivella jaspidea	m	m	–	–	–	–	–	–
O. mutica	–	–	–	–	–	–	n	–
Polinices duplicantus	m	–	–	–	–	–	–	–
Conus sp.	–	–	–	–	–	–	m	–
Freshwater shell- *Anculosa*	–	–	–	–	–	–	n	–
Copper	m	m	–	–	n	n	–	–
Hixton Silicified Sediment	–	–	–	?	–	n	–	–
Steatite	–	–	–	?	?	–	–	–
Catlinite	–	–	?	–	n	n	n	–
Bison	–	?	n	–	n	n	n	–
Plains ceramics (Mill Creek, Cambria)	–	n	–	–	–	–	–	–
Fireclay	m?	?	–	–	–	–	–	–
Mill Creek chert	m,n	m	n	n	–	–	–	–
References	Goldstein 1980b Perino 1971b, 1971c	Conrad 1972 Harn 1980b Henning 1967 Perino 1971b	Bennett 1945 Emerson pers. comm. Finney and Stoltman 1986	Barrett 1933 Griffin 1960b Maher and Baerreis 1958 Maxwell 1952 Porter 1961	Gibbon 1979 Griffin 1960b	Watrall 1974 Wilford 1945b	Tiffany 1982a Henning 1967 Fugle 1962	O'Brien 1978a Shippee 1972

m = mortuary contexts   n = nonmortuary contexts   ? = context unknown or identification uncertain

forms and includes ceramics in the Steed-Kisker, Mill Creek, Cambria, Red Wing, Spoon River, Rock River, Aztalan, and Apple River localities.

Some Mill Creek ware vessels also include copies of other Mississipian forms such as bowls, seed jars, beakers, bottles, and hooded bottles. Some of these vessels are red-filmed and/or polished, and several of the bowls also exhibit effigy heads similar to those found on Mississippian forms. Of particular significance is the fact that these forms appear stratigraphically earlier than Ramey Incised forms do at many sites. These forms, in particular bowls and seed jars, are also present at Over Focus sites in South Dakota and Glenwood Focus sites in southwestern Iowa. Their presence is presumably the result of interaction with Mill Creek (Tiffany, chap. 9).

The remaining materials represent additional items not generally associated with the indigenous cultures to the north. For example, the multiple-notched triangular projectile points are a distinctive type that have a wide geographic distribution that extends from the Upper Mis-

Table 4.5. Distribution of Ramey Incised and Powell Plain Ceramics Outside the American Bottom Region

Location	Material	Reference
Upper Great Lakes:		
Juntunen (2)	RI	McPherron 1967
Sand Point (40)	PP and RI	Dorothy 1980
Upper Mississippi Valley/Northern Lakes:		
Robinsons (3)	PP or RI	Salzer 1974
Burnett Co., Wi (1)	RI	Hall 1962
Silvernale (Cannon Junction) (6)	PP and RI?	Gibbon 1974, 1979; Griffin 1960b
Bryan (6)	RI	Gibbon 1974, 1979
Mero (5)	PP or RI	Lawshe 1947; Maxwell 1950
Cambria (7)	RI? and PP?	Knudson 1967
Eastern Wisconsin:		
Schultz (9)	RI	Hall 1962
Watasa Lake Swamp (4)	PP	Hall 1962
Pumpkinseed (8)	RI	Hall 1962
Hamilton-Brooks (9)	PP?	Hall 1967a
Manitowoc County (34)	PP?	Hall 1962
Aztalan (11)	PP and RI	Barrett 1933; Bleed 1970
Carcajou Point (12)	RI?	Hall 1962
Driftless Area:		
Hartley Fort (13)	RI	McKusick 1973
Mouse Hollow Rock Shelter (17)	RI and PP	Logan 1976
Mayland Cave (10)	PP	Storck 1972
Fred Edwards (35)	PP	James B. Stoltman, personal communication
Mills (16)	RI and PP	Bennett 1945
John Chapman (16)	RI and PP	Bennett 1945
Lundy (16)	RI? and PP?	Thomas E. Emerson, personal communication
Eastern Plains/Missouri River:		
Broken Kettle West (14)	RI	Ives 1962
Phipps (15)	PP?	Ives 1962
Kimball (14)	PP?	Henning 1969
Brewster (15)	RI and PP	Anderson 1981
Chan-ya-ta (15)	RI and PP	Tiffany 1982a
Coons (22)	RI	O'Brien 1978a
Vandiver Mound A (22)	RI?	O'Brien 1978a; Shippee 1972
Central Illinois River Valley:		
Kingston Lake (18)	RI	Simpson 1952
Dickson Mounds (18)	RI and PP	Conrad 1972; Harn 1980b
Eveland (18)	RI and PP	Caldwell 1967a
Frederick (21)	RI and PP	Perkins 1965
Lawrenz Gun Club (18)	RI and PP	Harn n.d. b
Lower Illinois River Valley:		
Schild (23)	RI and PP	Perino 1971b
Moss (23)	RI and PP	Goldstein 1980b
Audrey, Rapp, and seven other sites (23)	RI and PP	Conner 1985
Bell Farm (37)	PP	Braun, Griffin, and Titterington 1982
Wabash Valley:		
Collins (19)	PP?	Douglas 1976
Catlin (20)	RI	Winters 1967
Kaskaskia Valley:		
Kerwin (24)	RI and PP	Salzer 1963
Orrell (24)	PP	Salzer 1963
Hatchery West (24)	PP?	Binford et al. 1970

Table 4.5. (continued)

Location	Material	Reference
Bridges (24)	RI and PP	Hargrave et al. 1983
Marty Coolidge (26)	RI and PP	Kuttruff 1969
Central Mississippi Valley:		
Long (27)	RI and PP	Adams 1941
Kreilich (33)	RI and PP	Keslin 1964
Mansker (29)	RI	Piesinger 1972
Lower Ohio Valley:		
Angel (28)	RI	Black 1967
Kincaid (30)	RI	Cole et al. 1951
Turpin (37)	RI? and PP?	Griffin 1966
Green River Valley:		
Annis Mound (38)	RI and PP	Milner 1986a
Lower Tennessee Valley:		
Shiloh	RI	Bruce D. Smith, personal communication
Lower Mississippi Valley:		
Wickliffe (39)	RI	Kit W. Wesler, personal communication
Crosno (31)	RI	Williams 1954
Double Bridges (36)	RI	Williams 1968
Zebree (32)	PP?	Morse 1975
Banks Mound No. 3	RI? and PP?	Perino 1967
Lake George	RI and PP	Williams and Brain 1983
Shell Bluff	RI	Phillips 1970
Winterville	RI and PP	Williams and Brain 1983
Caddo Area:		
Spiro	PP	Brown 1971

( ) indicates map locations in fig. 4.3   RI – Ramey Incised   PP – Powell Plain   ? indicates uncertain attribution

sissippi Valley west to the Rocky Mountains (Davis and Zeier 1978) and south to eastern Oklahoma, where similar forms are referred to as Harrell points (J. Brown 1976). Certainly those multiple-notched Cahokia points that exhibit especially fine craftsmanship—such as those from Mound 72 at Cahokia (Fowler 1974)—may have been produced at sites such as Cahokia. Regardless of their source, these points appear to be a horizon marker for the period A.D. 1000–1200 in the Midwest.

Chert hoes are a distinct utilitarian item generally associated with the intensification of agriculture (Fowler 1969b) during the initial phases of Mississippian development. Although manufactured from a variety of different cherts such as Burlington and Kaolin, Mill Creek chert was the most popular raw material. Hoes occur in the greatest density between the Lower Illinois Valley south to northeast Arkansas (Morse and Morse 1983). Outside of this core area, Howard D. Winters (1981) has documented the distribution of all Mill Creek hoes. To the north their primary distribution (including the Lower Illinois River Valley) is at three mound centers (Aztalan, Mills, and Kingston Lake) and the Fred Edwards site, a small village in southwest Wisconsin.

Finely shaped bifacial Ramey knives have roughly the same distribution as hoes and are made from the same chert types. They are present in the American Bottom at a variety of sites, including mortuary locations and outlying farmsteads (Milner et al. 1984) and at sites north of the American Bottom. They are somewhat more common in the Spoon River sites than the hoes are, as well as being from mortuary contexts there.

Discoidals generally associated with Mississippian culture and the historic game of chunky made their first appearance during the Late Woodland (Kelly, Finney et al. 1984; Perino 1971b:112–16). Although they are common in the American Bottom, to the north they have a restricted distribution. They are present at Spoon River sites and at Aztalan and Collins. Their presence outside these centers is restricted to the Fred Edwards site (Finney and Stoltman 1986), a number of Mill Creek sites (Tiffany 1978), and sites in the Red Wing area (Link 1980a). Basically two types are present at these sites; the

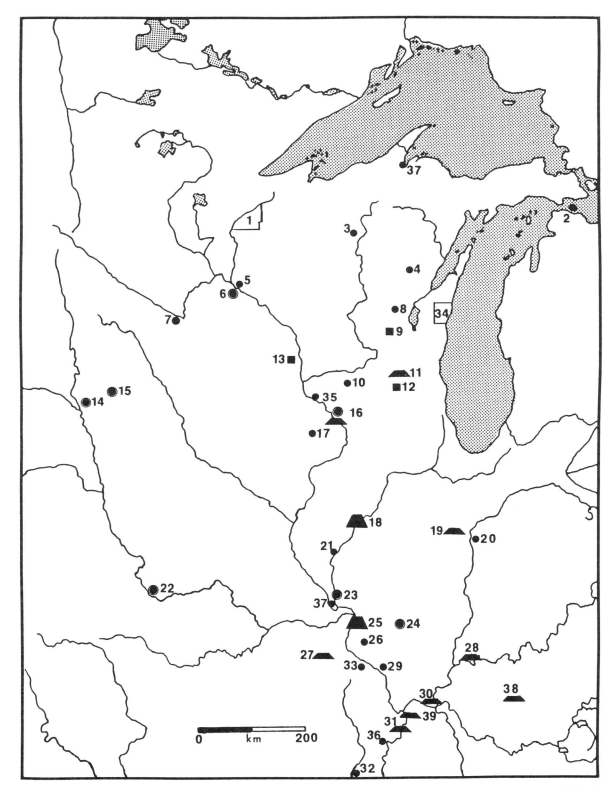

Figure 4.3. Sites with Ramey Incised and/or Powell Plain Ceramics: multiple mound centers and sites ▲; individual mound centers ▲; multiple sites ⊙; individual sites ● (see table 4.5 for key to sites).

biconcave type is generally associated with the Mississippian culture, whereas the biconvex "doorknob" types are presumably local types.

Earspools are a distinct ornamental artifact associated not only with the Mississippian culture but also with its Middle Woodland antecedents. Despite their affiliation with the Mississippian culture, they are not common at Mississippian sites in the American Bottom (Titterington 1938:8). These items have been reported from the Mississippian centers of Aztalan and Mills and from the Spoon River sites. Their distribution outside these centers appears to be restricted to some of the Mill Creek sites, where limestone and catlinite were used in their manufacture, and the Fred Edwards site. At the other sites copper, catlinite, steatite, bauxite, clay, and bone were also used.

Spuds or ceremonial celts or clubs are a distinct sociotechnic Mississippian artifact. A recent study of these artifacts (Pauketat 1983) has described three possible varieties along with their temporal and spatial parameters. The *round-bitted granitic spud* has been found in Wisconsin including Aztalan and at sites in Illinois including Jersey Bluff sites (Titterington 1947) in the Lower Illinois Valley. With the above exceptions, it is difficult to evaluate the context of this variety although it may appear early. The second variety, the *Cahokia ground chert spud*, is largely restricted to the American Bottom, although it has been recorded in mortuary contexts at Spiro (Hamilton 1952) and Crenshaw (Fowke 1896). The majority of these spuds from the American Bottom are manufactured from Kaolin chert, with Mill Creek chert second in importance (Pauketat 1983:5). The third type is the *long-stemmed spud*.

Marine shells are often found at Mississippian sites in the American Bottom (table 4.3) as well as at contemporary sites to the north and west (table 4.4). At least nineteen species have been identified from the Cahokia locality, but the most common shells are *Busycon perversum* and *Prunum apicinum* (Chmurny 1973:227). Although unmodified specimens occur, most were converted into ornamental artifacts, which include beads, conch columella pendants, gorgets, dippers, and long-nosed god masquettes (also crafted in copper and bone, see table 4.6). Although they are found in both habitation and mortuary contexts at most midwestern sites, in Steed-Kisker sites they appear to be restricted to mortuary contexts.

In contrast to the distribution of Cahokia products to the north, there is very little material from the north evident at sites in the Cahokia area. A few Plains-type vessels (Hall 1967a; Porter 1974) have been reported in the Cahokia area. Walthall's study of lead ore (1981) has documented the source for almost one-tenth of this mineral recovered from Mississippian sites in the American Bottom to be from the Upper Mississippi Valley quarries. Copper is present but rare, especially at sites outside Cahokia proper. In fact Mound 72 at Cahokia and the large mortuary mounds at St. Louis, East St. Louis, and Mitchell perhaps best illustrate that items such as copper were destined for the elite.

It has been suggested that the Plains area was the source of buffalo robes and dried meat (Alex 1981a). A recent study by Tiffany (1986b) provides substantial evidence that a surplus of bison meat and hides was available for trade. Bison scapula hoes and bracelets possibly of bison bone have been identified from the Spoon River area. Bison elements have recently been reported from the Lundy site in the Apple River locality (Thomas E. Emerson, personal communication, 1987). The only evidence of bison in the American Bottom is the portion of a skull recovered from the large mortuary mound at Mitchell in the 1870s (Howland 1877; McAdams 1881). Some teeth presently in the Museum of the American Indian have been verified as bison (Howard D. Winters, personal communication, 1987). In fact, most trade items at Cahokia-area sites at this time appear to have been traded from sources to the south (O'Brien 1972a). Ironically, like the American Bottom sites, coeval Mississippian sites to the south generally lack trade goods from the American Bottom. What went up river did not necessarily return downriver.

Discussion

The approximately two hundred years of interaction between Cahokia and its northern frontier was complex and incorporated both rapid changes through time among the participant cultures as well as geographic differences in the form of the contact. In this section I discuss the nature of this contact, the possible roles of Cahokia and its neighbors, and the applicability of the gateway model to describe this interaction. For our purposes the complex of centers in the American Bottom are treated as a single unit and the term *gateway locality* is used to conceptualize their single role in supralocal exchange. Cahokia is used in a generic sense to refer to the gateway locality.

Despite investigations at a number of American Bottom mound centers (Esarey with Good 1981; Gregg 1975b; Porter 1974) outside Cahokia, it is difficult to delineate their economic role within the settlement system. In local exchange, perhaps beginning as early as the Emergent Mississippian period (Kelly 1982), such major

Table 4.6. Long-nosed God Masquettes

Material	Location	Context	Reference
Shell:			
½ masquette	Dickson Mounds, Il. (3)	backdirt, pothunters hole	Harn 1972, 1975a
3 masquettes	Yokem Mounds?, Il. (4)	charnel house?	Bareis and Gardner 1968
1 short-nosed masquette	Yokem Mounds, Il. (4)	charnel house	Perino 1971c
2 masquettes	Crable site, Il. (3)	burial	Bareis and Gardner 1968
1 masquette—conch shell	mound near Emmons Cemetery, Crable site, Il. (3)	mound fill	Griffin and Morse 1961
2 masquettes	Booker T. Washington site, Il. (6)	burial	Perino 1966
1 masquette	Mero site, Diamond Bluff, Wi. (1)	unknown	Beadle 1942; Griffin 1960b:842; Lawshe 1947
1 masquette—*Busycon* sp.	Jones site, Ia. (14)	surface	Anderson 1975
½ masquette	Siouxland Sand and Gravel site, Ia. (15)	disturbed cemetery	Anderson et al. 1979
1 masquette—cf. *Busycon* sp.	cave, Muscle Shoals, Al. (11)	unknown	Holmes 1883a
2 masquettes	cave near Rogana, Tenn. (7)	unknown	Williams and Goggin 1956
2 masquettes	Shipps Ferry site, Ark. (8)	burial?	Davis 1969; Shoemaker and Shoemaker 1969
Bone:			
1 short-nosed masquette	site near Belleville, Il. (6)	burial?	Perino 1974
Copper:			
1 copper-covered wood short-nosed mask	Emmons Cemetery, Il. (3)	burial	Griffin and Morse 1961
2 masquettes	Meppen, Il. (16)	burial	Perino 1974
2 masquettes (incomplete?) and 1 possible nose	Aztalan site, Wi. (2)	surface	Barrett 1933
2 masquettes	"Big Mound," St. Louis Mound Group, Mo. (5)	burials	Williams and Goggin 1956
2 masquettes	Grant Mound, Fla. (13)	base of large burial mound	Goggin 1952; Moore 1894
2 masquettes	Gahagan site, La. (12)	burial pits in mound	Webb and Dodd 1939
2 masquettes?	Spiro site, Okla. (10)	one from burial	Brown 1976
2 masquettes	Harlan site, Okla. (9)	burial	Bell 1972
Representations as Ear Ornaments on Human Figures:			
bauxite? "Big Boy" pipe	Spiro site, Okla. (10)	unknown	Hamilton 1952
copper head plate	Spiro site, Okla. (10)	burial	Brown 1976
engraved shell	Spiro site, Okla. (10)	unknown	Hamilton, Hamilton, and Chapman 1974

( ) indicates map locations on fig. 4.4   ? indicates uncertainty of identification or context

centers might have served as central places where raw materials and commodities were redistributed through two possible mechanisms (Renfrew 1975): a central agent or a local market place(s). Porter (1969) has proposed that these mechanisms along with reciprocity were an integral part of the American Bottom Mississippian economy. Prentice (1983) has also suggested that cottage industries were a part of the economic system, especially among the fourth-line communities, although others question the evidence for such behavior (Pauketat 1987).

With regard to extraregional trade, Burghardt's gateway model and Cahokia present a number of parallel conditions. Perhaps the most compelling are in locational patterns and overall configuration. For example, Cahokia at approximately A.D. 1000 was situated on the northern fringe of Mississippian culture with a number of different

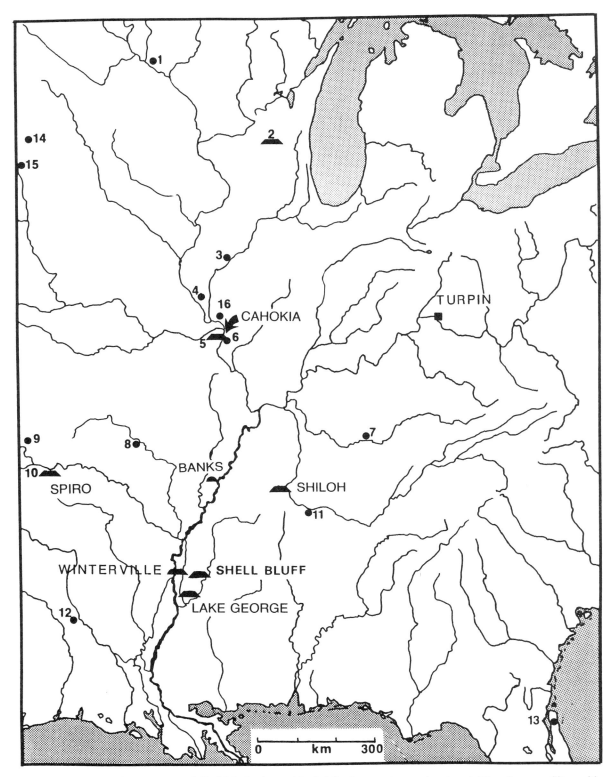

Figure 4.4. Sites with Long-nosed God Masks (see table 4.6 for key to site numbers) and Miscellaneous Sites with Ramey Incised or Powell Plain ceramics.

non-Mississippian societies to the north and northwest. By A.D. 1200 the Mississippian frontier had shifted further north, with a change in the overall configuration of the gateway and its hinterland.

Not only was there a clear demarcation between the cultures involved but also distinct physiographic differences. As stressed by Fowler, "there are few areas on the North American continent where such diverse zones are proximate to one locality" (1974:3). Cahokia was not only located at the northern end of the agriculturally and naturally productive American Bottom, but it was contiguous with the mineral-rich Ozarks to the southwest and the extensive riverine-incised Prairie Peninsula to the north. The American Bottom could provide necessary subsistence items, but it was necessary to turn to the adjacent uplands (specifically, to the Ozarks) for many of the other resources such as chert, salt, and lead (fig. 4.1), and perhaps for copper (Morse and Morse 1983).

Additionally, the Cahokia gateway locality was situated near the confluence of the Mississippi River and two of its major tributaries, the Missouri and Illinois rivers. These rivers were undoubtedly the primary avenues of transportation. Thus to the north of Cahokia was its fan-shaped hinterland or tributary area, while to the south was the core area of Mississippian culture. Cahokia in effect was positioned at the interface of two cultural and ecological areas and thus served to control the flow of goods and raw materials between the various participants.

Although the high population estimates for Cahokia (Gregg 1975a) may be questioned, the multiplicity of Mississippian centers and the large number of smaller settlements indicate not only a relatively large population for the region but also are evidence that the northern American Bottom may have been the most populous Mississippian area at this time. Because similar concentrations of population were evident at gateway cities historically, this is another similarity between Cahokia and the gateway model.

Wholesaling is another aspect of the gateway model; it refers to the selling or distribution of large volumes of products at a reduced price. Although this concept may extend beyond the level of Cahokia's economic complexity, in a sense it can be used to characterize the production and distribution of certain items to areas north of Cahokia. For example, a tremendous quantity of marine shell (Chmurny 1973) was transported to the Cahokia locality. A portion of this raw material was subsequentially converted, using a particular technology (Morse 1972; Yerkes 1983), into commodities such as beads and pendants for local as well as extraregional consumption. Ramey Incised and Powell Plain vessels comprise a second commodity group produced in the American Bottom and widely distributed to the north. These products may

be evidence of a possible group of specialists who produced such items for export specifically to the north. Or, these vessels may represent the rather fancy packaging used in the transportation of shell items. A few vessels have been recovered with marine shell contents in the Lower Mississippi Valley (Morse 1972; Pecotte 1972), suggesting their possible use for transporting shell.

Before proceeding further, it is important to emphasize that there are insufficient data at this time to actually specify which center(s) functioned as the gateway. Although Cahokia might represent the most logical choice because of its position within Fowler's (1974) settlement hierarchy, it is also possible that the second-line centers fulfilled this function and that Cahokia served as a central place. For example, the East St. Louis or the St. Louis mound groups may have functioned as gateway communities based on their proximity to the Mississippi River. This possibilty is reinforced by the discovery of three cache pits at East St. Louis in the 1860s (Rau 1869). These pits contained separate caches of Mill Creek hoes, marine shell beads, and boulders of "greenstone" and "hornstone" (Dongola chert?) (Snyder 1877) nodules. Another alternative gateway is the Mitchell site, which although several kilometers from the Mississippi River was connected to it by a series of sloughs. Mitchell is also positioned closer to the Missouri and Illinois rivers than any of the major American Bottom mound centers are. Further evidence in support of Mitchell's role as a gateway consists of several Plains vessels, catlinite, a bison skull, and copper recovered there. Finally, Pulcher, the southernmost of the large centers, is situated opposite the River des Peres and may have served, along with several other mound centers further south in the American Bottom (Porter 1974), as a gateway center to the Ozarks (fig. 4.1).

It is also possible that the location of the gateway within the American Bottom may have changed through time. For example, the initial gateway locality may have been established at the Pulcher site during the Lohmann phase and then shifted north to either the East St. Louis or St. Louis center during the Stirling phase. The final gateway center may have been at the Mitchell site by the Moorehead phase. Again, Cahokia may have functioned as the central place throughout the duration of this system.

As previously noted, Cahokia's hinterland extended from the Missouri River eastward to the northern Great Lakes and formed a fan-shaped tributary area in which raw materials and goods were funneled away from as well as toward the American Bottom. The majority of the items were being exported rather than imported, and the nature and extent of Cahokia interaction was very different between the western and eastern portions of this area.

The primary interaction for the western portion of the tributary area was with the Mill Creek settlements of northwest Iowa, where a clear trade relationship existed (Tiffany 1983; see also chap. 9). To the west the Over and the Glenwood settlements contained similar Mississippian vessel forms and large amounts of marine shell (Alex 1981a). The evidence for contact with Glenwood and Over foci settlements, however, is not as direct as that for the Mill Creek participants. Trade also apparently occurred between the Mill Creek and Cambria peoples (Henning 1967), and it appears that the Mill Creek settlements may have served as middlemen for Cahokia's northwest frontier.

The main Mississippian hinterland centers (i.e., Aztalan, Mills, and Collins) were restricted to the eastern part of the hinterlands. Presumably they were established by Cahokians and thus linked to the Cahokia gateway locality. They may have been, in effect, an extension of the Cahokia settlement system structurally similar to second-line centers in the American Bottom. At the same time, they appear to have been atypical parts of local settlement patterns. The exact magnitude and composition of the Mississippian populations involved at these centers cannot be determined at this time, but minimally there were sufficent numbers there for ceremonial purposes. Although others (such as Brown 1982) have urged us to examine alternative explanations (for example, the extent to which local populations organized such centers as a process of cultural emulation), one cannot readily ignore the existing patterns however tenuous.

In certain respects the northern expansion is very similar to one that occurred in the American Bottom during the tenth and early part of the eleventh centuries, when a portion of the population expanded into the interior along watershed divides between the Kaskaskia tributaries and the American Bottom (Woods and Holley, chap. 3; Koldehoff 1982b). This dispersal has been attributed to population increases, the concomitant loss of agricultural ground to the large mound centers, and the need to expand into new environmental niches. This expansion was possible due to the existance of an economic system in which necessary resources and goods could be obtained through centers on the bottom. The establishment of Cahokia's northern settlements can be viewed as the application of the same principle, with the Mississippian elite class's expansion into what were areas to the north inhabited only by dispersed Late Woodland populations.

The foregoing asssumes that the primary function of such centers was economic, although Hall states that exchange within the tributary area "may have been only partly economic and more importantly ritual as part of a system to foster intertribal relations beyond *the limit of enforceable Cahokia authority* (Hall 1975c:34; see also

chap. 1). One cannot deny the role of religion within the exchange networks any more than one can deny the role of the Catholic church in Spanish exploration of the New World and the economic basis for this adventure (Sauer 1969a). Certainly the various Mississippian motifs on items such as Ramey Incised jars had considerable religious significance (Emerson 1984a, 1989; Hall, chap. 1). However, the emphasis here is on the socioeconomic basis for such exchange.

It appears that such northern centers had at least two purposes. First, their primary purpose was to extract goods and raw materials for the elite class at Cahokia and its centers. Such items served to validate and reinforce positions of status within Cahokia society and thus were not for general consumption. Given the presence of copper (Barrett 1933) even from refuse deposits (Maxwell 1952) at Aztalan, it is possible that finished items were produced there (e.g. copper-covered earspools, beads) for sites in the south. For example, Mound 72 at Cahokia as well as the large mortuary mounds at the other mound centers may represent the destination of items such as copper. Some copper work may have been performed at Cahokia as well (Perino 1971b:138).

Second, these were places where local trade occurred, with the Aztalan inhabitants presumably dependent on Late Woodland populations for some of their subsistence items as well as other products such as ceramic cooking vessels. This could in part account for the large number of Late Woodland vessels at the Aztalan, Fred Edwards, and Collins sites. In turn, the Ramey Incised and Powell Plain vessels evident throughout southern and eastern Wisconsin and northeast Iowa were probably obtained at centers such as Mills and Aztalan. Thus these centers represent an adaptation to the north in which they served as permanent trading locations where local and supralocal exchange with the nonsedentary populations occurred. These patterns stand in contrast to Mississippian interaction to the northwest, where relatively stable agricultural populations in larger settlement units were evident. In such areas, trade rather than settlement characterized the Mississippian adaptive response.

This discussion has centered on the tributary area as though it was a static entity, although the character of this area changed quite dramatically between A.D. 1000 and 1200. Such changes point to the gateway model as a dynamic changing and developing entity (Burghardt 1971).

Not only were there possible changes in the location of the gateway center(s) in the American Bottom, but also similar changes were evident within the tributary area. Based on the ceramics and some stratigraphic evidence, it possible to delineate three stages within the tributary area (fig. 4.5). The first stage represents the

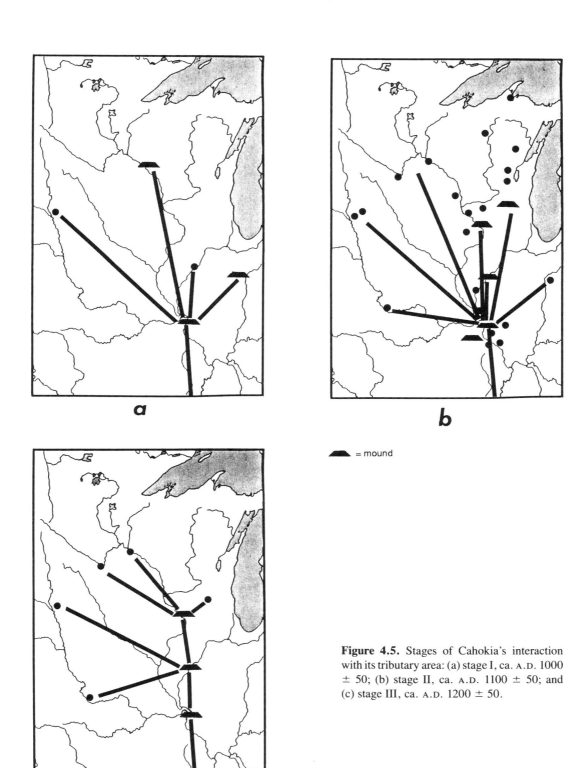

= mound

Figure 4.5. Stages of Cahokia's interaction with its tributary area: (a) stage I, ca. A.D. 1000 ± 50; (b) stage II, ca. A.D. 1100 ± 50; and (c) stage III, ca. A.D. 1200 ± 50.

initial contact with the Cahokia gateway locality at approximately A.D. 1000. As such it pre-dates any evidence of Ramey Incised ceramics, although an early form of Powell Plain may have been present. It is difficult to ascertain whether Aztalan was established at this time, although the Trempealeau and Collins sites appear to represent the earliest centers in their respective areas. There is little other evidence at this time for contact between Cahokia and the eastern portion of the tributary area except for contact with the Illinois Valley (McConaughy 1984). Contact with the Mill Creek locality was clearly evident by this time, with such connections initially noted by Hall (1967a:180). It is assumed that the red-filmed seed jars and bowls are local derivatives stimulated by contacts with the American Bottom, where such vessels were prevalent especially during the Edelhardt/Lindeman and subsequent Lohmann phases. In addition to the aforementioned ceramics, part of this trade involved marine shell and *Anculosa* shell beads from the Lower Ohio River drainage. The *Anculosa* beads appear to be absent later.

The second stage coincides with the Stirling phase and includes Mississippian developments in the Central Illinois River Valley with the Eveland site and the Aztalan site in southern Wisconsin. Presumably the other center, Mills, as well as the other complexes such as Steed-Kisker, Cambria, and developments in the Red Wing area were evident by this stage. Interaction with the Mill Creek settlements persisted, with this locality functioning as middleman especially with the other parts of the Plains area.

The final stage coincides with the Moorehead phase in the American Bottom and the Larson phase in the Spoon River locality. Cahokia's interaction with its tributary area was greatly diminished by the latter part of the twelfth century. This coincides with a northward shift in the Mississippian frontier and the emergence of the Spoon River locality as a secondary gateway center, thus competing with the Cahokia gateway locality. In fact the Apple River settlements may represent an attempt to extend the Mississippian frontier further north. Aztalan may have ceased to exist as a Mississippian settlement by this time. If the Spoon River locality is a secondary gateway, its tributary area may have been restricted to the Plains area with access through the Des Moines River. The Apple River locality then would have served as another secondary gateway with its tributary area to the north along the Upper Mississippi River toward the Red Wing locality.

Changes in the overall configuration of the gateway localities and tributary areas can be attributed to a number of factors. The widespread evidence of fortified settlements in the upper Mississippi River drainage during the twelfth century points to a highly competitive situation. In part this may be attributed to the emergence of a number of Oneota groups. Such developments were in part a result of their interaction with Mississippians throughout the tributary area, for whom subsistence changes following the adoption of corn as a major staple involved concomitant settlement changes at large permanent settlements. Presumably such settlement and subsistence changes indicate the extent of limitations placed on the settlement and subsistence systems by their nature and by the environmental niches available for exploitation. Thus such circumstances along with drought conditions produced by climatic changes of the Pacific episode (Baerreis and Bryson 1968) may have exacerbated the competitive character of these cultures.

The distribution mechanism for commodities such as marine shell and Mississippian vessels throughout the Mississippi Valley was probably traders similar to those observed by Hernando de Soto in the Southeast five hundred years later (Varner and Varner 1951:254). Presumably such traders were an integral part of Cahokia's economic system, but demonstrating their existence is very difficult archaeologically (see Adams 1974).

Long-nosed god masquettes may provide some insight into the presence of traders (see Hall's discussion in chapter 1). Since Williams and Goggin's (1956) study of the long-nosed god masquettes, the number of new masks recovered has almost tripled. Most of the masks are made of shell, with the greatest distribution from Cahokia north. In fact, there is a tendency for most of the shell masks to be restricted to the north, whereas copper masks exhibit a more southerly distribution with the exception of those recovered from the St. Louis group, Meppen, and Aztalan (fig. 4.4).

Griffin has noted that these masks appear about A.D. 1000 and that they are possibly representations of the "long-nosed god" of the Aztec *pochteca*, Yacatecuhtli, "who is sometimes portrayed with a prominant nose" (1967:190). Their widespread distribution in often remote places may be evidence of Early Mississippian traders operating throughout the Mississippi Valley. The tendency for them to be found in mortuary contexts may point to individual recipients who had established a partnership with the traders. As in most partnerships, this association probably dissolved upon the death of one of the partners. The mask may in part symbolize the partnership termination.

Although it is intriguing that these small masks may be in some way associated with traders, no historical connection exists between these masks and aboriginal traders in the southeastern United States, nor does there appear to be any direct evidence of their religious meaning in the ethnographic literature of the southeastern United States. Hall, however, has discussed (see chap. 1) Radin's

(1970:303) ethnographic work among the Winnebago in which there is mention in one of the origin myths of a man named He-Who-Wears-Human-Heads-as-Earrings. As pointed out by Hall, these earrings may represent the long-nosed masquettes present as ear ornaments on several of the items from Spiro (table 4.6). Presumably they exhibit some form of symbolism that might ultimately have its roots in the Mexican *pochteca* and their deity Yacatecuhtli.

Summary and Conclusions

The gateway model proposed for Cahokia provides one perspective of Cahokia's interaction with its neighbors to the north. The parallels with Burghardt's formulation include: (1) large populations at Cahokia and in the American Bottom on the northern edge of the Mississippian frontier at A.D. 1000 on a boundary between different ecological and cultural entities; (2) the development of Cahokia as a result of long-distance trade, especially early to the south and ultimately later to the north with a tributary area or hinterland that extended from the eastern Plains to the western Great Lakes; and (3) the emergence of several Mississippian centers in the tributary area and temporal changes in the area's overall configuration. These changes included a northward shift in the Mississippian frontier to the Spoon River locality and possibly as far north as the Apple River locality and coincided with the emergence of the Spoon River locality as a secondary gateway competing with Cahokia.

Thus the Cahokia gateway model, in terms of locational patterns and overall structure, is similar to that defined by Burghardt (1971). If it falls short, it is in terms of wholesaling. The primary items distributed to the north included marine shell items and Ramey Incised and Powell Plain vessels. These vessels served as a stimulus to changes in certain ceramic assemblages throughout the tributary area. Although perishable items such as bison meat and robes may have been transported to Cahokia, only a few items in relatively small quantities, primarily copper, appear to have been distributed further south. The establishment of Mississippian mound centers to the north and the distribution of Cahokia products and marine shell artifacts indicate Cahokia's or its satellites' role as a gateway center. Although these centers may have administered trade for local populations, I have suggested that they turned their attention to the north not for the benefit of local Mississippian populations in the American Bottom but to meet the social needs of the ruling classes at Cahokia and other Mississippian centers to the south.

In conclusion, one remaining parallel between Burghardt's gateway model and Cahokia provides some insight into Cahokia's demise: the emergence of competing centers in the frontier area. As previously noted, Missis-sippian settlements extended from Cahokia as far as the central Illinois River where a major Mississippian entity, the Spoon River culture, is centered (Conrad, chap. 6; Conrad and Harn 1972). Although the Eveland site may have been an early outpost of Cahokia, the Spoon River culture appears to have developed its own character. The number of items (e.g., bison scapula hoes, bison bone bracelets, and ceramics) derived from the Plains area to the west may indicate the manner in which the Spoon River centers were competing with Cahokia to the south. Likewise, the economic role of Cahokia and its satellites and the Spoon River centers were undoubtedly being altered through time as the cultural composition of the frontier area to the north and west was changing. Cahokia's demise, for example, may have simply been one in which the economic configuration of its frontier had changed dramatically. The gateway status of Cahokia's satellite would have diminished because of these changes, and the settlement system within the American Bottom reduced to a point that Cahokia would have simply served as a central place for the adjacent region. Many of the historic gateway cities such as Winnipeg have undergone similar alteration in their function as gateway centers shifting to central places.

No attempt has been made to relate the gateway model to other areas of Mississippian culture, although it provides a potential way in which to view extraregional exchange especially at the margins of Mississippian culture. Thus, for example, it might be applicable to early Mississippian developments at Macon Plateau in central Georgia and the earlier Plum Bayou center of Toltec (Rolingson 1982) in central Arkansas as well as the later Mississippian complexes such as Town Creek in North Carolina, Angel in southern Indiana, and Spiro in eastern Oklahoma. Critical to future work involving the use of this model is the need to examine in detail the context of the items traded, their quantification, and their identification. Such approaches will assist in understanding the complexity and variability in Mississippian economies. No longer can we afford to rely on concepts such as redistribution to characterize the entire range of differences extant in the term *Mississippian*.

NOTE

The term *fireclay* has been used in a generic sense in the figures instead of *bauxite* in referring to the various figurines recovered from the American Bottom. Dr. James Gunderson of Wichita State is currently working on the composition and source of the raw material used. Although the actual source is still not known, it appears that it is not bauxite derived from Arkansas. As noted by a pioneer archaeologist in the area, Gerald Fowke (Emerson 1982:12), these figurines are most likely made from fireclay from eastern Missouri, hence my use of the term.

ACKNOWLEDGMENTS

This paper is the outgrowth of a section of my dissertation on the development of Cahokia. I would like to thank George R. Milner and James W. Porter for encouraging me to publish this paper. Milner read and provided valuable suggestions on the initial draft. Others who took time to read and provide insightful comments include William Green, Dale R. Henning, and Joseph A. Tiffany. The author would also like to thank Thomas E. Emerson, James Gunderson, William Green, George R. Milner, Bruce D. Smith, James B. Stoltman, Kit W. Wesler, and Howard D. Winters for access to and the use of unpublished data. The editors of this volume are to be commended for their comments and their ability to reduce this paper to a manageable size. It is important to acknowledge the pioneer work of Robert L. Hall on the gateway concept and the general and often subliminal impact of his research on my presentation. Finally, I would like to thank my wife, Cricket, for typing the initial draft of this manuscript. However, none of these people should be held responsible for my speculations or any misinterpretations of the data.

PART TWO

———

The Northern Hinterlands

———

5

Patterns of Late Woodland/Mississippian Interaction in the Lower Illinois Valley Drainage: A View from Starr Village

KENNETH B. FARNSWORTH

THOMAS E. EMERSON

REBECCA MILLER GLENN

Although some excavations have been conducted at large settlements occupied after A.D. 800 in the Lower Illinois Valley, the late prehistory of the region is poorly reported except for studies of two substantial Mississippian cemeteries (Goldstein 1980b; Perino 1971b, 1973b). As a result, interpretations of Mississippian settlement remains from the lower valley have relied heavily on its intermediate location between two major nodes of Mississippian cultural development: the American Bottom population center to the south, with its associated monumental earthworks, and the smaller temple-town communities to the north in the Central Illinois Valley.

The Mississippian settlement history of the American Bottom and that of the Central Illinois Valley are discussed elsewhere in this book (pt. 1 and chaps. 6–7). One conclusion that can be drawn from these studies is that Central Illinois Valley Mississippian cultural traditions probably originated with American Bottom immigrants. Because the Illinois River waterway is the likely transportation route connecting the two areas, and because the Lower Illinois Valley is even closer to the American Bottom Mississippian heartland, it has been widely believed that lower valley Late Woodland populations were physically replaced by (or at least socially integrated into) American Bottom Mississippian cultural systems after about A.D. 1000.

This chapter explores the possibility that such assumptions are inaccurate. In three decades of nearly continuous field research in the Lower Illinois Valley, archaeologists have documented some three thousand prehistoric habitation and mortuary sites (see Farnsworth and Asch 1986: 326–27, 336). Several dozen of these sites have been excavated. Yet no Mississippian temple-mound centers are known, and even multiple-family villages are rare. The

most common Mississippian habitation remains from the region are scattered sherds recovered on primarily Late Woodland habitation sites. In contrast, final Late Woodland (Jersey Bluff phase) settlements in the southern half of the drainage number in the hundreds, and several are eight to twelve hectares in size. Late Woodland mound groups are abundantly distributed throughout the region as well. In this setting, the two large Mississippian cemeteries that have been excavated represent something of an enigma.

Because apparent Mississippian habitation sites are small and scattered, the region has been interpreted as a dispersed farmstead satellite community serving American Bottom population centers (Conner 1985; Goldstein 1980b). But it difficult to integrate the known large Mississippian cemeteries into this model, which also requires that we accept the sudden disappearance of a substantial Jersey Bluff population.

In the face of these contradictions, we propose an alternative model for late prehistoric culture change in the Lower Illinois Valley area: although many local Late Woodland settlement activities and Jersey Bluff ceramic styles of the A.D. 800–1000 period mirrored those of the northern American Bottom, Jersey Bluff settlements after A.D. 1000 remained largely unaffected by American Bottom Mississippian cultural developments, except in the realm of mortuary-related ritual. Recently assembled evidence from the Starr Village site in Macoupin Valley (fig. 5.1) suggests that Jersey Bluff cultural groups may have been present in at least portions of the Lower Illinois Valley drainage as late as A.D. 1200–1300.

In the following sections, we outline the regional distributions of Jersey Bluff and Mississippian artifact styles, present the radiocarbon-date evidence for a post–A.D. 800

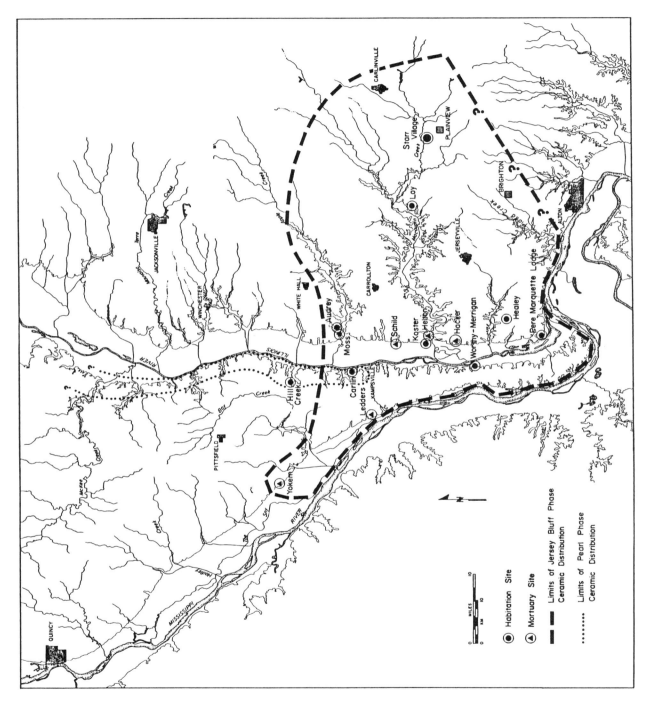

Figure 5.1. Lower Illinois Valley drainage showing stream valleys and archaeological sites discussed in the text. Dashed outline shows the approximate limits of regional Jersey Bluff ceramic distribution. Dotted outline shows the distribution of Pearl phase Mississippian settlements.

occupation chronology of the Lower Illinois Valley, and summarize and interpret the Starr Village data. Finally, alternative models of regional settlement during and after

so-called Emergent Mississippian times are discussed and evaluated.

The Jersey Bluff Phase

The Jersey County Bluff Culture was first defined by Paul F. Titterington (1935, 1943), a St. Louis medical doctor who for several years spent his summer vacations in the Lower Illinois Valley excavating Late Woodland blufftop mounds in Jersey County. Titterington's work all but excluded habitation sites, and pots were seldom found with the mound burials, so his trait-list studies do not discuss the ceramic assemblage of the Jersey Bluff phase in any detail. By 1943, with 852 excavated burials, he had recovered only fifteen vessels—including both Middle Woodland and Mississippian examples as well as Jersey Bluff and Early Bluff Late Woodland pots. In 1949 Robert Shalkop prepared a trait-list summary of artifacts from Titterington's Late Woodland mound excavations in Jersey County, also incorporating sparce data from surface collections at four Late Woodland bluff-base habitation sites (#19-21 and #41) and a three-meter test trench excavated in one of them. Shalkop applied the then-current McKern Taxonomic System to this trait-list summary to define what he called the Jersey Bluff Focus:

> Jersey Bluff is associated with the Lewis and Raymond foci of southern Illinois in a Bluff Aspect (MacNeish 1944), the scope of which is not precisely defined, but which is largely an Illinois aspect of the Tampico Phase. . . .
>
> The closest relative to the Jersey Bluff Focus probably is the Pere Marquette site, reported by Rinaldo (1937), and very close geographically. The burial mounds are quite similar and pottery from the village site even more so, with cord-marking below shoulders, lip notching, horizontal lugs, etc. (Shalkop 1949:1, 48).

By 1951 Walter Wadlow (who knew and worked with Dr. Titterington) was characterizing Jersey Bluff "cultures" as Late Woodland groups who preceded and were partly contemporary with the earliest Middle Mississippian peoples of the region: "evidence of some Middle Mississippi associations is present in some Late Jersey Bluff Sites. The work of Gregory Perino in Madison and St. Clair Counties discloses [that] a considerable time gap exists between the arrival of the parent tribes of this Jersey Bluff and the association noted in the late Jersey Bluff." Perino "found this Woodland pottery, which is identically the same as that of parent tribes of Jersey Bluff in eastern Jersey County, underlying those of the Cahokia Middle Mississippi" (1951:12).

Some confusion has entered the subsequent literature regarding the age and appropriate ceramic terminology

for the Jersey Bluff cultural phase. This may be due in part to the time depth encompassed by Titterington's original mound excavations. In 1952, with no discussion of his reasoning, James B. Griffin characterized Lower Illinois Valley Jersey Bluff ceramics as essentially anything following Hopewell and preceding Mississippian: "Jersey bluff pottery is very much like, but is not identical to, the Weaver pottery of central Illinois, Dillinger and Raymond of southern Illinois, and Canteen Plain and Canteen Cord Marked of the Cahokia area. By and large it is so similar to the Canteen pottery that I am calling it by that name" (1952b:15). In 1960 Stuart Struever noted that although the term *Canteen ware* had been accepted for pottery associated with Jersey Bluff mounds and villages in the Lower Illinois Valley, the term was becoming confusing and relatively meaningless. "At different times sherds of much the same cordmarked pottery have been called Weaver, Canteen, or Bluff, a fact that points up both the considerable variation in the form, paste, and tempering within this regional Late Woodland pottery, as well as the need for a more systematic study of it that will disclose developmental relationships with[in] the ware" (1960:63). By 1970 Griffin also recognized that the "Jersey Bluff focus" had been diluted to encompass essentially the entire Late Woodland period: "The time spread now . . . is so great for this Late Woodland unit from about A.D. 300 to about A.D. 1100 that several temporal phases need to be defined" (1970:10). Thus in his discussion of mortuary ceramics from the Knight Mound Group he designated a "Fox Creek" phase as "early" Jersey Bluff and called the associated pottery "Canteen" ware. For example:

> Mound C°1 is a representative of burial practices of a Late Woodland population which has been called Jersey Bluff for some years. Because of the decorative features on the Canteen Zoned Punctate vessel C°1-7, and the simple Canteen jars, either cordmarked or plain, it is reasonable to suggest that this mound is early in the Late Woodland sequence. There are none of the Canteen vessels with smoothed upper rims and small . . . lip lugs which mark the Late Woodland occupations close to the Early Mississippian period of around A.D. 1000 (Griffin, Flanders, and Titterington 1970:22).

In another recent report, Griffin discusses the origin of his "Canteen" ceramic terminology, contrasting it with "Jersey Bluff" pottery but leaving the waters muddied by failing to describe specific differences between the two: "There are three other types of temper represented in the [post-Middle Woodland] pottery from the Cahokia area. . . . The grit tempered pottery was named Canteen (after a creek flowing through the main Cahokia area north of U.S. 40), because I did not believe it was exactly the same as the Jersey Bluff pottery in the lower Illinois Valley" (Griffin and Jones 1977:463). Weaving this essentially unanchored Late Woodland terminology in and out of an increasingly general concept of Jersey Bluff has resulted in confused ceramic typologies in modern reports of investigations at Jersey Bluff sites. Perino, for instance, refers to the three cordmarked grit-tempered vessels he recovered from the Schild mound group as "Jersey Bluff ware" (1971b:65), but elsewhere he describes them individually as "Canteen Cordmarked" jars (Perino 1973b: 97, 100). He calls the isolated pottery sherds he recovered from pit fills at the site "Canteen Cordmarked" sherds.

In this chapter, following Moreau Maxwell (1959), Gregory Perino (1972), and recent consensus among Lower Illinois Valley researchers, the term *Jersey Bluff phase* has been used to refer to the final Bluff-culture occupants in the southern Lower Illinois Valley drainage (e.g., Maxwell 1959:27; Perino 1971b:65; Perino 1972: 310, 335–47), but the associated ceramic complex has not been formally defined from excavated habitation site assemblages. From illustrations and descriptions of the Canteen vessels found at the Knight mound group (Griffin, Flanders, and Titterington 1970), some of which are rocker stamped and many of which are clearly associated with terminal Middle Woodland or early Late Woodland burials, the Knight site Canteen ceramics date primarily to early Late Woodland times. Even if a Canteen ceramic series can be defined separately from other early Late Woodland (Weaver and White Hall) wares, the terminology should not be applied to the distinctive ceramics of the much later Jersey Bluff phase.

Characteristic Jersey Bluff ceramics are extremely hard-fired, thin-walled (usually 4–6 mm), shouldered conoidal jars varying in size from miniature vessels to large cauldrons. They are grit tempered, sometimes with grog temper added to the paste. The vessels are frequently a bright fleshtone orange to pink, but they may also take on an ashy gray-to-white tone. According to Porter (1963:9; 1974), the ceramic paste responsible for these distinctive colors is derived from weathered Pennsylvanian shales he calls Madison County Shale. This shale is distributed in Jersey, Calhoun, and Madison counties, Illinois, and St. Charles and St. Louis counties, Missouri.

The vast majority of these jars have simple flat-squared rims, although some are slightly flared toward the vessel exterior. Rim, neck, and upper shoulder areas are usually smoothed and undecorated, except for vertical or angled notching on the exterior, interior, or upper lip surface and occasional exterior-lip lugs. Lugs are used in single or double opposing pairs and may appear as simple flat-topped lip flares, small pinched nodes, or even larger lug appendages, some of which are bifurcated or perforated for suspension. Lugs and lip notching seem to be rare or absent on early Jersey Bluff jars, and they seem to become more common later in Jersey Bluff times (after A.D. 1000?). From the shoulder downward, vessels are cordmarked with cord-wrapped-paddle impressions. Individual cord impressions are narrow, closely spaced, and often obliquely overlapping. Jar shapes and shoulder location vary widely on individual vessels. Although Jersey Bluff jars are characteristically shouldered, some are more globular with a very narrow, rapidly constricting smoothed upper-shoulder zone. Others are more nearly cylindrical with their shoulder occurring very low on the vessel profile.

Bowls are more scarce, but do occur. Both shallow-profile shapes and deeper, rounded varieties are known. A nearly complete example excavated by Titterington is cordmarked over its entire outer surface (fig. 5.2; for illustrations of several complete Jersey Bluff vessels see Titterington n.d.; Shalkop 1949; Braun, Griffin, and Titterington 1982:41–42, 158).

Since the Titterington era, few Jersey Bluff habitation sites in the region have been excavated. The most extensive excavation was that undertaken at the Worthy-Merrigan site (Wettersten 1983), a multicomponent Woodland/Mississippian habitation site in the Illinois Valley trench. Unfortunately, Wettersten's study of ceramics from the site was limited to sorting grit-grog-mica temper combinations and cord-twist varieties in an attempt to seriate Late Woodland structural features. Wettersten also analyzed ceramics from the 1973 excavations at the Late Woodland Koster-East site. This work is unreported, but the focus of his study was similar to that at Worthy-Merrigan (see Wettersten 1983: appendix 1). Visual inspection of the Koster-East sherds indicates that they are largely Early Bluff Late Woodland types. Farnsworth's 1985 excavations at the Pere Marquette Lodge site in the Illinois Valley near the Illinois/Mississippi confluence also uncovered a substantial remnant of a Jersey Bluff village. Tabulation and analysis of the ceramics is currently underway. His 1971 excavations at the Loy site (situated on the Macoupin Valley bluffs twenty-three kilometers downstream from Starr Village) recovered a few Jersey Bluff pit features and two probable house structures, although the primary occupation at Loy was Middle Woodland. Analysis of the site's small Jersey Bluff assemblage is being incorporated into the Pere Marquette Lodge study. Less-extensive studies have also been carried out at two additional Jersey Bluff sites.

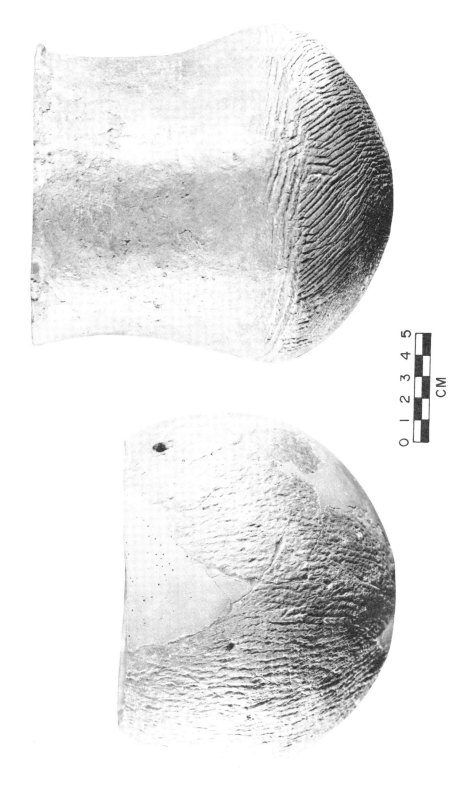

Figure 5.2. Jersey Bluff bowl (*left*) and jar (*right*) found in 1937 with an adolescent female burial in a blufftop mound at the southern juncture of the Illinois and Otter Creek valleys by Dr. Paul F. Titterington (Jy°69-93, McCarthy mound group: Titterington n.d.: book 4). Vessels are curated at the Illinois State Museum, Springfield.

The Healey site, located adjacent to a sinkhole in the dissected uplands five kilometers east of the floodplain, was subjected to limited feature excavation and controlled surface collection of pit feature contents brought to the surface after deep plowing in 1975. No report has been prepared on the results of this salvage effort. Finally, sixty-eight features were salvaged at the Carlin site in 1971 and 1972 prior to highway department rest-stop construction (Stoner 1972; Struever 1973). Carlin is a multicomponent Late Woodland site located at the base of the valley's western bluffs. Several features contained Jersey Bluff ceramics.

The locations of these sites are shown on fig. 5.1, together with an impressionistic estimate of the distribution of Jersey Bluff-style ceramics in the Lower Illinois Valley region. The southeastern limits of distribution (in the Alton area) are unknown, because this area lies beyond the limits of our survey studies. Although there are some differences in temper and perhaps lip-decoration attributes, nearly identical Late Woodland ceramics have been found at sites on both sides of this arbitrarily drawn line. Jersey Bluff-like ceramics in the northern American Bottom are called Peter's Station Cordmarked (Vogel 1975). The southern distribution limits of such Jersey Bluff-like vessels are unknown, but the distribution is well south of the dashed straight line shown on the map. In general terms, the line is more significant as an approximate northern boundary of local manufacture and widespread use of shell-tempered Emergent Mississippian pottery types at Late Woodland village sites. To the north of the line, the Late Woodland Jersey Bluff tradition appears to have continued essentially intact after A.D. 1000 despite the Mississippian emergence in the northern American Bottom during the Loyd, Merrell, and Edelhardt phases (ca. A.D. 800–1000).

To the west, distribution limits of Jersey Bluff ceramics are poorly known because comparatively few archaeological surveys or excavations have been undertaken in this area of the Mississippi Valley. Six Late Woodland mortuary sites have been excavated along the valley's eastern bluffs. The Yokem mound group (Perino 1972) is the northernmost such site to yield diagnostic Jersey Bluff ceramics. Only Yokem Mounds 4 and 5 produced Jersey Bluff remains; the other mounds in the group were built during an earlier "Yokem" phase, radiocarbon-dated from four dates at the site to between A.D. 770 and 910 (Perino 1972:375). Perino believes that the oldest of these four dates most accurately represents the age of the phase, but the Jersey Bluff vessels at the site may also be the result of a relatively late northward settlement expansion up the Mississippi trench from an earlier core settlement area centered on the southern Lower Illinois Valley. In any case, Jersey Bluff ceramics are present in two of the mounds, so the northwestern limits of known settlement distribution for the phase are tentatively drawn at Yokem.

The map estimate for the northern distribution limits of Jersey Bluff ceramics is more certain because this boundary area is situated in the midst of the Kampsville Archeological Center's Lower Illinois Valley research universe. The nature of late prehistoric settlement in the northern half of the Lower Illinois Valley is presently unknown. The area lies to the south of early Mississippian Eveland phase settlement distribution in the Central Illinois Valley, but there is little evidence for Late Woodland occupation here during Emergent Mississippian times.

Jersey Bluff Phase Chronology

There are few Jersey Bluff radiocarbon dates available from habitation sites in the Lower Illinois Valley drainage to test the possibility that late Jersey Bluff occupations here might be contemporary with the Moorehead and/or Sand Prairie phase occupation of the American Bottom. Currently, we have thirteen radiocarbon dates from only five sites (table 5.1). These include single dates run on carbonized material from excavated features at the Carlin site (Stoner 1972; Struever 1973), Healey site (see above), and Koster-North site (Houart 1971), four dates from excavated feature context at Loy, and six dates from excavated feature context at the Pere Marquette Lodge site. Seven of the thirteen dates are from features with only Jersey Bluff pottery. The remaining six contained some Mississippian sherds as well. At the Loy site, four of the excavated Jersey Bluff features yielded restorable sections of three Mississippian vessels. All are apparent American Bottom-style Stirling phase pots. At Pere Marquette Lodge, numerous Jersey Bluff features (some twenty of seventy) also produced shell-tempered sherds. In this case, only a few vessels—perhaps four or less—are of American Bottom Stirling phase manufacture. The remainder seem to be locally made shell-tempered variations on Jersey Bluff jar forms (Farnsworth, report in preparation). Some shell-tempered sherds were associated with pits in the only house floor uncovered at the site (a rectangular structure with wall trenches on three sides), and a small Schild Plain shell-tempered jar was found with the only burial. These two features were found forty-five meters apart at opposite ends of the excavation block. The other pits that contained both shell-tempered sherds and Jersey Bluff material were scattered apparently randomly among the numerous Jersey Bluff features in between, not clustered near the wall-trench structure as might be predicted if they represented a separate Mississippian farmstead component.

In addition to these thirteen habitation site dates, seventeen dates run on bone collagen from burials at four Lower Illinois Valley Late Woodland mound groups also fall in the A.D. 800–1300 era (table 5.2). Whereas the dates from Jersey Bluff habitation sites cluster between A.D. 800 and 1110, the mortuary site dates range from A.D. 825 to 1250 with nearly half falling between A.D. 1100 and 1250. Five additional collagen dates from probable Late Woodland burials in the Schild mound group

will be discussed in a later section because Schild also includes an extensive cemetery in which burials are accompanied by Mississippian grave goods.

All four of the Late Woodland mortuary sites with dated burials occur within the region of Jersey Bluff settlement distribution (see fig. 5.1). Although Late Woodland burials in this area seldom contain diagnostic grave goods that would help corroborate their cultural affiliation, the sparce artifact assemblage recovered from the four mound groups consists almost exclusively of Late Woodland-style arrowpoints, discoidals, pipes, and ceramics. All of the cordmarked, grit-tempered sherds and the few pottery vessels and vessel sections recovered from the mounds with post–A.D. 800 dates fall within the Jersey Bluff or earlier Bluff style ranges. (These include two bowls and three jars from Helton Mounds 22 and 47, a jar from Hacker Mound 2, and a jar from Ledders Mound 1.) The only exceptions to this pattern are a single shell-tempered sherd from the fill of Hacker Mound 3, a shell-tempered red-filmed bowl with a near-surface burial in Ledders Mound 1, and two sections of a single smoothed, shell-tempered jar with an extruded lip found in two stone-box graves near Helton Mound 47 (Conner 1984:221–22, 228–30, 241–42).

The Jersey Bluff radiocarbon dates listed in tables 5.1 and 5.2 are uncorrected, and recent high-precision dendrochronological calibrations of prehistoric variation in atmospheric C-14 content suggest some significant revisions in the probable age range of the samples (David L. Asch, personal communication, 1987; see Stuiver and Kra 1986). The earliest Jersey Bluff dates, those with C-14 ages of A.D. 880 to 950, are probably actually older

Table 5.1. Radiocarbon Dates from Jersey Bluff Features at Lower Illinois Valley Habitation Sites

Site	Date	Provenience	Lab No.
Carlin	A.D. 970 ± 70	Feature 24, level 1-2	ISGS-1434
Healey	A.D. 1070 ± 70	Feature 1	ISGS-1128
Koster-North	A.D. 980 ± 70	*Feature 2008b-c	ISGS-1205
Loy	A.D. 1080 ± 70	*Feature 9a	ISGS-1093
	A.D. 990 ± 70	Feature 64b	ISGS-1206
	A.D. 980 ± 70	Feature 19a-d	ISGS-1091
	A.D. 980 ± 70	*Feature 28x-y	ISGS-1209
Pere Marquette	A.D. 1110 ± 70	*Feature 16	ISGS-1586
Lodge	A.D. 1100 ± 70	*Feature 66	ISGS-1547
	A.D. 970 ± 70	*Feature 642	ISGS-1541
	A.D. 960 ± 70	Feature 27	ISGS-1585
	A.D. 950 ± 70	Feature 72, level 1P	ISGS-1582
	A.D. 880 ± 70	Feature 17	ISGS-1540

Note: Features with an * contained some Mississippian sherds in addition to Jersey Bluff materials.

Table 5.2. Radiocarbon Dates From Burials in Lower Illinois Valley Late Woodland Mound Groups

Site	Date	Provenience	Lab No.
Hacker Mound Group	A.D. 1190 ± 60	Mound 2, Burial 10	UCR-1389
(site report: Perino 1975)	A.D. 1160 ± 80	Mound 2, Burial 104	UCR-1392
	A.D. 1130 ± 80	Mound 3, Burial 2	UCR-1393
Helton Mound Group	A.D. 1220 ± 80	Mound 47-S2, Burial 3	UCR-1411
(site reports: Bielwaski n.d.;	A.D. 1200 ± 80	Mound 47, Burial 70	UCR-1413
Cheverud n.d.; Conner	A.D. 1170 ± 85	Mound 47-S2, Burial 15	UCR-1410
1984:222–31; Hinkes 1977;	A.D. 1090 ± 85	Mound 47, Burial 63	UCR-1409
Kerber 1982)	A.D. 930 ± 75	Mound 22 crematory	ISGS-257
	A.D. 920 ± 85	Mound 47, Burial 25	UCR-1412
	A.D. 825 ± 75	Mound 22 crematory	ISGS-258
Koster Mound Group	A.D. 1250 ± 100	Mound 4, Burial 8	UCR-1396
(site report: Perino 1973a)	A.D. 1200 ± 120	Mound 6, Burial 14	UCR-1407
	A.D. 900 ± 70	Mound 4, Burial 15	UCR-1397
	A.D. 860 ± 100	Mound 1, Burial 14	UCR-1394
Ledders Mound Group	A.D. 1060 ± 50	Mound 1, Burial 81	UCLA-1919G
(site report: Pickering n.d.)	A.D. 1000 ± 30	Mound 1, Burial 76	UCLA-1919F
	A.D. 960 ± 50	Mound 1, Burial 135	UCLA-1919H

Note: Listing includes all dates between A.D. 800 and 1300. UCR dates are from Conner (1984); ISGS and UCLA dates are from Tainter (1975).

than indicated, translating into calibrated dates that cluster between approximately A.D. 800 and 850. C-14 determinations of A.D. 950 to 1050 are likely to have an actual calendrical-year spread of from A.D. 850 to 1025. Radiocarbon ages of A.D. 1050 to 1150 once again collapse into an overlapping cluster of calibrated dates that group between A.D. 1025 and 1050. A.D. 1150 to 1250 C-14 dates calibrate out to corrected dates of A.D. 1050 to 1150. In contrast, dates between A.D. 1250 and 1300 spread across 150 years of actual calendrical time (from A.D. 1150 to 1300). These calibrations indicate that characteristic Jersey Bluff ceramics appear in the Lower Illinois Valley drainage soon after A.D. 800. From the limited chronological evidence, Jersey Bluff villages begin to receive occasional Stirling phase Mississippian vessels and, in the Illinois Valley itself, begin to produce some shell-tempered pots of their own by approximately A.D. 1000–1050. These dates are slightly earlier than the recent A.D. 1050–1150 age recently estimated for the Stirling

phase Mississippian occupation of the American Bottom (Milner et al. 1984), but the dates used by the FAI-270 Project were not calibrated against the dendrochronology curve.

The fact that our limited C-14 evidence has produced no post-Stirling Jersey Bluff dates from habitation sites in the Lower Illinois Valley region may well be fortuitous. Although over two hundred Jersey Bluff habitation sites are documented for the southern half of the Lower Illinois Valley drainage by unpublished site survey records on file at the Kampsville Archeological Center, only five such sites have been dated. All five were opportunistic rather than planned studies: the Loy site was excavated as part of a Middle Woodland settlement analysis project; Koster-North research focused on the site's buried Archaic horizons; Healey, Carlin, and Pere Marquette Lodge were excavated due to impending destruction from deep plowing, rest-stop construction, and lodge expansion.

Documentation of the Starr Village and Mound Group

The earliest recorded archaeological work at the Starr Village site (fig. 5.1) occurred over a century ago with the discovery there of a large, elaborately carved Mississippian human-effigy pipe of reddish-brown bauxite or Missouri fireclay (fig. 5.3). The circumstances of the pipe's discovery and the evidence for its association with Starr Village have been detailed by Farnsworth and Emerson (1989:23). The artifact, known as the Macoupin Creek Figure Pipe, depicts a crouching male with a rattle in his right hand. A snake or snakeskin is wrapped around his neck and his head is adorned with conch-shell and bead ear ornaments and a raccoon-pelt headband. The figure is an example of Cahokia-style stone effigies manufactured in the American Bottom between about A.D. 1050 and 1200, but was found with a burial in a stone-box grave. Stone-box graves in the American Bottom date to the early Sand Prairie phase (ca. A.D. 1250; Milner et al. 1984).

> While it is possible that Cahokia-style effigies were manufactured through the thirteenth century, it is highly improbable. The fertility and serpent symbolism associated with the Macoupin Creek Figure Pipe predominate during the Stirling phase Mississippian occupation of Cahokia. The stylistic and symbolic content of the Macoupin Creek figure are too closely similar to such classic Cahokia-style effigies as the Birger, Keller, Schild, and Rattler Frog to have been produced one or two centuries later. Thus, the view that the Macoupin Creek Figure Pipe is a curated heirloom seems most reasonable. Such items may have played an important role in religious activities

or represented symbols of status closely associated with elite social groups, and may have been carefully curated over fairly long periods of time (Farnsworth and Emerson 1989:23).

The pipe's Mississippian cultural affiliation and its stone-box-grave archaeological context are strikingly anomalous for the Macoupin Valley region. Extensive surveys of the valley conducted by Farnsworth between 1969 and the mid-1970s (Asch et al. 1978, 1981; Batura and Farnsworth 1981; Farnsworth 1973) indicate that the region was all but devoid of Mississippian settlement. After ca. A.D. 800, the valley and its margins and tributaries were extensively inhabited by Jersey Bluff-phase Late Woodland groups: nearly eighty Jersey Bluff habitation sites have been found scattered along much of the valley's 110-kilometer length (Farnsworth, unpublished Center for American Archeology survey records), and hundreds of burial mounds are known to occupy the valley-margin bluffs (e.g., Palkovich 1975). Most of these mounds are likely associated with the Jersey Bluff occupation, but a few are Middle Woodland in age (Farnsworth 1970, 1973). In contrast, evidence for Mississippian settlement in the Macoupin Valley drainage is limited to a single homestead-sized early Mississippian site located some fifty kilometers downstream from the Starr Village area.

In modern times, the bluff-top Starr Village and mound complex was first mapped and surveyed in 1953 by Harold Spencer, a Blackburn College art professor. At

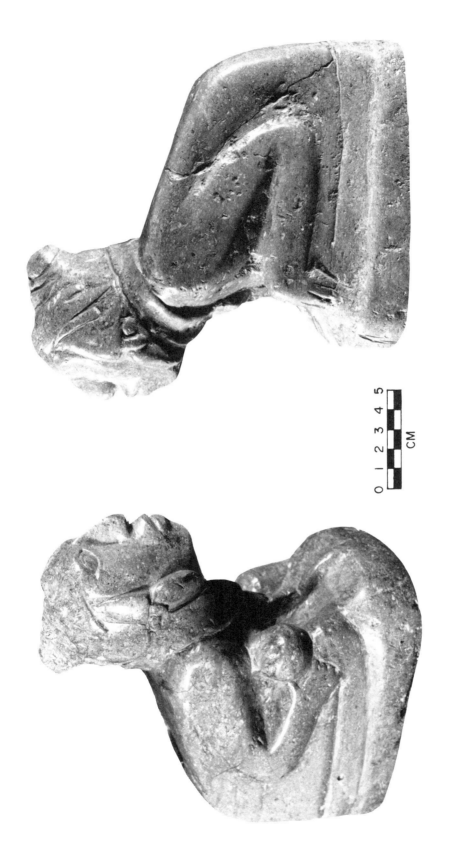

Figure 5.3. The Macoupin Creek Figure Pipe, recovered by Harris Thomas in a stone-box grave at the Starr Village site in the late 1870s.

that time, however, the site was not under cultivation. One of us (Glenn) visited the site in the late 1970s soon after it was cleared of trees for farming. She collected both Late Woodland and Mississippian artifacts from the surface and carried out small-scale test excavations in a number of areas. Farnsworth and Glenn returned to the site in 1983 to carry out mapping activities and conduct further controlled surveys.

The Starr Village site and its associated mound group are located atop the southern bluffs of Macoupin Valley in the NW quarter of section 29, Polk Township. The site overlooks a 1.3-kilometer-wide loop-meander area of the Macoupin floodplain containing a large backwater slough variously known as Meyers Lake or Bullard Lake (fig. 5.4). As recorded during surveys by Farnsworth and Glenn, the habitation area of the site extends over 1.4 hectares, covering much of the crest of a prominent bluff plateau whose 400-meter frontage drops steeply to the floodplain some twenty-five meters below. The site area is bounded to the east, west, and south by forested precipitous slopes of tributary drainages, except at a finger-like connecting bluff remnant near its southeastern corner along which most of the associated mound group is arrayed (fig. 5.5).

Outside the limits of the habitation area, fourteen possible mounds extend along the narrow C-shaped bluff-crest remnant connecting the village area to the remaining bluffline. These include Spencer's Mp°452 to Mp°463 and two possible small mounds between Mp°459 and Mp°460 (see fig. 5.6). At the time of his 1953 survey, Spencer mapped two additional large mounds (Mp°465 and Mp°466) found at some distance from the others, located in what we now know to be the midst of the village area. Today only Mp°466 is visible. He also assigned a mound number (Mp°464) to an area east of Mp°464 that had been excavated by the landowner as a watering hole for stock, because he found archaeological debris in backdirt associated with the pit. According to the 1953 survey form, he recovered "grit and shell tempered sherds, plain and cord marked, numerous flint flakes, various bone fragments including one molar, broken stone implements, [and an] abrading stone" from the disturbed area. The form indicates that he intended to write a report on the material, but this was apparently never done. The freshly cut watering-hole excavation was some sixty-eight by forty-four feet (20.7 × 13.4 meters) in diameter and five feet (1.5 meters) deep. Its approximate position is mapped in figures 5.5 and 5.6.

At the time of Spencer's survey, much of the village area was a pastured parkland, and although the two adjacent mounds near the center of this area were large (he recorded Mp°465 as being forty-four feet [13.4 meters] in diameter but less than two feet [0.6 meters] high; Mp°466

was sixty-five feet [19.8 meters] in diameter and four feet [1.2 meters] high), neither was obviously pitted or otherwise disturbed. Among the remaining smaller mounds in the forested area, all but tiny Mp°453 had suffered obvious pitting at the hands of relic hunters. Spencer carefully plotted the extent of pitting in each on plan maps that accompanied the survey forms he sent to the Illinois State Museum, and recorded the dimensions and height of the mounds themselves (table 5.3). These mounds (and the watering hole pit) were redesignated as Mp°7-°21 by the State Museum. The Illinois Archaeological Survey central site file designates the entire group as Mp-3.

In 1983 Farnsworth and Glenn were able to relocate mounds Mp°452 through Mp°463 and the two additional possible mound areas on the narrow forested bluff remnant adjacent to the Starr Village. Their arrangement closely approximated Spencer's detailed mapping, and thirty years later, they did not appear to have suffered much additional destruction. Because they were overgrown with vegetation and tangled underbrush, no new mapping was attempted.

In the village area, we found no visible remnant of either Mp°464 (the "watering hole") or Mp°465 (the lowest of the two adjacent large mounds). According to the current landowner, the site area was bladed free of trees and brush in about 1975 to prepare it for cultivation. At this time the swale remaining from the old stock pond ("Mp°464") was probably filled in. Also at this time a modern pond was built immediately north of the missing Mp°465, adjacent to the bluff crest. Apparently the combination of these two activities obliterated any aboveground evidence for Mp°465, which was less than two feet (0.6 meters) tall thirty years ago.

Glenn was first alerted to the fact that the Starr Village had been cleared and that quantities of archaeological ma-

Table 5.3. Dimensions of Mp°452-MP°463

Mound No.	Length	Width	Height
Mp°452	42	24	4.0
Mp°453	11	11	1.0
Mp°454	30	30	3.0
Mp°455	30	20	2.5
Mp°456	76	20	4.0
Mp°457	24	24	3.0
Mp°458	63	36	4.0
Mp°459	27	27	3.0
Mp°460	49	30	?
Mp°461	18	18	2.0
Mp°462	18	18	1.5
Mp°463	20	20	2.0

? = not recorded
Source: 1953 Harold Spencer survey (measured in feet).

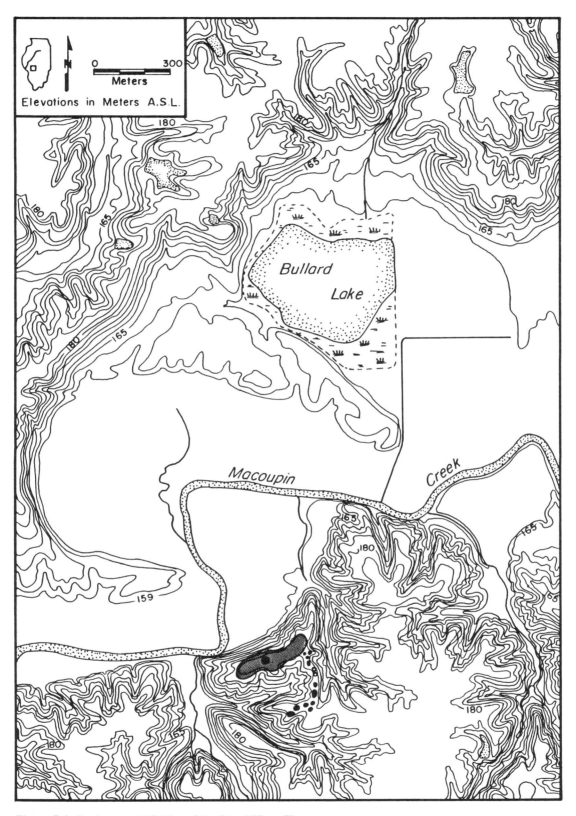

Figure 5.4. Environmental Setting of the Starr Village Site

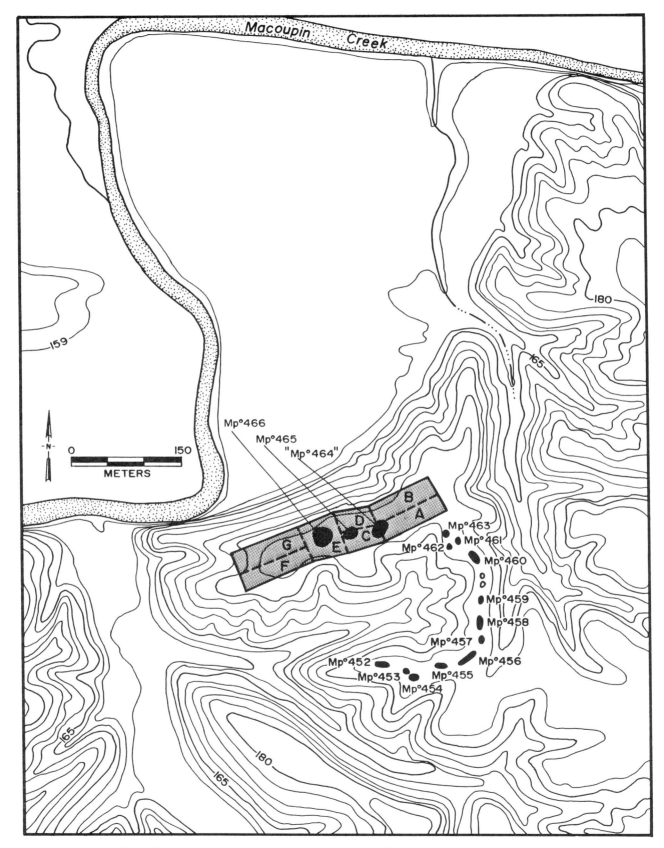

Figure 5.5. Starr Village Site and Mound Group Showing 1983 Surface-collection Subdivisions

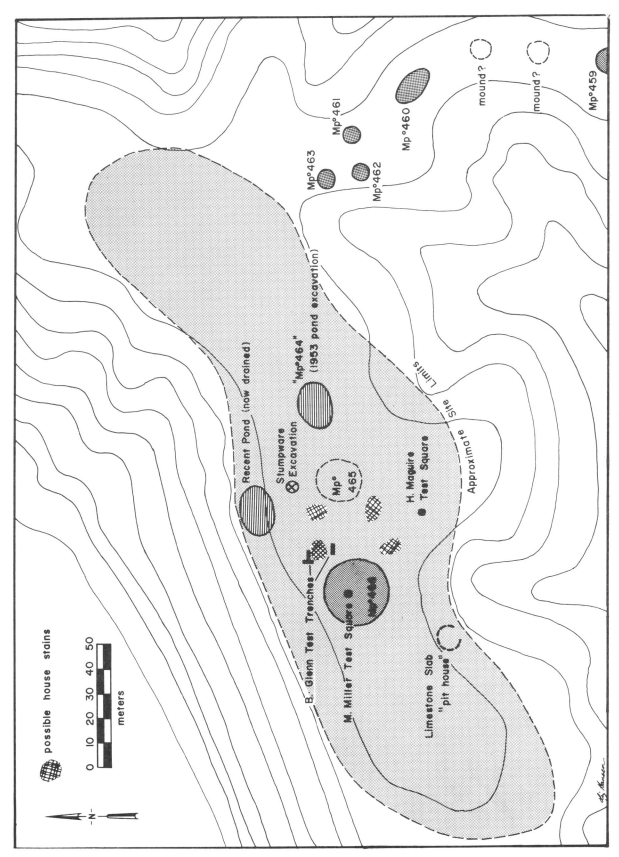

Figure 5.6. Sketch Map of Starr Village Showing Archaeological Features, Test Excavation Locations, and Areas of Modern Disturbance

terial were appearing on its surface by Harold Maguire, a collector who visited the site soon after the area was cleared in the mid-1970s and remembers that at the time Mp°466 appeared flat-topped "like a temple mound." Today its contours are more rounded as the result of plowing, although it still stands over four feet (1.2 meters) tall. In 1953 Spencer measured it at approximately sixty-five feet (19.8 meters) in diameter. Our paced-off estimates make its diameter closer to ninety feet (27.4 meters), but some of this difference is probably the result of plow disturbance. When the ground was first cleared, Maguire could see four dark house-sized stains to the east of Mp°466, in approximately the area between it and the missing Mp°465. He also noted an arrangement of sandstone slabs that he characterized as being the remains of a "pit house" on the south-facing slope to the southwest of Mp°466. He dug in this area and found it to contain quantities of general village debris including large pottery "slabs" and a mass of tempered raw clay.

According to local farmers, the pond seen by Spencer thirty years ago had been rebuilt from a pond originally excavated on the site with horse-and-scraper teams thirty years earlier. The first work reportedly exposed many human bones, which became incorporated into the dam of the pond. The approximate locations of all of these features are shown on figure 5.6.

1979 EXCAVATIONS

When Glenn first visited the site in the late 1970s, the only remaining obvious surface feature within the village area was Mp°466. From a 1930s photograph that shows the discoverer of the Macoupin Creek Figure Pipe posing with it at the site of his excavation (Farnsworth and Emerson 1989: fig. 4), it appeared that the stone-box grave he opened was located somewhere in the immediate vicinity of this mound, perhaps between it and Mp°465, or on Mp°465 itself (which may have been low enough to have escaped notice as a mound). In order to evaluate the site further, Glenn decided to excavate a series of test squares and test trenches in and around Mp°466. A four by four foot (1.2 × 1.2 meter) test square was dug to the southeast of Mp°466 in an area near where one of the possible house stains had been visible, but very little material was found below plowzone, and nothing was saved. A second four by four foot (1.2 × 1.2 meter) test square was excavated at the center of the large mound itself. This square was carried down completely through the mound until sterile subsoil was reached at its base. The mound fill yielded only occasional small chert chips and sherds, and again nothing was saved.

Glenn excavated two larger test trenches just east of the mound where Maguire had seen a second dark house stain. Her southernmost trench was two feet wide and

four feet long (0.6 × 1.2 meters); the trench to the north was T-shaped, with a four-foot-long (1.2 meters) east-west segment and a three-foot-long (0.9 meters) north-south addition at the west end. This T-shaped trench was narrower, perhaps only one and one-half feet (0.5 meters) wide. A substantial amount of unscreened artifactual material was saved from these trench excavations and is tabulated below. The southern trench yielded primarily ceramics (including a large restorable Jersey Bluff vessel section) and at its base revealed the squared edge of a dark feature outline that might have been part of a house pattern. The northern trench also produced quantities of both grit- and shell-tempered pottery sherds; at its base a large trash pit was uncovered (and excavated to a depth of about a meter), which contained numerous well-preserved animal bones and mussel shells. The faunal material includes eighty-six fragments of mussel shell (forty-one hinges) representing several flowing-water species characteristic of Macoupin Creek-like environments. No backwater-lake species were noted. Bone fragments were dominated by deer (n = 98) and box turtle (n = 18). Other identifiable bones included a raccoon mandible, two other small mammal bones, a cut turkey humerus, four unidentifiable bird or small mammal bones, and one fish bone (sucker family). The collection also contains two human bones (fragments of a skull and an innominate) and a section of the inner whorl of a marine shell.

A final excavation was undertaken by Maguire between Mp°465 and the most recent pond, where he had found a large restorable section of a grit-tempered stumpware vessel on the surface. Stumpware is all but unknown in the Macoupin Valley region, and an area about 2.5 meters in diameter was shoveled out in a search for more pieces. The excavations uncovered a refuse pit containing some additional sherds of the stumpware vessel as well as two rim sections from a second stumpware vessel. The approximate locations of the test squares, test trenches, and stumpware excavation are shown in figure 5.6.

1983 CONTROLLED SURFACE-COLLECTION STUDIES

In May 1983 Farnsworth and Glenn visited the site and conducted an intensive day-long surface-reconnaissance, mapping, and artifact-collection study. Glenn returned twice after heavy rains, adding substantially to our surface artifact assemblage. The seven surface-collection subdivisions used within the site area (designated A through G) are shown in figure 5.5.

DESCRIPTION OF DIAGNOSTIC ARTIFACTS

Lithic and ceramic artifacts recovered from Starr Village fall largely into two groups, those associated with local

Table 5.4. Chipped and Ground-stone Tools Recovered from Starr Village Surface Studies and Test Excavations

	1975–82 SURFACE	1979 TRENCH	1983 AREA A	1983 AREA B	1983 AREA C	1983 AREA D	1983 AREA E	1983 AREA D+E	1983 AREA F	1983 AREA G
Chipped-stone Artifacts										
Flake arrowpoints [22]	12	–	1	–	2	1	2	2	2	–
T-shaped drills [6]	3	–	–	–	–	–	1	1	–	1
Drill on flake blade [1]	–	–	1	–	–	–	–	–	–	–
Small bifaces [4]	?	–	1	2	–	–	–	–	–	1
Refined biface fragments, Mill Creek chert (Ramey Knife?) [2]	–	1	–	–	–	–	–	–	1	–
Small unifaces [2]	?	–	2	–	–	–	–	–	–	–
"Thumbnail" scrapers [2]	–	–	–	–	–	–	1	–	1	–
Hoe chip, Burlington chert [1]	–	1	–	–	–	–	–	–	–	–
Archaic points and refined biface fragments [7]	4	–	–	1[a]	–	–	–	1	1	–
Early/Middle Woodland points [3]	3	–	–	–	–	–	–	–	–	–
Ground-stone Artifacts										
Celts [8]	4[b]	–	1[c]	2[d]	–	–	–	–	1[e]	–
Igneous manos and fragments [3]	?	–	–	1	–	–	–	–	1	1
Grooved sandstone abraders [2]	–	–	–	–	–	2	–	–	–	–

[a] found in bluff-face roadcut adjacent to north edge of Area B
[b] one is a large poll fragment only
[c] a ground fragment of blade surface only

[d] one found in bluff-face roadcut adjacent to north edge of Area B
[e] poll fragment only

Late Woodland Jersey Bluff phase occupations (ca. A.D. 800–1250?) and those associated with the Moorehead or Sand Prairie phase Mississippian occupation of the American Bottom. Mississippian diagnostic artifacts at the site are primarily pottery sherds. The majority of these can be identified as late Moorehead or early Sand Prairie phase types (ca. A.D. 1200–1300). Among lithic artifacts, fifty-three probable Late Woodland or Mississippian chipped-stone and ground-stone tools were recovered by the combined survey and test excavation work at the site between 1975 and 1983 (table 5.4). Tables 5.5 through 5.7 list 1,587 grit-tempered Jersey Bluff sherds and 259 shell-tempered, limestone-tempered, and grog-tempered Mississippian sherds found at the site during this same period.

The Starr Village stone tools (table 5.4) are primarily those that would be expected in a Jersey Bluff assemblage. For instance, all twenty-two flake projectile points (fig. 5.7) are corner-notched and side-notched types that fall generally into the Klunk Side-Notched, Koster Corner-Notched, and Schild Spike forms defined by Perino as regional Late Woodland arrowpoint styles (1985:209, 211, 346). However, they are also very simi-

lar to characteristic Moorehead phase projectile points recently illustrated by Milner et al. (1984:177). The only strong candidates as diagnostic Mississippian stone tools are two refined biface fragments of Mill Creek chert, which may be midsections from Ramey knives. The single hoe-sharpening flake recovered from the site is local Burlington chert rather than Mill Creek chert. More generally, all of the identifiable chert debris appears to be local Burlington material. The several squared-poll celts recovered (fig. 5.8) are also characteristic local Late Woodland forms. Three of the five complete examples shown in figure 5.8 are pitted on their mid-reverse face, indicating they were used as hammers as well as chopping tools.

Table 5.4 also lists ten Archaic, Early Woodland, and Middle Woodland points and refined biface fragments that were recovered from the village area between 1975 and 1983 (see fig. 5.9). From their temporal spread, these points most likely represent isolated hunting losses at the Starr Village locale during the 8,000 years prior to its Jersey Bluff occupation.

From the pottery sherd assemblage, there is some slight evidence (not listed on tables 5.5–5.7) for a pre–

Table 5.5. Ceramics from Glenn's 1979 Test Excavations
and All Pre–1983 Surface Collections[a]

Sherd Category	Sherd Count
Jersey Bluff Rims (smoothed, grit tempered):	
squared, unnotched	37[b]
flared, lip-notched	13[c]
flared, unnotched	8
everted-squared, lip-notched	2
everted-squared, unnotched	2
Jersey Bluff Body Sherds (grit tempered):	
smoothed upper shoulder/neck	134
cordmarked	312[d]
type indeterminate sherdlets (probable J.B.)	18
Total	526
Stumpware (grit and grog tempered)	7[e]
Mississippian Sherds (shell tempered)	
Cahokia Cordmarked:	
rim w/ interior red-orange slip	14
body sherd w/ interior red-orange slip	33
rim w/ plain/eroded interior	8
body sherd w/ plain/eroded interior	25
Black Burnished Plates:	
Wells Incised rims	4
plain rims	5[f]
Other:	
Juice Press (base)	1
narrow-mouth bottle (rim)	1
bowl (interior/exterior red-slip rim)	1
burnished everted rims (Powell/Ramey?)	3[g]
burnished body sherds	35
center-drilled circular sherd disk	1
crude plate rim ("salt pan"?)	1
type-indeterminate smoothed body sherds	34[h]
Total	166
Mississippian? (not shell tempered):	
limestone temper, cordmarked body sherds	7
limestone temper, smoothed body sherds	1
grog temper, smoothed body sherds	1

[a] Approximately 80–90% of these tabulated sherds were collected from R. Glenn's two 1979 test trenches (see fig. 5.6).

[b] Four have lip-flare lugs; one has massive notched, drilled lug (see fig. 5.11).

[c] Includes large restored vessel section with seventy-two associated unrestored body sherds (not counted above); found by R. Glenn in her southern test trench.

[d] Includes twenty-one sherds with unusually sandy paste.

[e] Includes the two restorable sections found by H. Maguire north of the now-leveled Mp°465 (see fig. 5.6, fig. 5.12).

[f] Four have interior red slip.

[g] One is incised (Ramey Incised?); the second is a shoulder with a loop handle.

[h] Four have an exterior red slip; one is combed.

Jersey Bluff Late Woodland encampment at Starr that may have contributed stone tools to the tabulated assemblage. Six thin, grit-tempered, cordmarked body sherds and two thin, grit-tempered rims collected from the site surface appear to date to earlier Late Woodland (Early Bluff phase?) times. One of the rims is smoothed and slightly flared. The other has a cordmarked exterior and cord-wrapped-stick impressions on the interior lip. Four of the eight sherds (including both rims) were collected during the controlled surface pick-up. Three were found in Area F and one in Area E. Beyond these eight sherds, only two other ceramic objects are excluded from tables 5.5–5.7: a type-indeterminate untempered "toy" pot rim collected prior to 1983, and a small basal bowl fragment of a clay elbow pipe found in Area C.

STARR VILLAGE JERSEY BLUFF CERAMICS

As listed in tables 5.5–5.7, over 86% of the 1,587 recovered sherds are grit-tempered Jersey Bluff forms. The Jersey Bluff ceramics from Starr Village form a tightly homogeneous assemblage. The sherds from rim, neck, and upper shoulder areas of vessels are smoothed. In profile, the rims are either squared-vertical, everted-squared, or flattened and flared; two rims are everted and rounded (figs. 5.10 and 5.11; tables 5.5–5.7). Among 115 rims, twenty-nine (25%) have interior or exterior lip notching; eight (7%) have lugs.

Several fragments of grit-tempered "stumpware" vessels have also been recovered from Starr Village. These enigmatic ceramic objects have long been known and remarked upon in the American Bottom area (Titterington 1938), where they tend to be found in Emergent Mississippian contexts and are characteristically grog tempered. Stumpware vessels are thick funnel-shaped objects with cordmarked or smoothed-over cordmarked exteriors and two footlike projections at their narrow ends. Several possible functions have been proposed for these curious objects. Howard D. Winters suggests that from frequent smudging of their surfaces, stumpware vessels may well have been "fire dogs" (personal communication, 1987). "O'Brien (1972a) suggests possible use as incense burners. Porter (1974) suggests probable use associated with cooking areas. Kelly (1982) suggests that the thinner-walled stumpware vessels may have served as funnels, probably used in the production of lime or lye, or they may have been multifunctional. The differences in cavity size may be a reflection of the varied functions of this unique vessel type" (Emerson and Jackson 1984: 73).

Although fairly common in the American Bottom, stumpware is all but unknown in the Lower Illinois Valley

Table 5.6. Ceramics from Farnsworth and Glenn's 5/15/83 Controlled Surface Collection (Areas A–G).

	AREA A R.G. 30 min	AREA B K.F. 30 min	AREA C R.G. 20 min	AREA D K.F. 20 min	AREA E KF+RG 15 min	AREA F R.G. 20 min	AREA G K.F. 20 min
Surveyor *Survey Time*							
Jersey Bluff Rims (smoothed, grit tempered):							
squared, lip-notched	1	–	–	–	–	–	–
squared, unnotched	1	5[a]	2	5	4[b]	–	6[a]
flared, lip-notched	1[c]	2	1	1	1	–	–
flared, unnotched	–	–	–	1	–	2	1
everted-squared, lip-notched	–	–	1	1	1	1	1
everted-squared, unnotched	–	–	–	1	–	–	–
everted-rounded (unnotched)	–	–	–	–	–	2	–
Jersey Bluff Body Sherds (grit tempered):							
smoothed (upper shoulder/neck)	20	54	34	61	21	26	71
cordmarked	23	99	42	102	63	19	81
type indeterminate sherdlets (probable J.B.)	6	16	6	11	10	4	14
Total				825			
Stumpware (grit and grog tempered)	1	5					
Mississippian Sherds (shell tempered)							
Cahokia Cordmarked:							
rim w/ interior red-orange slip				3	1		
body sherd w/ interior red-orange slip				10[d]	2		
rim w/ plain/eroded interior				–	–		
body sherd w/ plain/eroded interior				5	3		
Black Burnished Plates:							
Wells Incised rims				3	1		
plain rims and body sherds				1	1		
Other:							
bowl (interior/exterior red-slip body)[e]				1	1		
horizontal incised rim w/ interior red slip				1	–		
smoothed rim with everted lip				1	–		
burnished body sherds				2	–		
type indeterminate smoothed body sherds				–	4		
Total				40			
Mississippian? (not shell tempered):							
limestone temper, cordmarked body sherds				1	–		
limestone temper, smoothed/eroded body sherds				6	–		
sand tempered body sherd, interior red slip				1	–		
grog temper, smoothed/eroded body sherds				2	2		

[a] one with lip-flare lug
[b] two with lip-flare lugs
[c] very thin "toy" vessel sherd

[d] one with loop handle fragment
[e] Area D specimen is shell tempered (Cahokia Red Filmed); Area E specimen is grog tempered (Merrill Red-filmed)

drainage. In paste and temper, the Starr Village fragments mirror Jersey Bluff ceramics, except that there is an added element of grog in the grit-tempered paste. As noted above, restorable sections of two stumpware vessels were recovered from a pre-1983 Starr Village test square excavation by Maguire (fig. 5.12). Six additional stumpware fragments, including a complete "foot" section, were recovered from Areas A and B by our controlled surface collection (table 5.6).

STARR VILLAGE MISSISSIPPIAN CERAMICS

Although few in number (259 sherds; 14% of the ceramic assemblage), the Mississippian sherds from Starr

Table 5.7. Ceramics from Glenn et al. June-July 1983 Controlled Surface Collection (Areas A–G).

Survey Time[a]	AREA A 30 min	AREA B 20 min	AREA C 30 min	AREA D and E 20 min	AREA E 30 min	AREA F 30 min	AREA G 20 min
Jersey Bluff Rims (smoothed, grit tempered):							
squared, lip-notched	–	–	–	1	–	–	–
squared, unnotched	1	1	–	2	2	2	1
flared, lip-notched	1	–	–	–	–	–	–
flared, unnotched	–	–	–	–	–	–	–
everted-squared, lip-notched	–	–	–	–	–	–	–
everted-squared, unnotched	–	–	–	–	–	–	–
Jersey Bluff Body Sherds (grit tempered):							
smoothed (upper shoulder/neck)	16	6	7	17	17	4	4
cordmarked	20	17	14	27	41	11	9
type indeterminate sherdlets (probable J.B.)	2	–	–	–	–	–	–
Total				223			
Mississippian Sherds (shell tempered)							
Cahokia Cordmarked:							
rim w/ interior red-orange slip				2	2		
body sherd w/ interior red-orange slip				–	2		
rim w/ plain/eroded interior				1	–		
body sherd w/ plain/eroded interior				1	5		
Black Burnished Plates:							
Wells Incised rims				1	–		
plain rims and body sherds				1	1		
Other:							
smoothed rim with everted lip				–	–	–	1 [b]
type indeterminate smoothed body sherds			2	7	5[c]		
Total				31			
Mississippian? (nonshell tempered):							
limestone temper, smoothed/eroded body sherds				–	1		

[a] Survey times estimated after the fact   [b] Eroded (Powell Plain?) rim with interior red slip. Found near the western edge of Area E.
[c] Two may have eroded exterior red slip

Village include several vessel forms identifiable as classic American Bottom types. Among 147 sherds that can be attributed to a specific vessel form, 117 (80%) are Cahokia Cordmarked jars and eighteen (12%) are probable Wells Incised plates (fig. 5.13), both known to date to late Moorehead and Sand Prairie phases in the American Bottom (Milner et al. 1984:173–81). Moreover, these vessels are physically indistinguishable from their American Bottom counterparts and may have been manufactured there and transported to Starr Village. A distinctive attribute of the Cahokia Cordmarked vessels at Starr is that twenty-two of twenty-nine rims have interior red slip (76%), while forty-seven of eighty-six body sherds have a similar red-slipped interior. Surface erosion on the few rims lacking a visible red slip leaves open the possibility that many or all of them were originally slipped, and thus that all Cahokia Cordmarked vessels imported to the site were originally tinted red on at least their upper interior surfaces. These vessels also form an unusual (chronologically tight?) assemblage in that the everted portion of the rim is generally narrow in the range of variation of the type (fig. 5.14). This may indicate a late Moorehead rather than Sand Prairie affiliation for the assemblage (Milner et al. 1984:176).

In comparison to ceramic assemblages from Sand Prairie phase Mississippian sites in the American Bottom, the shell-tempered pottery collection from Starr Village is unusually homogeneous. It also seems to be distinctly shifted toward the "fine china" end of the spectrum of vessel quality. Over ninety percent of the assemblage is made up of fragments of interior red-slipped jars or burnished/incised plates.

Metric data on Cahokia Cordmarked rims from Starr Village are summarized by Morgan (1985:37–52) in

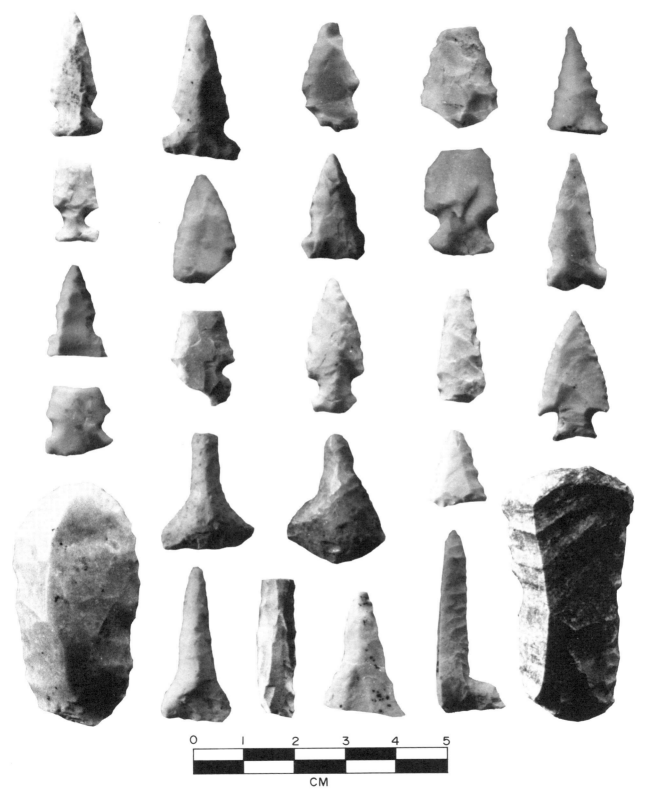

Figure 5.7. Late Woodland Projectile Points, Drills, and Scrapers from Starr Village

Figure 5.8. Ground-stone Celts from Starr Village

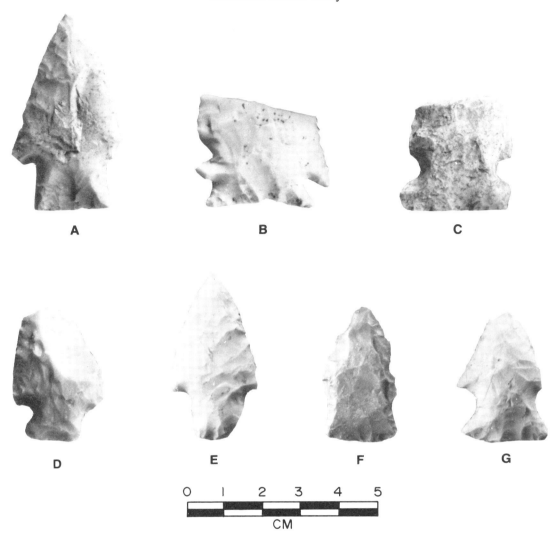

Figure 5.9. Archaic and Early/Middle Woodland Projectile Points from Starr Village: (a) Hardin Barbed, (b) Kirk Cluster, (c) Godar, (d) Table Rock, (e) Belknap, (f) hornstone Norton (reworked), and (g) Gibson.

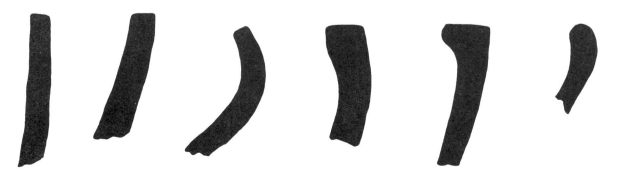

Figure 5.10. Characteristic Rim Profiles of Starr Village Jersey Bluff Ceramics (rounded lip at far right is one of only two examples from the site)

Figure 5.11. Jersey Bluff Rim Sherds from Starr Village

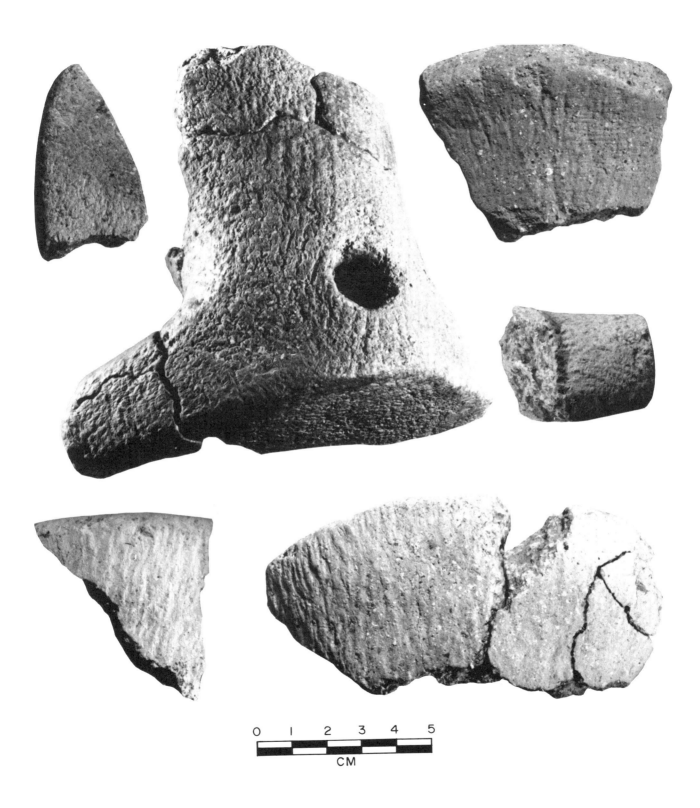

Figure 5.12. Stumpware from Starr Village

Figure 5.13. Mississippian Rim Sherds from Starr Village: (a-g) Cahokia Cordmarked, (h-j) Wells Incised, (k-l) Powell-Ramey?, (m-o, q-s) miscellaneous shell-tempered sherds, (p) possible juice press or funnel.

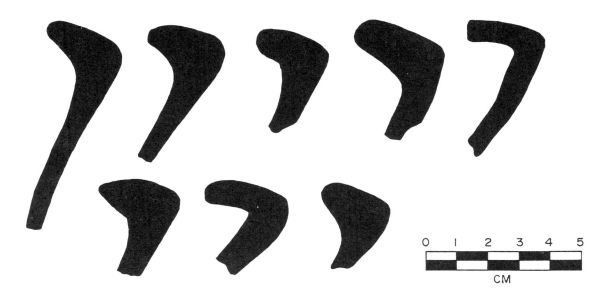

Figure 5.14. Characteristic Rim Profiles of Starr Village Cahokia Cordmarked Vessels

comparison with sherds from both the Hill Creek site in the Lower Illinois Valley and the Julien site in the American Bottom. Morgan's study of rim height, rim angle, and adjusted lip length for the Starr material shows that the sherds are slightly shorter with greater rim angles than those from Hill Creek (Morgan 1985: fig. 2.11, tables 2.5–2.8). However, these measures produce conflicting estimates of the site's chronology with respect to the other studied Mississippian components (Morgan 1985:49). This may be because the Cahokia Cordmarked ceramics at Starr are part of an unusual functionally specialized assemblage (discussed below).

According to a recent study by John E. Kelly (1984), Wells Incised ceramics first appear in early Moorehead times. These "Wells Broad-Trailed bowls" have everted rims diagonally incised with broad parallel lines. By late Moorehead times, broad-trailed plates appear. Rims of these vessels have incised motifs consisting of multiple diagonal lines or simple chevrons (like those from Starr Village, see fig. 5.13). During the subsequent Sand Prairie phase these are replaced by Wells Fine-Incised plates, whose 1–2 millimeter incising was characteristically scratched into dried or already fired rim surfaces.

The radiating incised-line patterns on Wells Incised flaring rims are generally viewed as sunray or "sunburst" patterns surrounding the central serving portion of the vessel, thought to represent the sun circle itself. In the American Bottom, fragments of these plates are found in habitation areas associated with mound centers, perhaps concentrated where "social and religious gatherings" occurred (Kelly 1984:15). "Whether the usage of the decorated plates was restricted to certain ceremonies such as the Green Corn Ceremony is difficult to ascertain. The uniformity of design motifs over a large geographic area does indicate a level of interaction that extended beyond one's own house or community and beyond regional barriers" (Kelly 1984:25).

Most of the remaining typable vessels also fit chronologically within a late Moorehead/Sand Prairie assemblage (fig. 5.13). These include three sherds from interior/exterior red-slip bowls and single sherds from a narrow-mouth bottle, juice press or funnel, and probable salt pan. Three additional distinctive rims have an unknown Mississippian temporal affiliation: a vertically incised rim with interior red slip and two everted smoothed rims. The only sherds that may be out of place in the assemblage are three thin, burnished-gray everted rims collected prior to the 1983 work (table 5.5), which appear to be from Powell Plain or Ramey Incised vessels. Powell and Ramey ceramics most typically date to earlier Stirling phase Mississippian times (ca. A.D. 1050–1150), but they are found in Moorehead phase contexts as well (Milner et al. 1984:175).

DISTRIBUTION OF DIAGNOSTIC ARTIFACTS

Distribution of Jersey Bluff and Moorehead/Sand Prairie phase artifacts at the Starr Village site are dramati-

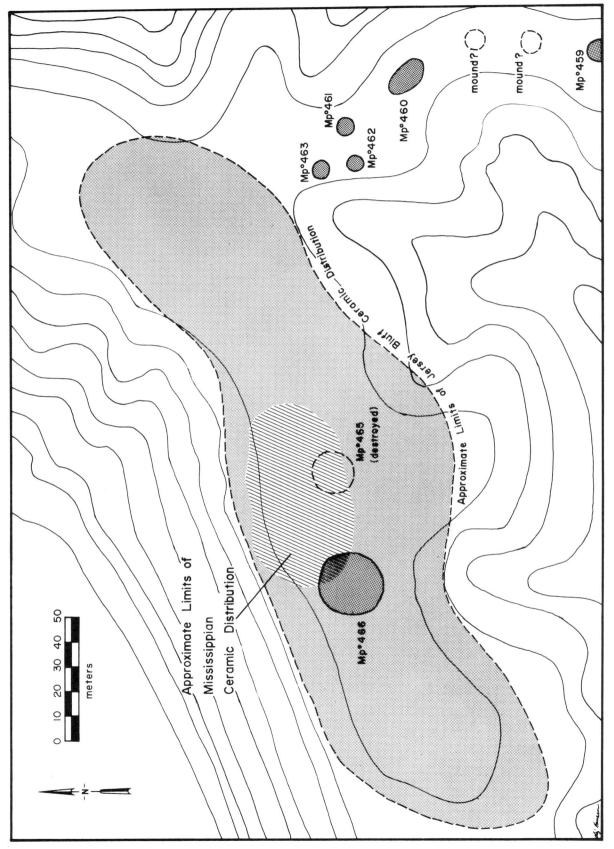

Figure 5.15. Schematic Distribution Map of Jersey Bluff and Mississippian Ceramics at the Starr Village Site

cally different (table 5.6; fig. 5.15). As described earlier, our controlled surface-collection study divided the 1.4-hectare habitation area into seven survey zones (fig. 5.5). Jersey Bluff ceramics and stone tools were widely distributed over the entire site area, with somewhat increased concentration of material in the vicinity of Mp°465 and Mp°466. In contrast, all Mississippian artifacts recovered from surveys and test excavations at the site were localized within a 0.16-hectare (less than 30 × 60 meters) scatter in Areas D and E, in the immediate vicinity of the two mounds.

The strong impression produced by these distribution patterns (and by the exotic nature and fine quality of many of the Mississippian artifacts recovered) is that the Mississippian materials do not represent a habitation site scatter so much as a small activity area within the Jersey Bluff village, associated with the mounds and contemporary with the Jersey Bluff occupation. It should be noted, however, that Woods and Holley (chap. 3) have documented a pattern of late Mississippian small-site upland settlement in the Wood River drainage to the south of our regional study area. It is remotely possible that the Mississippian remains at Starr represent a northern extension of this settlement pattern.

Starr Village Chronology and Site Interpretation

The data from Starr Village provide us with our first evidence for the longevity of Jersey Bluff occupation in the Lower Illinois Valley region. Although professional excavations are obviously needed at Starr Village and we as yet have no radiocarbon dates from the site, a distinctive cluster of datable Mississippian features and artifacts has been found there in an otherwise Late Woodland habitation setting. These include one and perhaps two nonmortuary platform mounds, a stone-box-grave burial containing the Macoupin Creek Figure Pipe as a grave offering, two fragments of probable Mill Creek Ramey knives, a marine shell columella, and hundreds of shell-tempered pottery sherds that belong to a late Moorehead or early Sand Prairie assemblage stylistically indistinguishable from American Bottom assemblages. The Macoupin Creek Figure Pipe may be anomolously early, since such pipes date to the Stirling phase in the American Bottom (Emerson 1982). But this particular artifact was recovered from a stone-box grave, which in Illinois is an unambiguous Sand Prairie phase mortuary feature (Griffin and Jones 1977; Milner 1983), so it was most likely an heirloom. The carved figure is an outstanding sculpture, and its survival for a hundred years or more into Sand Prairie times is easy to imagine.

Together these artifacts seem to argue in favor of a Sand Prairie or late Moorehead phase date for the Mississippian presence at Starr Village. From the American Bottom chronology (Milner et al. 1984), the Starr Mississippian materials would date to approximately A.D. 1200–1350. Because the Mississippian artifacts at Starr consist of a restricted range of high-quality items and are concentrated in less than a 30 × 60-meter area adjacent to a possible platform mound (perhaps between two platform mounds bracketing a rectangular configuration of four house-sized structures and the stone-box grave that contained the Macoupin Creek Figure Pipe) in the midst of a 1.4-hectare Jersey Bluff village, we hypothesize that the Jersey Bluff occupation in this area of the Macoupin Valley was thriving as much as two hundred years after the most recent radiocarbon date for Jersey Bluff phase habitation sites in the region. At this time, the Starr Village Jersey Bluff inhabitants had incorporated significant elements of American Bottom Mississippian ritual (perhaps associated with mortuary ceremonialism) into their Late

Table 5.8. Tabulation of Surface Pottery Sherds from Macoupin Valley Sites with Shell-Tempered Mississippian Ceramics

| Site | Jersey Bluff | Mississippian | | | |
		plain/burnished	cord-marked	Cahokia Cordmarked	Wells Incised
Berry	3	1	–	–	–
Bierman	21	1	–	–	–
Carlinville	**3**	–	–	1 (r)	–
Cottonwood Creek	–	1 [a]	–	–	–
Crib	17	1	–	–	–
Fillager	127	2	–	–	–
George	**12**	–	**3**	–	–
Green Persimmon School	43	3	–	–	–
Griswold	3	3	–	–	–
Kemper	**114**	**4**	**2 (1r)**	**1**	–
Krueger	111	1	–	–	–
Lost Mississippian Pot	(Isolated Cahokia Cordmarked rim section; not found on habitation site)				
May complex [b]	375	5	–	–	–
Park	11	2	–	–	–
Pregler	5	1	–	–	–
Randolph	**11**	**1**	**7 (2r)**	**3 (1r)**	–
Shanks	–	117	–	–	–
Ward	89	3	–	–	–
Wines Branch	12	1	–	–	–

[a] Only sherd from site.
[b] Includes three adjacent surface scatters ("May", "Trestle", and "Bernstein") that are probably all part of a single site complex.
r = interior red slipped sherd

Woodland life-style and had imported American Bottom Mississippian artifacts into Macoupin Valley to support these ceremonial activities.

To our knowledge, the Starr Village pattern is regionally unique. The presence of high-quality late Mississippian artifacts in a ritual precinct within a Jersey Bluff village is not a pattern noted at any other Macoupin Valley Jersey Bluff site, several of which have large associated mound groups. A few shell-tempered sherds are known from nineteen of the Jersey Bluff sites in the valley, but these largely seem to reflect a Loy-site pattern of occasional transport of early Mississippian vessels into the region, probably in the context of infrequent trade interaction (table 5.8). A single glaring exception to this pattern is the Shanks site. Shanks is located only eight kilometers east of the juncture of the Macoupin and Illinois valleys and may be related to a cluster of sites there which have unusually high percentages of Mississippian

sherds (see table 5.9, discussion below). Starr Village is the only regional Jersey Bluff occupation with evidence of platform mounds or on-site Mississippian ritual activities, although four of the other Macoupin Valley Jersey Bluff sites listed in table 5.8 have produced a few Cahokia Cordmarked sherds similar to the Mississippian assemblage from Starr. (These sites are indicated in boldface in the table.)

Possibly by A.D. 1250–1300 the Jersey Bluff occupants of Macoupin Valley were clustered in the vicinity of Starr Village, which served as their ritual/mortuary center. Alternatively, Starr may be evidence of some regional ritual "freedom of choice" in Late Woodland times, perhaps representing a situation in which residents of one village embraced elements of late Mississippian ritual while surrounding village/mortuary centers held to a more traditional Late Woodland ritual pattern.

Regional Settlement Interpretations

The American Bottom has been characterized as the northern frontier of the Middle Mississippian heartland (e.g., Smith 1984b), and several models have been proposed to explain Mississippian interaction with more northerly indigenous groups and apparent Mississippian settlements to the north of this American Bottom frontier. While scholars differ in viewing dramatic Mississippian developments in the American Bottom as evidence for the appearance of a primitive theocratic state (see Gibbon 1974:136; see also chap. 11), complex hierarchical chiefdom (Hall, chap. 1; Lathrap and Porter 1985), or series of competing chiefdoms (Emerson, chap. 12), they generally accept the view that construction of monumental public works, development of widespread trade networks, and proliferation of economic specialization at Cahokia and its surrounding temple-town centers was politically organized and legitimized by a pan-regional religious authority. Far from being separate entities, Mississippian religious and political systems were intimately entwined. This has given rise to a complex web of competing theories of northward Mississippian ideological expansion and migration:

(1) Mississippianization of northern local groups was the result of contacts and proselytizing by missionaries representing the American Bottom theocracy. In this view, contacts and supernaturally ordained alliances were made with local tribal elite by religious emissaries of Mississippian culture who traded in ritual ideas and paraphenalia (Gibbon 1974, see also chap. 11; Hall 1975a, see also chap. 1; Riley and Apfelstadt 1978; Stoltman 1986).

(2) Interaction with northern groups was missionary-like and based in ritual, but was motivated by more mundane political and economic needs to stabilize tense intertribal relations along trade routes and to cement ties with trading partners (Conrad, chap. 6). This may have taken the form of some sort of adoption rite creating the fiction of blood relations between tribal leaders and Cahokia elite (see Douglas 1976:100, 285; Hall 1980, see also chap. 2).

(3) Relationships with northern groups were much more explicitly economic, involving both contact and settlement. Cahokia and/or one or more of its surrounding temple-town centers served as a "gateway" trade center that controlled major transportation routes on the northern Mississippian frontier (see Fowler 1974; Hall 1967a; Kelly, chap. 4; Porter 1969, 1974). Transient traders and trading stations were established in northern tribal areas to support the flow of desired goods and raw materials into the American Bottom and further south. This perhaps involved an attempt to extend Cahokia governing boundaries by its ruling elite (Harn 1975b:429). Trade materials may have been exotic items that served to reinforce the status of Cahokia's elite (Walthall and Struever 1985; Kelly, chap. 4), or were perhaps more mundane goods such as buffalo robes and meat (Alex 1981a; Tiffany 1986b), forest products (Conrad, chap. 6), agricultural products, dried game or fish, and lithic resources (Conner 1985).

(4) Northern interaction, although primarily economic in impetus, was more passive and had a major export focus. In this view, northern tribal groups locally Mis-

sissippianized themselves through the desire to acquire high-quality Mississippian material goods ("keeping up with the Joneses"). Eventually this expanded into northern tribal efforts to emulate the political, religious, and economic sophistication of their famous "big city" neighbors to the south (see Moffat, chap. 13; Smith 1984b).

(5) Mississippianization of northern tribal groups was accomplished through the establishment of pioneer settlements of American Bottom emigrants, primarily during the Stirling phase (see Griffin 1960b). These emigrants may have been invited, or at least cordially received, by local groups wishing to expand previously established Mississippian trade and social ties (see Conrad, chap. 6). Mississippian settlers likely left the Cahokia area as the result of economic or population pressures, presumably due to the limited availability of agricultural land or other American Bottom subsistence-productivity stresses. Two scenarios have been proposed regarding the political atmosphere of such immigrations and the course of local Mississippianization following the arrival of the emigrants:

(a) Mississippian settlers maintained their political ties with Cahokia and served as a conduit of Mississippian culture and material goods to local tribal groups (see Conrad, chap. 6; Gardner 1973a; Hall 1980:448).

(b) Alternatively, the Mississippian settlers may have been refugees from American Bottom political unrest. Emerson (chap. 12) offers a compelling argument for the possibility of competing local Stirling phase chiefdoms during the rise of Cahokia and sees evidence of refugees from such conflicts migrating northward (Lundy site study, see chap. 8). In this model, the pioneers would sever ties with the American Bottom when they left, and their subsequent Mississippian culture change and the Mississippianization of local tribal groups they influenced would be independent of Cahokia interaction.

As this book demonstrates, sound evidence can be gathered in support of many of these ideas, and it may well be the case that Mississippianization of northern tribal groups was the result of a complex fabric of interactions and migrations that situationally involved several of the scenarios presented above. For instance, Douglas (1976:97) argues that Cahokia-controlled settlement expansion extended as far north as Peoria. Further north, interaction was restricted to contact with "merchants" or "missionaries." Kelly (chap. 4) presents a sequential scenario for the Central Illinois Valley that includes American Bottom trade contact in Emergent Mississippian times, then Stirling phase arrival of settlers with allegiance or ties to the Cahokia gateway center, and eventual establishment of a secondary gateway center in the Spoon River locality that was an independent Cahokia competitor (see also Conrad, chap. 6). To the north of

Illinois, Stoltman (1986:28–31) proposes a pattern of four distinct "culture contact situations" for Iowa, Wisconsin, and Minnesota. The Mississippianization debate is far from resolved. As Hall laments: "Cahokia was a cultural pump that seems to have mediated various kinds of interareal contacts and exchanges in ways at which we can only guess" (see chap. 1).

EVIDENCE FOR MISSISSIPPIAN SETTLEMENT IN THE LOWER ILLINOIS VALLEY

Via the Illinois River, the Lower Illinois Valley is the principal avenue to central and perhaps northern Illinois for Mississippian settlers, missionaries, or traders. Yet the Lower Illinois Valley and its tributary stream systems are curiously devoid of evidence for any substantial Mississippian presence. Both Goldstein (1980b) and Conner (1985) have evaluated regional survey data for Mississippian settlement, and they reach similar conclusions: with the exception of one Stirling-age village (the Audrey site), all of the Mississippian sites recorded during more than twenty years of regional surveys and excavations are small homesteads. Goldstein's cursory search of the regional survey files for the entire drainage reportedly revealed seventy-two such sites, each identified by the presence of three or more shell-tempered sherds. In her opinion, these sites tended to be linearly spaced along valley margins with a "relatively even distance" between individual sites (1980b:23).

Conner's more detailed site-file search was limited to the Illinois trench itself. Here, he documented thirty-eight Mississippian sites, including eleven Stirling-age components and eleven components dating to the Sand Prairie phase. Site distribution patterns revealed by this temporal subdivision are anything but "linearly spaced" along the valley. From Conner's discussion and map (1985:216–17), it is clear that sites with American Bottom-like Stirling ceramics are restricted to the southern half of the Lower Illinois Valley and are found primarily in a grouped cluster along twelve miles of eastern bluffline bracketed by Apple and Macoupin creeks. In contrast, sites with Sand Prairie-age ceramics occur only in approximately the northern half of the Lower Illinois Valley along its western bluffline (see fig. 5.1). The "Pearl phase" ceramics from these sites are locally made, but have obvious stylistic affinities with Central Illinois Valley Larson phase vessels. As Conner points out, "It may . . . be that the focus of extraregional interactions changed through time, shifting from the American Bottom to the Central Illinois Valley" (1985:218).

Goldstein, following Perino, believes that these sites were small "conveniently located" exploitative farmsteads that helped support the "more urban" American

Bottom or Central Illinois Valley Mississippian population. Conner essentially agrees:

> While many archeologists have thought that the lower Illinois Valley has few Mississippian sites, Gregory Perino has long argued against this position, despite the scarcity or absence of large sites. He believes (personal communication) that Mississippian people in the lower Illinois Valley were primarily farmers, and that many small farmsteads were occupied instead (Goldstein 1980b:22).
>
> [T]he lower Illinois Valley region was a resource procurement area for Mississippian people, occupied by a series of farming communities that may have helped to support the more urban Mississippian population. . . . [I]t appears that this region, with smaller sites and fewer artifact forms and activity areas, represents the lower level or echelon in the Mississippian settlement hierarchy (Goldstein 1980b:23).

> On the whole, Goldstein's conclusion that the lower Illinois Valley served primarily as a resource procurement area with redistribution to the American Bottom or the central Illinois Valley seems likely. These resources may not have been limited to agricultural products. They may have included dried meat, dried fish, skins, chert, and other items (Connor 1985:18).

The Goldstein model is essentially a variation on Mississippian-northward-expansion model 3 above (establishment of traders or settlements in adjacent areas to control access to desired goods and raw materials), with an added wrinkle. In this case, the unstated assumption is that by the Stirling phase the Lower Illinois Valley trench was available for farmstead colonization by Mississippians, presumably because the extensive local Jersey Bluff Late Woodland population was willing to "make room" for a few Mississippian farmers, or for some reason had retreated into tributary valley regions to the east, or had abandoned the region altogether. Kelly (personal communication, 1983) has suggested that the Lower Illinois Valley may have been depopulated because its Jersey Bluff people were magnetized into the Cahokia area by Mississippian cultural developments, and once there were incorporated into the new American Bottom religious and socioeconomic system. Hall (1966) has voiced a similar opinion: "The evidence suggests that Woodland peoples were being drawn into the Mississippian orbit at Cahokia over a period of perhaps three or four centuries and that the face of Mississippian culture itself was also changing in response to this interaction" (quoted in Hall 1975a: 18). A variation on this assumption has been provided by Perino: "I believe that a relatively small group of Mississippians were instrumental in effecting the acculturation of Jersey Bluff groups into a Mississippian way of life" (1971b:141). In this view, although most of the extensive Jersey Bluff population would have disappeared

(perhaps drawn in by the Cahokia "magnet"?), the small Mississippian farmsteads may have been manned by acculturated Jersey Bluff folk.

Goldstein supports her view that the Lower Illinois Valley was the farm belt for Cahokia and Dickson Mounds by showing that lower-valley Mississippian sites are located primarily on fertile bottomland soils that would be rich agricultural lands (Goldstein 1973). She characterizes this prime farmland area as "richer and wider" than that of the American Bottom or Central Illinois Valley, and points out that it is "conveniently placed between the two" (1973:21–22). This model of detached Lower Illinois Valley farmsteads, if accurate, would be unique in the Mississippian settlement world. Mississippian farmsteads elsewhere are organized hierarchically and are found in the immediate vicinity of more complex settlements (Conrad, chap. 6; Emerson and Milner 1981, 1982).

Regardless of the model's internal strength, the idea that the Lower Illinois Valley was colonized in Mississippian times to provide hinterland farmstead resource support for population centers in the Cahokia area or the Central Illinois Valley does little to explain the presence of the larger Audrey site and its associated Moss cemetery at the mouth of Apple Creek valley, or the massive Schild cemetery fifteen kilometers south of Audrey, which produced "nearly 300 Mississippian period skeletons" (Perino 1971b:4). The Audrey site (Cook 1982, 1983a, 1983b) is an three-hectare village; the Moss cemetery, a kilometer to the west, contained some forty-five Mississippian burials (Goldstein 1980b).

Unreported Audrey site excavations have encountered at least seven wall-trench-in-basin house floors, over 100 pit features, two possible stockade segments, and a plaza. Howard D. Winters, an archaeologist familiar with the Audrey site fieldwork, notes that one of the structures excavated there was very large and looked nonresidential. He points out that such "ground level structures often preceeded the construction of pyramidal mounds." In Winters's view, "Audrey . . . seems to have been occupied only for a short time and to have been more complex than farmsteads or hamlets, or even the simpler villages. It is perhaps the most complex Mississippian site between . . . Beardstown . . . and the mouth of the Illinois" (letter to the senior author, 26 May 1987). Stylistically, Audrey Mississippian artifacts are closely similar to Stirling phase materials (A.D. 1050–1150) from the American Bottom. No platform or other mounds are associated with the Audrey village.

The Schild cemetery was excavated in 1962 by Gregory Perino (Perino 1971b, 1973b; Goldstein 1980b). Although it produced hundreds of skeletons buried with classic Stirling phase American Bottom pottery vessels and other artifacts, no associated Mississippian village or town site could be located. However, according to Perino (1971b:4) a small "temple mound" is situated on a nearby bluff-base area of the adjacent Illinois floodplain, "and the mound shows evidence of having supported a structure that burned." Interestingly enough, when the area surrounding the mound was bulldozed for highway fill in the early 1940s "[a] number of Late Woodland refuse pits were found, and all were included in the road fill."

There are seven post–A.D. 700 radiocarbon dates from Schild. These dates directly overlap the C-14 age determinations for Jersey Bluff village occupations (table 5.1) and Late Woodland mortuary sites (table 5.2). From the occasional diagnostic mortuary artifacts in Schild Mounds 1-9, Perino (1973b) interprets all of their interments as Late Woodland. For instance, all three pottery vessels recovered are identified as Jersey Bluff (Perino 1971b:64–65). From abundant associated grave goods, the nonmounded Knoll A and B cemetery adjacent to Mound 9 is interpreted as Mississippian (Perino 1971b).

None of the dated burials from the Schild Late Woodland mounds were accompanied by diagnostic grave goods. However, Burial 11 in Mound 2 was adorned with a marginella-shell necklace and the grave fill contained a side-notched arrowpoint fragment and two cordmarked Late Woodland sherds. The UCR collagen dates were run by Conner (1984) and the UCLA dates by Tainter (1975):

A.D. 1050 ± 70	(Mound 2, Burial 31)	UCR-1401
A.D. 970 ± 80	(Mound 1, Burial 34)	UCR-1399
A.D. 870 ± 90	(Mound 2, Burial 11)	UCR-1400
A.D. 820 ± 50	(Mound 3, Burial 34)	UCLA-1919c
A.D. 795 ± 50	(Mound 9, Burial 5)	UCLA-1919a

Perino also submitted charred wood, bone, corn, and hickory-nut fragments from two of the three cremated burials in the Knoll A-B (Mississippian) cemetery area to the University of Michigan radiocarbon lab (Perino 1971b:135–36). Burial 122 (Knoll A) included a "small limestone tempered jar" (surface treatment not described) and a St. Clair Plain jar with "animal-like" effigy loop handles (Perino 1971b:29). Burial 275 (Knoll B) had no diagnostic artifacts but included "corn kernels fused together in part of a charred woven reed basket" (Perino 1971b:61). The Michigan dates are:

| A.D. 1200 ± 110 | (Knoll A, Burial 122) | M-1394a |
| A.D. 930 ± 110 | (Knoll B, Burial 275) | M-1393 |

From ceramic styles associated with burials in the cemetery at large, Perino believes that an average of these two dates (A.D. 1065) "should produce the correct period in which these people lived" (1971b:136). In light of the Schild Late Woodland mound dates, the shifts from mound to cemetery interments and from characteristic

Late Woodland to Mississippian grave goods at the site seem to have occurred at about A.D. 1050.

Although neither Conner nor Goldstein addresses the Audrey site issue directly, it may be assumed they view this larger village as a support community for the area's scattered Stirling farmsteads, as perhaps it was. Further evaluation of this possibility is hindered by the fact that several seasons of field school excavations at the site between 1975 and 1985 remain largely unstudied and unreported. The Schild cemetery is more perplexing given the Goldstein hinterland-farmstead model. Schild is located in the midst of the Stirling phase farmstead distribution documented by Conner's settlement distribution study, and he sides with Goldstein in its interpretation: "In the case of the earlier occupation, there is even a regional mortuary center at the Schild site. Goldstein (1980b:126) originally proposed this idea, and it is certainly supported by the fact that Schild is close to the center of the main distribution of earlier Mississippian sites. No such regional mortuary-ceremonial sites are known for the later occupation" (Conner 1985:219).

This answer glosses over the fact that the local Audrey village has its own cemetery (with forty-five burials that could in themselves account for much of any scattered Stirling homestead population). Moreover, if Stirling phase settlers had close tributary ties to a nearby urban center, it is conceivable that the rural farmers would carry their dead to the ritual center for burial. In the Goldstein model, 300 Mississippian interments at an apparently isolated Schild cemetery is inexplicable.

Several studies of late prehistoric skeletal populations from Lower Illinois Valley mortuary sites support the view that local Jersey Bluff people were not physically replaced by incoming Mississippian settlers. Two recent doctoral dissertations evaluate a series of craniometric measurements (Droessler 1981) and nonmetric cranial/mandibular attributes (Konigsberg 1987) of Late Woodland versus Mississippian burials at Schild and other local mortuary sites. The authors conclude that these burials represent members of a single biological population or "lineage" (Konigsberg 1987:185): "[T]he biological distance results support a model of biological continuity within the region from Late Woodland through Mississippian times, with very limited immigration, if any, accompanying the transition to a Mississippian way of life" (Droessler 1981:194–95).

Two earlier studies of the Schild site burials by Jane E. Buikstra (1975, 1977) predicted the Droessler and Konigsberg results. From her 1975 analysis of nonmetric skeletal traits, Buikstra concluded that "the major cultural change here, whatever it is, is *not* associated with an initial alteration in either population composition or breeding patterns" (1975:13).

These conclusions are in sharp contrast to those reached by Blakely for the Central Illinois Valley. His doctoral study of biological distance between Late Woodland and Mississippian skeletons from Dickson Mounds concludes that the Mississippians were not direct descendents of the area's local Late Woodland inhabitants, and thus that Mississippian people and Mississippian culture arrived from outside the region (Blakely 1973:155). Although biodistance studies do not support arguments for Mississippian immigration into the Lower Illinois Valley, Droessler assumes that the area's resident Late Wood-

land groups underwent a "transition to a Mississippian way of life" at the same time they began to use Mississippian mortuary artifacts. Buikstra (1975) wisely avoids such assumptions about the direction or extent of Late Woodland culture change accompanying the new pattern of placing high-quality Mississippian burial goods with the dead. However, she does note that there is some biological evidence for an associated change in residence pattern at this time (from matrilocal to patrilocal residence rules).

A Revised Model of Lower Illinois Valley Mississippian Settlement

The key to a balanced assessment of Mississippian settlement in the Lower Illinois Valley is the extensive Late Woodland Jersey Bluff phase population distributed across at least the southern half of the drainage after A.D. 800 (see fig. 5.1). Although there has been no formal settlement study to document the extent or density of Jersey Bluff site distribution in the region, unpublished survey records on file at the Kampsville Archeological Center indicate that nearly 100 Jersey Bluff habitation sites and well over 300 probable Jersey Bluff burial mounds are known from Macoupin Valley alone. In the southern Lower Illinois Valley trench, Jersey Bluff mortuary sites are at least equally common (Farnsworth and Neusius 1978; Shalkop 1949; Titterington 1935, 1943; Wadlow 1951:13). In this area of the valley, several known Jersey Bluff habitation sites have surface scatters that cover eight hectares or more, much larger than any settlement of earlier times. Study of one such twelve-hectare Jersey Bluff "town" (which has also produced Stirling-era Mississippian remains) was the original impetus for initiating the Koster site excavations, later refocused on buried Archaic horizons in a small area of the site (Struever and Holton 1979:9–11).

The few radiocarbon dates we have from Jersey Bluff sites along the Illinois Valley itself cluster largely between A.D. 850 and 1100. In Macoupin Valley, the data from Starr Village point to a Jersey Bluff occupation there at A.D. 1200 or later. From the wide distribution of Jersey Bluff sites and these early glimmerings of a settlement chronology, it appears that the bulk of Jersey Bluff phase occupation is contemporary with the dramatic Stirling phase Mississippian developments in the American Bottom, and that the southern Lower Illinois Valley drainage housed an extensive Jersey Bluff population. From the data at hand, we must disagree with implied arguments for Stirling phase farmstead occupation of an essentially depopulated valley. Chronologically, it also seems un-

likely that Hall's model of regional Late Woodland groups being physically drawn into the American Bottom and the Cahokia "socio-political fabric" (Hall 1966, 1975a) can seriously be applied to Lower Illinois Valley populations. Perhaps the northern American Bottom was depopulated by such an urban population shift and Late Woodland Mississippianization, but even there the process seems to have been a slow one. From seven American Bottom radiocarbon dates of A.D. 1040 to 1185 on Late Bluff features lacking Mississippian ceramics at Cahokia and nearby sites, Hall identifies

> a late Late Woodland "Bluff" segment within the greater Cahokia community and within Cahokia itself which may be operating as a part of Cahokia society but which is outside of the Cahokia Mississippian tradition in the formal-stylistic sense. In 1966 I wrote, "This complex forms enclaves within the Cahokia area during Old Village times and may have contributed to the formation of Trappist Phase [now Sand Prairie Phase] Mississippian" (Hall 1966). By Old Village I meant then what we would now call Stirling Phase. . . . I would see this as an instance of Woodland peoples being integrated into the socio-political fabric of Cahokia society at a faster rate than they were being assimilated to the Cahokia Mississippian tradition in the formal-stylistic sense (1975a:22–24).

If the Lower Illinois Valley was heavily populated with Jersey Bluff villages and farmsteads during Stirling phase Mississippian times, evidence for regional Mississippian settlement can be viewed in a different light. Closer scrutiny of the Mississippian "farmstead" sites postulated by Goldstein and Conner should reveal the majority to be Jersey Bluff habitations that also yield occasional Stirling phase Mississippian sherds. This can be interpreted as evidence for Jersey Bluff trade interaction with the American Bottom, not extensive Mississippian farmstead settlement of the Lower Illinois Valley.

As an initial test of the model, surface-collected sherds

Table 5.9. Tabulation of Surface Pottery Sherds from Goldstein's (1973, 1980b) Lower Illinois Valley Mississippian Sites, Excluding Macoupin Valley Sites (see table 5.8)

Site	Late Woodland Jersey Bluff	Late Woodland type Indeterminate	Mississippian plain/ burnished	Mississippian cordmarked	Mississippian Cahokia Cordmarked	Mississippian Wells Incised	Site	Late Woodland Jersey Bluff	Late Woodland type Indeterminate	Mississippian plain/ burnished	Mississippian cordmarked	Mississippian Cahokia Cordmarked	Mississippian Wells Incised
Audrey	(Massive surface collections including quantities of both Jersey Bluff and Mississippian ceramics)						Hobson	–	7	3	–	–	–
							Kanallakan	41	11	8	–	–	–
Big Bear	16	3	1	–	–	–	**Kiel**	**25**	**15**	**16**	**8**	**–**	**–**
Blackerby	**199**	**52**	**37**	**36**	**1**	**1**	Knight	–	171	16	–	–	–
Bluffdale-							Koster	(Massive surface collections including quantities					
Russell	45	–	20	–	–	–		of both Jersey Bluff and Mississippian ceramics)					
Brownie							**Lawson**	**–**	**–**	**27**	**94**	**2**	**3**
Bickers	3	5	4	–	–	–	Levis	22	60	82	–	–	–
Byrns South	**–**	**1**	**–**	**1**	**–**	**2**	Levis Culvert	4	7	8	–	–	–
Camerer	–	1	8	–	–	–	Meyer I	51	15	5	–	–	–
Clinton Smith	19	–	3	–	–	–	**Morgan**	**18**	**114**	**12**	**27**	**4**	**1**
Closser	205	132	411	–	–	–	**Mound House**	**–**	**102**	**14**	**2**	**1**	**–**
Cole Creek	4	4	1	–	–	–	**Rapp**	**–**	**68**	**160**	**303**	**49**	**10**
Cypress Land	**–**	**–**	**–**	**3**	**1**	**–**	Reif	7	–	3	–	–	–
Dependahl	8	–	5	–	–	–	Sand Branch	89	13	7	–	–	–
Duncan Farm	2	10	2	–	–	–	Schallenberg	–	–	3	–	–	–
Fisher	**3**	**–**	**1**	**5**	**1**	**–**	**Springer**	**15**	**25**	**4**	**2**	**–**	**–**
Froman							**Stillwell II**	**–**	**9**	**9**	**10**	**1**	**–**
Holtswarth	134	240	6	–	–	–	**T.B. GOK**	**1**	**4**	**100+**[a]	**–**	**10**[a]	**–**
Gans	**–**	**–**	**5**	**8**	**2**	**–**	Titus	19	69	104	–	–	–
German	1	–	3	–	–	–	Tom Collins	1	2	6	–	–	–
Gettings	7	–	1	–	–	–	Upper						
Golden Eagle	**90**	**–**	**–**	**2**	**1**	**–**	Macoupin	10	16	32	–	–	–
Gourley	**–**	**6**	**4**	**14**	**2**	**1**	Walkerville	8	8	6	–	–	–
Harlin	28	–	2	–	–	–	Woodville	26	16	38	–	–	–
Hazelwonder I	**–**	**10**	**3**	**6**	**1**	**–**							

[a] These sherds represent two restorable vessel sections found by workers excavating a house foundation in Kampsville. Two Center for American Archeology excavation seasons at this primarily Middle Woodland site have produced only eight additional shell-tempered sherds (Kraus 1980:53).

from the Lower Illinois Valley sites Goldstein identified as "Mississippian" (1973: appendix 1) were retabulated to identify any associated Jersey Bluff ceramics. At the outset, an isolated cluster of twelve sites situated 114–20 kilometers upriver from the valley mouth were excluded from consideration. These include the Walsh site and eleven nearby sites (Bartley, Camp Creek Bridge, Clytus, Dawson, Hall, Josiah, Lanier, Markert, McPhail, Orpha, and Thompson Hill) that are more properly considered as elements of the Central Illinois Valley Mississippian settlement system (see Conrad, chap. 6). Goldstein's list also contained eleven Macoupin Valley sites, all of which are included in table 5.8. Three further sites are excluded from the present study because no Mississippian sherds could be found in their ceramic collections (Bixby, Daniels, and Lyons). Finally, Center for American Archeology collections from the Kamp site are on loan to Rutgers University and not available for restudy.

Struever's (1960) report of excavations at Kamp makes no mention of Mississippian sherds at the site.

Surface ceramics from the remaining forty-five sites are listed in table 5.9. The "Late Woodland type indeterminate" column includes primarily grit-tempered, cordmarked body sherds that may be fragments of Jersey Bluff vessels, but which lack diagnostic Madison County Shale pastes. Sites with only smoothed or burnished shell-tempered sherds, associated with earlier Lohmann and Stirling phase Mississippian developments in the American Bottom, are listed in regular type. Those producing Cahokia Cordmarked and Wells Incised sherds associated with the local Pearl phase (Conner 1985) and with the later Moorehead and Sand Prairie phases in the American Bottom are listed in boldface.

Sixteen sites in table 5.9 have produced Cahokia Cordmarked and Wells Incised ceramics. All but three fall within Conner's Pearl phase settlement distribution as shown on figure 5.1. Two of the three exceptions are widely separated sites in the Mississippi Valley: the Golden Eagle site is situated eight kilometers upstream from the Illinois/Mississippi River confluence at the southern edge of Jersey Bluff settlement distribution; the Gans site is located near the mouth of a small tributary valley more than fifty-nine kilometers further upstream at the western edge of Jersey Bluff settlement distribution. The third exception is Kiel, located at the western Illinois Valley bluff base some sixteen kilometers upstream from the Illinois/Mississippi confluence. The few Mississippian sherds at Golden Eagle and Kiel may represent ephemeral American Bottom late Moorehead/Sand Prairie phase occupations or a few trade vessels. The Gans site is located in a largely unsurveyed region and is associated with an unknown Mississippian cultural phase.

All of the remaining sites in table 5.9 have produced Stirling or pre–Stirling era smoothed and burnished Mississippian sherds. Two of these sites (Audrey and Koster) have been the subject of extensive surface and excavation studies and their surface ceramics were not retabulated. The Koster site is an apparent example of a massive Jersey Bluff village that produced only occasional Mississippian materials (Houart 1971; Struever and Holton 1979). According to Houart: "The Jersey Bluff component at Koster was apparently the most extensive of the six components found in the 1969 excavations. Jersey Bluff pottery is found over the entire North Field and over the remainder of the 25-acre site. . . . Mississippian pottery occurs at Koster in the upper levels of six test squares. No attempt was made to classify the Mississippian pottery into series or types since only 23 sherds were recovered" (1971:9, 10). The Audrey site situation is less clear. Although unpublished surface-survey maps on file in Kampsville show that the largest component at the site is a seven-hectare Jersey Bluff village, the results of several excavation seasons there also seem to demonstrate that Audrey is the region's most creditable candidate for a small transplanted Stirling phase Mississippian settlement (Cook 1982, 1983a, 1983b; Howard D. Winters, letter to the senior author, 26 May 1987).

All of the sites listed in tables 5.8 and 5.9 that have yielded Stirling-era Mississippian sherds fall within the regional distribution limits of Jersey Bluff settlement as shown in figure 5.1. Moreover, the great majority of these sites have produced far more Jersey Bluff/Late Woodland sherds than Mississippian sherds, lending support to the hypothesis for Jersey Bluff trade and interaction with American Bottom Stirling phase groups rather than Mississippian farmstead settlement of the Lower Illinois Valley.

There are a few exceptions to this pattern, which can be grouped into two settlement clusters along the eastern bluffline of the southern Lower Illinois Valley. The northernmost group is anchored by the Audrey site at the mouth of Apple Creek Valley, and by two adjacent small scatters that may represent specialized activity areas for Audrey inhabitants: Closser and Camerer. The Closser site, for instance, is located in a frequently flooded zone within an Apple Creek loop meander that may only have been seasonally occupiable. Test excavations there by the senior author in 1971 produced no subplowzone artifacts or features, largely because frequent flooding had caused extensive deflation (and thus progressively deeper plowing) of the artifact-bearing surface soil zone. The Bluffdale-Russell site, five kilometers south of Audrey, has also produced an unusually high percentage of shell-tempered sherds among its Jersey Bluff assemblage, as have the adjacent Levis and Levis Culvert sites one and one-half kilometer further to the south. The shell-tempered sherds at the Levis sites are thick, unburnished, and relatively crude, and may pre-date Stirling times or represent local Late Woodland attempts to mimic shell-tempered ceramic technology.

The second settlement cluster at which Mississippian sherds are unusually numerous is located near the mouth of Macoupin Valley about twenty kilometers south of the Audrey site. The group includes the adjacent Titus and Upper Macoupin sites at the valley mouth, the Shanks site overlooking Macoupin Creek eight kilometers to the east, and the Woodville site in the uplands four kilometers to the north. The Koster site is also located in the midst of this settlement group, so if James Brown is correct in his impression that there is more to the Koster Mississippian occupation than meets the eye (personal communication, 1987), then it too can be added to the cluster.

It should be emphasized that the surface collections from eight of the ten sites in these two clusters (all but Camerer and Shanks) also contain Jersey Bluff ceramics, and that many of them have produced substantial numbers of Jersey Bluff sherds. The reason that relatively higher percentages of shell-tempered ceramics occur at these few sites is unknown. Because of the near absence of diagnostic material from the four sites in table 5.9 that have produced only a few shell-tempered sherds and little or no Late Woodland material, they also are enigmatic (German, Schallenberg, T.B. GOK, and Tom Collins). Hopefully, future collections from these sites will clarify their status.

Perino's Schild site mortuary data (Perino 1971b, 1973b) provide fuel for speculation that the reason so little Stirling Mississippian material is found at most Jersey Bluff habitation sites is that this material was imported largely as ritual/prestige items that ended up as mortuary furniture. Schild produced over 230 Late Woodland burials (Perino 1973b) and nearly 300 skeletons with Mississippian artifacts (Perino 1971b). As discussed above, there is no regional evidence for Stirling phase Mississippian settlements to support this mortuary; however, a nearby bluff-base village area destroyed by highway construction in the early 1940s contained a small temple mound and Late Woodland, not Mississippian, village refuse (Perino 1971b:4).

From his mortuary excavations at Schild, Perino observed that

> [Mississippian] vessels were confined to remarkably few forms when compared to the great number of forms found at Cahokia (1971b:64).
>
> Late Woodland ceramics and mortuary traits . . . were blended in with the more spectacular Mississippian wares, mortuary ceremonialism, and civic processes. . . . [M]ortuary and ceremonial customs evolved rapidly at the Schild site from a Late Woodland culture toward a classic Mississippi definition (1971b:136).

Perhaps Schild and its adjacent Late Woodland (town?) site are evidence for Stirling-era Mississippianization of Late Woodland ritual similar to that seen during later Moorehead/Sand Prairie times at Starr Village. If so, this Mississippianized mortuary pattern does not seem to have been shared by nearby contemporary communities. Burials of A.D. 1000–1200 at the Hacker, Helton, Koster, and Ledders mound groups show no evidence of Mississippian cemetery organization and are all but devoid of Mississippian grave goods (Conner 1984:222–31; Hinkes 1977; Kerber 1982; Perino 1973a, 1975; Pickering n.d.). Perhaps some late Jersey Bluff communities were more closely tied to Mississippian ritual systems (and trade?) than others were. Alternatively, two regional (hierarchical?) mortuary-related religious options may have existed at the time in the Lower Illinois Valley, one promoting Mississippian mortuary practices and burial goods and the other adhering to traditional Jersey Bluff patterns of mortuary ritual.

The Audrey site complex (including the nearby Closser and Camerer sites) clearly does not fit into a regional model of Jersey Bluff settlement with Mississippian trade interaction and Mississippianized ritual. Audrey and its adjacent Moss cemetery are located near the mouth of Apple Creek Valley some fifty kilometers above the Illinois/Mississippi River confluence. Although results of excavations at the site are largely unreported, it seems to represent a bona fide isolated Stirling phase Mississippian village in the middle of the Lower Illinois Valley. Two interesting aspects of the site's location may bear on its eventual interpretation: (1) There is a large (ca. seven hectare) area of Jersey Bluff surface scatter at Audrey, which completely encompasses the three-hectare Mississippian scatter. Moreover, Audrey is situated at the northern limits of regional Jersey Bluff site distribution,

and the Mississippian occupation there may be some kind of border or boundary settlement. (2) This being the case, it is curious that no Stirling-age Mississippian settlements are known along the fifty kilometers of Illinois River valley that separate Audrey from the southernmost Eveland phase settlements of the Central Illinois Valley.

Substantial Mississippian settlements are established in the Central Illinois Valley during Stirling phase times (the local Eveland phase; see Conrad, chap. 6). It may well be the case, as earlier postulated by Conrad (1973:6–7) and Emerson (1973:28), that while the dense Late Woodland population of the Lower Illinois Valley precluded actual Mississippian settlement there, far lower population densities in the central valley attracted American Bottom immigrants farther north. Although the southern lower valley may have been largely unavailable for Mississippian settlement, the river itself was apparently an unrestricted transportation artery. Jersey Bluff population densities cannot explain the apparent absence of Stirling/Eveland Mississippian settlement in the northern half of the Lower Illinois Valley, however. This area lies beyond the limits of known Jersey Bluff settlement, but we have no evidence for dense non–Jersey Bluff Late Woodland occupations along this stretch of valley during emergent Mississippian times. If Emerson's view of American Bottom immigrants as political dissidents is correct (see chap. 12), perhaps this relatively empty zone served as a buffer between the Jersey Bluff-Stirling trading partners and breakaway Eveland groups. Early historic Spanish accounts record the existence of such buffer zones between aboriginal groups in the Southeast (Swanton 1911).

By Moorehead/Sand Prairie phase times in the American Bottom, trade contact with the Lower Illinois Valley itself had ceased. There is strong evidence that Mississippian farmsteads or homesteads actually appeared in the valley at this time (Conner 1985), but ceramic style ties—and thus the probable origins of population movement—for this Pearl phase occupation are with Larson phase settlements in the Central Illinois Valley, *not* with the Moorehead or Sand Prairie phase inhabitants of the American Bottom. So far as is known, the distribution of these small sites is limited to approximately the northern half of the Lower Illinois Valley trench (see Conner 1985:215–19). They are not known to occur in the large tributaries to the east of the Illinois River, and none have been found to the south of the northern limits of Jersey Bluff settlement distribution (see fig. 5.1). The Pearl phase is only dated at the Hill Creek site (Conner 1985:7, 12–13), where five radiocarbon dates suggest an occupation of approximately A.D. 1190. The absence of Pearl phase sites in the Jersey Bluff settlement area of the southern Lower Illinois Valley may be evidence that Jersey Bluff inhabitants continued to dominate this area at the end of the twelfth century. The only evidence to the contrary consists of eight cordmarked, shell-tempered body sherds from the Kiel site, located nearly forty kilometers south of the Pearl phase settlement distribution in the southern Jersey Bluff settlement area. These sherds may minimally represent a single late Moorehead/Sand Prairie phase trade vessel from the American Bottom.

Finally, in the Macoupin Valley, we have compelling evidence for a thirteenth-century Jersey Bluff occupation at the Starr Village site. Here in the tributary uplands, there is a continued focus on American Bottom Mississippian interaction, primarily in the context of apparent Mississippianization of Late Woodland mortuary ritual. We lack similar evidence for American Bottom late Mississippian ritual ties at Jersey Bluff sites in the Illinois trench itself, but few such sites have been studied. Notably, there is a move from floodplain to upland settlements in the American Bottom in Sand Prairie times (Woods and Holley, chap. 3; Emerson, chap. 12), and Starr Village may indicate a similar trend for the Lower Illinois Valley.

ACKNOWLEDGMENTS

The radiocarbon-date sequences discussed in this chapter are drawn primarily from two sources: habitation-site dates being assembled and evaluated by David Asch for eventual inclusion in "A Radiocarbon Chronology of West-Central Illinois"; and mortuary-site dates assembled by Michael Conner for his doctoral dissertation (Conner 1984).

The authors would like to thank several colleagues including David Asch, James Brown, Jane Buikstra, Lawrence Conrad, Harold Hassen, John Kelly, John Walthall, Michael Wiant, and Howard Winters for thought-provoking discussions and insightful written criticism as this article was being developed. Kelly in particular made special efforts on many occasions to try to show the senior author the error of his ways and was always ready to respond to our requests for data and perspectives on the late prehistory of the American Bottom.

The senior author is also indebted to Illinois State Museum director R. Bruce McMillan, assistant director for research Bonnie Styles, and anthropology curator Michael Wiant for providing research associate study space and access to records, collections, and library facilities in Springfield during the course of this project.

The very fine maps and photographic prints accompanying this chapter are the work of Liz Hansen at the Kampsville Archeological Center. The artifact photos were taken by the senior author.

6

The Middle Mississippian Cultures of the Central Illinois Valley

LAWRENCE A. CONRAD

The dominant elements in the Central Illinois Valley Middle Mississippian cultures are derived from the American Bottom region through the mechanism of population movement. Evidence indicating this includes the simultaneous introduction of new ceramic, artifactual, and architectural complexes while the previous ones were present in unaltered form; the introduction of a concept of theologically based coercive force that was unknown among the indigenous Late Woodland bands, but existed at Cahokia (e.g., sacrifice of in-group members); and the sudden appearance of physically distinct people.

The initial light influx of new people from the Cahokia area was during Lohmann times at ca. A.D. 1000–1050. Because this Lohmann phase influx is known only from a farmstead at the Rench site (McConaughy, Jackson, and King 1985) and a single shoulder sherd from the Weaver-Betts site, few people seem to have been involved. The immigration that led to the Mississippianization of the region occurred during Stirling times (A.D. 1050–1150) and the evidence of that movement is more abundant. (All dates used in this chapter are based on uncorrected RCYs.)

When the Mississippian people moved into the region, they encountered at least two indigenous Late Woodland groups. One population, identified with the Maples Mills phase (Cole and Deuel 1937:191–98), were making single cord-impressed Canton ware ceramics (Fowler 1952) similar to those found from Lake Michigan through central Illinois to the Dakotas and Nebraska. Maples Mills sites are found throughout the wooded portions of west-central Illinois. They range in size from substantial occupations on the Illinois and Mississippi rivers to small camps on the prairie edges (Conrad 1981, fig. 20; Conrad 1988; Conrad, Gardener, and Alford 1984; Esarey 1988a). These habitation remains and the limited number of mortuary sites along the river bluffs that sometimes evolved into sizable mound groups suggest highly mobile bands congregating seasonally to exploit river resources and sharing burial sites.

The uniformly meager grave goods at the Maples Mills phase Gooden site, where almost 100 burials were excavated (Cole and Deuel 1937:191–98), most frequently consisted of unworked mussel shells, followed by smaller numbers of Mounds Stemless II and III (Winters 1963: 29) projectile points, *Anculosa* sp. shell necklaces, ceramic jars, and a single shell spoon. Excluding mussel shells for which placement data are unavailable, artifacts were found with approximately 15% of the burials. None of the burials had an abundance of furniture and the items found are not sociotechnic in nature. Such an assemblage is consistent with the assumption that the people were organized into egalitarian bands.

Another Late Woodland group, the Bauer Branch phase people (Green 1976), seems to have restricted itself generally to the interior and to have had little Mississippian contact, at least in the Spoon River area. Bauer Branch people predominated, however, in the valley south of the area of Spoon River occupation and may have been ancestral to the La Moine River phase inhabitants.

Although the geographic range of the putatively Weaver-derived Sepo people (Harn 1975b:417), another possibly relevant Late Woodland ethnic group in the Spoon River area, may be disputed, it seems that they were less likely than Maples Mills or Bauer Branch phase people to venture from the immediate river valley areas. No late pre-Mississippian Sepo habitations have been recognized and few, if any, burials pre-dating the Stirling phase Mississippian intrusion have been recognized at Dickson Mound (Harn 1975b). If there is an immediately pre-Mississippian Sepo lithic assemblage, nothing is known of it. In fact, there is no firm evidence that the Sepo people associated with the Eveland phase were descended from the earlier (ca. A.D. 600) Sepo people. It could be as easily argued that they arrived with the

Stirling emigrants. Most likely the Sepo ceramic complex is a result of Mississippian impact on indigenous Woodland peoples that is strictly coeval with the Eveland phase Mississippians.

Mississippian Sites in the Central Valley

The 210-kilometer stretch of the Illinois River Valley between Meredosia and Hennepin has traditionally been called the Central Illinois Valley. Because Alan D. Harn (1978:237–41) has provided a readily accessible description of the natural history and physiography of the region, the present discussion focuses on the distribution of the Middle Mississippian sites within the valley. These sites occur along the length of the Central Illinois River Valley south from just above Peoria (fig. 6.1), but most of the information available is from those in the central portion. As discussed below, there are significant differences between sites in the northern portion of the region and those in the south.

At least seven temple towns, characterized by platform mounds, are spaced from thirteen to twenty-six kilometers apart along the Central Illinois Valley. From north to south these temple towns are Hildemeyer or Ten Mile Creek, Kingston Lake, Orendorf, Larson, Crable, Lawrenz Gun, and Walsh. Four of the northern five have single modest platform mounds, whereas Hildemeyer, Lawrenz Gun, and Walsh have several mounds apiece.

Most Middle Mississippian habitation sites are situated near the Illinois River bluff edge. Some, including three of the temple towns (Hildemeyer, Kingston Lake, and Lawrenz Gun), are in the lowlands. A few sizable permanent settlements are located on the lower reaches of the Spoon River (Harn and Weedman 1975) and approximately twenty stream-valley kilometers up Big Creek, the last main tributary of the Spoon. In fact, judging from surface collections, there may well have been permanent habitation sites more than eighty-five river-valley kilometers up the Spoon River.

Madison points and notched variants were common on a survey transect of the Spoon River Basin that crossed the river valley thirty-five kilometers above its mouth, suggesting either the utilization or occupation of this interior area by Mississippian groups. Similar point types were much less common in the upper La Moine Basin and along the Mississippi Slope between Carthage and Quincy (Conrad 1981:225–47). However, the recovery of Mississippian jar fragments, shell beads, and arrowpoints, in association with a human tooth, near the confluence of the East and West forks of the La Moine indicates Mississippian burials and presumably a habitation in the vicinity.

These site locations, like those of most west-central Illinois Mississippian sites, correlate closely with the occurrence of grey-brown alfisols or alluvium bounded by alfisols (see U.S. Department of Interior 1970:86–87 for a map of these soils). Like the alluvium, alfisols formed under deciduous forests are quite fertile. The general lack of such soils along much of the left bank of the Illinois River probably explains the almost total absence of Mississippian sites. While prairie soils are more fertile than alfisols, the prairie sod could not be broken with Indian tools. Harn (personal communication, 1985) has suggested that the presence of a prairie immediately below the mouth of the Spoon River was probably the limiting factor in Larson phase expansion into that area.

Two geographical variants of Central Illinois Mississippian culture can be recognized. These are a northern Spoon River culture and a southerly La Moine River culture, each to some degree associated with the river basin for which it is named. The Spoon River culture has been the more extensively studied beginning with the University of Chicago (UC) field schools and Cole and Deuel's (1937) pioneer summary, through the initial classificatory attempts of Wray's (1952) Garren and Spoon River foci, to the more recent four-phase sequence in use since the early 1970s. This chapter builds upon, expands, and clarifies this most recent sequence.

The Spoon River culture includes the four northernmost temple towns of Hildemeyer, Kingston Lake, Orendorf, and Larson. Chronologically, three major phases have been defined, including an Eveland phase (A.D. 1050–1150), Orendorf phase (A.D. 1150–1250), and Larson phase (A.D. 1250–1300). The Eveland phase has been subdivided into an initial Waterford subphase (A.D. 1050–1100) and a final Wolf subphase (A.D. 1100–1150) on the basis of recognizable internal ceramic style development. The Larson phase is followed by a less clearly defined Marbletown complex (A.D. 1300–1400?). I have refrained from designating Marbletown as a "phase" because we presently lack sufficient information to present a complete definition and, instead, have opted for the less rigid classificatory term *complex* (Wood 1961:5).

In earlier synthetic attempts, the southern temple towns of the Central Illinois River Valley were the most difficult to deal with both because they were poorly known and because their material culture appeared to be distinctly

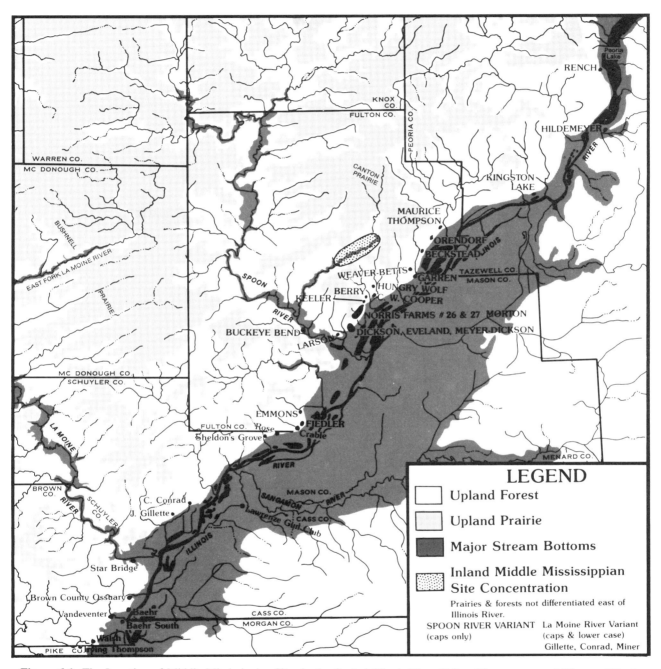

Figure 6.1. The Location of Middle Mississippian Sites in the Central Illinois River Valley. Map courtesy of Western Illinois University.

different from the towns to the north. In this paper I have collected sufficient data to argue that these southern towns do, in fact, form a separate polity that I have designated the La Moine River culture.

The three temple towns to the south of the mouth of the Spoon River—Crable, Lawrenz, Walsh, and their outlying sites—comprise the remains of the La Moine River culture. To some extent the early history of the La Moine River peoples parallels that of the Spoon River peoples. The initial influx of Cahokia Mississippians is marked by the Gillette phase (A.D. 1050–1150), followed by a poorly understood period contemporary with the Orendorf/Larson horizon (A.D. 1150–1300). The Crabtree phase (A.D. 1300–1375) is the climax of local Mississippian development with the subsequent and, perhaps in part contemporary, Crable phase (A.D. 1375–1450) marked by cohabitation with Oneota peoples. Only controlled excavation and analysis of these sites can confirm the validity of these suggestions.

The Spoon River Culture

The Spoon River culture was the first Mississippian manifestation to be extensively investigated with modern archaeological techniques (Cole and Deuel 1937). As Harn (1978:233–36) has detailed the early history of Spoon River studies through the 1960s, the following paragraphs outline some of the more important events in the succeeding years.

In 1970 Harn excavated approximately 0.18 hectares (2.25%) of the eight-hectare Larson site for the Illinois State Museum (ISM). During the 1971 season Thomas E. Emerson and I excavated a trench in the C. W. Cooper site, a multicomponent site with distinct Spoon River and Oneota occupations, examined a wall-trench structure at the Spoon River V. L. Trotter site, and performed the initial testing at Orendorf. Subsequently, between 1971 and 1978, nine hectares of the Orendorf site were excavated (Esarey and Conrad 1981) under the auspices of the Upper Mississippi Valley Archaeological Research Foundation (UMVARF) and Western Illinois University (WIU).

During the early 1970s the U.S. Department of Interior and the Illinois State Historic Preservation Office supported surveys by the ISM, Illinois State University, and UMVARF that gathered data on the Middle Mississippian presence in the Central Illinois Valley as part of the Historic Sites Survey program. Between 1976 and 1978 WIU conducted a survey of a ninety-mile-long, two-mile-wide transect of upland west-central Illinois for the Illinois Department of Transportation that provided data on Mississippian occupations in the central Spoon River Basin and evidence of their paucity in the upper La Moine River Basin (Conrad 1981:224–50).

Also during the 1970s, radiocarbon dates were run from the Eveland, Orendorf, Larson, Cooper, and Crable sites.[1] These dates provided a more refined chronology than had been available previously (Bender, Bryson, and Baerreis 1975).

During this same decade I synthesized the Spoon River data by revising the summary and conclusions of a report on the 1966 ISM excavations at Dickson Mounds (Conrad 1967). I have revised it several times since, but in the past, the pace of data collection made the revisions obsolete before they could be published. The preliminary report on Dickson Mound (Harn 1971b) was published and my masters thesis on the 1966 excavation at Dickson Mound was submitted to the University of Wisconsin at Madison (1972). Other papers, which explored some of the questions dealt with here, were delivered at the Central States Anthropological Society meeting in St. Louis in 1973 (Conrad 1973; Harn 1973). Harn's paper was reworked, expanded, and published (Harn 1975b). Some of the ideas initially expressed in my paper are included below and in a recent discussion published elsewhere (Conrad 1989). Robert L. Blakely (1973) completed his study of a large sample of burials from the Dickson Mound in the fall of 1973. In 1978 Harn published a major paper on the Larson phase Spoon River settlement system (Harn 1978).

Fieldwork in the 1980s has been more limited. Harn (1983) has investigated some smaller outlying sites of Larson. WIU has been able to examine summarily approximately forty hectares of Orendorf's immediate hinterland after topsoil removal but before strip mining; to excavate a small portion of the C. W. Cooper site, including a number of early Spoon River culture pit features; to test one of Orendorf's outlying sites; and to initiate excavations in the Orendorf burial mounds. In addition WIU's Middle Mississippian program has benefited significantly from the collections and observations of amateurs, particularly along the middle Spoon River and the lower Central Illinois River. One result of this cooperation was an excellent aerial photograph of the Star Bridge site (fig. 6.2), an approximately 200-building burned village near the mouth of the La Moine.

In the 1980s analysis and publication of Spoon River data has included Harn's (1980b) revision of his report on the Dickson excavation at Dickson Mounds utilizing Don Dickson's recently discovered field notes, and WIU and UMVARF have published a collection of six papers

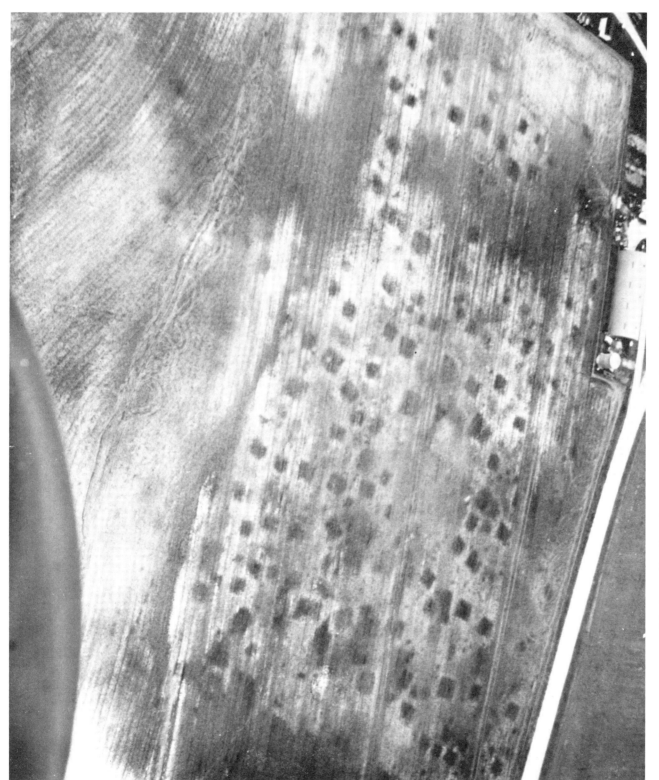

Figure 6.2. Aerial Photograph of the Star Bridge Site. Photo courtesy of Western Illinois University.

analyzing various aspects of the Orendorf data (Esarey and Conrad 1981). There have been a number of papers delivered at meetings, including the predecessor of this one and Harn's chapter in this volume. Duane Esarey has made important studies of spider gorgets (1987) and negative-painted pottery (1988b), while Kelvin Sampson and Esarey (1988) have summarized the Mississippian use of sheet copper in the region.

EVELAND PHASE (ca. A.D. 1050–1150)

The Eveland phase can usefully be divided into two sequential subphases on the basis of ceramic changes. The Waterford subphase presumably dates from A.D. 1050 to 1100 and represents the initial intrusion of Cahokia-based Stirling phase immigrants into the Central Illinois Valley. The material from the Eveland site and Dickson cemetery is considered the type collection for this subphase. The subsequent poorly understood Wolf subphase (A.D. 1100–1150) marks the first visible signs of the development of the unique Spoon River ceramic assemblage.

Waterford Subphase (A.D. 1050–1100)

WATERFORD SUBPHASE SITES. Stirling phase ceramics are known from more than twenty sites in the Central Illinois Valley. Although other sites provide details, the Eveland-Dickson, Garren, and Kingston Lake sites provide the primary basis for the following interpretation of the advent of Middle Mississippian culture in the Central Illinois Valley.

The most thoroughly investigated site evincing a substantial Cahokian intrusion is the Eveland site (ISM Fv900) (Caldwell 1967a, 1967b) located on a terrace along a now-abandoned stream channel at the base of the Illinois River bluff. The site, which covers slightly more than a hectare, consisted of ten or eleven buildings including two large council houses, two large sweat lodges, a cross-shaped building, and four or five dwellings with associated storage pits. Several of the dwellings superimposed one another and were superimposed, in turn, by a large council house. Therefore, there were apparently no more than seven or eight buildings including four private dwellings at the site at any one time.

Three of the public buildings warrant special description. The best-preserved structural remains at the site (Structure 2) are those Caldwell (1967b) referred to as an earth lodge. It was a rectangular building with a floor area measuring approximately 11.9 × 16.3 meters with an entry ramp at least 7.4 meters long extending to the south. Pairs of broad, deep wall trenches on the ends and shallower trenches on the sides were dug along the walls of a deep house pit. The house floor sloped gently toward the middle. A well-prepared, slightly elevated, square

clay hearth lay just to the southwest of the center of the floor. The charred logs on the floor represent the remains of a substantial peaked roof.

Caldwell (1967b:141) interpreted this building as an earth lodge and there are several indications that it may have been at least partially earth covered. The preservation of the roof timbers is in itself an unusual occurrence, as they normally burned completely before the walls collapsed (but then, most roofs were not as substantial as this one). Two substantial borrow pits to the west and south of the structure may have provided earth to cover the roof. Caldwell felt that the fill of the house pit may have been earth from the roof because it did not appear to have washed in. Yet it seems there should have been a fabric of branches and perhaps matting preserved above the timbers had there actually been an earth layer over the roof. There is good ethnological reason to believe this building was a combination "chief's house"/council house.

An even larger council house, measuring 16.3 × 23.8 meters, probably served a similar function at a different time. It also had an extended entryway evinced by two wall trenches set 60 centimeters apart and extending 50 centimeters from the south wall near the west end.

Structure 1 was apparently a large (4.7 meters in diameter) sweat lodge with a 52-centimeter-wide and 45-centimeter-deep cylindrical fire pit just south of the center. The pit had a 10-centimeter-high, plastered rim and a post hole in the bottom. The floor was set 45–60 centimeters deep and surrounded by a 45-centimeter-deep wall trench measuring from 15 centimeters to 24 centimeters wide. Two flat-bottomed, slightly belled storage pits and three hemiconical pits that Caldwell called "cubby hole pits," assuming they were under beds, were dug around the walls. Caldwell (1967a) drew a parallel between these remains and the historic, thatched, conical, bent-pole houses of the Caddoan speakers of the southern Plains.

Structure 6 was a cross-shaped building composed of five rooms, each just under 2.5 meters square. The exterior walls were placed in a combination of wall trenches and individual post holes and the interior walls were of single-post construction. Most of the interior wall of the south wing was plastered with daub. A prepared hearth was located just off center in this building, but a later post hole had been cut through it and the earlier post hole was used as a fireplace. Material on the floor and in pits included, among other trash, an ear of corn, a cache of hickory nuts and corn kernels, ceramics including a miniature jar, and a fragmentary clay discoidal. This building may have been a fire temple.

Waring (1968) has gathered abundant evidence to link the equal-armed cross to the sacred fire of the southeastern tribes and has also gathered numerous accounts of such fires being maintained in public buildings. He also (1968:54–56) discusses the use of separate storage chambers for ritual paraphernalia among the Creeks. Assuming one of the arms (presumably the south one with the heavily plastered inner wall) was an antechamber that insulated the fire and the center room (which had two heavily burned fireplaces) was the room set aside for the fire, that would have left three storage chambers. The fact that nothing of a ritualistic nature (with the possible exception of a pile of maize and hickory nuts, a crushed fine Powell Plain jar, and the minature jar [medicine pot?] in the south arm and a clay discoidal in the central chamber) was found in the building may indicate only that the rooms had been cleaned out before burning. Harriet Smith's smaller and apparently slightly earlier cross-shaped building under the Murdock Mound at Cahokia seems not to have had separate rooms and the report (Smith 1969) does not mention a hearth. The much smaller example on the plaza of Settlement D at Orendorf had a hearth and a renewed floor (or a collapsed, unburned daub wall?) in one wing but no interior wall posts.

The domestic structures were rectangular wall-trench buildings set in shallow basins. They ranged in size from 7.1 × 4.2 meters to 8.5 × 5.6 meters. Additional features of the site include a group of eleven pits both superimposed on and to the south and east of Structure 1, a group of six pit features scattered from nine to eighteen meters west of Structure 2, and two lines of posts in the area of Structure 5.

The Garren site (Fv920), located at the point where Duck Creek enters the Illinois floodplain, represents a contact situation involving Stirling phase Mississippians and Maples Mills phase indigenes. Wray describes the site as consisting "of one or more lines of houses along the edge of the Old Hopewell village [at the bluff base]. Remnants of their pottery are fairly well limited and indicate a small and rather compact village" (Wray and MacNeish 1958:118). Wray excavated two or three of these buildings (Wray and MacNeish 1958:43, 83) and says fire and refuse pits were located inside and outside of the rectangular wall-trench structures.

Although the multimound Kingston Lake site was destroyed years ago by quarrying, it has contributed important information on burial patterns and ceramic styles of the initial Middle Mississippian occupation of the Central Illinois Valley. Our ability to say anything about this site is a tribute to the amateur members of the Peoria Academy of Sciences, who salvaged what they could of the site over a number of years beginning in 1932 (Simpson 1937, 1939, 1952).

ECONOMY. At this point, little detailed information is available on the subsistence practices of the Eveland

phase inhabitants of the Central Illinois River Valley. Based on what we know of Cahokia subsistence and the more abundant evidence from the succeeding Orendorf and Larson phases, the Eveland phase immigrants were probably maize horticulturists who gained most of their subsistence through hunting, gathering, and fishing.

CERAMICS. Three ceramic wares made up most of the Eveland site assemblage and were distributed in a seemingly uniform pattern throughout the building and pit features. One was Sepo ware (Harn 1975b) that usually occurred as relatively small jars, miniature bowls, and pinch pots. Another was the sandy Eveland ware (Caldwell 1967b:139) made in Middle Mississippian jar forms. The final major ware represented an American Bottom Middle Mississippian Stirling phase component. This pottery included Powell Plain and Ramey Incised jars with low rolled rims and occasionally with handles with two pronounced nodes extending above the rim; beakers with very high interior/exterior polish and extremely fine shell tempering; and at least one example each of a short-necked water bottle, a hemispheric bowl, a handled beaker, and a Ramey decorated seed jar. St. Clair Plain sherds were also present.

Some vessel fragments from Feature 21 warrant special mention. Among other sherds, including a high-quality Ramey Incised sherd and an untempered small ceramic spoon, was a fragment of a markedly constricted, presumably vertically compound, vessel and a fragment of a castelated rim that may be from a bowl. Strikingly similar sherds were recovered from a pit at the C. W. Cooper site in 1971. It is by no means certain these sherds represent single vessels, but the co-occurrence is interesting. A Monks Mound Red vessel of similar form was found at the Kingston Lake site.

Another ceramic assemblage that warrants special mention is the one from Feature 10A, a pit feature intruding into a borrow pit east of Structure 2. Ceramics in this feature included some relatively sloppy ("second generation") Ramey Incised, a well-made deep bowl with nodes that may represent a stylized marine shell, and a sherd with cordmarking below the shoulder and a plain surface above it. This latter pottery type is called Dickson Cordmarked in a Larson (Harn 1980b:21–22, fig. 27D362) or late Orendorf (Conrad, Good, and Jelly 1981:137–41) context, but seems to be absent during most of the Orendorf phase. It is found with some regularity at the Lundy site in Jo Daviess County, Illinois, which appears to be contemporaneous with or slightly postdate the Eveland phase (Emerson, chap. 8). Perhaps this type was reintroduced into the Illinois Valley from northwestern Illinois during late Orendorf times.

Other sherds from Eveland include a few small fragments of Canton ware, Chamberlain Incised, McVey Pinched Fillet, McVey Tool Decorated, and Beckman Tool Decorated-like vessels (Henning 1967). As mentioned, all of the cultural material seems to be uniformly distributed throughout the site and everything suggests a relatively short period of occupation. Some of the pottery was decorated with rather crude Ramey designs, and it is possible that Joseph R. Caldwell (n.d.) is correct in his assessment that some of the pit features represent a later period with locally modified Ramey Incised (presumably Wolf subphase). However, if this is the case, the later occupation accounted for only a few pit features and none of the buildings.

The Garren site ceramics were previously described by Wray and MacNeish (1958) and those that remain in the Dickson Mounds collections are presented in table 6.1 and figure 6.3. The material from House 1 includes sherds from nine different Ramey Incised and three Powell Plain jars as well as rim sherds from four additional vessels of one or both of these types. Other identifiable Mississippian sherds include single rimsherds from a beaker, a deep bowl, and a small seed jar. A large handle with a vertical groove producing two nodes on top and seven plain body sherds complete the inventory of Mississippian sherds. Although Wells Incised sherds were described by Wray and MacNeish, none have been relocated in the Dickson Mounds Museum collection.

In addition to sixty plain shell-tempered body sherds, "Square 19" produced sherds of from four to six Ramey Incised jars, two St. Clair Plain jars, one cambered rimmed jar, and a thick plain deep bowl.

All of the vessels of the Powell-Ramey series as well as a beaker and seed jar from this building are of high quality. In fact, the seed jar is tempered with such fine shell that it was probably this vessel to which Wray (1952: 156) referred when he listed Monks Mound Red as being present at the site.

Wray must have meant that the Mississippian ceramics were not comparable to the best at Cahokia when he said, "These wares are less well fired and more porous than those from Cahokia, although they are within the range present at the site" (1952:156). Although some ceramics from the American Bottom are thinner and more elaborately decorated, it is unlikely that any are significantly better fired or less porous than several of the vessels represented in this collection. It is noteworthy that most of the Ramey Incised vessels left in the Garren collection are decorated with chevrons.

Woodland material from House 1 includes eight Maples Mills and two Sepo sherds. Hybrid sherds include three that may be from the same shell-tempered vessel of a Canton ware form and decoration and one-quarter of a small, grit-tempered, very shallow bowl with a bird effigy on one end.

Table 6.1. Eveland-Phase Ceramics from the Garren Site

Provenience:	Wray and MacNeish			Dickson Mounds Collections	
Ceramics	House 1	House 2	House 3	House 1	Sq. 19
Hybrid types	7	1	0	2	0
Canton ware	0	0	0	8	0
Sepo ware	0	0	0	2	0
Maples Mills Cordmarked	27	17	0	0	0
Monks Mound Red	1	0	0	0	0
Cahokia Red-Filmed	0	0	2	0	0
Ramey Incised	31	20	2	9	6
Powell Plain	9	3	14	3	0
Powell Plain/ Ramey Incised	0	0	0	4	0
St. Clair Plain	220	149	24	0	2
Plain Bodysherds (shell tempered)	0	0	0	8	60
Tippets Bean Pot	0	0	2	0	0
Beaker	0	0	0	1	0
Deep bowl	0	0	0	1	1
Seed jar	0	0	0	1	0
Jar handle	0	0	0	1	0
Cambered rim	0	0	0	0	1
Total	297	190	43	39	70

Sources: Wray and MacNeish (1958) data is from their table 1. Dickson Mounds Collection information is from personal observation by the author. As of this writing, the only materials located from this site in the Wray collection at Dickson Mounds Museum are forty-three sherds from House 1 (the remainder were apparently loaned and not returned) and seventy-one sherds from "Square 19."

Of the thousands of Kingston Lake village sherds that have found their way into public repositories, very few can be assigned to the Eveland phase. Due to the limitations under which the excavators worked, it can only be assumed that if there were Eveland phase habitation features at the site, they were not plentiful. Wray describes a mound on the northwest edge of the village that was destroyed for fill. He says, in part, "Excavation revealed a number of poorly preserved burials which were either secondary or flexed. Two of these had Spoon River pots but one had fragments of a large Maples Mills vessel. Some of the sherds clearly revealed a blending of Maples Mills and Old Village [Wray always refers to Eveland phase Mississippian as Old Village] traditions" (n.d.:6). Although these collections have not been relocated, it seems that they represent an Eveland phase contact situation.

The principal hallmark of the Stirling phase in the American Bottom is the Powell-Ramey ceramic series (Fowler and Hall 1975:6; Milner et al. 1984:168). Jars compose by far the most common group of vessels, and bowls compose the second largest group. Beakers, water bottles, seed jars, "funnels," and stumpware are

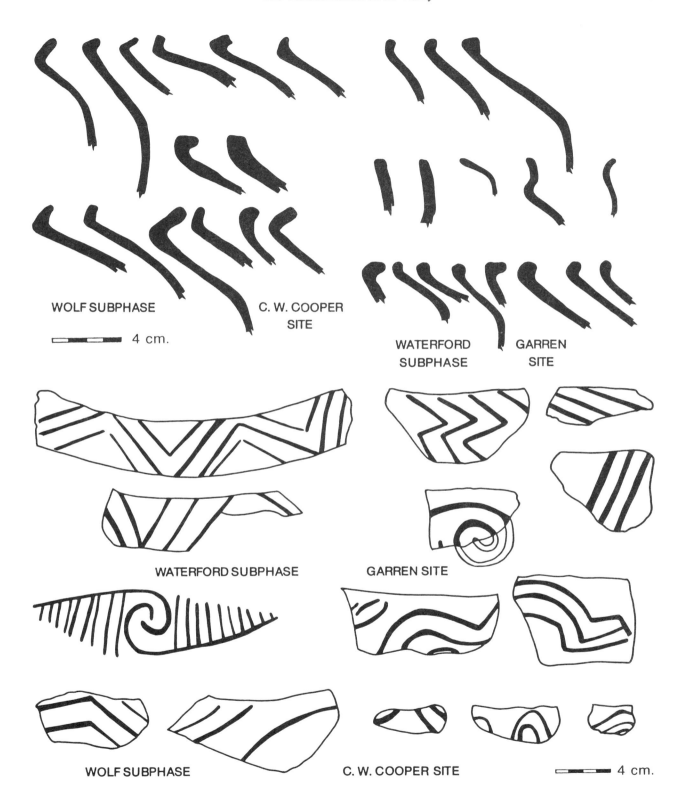

WOLF SUBPHASE   C. W. COOPER SITE

4 cm.

WATERFORD SUBPHASE   GARREN SITE

WATERFORD SUBPHASE   GARREN SITE

WOLF SUBPHASE   C. W. COOPER SITE   4 cm.

Figure 6.3. Eveland Phase Ceramics

present but are relatively rare. Jar shoulders are normally relatively sharp but with time are increasingly more likely to be rounded than hyperangular. Also through time, rims are more likely to be angled than rolled or everted, although the latter forms are not uncommon later. Extruded lips are much less common than they are in Lohmann phase collections. Limestone tempering is rare but does appear (Milner et al. 1984:168). With the exception of "funnels" and the enigmatic stumpware, all of the Stirling phase ceramic forms are in place at Eveland-Dickson. It is unlikely that the shell-tempered assemblage from Eveland-Dickson, Garren, and Kingston Lake could be sorted from shell-tempered Stirling assemblages from the American Bottom.

At Eveland-Dickson and Garren there are grit- or sand-tempered imitations of Early Mississippian jars and beakers, and at Garren there are shell-tempered imitations of Canton ware, a Canton ware vessel with loop handles, and an awkward grit-tempered imitation of a duck effigy bowl. These vessels are obviously attempts by apparently capable local potters to imitate Middle Mississippian artisans, even though they fall short of the mark. The suggestion that the beautiful shell-tempered ceramics so common at these sites are the result of local imitation certainly presumes that the Sepo and Maples Mills potters were able to replicate the fine points of shell-tempered ceramic technology and Mississippian forms and ignores abundant evidence to the contrary. If Eveland phase Mississippian ceramics were not locally made by people trained by Mississippian potters, they were most certainly imported; however, thin-section studies indicate they were locally made (James B. Stoltman, personal communication, 1989).

NONCERAMIC ARTIFACTS. The artifactual material from Eveland is quite varied, but generally not exceptional. Noteworthy items include a Mill Creek chert knife fragment, a heavily worn microdrill, a bison scapula hoe, and a piece of galena. No copper or marine shell was noted, although it is common in the associated Dickson cemetery. Woodworking tools were confined to a single broken, unfinished celt and a polished stone adze, while chert excavating tools were absent. There was an abundance of chert working debris and a number of arrowpoints ranging from crude triangles to well-made, rather large specimens with single sets of side notches and a single basal notch. Several points were noted with abbreviated lateral notches above a single set of pronounced side notches. End and side scrapers were common.

The approximately 250 Eveland phase burials from the Dickson site included a number of finely made, notched (in some cases multiple notched) triangular points as well as simple Madison points, and there is little reason to doubt that the mental template for these was Cahokia derived. Large knives of Mill Creek chert, stone discoidals, stone and wooden ear plugs covered with copper, and marine shell and bone artifacts were recovered from Dickson. The Garren lithic material is not currently available for examination, but Wray's sketches show a number of triangular points with widely differing numbers of notches. Although some of this material seems to be within the range of workmanship of the people who made the Mounds Stemless points, much of it is not. Admittedly, some of these items such as marine shell beads, Mill Creek chert blades, and copper-coated ear plugs were traded to non-Cahokian groups, but it seems unlikely that foreign-made projectile points would be as common as Cahokian points were at Eveland and apparently at Garren.

MORTUARY COMPLEX. The approximately 250 Eveland phase burials that were excavated from the Dickson Mound on the bluff above the Eveland site were endowed with a wide range of burial furniture.[2] Ceramics included Sepo, Eveland, and Canton ware jars, and a shell-tempered ware including the Powell-Ramey series, beakers (some with handles), wide-mouthed bottles, effigy bottles, miniature vessels, a cambered-rimmed, lobed vessel, and a deep effigy bowl. Mill Creek chert knives; stone discoidals; ear spools of wood and of stone covered with copper foil; tool caches; notched and unnotched triangular points; shell spoons; *Marginella* sp., *Olivella* sp., and a variety of cut marine shell beads on necklaces, sashes, head bands, and forelocks; *Busycon* sp. and fresh water shell pendants; arm rattles; cougar canine ear pendants; bone hair pins; and shell spoons were frequently placed in the graves. There seems to be no significant difference in access to status-validating objects between those people buried with Mississippian, Sepo, or hybrid Eveland wares.

Most burials were in a supine or semiflexed position, but bundled interments were not uncommon; partial cremation was rare. Aboriginal exhumation of complete or partial skeletons was not uncommon, and grave goods were often left behind. An elaborate burial feature including among other elements four supine headless adult male burials on the bottom of a rectangular grave with a Mississippian or Woodland vessel at each shoulder (fig. 6.4) has been described elsewhere (Conrad 1984, 1989:102–3, fig. 6; Harn 1975b:427–38). The final feature that requires mention is the small truncated pyramid that seems to date from this period. As the top of this structure has not been excavated, no definite statement concerning its use is possible, but it was probably topped with a charnel house (Conrad 1967, 1972).

No cemetery was located that could confidently be associated with the Garren village, but the Maples Mills cemetery (Fc911) found by Wray above the Garren site

Figure 6.4. Retainer Sacrifices at Dickson Mounds. Photo courtesy of Illinois State Museum.

may have some relevance here because it had a Canton ware vessel with loop handles associated with the burial of a child (Wray and MacNeish 1958). The Beckstead mound 4.8 kilometers up the bluff was built at about this time. It yielded twenty-two extended, semiflexed, flexed, and bundled burials and one loop-handled Powell Plain jar, one strap-handled Ramey Incised jar, and two strings of marine shell beads. The Maurice Thompson Mound located just over 4.8 kilometers further up the bluff yielded flexed, bundled, and cremated burials and Powell, Ramey, and St. Clair Plain sherds along with unidentified Late Woodland sherds as well as a "Jersey Bluff" discoidal (Perino 1971b), a metapodial awl, a bone pin, and a shell bird effigy pendant. These mounds differed from Dickson in that mortuary goods were uncommon and those present were not of the value of many of the status-validating items at Dickson.

By far the most revealing features from the Kingston Lake site are two burial pits excavated by Robert L. Poehls and Anson Simpson in 1933 and 1934. One grave was a rectangular bark-lined and bark-covered pit that contained three extended burials oriented to the west. The southernmost skeleton, that of an adolescent, showed evidence of scalping, and the other two skulls were absent. Single unnotched triangular arrowpoints were found beneath each scapula of the scalped individual, and a copper-coated wooden ear plug was inside the left arm of the middle person. Other material from the grave included a 2.8-kilogram double-cupped discoidal and three pitted stones (Poehls 1944).

The second grave contained two extended burials with heads to the south. One had a sleeve of 694 marine shell beads on the right arm, a 30.5-centimeter-long chert blade, a 2.5-centimeter quartz crystal bead and, at the feet, twenty-one side-notched triangular points. The second individual had a fine Ramey Incised jar and a sandstone needle sharpener at the head and a handled beaker and a Monks Mound Red vertically compound jar at the feet. Wray (n.d.:7) is in error in referring to this vessel as being composed of very fine shell-tempered paste; it is a red, limestone-tempered paste. Between the burials were four copper hemispheres (Poehls 1944; Simpson 1937, 1939, 1952). Given our limited evidence from Kingston Lake, the social status of these individuals is uncertain although clearly it was one of importance. It is possible that these people were members of the paramount lineage or, perhaps, high-ranking retainers and their subordinates. At this time members of the ruling lineage may have been ultimately interred at Cahokia.

It is during the Waterford subphase that there is the first evidence for retainer sacrifice in the Central Illinois Valley. The best example of this practice is the mass grave of four headless men at Dickson. The similarity to a burial in Mound 72 at Cahokia (Fowler 1974)—four headless adult males, each with arms slightly akimbo and overlapping those of the adjacent burial—is striking. I reject the suggestion that these men might be war captives or group members killed in battle whose heads and hands were removed by the enemy before their bodies were recovered, although this latter interpretation might be appropriate to explain the scalped individual and two decapitated individuals buried at Kingston Lake.

The inclusion of the four headless males in Mound 72 in association with a high-ranking central figure and scores of clearly sacrificed female retainers strongly indicates that the males too were sacrificed in-group members. Given the striking similarity between the Dickson and Mound 72 headless burials, a similar explanation at Dickson seems inescapable. The double burial at Kingston Lake cannot be demonstrated to have involved retainer sacrifice. It may represent the chance death and joint burial of two adults. However, the similarities in pattern and age between the Dickson mass grave and the one at Kingston Lake lend circumstantial weight to the case for retainer sacrifice there as well.

It may be argued that it is difficult to prove that the burials at Dickson and at Kingston Lake represent the sacrifice of in-group members. A similar argument might be made regarding the headless burials and pits containing scores of young women in Mound 72 at Cahokia. However, given the ethnohistoric evidence for such customs among late prehistoric peoples of the Southeast combined with the archaeological contextual data, the practice of in-group retainer sacrifice among Central Illinois Valley Mississippian peoples seems clear.

The presence of in-group retainer sacrifice is a strong argument for the presence of high-ranking people in the community. There is no suggestion that Bauer Branch or Maples Mills societies had moved beyond a band level of organization before the appearance of the high-quality Powell-Ramey ceramic series. The beginning of the short-lived Powell-Ramey ceramic horizon and the practice of retainer sacrifice appear simultaneously in the Central Illinois Valley. Because it is unlikely, given what we know of band-level societies, that a member of an egalitarian band could rise to a position warranting retainer sacrifice, it suggests the presence of both a new, intrusive social system and a new population. This new system led the Late Woodland people in the Central Illinois Valley to believe that it was reasonable to die in order to accompany others in death.

Finally, Robert L. Blakely (1973; personal communication, 1984), in analyzing the Dickson cemetery, has concluded that there were sharp physical differences between the Sepo people and the people buried with the Stirling ceramics, and that these differences were much sharper than the differences between the Sepo population and the subsequent Larson phase Spoon River population. This is to be expected if the later population was descended from the two formerly disparate populations.

EXTERNAL CONTACTS. During all of the Eveland phase, the Spoon River area was probably politically subordinate to Cahokia, which was certainly its main trading partner. Much of what came into the area from Cahokia consisted of politico-religious paraphernalia, including shell long-nosed god masquettes, copper-covered stone and wood ear plugs, probably a few large human effigy pipes of Arkansas bauxite, and large chert blades. Special ceramics including the Monks Mound Red jar from Kingston Lake were also part of this trade. The most common imports were marine shell beads.

Another extraregional element at this formative time and later in the Spoon River period is from the Middle Missouri Basin. It is evinced by the occurrence of a bison scapula hoe and Foreman series and other clearly western ceramics at the Eveland site and probably by the sharing of notched triangular points by inhabitants of both areas (they are not ubiquitous in the Mississippian area). The Plains influence on Cahokia and the Spoon River culture as seen in the similarities in point types, bone bracelets, and bird-wing fans as well as in the presence of imported ceramics and bone tools has been discussed elsewhere (Conrad 1972; Conrad and Harn 1976).

OVERVIEW. People from the American Bottom area apparently moved into the Illinois Valley and were instrumental in the formation of the Middle Mississippian societies in the Central Illinois Valley. Given this population movement, it would be valuable to know its size and cause. Although there are few Eveland phase sites known in the area and all are seemingly small, there could have been a substantial foreign population involved. The Waterford subphase Mississippians were distributed across the landscape in dispersed villages, with nodal centers such as Eveland and perhaps Kingston Lake serving as focal points. Such dispersed villages were common in the American Bottom at this time (Emerson and Milner 1981, 1982) and among the Natchez (Swanton 1911:45–45, 158), for example, during the early historic period.

As yet there is no evidence of towns or compact villages such as those in the American Bottom. Dispersed villages are difficult to identify because of the limited area of light debris scatter that normally characterizes their components and the tendency of shell-tempered pottery to disintegrate rapidly in the plowzone. Nineteen years ago it seemed reasonable to suggest that Stirling phase Mississippians had left the American Bottom "largely unoccupied" except for the major towns (Harn 1971b: 36), but recent highway excavations have demonstrated the existence of numerous dispersed villages in the hinterlands (Milner et al. 1984). There could be scores or even hundreds of Eveland phase sites in the Central Illinois Valley that have gone undiscovered or unrecognized.

If the number of people involved was small, emigration was probably not a release valve for population pressures in the Cahokia area, nor evidence of a search for new fields to augment exhausted farm lands. The generally low number of recovered flint hoes and hoe fragments implies that the Cahokia agricultural took kit was not transplanted into the Spoon River area, but it may have been adopted further south in the La Moine River area, where Mill Creek hoes are much more common, at least on a later horizon. If these two reasons can be excluded, it seems most likely that the intention was to plant a colony to ensure access to some resources in the area.

The only available resources other than farm land of value to the American Bottom would have been forest products. There is evidence that the large population in the American Bottom had degraded the environment to a marked degree and that they were importing wood (Porter 1974:133–36). Likewise, large deer populations would have been economically incompatible with extensive corn fields and deer were seemingly not a major component in the Cahokian diet, at least of the rural people (Kelly and Cross 1984:231–32). The Illinois Valley could have provided a wide range of plant and animal products including wood and venison, and the much higher numbers of arrowpoints and hide scrapers in the Illinois Valley strongly suggest more active animal procurement in the area. The paucity of arrowpoints in the American Bottom has been recently illustrated by the excavation of five small habitation sites that produced only eleven arrowpoints in Stirling phase context (Emerson 1984c: 243; Johannessen 1984b:266; Milner and Williams 1983: 95; Milner and Williams 1984:104; Prentice and Mehrer 1981:51). However, the possible use of cane arrows in the American Bottom cannot be discounted. Arrowpoints are much more frequent in Eveland phase context.

Another possible explanation for the movement of groups into the area is political. In a complex society such as that of the American Bottom there may have been other pressures beside population that caused members of the ruling lineage, assuming only members of the ruling lineage warranted retainer burials such as those at Dickson Mounds, to leave Cahokia. Because we know that members of the Natchez ruling lineage held many of the offices in the principal town (Swanton 1911) and were chief officials in at least some of the outlying villages (Cadillac 1947:80; Swanton 1911:219-20), we could infer that a member of such a lineage might have led an enterprise to bring the rich outlying area into Cahokia's orbit and might have subsequently administered it.

It is apparent that armed conquest played no part in the introduction of Mississippian culture into the Central Illinois Valley. Assuming that the scalped and decapitated burials at Kingston Lake and Dickson represent retainer sacrifices, there are no skeletons from this time suggesting violent death or weapon-inflicted wounds. There is no evidence of fortifications, thus suggesting that the Mississippians were welcome, perhaps even invited. The rapidity and degree to which Mississippian culture was accepted might indicate that the Sepo people and at least some of the Maples Mills and presumably Bauer Branch people had voluntarily decided to become Mississippians. Given that the Woodland groups thinly populated the area, there was room for more people and the Mississippians had much to offer, including a perceived advanced knowledge of maize agriculture, which could increase the carrying capacity of the area to more than offset their own needs.

Waterford subphase habitation sites have been found in both the uplands and the bottoms. Cemeteries were both mounded and unmounded. It appears that people with high status as indicated by ear plugs, large blades, large quantities of marine shell beads, and, in one instance, a copper-over-wood imitation chert blade were buried in restricted areas such as Eveland. Lower-status people were often buried in cemeteries such as at the Dickson, Beckstead, or Thompson sites in mounds with nothing more than a ceramic jar or a string of beads and usually not even that. At Dickson, high-status-indicating objects were recovered with flexed, extended, and bundled burials. Sepo, Eveland, and Mississippian wares were associated with these objects. This seems to indicate that the Mississippians and the indigenes were soon integrated into a single society ruled by a semidivine lineage. It is not known how long this period of integration lasted, but it seems from the presence of very high quality Powell and Ramey ceramics that it was not more than a few decades and perhaps less.

The Wolf Subphase (ca. A.D. 1100–1150)

An Early Mississippian ceramic assemblage that is clearly younger than that present at Eveland and Garren was collected at the Charles W. Cooper site. Although there are some high-quality Ramey Incised and Powell Plain sherds from the site and a limestone-tempered seed jar from the adjacent Sister Creeks site, they are rare and have not been found in context. The excavated material is coarser in every aspect and must be considered degenerate Ramey Incised and Powell Plain. This material is considered the type collection for the Wolf subphase of the Eveland phase. Certainly the majority of vessels from this assemblage are Powell Plain jars followed by Ramey Incised jars, but it is probable that polished black deep

bowls, seed jars, high-quality beakers, and bird effigy bowls from the site are attributable to this phase. As illustrated in figure 6.3, most of the Ramey designs are rectangular, but some are curvilineal, including a fairly well executed feathered scroll and two examples of what may be stylized weeping eyes.[3] The Sepo and Eveland wares have dropped almost completely out of the ceramic assemblage by this time.

McGimsey et al. (1987:37–63) describe a burned house of this subphase with an intact floor assemblage and associated features from a site on a low terrace of the Illinois River at Liverpool.

ORENDORF PHASE (ca. A.D. 1150–1250)

ORENDORF PHASE SITES. Assuming that the Kingston Lake platform was not built during Eveland times, Orendorf is as early as any recognized town in the Central Illinois Valley and played a critical role in model formulation of town interrelationships.[4] Orendorf was not alone in the valley, but the phase definition is based primarily on this site and its satellites. Orendorf phase material is abundant at the Emmons Village site and there are jar and plate fragments from the Kingston Lake site that fit comfortably into the Orendorf series. However, the size of the Orendorf phase component at Kingston Lake is unknown.

The Orendorf site is located on a naturally defensible finger of land on the thirty-meter-high Illinois Valley bluff edge. Substantial portions of three of the postulated five settlement locations composing the site have been investigated. Sharron K. Santure (1981) has analyzed two of these: B/C and C. Settlement B/C was located east of and partially under Settlement C. Approximately one-fourth of it was mapped and a slightly smaller portion was completely excavated. Santure tentatively assigned forty-six buildings to the excavated portion of this settlement on the basis of stratigraphy and orientation. She estimated it covered approximately one hectare in its earlier stage and had a public square with at least one large building fronting on it. A separate simultaneous study of the minority cordmarked ceramics from Settlements B/C and C (Conrad, Good, and Jelly 1981) found that in the area excavated, cord-wrapped-paddle stamping over fabric marking was confined almost exclusively to this earlier settlement, whereas cord-wrapped-paddle stamping without underlying fabric marking and cord-wrapped-stick cordmarking were virtually absent from B/C but common in C.

Settlement C was oriented about 45° east of north and measured approximately 110 × 180 meters and had a light fence with interior "sentry boxes" along at least the southwest side. Sections of bastioned palisades were located within the area of overlap between B/C and C, but as of yet they have not been related to either settlement. A bastioned redoubt measuring 57.6 × 46.2 meters was located approximately fourteen meters west of Settlement C. Only three large storage pits (located in the exact center) and one possibly associated building were within the enclosure. It overlaps the area of Settlement D and was oriented 80° east.

Santure estimated that approximately ninety private dwellings (with additional public buildings fronting on the plaza) made up Settlement C in its earliest stage and that perhaps 400–500 people lived within the settlement. Individual dwellings became larger and more square through time, but public buildings on the plaza grew generally smaller and perhaps more numerous. By far the largest building in Settlement C was approximately 25 × 16 meters. It had a very narrow, extended entry way in the center of the southeast wall. An earlier or later stage of construction on this location had a heavily puddled clay hearth near one end on the median line. A large building fronting on the west side of the plaza had a fifteen-centimeter layer of clean soil packed above an earlier floor and a fireplace that had evidence of having been cleaned and renewed with sand seven times. Excess sand was spread in the immediate vicinity of the hearth.

There is no suggestion of streets or courtyards, but the frequent occurrence of two or even three building stages on the same spot as well as multiple superpositions of storage/refuse pits in very restricted areas suggests a relatively firm concept of land use rights within the town.

Three of the structures fronting on the plaza show six or more construction stages, with the later structures being considerably smaller. The later presence of several similar smaller structures, perhaps men's club houses, around the plaza may suggest a division among distinct groups of political authority that had previously been held by a common council evinced by the earlier larger buildings. Because the council house was probably also the political leader's home, the shift may suggest a decline in that individual's authority.

Settlement D at Orendorf, which was located approximately seventy meters southwest of Settlement C, has the clearest community plan, but its exact relationship to the various occupational phases in Settlement C in unclear. Tentative archaeomagnetic dates, large council houses, the presence of a cruxiform building, and the virtual absence of cordmarked pottery argue for an early date. Its position on the west edge of the site, the apparent absence of curvilinear elements on pottery, and the fact that the entire town burned and was not reoccupied argue for a later date. At present the dating question is unresolved.

Settlement D (fig. 6.5) consists of a 203 × 244-meter stockaded area oriented 123° east along a restricting bluff finger. Two rows of burned buildings extend fifty-two meters beyond the southwest end of the stockaded area. There is no obvious difference in the material immediately within and immediately without the stockade. Approximately ninety-six buildings were arranged around a plaza, which originally measured 116 meters square but which had been expanded to 133 meters long by the time the town burned. The charred stump of a hickory pole was found in the center of this plaza. The bastioned stockade had been expanded twice. A substantial rectangular building attached to a 9.14-meter in diameter circular building behind it had originally fronted on the center of the northwest side of the plaza. After the plaza was expanded, these council houses were replaced by a 9.75 × 8.84-meter building with a porch and a subterranean floor. A large circular council house measuring 15.25 meters in diameter, with its extended entry way facing west, stood on the southeast corner of the plaza. The population of Settlement D is estimated at approximately 425.

A loose cluster of about five buildings was found approximately fifty meters northwest of Settlement C, but the small collection recovered from them did not allow a determination of their affiliation. Superficial examination of several hundred acres of the site's immediate hinterland after topsoil removal prior to "development" by strip mining located no other isolated buildings, although some were known to exist about forty meters southwest of Settlement D.

Of the 286 excavated building stages on 184 building sites (excluding the sentry boxes) of Settlements B/C and C, all but two were of wall-trench construction. The other two were of single-post construction; one rectangular building on the extreme northern corner of the site was apparently a dwelling, whereas a small (3-meter diameter) circuloid structure on the northwestern edge of the settlement probably was not. The measurements given in table 6.2 (after Santure 1981) illustrate size and width/length ratio trends for Orendorf phase dwellings during the period of occupation of Settlements B/C and C.

The architectural picture of Settlement D is much more varied than that of Settlement C. The most obvious dif-

Table 6.2. Orendorf Phase Structure Sizes, Orendorf Site

Period	N	Mode Size range (m²)	Mode	Width/ Length
B/C	42	4.64–37.2	(9) 11.6–13.9	.7022
Early C	31	6.97–23.2	(8) 18.6–20.9	.7603
Middle C	30	6.97–34.8	(7) 18.6–20.9	.7842
Late C	19	11.6–27.9	(4) 16.3–18.6	.8075
			(4) 25.5–27.9	

Source: Santure 1981

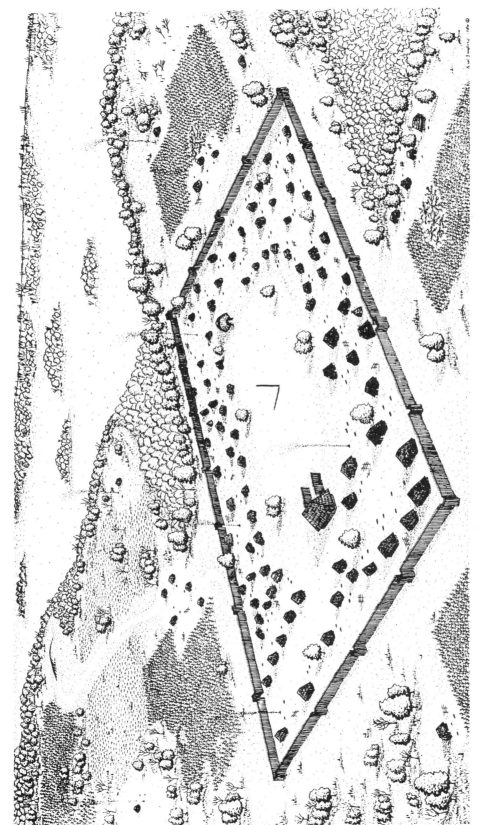

Figure 6.5. Artist's Rendering of Settlement D at Orendorf. Drawing by Kelvin Sampson, courtesy of UMVARF.

ference is the presence of three circular council houses ranging in diameter from 7.62 meters to 15.25 meters. The largest was supported by a large central post in a ramped pit with lenses of sand in the fill; the second was supported by numerous interior posts; and the smallest one was too poorly preserved to allow a description. Each of the two better-preserved buildings had a narrow gap in the wall trench for the door and the larger one had an extended entry way. If any of these buildings were set in pits they must have been very shallow. Single circular buildings on opposite sides of the town may have been small (less than three meters in diameter) sweat lodges or female isolation huts. Both had simple fireplaces without evidence of intense burning and one had a small amount of burned limestone. There was a cruxiform structure on the plaza in Settlement D. Two rectangular buildings of single-post construction, one with a shallow pit and one without, were excavated on the west side of town.

The vast majority of the buildings in the town were simple rectangular wall-trench dwellings, most of which were set in shallow flat-bottomed pits arranged in rows (but not streets) conforming to the shape of the stockaded enclosure. These buildings ranged in size from approximately 3.7 × 3.7 meters to 7.3 × 6.1 meters, with the average size being closer to the larger extreme. The estimated mode ranges from 16.35 to 19 square meters. A random sample of twelve presumed domestic structures had a width/length ratio of roughly 0.86 and one had two small alcoves. In the scores of burned buildings excavated at Orendorf, nothing resembling a bed or wooden bench was found.

Very little is known concerning Orendorf's hinterland. WIU's 1984 summer field school excavated one building, several associated pit features, and apparently associated burials in an Orendorf phase hamlet approximately five kilometers up the bluff from the site. The analysis has yet to begin on this material. Wray also excavated relevant structures, features, and burials at the Weaver-Betts site above the Weaver site (Wray and MacNeish 1958). These too await analysis.

ECONOMY. Harn (1978:259; 1980b:82) has consistently minimized the importance of Spoon River maize production while emphasizing the undoubtedly heavy amount of hunting and foraging. The data available for Orendorf (Blake n.d.; Emerson 1981; Paloumpis 1981, 1983; Speth 1981) does not support this position. Leonard Blake's preliminary analysis of 190 flotation samples from the site has identified corn in approximately 150 samples, hickory in ninety-four, walnut in nine, hazel in seven, *Polygonum* sp. in four, *Chenopodium* sp. in four, pecan in three, sunflower, domestic bean, and maygrass in two each, and squash and an unidentifiable tuber in one each.

Clearly maize was common and important at Orendorf. This is even more evident when the virtual indestructability of charred hickory nut shell is considered. Preliminary analysis of C-13 values by Jane E. Buikstra (1989) and George R. Milner of human skeletal material suggests that maize was more important in the diet of Orendorf inhabitants than of the other late prehistoric people studied. There can be no reasonable doubt that maize was important to all Middle Mississippian groups in the Central Illinois Valley. Although maize was seldom if ever the mainstay of Middle Mississippian diet, it was apparently the critical variable in allowing larger population size and concentration and in eroding their health (Milner 1982:31).

In his ongoing study of the Orendorf ungulates, Thomas E. Emerson has identified a minimum of 178 deer in the approximately two-thirds of the sample analyzed. He concluded, "Based on the Orendorf data it appears at this time that the economic pattern and seasonal population shifts may closely resemble the pattern described by Swanton (1946:256–57) for the southeastern United States" (1981:178). Andreas Paloumpis (1983:91) concluded that most of the 2,900 individuals representing thirty-six species of fish in the sample he examined were gathered from oxbows, sloughs, and backwater lakes. Janet M. Speth (1981:185) demonstrated that turkeys and waterfowl were the most important avian food sources. The evidence suggests that at Orendorf the economy was typically Middle Mississippian (see Smith 1985b:68–72).

Another suggestion, that the Spoon River people had a "mundane life style more closely aligned with that of the western Prairie and eastern Plains" (Harn 1975b:430), does not adequately take into account the evidence that their economy was based on deer, fish, waterfowl, and maize, whereas subsistence in the central Missouri Basin was based principally on bison and maize. It has even been suggested that Spoon River people may occasionally have hunted bison on the Plains. However, their day-to-day life-style is clearly Mississippian, and the resemblance to that of the Plains is only to the degree that the contemporary cultures of the Missouri Basin resembled Middle Mississippian.

CERAMICS. There are some major differences between the ceramic assemblages of the Eveland and Orendorf phases. Sepo ware was essentially nonexistent and Ramey Incised very rare in Settlement C, where Ramey Incised represented two of an estimated minimum of 10,000 vessels in the WIU collection. Both wares were absent in Settlement D. Powell Plain jars were frequent occurrences in Settlement C but had higher rims and were not so common nor so fine as Powell Plain in Eveland phase contexts. Shell-tempered cordmarked, Dickson Plain, Dickson Cordmarked, Dickson Trailed (see

Harn 1971b for discussions of the latter three types), and probably plates made their earliest appearances in any quantity at Settlement B/C or C.

The most common vessels at Settlement C were plain jars, which represented 45% of the ceramic assemblage (Santure 1981), while trailed jars composed 15% and cordmarked jars made up 9%. Plain bowls and decorated bowls composed 11% and 2.9% respectively. Plates, beakers, water bottles, and miniature vessels made up 4.5% each. The usual jar decoration in the sample analyzed to date was the nested chevron with lesser occurrences of curvilinear and scroll designs, and oblique parallel lines (fig. 6.6). The curvilinear and pseudo-scroll designs are the hallmark of the Orendorf series. They are obviously Ramey derived and occur rarely if at all in the Larson phase. Such Larson ceramic elements as the Dickson series, line-filled triangles, and tridactyle handles were present in small quantities at Settlement C. It appears that larger vessels were incribed slightly more than half of the time, whereas smaller jars were less frequently decorated.

The paucity of effigy handles from the Orendorf site suggests that most deep bowls were plain. Except for one long-eared mammal (a deer?) from Settlement C and a raptor head from Settlement D, the few effigies recovered were either ducks or too stylized or eroded to identify. Deep bowls were often coated with a polished black or red wash. The different colors are actually a result of firing rather than of different composition. Shallow bowls were usually more carelessly finished but were often decorated with opposing bifurcated lugs or, rarely, with effigies.

Plates usually were well finished, often polished, and had a fairly wide range of rim widths (fig. 6.7). Many were trailed, incised, or engraved with nested meanders, arcs, chevrons, or triangles. Triangles were single, nested, or line filled.

Three basic beaker forms were present: the constricted-sided Spoon River beaker, the barrel-shaped beaker, and the straight-sided Tippets Bean Pot. Most beakers had a plain surface, but some had polished red or black surfaces. A small percentage were tempered with exceptionally fine shell and apparently grog and limestone and were decorated with engravings after red washing. These vessels may have been imported. Beaker handles were either plain cylinders or were in the form of bird beaks or fists and arms.

Locally made water bottles were either short or medium necked or were hooded. Some of the hooded bottles were decorated with effigy human or owl heads. Almost all had a marked concavity in the bottom for added stability.

The limited representation of plates, beakers, and water bottles in the assemblage probably reflects their less rigorous use or in the case of plates, their more durable form, than their actual proportion in a functioning assemblage. This thesis seems to be borne out by their presence in assemblages on the floors of burned houses. Deep bowls, beakers, and water bottles are also more common in mortuary contexts than in midden deposits, whereas large jars are never found there and plates are infrequent. Seed jars and imported salt pans are rare occurrences in this assemblage.

NONCERAMIC ARTIFACTS. It is not practicable to list all of the items utilized by these people to cope with their environment, both in the physical and social sense, but a few that have utility in characterizing the Orendorf phase include: large sandstone effigy pipes, often stylized representations of birds and more rarely mammals or realistic humans; discoidals of the Jersey Bluff and Cahokia types (Perino 1971b:115), some of the latter of which are perforated; and large, poorly fired, perforated, truncated ceramic cones, which may have been loom weights.

The long, wide Cahokia points (Perino 1968:12–13) are not found at Orendorf or its surrounding sites, although smaller, less elaborately made ones along with Harrell (Bell 1958:30–31), Washita (Bell 1958:98–99), Huffaker (Bell 1960:58–59), and Madison (Perino 1968: 52–53) points are. The finest point examples are found as burial furniture. The field and initial lab impressions of the material from Orendorf suggest that a large percentage of the points were not triangular and there was a surprising amount of corner notching.

MORTUARY COMPLEX. The Orendorf phase burial complex is characterized by extended interments in cemeteries and cemetery mounds on or near the Illinois River bluff. Mounds were built in definite stages, not as minimounds over individual corpses. Graves were frequently dug into these stages, often cutting through earlier burials. Importance was attached to solarly derived axes (i.e., summer or winter solstices or 90° off these axes), and crowded plots of burials on nearly the same axes were built up (Conrad 1967, 1972). Although most burials were extended, there were in decreasing frequency disarticulated bundle and pile, semiflexed, flexed, and possibly cremated burials. The only carefully excavated Orendorf phase burial sample is that from the Dickson Mound and from ongoing work at Orendorf. In the Dickson sample (which is presumably actually early Larson phase, but so far as can be determined is virtually identical to the sample collected by Wray at the Weaver-Betts site), only one of the eight disarticulated burials was unassociated with remains of a second individual and all three disarticulated adult burials were associated with subadults accompanied by prestige items. It is not apparent if a retainer was involved in these cases or if the

JARS

Figure 6.6. Orendorf Phase Jars

PLATES

SHALLOW BOWLS   4 cm.

Figure 6.7. Orendorf Phase Plates and Shallow Bowls

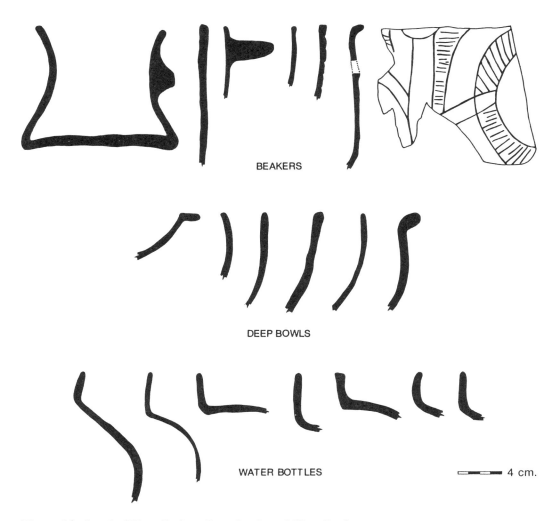

Figure 6.8. Orendorf Phase Beakers, Deep Bowls, and Water Bottles

corporeal remains of adults from a charnel house were placed with immature people of status (Conrad 1972).

Approximately one-half of the burials had associated grave goods, ranging from flake knives to rare caches of imported items. The items found in graves almost duplicate the list of items found in habitation contexts. Of course, some classes of artifacts, particularly ornaments of copper and marine shell, were found almost exclusively in graves, while others, such as block pipes and plates, were seldom found. Mutually exclusive groups of burial furniture (marine shell versus ceramics) are characteristic of the burial assemblage of the latter part of this phase. Two Orendorf phase cemeteries at the Weaver-Betts site, Fo228 and Fo914, excavated by Donald Wray (Wray and MacNeish 1958) were also characterized by these mutually exclusive categories, as was the roughly contemporary Moorehead phase Kane Mounds site above the northern end of the American Bottom (Melby 1963).

The association of badges of office with the skeletons of children seems to indicate the assignation of status on the basis of kinship (Conrad 1972).

Harn's study of the Dickson Mound suggests that there was a gradual decrease in the quantity of grave goods and a greater emphasis on utility items at the expense of status indicators as time went on (Harn, personal communication, 1975).

There are three major sources of information on the mortuary customs at the Orendorf site proper: ongoing UMVARF/WIU excavations in the burial mounds east of the habitation area; unsystematic and unreported controlled excavations in the burial mounds; and UMVARF/WIU excavations in the habitation area.

Since 1986 an UMVARF/WIU field school has been working in a large (approximately 65 × 25 × 1 meters) burial mound at the site. More than 160 burials and the disturbed bones of many more have been exposed in the approximately one-tenth of the mound excavated thus far. Some of these burials had been partially disturbed by looters. The recorded burials were of both sexes and all ages arranged in distinct cemeteries. The most common burial mode was extended supine in a single grave, but others were flexed and bundled, and multiple burials were common. Ceramics consisting of numerous jars (including those with sharp shoulders indicating an early Orendorf age and one lobed and one cambered specimen), two handled beakers ("Tippets Bean Pots"), and one narrow-rimmed plain plate were the most common class of grave furniture. Other grave goods included shell spoons, *Busycon* pendants, marine shell beads, cougar teeth, bone pins, arrowpoints, single celts or battle axes of polished limonite, flaked and ground Mill Creek chert, fishhooks, tool kits, galena, and a possible medicine bag. Some corpses were interred with both ceramics and marine shell, unlike those at Weaver-Betts. None of the burials excavated so far seems to be of a community leader.

Unsystematic and unreported controlled excavations in the mounds and cemeteries in the Orendorf burial mounds provide some data not available from UMVARF/WIU work on this portion of the site. Relic collectors have excavated ceramic jars, shallow bowls, short-necked and owl effigy water bottles, beads and pendants of marine shell, mussel shell rattle anklets, bone pins, copper-over-wood and copper-over-catlinite ear plugs, a deer jaw sickle, a bone gorge, fishhooks, galena, quartz crystals, and a cache including a large Mill Creek chert spade, a Kaolin chert notched hoe, a Burlington chert pick, a bone harpoon head, and several socketed conical bone points. This cache was reportedly buried with a bundle burial lacking a skull. In the Dickson Mound site skulls were apparently never interred with disarticulated burials of adult males at this time. The suspicion that these skulls were probably curated is apparently supported by the finding of disproportionate numbers of skull fragments relative to other human bones in the midden at Orendorf (Witzig-Hofsess 1983).

The charnel house excavated at the Orendorf site by UMVARF was built on a 46-centimeter-high, clay-covered ellipsoid platform measuring 6.8 meters along the long axis (which was the vector for the winter solstice) and 4.8 meters wide. The building itself measured 5 × 3 meters. It was constructed of substantial logs that sloped in at a 45° angle, apparently to form an ellipsoid tepee-like structure. The exterior and the floor were covered with hickory bark.

Although vandals had destroyed virtually all of the structure's floor, a few observations are possible on the basis of the intact areas and the materials recovered from the fill of the vandals' pits. It is apparent that several indi-

viduals of various ages were placed on the floor and in at least one case underlain by two mats (Witzig-Hofsess 1983). *Marginella* sp. and large disc beads cut from the outer whorl of marine gastropods were placed in the structure. Data concerning burial position or the arrangement of corpses are lacking. The building was destroyed by fire and covered over with a substantial cap of earth while still burning.

Five articulated burials were found in the Orendorf habitation area. One tightly flexed individual was in a pit intruding into a burned house in Settlement C and may not have been a Middle Mississippian burial. The remainder were in Settlement D. Two were in graves in the floor of a building that was later used as a dump, an extended burial was on the floor of a small burned building adjacent to the public building at the head of the plaza, and the last was in a grave at the edge of the plaza. The latter two burials were the only ones with furniture. The fourth one included several cobbles that may have been milling stones, but they may also have been weights for a covering. The burial on the plaza had a pipe, a wooden rattle, a bone pin, a copper-faced ear plug, and a small piece of fresh-water shell.

EXTERNAL CONTACTS. The presence of fortifications at Orendorf indicates that some of its external relations were not positive. Although its adversaries have not been identified, it is likely they were other Middle Mississippian groups in the valley. Both of these observations seem to be confirmed by the finding of Mississippian arrowpoints in a fatal context in the mound excavations. If this is the case, it would indicate that Cahokia no longer had firm control of its former colonies, because if it had such control it would probably have prevented such conflicts.

Most of the exotic southern materials found in Orendorf phase sites probably still moved through the Cahokia area. They include: *Busycon* sp., *Olivella* sp., and *Marginella* sp. shells from the Florida coasts; Bell Plain human and owl effigy water bottles, effigy marine shell dippers, and Mound Place Incised bowls from the Central Mississippi Valley; Kaolin and Mill Creek cherts from Union County, Illinois, in the form of spades, hoes, and knives; and engraved-over-red-slip beakers and perhaps salt pans from the American Bottom area. The virtual absence of manufacturing scraps of marine shell and exotic cherts suggests that trade was in finished objects. Southern influence is also seen in the Braden-style (Phillips and Brown 1975) human face engraved on a pipe of local stone from Settlement D, in the weeping eyes on another pipe from the same area, and in the bead ensemble, including forelock and sidelock beads from an Orendorf phase (or perhaps immediately post-Orendorf phase) burial in the Dickson Mound. No other discernible Southeastern Ceremonial Complex material, which is not ubiquitous for

Mississippian assemblages, is known from an Orendorf phase context.

Overland trade with the Missouri Basin likely produced the bison bones including scapula hoes, a horn and skull scoop, and a ball-joint hide softener from the Orendorf site. The copper presumably from the north and catlinite from the west forming a set of ear plugs from the same site may have been combined at Cahokia and then imported. Bird-wing fans have been noted only during this phase and the early Larson phase of the Spoon River culture but were probably used earlier as they were to the south (Perino 1971b:102) and also later. While such fans are common from the Illinois and Mississippi rivers west, they are extremely rare to the east and may be a Plains-derived trait, but they may have been introduced to the Plains from the Cahokia sphere. Bone bracelets are probably of western origin, but their ultimate derivation from the eastern proto-Iroquoian groups cannot be ruled out. These artifacts have been recorded only in Orendorf and early Larson phase contexts in the Spoon River area.

It has not been established whether the copper for the beads and foil occasionally found in Orendorf contexts originated in quarries in the Lake Superior region, in local glacial till, or at some southern source. It is likely that the galena in use at this time originated in the general area of northwestern Illinois, because this is the source area for three of the four Mississippian samples analyzed by Walthall (1981:41, 55) for the Central Illinois Valley.

OVERVIEW. In the early 1960s six Middle Mississippian towns were recognized. At that time, the Orendorf burial mounds were not recognized as a town. An examination of notes made twenty years earlier by people who had trenched the largest mound at the site convinced me that this was a platform mound. On that basis I included Orendorf as a town site, thus creating the sequence of seven more or less evenly spaced towns. Originally, I envisioned an organized establishment of contemporary towns at an early date and led some astray with this idea (see Caldwell 1967a). This hypothesis was based on limited data; the situation was obviously more complex than that and the importance of the spacing may have been exaggerated.

It is now clear that Orendorf and Larson were sequentially occupied and none of the towns, except perhaps Orendorf, has a major Eveland phase occupation. The relationship, if any, between the Orendorf-Larson population and the two northernmost towns (Kingston Lake and Hildemeyer) is unclear and the same is true for the lower towns (Crable, Lawrenz Gun, and Walsh). The spacing of the towns is probably related to the distance to agricultural fields and other necessary resources, the presence of other populations, and the previous depletion of resources by former occupations. It is now clear

that numerous factors influenced town placement in the valley.

LARSON PHASE (ca. A.D. 1250–1300)

LARSON PHASE SITES. The Larson site and its outliers seem to have been built by the descendants of the Orendorf community after they abandoned that site complex. It is not certain that this movement was direct. The Wray collection from the Weaver-Betts village site above the point where Duck Creek enters the Illinois floodplain may represent an intermediary occupation.

Although more resources have been expended on the study of the Orendorf site than on the Larson community, most have been directed toward salvaging the endangered portions of the town. The available resources for Larson have been more uniformly applied. Consequently, the Larson site itself is not as well known as Orendorf, but we have more raw data on the Larson hinterland. The settlement system is known from excavations at the Larson site (Harn and Baerreis n.d.; Harn 1978:251–54; Harn n.d.a, n.d.b), Fouts village (Cole and Deuel 1937:111–19), Myer-Dickson (Harn 1974), Morton (Harn 1983), Berry (Conrad 1970), Norris Farms sites 26 and 27 (Harn 1983; also see chap. 7), and the Hungry Wolf site (Conrad 1971), as well as from extensive casually structured survey (see Harn 1978:243), more formal survey (Conrad 1981), and aerial photography (Harn 1978:251; Harn and Weedman 1975). Mortuary practices are known from the Dickson Mound (Cole and Deuel 1937:120–26; Conrad 1972; Harn 1971b, 1980b) and the Morton Mounds (Cole and Deuel 1937:69–108), especially Fo14.

The Larson site is a rectangular, stockaded settlement aligned with the winter solstice and covering approximately eight hectares on the bluff overlooking the confluence of the Spoon and Illinois rivers. A platform mound measuring approximately 60 × 60 meters and perhaps 5 meters high with a ramp ascending the east side stood on the northwest side of a 150-meter-square plaza that was bordered on the other three sides by houses. The stockade, apparently without bastions, was set in a shallow trench. Borrow pits and cemeteries were located to the north and southeast of the site, while widely spaced buildings were scattered over an expanse much greater than the densely packed stockaded area (Harn 1978:251–52).

Excavations at Larson revealed approximately 100 structures on over sixty building sites, most of which were subjected to very limited excavations, and over 300 pit features. All structures but one were rectangular, ranged in size from approximately 3 × 3.9 meters to 4.2 × 6 meters, and were aligned with the sun's path at winter solstice, 90° off the azimuth of the winter solstice, or east-west. The east-west structures were the youngest in the cases where superposition occurred. Many of the buildings had interior hearths. One circular building, presumably a sweat lodge, was excavated at the site (Harn and Baerreis n.d.). The limited number of building types probably reflects more of the limited excavation than of a reduced variety of building types in the town.

Data on the community plans of three of Larson's outlying settlements are available. The data from a fourth, the Berry site, are too fragmentary to be of much value. Discontinuous, although in some areas extensive, excavations at the Myer-Dickson site suggest that it was a loosely organized collection of private and public buildings, square grounds, and open spaces extending over more than forty hectares along the Illinois River bluff around Dickson Mounds. One square ground was surrounded by perhaps twenty apparently private structures and a very large (14.6 × 24.7 meters) building seemingly aligned with the summer solstice. Five massive posts along the axis of the building were set in large pits with insertion ramps (Shields 1969).

Due to a fortunate set of circumstances, it was possible to make what appears to be a nearly complete plan of the Buckeye Bend site using aerial photography and surface measurements. Seventy-three rectangular midden spots that are obviously house pits form a open rectangle with the two largest spots facing each other across the "square." A number of the spots representing buildings of unknown function measured less than three meters across. The village was located on a low terrace on the Spoon River and the microrelief to some degree appears to have dictated the location of the structures. Eleven additional structures were located on a low ridge a short distance from the main village (Harn and Weedman 1975).

The third Larson phase site for which we have good settlement pattern data is the Fouts site, for which there is a plan of the fifteen house pits (Cole and Deuel 1937: fig. 16) and some details from the excavation of three of them (Cole and Deuel 1937:111–19). The house pits scattered over approximately four hectares are grouped in apparently nonrandom clusters of two (n = 1), three (n = 3), and four (n = 1). It is possible that the cluster of four actually represents two clusters of two, but the bilateral symmetry of the arrangement suggests that they were meant to face each other across a small courtyard. With the exception of a broad crescent arrangement that excludes the cluster of four, no patterning of arrangement is discernible. The remaining four house pits are located about ninety meters from the rest across a ravine.

One of the clusters of three buildings was excavated. The buildings all measured about 4.8 × 6.6 meters and were roughly in line. The floor of the central building contained four pit features and a large hearth, while the other two buildings had only single hearths placed slightly off center (Cole and Deuel 1937: fig. 23). These three buildings may represent the holdings of an extended or polygynous family that used the central building for cooking and storage and the other two as dwellings, but that has not been demonstrated. In this volume Harn (chap. 7) provides information on three other buildings or small groups of buildings and their associated pit features. In my view the Larson community data are best viewed as indicative of a dispersed village pattern in association with a central town that may have been used by most people during times of strife or ceremony.

SETTLEMENT SYSTEMS AND ECONOMY. Harn (1978: 252) has interpreted the data from the Larson community as indicative of a population amalgamation in the central town in the winter and a dispersal during the period from early spring to fall. Such a settlement system was practiced in the historic East only by the Huron and then only during the Iroquois wars (Trigger 1969) and would be the antithesis of the commonly known ethnographic pattern. Resolution of the problem is hampered by the fact that there was at least some occupation of the principal town during the summer and of the hinterlands during the winter, the relatively small samples available, the general lack of understanding of storage pit longevity, the few good winter indicators available to us, and the fact that nonwinter foods were stored for use during the winter. As elsewhere, the overriding problem with attempts to understand and describe the Larson phase is the almost total lack of reports and primary data gathered since 1932.

Subsistence patterns resembling those of the previous Orendorf phase with a continuing dependence on maize horticulture, hunting, fishing, and gathering are to be expected but can only be confirmed by conducting and presenting detailed analyses as opposed to field impressions.

CERAMICS. The major differences between the Orendorf and Larson phases were the growth in the percentages of cordmarked ceramics, the virtual disappearance of scrolls as decorative elements, and the increase in popularity of the Dickson series. Plates and bird and mammal effigy deep bowls became more common and plate rims became wider in most cases. Cordmarked water bottles occasionally occurred and "funnels" appear rarely. Plate rims were often decorated with line-filled or nested triangles as were occasionally jars. These motifs appeared on similar vessels during the Orendorf phase but became increasingly common later.

Published sherd counts are available for only three Larson phase structures and associated features, F'664 F, G, and H (Cole and Deuel 1937:118–19). There were 664 sherds, of which 179 (27%), were cordmarked. Cole and

Deuel estimated that 106 vessels were represented. When just rim sherds are considered, fourteen of forty-one were cordmarked. Vessel forms included: rounded-shouldered jars (40%), plates (36%), shallow bowls (12%), angular-shouldered jars (8%), water bottles (2%), and miniature vessels (2%). If the sherd count is assumed to reflect the percentages of vessels, approximately one-half of the jars were cordmarked; unfortunately, the percentage of plates suggests that this is a nonrepresentative sample.

NONCERAMIC ARTIFACTS. The only significant changes in the nonceramic artifact assemblage seem to be a shift in preference from block pipe effigies portraying water birds to those portraying frogs and the apparent disappearance of bison bone artifacts, except possibly for bracelets.

MORTUARY COMPLEX. There is usable mortuary data from three Larson phase sites: Dickson, Morton, and Berry. The burial customs of this phase seem to resemble those of the preceding phase with one important exception: the mutually exclusive categories of burial furniture (i.e., marine shell versus ceramics) break down. There are also differences in the axes preferred for burial orientations during the Orendorf phase (as represented in the possibly early Larson phase submound burials at the Dickson Mound) and the Larson phase as represented by the original Dickson excavation. At the Dickson Mound sunrise angles at the solstices and 90° off these angles were popular determinants of burial orientation with the cardinal directions playing a minor role (Conrad 1972; Harn 1971a:57–59). At the Berry site, of the twenty-seven identifiable burials twelve were oriented generally east-west, ten north-south, four northeast-southwest, and one northwest-southeast (Conrad 1970). Virtually all burials made during this period were either dorsally extended or disarticulated, although a few were partially disarticulated and some may have been flexed or partially flexed.

Although Harn has observed that Larson phase burials at Dickson were normally less well supplied with artifacts in general and status-indicating artifacts in particular than in earlier phases, there was at least one important exception. Burial 1,000, a sixty-year-old male, had the following nonperishable items interred with him: a copper gorget with a circle and cross design; a large Kaolin chert knife; 372 marine shell beads, including forelock beads; a cache of twenty-three fabricating tools, which included ocher, marine shell, and chert; and nine notched and unnotched triangular points.

Cole and Deuel (1937:83–84) describe the richly furnished Larson phase burial of a cripple from Morton. Although Cole and Deuel (1937: fig. 20) indicate that the Mississippian burials at F°14 were oriented with the cardinal directions, the original field map makes it clear

that this was idealized for the published map. Almost all of the undisturbed primary burials from Berry had associated artifacts including, in some cases, such items as engraved-over-red-slip beakers with bird effigy tabs or a Kaolin chert dance sword (Conrad 1970). Projectile points from graves are generally much finer than those from habitations. Burials have been plowed out of the Larson platform mound but we have no other data concerning them except that a calcite effigy turtle(?) head pipe was apparently associated.

EXTERNAL CONTACTS. All of the trade materials known for the Orendorf phase have been documented for the Larson phase except bison bone, Mound Place Incised pottery, and catlinite. A tripartite water bottle excavated by vandals from the Keeler mounds between the Morton and Berry sites presumably originated in the Central Mississippi Valley and the funnels may have too.

Southeastern Ceremonial Complex influence (Conrad 1984, 1989) can be seen in the circular copper gorget decorated with the circle and cross on Burial 1,000 at the Dickson Mound, in the fenestrated circle and cross marine shell gorgets from Larson, and perhaps in the massive sandstone frog and human effigy pipes, a cross-hatched sandstone tablet, and the Kaolin chert flared-bitted spatulate from the Larson site. Two red-slipped beakers with engraved serpent symbols on the sides and avian tabs probably symbolize fertility. The absence of influence from the south other than from the southeast Missouri–northeast Arkansas area may reflect a reduction in the vitality of Cahokia. The absence of bison bones (with the possible exception of bison rib bracelets) and the disappearance of Mill Creek culture influence on Spoon River ceramics during the Larson phase may be a result of an expanding Oneota tradition. However, a seemingly Plains-derived vessel was recovered in a Larson phase building on the slope above the Eveland site.

OVERVIEW. It is by no means clear what became of the inhabitants of the Larson area. In fact it is not clear when they left, although the radiocarbon dates suggest a short occupation of the Larson site. If these dates actually reflect the span of occupation of the site, it may be that there was a period, during which Dickson series pottery was still in vogue, when the population was dispersed without a town site. Dating some of the small sites might shed light on this question. There seems to have been a major Larson phase, as defined by the presence of Dickson series vessels, occupation at Kingston Lake and, according to Harn (1978:246), Hildemeyer, but it is not known whether these occupations were contemporary with or later than those in the Larson-Dickson area. Harn (1978:246, 247) considers Walsh and Lawrenz Gun Club to be Larson phase towns, apparently later for the most part than Larson and earlier for the most part than

Crable. In fact he suggests that these towns may have been occupied by populations abandoning Kingston Lake and Larson (Harn 1978:242). There is, however, evidence to suggest that this scenario is unlikely for reasons that will be developed below.

MARBLETOWN COMPLEX (ca. A.D. 1300–1400?)

MARBLETOWN COMPLEX SITES AND ECONOMY. There are three known sites in the Fulton-Schuyler county line area that may be related and that may represent the closing portion of the Spoon River culture. One of the difficulties in interpreting these sites is that they lie within the boundary zone between the Spoon River and La Moine River cultures. I have suggested the name Marbletown complex to characterize this material. Two of the sites, Rose Mounds and Emmons Cemetery, are known only from brief burial excavation reports; the Fiedler site is known from a brief report on a habitation area and a mound group.

CERAMICS. Concerning the ceramic assemblages of these habitation and burial areas, it can be said they include cordmarked jars and plates very similar to those from Larson but not Oneota ware, Crable plates, or typical Dickson series pottery.

Burial vessels are not as sensitive chronological indicators as are domestic ceramic assemblages, due to their more limited numbers and range and the conservatism in ideas concerning the standard burial jar.

A comparison of the Middle Mississippian jars from the Fiedler mounds (Morse, Schoenbeck, and Morse 1953:34), Rose Mound 13 (Griffin and Morgan 1941: plates 31 and 32), and the Emmons Cemetery (personal observation) with the Larson phase material from the Dickson excavation in the Dickson Mound (Harn 1980b: figs. 17–29) and the ISM excavation in earlier Larson phase areas (Conrad 1972: pl. 10) shows the former jars to be shallower and to have higher rims than the latter. Fiedler, Rose, and Emmons burial jars also seem to be shallower than the Crable burial vessels pictured by Hale G. Smith (1951: pl. 8), most of which are Oneota, and than the Crable Middle Mississippian jars in the WIU Morse collection. The Fiedler, Rose, and Emmons rims are similar to the Oneota rims.

The handles on the three jars with handles from Fiedler and the one from Rose tend to be more pronounced and to form a more perfect arc than do those from Dickson. Similar handles occur on some of the Oneota and Middle Mississippian jars from Crable, but most are not both pronounced and round. The angle of the photograph (Hoffman 1960: fig. 49) of the cordmarked-to-the-shoulder jar from the Irving Thompson site, in Brown County, makes it difficult to be certain, but it appears that

the single remaining handle is both round and prominent. This is not the case with the three handled jars pictured by Snyder (1962: plates 25 and 28) from the Brown County Ossuary, a La Moine River variant site in Brown County. No notice was made of this characteristic of the handles on the Emmons Cemetery jars. Two of the jars from the Emmons Cemetery are cordmarked to the shoulder and have broad, low arcs above the shoulder. This suggests to me a degenerate form of Dickson Trailed and probably a post-Larson Spoon River affiliation. Cordmarked jars occur at all of these sites except the Fiedler cemetery. There is one narrow-rimmed plate recorded from the Emmons Cemetery. It is approximately 5 centimeters high and 23 centimeters in diameter. Although more detailed analysis is needed, the jars from Fiedler, Rose, and Emmons appear to be more like each other than they are like either Larson phase or La Moine River variant jars.

NONCERAMIC ARTIFACTS. There are not enough data available in the literature to allow a discussion differentiating the nonceramic assemblage of the Fiedler, Rose, and Emmons sites from that of others, except that the Fiedler site seems to be the only Spoon River site with Mill Creek chert dance swords. Such comparisons as are possible for burial furniture are made below.

MORTUARY COMPLEX. Burials were interred in mounds and cemeteries. The only formal cemetery for which information is available is the Emmons Cemetery (Morse, Morse, and Emmons 1961). At the time of the preliminary report, eighty-three burials had been excavated from an area approximately 16 meters square just below the edge of the bluff. With the exception of five flexed, one semiflexed, and one bundle burial, all seem to have been extended. Of these, sixty-six were oriented to the south and four on the northern and southern sides of the cemetery were oriented "east to west." The population included fifty-three adults, eight children, and sixteen infants (the remaining six had not been completely excavated at the time the report was written). Morse, Morse, and Emmons provide considerable detail on burial associations, which need not be repeated here. It is clear that the cemetery was very rich by local standards, with fifty-five pottery vessels (some of which were probably imported), a marine shell vessel or dipper, the front of a copper-covered-wood, short-nosed god effigy rattle that had probably been incorporated into an elaborate headdress, other fragments of the suggested copper-covered-wooden headdress, seven copper-covered-wood or stone ear plugs, six conch shell pendants, a pair of barrel-shaped forelock beads, a necklace of cut marine shell beads, a necklace of pearl beads, six bone and pottery hair rings, a sheet copper fragment, a set of drilled mussel valves (rattle?), six bone pins and/or awls, a bone scarifier set, three lumps of calcite, twenty arrowheads, two bifacial knives, twelve flake knives, four chert scrapers, and twelve shell spoons.

The richest burial was in the center of the cemetery. This burial has been discussed in detail elsewhere (Griffin and Morse 1961), but it is appropriate to briefly note it here. It was that of a forty-six-year-old man with pronounced osteoporosis of all vertebrae who had been buried in a one-meter-deep rectangular grave. A smoothed-over-cordmarked bowl and a shell-tempered, red effigy bowl with both appendages missing were buried at his head along with a shell spoon. A side-notched triangular point was on the left elbow and a flake knife was at the right wrist. A twelve-centimeter-high wooden rattle portion with a well-sculpted representation of a human face with galena painted weeping eyes, a stepped crown headdress, and a concave back was found on the individual's upper thorax. It is thought to have been a portion of a rattle similar to one from the last stage of Etowah Mound C (Larson 1957) but incorporated into a headdress. Identical elements are pictured for Spiro (Phillips and Brown 1975: pl. 17) and the Malden Cache from southeast Missouri (Fowke 1910). Four *Busycon contrarium* shells running in a diagonal line across the thorax of the burial may have been directly associated with the effigy. Four fragments of copper-covered-wood and three copper-covered-limestone ear plugs lying in the area of the knees are interpreted as possible headdress fragments. The corpse wore copper-coated wooden ear plugs at the time of interment.

The burial area at the Fiedler site (Morse, Schoenbeck, and Morse 1953; Morse, Morse, and Emmons 1961:139–40) consisted of thirteen mounds ranging in size from 3.0 to 3.6 meters (n = 3) to 12 meters (n = 1) with most (n = 9) averaging about 7.5 meters across. Excavations ranging from test pitting to almost total excavation were carried out in ten of these mounds, and thirty-six extended burials were excavated from and between them. One of the mounds (A) yielded no burials, even though it was almost completely excavated and had a submound humus zone, and another (B) yielded a single adult female without burial furniture on the old sod line after extensive excavation. Other mounds contained several individuals of all ages and both sexes in the portions excavated. Most burials were in submound pits, often with several corpses in the same pit, but burials resting on the old humus line were common. Remains in the mound fill were rare and these probably were in graves dug from the surface.

There was a strong preference for orienting burials to the cardinal directions. Half were oriented to the west; four to the south; three to the east; and one to the north. Burial furniture consisted of ten ceramic vessels including jars (n = 4), beakers (n = 3), bottles (n = 2) and a duck effigy bowl, two bifacial chert knives, two flake

knives, a triangular point, a shell spoon, a bone hair pin, a fragment of a platform pipe, a marine shell effigy canine tooth, and a 43-centimeter Mill Creek chert dance sword. With the exception of the dance sword, which was the only artifact associated with the adult male with whom it was buried, everything known about the groups suggests a cemetery of fairly low status individuals.

The Rose mound "group" consisted of nineteen mounds in two groups. One group of thirteen included two overlapping low, flat, circular mounds (12 and 13) with Middle Mississippian burials. Mound 12 yielded a single extended adult burial identified as a male with his head to the west. He had a flake scraper at his right wrist and a set of mussel shell (*Lampsilis ovata*) rattle anklets (which are normally associated with females).

Mound 13 yielded all or part of nineteen skeletons in fifteen burials. Of these at least one appears to be Red Ocher and several appear to be Late Woodland. Based upon artifacts or placement above Middle Mississippian artifacts, at least seven (1, 1a, 1b, 5, 5a, 13, and 15) were Middle Mississippian burials, and others probably were. Of the seven, four were adults, two were infants, and one was a child; six were extended and one adult was flexed. Three were oriented toward the southwest, two to the southeast, and two to the northwest. The flexed burial was oriented to the northwest.

Grave lots included an owl effigy water bottle, a handled beaker, and a plain burial jar with Burials 1, 1a, and 1b; at least nine copper-covered-wood hemisphere anklets on Burial 5, an adult; copper-covered flat pieces of wood (over the pelvis), a *Busycon* sp. columnella pendant, a *Lampsilis ovata* shell spoon, and a flake knife (under the ball of the left femur) with Burial 5a, a child; and a short-necked water bottle near the skulls of both burials. Burial 15 had a crude notched triangular point, and Burial 13 had no nonperishable furniture but overlay Burial 15 (Griffin and Morgan 1941:22–28, plates 25–31).

Emmons, Fiedler, and Rose were similar in that burials at all three sites frequently had flake tools near the wrist and one burial at both Rose and Emmons had unidentifiable copper-covered flat pieces of wood over the pelvis. The placement of flake tools at the wrists was also a common characteristic of mortuary behavior during early Larson times at the Dickson Mound (Conrad 1972:137). Rose, Crable, and Dickson also had rattle anklets, but Emmons and Fiedler did not. The Emmons burials were usually oriented with their skulls to the south; the Fiedler burials tended to be oriented to the west; and those at Rose were oriented to the southwest, southeast, and to the northwest. The variation in orientation was probably related to social rather than political or chronological factors (see Binford 1971).

Emmons resembled Crable in that both had structured cemeteries with the richest burial near the center. They differed markedly, however, in the presence/absence of most status items including Mill Creek swords, gorgets, shell dippers or bowls, maces, and copper-covered wooden human faces. The notable resemblances between Fiedler and Crable were the presence of Mill Creek dance swords in both and the tendancy of burials to be placed in submound pits or on the old humus line with very few in the mound fill. The Fiedler swords (Morse, Schoenbeck, and Morse 1953: fig. 15) are the most northerly recorded examples of such blades, but they are fairly common at some La Moine River sites including Crable. Blades about thirty centimeters long have been found at Berry (Conrad 1970) and Kingston Lake (Simpson 1939:12), but they are relatively broader than the Crable and Fiedler blades and are not of Mill Creek chert. Mill Creek chert dance swords as opposed to Ramey knives probably were not available until post-Larson times. The major difference between Emmons, Fiedler, and Rose on one hand and Crable on the other was the presence of Crable plates and Oneota material at Crable but not elsewhere.

EXTERNAL CONTACTS. There are a number of vessels from the Emmons Cemetery, including an owl effigy stirrup-necked bottle, an owl effigy hooded bottle, a deep bowl with an inward facing rattle effigy head (Morse, Morse, and Emmons 1961: fig. 77), and one of a set of two conjoined jars that probably originated at least in inspiration in the Middle Mississippi Valley, as did the Fiedler swords. A small fragment of embossed sheet copper with an indeterminate design from Emmons probably originated in the same area. According to Baker (1941:60), the *Lampsilis ovata* shells used in the rattle anklets in Rose Mound 12 must have been derived from the middle Ohio River. It is likely the copper-covered-wood and stone ear plugs from Emmons and the unidentified copper-covered-wood objects from Rose and Emmons were also imported, but their source is presently unknown. Unfortunately, the same must be said for the Emmons mask.

OVERVIEW. The most parsimonious interpretation of the available data is that Rose Mounds, Fiedler mounds and village, and the Emmons Cemetery represent the late Spoon River culture. Until such time as this material is better understood, I propose the term *Marbletown complex* for convenience of discussion. The absence of shell gorgets and Mill Creek blades among the high-status burials at Emmons may be an indication that the people of Emmons did not hold the offices or affiliations that dance swords and gorgets symbolized. Further refinement of the situation must await a more detailed study and description of the data at hand and probably the gathering of considerably more data. Survey and testing of habitation sites between Larson and Crable are essential to clarifying the La Moine–Spoon River cultural boundary and the question of late Spoon River cultural development.

La Moine River Mississippian

Although I have assumed for a number of years that the people responsible for the multimound centers in the lower Central Illinois Valley represented a different polity than that of the Spoon River peoples living in Fulton County, it was only while gathering data for this paper that it became apparent to me how different their assemblages really are. A parallel sequence for a separate polity and distinct Middle Mississippian variant seems to be the best explanation for this difference. However, the quality of the data available for this putative variant does not preclude an explanation involving earlier Spoon River sites being masked by post-Larson Spoon River occupations. The term *La Moine River variant* is proposed to distinguish this material. Known La Moine River temple towns include Crable, Lawrenz Gun, and Walsh. Other sites include J. Gillette, C. Conrad, Baehr South, Star Bridge, Vandeventer, and Brown County Ossuary, among others.

The earliest report of Mississippian archaeology in the region is Cyrus Thomas's (1894:118–20) report of Colonel Norris's 1882 or 1883 visit to the Welch site (now called Walsh) where he mapped and tested its mounds and "hut rings."

In 1908 Snyder (1962) reported on the Brown County Ossuary (also known as the Crabtree site). The next relevant scholarly report was Hale G. Smith's (1951) Crable report, followed in 1960 and 1969 by Dan F. Morse's very brief reports on the same site and Margaret L. Hoffman's (1960) report on the Irving Thompson site in northern Pike County. With the exception of some very brief Historic Sites Survey reports (e.g., Holstein, Fairchild, and Shields 1975; Stephens 1972), notes by the Morse family on Crable, and a note by Mary Hanning (1979) on an air photo of the Star Bridge site, that is the sum total of scholarly reports of fieldwork on Middle Mississippian sites in the area. As-yet-unreported scholarly work in the area includes two field school seasons' work at Crable by the University of Illinois at Chicago in 1969 and 1970 and Dickson Mounds' excavations of a farmstead at the C. Conrad site in 1971. Other reports are confined to collectors' descriptions of their acquisitions from plowed or looted sites. There is not one percent as much controlled data available for the La Moine River variant as for Spoon River, but some artifacts have been preserved and they are certainly worthy of analysis.

GILLETTE PHASE (A.D. 1050–1150)

The limited evidence available suggests a scenario similar to that in the Spoon River area for the origins of the La Moine River variant of Middle Mississippian. Canton ware jars with loop handles from Maples Mills mounds at the Emmons site and at a habitation on a natural levee of the Illinois River (Esarey 1988a), a fragment of a Mississippian kneeling human pipe from the fill of a Late Woodland mound near Sheldon's Grove, and mixed Late Woodland and Powell Plain ceramics in pit feature at the C. Conrad site in Schuyler County indicate a blending of Mississippian and Woodland traditions. It may ultimately be determined that the predominance of the Bauer Branch versus Maples Mills people in this stretch of valley is a major source of difference between Spoon River and La Moine River Mississippians.

GILLETTE PHASE SITES AND MORTUARY COMPLEX. The type site for this phase is the J. Gillette Cemetery on the bluff in Schuyler County, where a collector excavated a number of graves and recovered, among other things, a copper-covered-cedar imitation flint blade of the same type as those from Spiro (J. Brown 1976:189, 193; Hamilton 1952:87) and Eufaula (Orr 1941), copper-covered-wood ear plugs, a vertically compound Ramey Incised vessel, marine shell beads, and fine side-notched arrowpoints. The nature and quantity of material from this site suggest that it was the cemetery for the administrative center of a dispersed village. Several other sites in the area, including Star Bridge and Lawrenz Gun Club, have yielded a few Powell Plain or Ramey Incised sherds.

ORENDORF AND LARSON HORIZON
(A.D. 1150–1300)

Harn (1978:246) has pointed out that trailing on jar shoulders is absent in the lower part of the Central Illinois Valley. Although not strictly accurate, this is an important observation and is a significant difference between the two variants' assemblages. The Hanning collections from Lawrenz Gun and Star Bridge sites at WIU contain a substantial number of plain jar rim sherds and two trailed ones that would not be out of place in the Orendorf assemblage. Similarly, several plate fragments are comparable to Orendorf plates in rim width, profile, finish, and decoration.

Orendorf horizon plain jars are moderately well represented in the Hanning collections from Lawrenz Gun and to a lesser extent at Star Bridge (also known as the Snyders site). A small percentage are decorated with nested chevrons or parallel oblique lines. Several narrow-rimmed plates from Lawrenz Gun with broad trailing are similar to those at Orendorf. Several narrow-rimmed plates in the Vandeventer family collections at WIU from Walsh, some of which have broad trailing, probably date from this horizon. This horizon in the lower Central Valley is not defined well enough to warrant suggesting a phase name.

ORENDORF AND LARSON HORIZON SITES AND ASSEMBLAGES. The Lawrenz Gun site may have become a town at this time, but firm evidence is lacking. The site has never been properly defined, but it is said to be quite large and to have four large mounds or sand dunes. People who have dug there report that it has substantial midden deposits interspersed with sterile layers. Items of interest from this site of uncertain age in the Hanning collection at WIU include fragments of several funnels of coarse paste (see Esarey with Good 1981: fig. 3.20); two salt pans; several beakers and shallow bowls with engraved-over-red-slipped solstice symbols, ladder designs, and/ or highly stylized lip tabs; several good Mound Place Incised imitations; a three-millimeter-thick cup; numerous beakers of varying ceramic quality; short- and medium-necked water bottles; deep bowls; and effigy bowls with modest solid bird heads.

Presumably some of the shell-tempered cordmarked jars; the plates decorated with line-filled triangles; the coarse and fine deep bowls, including effigies; the beakers; and perhaps the large cordmarked water bottle in the Hanning collection from Lawrenz Gun date to the Larson time period. Similar assemblages could be found at the Walsh, Star Bridge, and Baehr South (ISM Brv75, located about one kilometer south of the more well known Middle Woodland site) sites, although the major occupations are later. A Dickson Plain jar with a plain shoulder from the Irving Thompson site (Hoffman 1960: fig. 14) likely dates from this period.

Nonceramic items from the Lawrenz Gun site include a variety of projectile point forms (approximately one-half of which are unnotched triangles), a small human effigy of marine shell, large fluorite beads, a few discoidals, a bone scarifier set, *Marginella* sp. beads, two drilled human teeth, and a cache of forty-four Mill Creek chert spades.

CRABTREE PHASE (A.D. 1300–1375)

CRABTREE PHASE SITES. This was apparently the period of major occupation at sites such as Lawrenz Gun and Walsh, which probably functioned as towns during this period. Thomas (1894:119–20) has provided an early description of the Walsh site.

An extremely productive but little known site of this phase is the Vandeventer site in Brown County. It is said that house pits are still visible, and little if any of this site has been cultivated. The site is best known for its extensively looted cemetery. Star Bridge was completely burned at this time, and following a deep plowing episode we were able to get an excellent photograph (fig. 6.2) that revealed it as a large, compact village with a square ground and apparently a fortification, but without mounds.

CERAMICS. It is during the Crabtree phase that the ceramic assemblage in the La Moine River culture is most striking. Lawrenz Gun, Star Bridge, Walsh, and Baehr South all evidence a proliferation of high, broad-rimmed plates with incised designs, usually involving line-filled or more rarely cross hatching-filled triangles, but not infrequently depicting what must be sun symbols composed of nested arches or circles with triangular rays. Of course a plate encircled with triangles is also a sun symbol. The circle and cross and the ladder design also occasionally appear. There are fragments of two deep-rimmed plates from Walsh in the Vandeventer family collection at WIU and in the Dickson Mounds collection. The Hannings' personal collection from Star Bridge includes a plate rim with an incised raptoral bird's head with a forked eye. Their collection from Lawrenz Gun at WIU also includes a plate rim fragment depicting a beautifully executed raptor or falcon dancer showing the lower half of an elaborate wing and two toes with pronounced talons (Conrad 1989:fig. 13). A more complete fragment of the same design from Baehr South was recently reported sold on the antiquities market. Most of the rest of the assemblage for this period is made up of shell-tempered cordmarked jars; large deep bowls, more frequently cordmarked than previously; and deep effigy bowls, often with very large rattle effigy bird and mammal heads.

Most of the approximately forty burial jars examined from Vandeventer were of mediocre workmanship and decorations were confined to a single tridactyle handle and a single instance of crude pendant archs. Water bottles were common and included plain, long- and short-necked forms of widely varying sizes, and two poorly made stirrup water bottles—one with a crude effigy face at the spout, and another with an engraved ladder design on the neck and red painted examples. The two plates represented were decorated with incised triangles. B. W. Stephens (1958) illustrates six beakers from the site, one of which is decorated with a ladder motif and another has incised flying birds on the exterior. The one that is completely visible in the illustration has a circle and cross

on the torso and apparently a forked eye. Among the specimens from the site in the Morse collection at WIU is one with engraved solstice symbols. Other material from this site is illustrated in an unsigned article (Anonymous 1948). One gets the impression that there was an uncommonly large number of beakers in this cemetery.

NONCERAMIC ARTIFACTS. Surface collections of projectile points from the Star Bridge site revealed that approximately nine-tenths were unnotched triangles and the other tenth may be attributable to the earlier Mississippian occupations. About one percent of the points from this site are Huffakers.

Walsh has produced a Mill Creek chert mace handle and sections of Mill Creek chert dance swords. More than half of the points are unnotched and many are exceptionally crude flake points. The site owners' large collection includes a very wide range of points of highly variable quality.

Apparent differences in the site assemblages may be due to collecting pressures in some cases and to multiple occupations in others, but it is worth noting that the Walsh site apparently does not produce hoes of any kind, even though the owners guard it closely and collect it heavily.

MORTUARY COMPLEX. The famous Brown County Ossuary (or Crabtree site) described by Snyder (1962) is a burial mound of the Crabtree phase, probably for Baehr South. According to Snyder, a number of articulated adult burials were placed on the ground surface with heads pointed in a variety of directions (I doubt they were in circles with their feet to the center, as Snyder suggests). A mass of disarticulated bones including skulls and limb bones measuring an estimated 24 × 7.6 × 0.3 meters was then placed directly on top of them. Snyder estimated that more than 350 individuals were represented. This mass was then covered by a 20–25-centimeter layer of gravel and fine soil which formed a "mortar." A loess mound approximately 1.5 meters high was then built over the spot.

Material recovered from the mound included over a hundred unbroken plain and effigy jars; deep bowls; plain, noded, and effigy water bottles; plates including at least one Crable plate; at least one conch effigy vessel; "many more" broken vessels; hundreds of *Marginella* sp. beads; two spider gorgets; several annular gorgets; a dozen or more long bone awls; mussel shell spoons; a fluorspar bead; several quartz crystals; a small piece of sheet copper; and fourteen arrowpoints (Snyder 1962:224–25, plates 24–26, 28).

Burials from the Walsh site are recovered from the mounds and the village area, particularly in the plaza. Marine shell beads, a fenestrated cross gorget, and a large marine shell dipper have been plowed from these graves.

No responsible investigation has been carried out at the Vandeventer site, but vandals have removed large quantities of material from the cemetery, including well over a hundred (and quite possibly over 250) ceramic vessels such as plain and cordmarked jars, water bottles, bowls and plates, an exceptionally large number of beakers, numerous Mill Creek and a few Kaolin chert blades, a chert spatulate celt, hair pins, shell and pearl beads, *Busycon* pendants, large and small marine shell annular gorgets and circular gorgets with engraved crosses, a fragmentary copper falcon plate, pottery and stone elbow pipes, a bone scarifier, and shell spoons with decorated handles.

A vandal removed two small marine shell annular gorgets and a twenty-five-centimeter Mill Creek knife from graves near Crabtree in 1982 (Anonymous 1983).

CRABLE PHASE (A.D. 1375–1450)

The Crable phase is the best known phase of the La Moine River culture, yet it may have been the least typical of the Middle Mississippian developmental sequence. The Crable phase was marked by the appearance of Oneota Bold Counselor-phase immigrants from the north (Conrad and Esarey 1983) and seems to have been characterized by a period of dramatic political and social instability in the Central Illinois Valley.

CRABLE PHASE SITES. There are more data available for the Crable site than for any other La Moine River variant site, but that is not to say the site is well understood. Morse (1960, 1969) has summarized the available data from the site; Hale G. Smith (1951) has described the University of Chicago's (UC) work there; and Edgar S. MacDonald, one of the vandals who plundered its cemeteries (1950), has left reminiscences of their activities. Because these sources are widely available, only a brief overview will be given here.

In a recent paper discussing Oneota culture in west-central Illinois (Conrad and Esarey 1983), the site was described as follows:

The Crable site is located on a bluff finger measuring about 3,000 m long and from 61 to 460 m wide overlooking Wilson Creek. The crest is about 48 m above the Illinois River bottom lands with the last 30 m being a steep bluff. Village debris is reportedly scattered over approximately 30 ha in several areas of concentration with by far the densest being the roughly four to six ha known as "Mound Field" (Fv891), where the midden is reported as being as deep as 0.9 to 1.2 m. There is a natural spring in this area of the site. A platform mound (Fo898) which was originally probably more than 4.5 m high and roughly 15 m on a side stood near the center of the concentration on the northeast edge of a plaza of unreported size. A trench cut into this mound by Indiana University revealed evidence of a 14.3 meter-in-diameter, premound, single-post struc-

ture, three building stages and sand-covered floors in the 1.8 m of mound remaining in 1964 (Morse 1969:65). A group of four hemispherical burial mounds and a cemetery were located on a bluff spur approximately 330 m northeast of the platform mound while another cemetery, Trail Ridge Cemetery or cemetery number three was located approximately 230 m northeast of it. The Signal Ridge Cemeteries (numbers two and four) were approximately 280 m southwest of it.

There is virtually no hard data available on the Crable site habitation area. A report of more than a century ago (Chapman and Co. 1879) mentions cup-shaped depressions which must have been house pits and the University of Illinois at Chicago excavated approximately thirty-five features and four houses, including one burned rectangular, wall trench structure which had been rebuilt six times. Storage/rubbish pits were numerous and frequently large. MacDonald (1950:18) indicated they averaged about 1.5 m in diameter and from 0.9 to 1.8 m deep. Another vandal reports a deep pit large enough to hold himself and his shaker leaving room to work. The four pits excavated at the site by the UC were all about 0.6 m in diameter (H. G. Smith 1951:5, 8). The depth of the midden in a relatively restricted area suggests the habitation area was enclosed by a stockade.

The Sleeth site (ISM Fv148), the only other known Crable phase site, is a rectangular village measuring approximately 150 meters on a side located on the Illinois River bluff approximately thirty-five kilometers upriver from the Crable site. The rectangular pattern and the very sharp edge of the dense midden suggest that the site was stockaded. No excavations have been conducted at this site, which was occupied by both Middle Mississippian and Bold Counselor Oneota people.

ECONOMY. Paul W. Parmalee (n.d.) recorded twenty-one species of mussels, and a minimum of eleven species of fish, five species of turtles, sixteen species of mammals, and twenty-three species of birds among the unfloated faunal remains that he examined from Crable. Maize kernels have been observed in the pit features. The number and size of the storage pits suggest very large quantities of food were being stored.

A surface collection of faunal remains that I made at the Sleeth site and sent to Parmalee in 1965 yielded forty-six mussel shells of nine species as well as bones of five species of fish, seven species of turtles, three species of birds, and six species of mammals in addition to those of humans. Deer were represented by 206 bones of at least fourteen individuals, whereas elk were represented by twenty-three bones of at least two individuals. Again, it seems safe to assume a broad spectrum exploitation of the natural environment combined with corn, bean, and squash cultivation.

CERAMICS. The Morse family Crable collection at WIU includes an estimated 8,000–10,000 sherds, of which approximately 550 are Bold Counselor Oneota. This includes plates with trailed-line and punctate designs as well as all of the Mound Place Incised-like deep bowls without obvious effigies. Such bowls are very common in the area's Bold Counselor assemblages. Allowing for roughly half of the surface of Oneota vessels being undecorated, an estimate of 1,000 to 1,200 Oneota sherds in the collection seems appropriate. If this collection is representative, it is probable that about 85%–90% of the ceramics at Crable are Middle Mississippian.

Perhaps one-tenth of those were made earlier than the Crable phase. The Crable phase Middle Mississippian ceramic assemblage (figs. 6.9–6.10) consists of large quantities of cordmarked (202 rim and shoulder sherds in the surface collection) or plain jars (n = 96); fine and coarse plain (n = 473), or coarse cordmarked (n = 94) deep bowls; a high percentage of plate rimsherds (n = 592), usually the wide rimmed "Crable Deep Rimmed Plate" most often with incised decorations (fig. 6.10); and small quantities of water bottles (often cordmarked or red painted) and beakers (at times engraved over red slip). The counts for rim sherds cannot be converted into accurate percentages, because cordmarked jars were usually larger than plain ones and therefore produced more rimsherds, and plates had a much larger proportion of easily recognized rim than did jars or bowls.

There are forty-seven ceramic effigy heads in the Morse collection, including seven fragmentary hollow ones that must have been rattles. Thirty-two of the thirty-five identifiable specimens are combed birds, apparently wood ducks (*Aix sponsa*), one is a horned owl, one is a mammal with prominent ears, and one is an open-mouthed frog(?). There is considerable variability in the quality of these heads (see Morse 1960: fig. 64). Most are modeled in the round, but a few are flat. It appears that they usually faced out. With the exception of five incised plates with punctates, no evidence of an amalgamation of the Oneota and Middle Mississippian ceramic traditions has been noted.

The ceramic sample from Sleeth consists of 188 identifiable shell-tempered sherds collected at three different times. The largest and best sample represents a total pickup and is in the Illinois State Museum collection at Dickson Mounds. With the exception of sherds from two bottles (1.1%) and from four possible beakers (2.2%), the assemblage is composed of bowls (51.8%), jars (27.5%), and plates (17%).

Of the ninety-eight bowl sherds, fifty-four (55.1%) are plain. Of these, two have plain, two have bifurcated, and one has a double notched lip tab. Nineteen (19.4%) are plain except for lip stamping; nine (9.1%) are the Bold Counselor variety of Mound Place Incised-like; one (1%) has an arch and punctates; twelve (12.2%) are cord-

marked; and three (3%) have inflected lips. Of the jars, thirty (57.7%) have trailed-line and punctate designs and of these three have loop handles. Eighteen (34.6%) are cordmarked and only one (1.9%) is plain. The remaining three (5.8%) are miniatures, two of which are plain and one of which is cordmarked (Conrad and Esarey 1983).

The ratio of Oneota to Middle Mississippian jars seems to be approximately seven times as high as at Crable. It is clear that controlled excavations are desperately needed at Sleeth (Conrad and Esarey 1983).

NONCERAMIC ASSEMBLAGE. For the most part it is not possible to separate the Oneota from the Middle Mississippian nonceramic utilitarian artifacts in the Crable collection. The vast majority of the arrowheads are unnotched triangles, as is the case with the slightly earlier Middle Mississippian assemblages immediately to the south of Crable and the other Oneota assemblages in the valley. The numerous scrapers, celts, adzes, knives, drills, and discoidals in the collection cannot be sorted, but it is probable that the eight "hoes," two chisels, three knives, one end scraper, and nine indeterminate fragments of Mill Creek chert are attributable to the Middle Mississippian component. This Mill Creek chert collection is larger than that from any known Spoon River site except perhaps from the Emmons Village.

In addition to a large sandstone rabbit pipe, probably attributable to the Middle Mississippian occupants of the site, the Morse collection includes twelve pipes or pipe fragments of a general elbow form. Six are of stone and six are ceramic. None is catlinite. Four have moderate but obvious "prows" extending beyond the bowl opposite the stem and three have very pronounced extensions; the other two are too badly damaged to classify. On four of the specimens, the bowl rises at an oblique angle. Although the bowls on these pipes usually flare, occasionally abruptly, there are none that could be called a disc pipe. In fact none of these pipes would warrant special comment if found on the floor of a Spoon River Middle Mississippian house.

Worked antler seems to separate the Crable nonceramic assemblage from other Middle Mississippian assemblages and links it with Bold Counselor-phase Oneota (Conrad and Esarey 1983). Antler items are common at Crable and C. W. Cooper, one of two known pure Bold Counselor Oneota habitation sites, but rarely do contemporary Middle Mississippian assemblages include elk antler hoes and socketed arrowpoints. The Crable assemblage contains an abundance of pressure flakers and handles, including an L-shaped scraper handle duplicated at Cooper and Morton. The range of most bone tools from the collection would fit comfortably in either a Middle Mississippian or an Oneota assemblage, but the deer toe arrowheads would be rare in the former.

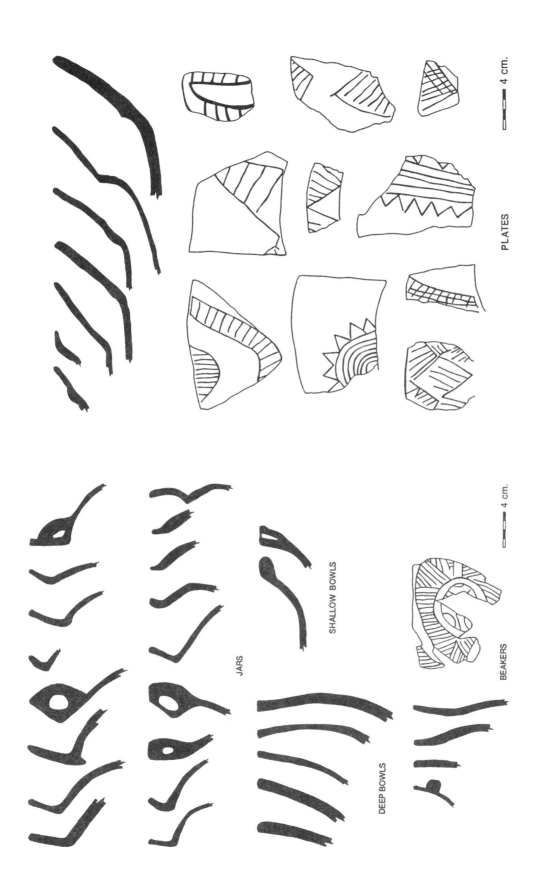

Figure 6.10. Crable Phase Plates

PLATES

4 cm.

Figure 6.9. Crable Phase Jars, Bowls, and Beakers

JARS

SHALLOW BOWLS

DEEP BOWLS

BEAKERS

4 cm.

By far the most common nonceramic artifacts from Sleeth are arrowheads. One collector gathered more than 2,000 over several years. Of the seventy-two examined from the collections under discussion, all but two (2.8%) are unnotched. A detailed analysis has not been done, but there is clearly considerable variety in these points. Most are relatively crude but some are rather fine. There is considerable variety in width/length ratio, in angularity, and in basal form.

There is also considerable variety in the seventeen end scrapers from Sleeth, but most are quite crude. It is difficult to know whether to assign most of the small knives to the component under discussion or to one of the several earlier Archaic and Woodland components lightly represented at the site, but one seems to be a good example of a hump-backed knife (Munson and Munson 1972).

Similarly, the three fine drills or gravers might be assignable to any of the assemblages at the site. Two flat sandstone disks are probably discoidals associated with the Oneota/Middle Mississippian occupation. Two spindle whorls, a fine schist chisel, a shell hoe, a small marine shell fragment, a broken block pipe, and a peculiar pipe resembling a bent trumpet are all probably from this occupation as well.

MORTUARY COMPLEX. Most Crable burials were interred in cemeteries, but some were in mounds and others were in graves or converted storage pits and abandoned houses in the town. The only detailed report of burial excavations at the site is Hale G. Smith's (1951) account of UC's work of 1933. Excavations were conducted in three mounds and a cemetery. The first mound (Fo892), which was circular and measured 9 meters in diameter and 75 centimeters high when excavated, was immediately adjacent to the habitation area. The construction sequence included removing most of the sod, beginning the building of the mound, the interment of one corpse, the completion of the mound; and the final interment of a second corpse. Both burials were extended in graves 1.2–1.5 meters deep without grave goods.

Excavations in Fo894 produced all or parts of twelve burials, five of which were disturbed. According to Smith, the majority of these burials were in submound graves of more or less uniform depth but at least one, the only flexed burial, was in the mound fill. All six undisturbed adults burials had grave furniture, but the one undisturbed infant burial had none. Excluding sherds and shells that may have been rubbish in the fill, grave lots included a rectanguloid, two-hole marine shell gorget; a knife fragment, a graver, and red ocher; two bone needles or hair pins; a flint graver; a pointed piece of elk antler and a hammerstone; and two small triangular points.

UC excavators removed thirty-two burials from Fc896, but vandals apparently removed many more. As Morse

points out (1960:126), almost all of those for which a determination can be made were oriented toward the south or west. All of those excavated by UC and most of those noted by the MacDonalds were extended. Dan F. Morse (1960:126) reports a cemetery of bundle burials had not been looted due to its lack of artifacts, but it may not be Middle Mississippian.

All ages and both sexes were represented in Fc896. Of the twenty-four undisturbed burials for which we have data, ten had grave goods including projectile points (singly and in a cache of eight), flake knives and scrapers, bifacial(?) knives, a bone ring, a cut antler tine, two small jars, and a set of thirty-two rattle anklets of mussel shell. Adults had burial furnishings more often than infants. MacDonald (1950:17) indicates that the material from this cemetery was comparable to the material from the others at the site. If this was the case, it would appear UC's excavations were in a poor section of the cemetery. Smith (1951) provides no information on the structure of Fc896, but plate 2a shows a row of six extended burials and MacDonald says, "In all the cemeteries we found the center contained the most culture. As we neared the outer edge very few artifacts were found and one of the notable characteristics was, that all the burials were extended and seemed to form a complete ring around the outside of the burial grounds. No artifacts were found with these skeletons" (1950:17). This situation is in some ways reminiscent of the Emmons and Norris Farms No. 36 cemeteries, where the highest status burial was in the center, but peripheral burials also had furniture (Morse, Morse, and Emmons 1961; Santure, Harn, and Esarey 1990). The preference for a southerly orientation is another common trait for Emmons and Fc896.

The only clue to the numbers interred in these cemeteries is MacDonald's statement (quoted in Morse 1960: 126) that there were 200–300 burials in the largest cemetery. It seems safe to assume there were fewer than 1,000 burials in the four cemeteries and the mound group. These burials yielded a minimum 240 vessels, not counting broken ones thrown back. Although Smith (1951:19) says that the pottery removed from the cemeteries by Glen McGirr was approximately evenly divided between Oneota and Spoon River vessels, this is apparently based on the assumption that all shallow bowls and all deep-rimmed plates were attributable to Oneota. Observations on the various collections from the cemeteries indicate only that the collectors tended to specialize in either Middle Mississippian or Oneota vessels. The Morse surface collection from the town suggests a ratio of approximately ten Mississippian vessels to each Oneota one at the site.

Both MacDonald (1950:18) and Morse (1969:64) report burials with grave furniture, including ceramics and marine shell beads, in storage or house pits in the town.

All that is known of the mortuary complex at Sleeth is that human bones have been plowed from the midden.

EXTERNAL CONTACTS. In addition to ceramics, the Crable graves produced an abundance of the various tools, weapons, and ornaments normally associated with Middle Mississippian burials in the area, but it is the imported material that has generated the most interest. Imported artifacts that originated in the Middle Mississippi Valley can be divided into three main categories: pottery, stone, and shell. Pottery includes at least two tripartite water bottles, a pair of conjoined jars, and a fluted Bell Plain bottle (Smith 1951). Stone artifacts include at least six blades ranging from 24 to 39 centimeters long. Morse reported (1960:126) one of these blades to be white, three as gray, and one as a yellowish quartz-like flint (Kaolin?). The one in the WIU collection is of Mill Creek chert, and it is likely most of the others are also. One ground Kaolin chert mace was recovered from the site (Smail 1952) and there were rumors of a second one. Several marine shell gorgets decorated with spiders (some of which were much finer than others), fenestrated crosses, and a stepped-cloud motif were confidently assigned to the Central Mississippi Valley in earlier drafts of this paper, but Duane Esarey (1987) has demonstrated that many if not all of the spiders, at least, were very likely locally made, as were the negative painted vessels (Esarey 1988b). A crudely engraved bird gorget may also have been locally made (Morse 1960).

As indicated above, the lower portion of the Central Illinois Valley was occupied by people other than those of the Spoon River variant for a comparable period of time. On the Stirling-Eveland time horizon, the whole area clearly interacted with Cahokia, as the presence of high-quality Ramey Incised pottery indicates. This may also have been the source of the copper-faced-stone ear plugs and the marine shell beads and annular gorget. However, the source of the copper-over-wood imitation chert blade from the Gillette site is problematical. Such items are reported from only Spiro and Eufaula in Oklahoma, but they may have been introduced into the Caddoan area from elsewhere.

There is no evidence to suggest that Larson phase people gave rise directly to those at Crable, even though I used to "know" they did. There seems to be a gap of about 75–100 years between the occupations at Larson and Crable. This would be time for considerable evolution, but there are no known intermediate assemblages. However, this gap may be a dating problem and the apparent lack of intermediate assemblages may be due to my relative ignorance of the cultural evolution of the Larson phase. During the Crable occupation, much of the Spoon River area was apparently occupied by Bold Counselor Oneota people. Therefore, it is appropriate to consider evidence of connections between the central and lower Central Illinois Valley as evidence of external contact.

There are several plate rims from Star Bridge and Lawrenz Gun that would fit into the Orendorf assemblage, but this may simply be parallel evolution. It is more likely, however, that the two Dickson Trailed sherds from Lawrenz Gun represent vessels from the Larson area.

A thick, crudely done effigy of a combed bird head from an Oneota feature at the C. W. Cooper site is identical to some from late La Moine River variant sites and probably indicates contact between the two traditions. Several Middle Mississippian vessels, a fine discoidal, and a small Mill Creek chert dance sword, probably obtained from Crable or a Crabtree phase site, were recently excavated from a Bold Counselor Oneota cemetery at the Morton site by the ISM (Santure, Harn, and Esarey 1990). Whether or not the La Moine River people had any responsibility for the large number of violent deaths in the contemporaneous Morton Oneota population is unclear, but it seems unlikely. A trailed-over-cordmarked sherd from Sleeth, incised plate sherds from Plum Island below Starved Rock (Fenner 1963: pl. 24a, b), and shell-tempered cordmarked sherds from Zimmerman in the same area (Brown 1961:45) probably indicate connections between those areas during the fourteenth or fifteenth centuries, and a low, constricted-sided beaker from the Fisher site at the confluence of the Des Plaines and Kankakee rivers (Langford 1927) probably indicates contact as well.

Mill Creek chert from Union County, Illinois, is much more common on La Moine River sites than on Spoon River sites. The spade cache from the Lawrenz Gun Club site (reported as Mound Lake by Miller 1958) contains more Mill Creek chert than is known from all of the Spoon River sites combined. Although no other site in the area has produced such a quantity of this material, it seems that all of them yield it in the form of spades, small unnotched hoes, mace fragments, long slender blades, and/or Ramey knives. Kaolin chert tools are much more rare. Like Mill Creek chert, this material also originated in Union County, Illinois, and until perhaps A.D. 1250 probably moved into the Illinois Valley via Cahokia.

Other commodities originating in the area between Cahokia and the Missouri Boot Heel and finding their way into the Central Illinois Valley probably include salt pans and thick funnels. Fluorspar for beads must have originated in southeastern Illinois or adjacent areas of Kentucky and moved into the Illinois Valley after the decline of Cahokia. The shell human effigy recovered from the Lawrenz Gun site may have been locally made. A cursory examination of the literature has produced only two other marine shell full human effigies. The specimens are from Spiro (J. Brown 1976: fig. 79a, b; Duffield 1964:

pl. 13) and bear little resemblance to the one from the Lawrenz Gun site.

There is an abundance of southern trade material from the Crable phase and it is noteworthy that all of it except the marine shell probably came from a 400-river-kilometer stretch of the Central Mississippi Valley between the declining or abandoned site of Cahokia and the southern border of the Missouri Boot Heel or the lower Ohio Valley. Whereas many if not all of the Central Illinois Valley gorgets may have been locally made, the remaining spider gorgets of the McAdams style are distributed from the Cahokia vicinity (although apparently not from the site) to Henry County, Tennessee, on the Tennessee River (Esarey 1987; Holmes 1883b:286–89; Phillips and Brown 1975:175). The stylistic uniformity among the Illinois Valley gorgets on the one hand and those from Cakohia south on the other hand demonstrates the close ties between the two regions.

Among the other specimens indicating these links is a "stepped cloud" motif on one Crable gorget that is similar to another one from the St. Marys Cemetery, which also produced two spider gorgets (MacCurdy 1913: figs. 64, 67, 68). There is at least one good fenestrated cross gorget from Crable (Morse 1969: pl. 36). Except that the Crable specimen is scalloped around the edges, it is similar to one illustrated by Holmes from Union County, Illinois, and perhaps one from near Charleston, Missouri (Holmes 1883b: pl. 51). The engraving on the bird gorget from Crable (Morse 1960: fig. 61) is not very similar to any located in the literature and the engraving is not of a quality that would preclude its being locally done by a nonspecialist.

Several lines of evidence demonstrate that the lower Central Illinois Valley was interacting at least indirectly with the lower Ohio and Cumberland valleys. The most conclusive evidence is the fluorspar bead from the Brown County Ossuary and those from Lawrenz Gun Club. Fluorspar occurs in extreme southeastern Illinois and adjacent portions of Kentucky but apparently does not outcrop in Illinois. If we assume that the best outcrop would have been the one first mined by Euro-Americans, one in Crittendon County, Kentucky, would be the most likely source (see Bastian 1931:9–10).

Another line of evidence is the small annular shell gorgets from Crable, Brown County Ossuary, and perhaps near Baehr South (Anonymous 1983; Morse 1960: 13; Snyder 1962: pl. 25). They have few close analogues in the Middle Mississippi Valley (Williams 1954). They are common in the Fort Ancient cultures of the Ohio Valley (see Griffin 1943: plates 44, 98) and occur in Will County, Illinois (Skinner 1953: fig. 1) and at Spiro (J. Brown 1976:399, 104, fig. 81).

Finally, there is the deep-rimmed plate, so common at Crable but so uncommon elsewhere in Illinois. A few examples are known from Walsh, Cooper, Sleeth, and Morton/Norris Farms No. 36 and one is pictured by Snyder (1962: pl. 25, fig. 1) from the Brown County Ossuary. There is a large incised fragment of one from the First Terrace of Monks Mound at Cahokia. The only other site at which such plates could be said to be common is the Angel Mounds site at Evansville, Indiana, where they are referred to as "wide rimmed plates." At Angel many and perhaps most are negative painted. Although there are a few dramatic Southeastern Ceremonial Complex motifs such as woodpeckers or bilobed arrows on these painted plates, most (nearly 98%) are decorated with geometric designs forming a radiating circle. The variations on this theme seem to be more numerous and often more elaborate than those at Crable, but the available report (Curry 1950) is not of a nature that allows quantitative discussion. Angel and Crable share line-filled triangles radiating from the well of the plate and straight lines extending across the rim from the well to the lip and bracketed by horizontal elements. A variety of sun circles including circles and crosses appears on plate rims at both sites and on more standard plate forms on Crabtree phase sites. The circle and cross motif also appears on contemporary Bold Counselor Oneota jars.

Gates P. Thurston collected several of these plates in the Nashville region (see Cox 1985:144–46) at least one of which was negative painted (Thurston 1897: fig. 14). Finally, a deep-rimmed plate is known from the Madisonville site near Cincinnati (Griffin 1943:142).

Esarey (1988b) has demonstrated that the negative-painted pottery from the Central Illinois Valley was almost certainly made there and should not be listed as exotic. On the other hand, the technique was clearly not independently invented there. Although negative-painted ceramics occur occasionally from Mobile Bay to Lake Winnebago and from the eastern edge of the Great Plains to central Georgia, they are common only in two areas (which may actually be a single area): from southeast Missouri up the Ohio to soutwestern Indiana and in the Cumberland Basin (Williams 1979). Therefore, negative painting, which is more common in late Mississippian and Oneota sites in the Central Illinois River Valley than in any area other than these two, can be viewed as another link between the Central Mississippi–Lower Ohio–Cumberland region and the study region.

Rare salt pan sherds from the Crable and Walsh villages and the Bell Plain effigy bowls, conjoined jars, reduplicate vessels, and tripartite water bottles from the Crable cemeteries (Smith 1951: pl. 7) could all have originated in the Central Mississippi Valley.

Middle Mississippian Cultures of the Illinois Valley

The Spoon River culture was one of the major sources for the original definitions of Middle Mississippian as something other than a ceramic tradition (e.g., see Griffin 1985:48–51) and it still fits well within most modern definitions (see Conrad 1989; Griffin 1985; Smith 1985b [compare Smith with section on Orendorf economy]). It is indicative of how archaeological perceptions can vary that Muller and Stephens (chap. 17) suggest that the Spoon River culture is not truly Middle Mississippian. Elsewhere Muller has suggested that the term *Mississippian* "return" to the status of the designation of a ceramic tradition (1978b:312). He also laments "fruitless discussions over the classifications of cultures in the Southeast" and indicates it seems fruitless to expend much energy debating whether or not a particular "complex" is Mississippian (1978b:313). Both positions are defensible; however, excluding what is arguably the most important manifestation in the formation of the term *Middle Mississippian* while continuing to use the term is not.

The concept of the Middle Mississippian is, of course, an archaeological construct and its applicability depends on the researcher's orientation. If one element of the definition gives the northern limit of Middle Mississippian as the "Cypress" line or the American Bottom or is based on environmental characteristics typically associated with the Southeast, then by definition none of the stratified, agricultural village peoples of Cahokia's northern hinterlands can be called Middle Mississippian. However, no one has devised a definition of Middle Mississippian that includes the late prehistoric societies of the Midsouth and excludes those of the Central Illinois River Valley on any but arbitrary grounds.

Although the Spoon River and La Moine River Mississippian variants are frontier Middle Mississippian cultures, *they are clearly not marginal*. Their basic economy, architecture, towns, and fortifications seem to have been quite similar to those of contemporary groups of the Midsouth. Although there is some dispute concerning the season of occupancy of the central town in the Larson community, the settlement patterns seem comparable to what is known of most undisputed Middle Mississippian societies. The tool assemblages are basically similar to those of the American Bottom, except bison scapula hoes were the norm during the Eveland and Orendorf phases of Spoon River. The assemblages may indicate less wealth to expend on chert digging tools or less need for such durable tools (at least in Spoon River), and of fewer craft specialists and more hunting. These minor differences do not warrant placing them on the other side of a major cultural divide.

Ceramics have traditionally been given considerable weight in assessing cultural relationships. Clearly the Illinois Valley vessel forms are what one would expect in a Middle Mississippian assemblage, since they are quite similar to those of the contemporary American Bottom phases at Cahokia. For example compare figures 6.6–6.8 to Milner et al.'s (1984) figure 64a–h for an illustration of the similarities between Orendorf and Moorehead phase ceramics (Fowler and Hall 1975; Milner et al. 1984). The major difference in the assemblages seems to be in the manner of decoration. For example, Ramey Incised and Mound Place Incised are quite rare at Orendorf as are shell-tempered cordmarked jars. Funnels seem to be absent. The apparent absence of effigy water bottles in Moorehead phase deposits is probably related to sample size.

Available evidence also suggests strong similarities in sociopolitical organization and religion between the two areas. Reference has already been made to the presence of mutually exclusive categories of marine shell and ceramics with burials in both areas during Orendorf phase times. Although the meaning of this dichotomy is not clear, it seems likely that it reflects similar beliefs in both cases. Judging from the burials and assuming that presence and absence of various classes of burial furniture indicate various societal positions, the Spoon River and La Moine River societies were nonegalitarian and had some inherited positions.

Available evidence also suggests that the people in the Central Illinois Valley were participants in the pan-southeastern religion often referred to as the Southern Cult or the Southeastern Ceremonial Complex (Conrad 1989). No members of the highest Middle Mississippian social stratum with whom the more elaborate items are normally associated have been found in the Illinois Valley, but numerous traits of this complex have been. These items have appeared at several sites of different periods throughout the region. Elements include the cross, circle and cross, sun symbols, forked eyes, elaborate falcons on plate rims, circular gorgets of copper and shell, at least two "falcon plates," ear plugs, maces, chert spatulates, dance swords, kneeling human pipes (including one of bauxite), a feline pipe, discoidals, marine shell dippers and ceramic imitations thereof, a copper-over-wood imitation chert blade, beaded forelocks, a human head effigy rattle headdress element, long-nosed and short-nosed god masquettes, and the bead ensemble associated with "falcon dancers."

Waring (1968:57–58) has briefly summarized the historic and prehistoric Middle Mississippian practice of renewal of fireplaces, buildings, square grounds, and mounds through the addition of layers of earth or sand, and Swanton (1928:546–614) has presented detailed descriptions of several Creek busks that mention cleaning the ashes from the old fireplaces at this time and several notations of relining them with earth (1928:581, 591) or sand (1928:605). A similar pattern is present in the renewal of the floor with a thick layer of pure loess and the multiple alternating thin layers of ash and sand in the hearth of the plaza-front building at Orendorf and the evidence of sand layers on the floors of other public buildings. Although renewal ceremonies were practiced widely throughout eastern North America, the only one outside of the Southeast of which I am aware that involves the cleaning of hearths is a war ceremony of the Pawnee (Murie 1981:149), a group with strong southeastern ties.

There is overwhelming evidence that the Spoon River and La Moine River cultures were Middle Mississippian with much more in common in every respect with similar groups in the Midwest, Midsouth, and Southeast than even with surrounding people in the upper Illinois River Valley (Brown et al. 1967; Fenner 1963; Langford 1927) or in Iowa. That there is some confusion on this point is a serious indictment of those of us who have been more resourceful at gathering data than at disseminating it. The rectification of this situation must take a higher priority in the future.

NOTES

1. These dates were provided through the courtesy of the late David A. Baerreis and the Center for Climatic Research of the University of Wisconsin and with the cooperation of the ISM, UMVARF, and the University of Illinois at Chicago (U of I-C).

2. I am indebted to Alan D. Harn for much of the data on Eveland phase burials in the Dickson Mound.

3. It is known that rectangular designs gradually displaced curvilinear ones on Spoon River ceramics, and it may be that they originated at Eveland insofar as the upper Central Illinois Valley is concerned. The increased frequency of rectangular designs in the selected sample from Garren may indicate that site is slightly later, even though the pottery is of high quality.

4. During the summer of 1971 Thomas E. Emerson and I tested the Orendorf site and initiated a project that continued seasonally until October 1978. This project ultimately excavated a total of nine hectares that included roughly seventy percent of two town sites and one-quarter of a third town. Institutions involved included the University of Wisconsin, the Upper Mississippi Valley Archaeological Research Foundation, and Western Illinois University (Esarey and Conrad 1981).

ACKNOWLEDGMENTS

In the field, laboratory, and library research for this paper and in the actual writing and production of it I have had the assistance of many people. Some of them must be thanked generically such as the people who gathered the raw data, the site owners, and the people and organizations who provided the financial and logistical support for much of the work. Institutions that provided access to the relevant materials under their care include the Dickson Mounds Branch of the Illinois State Museum, Lakeview Center Museum, and Western Illinois University.

Numerous colleagues have provided helpful comments on various versions of this paper, but Duane Esarey and Alan D. Harn must be singled out as the most helpful. Much of the Larson phase raw data used here was generated by Harn, and he has been very generous in his provision of data and with his constructive criticism. Duane Esarey and I have spent countless hours in stimulating and productive discussions on the topic and in the examination of collections in the last ten years. His careful reading of various drafts of this manuscript resulted in numerous changes that I feel improved it. Thomas E. Emerson with his familiarity with the archaeology of the American Bottom, the Central Illinois River Valley, and northwestern Illinois has been very helpful in my attempts to understand Central Illinois Valley Mississippian archaeology, but his greatest contribution has been in keeping my feet to the fire until I finally finished this essay. James A. Brown and James B. Griffin also provided helpful comments on drafts of this paper.

Insofar as the actual production of the manuscript is concerned, I am indebted to Melissa White and Sally Hodgson for word processing, Jeff Maddox and Scott Minor for cartography, Cindy Balek for drawing the original rim profiles, Susan Roop for inking the original ceramic drawings, Linda S. Alexander for preparing the final artwork, and to Tom Emerson, Duane Esarey, Mary Hanning, Barry Lewis, David Nolan, Kelvin Sampson, and Sharron Santure for editorial comments. Of course, any misuse of their assistance is totally my responsibility.

7

Comments on Subsistence, Seasonality, and Site Function at Upland Subsidiaries in the Spoon River Area: Mississippianization at Work on the Northern Frontier

ALAN D. HARN

Since the turn of the century, accumulating information on the developing socioeconomic impact of Cahokia on contemporaneous cultural systems throughout the Midwest has led researchers to focus on the phenomenon called Mississippian. As innovations with roots in the Cahokia Mississippian heartland spread to the north and west, all indigenous Woodland lifeways were affected to some degree. Much has been written about these patterns of Mississippianization in the upper Midwest (see Emerson, chap. 12), traditionally focusing on the identification of Cahokia-derived trade items and other more intangible elements of Mississippian cultural inspiration.

For the most part, emphasis has been placed on excavation and study of the larger Mississippian sites on the northern frontier, especially towns and large villages, so that the resulting information is frequently biased toward sites that most closely approximate the model of Mississippian usually synonymous with the terms *structured, urban,* and *agriculturalist.* Only in recent years has excavation of smaller site classes been undertaken to provide insights into the degree that Mississippian cultural organization pervaded patterns of daily living. Although there is clear evidence that Mississippian occupations in the Central Illinois River Valley participated wholeheartedly in many aspects of the Cahokia version of Mississippian (Conrad 1984), the degree of sociopolitical similarity that was shared between the regions and the degree that participation in the Mississippian movement affected their secular existence often seems to contrast markedly (Harn 1975b). Yet careful examination of the data often reveals that many of these differences may have provided adaptive flexibility that allowed the Mississippian system to prosper and function in areas that otherwise might have been marginal to its established or idealized subsistence, economic, and political strategies.

In the 1960s and early 1970s, explorations at several related mortuary and habitation sites provided the first insights into subsistence, seasonality, and settlement patterning for post–A.D. 1200 Mississippian populations in the Spoon River area of Illinois (Harn 1970, 1978). These studies suggested that local Larson phase Mississippian populations consisted of nucleations of interrelated sites that were sometimes seasonally distributed within the region. The resulting settlement pattern was viewed as representing an expediently interrelated extractive system that somewhat opposed the rigid sedentism and its complexly interrelated sociopolitical organization that is usually identified with the Cahokia Mississippian movement. In general, it was proposed that much of the local Larson phase population was dispersed into a variety of biotic zones during warmer weather and often consolidated at the central town during the colder months (Harn 1978, n.d.b).

Development of an explanatory model for this settlement pattern was greatly influenced by excavations at two major sites, Larson, the central town for the Spoon River core area, and Myer-Dickson, a nearby large village. Data from the smaller units of occupation, the "camps" and activity stations, were meager and generally insufficient to support the site function and seasonality hypotheses (Harn 1978:262).

New data relevant to life patterns at dispersed Mississippian homesteads on the northern Mississippian frontier have recently been generated by a program of excavation and detailed surface survey, mapping, and aerial photography at six small sites in the Illinois River bluff-edge zone between Coal and Dickson creeks some three kilometers upriver from the Larson site. Newly deforested and previously neither farmed nor exposed to relic collecting, these sites are without local precedence in their general material integrity and preservation of physical features. They represent what is probably the last opportunity in the Spoon River core area to analyze extinct cultural patterns that are unbiased by decades of selective artifact collecting and relatively undisturbed by farming and erosion.

The pristine condition of the various artifact scatters provides an unusual opportunity to isolate occupational patterning that frequently indicates restricted spatial aggregation of the various cultural components within each site. This was especially evident with the Mississippian occupations, as virtually all ceramics and a high percentage of triangular arrowpoints and end scrapers were clustered within areas of less than 500 square meters. Dark soil stains representing house basins were clearly evident within two of these artifact clusters, suggesting that similar concentrations might indicate the remains of discrete homesteads. Although none of the Norris Farms Project sites was totally excavated, complete activity units were exposed at three locations. Analyses of the artifacts, features, and physical composition of the sites have been completed, and sufficient faunal and floral analyses have been conducted to suggest preliminary subsistence trends and yield certain insights into the role Cahokia played in the Mississippianization of the Illinois River Valley.

The Norris Farms Archaeological Project

One farming corporation, The Norris Farm, owns some 5,000 hectares of land adjacent to Dickson Mounds, and with it more than seventy archaeological habitation sites and burial mounds. In the late 1970s, The Norris Farm initiated a project of levee construction and land reclamation that resulted in the development of nearly 250 hectares for row crops and exposed a number of new archaeological sites. Several of these sites were either destroyed or badly damaged. A coordinated effort between the landowner and Dickson Mounds Museum allowed detailed site survey work to be carried out over all reclaimed land tracts and excavation to be undertaken of the more critical or damaged areas. The Norris Farm's continued support and contribution of heavy equipment and equipment operators is greatly responsible for the success of the archaeological project. The work described herein was accomplished over a three-year period between 1980 and 1982.

The Setting

The study area is situated on the western blufftop of the Illinois River, three kilometers upstream from its confluence with Spoon River (fig. 7.1). It is bordered on the west by Dickson Creek and is bisected by Coal Creek, two first-order streams. The sites under consideration are positioned within the first 500 meters behind the Illinois River bluff edge on flat upland heavily dissected by ravines and small stream valleys. The two valleys are so near and dissection of the landscape is so advanced that a series of interconnected, narrow interfluvial ridges and plateau fingers have resulted, each generally less than 100 meters wide. The surface of the study area developed under forest and is a brownish yellow-grey silt loam of the Seaton-Fayette-Stronghurst association (Fehrenbacher, Walker, and Washer 1967; Smith et al. 1932). Agricultural productivity of this soil is very high. Second-growth oak, hickory, elm, black locust, and honey locust covered much of the area at the time of excavation, but oak and hickory probably dominated the vegetation during Mississippian times, as it still does in the uncultivated ravines.

Most of the small Mississippian sites located to the west of Coal Creek are positioned on the east edge of plateau fingers overlooking steep-sided ravines. Available tillable land adjacent to these occupations is usually restricted by bordering ravines to areas less than two hectares in extent. One site, Norris Farms No. 24, is positioned at the juncture of several drawheads, has a larger potential occupation area, and has an occupational scatter that suggests the presence of as many as four or five structures. All of these sites are positioned to the west of F^{v}66, a primary Mississippian village of perhaps eight hectares that fronts the Illinois River bluff. Across Coal Creek to the east, the Morton homesteads are situated about 800 meters southwest of the main Morton village on such a narrow ridgetop that very limited space for gardening would have been available. Except for the short span across the Coal Creek valley, none of these sites is more than 200 meters from any other. All are positioned along a 1.5 kilometer strip of blufftop representing approximately thirty-one hectares of habitable land surface.

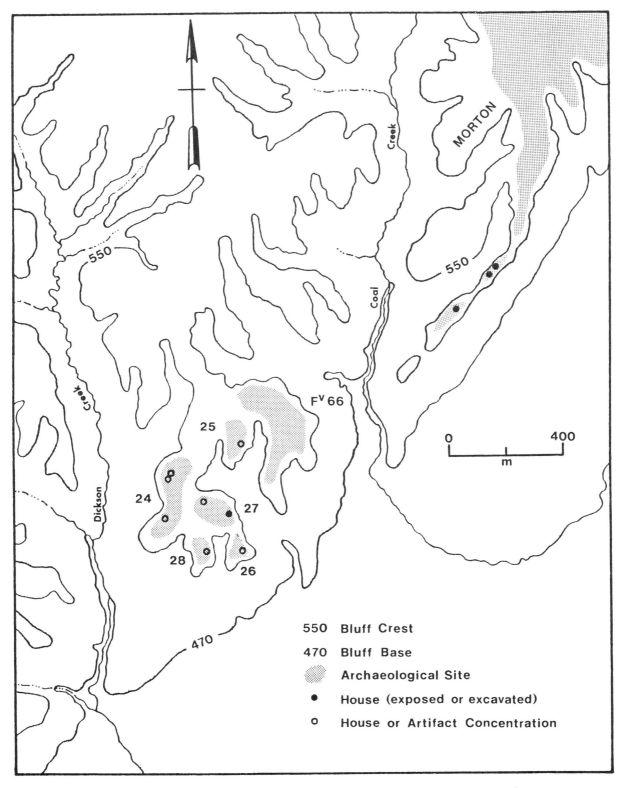

Figure 7.1. The Distribution of Certain Larson Phase Sites within the Norris Farms Archaeological Project

Methodology

Two sites exposed by land reclamation, Morton and F^{V}66, had been previously recorded and, in the latter instance, farmed for a number of years. The entire damaged area at the Morton mounds and habitation complex was excavated. No appreciable damage was evident in the case of F^{V}66 and—aside from pedestrian examination, aerial photographing, and a surface pickup—it received no further archaeological attention. The seven other sites recorded on the blufftop to the west of F^{V}66 were similarly examined and photographed; and detailed, controlled surface collections were made with piece-plot mappings of all tools, ceramics, and animal remains. Analysis of these assemblages suggests the presence of prolonged Archaic occupations, as well as short-term Woodland and Mississippian occupations.

Most of these sites were undamaged by land clearing and should remain relatively so since the area is under a minimum-tillage farming program. Portions of the Morton mound group and habitation area and a large section of the Norris Farms No. 26 site were damaged to a degree that salvage excavations were required. A third site, Norris Farms No. 27, was also excavated because it had a shallow house basin and nearby dump accumulation that would have been destroyed by even the most subtle of farming activities.

The Excavated Sites

MORTON MOUND GROUP AND HABITATION AREAS

The southern extension of the Morton site was damaged by bulldozing during the construction of a terrace to check heavy soil erosion across the bluff face. Portions of four Red Ocher burial mounds and a 335-meter strip of habitation area between Mounds 5 and 11 were heavily damaged (White and Seider 1980). In addition to various pit features and burials pertaining to earlier occupations, six Larson phase Mississippian storage pits and evidence of three houses or house construction sites were recorded. However, two of these apparently were abandoned early in their building stages, and the third was not excavated because it was protected from further construction disturbance. Faunal and floral recovery from this site was poor.

NORRIS FARMS NO. 26

Approximately sixty percent of the Norris Farms No. 26 site was deforested. Although occupational debris was scattered over the entire surface of the exposed area, excavation revealed that all subsurface Mississippian features were clustered in a small area of less than forty square meters on the eastern site edge. One, or perhaps two, house depressions lay in the undamaged wooded area to the east and southwest of this concentration but were not excavated. A series of twelve overlapping pit features under a large, shallow midden-filled depression were found that represent an uninterrupted cultural sequence from Sepo phase (Late Woodland) through Larson phase occupations. Artifact recovery and the quantity and preservation of faunal and floral remains were excellent.

NORRIS FARMS NO. 27

The entire area surrounding the structure at Norris Farms No. 27 was excavated, exposing the house, fourteen associated storage pits, three external cooking areas, and the dump site for the topsoil from the original house basin excavation. The structure was burned and had a large inventory of tools remaining in situ on the basin floor. The single internal storage pit was empty when the house burned, but the external features produced an excellent sample of well-preserved faunal and floral remains.

Distributional Patterns of Cultural Elements

PHYSICAL FEATURES AND TOOLS

Distributional patterns of certain cultural elements are shared by virtually all six small Mississippian sites under consideration. Among these are: restricted spatial aggregation of cultural materials; restricted availability of adjacent habitable land; physical placement of the site nucleus with respect to landform; presence of single or small numbers of structures; and an artifact inventory that includes similar ceramics, arrowpoints, knives, and scrapers. In addition to these items, all excavated sites produced storage facilities, fishing equipment, spokeshaves, slot abraders, paint pigment, and lithic reduction tools. Polished chert hoe flakes were found only at Norris Farms sites 26 and 27, but increased sample sizes from the other sites might produce additional horticultural elements. Inclusion of examples of tools held in common by two of the three excavated sites would significantly increase the scope of tasks performed. From the available tool inventory, it is postulated that butchering, processing, cooking, storing, woodworking, painting, and lithic reduction were common pursuits at all homesteads. Additionally, each small site served as a base for foraging, hunting, and fishing in nearby biotic zones.

FAUNAL AND FLORAL REMAINS

The low incidence of faunal and floral remains in surface collections generally negates broad intersite collations of subsistence data, only allowing comparisons among our three excavated sites. The small Morton site sample makes any interpretation speculative, although fish, mussels, and other aquatic fauna are represented in the sample, as are small amounts of deer, small mammals, birds, corn, and nutshell. Warm weather occupation is suggested by this assemblage.

At Norris Farms No. 26, the early Larson phase features contain abundant remains of aquatic resources, primarily fish. Bones of small animals, migratory birds, and some deer are also present, along with corn and nuts. Although fish are still present in large numbers, chronologically later Larson phase pit features suggest a steadily increasing emphasis on large animal procurement dominated by adult and late-adolescent whitetail deer. As the latest midden feature developed over the abandoned pit areas, greater emphasis seemed to be placed on deer hunting and nut gathering. Fish, small animals, birds, and corn are no longer present in any numbers. Although these criteria are interpreted as reflections of changing subsistence strategies, they may also reflect seasonal occupational emphases that shifted from late summer and early fall to late fall and winter. Neither can intrasite changes in waste disposal patterns be completely ruled out to explain these fluctuations.

Norris Farms No. 27 yields a contrasting occupational emphasis. Its house and associated pit features contained seeds of summer-ripening plants, bones of immature animals, fish, snakes, and a variety of other warm weather

fauna. The presence of a few nuts suggests that occupation probably extended into early fall. Horticulture was indicated by the presence of chert hoe flakes and small quantities of corn and beans. All cooking areas were external, typical of other summer residences of Spoon River Mississippian peoples (Harn 1974). As evidenced by the mature Larson phase ceramics, this occupation may have been the latest in the area, probably postdating the others by a generation or more and being contemporaneous with the main occupation of the Larson town.

GROUP SIZE, COMPOSITION, AND OCCUPATIONAL DURATION

Little can be said positively about group size, composition, and occupational duration for most of the sites. Without additional excavation, there is not sufficient evidence of what this particular settlement pattern represents. Although it is possible that all of these sites were contemporaneous, it is equally conceivable that they represent a continuum of succeeding short-term occupations by the same households. All sites may have been characterized by a single structure or, in one instance, a small group of structures occupied by nuclear families. The initial small house at Norris Farms No. 27, which was adequate for two or three individuals with 14.7 square meters of floor space, was enlarged to 26.3 square meters apparently as family size increased. In addition to adult males and females, children were probably present at all three excavated sites. The presence of children at these sites is based on the recovery of small ceramic jars, which are almost exclusively associated with children in nearby mortuary contexts (Harn 1980a, n.d.a).

At Morton, two of the three buildings were abandoned during construction, and the paucity of pit features and occupational debris would argue for a brief period of habitation. In contrast, Norris Farms No. 26 appears to have been sporadically occupied for several generations, perhaps by descendants of the original founders, based on a particular pattern of atypical jar rim configuration that appears to be evidenced throughout the developing Mississippian ceramic sequence. Although the house at Norris Farms No. 27 had been enlarged once, the associated occupational scatter was negligible, and the fourteen associated pits may suggest that new storage facilities were dug yearly over a period of four or five seasons.

Summary

The Norris Farms Project provides new insights into the structure of thirteenth-century Mississippian lifeways through analysis of surface features, artifact distributional

scatters, and excavations at six small Larson phase Mississippian settlements in the Spoon River area. Major activity units at three sites were exposed that could be viewed as essentially complete, but none of the sites was excavated in its entirety. Likewise, although final analysis has been completed of the artifactual materials, features, and physical composition of the sites, and sufficient faunal and floral remains have been examined to suggest certain preliminary trends, the final report of these investigations is still in preparation.

For the most part, these small bluff-edge Mississippian settlements probably represent seasonal reoccupations by nuclear families and existed for only a few years. If houses were rebuilt, they were apparently superimposed in their own basins, and there was no significant increase in group size through intragroup fission and lateral expansion of the homestead. Perhaps as a result of a particular strategic location, some sites experienced sporadic reoccupation through many generations with functional emphases shifting in response either to changes in available natural resources or to adjustments in nutritional requisites. The settlement pattern does not appear to be highly structured in terms of corporate organization. It is probable that such homestead dispersal in the vicinity of large villages simply represents a flexible compromise between the need to disperse in order to obtain suitable gardening plots and the need to retain access to the social aspects and protection of the larger settlement.

A primary requisite for a majority of the sites was immediate availability of a small, relatively flat land area. If these tracts were for gardening, the restrictive areas circumscribed by bordering ravines indicate that each family was probably responsible only for its own horticultural production. The spatial patterning of the occupational scatter at Norris Farms No. 27 may constitute a classic example for Spoon River Mississippian farmsteads. Most of the diagnostic artifacts occurred in close proximity to the burned house on the southeast site edge, with some scatter extending to the north and west along the ridge margins. These extensions partially encircled an area of perhaps 0.25 hectares that was nearly devoid of tools and had no ceramic scatter. A ground-stone celt, broken at the bit, lay at the eastern edge of this barren tract, and hoe flakes occurred along its south margin. Viewed collectively, these items may indicate that a portion of the flat had been cleared and used for gardening. Had this tract been in mature forest, clearing would have involved a significant labor expenditure, perhaps further underscoring the importance of horticulture to the local group.

Although gardening activities may have been associated with most of the homesteads, a wide variety of hunting and foraging activities was concomitantly pursued. Ceremonial equipment and related items of ornamentation are notably absent in the artifact assemblages, and indications are that the physical composition of the tool kits is more restricted than at the larger sites. Yet the artifact assemblages in evidence at these six small habitation loci support a previous proposal (Harn n.d.b) that a wide variety of technological activities transpired at small bluff-edge Mississippian sites. They were not just farmsteads. Such technological variability probably correlates directly with the central positioning of these sites among a number of natural resource zones. Great functional variability would not be expected at bottomland or interior upland camps, for example, because of the specifically restricted natural resource availability.

Analysis of these small sites reveals that, although their function seems to differ markedly from the "structured, urban, agriculturalist" concept usually associated with the Cahokia Mississippian movement, their function and purpose do not appear to differ significantly from similarly sized occupations peripheral to the Cahokia site itself (Emerson, Milner, and Jackson 1983:179–207; Milner and Williams 1984:187–200). The data support the interpretation that adaptive strategies on the northern Mississippian frontier that do not include intensive agriculture and massive population consolidation are equally as important in the perpetuation of the Mississippian movement as those that do. Unintentional as they might have been, such strategies would have allowed indigenous populations the cultural comfort of retaining established subsistence patterns to build upon while they adapted other attractive elements of the Mississippian movement to their lifeway. Allowing marginal groups to "ease into" mainstream Mississippian probably resulted in a much greater conversion rate among the indigenous populations than did any structured sociopolitical reformation.

Although the nuclear families occupying the Norris Farms homesteads were spatially isolated and domestically independent, they were undoubtedly participants in a broader sociopolitical network. The nearby F^{V}66 village may have served as a seasonal base for the dispersed early Larson phase Mississippian homesteads between Coal and Dickson creeks, whereas the larger Morton village site may have functioned similarly for those sites to the east. However, both F^{V}66 and the western scatter of homesteads could have been extensions of the major Morton site. Even less clear is the relationship of these site groupings to the primary ceremonial center at Larson. The focus of activities at the Norris Farms Project homesteads and their seasonal variability of occupation are compatible with those projected for Myer-Dickson, the only excavated village near the Larson site, while contrasting markedly with the occupation of that town (Harn 1974, 1978, n.d.b). However, only Norris Farms No. 27 seems late enough to have been contemporaneous with the main occupation of Larson. Recent excavations at the Morton village produced a number of burned early Larson phase houses that are probably coeval with the five other Norris Farms homesteads under consideration (Santure, Harn, and Esarey 1990). However, in direct contrast to the situation at the Myer-Dickson village, internal house features and faunal and floral remains at Morton indicate year-round occupancy. In this light, it is possible that the ancillary settlements in the Morton site area represent seasonal occupational dispersal from the main village, much as villages were dispersed from the town during the later Larson phase.

It is probable that the early Larson phase settlement system evidenced around the Morton site in the Coal and Dickson creeks vicinity waned before the rise of the Larson site as the primary Mississippian center for the Spoon River core area. Indeed, it is conceivable that the erection of the fortified town at Larson resulted via population relocation from the Morton site vicinity, possibly in response to increased levels of social stress. Although support is thus offered for specific functional and seasonal aspects of our initial settlement pattern model (Harn 1978, n.d.b), conclusive evidence for the myriad of intersite social and economic relationships will only be generated by examining a broader spectrum of ancillary sites in a variety of other physiographic situations throughout the Larson site area.

Previous studies have demonstrated many direct Cahokia Mississippian influences that underlay the Mississippianization of the Central Illinois River Valley (see Conrad, chap. 6), but most were influenced by excavations undertaken at the larger ceremonial centers and mortuary sites. Such biased data have sometimes portrayed the secular Spoon River Mississippian existence as either mirroring Cahokia or as differing significantly from that of coeval occupations in that region. However, the continued dependence by researchers on the tripartite concept of structured corporate society, urbanism, and agriculture as a barometer of relative Mississippianness (Muller and Stephens, chap. 17) has a tendency to mask the identification of many more subtle post–A.D. 1200 Mississippian cultural influences throughout the Cahokia Mississippian frontier. That individual elements of this tripartite concept are not always present even in classic Mississippian occupations within the central Cahokia sphere is now being recognized (Emerson, Milner, and Jackson 1983:179–207; Milner and Williams 1984:187–200). Thus the widely variable Mississippian settlement patterns of the Illinois River Valley are not unique among occupations on the northern Mississippian frontier.

As long as there is variation in landform, habitat, available adaptive niches, human populations, and social hostilities, one should expect an infinite range of variability in the interrelationships between them that are ultimately reflected in local settlement, subsistence, and sociopoliti-

cal patterns. Thus the primary differences between the small Spoon River Mississippian settlements under discussion and similar sites in the Cahokia sphere resulted more from casual adjustments to differing landscapes than from structured societal divergencies. The kinds of activities pursued in both areas were quite similar despite their often differing physiographic locations selected for bases of operations. Both groups were carrying on established Mississippian traditions that were being adapted to local environments in ways that would best minimize energy expenditure.

Differences in social organization and complexity between the Cahokia and Spoon River areas exist, but how important should these differences be viewed in determining relative Mississippianness? The degree that peoples in both areas were structurally organized as competitive cultural entities probably pertained more to their individual need or lack of it to defend or maintain support territories (Smith, ed. 1978) than it pertained to their collective interest in being recognized as classic or less classic Mississippians. Similarly, the somewhat differing levels of sociopolitical organization between the two areas is probably indicative of differences in dealing with differing levels of internal social order.

The seasonal variability of site occupation, dispersed settlement patterns, and lower levels of horticultural production in the Illinois Valley are often viewed as deviations from the Mississippian norm (see Muller and Stephens, chap. 17). However, recent work at smaller site classes in the vicinity of Cahokia now complements data from the Norris Farms Project to suggest a degree of similarity between the two areas in terms of variable subsistence base, settlement dispersal, and seasonal occupation that is equitable with their previously recognized close sociopolitical relationship. Such findings tend to further diminish the perceived differences between Cahokia and other Mississippian occupations on its northern frontier.

ACKNOWLEDGMENTS

Comments on this paper were provided by Michael Wiant and Bonnie Styles of the Illinois State Museum. Analysis and preliminary observations of the faunal remains from several Norris Farms Project sites were provided by Bonnie Styles and Neal Woodman. Floral remains were analyzed by Francis King and Katherine Eggan. Access to the sites was generously provided by the landowner, The Norris Farm. Considerable volunteer time on the project was contributed by many staff members of Dickson Mounds Museum and the Illinois State Museum, and by Matthew Greby, our archaeological neighbor. Especially acknowledged are the efforts of Nicholas Klobuchar, often the sole crew member on the project. Funding for portions of the research was provided by the Illinois State Museum Society.

8

The Apple River Mississippian Culture
of Northwestern Illinois

THOMAS E. EMERSON

The Apple River Focus of northwestern Illinois has played a central role in discussions of the northward spread of Middle Mississippian culture and the relationship of Mississippian and Oneota cultures in the Upper Mississippi River Valley. Early excavations by the University of Chicago at such sites as Mills Village, John Chapman, and Savannah Proving Ground produced collections of Mississippian materials that provided the basis for a series of often conflicting interpretations on the cultural associations of the Apple River Focus. The focus has been variously viewed as (1) a product of cultural contact between Middle Mississippian and proto-Oneota groups (Bennett 1945:viii), (2) contact between late persisting Trappist groups and fully developed Oneota cultures (Bennett 1945:viii), (3) the in situ evolution of a

Middle Mississippian group into an Upper Mississippian one (Griffin 1960b:835–38), and (4) most recently, as an early Oneota manifestation influenced by southern Mississippian groups (Stoltman 1983:240).

Recent work by the Center for American Archeology (CAA) at the Lundy site (11Jd140) in Jo Daviess County on the Apple River and a reexamination of the University of Chicago collections have provided new insights into the nature of the Apple River Mississippian culture. This paper summarizes the new data from the Lundy site, reviews the previous work by the University of Chicago, examines past interpretations, and presents a new perspective of the Mississippian culture in the Apple River region.

Environment

The Apple River Valley is in the extreme southern portion of the Driftless Zone. The zone (Martin 1965) covers the extreme northwestern corner of Illinois, the northeastern and southeastern fringes of Iowa and Minnesota, and the majority of southwestern Wisconsin. Almost 38,800 square kilometers are encompassed within its boundaries. As is implicit in its name, this zone was untouched by the Late Pleistocene glacial activities that so strongly modified the surrounding landscape. Thus the Driftless Zone with its weathered topography of deep river valleys, rocky precipices, and narrow hogback ridges is physiographically unique in the Midwest.

The vegetation patterns of the Driftless Zone reflect its

distinctive and diverse topography. The southern boundary of the zone lies along the northern edge of the Prairie Peninsula (Transeau 1935), which was dominated by prairies of giant bluestem grasses. It is a region characterized by meadows, partially forested floodplains, mixed forest hillslopes, and a scattering of xeric blufftop forests and hill prairies (Curtis 1959).

The southern portion of the Driftless Zone falls into Cleland's (1966:11–12) Illinoian Biotic Province. It is clear that a vast and extremely diverse faunal and floral assemblage was present for prehistoric exploitation in this zone and its surrounding environs.

Mississippian Site Excavations

THE APPLE RIVER FOCUS SITES

In 1932 the University of Chicago tested three Mississippian sites on the Apple River near Hanover in Jo Daviess and Carroll counties, Illinois (fig. 8.1)—Mills Village (11Jd11), John Chapman Village (11Jd12), and Savannah Proving Ground Village (11Ca226). The analysis of these excavations was later undertaken by Bennett (1945). In his opinion, the recovered material included an inseparable mixture of Middle and Upper Mississippian traits. Because these represented two separate phases in the Midwestern Taxonomic System, Bennett was faced with a problem of classification. To solve it he created a "floating focus," which grouped all of these sites into the Apple River Focus.

Mills Village was the most important site tested during these investigations. Located on a raised spur of land enclosed by a meander of the Apple River, it contains a village area, a truncated pyramid mound, and two conical mounds, all of which can be associated with the Mississippian occupation. Slightly to the west of these features are a large circular depression and a string of seventy-two conical mounds of uncertain cultural affiliation (fig. 8.2).

As part of their research at Mills, the University of Chicago excavated a three-meter-wide trench through the pyramid mound (Mound 1). This was expanded to a width of ten meters in the central flat top area of the mound. Although badly eroded, the mound still rose 2.5 meters above the surrounding field. Its base covered an area about twenty-four meters in diameter and the flat top about eleven meters. Excavations revealed that before the mound was constructed the topsoil had been removed down to the sandy yellow subsoil. Ten pit features were found, apparently originating at the surface of this sandy layer, although some may have been dug after a layer of mound fill had been deposited. These deep round pits contained village refuse such as flint chips, potsherds, mussel shells, and faunal remains.

On this sandy subsoil base, sand, loam, and clay mound strata formed more or less distinct layers and were overlain by a layer of black clay and loam in which some evidence for packing was observed. Above this black layer and forty centimeters below the present surface, a hard, yellow clay floor was encountered. Although there seemed to be some evidence for the burning of a structure at this level, no post molds were found. The last stratum from the top of the floor to the present ground surface consisted of a hard loamy clay. Village debris such as faunal remains (deer, beaver, fish, turtle, dog, and bird), eight-rowed corn, ash lenses, lithic material (including two unnotched triangular points), bone im-

plements, and a *Busycon perversum* columella pendant were found throughout the mound fill. Also recovered in the fill and apparently in the refuse pits were "randomly distributed" sherds of a Mississippian nature that Bennett included with the village material for the purpose of analysis (1945:134).

About thirty meters west of the truncated pyramid mound is a large conical mound (Mound 2) through which pioneer archaeologist W. Nickerson excavated a four-meter-wide trench sometime between 1895 and 1901. Bennett's (1945:135) description of this mound and its internal construction are taken from Nickerson's detailed notes. As in the case of Mound 1, the topsoil had been removed and Mound 2 construction began on the sandy yellow subsoil. The subsoil was covered in the center of the mound by a thin irregular clay floor, which was penetrated by a line of postholes apparently representing one wall of a rectangular structure. An irregular pit in the mound center contained assorted debris. Clay and sand strata formed the overlying mound fill. This, in turn, was covered by a hard, black clay stratum. Loamy clay overlaid the black clay and formed the final covering of the mound.

Mound 2 measured three meters high and eighteen by twenty meters at its base. It may have been a truncated pyramid mound that was eroded to a conical form, but Bennett was not able to test this hypothesis in his analysis of Nickerson's notes. Village debris was found throughout the mound fill and it included mussel shells, shell-tempered pottery, faunal remains, and lithics. Nickerson noted that at two points above the clay floor he found matting and an organic stain that he postulated may represent the remains of burials.

The conical mound (Mound 3) is located twenty-four meters to the south of Mound 2. Although mostly eroded away by the river, Nickerson observed that its features were similar to those of Mound 2 (Bennett 1945:136).

Slightly to the west of Mound 2 is a large circular depression, which measures 2.7 meters deep and forty-four meters in diameter. Bennett (1945:136) points out that this may represent a borrow pit used in the construction of the large mounds or it may represent a Woodland feature such as the elliptical enclosure at the nearby Aiken Group. Although the University of Chicago did not examine the depression, they did excavate several of the seventy-two small conical mounds to the west of the Mills Village site. These mounds were constructed on the sandy subsoil from a homogeneous sandy loam fill. They contained large quantities of flint chips and shell-tempered pottery identical to that associated with Mills Village.

Based on surface debris, the village occupation area ap-

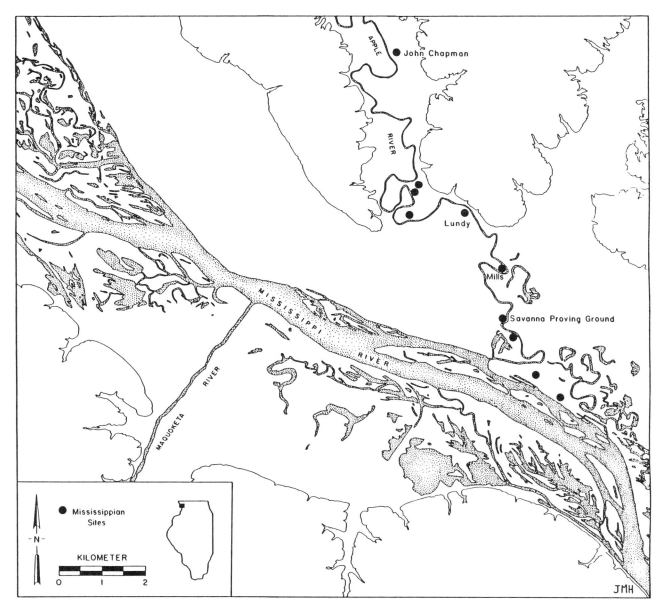

Figure 8.1. Mississippian Sites on the Apple River

pears to begin about thirty meters to the east of Mound 1 and to cover the entire end of the spur, an area of about 4,000–5,000 square meters (fig. 8.2). Nine test pits, each 1.5 by 3 meters, were excavated in the village area by the University of Chicago crews. On examining the placement of these tests, it appears that all were on the periphery of the village occupation. This may account for why largely undifferentiated midden deposits were encountered in the excavations. Three refuse pits, two irregular fireplaces, a cache of mussel shells, and "a house floor

or pottery making area" were excavated. The house floor, located in Test Pit 6, consisted of sand, clay, and charcoal "beaten together." A prepared, baked oval fire basin and a burned, irregular hearth filled with ashes were also present. Although a few scattered postholes were noted, it was not possible to delineate a structure outline. All of the test pits were excavated in 7.5-centimeter levels to determine if stratigraphy was present. None was discovered. Although not specifically stated, it appears that some of the test pits revealed midden deposits up to 0.75

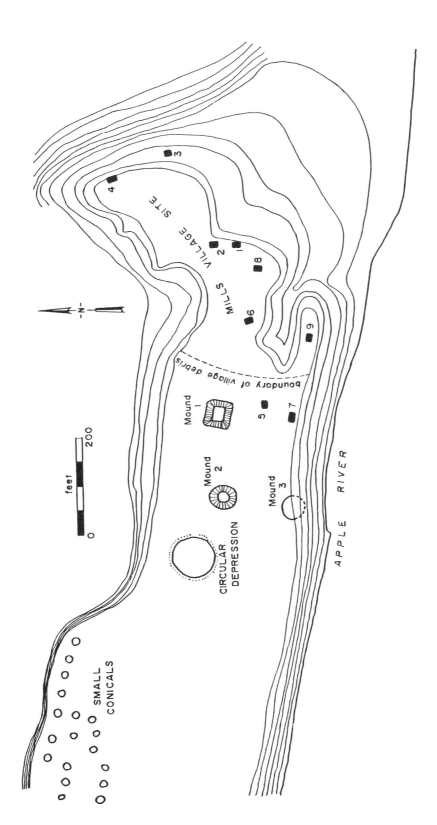

Figure 8.2. The Mills Village Site. University of Chicago test squares are shown in black (modified from Bennett 1945: fig. 22).

meters thick. At least some of the refuse pits reached 1.7 meters in depth (R. Adams, field notes for week ending Wednesday, 27 July 1932).

As mentioned earlier, Bennett (1945) interpreted the ceramics from the Apple River Focus sites as representing a mixture of Upper and Middle Mississippian stylistic traits. At the Mills site, it is specifically stated that there is no differentiation between the ceramics in the different strata, but rather there was a homogeneous deposit of shell-tempered pottery.

In terms of the traits (table 8.1) listed by Bennett, the dominant vessel at Mills was a jar with either an everted or outcurving, undecorated rim (fig. 8.3). The abundance of plainware sherds is borne out by Bennett's figures. He lists 1,615 plain, 100 incised, and 96 cordmarked sherds. Incision as a mode of decoration was present in all jar rim and body categories (Bennett's use of the term *incision,* although followed here, is more aptly viewed as trailing). Incised patterns on angular shouldered vessels were limited to the area above the shoulder; the patterns sometimes extended below the shoulder on vessels with rounded shoulders. According to Bennett (1945:141), the most common incised motif is concentric festoons or arcs on the shoulder. A variation of this consists of several arcs enclosing a panel of vertical lines. However, an examination of the illustrations of sherds from Mills, indicates that at least some had incised chevron motifs (e.g., pl. 25e, f and pl. 26b, i).

Cordmarking was the least prevalent surface treatment.

Table 8.1. Ceramics Recovered by the University of Chicago from the Mills Village Site (modified from Bennett 1945:139–41)

JAR RIMS	Everted	Outcurving	Thickened Upper Rim-Lip
Cord paddled	2	3	0
Plain	34	29	12
Incised	11	5	4
	47	37	16
JAR SHOULDERS	Angular	Rounded	No Shoulder
Plain	6	3	3
Incised	17	3	7
Cord paddled	0	0	2
Small fragments	3	0	0
	26	6	12

BOWLS – 18 large, shallow bowls, with very thick to thin vessel walls; smoothed interiors, and rough exteriors; similar to "salt pan" types 4 small to medium bowls; smoothed interior and exterior.
PLATE – One possible convex-rimmed, plate sherd.
WIDE-NECKED WATER BOTTLE – Sherds from 2 vessels.
MINIATURE VESSELS – 5 wide-necked bottles and 2 bowls.

Other jar characteristics consisted of the predominance of rounded lips. On some sherds of thickened rim variety, a flattened lip was present. Handles included six of the strap kind, four loops, and three intermediate. Two strap handles had earlike projections at the junction of the handle and rim. Four lugs were identified on everted rims.

Only five sherds showed the presence of a red slip; each of those sherds represents a distinct vessel. One was a clenched fist, bean pot handle with a rivet attachment. Three were bowls, two of which bore incised, cross-hatched designs. Although not distinguished as such in the text (Bennett 1945:139), from the label on plate 29c, it would appear that the two cross-hatched, red-slipped "bowl" sherds are actually beakers. The last vessel was a wide-mouth jar with an overturned lip (thickened).

All of the red-slipped sherds have a very fine shell-tempering. This is distinct from most of the Mills sherds, which have what Bennett (1945:138) calls Paste Type 1, typified by large shell particles and a moderately dense, laminated paste. The tempering of the red-slipped sherds resembles Bennett's Type 2 paste with its fine shell particles and dense, compact texture. Type 2 paste occurs in two vessel forms at Mills, the small bowl and the wide-necked water bottle. In each case, it is the only paste used for these forms. Bennett (1945:138) suggests that the temper difference is due to a distinction between utilitarian ware (Type 1) and decorative ware (Type 2).

In addition to the excavated material, the university field parties also examined ceramics collected from the Mills site by the family who owned it. Included in this collection were several kinds of artifacts not found by the excavators. These include fragments of two four-lobed jars, a rimsherd with an incised, interlocking rectilinear scroll motif, several sherds decorated with a scroll motif, two loop handles, as well as some pipe bowl fragments (Bennett 1945:144).

Of the nonceramic artifacts recovered, projectile points and scrapers were by far the most common (Bennett 1945:142–44). A total of thirty-one small triangular points were found. Only two of these were notched, one side notched and one side and basally notched. The remainder were simple, generally isosceles points. A total of fifty-one scrapers were found, most of which (n = 41) were snub nosed. Few knives, bone tools, and abraders were found, as were some *typical* Mississippian items such as shell hoes (n = 1), celts (n = 4), and earspools (one-half of convex copper earspools perforated in the center). The surface collections made by the Mills family contained two expanding-blade chert hoes, a single axe, an equal-arm, obtuse-angle pipe of sandstone, two enlarged head drills, and a knife.

The Mills site is the largest and most important Mis-

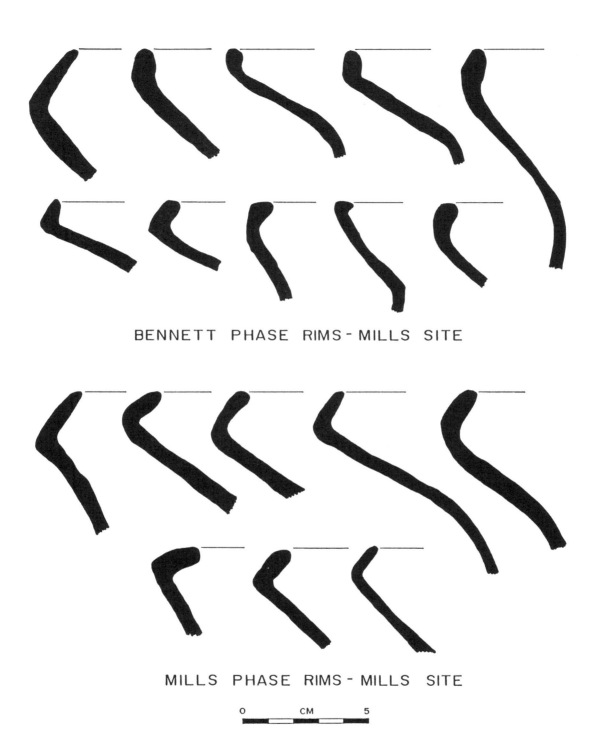

Figure 8.3. Bennett and Mills Phase Rim Profiles from the Mills Village Site

sissippian site on the Apple River, but information is also available from two other local sites that were tested by the University of Chicago. The John Chapman Village site is located 4.8 kilometers north of Mills on the east bank of the Apple River. This site, which was interpreted to be a campsite or farmstead, is located between two shallow gullies that lead from the bluff to one of the river terraces. Seven test pits revealed two circular, stone fireplaces containing bones, shell, and a deposit of burned mussel shells, near which a shell hoe was recovered.

The John Chapman site ceramics (fig. 8.4; table 8.2) are similar to the Mills material and show an even heavier emphasis on plainware, with 654 plain surfaced, 27 cord-paddled, and 9 red-slipped (two of which are incised rims) sherds. Although few incised sherds were found in the excavations (Bennett 1945: pl. 23), a local amateur collection contained several sherds with concentric festoons and chevrons (Bennett 1945: pl. 25). Paste Type 2 is again the minority paste (10 sherds compared with 672 of Type 1) and is found in the red-slipped sherds, the bowl form and the bottles.

Few nonceramic artifacts were recovered. The specimens include a number (not given) of large isosceles points, four snub-nosed scrapers, one shell hoe, and one incised, stone (bauxite?) earspool.

Recent work at the John Chapman site by Ferrell Anderson has produced evidence that raises questions concerning the earlier interpretations of the site (personal communication, 1985). Anderson's observations and surface collections indicate that the site covers several hectares, has a fairly high density of materials, and may contain a plowed-down mound. Potsherds are homogeneous and include several hundred body sherds and several dozen low-rimmed, jar rim sherds. Jar shoulder decorations include a weeping eye, feathered scroll, nested arcs, and multiple, vertical, parallel line motifs. Vessel shoulders are equally divided between smoothed and smoothed-over, cordmarked surfaces. All of the observed shoulders are angular. The body sherds are predominantly plain, but about one-quarter are cordmarked. Few polished, red-slipped, or trailed body sherds occur.

The lithic assemblage includes twenty triangular points (six notched), fifteen end scrapers, and three celt fragments. The site has also reportedly yielded many shell beads and a *Busycon* shell "cup" with the columella removed.

It is clear from Anderson's information that the site is not the simple farmstead that earlier investigators envisioned. John Chapman appears to represent at least a multihectare village and may be a single mound center.

The other Apple River Focus site is the Savannah Proving Ground Village site, which lies about 2.4 kilometers southeast of the Mills site. Eight test pits were excavated by the University of Chicago here, but little material was found and the site was interpreted as an occupation of short duration. The ceramic assemblage (table 8.3) consists mostly of jars with everted rims and incised decoration. Handles were mainly of the loop variety. Some lugs, which were similar to those at Mills but not quite so

Table 8.2. Ceramics Recovered by the University of Chicago from the John Chapman Village Site (modified from Bennett 1945:147–48)

JAR RIMS	Everted	Outcurving	Thickened Upper Rim-lip
Cord paddled	1	0	1[a]
Plain	4	11	13[b]
	5	11	14

a – erect rim;   b – slightly outcurving rims.

JAR SHOULDERS	Angular	Rounded
Plain	7	9
Incised	1	0
Cord paddled	3	2
	11	11

OTHER JAR ATTRIBUTES – Lips are predominantly rounded; a few are flattened. The collection includes one loop handle and one intermediate strap handle.

BOWLS – 8 sherds of large shallow bowls with smoothed interiors and rough exteriors; Paste Type 1; lips rounded, and slightly thickened; one specimen has smoothed-over cord-paddling on exterior.

SEED BOWL – 1 sherd of Type 1 paste, but carefully smoothed.

VARIANT BOWL – 1 crude Paste Type 2 specimen; wide, flat rim; lip has projection shaped like a terrace with two steps.

BOTTLES – 4 specimens, form seems to be a short, wide necked vessel with thinned lips; 1 red-slipped sherd has a thickened lip; 2 polished, black sherds are of Paste Type 2; 1 sherd is Type 1.

Table 8.3. Ceramics Recovered by the University of Chicago from the Savannah Proving Ground Site (modified from Bennett 1945:150–51)

JAR RIMS	Everted	Outcurving
Cord paddled	3	0
Plain	1	0
Incised	11	2 (small)
	5	11

JAR SHOULDERS	Angular	Rounded
	2	–

OTHER JAR ATTRIBUTES – Lips are rounded. The collection includes five loop handles and two intermediate strap/loop handles. Lugs are flange-like protrusions on vessel lips; they are similar to, but less developed than, the lip-lugs of the Mills and Aztalan pottery.

BOWL – Plain, wide, shallow bowl, similar to the Mills and Chapman "Form 4."

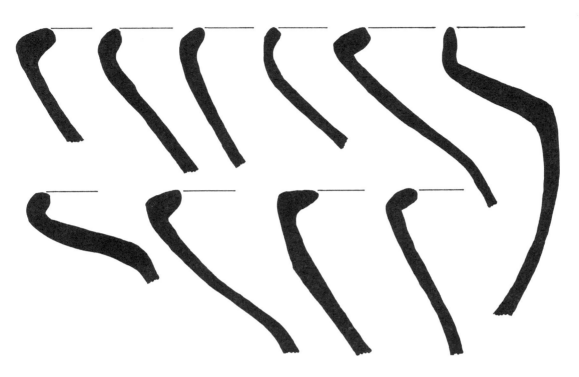

BENNETT PHASE RIMS - LUNDY SITE

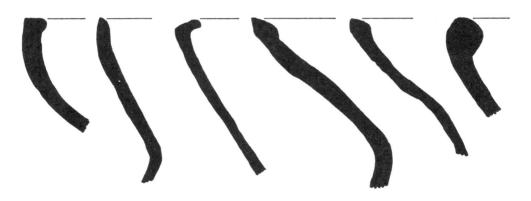

BENNETT PHASE RIMS - JOHN CHAPMAN VILLAGE

0   CM   5

Figure 8.4. Bennett Phase Rim Profiles from the Lundy and John Chapman Village Sites

prominent, were present. The most common motifs were double line festoons with convex areas filled with vertical lines. These are often impressed to the extent that cameos are produced on the vessel interior. One red-slipped bowl sherd (Bennett 1945: pl. 29d) is decorated with an open cross-hatching similar to that found at Mills. Most (n = 537) of the sherds are plain, seventy-six are incised, and eight are cordmarked. One sherd was decorated with a "feathered" simple scroll (Bennett 1945: pl. 27a). All of the recovered ceramics have Type 1 paste.

Four snub-nosed scrapers, a large, crude, triangular point with side and basal notching, the tip of a triangular point, two knives, a drill, and an abrader comprised the entire collection of nonceramic material from the site.

THE LUNDY SITE

The Lundy site (11Jd140) is located on a small ridge in the floodplain of the Apple River two kilometers northwest of the Mills Village site and three and one-half kilometers upstream from the confluence of the Apple with the Mississippi River. The occupation area, based on surface debris, covers about 1.4 hectares along the crest and slopes of a one-meter-high ridge. The northern end of this ridge is truncated by the present channel of the Apple River.

Initial surface collections at the site (Edging, Meinholz, and Berres 1982) revealed a high density of artifacts. Almost 6,000 items were recovered from a fairly restricted area. In addition to numerous shell-tempered ceramics, the collection yielded many triangular projectile points, scrapers, drills, bifaces, hammerstones, cores, and abraders.

Because the site locus was to be affected by a bridge and road relocation project, a series of archaeological excavations were carried out there in 1982. CAA crews opened an L-shaped excavation block (Block I) of about eighty square meters along the central ridge crest and exposed a structure and twenty-six pit features. Twenty of these features were excavated before freezing soil conditions forced an end to the work. During the following summer, the remaining six features were removed by volunteers from the Western Illinois University field school. In 1983 CAA crews opened an additional 1,000-square-meter area to the north of Block I. Block II revealed two separate clusters of pit features, one containing nine features, and the other ten. The excavations at the Lundy site yielded a total of one structure and forty-five pit features, all of which are associated with the Mississippian component.

Structure 1 was first recognized by the presence of a large, irregular, house basin stain in the northern end of Block I. Portions of the basin, which had been dug on the crest of the ridge, had been destroyed by plowing. When the remainder of the house fill was removed, a rectangular wall-trench structure, measuring 3.4 by 5.4 meters, was discovered. The wall of the structure had been constructed by excavating wall trenches into which individual posts had been driven, often to a point well below the base of the trench. In areas where the wall trench had been removed by plowing or excavation, only these individual post molds still remained. A second set of post molds were exposed when the floor level of the first structure was cleared. These single-post walls paralleled the southeastern and southwestern walls of the wall-trench structure and formed an interior space with an area of 3.5 by 2.5 meters. It is not known whether these single post walls represent a former structure that was later expanded or are interior walls of the larger wall-trench structure.

The excavated pit features are primarily shallow basins ranging up to two meters long and from five to twenty-five centimeters deep. About two-thirds of the features fall into this category and characteristically contain low densities of archaeological debris. These pits may be associated with processing rather than storage. The remaining pits are large and deep with straight or slightly belled walls and flat to rounded bottoms. These features, which range in depth from about forty-five to eighty-five centimeters and in width from about one to one and one-half meters, probably represent storage pits. Such features usually contain a high density of archaeological debris, often displaying multiple shell, ash, charcoal, or bone lenses.

Only the analyses of the Lundy ceramic and faunal assemblages have been completed to date. Although the statements made here should therefore be viewed as preliminary, it is unlikely that future analysis will substantially alter the conclusions presented here. Among the recovered artifacts are several hundred chipped- and ground-stone tools, several thousand pieces of chert debitage, and over 2,000 shell-tempered potsherds. Plain, triangular projectile points and snub-nosed scrapers are the most common stone tools. Other items include bits of copper and galena, a copper bead, a stone ear plug, and bone tools such as awls and a fishhook.

Preservation of organic remains was moderately good and a substantial number of both faunal and floral remains were recovered. Examination of these remains (Colburn 1990) indicates that the bones of deer and elk were plentiful, fish were common, and bird and small to medium mammals were present. Of special interest was the recovery of bison long bones, indicating a limited exploitation of that species. Shellfish must have been frequently collected since a number of the excavated pits had large shell lenses in their fill. Maize, squash, and nuts were noted to be present in the floral assemblage (Nancy Asch, personal communication, 1986).

The potsherds are the crucial portion of the Lundy site assemblage for understanding the development of Mississippian culture in the Apple River area and its relationship to the surrounding region. The author has examined all of the ceramics recovered from the Lundy site and the trends described below are based on the analysis of rim and shoulder sherds of 136 vessels.

Viewed as a whole, the ceramic assemblage is almost completely shell-tempered. The temper particles range in size from fine to coarse. Most sherds appear to have been smudged black on their exterior surfaces, and the remainder have a reddish tan surface. Several sherds are red slipped. Shoulders are generally more angular than rounded. The overall appearance of the ceramic assemblage resembles that found in the American Bottom during the Stirling and early Moorehead phases.

Three vessel forms—jars, bowls, and seed jars—have been identified. Jars comprise 86% of all vessels, 12.5% are bowls, and the remaining 1.5% are seed jars. Jar rim forms have been segregated into three categories (defined in Emerson and Jackson 1984): inslanting, flared, and straight (fig. 8.4). Inslanting rims are present on 40% of the Lundy site jars. Lip forms on these inslanting jars are more often everted or extruded than rolled. Of the remaining jars, 38% had flared rims, while 22% were straight. This distribution of rim forms compares favorably with assemblages from Stirling phase sites in the American Bottom.

Although the Lundy site jar rim forms are clearly similar to the Stirling forms to the south, there are a number of stylistic differences that clearly distinguish the ceramics of the two regions. Perhaps the most distinctive of these is the use of cordmarking in the Lundy assemblage. About seven percent of the Lundy site jars are cordmarked on their bodies or shoulders. Most commonly, the jars are cordmarked to the shoulder, which is then smoothed and left plain or is decorated with incised motifs. Cordmarking is sometimes noted on the actual shoulder, but it is always at least partially smoothed over. Another characteristic of the Lundy assemblage is the extensive use of incising. Thirty percent of the jars have incised shoulders (Stirling phase assemblages probably have fewer than ten percent incised jars in an average collection). The incised decorations are dominated by rectilinear motifs, most commonly nested chevrons, but occasionally with horizontal lines linking them together. Curvilinear motifs such as scrolls are uncommon. Another decorative trait in the Lundy assemblage is the use of lip notching. Nine percent of the jar lips are notched. These notches range mainly from sharp angular indentations to occasional, broad, shallow depressions.

The overall impression of the Lundy ceramic collection is of a ceramic tradition in which Middle Mississippian Stirling phase vessel forms were being decorated in a locally developed style. This local style includes the common use of incising on shoulders, cordmarking on jar bodies, and lip notching.

The estimated age of the Lundy occupation is based on ceramic comparisons and radiocarbon determinations. As noted above, the Lundy vessel forms are comparable to vessels of the Stirling and early Moorehead phases in the American Bottom, which would date to between A.D. 1050 and 1200. Three uncorrected radiocarbon dates of A.D. 1010 ± 70 (ISGS 1315), A.D. 1040 ± 70 (ISGS 1092), and A.D. 1150 ± 70 (ISGS 1307) have also been obtained for the site. Based on these two lines of evidence, it is inferred that the Lundy occupation occurred at roughly A.D. 1100.

Previous Interpretations of Apple River Mississippian Culture

The Apple River Focus has played an important role in many discussions of Middle Mississippian development and spread into the Upper Mississippi River Valley and its relationships to both Oneota and Late Woodland cultures in the area. John W. Bennett, however, was equivocal in his explanation of the nature of the influences that had created the Apple River Focus. He states "that the appearance of Upper Missipsippi (sic) traits in Apple River pottery is not the result of Oneota 'influence,' but is rather an internal 'development toward' an early Upper Mississippi type. This interpretation requires the development of Upper Mississippi in Illinois, from an Old Village–Early Trappist base, with developed Oneota returning to Illinois at a much later date to influence late Trappist at Crable" (1945:viii). However, by the time his publication of the Jo Daviess research had gone to the presses he had changed his mind:

> The author is no longer confident of this (previous) interpretation, which is predicated upon a lengthy duration for Trappist. Two alternatives may be suggested: (1) Upper Mississippi developed earlier than heretofore believed, and was contemporaneous with Middle Mississippi during a great portion of the history of the latter phase. Thus the Upper Mississippi tendencies in Apple River represent influence from an earlier, more generalized Upper Mississippi culture, rather than having a part in the origin of Upper. (2) Middle Mississippi cultures have a considerably longer history than is usually thought, and the Apple

River sites do indeed represent the beginnings of Upper but at an earlier stage of Middle than believed. The author at present inclines toward the first view, but must confess that his opinion is based on meager evidence (1945:viii).

Bennett's final interpretation was that the Apple River Focus represented a culture contact situation between Oneota and Middle Mississippian peoples. The derivation and affiliations of the Oneota-related traits was never clear to Bennett, but there was little doubt as to the nature of the Middle Mississippian traits. Mississippian ceramic types such as Powell Plain, St. Clair Plain, and Ramey Incised, as well as vessel forms such as water bottles, bowls, seed jars, and bean pots were clearly part of the Apple River Focus ceramic assemblage. Bennett notes (1945:154) that the Mississippian wares of the Apple River Focus were reminiscent of both Old Village and Trappist forms. He went on to suggest that the angular-shouldered incised ceramic forms from Apple River showed a closer relationship to similar types from Aztalan than to those from Cahokia.

James B. Griffin (1960b:835–38), in his review of Mississippian cultures in the Midwest, disagrees with Bennett's interpretation. Based on views formed in the late 1930s (Griffin, personal communication, 1986), he suggests that the Apple River sites represent a developmental sequence from Middle Mississippian to incipient Oneota. The earliest aspect of this sequence is formed by the ceramic assemblage present at the Mills site, which Griffin sees as strongly Old Village-like. He also feels, however, that many of the ceramic forms at Mills are intermediate in nature with rims that are halfway in height between the high outslanting Upper Mississippian rims and the low rolled rims of such types as Ramey Incised and Powell Plain. In addition there are handles that represent neither the broad-strap Oneota form nor the small loop or rope variety of Old Village. There are no distinctive Oneota motifs present at Mills.

Griffin interprets the John Chapman site ceramics as a mixture of Late Woodland and Old Village types similar to the Aztalan pattern. However, the Aztalan analogy should not be pushed too far since at John Chapman only 7 of 700 sherds are Late Woodland (Bennett 1945). That there was some interaction between Mississippian and Late Woodland groups at John Chapman is indicated by the presence of a grit-tempered rim sherd displaying a cordmarked body, angular shoulder with punctates, and a trailed chevron design on the smoothed shoulder (Bennett 1945: plate 22f). Although the projectile points found at John Chapman are not discussed by Bennett, Griffin states that Cahokia notched points outnumber the plain triangular points almost two to one.

In discussing the Savannah material, Griffin sees few Old Village traits and contends that most of the pottery is rather Oneota-like. He notes that the design motifs are strongly curvilinear rather than being more rectilinear as in the typical Oneota designs. Savannah represents, according to Griffin (1960b:836), a transitional complex just on the verge of becoming completely Oneota.

The most recent interpretation of the Apple River Focus sites has been put forward by James B. Stoltman (1983) in his review of the prehistory of the Upper Mississippi River Valley. Although noting the presence of signs of Cahokia influence such as Ramey Incised and Powell Plain pottery, stone hoes, notched and unnotched triangular projectile points, and platform mounds in the Apple River sites (Stoltman 1983:236–37), he suggests that these same sites contain components of an early temporal variant of the Oneota culture (1983:239–40). Stoltman describes this early Oneota culture as follows:

> Early, circa A.D. 1050 to 1200, characterized by signs of Cahokia influences (e.g., low, rolled rims, angular shoulders, loop handles, and continuous curvilinear incised motifs); before this period ended, vessels with higher rims and more rounded shoulders along with discontinuous rather than continuous, interlocking curvilinear scroll motifs had appeared (what Hall 1962:169–71 defined as Diamond Bluff Trailed); sites with occupations during this period include *Mills*, *Chapman*, and *Savannah* in Illinois (Bennett 1945:137–53), Silvernale and Bryan in Minnesota (Anfinson 1979:183–90; Blessing 1967), and Diamond Bluff and Armstrong in Wisconsin (Lawshe 1947; Maxwell 1950; Hurley 1978). I would most emphatically not include all of these components in a single phase, although it is impossible at the present time to disentangle the taxonomy of these complexes (1983:240).

The interpretations by Bennett, Griffin, and Stoltman focused primarily on the Middle Mississippian–Oneota relationship that may be involved in the Apple River Focus. The central research question has been whether the Apple River Focus represents a Middle Mississippian culture evolving into or merely in contact with a Oneota culture. Major obstacles that have hampered the resolution of this question have included: (1) the limited nature of the data from the Mills, John Chapman, and Savannah sites; (2) researchers' inability to sort out the multicomponent Mills Village collections; and (3) the lack of large comparative collections that illustrate the full range of Oneota and Middle Mississippian ceramic variation.

Recently, a number of these obstacles have been removed or at least partially ameliorated. The Lundy site excavations have provided a substantial body of data from a single-component Apple River site. The existence of this large, unmixed Mississippian assemblage has provided new insights into the prehistory of the Apple River Mississippian culture. Equally important has been the appearance of new information on Stirling and Moorehead phase Mississippian sites in the Cahokia region (i.e., Emerson and Jackson 1984; Mehrer 1982; Milner and Williams 1983, 1984; Milner et al., 1984). These excavations have provided detailed information on large Old Village ceramic assemblages (outside of Aztalan) for comparison with those of the Apple River sites. The availability of this information means that discussions of

Middle Mississippian ceramics in the Upper Mississippi River Valley need no longer be confined to the presence or absence of such traditional types as Ramey Incised or Powell Plain. The fuller understanding of Mississippian ceramic variation provided by the American Bottom materials is important to the correct interpretation of the Apple River Mississippian ceramic sequence.

New Interpretations

A REVIEW OF THE DATA BASE

The Apple River Mississippian manifestation is a valid cultural entity within the Middle Mississippian tradition. Research has demonstrated that the culture has its own internal developmental sequence that, while it parallels those of other Mississippian cultures in the region, is recognizable as a discrete entity. The prehistory of the Apple River culture appears to follow closely the pattern documented for the Middle Mississippian Spoon River culture of the Central Illinois River Valley. It is possible that similar cultural and historical factors were operating in each region.

One of the valuable contributions that recent research has made to our understanding of the Apple River culture is how to separate the "inseparable" mixture of Middle Mississippian and Oneota traits that characterized the Apple River Focus. As demonstrated in earlier portions of this paper, the Middle Mississippian–Oneota ceramic question is largely spurious. The Lundy information and the reexamination of the previous collections indicate that the early ceramic assemblages of Apple River culture are Middle Mississippian with some incorporation of Late Woodland traits. Only in the later portion of the Apple River ceramic sequence is there a possibility of minor Oneota influences. It is instructive to remember when discussing Apple River culture–Oneota relationships that there are no known large Oneota sites in Jo Daviess County and any Oneota presence there appears to be marginal. On the basis of present knowledge, I would argue that the Apple River Focus as some Middle Mississippian and Oneota hybrid taxon is not supported by the archaeological data base and should be abandoned.

From my perspective, the cultural associations, chronological, and taxonomic relationships of the Apple River Mississippian sites can best be understood through the delineation of two sequential Mississippian phases, the Bennett and Mills phases, which are defined below.

BENNETT PHASE (A.D. 1050–1200)

The Bennett phase was defined on the basis of the collections from the Lundy and John Chapman sites. This information was subsequently utilized to delineate the Bennett phase component at the multicomponent Mills Village site. The phase was named in recognition of John W. Bennett's contribution to the Mississippian archaeology of the Apple River area. The cultural and chronological correlate of the Bennett phase in the American Bottom is the Stirling phase, although relationships can also be observed to the earlier Lohmann and later early Moorehead phases. In the Spoon River culture, the correlation is with the Eveland and early Orendorf phases, although Bennett phase influences may persist into the later Larson phase. To the north, this phase is on the same time horizon as the initial Mississippian components at Bryan, Silvernale, Diamond Bluff, Carcajou Point, and Aztalan. The phase's chronological placement is based primarily on the correlation of vessel forms with the above areas and supported by the A.D. 1010 ± 70, A.D. 1040 ± 70, and A.D. 1150 ± 70 radiocarbon determinations from the Lundy site.

The Bennett phase ceramic assemblage is distinctive, but it includes vessel forms that are commonly associated with early Middle Mississippian culture throughout the Midwest. Jar forms predominate and bowls are common. Seed jars, water bottles, and beakers have been recovered but are uncommon. The characteristic jar forms are inslanting with angular to slightly rounded shoulders (figs. 8.3 and 8.4). The low rim forms include extruded, everted, rolled, vertical, and flared lips. Jar decorations include the frequent use of incised, feathered scrolls. Cordmarking to the shoulder and lip notching are also significant jar decorative attributes. Loop handles occur in small numbers. Bowls are the second most common vessel form and are most often deep and straight-sided. Bowl exteriors may be either smoothed or cord-roughened. Bennett phase ceramics are often fired in a reducing atmosphere, but oxidized sherds are not uncommon. The dark gray paste in the reduced vessels is frequently emphasized by black smudged exteriors, less frequently by black slipping. Polishing of exterior surfaces occurs. Red-slipped exteriors are rare. All of the examined vessels use shell as the tempering agent. As a general rule the shell is finely crushed; however, examples of coarsely crushed shell temper are present.

Mississippian lithic assemblages are typically undiagnostic and that of the Bennett phase is no exception. Snub-nosed scrapers and triangular projectile points are common. Most projectile points are unnotched triangles, but notched "Cahokia" points do occur. Other artifacts such as earspools, celts, hoes, and sandstone abraders are present as well as such exotic materials as copper, hematite, and galena.

On a larger scale, truncated pyramid and large conical mounds, plazas, wall-trench structures, and possibly small conical mounds (such as those at Mills Village) appear to be associated with the Bennett phase. The phase represents a fully Middle Mississippian culture with all of its associated social, political, material, and religious trappings.

SPECULATIONS ON BENNETT PHASE ORIGINS. The initial Middle Mississippian settlement in the Apple River drainage was probably located on the protected terrace spur at the Mills site and was established by peoples possessing a late Lohmann or early Stirling phase material culture. At present this settlement is best characterized as a site unit intrusion from the south and is amply represented in the ceramics of the Bennett phase component at the Mills Village site. This intrusion could have occurred as early as A.D. 1000 (i.e., at the beginning of the Lohmann phase [Milner et al. 1984]), but it probably took place slightly later, perhaps about A.D. 1050. There is some evidence to suggest that the initial settlement may have consisted only of a village area at Mills, although the first construction of the ceremonial precinct and associated mounds must have commenced shortly thereafter.

Mound enlargement and perhaps new mound construction probably continued throughout the Bennett phase and the ceremonial precinct as we now see it was completed by the end of the phase. The Mills Village may have reached its maximum size and achieved its formal arrangement of village, plaza, two(?) pyramid and one conical mound by the second half of the Bennett phase. It is possible that the seventy-two small conical mounds at Mills Village are associated with this phase, but the only supporting evidence for such an association is Bennett's (1945:136) comment that the fill of the several tested conical mounds contained a mixture of shell-tempered ceramics and other cultural debris.

Although there is no evidence bearing on the question one way or the other, Mills Village may have been lightly fortified during this time. The site is located on a terrace spur that is naturally protected on three sides by steep banks. A light fence may have been placed across the neck of the spur to offer some protection. I would stress the fact, however, that the Apple River people did not appear to maintain a strong defensive posture and their dispersed population suggests a basically peaceful situation.

It may be possible to delineate an internal developmental ceramic sequence within the Bennett phase. The Mills Village site component seems to include a high number of black, polished, Middle Mississippian vessels with little use of either lip notching or cordmarking. The Lundy site, and perhaps John Chapman, have higher numbers of cordmarked and lip notched vessels, which may indicate a slightly later placement within the Bennett phase.

The pattern of ceramic development that characterizes the Bennett phase is one marked by the increasing incorporation of indigenous Late Woodland traits into the ceramic assemblage. The diagnostic traits of this influence include the use of cordmarking on jar bodies and bowls and the use of lip notching on jar rims. Lip notching has often been treated as evidence of Oneota influences. In this instance I prefer to interpret it as derived from the Late Woodland trait of cord-wrapped stick impressions on rim lips. The concept is the same in both the Late Woodland and Apple River ceramics, the only difference is the instrument used to make the impressions. The sharp, angular Apple River notching is also easily distinguished from the typical, shallow, broad Oneota notches. The association between Oneota and Apple River notching may simply be that they are both derived from the same Late Woodland base.

There are also a number of specific sherds from Bennett phase contexts that demonstrate a mixture of Late Woodland and Middle Mississippian traits. At Mills Village, for example, a Late Woodland, grit-tempered, cordmarked sherd decorated with incised lines was recovered (Bennett 1945:142). A classic grit-tempered Late Woodland shoulder sherd with a trailed chevron design is illustrated by Bennett (1945: pl. 22f) from the John Chapman site. To date, the Lundy site collection has yielded a Mississippian shell-tempered rim that is decorated with a band of vertical cordmarking on the exterior neck above a smoothed shoulder, four shell-tempered vessels with horizontal single cord impressions on the neck area, and a shell-tempered shoulder(?) sherd decorated with single cord-impressed cross-hatched design above a band of horizontal cordmarking. Two grit-tempered Mississippian rims were also recovered from the Lundy site. The incorporation of such Late Woodland traits into the ceramic assemblage is one of the characteristics that serves to distinguish the Bennett phase and the Apple River culture in general from other local Middle Mississippian groups.

Although there has been no systematic archaeological survey of the Apple River drainage, work by the University of Chicago teams and by the University of Wisconsin-Milwaukee (Dudzik 1974) did locate a number of small

Mississippian sites in the general vicinity of Mills Village. Only the John Chapman and Lundy sites can be definitely associated with the Bennett phase. The available data suggests that the Bennett phase settlement pattern is one that consists of a central temple town (Mills) surrounded by farmsteads and small villages. Representative sites include John Chapman and Lundy. Although very limited, our evidence suggests that all such outlying sites are located within a short distance of the central town (e.g., Lundy is 2 kilometers and John Chapman 4.8 kilometers from Mills). Whether smaller sites were occupied seasonally or permanently is not known, but I would favor the later pattern. The exact role of the possible single-mound John Chapman village in such a system will remain somewhat unclear until more information is available on the site.

In summary, the Bennett phase marks the initial intrusion of Middle Mississippian peoples into the Apple River region of northwestern Illinois about the middle of the eleventh century A.D. These settlers brought with them the full panoply of Mississippian society and religion and established the central temple town at Mills Village. An important aspect of this phase was a fairly high level of interaction with the local Late Woodland populations. This interaction is reflected in the increasing incorporation of Woodland traits into the Bennett phase ceramic assemblage. One of the most significant results of this reexamination of the data has been the demonstration of the absence of any Oneota influences in this phase. The ultimate fate of the Late Woodland peoples is unclear. They may have been incorporated into the Middle Mississippian Apple River culture or they may have simply moved out of the area. Whatever the cause, Late Woodland influences diminish at the end of the Bennett phase and the subsequent Mills phase was characterized by a new set of external stimuli.

MILLS PHASE (A.D. 1200–1300)

The Mills phase collections are represented by the late component at the Mills Village site and, perhaps, the Savannah Proving Ground site. The phase is named for the Mills component. Although the Savannah component is tentatively included in the phase, so little of the ceramic assemblage is available for study that it cannot serve as a type site.

External correlates of the Mills phase are the late Moorehead and early Sand Prairie phases (about A.D. 1200–1400) in the American Bottom region, the late Orendorf and Larson phases in the Spoon River culture, and the various Oneota groups of Iowa, Minnesota, and Wisconsin. The chronological placement of this phase is based on correlations with the vessel forms of the Spoon

River and American Bottom Mississippian cultures. The beginning date of A.D. 1200 can be well supported, but the A.D. 1300 ending date is tentative.

The ceramics are primarily jars with the high everted rims that typify later Mississippian ceramic developments to the south (fig. 8.3). The jars are inslanting with rounded shoulders; some jars possibly had globular bodies. Bowls are the only other common vessel forms and appear to resemble closely those of the previous Bennett phase. A few beakers are present, as is one possible plate.

Trailed shoulder designs on jars consist primarily of nested arcs with the interior space filled with vertical lines. Broad lip tabs are common, but lip notching does not occur. Interestingly enough, body cordmarking also seems to be virtually absent. Only two vessels are cordmarked, one from Mills Village (Bennett 1945: pl. 33) and one from Savannah (Bennett 1945: pl. 27h). Both specimens are classic examples of Cahokia Cordmarked and are very different from the cordmarked vessels associated with the Bennett phase. Jar surfaces are smoothed. Handles range from wide loop to true strap forms, occasionally with eared projections.

The bowls of this phase are similar to those of the Bennett phase in having cordmarked or smoothed exterior surfaces and in being generally deep and straight sided. Mills phase ceramics are more often oxidized than reduced and have the typical reddish paste of vessels fired in an oxidizing atmosphere. Polished surfaces are absent, or at least rare. No examples of red or black slipping are known. The ceramics are consistently shell-tempered. There appears to be a slight increase in the use of coarsely ground shell temper, but most sherds still have fine shell temper.

The Mills phase lithic assemblage is poorly known, but snub-nosed scrapers and unnotched and notched triangular projectile points are present. It is possible that such items as earspools, celts, hoes, and sandstone abraders continue into this phase.

As now understood, the Mills phase continues a number of patterns begun during the Bennett phase. For example, I believe that the Apple River culture continued to participate in the broad Mississippian pattern of ceramic change that pervaded the Midwest between A.D. 1000–1300. The ceramics of this phase are all of the high rim everted form, but there are also examples of the shorter everted rim forms that are so typical of the earlier Moorehead phase in the American Bottom. In other words, there does appear, in the Savannah Proving Ground and the Mills Village late component, to be evidence that the entire ceramic developmental sequence from low through high rims occurs in the Apple River culture. A parallel developmental sequence has been demonstrated to exist both in the American Bottom (Milner et al. 1984) and the Spoon River (Conrad and Harn 1972; Conrad, chap. 6) Mississippian cultures.

The settlement pattern of the Mills phase may mirror that of the earlier Bennett phase. There is a major Mills phase occupation at the central temple town of Mills Village and one small occupation at the Savannah site 2.4 kilometers downriver in Carroll County. Material density at the Savannah site was very low and the site probably represents a short-term farmstead. Impressionistically, it may be that the Mills phase population was clustered at Mills Village and only a few outlying sites. Until a systematic survey of the area is undertaken, the settlement pattern will remain speculative.

Perhaps one of the major shifts that is observable from the Bennett to the Mills phase is a change in the nature and the direction of external influences. The dominating influences in the Bennett phase are from the Mississippian groups of the American Bottom and Spoon River and from the indigenous Late Woodland population. The Mills phase is marked by a decrease in the strength of southern influences. Although the ceramic developmental pattern within the Apple River culture generally parallels that of the American Bottom, the strength of this resemblance is much less in the Mills than in the Bennett phase. Interaction with the American Bottom appears to be at a low point during this phase and the number of ceramic vessels directly recognizable as Cahokia types are conspicuous by their absence.

Another stylistic change that marks the beginning of the Mills phase is the disappearance of all evidence of Late Woodland ceramic traits. Cordmarking is absent from the Mills phase vessels with the possible exception of its limited use on bowl exterior surfaces. The only cordmarked vessels associated with this phase are two Cahokia Cordmarked jars that probably represent imports from the south. The other trait that is now missing from the late Apple River culture ceramics is lip notching. Although neither cordmarking nor lip notching were numerically important aspects of the Bennett phase ceramic assemblage, they certainly were major contributions to its distinctiveness and were important distinguishing characteristics of this local variant.

The disappearance of Late Woodland influences at the beginning of the Mills phase may be explained in several ways. Conrad and Harn (1972; Harn 1975b; Conrad 1973) have argued in reference to the Central Illinois River Valley that the intrusive Mississippian culture absorbed the local Late Woodland culture to produce the hybrid Spoon River peoples. A similar process could have taken place in the Apple River region. There is also the possibility that the expanding Apple River peoples may have eventually pressured the Late Woodland groups

out of the region. On a broader scope, Guy E. Gibbon (1972) has suggested that many of the Late Woodland Effigy Mound people were transformed into Oneota by Mississippian influences. The evidence from the Apple River sites is not sufficient to reach any conclusions as to the fate of the local Late Woodland peoples. I would tend to accept either of the first two explanations as being the more likely. Given the lack of local Oneota populations in northwestern Illinois, Gibbon's transformational model does not seem specifically applicable to the Effigy Mound people in this region.

One of the most dominating characteristics of the Mills phase is its insularity. The phase is marked by a general decrease in the interaction with the Middle Mississippian groups to the south and with the local Late Woodland inhabitants. What is less clear is the relationship of the Mills phase peoples to their more northerly Oneota neighbors.

As previously interpreted, the Apple River Focus was an inseparable blend of Middle Mississippian and Oneota traits. It has been demonstrated that the Bennett phase has no traces of Oneota traits. The nature of the Mills phase–Oneota relationships is not so clear. Many of the Mills vessel forms, paste and surface characteristics, and to some extent the decorative motifs have what some researchers would interpret as a Oneota feel to them. Yet attempts to isolate these presumed Oneota traits and associate them with a known archaeological culture have not been very successful. Bennett recognized this problem in this original analysis and states, "The Upper Mississippi elements in these sites, particularly Savannah, constitute a more difficult problem. The similarities cannot be ascribed to any single manifestation, being reminiscent of various Upper Mississippi manifestations, with Oneota perhaps the closest" (1945:157). Griffin commented much to the same effect on this material:

> The Savannah village site, on the other hand, has a small proportion of features of the pottery which are Old Village, but most of the pottery is close to Oneota in vessel shape and surface treatment. The designs, including a scroll, are still strongly curvilinear. This pottery complex is not quite Oneota but is only a short distance from it. The Savannah site should not be regarded as a component of a focus which would include the Chapman and Mills sites, nor should it be regarded as a part of an Orr Focus. It is a distinctive transitional unit (1960b:836).

Neither Bennett, Griffin, nor the numerous authors who have commented on the late prehistoric Apple River ceramics have been able to associate them with a specific Oneota manifestation. This is most instructive. The majority of the traits that are being examined are very generalized in character and are shared by most of the late Mississippian groups throughout the Midwest. Traits such as high rim forms, unpolished surfaces, broader handles, less skillfully executed design motifs, and a tendency toward globular vessels do subjectively have a Oneota look to them, but these traits are also common in late Middle Mississippian ceramics and therefore cannot be used to argue for specific Oneota affiliations. It should also be noted that, popular opinion not withstanding, snub-nosed scrapers and unnotched triangular points are not characteristic only of Oneota, but are found in most northern Middle Mississippian assemblages, including those of the Apple River cultures. Lip notching could also be construed as arguing for Oneota influences, but as shown previously in this chapter lip notching is confined to the earlier Bennett phase and is most likely derived from Late Woodland design concepts. It does not seem possible at this time to isolate any specific Oneota traits in the Mills phase.

The most expeditious explanation for the Mills phase is that it evolves out of the previous Bennett phase. Such a ceramic development is supported by the presence of rim forms in the Mills phase ceramic assemblage that are intermediate between the earlier low and later high rim forms. There is also a continuance of some of the design motifs from the Bennett phase, most notably the nested arcs with vertical lines in the interior space. The lithic assemblage of scrapers and triangular points continues. The major Mills phase occupation is at the Mills Village temple town, which suggests that the group was still utilizing the village and ceremonial precinct and continuing the social, political, and religious pattern of their ancestors.

The Mills phase represents a very localized variant of the Middle Mississippian culture that is confined to the Apple River drainage. It can best be explained as the cultural assemblage of peoples descended from those who were previously recognized as the Bennett phase. Some of its ceramic traits may be the results of generalized Oneota influences, but such influences do not appear to have any significant effect and are not readily identifiable. As a final thought on this topic it is instructive to consider that there are no significant Oneota populations known to be in northwestern Illinois and I would conclude that the question of Oneota–Mills phase relationships may be a moot one. The Mills phase is associated with the Middle Mississippian, not the Oneota tradition. The phase appears too late to play any meaningful role in Oneota evolution and is too localized to have received any significant Oneota influences.

External Relationships of the Apple River Culture

Although Apple River Mississippian culture clearly has an internal developmental history all of its own, it is also obvious that it participated in the broader Mississippian cultural development observable throughout the Midwest. It is useful at this point briefly to take note of the Apple River culture's relationship to the other surrounding Mississippian groups.

Central to any discussion of Mississippian relationships in the Midwest is the role of the Mississippian groups centered in the American Bottom. Griffin (1960b) has interpreted the cultural assemblage of the Apple River sites as providing evidence for the northward migration of Cahokians. I have no trouble accepting the view that the American Bottom was the ultimate source of the early Mississippian settlers who moved into the Apple River area; however, it has yet to be conclusively demonstrated that this is the case.

The proposal that the Apple River area was settled by migrants from the American Bottom begs the question as to the purpose of such a movement. The presence of Middle Mississippian peoples in the Apple River region is only one aspect of the broader pattern of Mississippian expansion that took place in the eleventh century A.D. through the northern Midwest. A number of explanatory models have been proposed to account for this phe-

nomena. Gibbon (1974) has seen this expansion as part of a broad extractive system tied to the formation of a theocratic state at Cahokia. Somewhat along the same lines, Conrad (1973) has developed the argument that the Mississippian Spoon River culture came into being as the result of a migration of American Bottom elite into the Illinois River Valley to exploit the local resources for the advantage of the homeland. Variations on these themes have been suggested by other researchers, including suggestions that some northern sites may have been established for the control of specific resources (i.e., Aztalan for copper or the Apple River sites for galena [the latter theory being rather difficult to sustain given Walthall's (1981:37–44) demonstration that Cahokia received its galena from the Missouri sources]).

Conversely, it may have been a combination of population pressure, restriction of resources, and the appearance and dominance of the more northerly adapted eight-row maize in the tenth century A.D. that led to the sudden outpouring of peoples from the American Bottom (Hall 1980). I believe (as discussed at length in chapter 12) that much of the out-movement from the American Bottom may have been tied to population pressure and political fragmentation. It would seem that a viable model for explaining the northern expansion would include the movement by splinter political/kinship groups out of the more contentious and densely occupied Cahokia locality. This model is predicated on the belief that the American Bottom in the eleventh through thirteenth centuries A.D. can be most economically explained as a series of competing chiefdoms located at such centers as Cahokia, Mitchell, Pulcher, East St. Louis, and the St. Louis mound centers. At times these chiefdoms may have been integrated into larger political and religious entities and at other times fragmented into conflicting petty chiefdoms. Such a system would have provided a ready supply of minor lineages which could clearly improve their lot by migration to the northern frontier areas that were sparsely occupied by Late Woodland groups. It would also seem that this model is more in keeping with the ethnohistoric record for North American chiefdoms. The explanation that some of these northern migrants are dissidents from the American Bottom may also be more compatible with the subsequent developmental pattern that we see in the Spoon River and Apple River cultures. In both cases, after the initial appearance of American Bottom material culture, the local culture very rapidly departs from the American Bottom pattern. This suggests that there is minimal contact between these and the American Bottom groups, as one might expect if the original settlers were dissidents. In this regard it may be very important that during the lifespan of the Apple River culture, galena from Jo Daviess County moved into the Spoon River culture and down into the Tennessee River Valley, but seldom into Cahokia (Walthall 1981).

There is little doubt that the American Bottom Mississippian ceramic sequence is useful in establishing chronological parameters for the Apple River culture despite what might be considered as rather intermittent interaction between the two areas. The earliest date for the appearance of Middle Mississippian traits on the Apple River could not have been earlier than the Lohmann (A.D. 1000–1050) or Stirling (A.D. 1050–1150) phases at Cahokia, since it was this later phase that saw the first common use of Ramey Incised and classic Powell Plain types. Although both Cahokia Cordmarked and Tippets Red Film Incised may be present by the end of the Stirling phase, they do not become common until the following Moorehead phase (A.D. 1150–1250). Their presence in Apple River assemblages would presumably date to this later time. On the basis of the rather general correlation of ceramic types, it can be suggested that the earliest settlement in the Apple River region could have taken place about the middle of the eleventh century A.D. and that contact between the two areas probably continued sporadically into the late Moorehead/early Sand Prairie phases based on the presence of such characteristic Cahokian types as Tippets Bean Pots and Cahokia Cordmarked jars.

An interesting aspect of the Apple River culture is the similarity it bears to Spoon River culture of the Central Illinois River Valley. I have discussed these similarities in the past (Emerson 1973:48–49), but given the new data and the limited circulation of the previous paper, they are worthwhile enumerating here.

> In both areas, Powell Plain type rim sherds are found in intermediate forms between rolled and everted shapes. The elaborate scroll motifs are missing on Ramey Incised, instead rectilinear motifs prevail. Lobed jars, incised cross hatching, clenched fist effigy bean pot handles, nested arcs with descending trailed lines, dominate use of rectilinear motifs, abundant use of end scrapers, the predominance of unnotched triangular projectile points over notched, and eared projections on the top of handles are present in both the Apple and Spoon River Cultures (Emerson 1973:48).

This list represents a sampling rather than an exhaustive listing of shared traits between the two areas, but it does demonstrate their overall similarities.

Perhaps the most startling revelation of the newly excavated material from the Lundy site is the presence of ceramic forms that have an extremely close resemblance to the Spoon River Dickson ceramic series. In the Spoon River region the types Dickson Trailed, Cordmarked, and Plain are associated with the Larson phase, which dates to about A.D. 1250–1300. They are also found with such Cahokia types as Cahokia Cordmarked, Wells Incised, and St. Clair Plain (Harn 1980b:21–22). Similar ceramics recovered from Lundy differ only in having slightly lower rim forms and are associated with earlier Cahokia types such as Ramey Incised and Powell Plain rather than the later forms. The Lundy forms appear to take chronological precedence over the Dickson series from the Spoon River, but Lawrence Conrad (personal communication, 1984; chap. 6) recently identified a Dickson Trailed vessel from an Eveland phase context. This find suggests that the Dickson series may be as early in the Spoon River Valley as it is at Lundy. In 1973 I suggested that the relationship of many of the observed traits were so close between Spoon River and Apple River that the later may have been settled by migrants from the former area. I no longer hold that view. It appears that the best explanation for the similarities between the two areas is parallel development within the broad Mississippian pattern bolstered by frequent interaction. The similarities between the Lundy and Dickson series ceramics are so close that it is difficult not to derive the later from the former. Perhaps this contact between the areas was bolstered and sustained by the galena trade and a mutual relative isolation from the Mississippian groups in the American Bottom.

The relationship of the Apple River culture to the more northerly Mississippian sites is less clear. In the past many of these sites have been unsystematically collected, tested, and excavated, but seldom has the material obtained been reported in even a cursory manner. S. Barrett's work at Aztalan (1933) stands in stark contrast to the more typical archaeological investigations of Mississippian sites in the upper Midwest. Later significant investigation and reporting was performed by Hall (1962) at Carcajou Point. This was followed by Gibbon's (1979) report on the Mississippian materials from the Red Wing area. This work contained the first thorough reporting of the material culture of the important Bryan and Silvernale sites that Wilford had collected some twenty to thirty years earlier. Past interpretations of the nature of the Mississippian intrusion into the northern Midwest have been severely hampered by the lack of carefully described and reported materials, limited collections, poor data collection procedures, and a lack of good comparative information from the Mississippian heartland to the south. It just the last few years, this picture has changed drastically. In 1974 Dr. Robert Alex conducted sizable excavations at the Diamond Bluff site and that material is now in the process of being analyzed by Roland Rodell at the University of Wisconsin-Milwaukee. Barrett's Aztalan collections are being reanalyzed by John Richards at the University of Wisconsin-Milwaukee. This study will provide data that is directly comparable with the new results from other ongoing research. Dr. Clark Dobbs, University of Minnesota, has just completed large-scale excavations at the Bryan site and is undertaking similar work at the Silvernale site. Over the next few years the results of this work will be forthcoming.

Given the fact that such critical sites as Aztalan, Diamond Bluff, Bryan, and Silvernale are currently being analyzed, it would be premature for me to attempt to make anything other than general comparisons between those materials and the Apple River culture. Of the northern sites, the one that bears the closest relationship to the Apple River culture is Aztalan. The similarities between the two go far beyond that of ceramic forms and temple mounds. Perhaps the critical point is that both represent Middle Mississippian groups with their full regalia of social and religious paraphernalia interacting mainly with the surrounding Late Woodland groups and to a limited extent being acted upon by it. The nature of the Late Woodland–Mississippian interaction in each region seems to have taken a very different course. In the Apple River area this interaction appears fairly peaceful, long-term, and resulted in the possible acculturation of some of the Late Woodland population. The pattern appears to be similar to that observed in the Spoon River culture. At Aztalan, as we now understand it, the occupation seems to represent a fortified site unit intrusion into a hostile area. The exact nature of Late Woodland–Mississippian interaction at the site is not well understood, but it appears to have been short-term and possibly ending in the destruction of Aztalan. The nature of the local settlement pattern in each case reflects the differing situation well. Aztalan is not known to have any associated farmsteads or hamlets while the comparable Mills site has a number of small outlying sites scattered across the countryside.

When one considers the relationship of the Apple River culture to such outlying areas as Carcajou Point, Silvernale, Diamond Bluff, and Bryan, a different picture emerges. It is clear from examining the ceramic material from these sites that they are related closely to the low rim forms at Apple River, yet at the same time are local variants. As an illustrative example, we can look at the Carcajou Point data reported by Hall (1962). It is from these data that Hall defined the Koshkonong Focus that he sees as a parallel cultural development with the Apple River and Silvernale foci out of a previous "Old-Village" base. As defined, the Koshkonong Focus reflects the Mississippian-Oneota ceramic mixture that traditionally has been attributed to the Apple River Focus. The earlier portion of the focus (Hall 1962, 2: 120–21), which began about A.D. 1000, is seen here as contemporaneous with the Bennett phase. The latter portion of the Koshkonong Focus, which continues into the fifteenth century A.D., is at least partially contemporaneous with the Mills phase. The early Koshkonong Focus and the Bennett phase share such traits as shell tempering, low-rimmed vessel forms, lip notching, frequent trailed shoulder decorations, and loop handles. Ceramic traits such as high rim forms are common in the middle Koshkonong Focus and Mills phase materials. Such resemblances are not interpreted here as indicative of close relationships between the Apple River and the Koshkonong Focus groups, but rather are instructive of the shared pattern of Mississippian ceramic development that is co-occurring throughout the upper Midwest at that time (as has long been argued by Griffin). I would suggest that similar patterns will be observed in the Bryan, Silvernale, and Diamond Bluff assemblages when they are analyzed.

Summary

Early excavations and analysis of materials from north-western Illinois Mississippian sites by the University of Chicago led to the recognition of the Apple River Focus (Bennett 1945). As defined, this was a "floating focus" combining an inseparable mixture of Upper and Middle Mississippian traits. Although subject to various reinterpretations by scholars, the exact nature of the Apple River Focus could not be delineated until additional information was obtained. The recent excavations at the Lundy site provided this essential information.

The reexamination of the Apple River materials from the Mills Village, John Chapman, and Savannah sites in light of the data from the Lundy site, the American Bottom, and the Spoon River culture demonstrated that the Apple River culture was an integral part of the Middle Mississippian tradition. The Apple River Focus can no longer be treated as a hybrid Upper-Middle Mississippian taxonomic unit. It has been replaced by the sequential Bennett and Mills phases defined in this paper.

The Apple River Mississippian culture is part of the broad Mississippian pattern that encompassed much of the Midwest. Its development paralleled that of the American Bottom and Spoon River regions. Yet within this broader pattern it must be recognized that the Apple River culture possessed its own individual developmental sequence and should be understood first as an independent cultural entity. The Bennett phase is marked by strong similarities to the American Bottom in its ceramic forms, but one of its diagnostic traits is the presence of a strong ele-ment derived from the local Late Woodland cultures. The following Mills phase sees increasing localization of the Apple River culture. Ceramic resemblances to surrounding groups became very generalized with few specific shared traits. It is the ceramic patterns observed in the Mills phase that some researchers have suggested to be Oneota-like or incipient Oneota. It is argued here that such trends were not specifically Oneota, but were part of the broader pattern of Mississippian ceramic development in the Upper Mississippi River Valley. Finally, it was concluded that the Apple River culture is a local variant of Middle Mississippian tradition that existed within a fairly isolated context within the Upper Mississippi River Valley and that is best understood in terms of its own developmental culture history.

ACKNOWLEDGMENTS

The excavations and research that formed the basis of this chapter were funded by the Illinois Department of Transportation through the efforts of Dr. John Walthall. Mr. Kenneth Farns-worth, Kampsville Archeological Center, provided the opportunity for me to conduct this project. The continued support of both of these individuals has been crucial to the success of this endeavor. Numerous archaeologists including James B. Griffin, Lawrence Conrad, R. Barry Lewis, John Kelly, and Kenneth Farnsworth have commented on aspects of this paper. Especially important have been comments and historical insights provided by Dr. Griffin. The assistance and efforts of all of these individuals are appreciated.

9

Models of Mississippian Culture History in the Western Prairie Peninsula: A Perspective from Iowa

JOSEPH A. TIFFANY

Through the years several interpretative models have been proposed to explain Mississippian interaction with non-Mississippian cultures in the western Prairie Peninsula and the role Mississippian culture had in the development of non-Mississippian societies. In this chapter the nature of Mississippian contact and interaction with western Prairie Peninsula cultures is analyzed by reviewing previous explanations of the Mississippian "presence," as well as examining the distribution of various Mississippian artifacts within the region.

Much of what is presented is based on Dale R. Henning's (1967, 1982) comprehensive reviews along with the work of Robert A. Alex (1971), Robert L. Hall (1967a), and Guy E. Gibbon (1982). A descriptive-classificatory approach (Willey et al. 1956) is used in discussing and interpreting the available data. Emphasis on cultural-historical reconstruction is appropriate given the present state of knowledge of most of the prehistoric cultures to be examined. Such an approach is a necessary prerequisite for development of explanatory or processual models.

As Henning (1967) and James A. Brown (1982) have noted, "discussions of Mississippian immediately involve problems of definition" (Henning 1967:184). As the term *Mississippian* is used in Iowa and the eastern Plains border, it refers to Middle Mississippian culture as delineated in the Cahokia site sequence. The period of time under consideration is A.D. 900–1200, or roughly, the Fairmount (A.D. 900–1050), Stirling (A.D. 1050–1150), and the Moorehead (A.D. 1150–1250) phases (Fowler and Hall 1975:3–7). Mississippian culture can be characterized by distinctive shell-tempered pottery forms, intensive maize agriculture, and a nucleated settlement pattern consisting of communities of varying sizes. Mis-

sissippian sites are often fortified and contain rectangular wall-trench houses of wattle-and-daub construction. Flat-topped pyramidal mounds are commonly associated with Mississippian sites (Griffin 1967; Smith 1978:479–98; Stoltman 1978:725). The Mississippian temple-plaza community pattern is interpreted as representing socially stratified societies in which territoriality and ownership of land were emphasized (Griffin 1967:189; Stoltman 1978:725). Extensive trade networks involving marine shell, salt, and copper are in evidence among Mississippian and non-Mississippian cultures (Griffin 1967:190). Additional evidence for Mississippian contact with western Prairie Peninsula cultures, perhaps errantly attributed to Cahokia, includes artifacts and motifs associated with the Southeastern Ceremonial Complex or Southern Cult (Waring and Holder 1945).

As Henning (1967:185) states, the Mississippian presence in the Prairie Peninsula is identified by ceramic decoration and technology, Mississippian settlement patterns and village organization, and iconography and artifacts reflecting Mississippian religious beliefs. A number of different models have been developed to explain the Mississippian material culture found in these complexes. In order to organize these interpretative models, a classification of the various types of cultural interaction is utilized. Willey et al. (1956) classified culture contact situations on the basis of the nature of the contact and its results. The authors distinguished two kinds of intrusive elements, site-unit intrusions and trait-unit intrusions, which they defined as follows: "A site-unit is a site or an occupation level in a site, which is sufficiently homogeneous to be regarded as representing the culture of a single place at a single time (i.e., a component in the McKern terminology). A trait-unit is an object modified or transported by human agency, a stylistic or technological feature or complex, or a characteristic archaeological association" (1956:7–8).

This descriptive approach is useful given the present knowledge of Mississippian influences on late prehistoric cultures in Iowa and in the western Prairie Peninsula. It does not specify nor imply any particular process or combination of processes of cultural change.

One of the weaknesses of the migration and in situ models to be presented is that researchers have tended to treat the processes of culture change and interaction associated with each class of interpretative model as mutually exclusive, which may not be the case. Furthermore, the use of anthropological concepts such as diffusion or acculturation to interpret archaeological data can be misleading because these concepts are imperfectly defined with respect to material culture ethnographically. With these thoughts in mind, the remainder of this article will be devoted to reviewing the evidence for Mississippian culture in Iowa.

Interpretative Models

There are no Mississippian sites in Iowa. Nonetheless, several prehistoric cultures in the western Prairie Peninsula exhibit various levels of Mississippian contact, interaction, and influence. Among these are the Mill Creek culture and Great Oasis Aspect of northwest Iowa, the Glenwood culture of southwest Iowa, the Late Woodland period Hartley phase of northeast Iowa, and the Oneota tradition which is statewide in extent (fig. 9.1).

There are two categories of interpretative models regarding the origins of these cultures and Mississippian culture as it developed at the Cahokia site (Gibbon 1982: 85). In the migration models proposed by Griffin (1946, 1960b) Mississippian peoples moved northward during the Stirling phase of Cahokia up the Mississippi Valley. This migration is represented by several sites with Mississippian settlement patterns and material culture in association with local/regional cultural sequences. These complexes include the Apple River culture in northwestern Illinois (Emerson, chap. 8), the Spoon River culture of the Central Illinois Valley (Conrad, chap. 6), Aztalan in south-central Wisconsin (Goldstein and Richards, chap. 10), and the Silvernale phase sites in the Red Wing area of southeastern Minnesota (Gibbon, chap. 11). According to Griffin, the Oneota tradition developed from this Mississippian base after A.D. 1300 as a result of either adaptation by Mississippian groups to the northern deciduous forest habitat, climatic deterioration, or both. Mill Creek culture was seen by Griffin as a result of migration of Mississippian peoples from Cahokia through Aztalan and the Cambria site (21BE2) on the Minnesota River in southwest Minnesota into northwest Iowa. In a later article, Griffin postulates a broader, more general migration of Mississippian peoples from Cahokia ca. A.D. 1000 wherein Mississippian groups "moved up the Illinois to the Peoria area, up the Mississippi into Wisconsin and eastern Minnesota, and up the Missouri to Kansas City, Sioux City, and into South Dakota" (Griffin 1967:189; also see Emerson, chap. 12, for a discussion of this topic).

The other category of interpretative models regarding Mississippian interaction in the Upper Mississippi Valley involves some form of in situ development. James A. Ford and Gordon R. Willey (1941) and Gibbon (1972) suggest that Oneota developed out of resident Woodland groups as a result of Mississippian contact and acculturation. Researchers working with the Mill Creek culture since the early 1960s have presented essentially the same viewpoint for this manifestation. They suggest that Mill Creek developed out of resident Late Woodland period cultures such as Great Oasis and is part of the Middle Missouri tradition. They also note that the presence of Mississippian material culture in Mill Creek sites is a result of contact with and acculturation to aspects of the Mississippian lifeway (D. Anderson 1969; Henning 1968, 1971b; Tiffany 1982a).

Both migration and in situ models have been used to explain the presence of Mississippian cultural traits in the eastern or Nebraska variant of the central Plains tradition. The Glenwood culture, and the Nebraska variant of which it is a part, also developed from a local Late Woodland period base. The presence of Mississippian material culture in Nebraska variant sites is explained as the result of Mississippian contact and influence (W. Wedel 1959: 129, 535, 560–61, 564–65). Waldo R. Wedel (1940) and Patricia J. O'Brien (1978a, 1978b) suggest that the Steed-Kisker complex in the Kansas City area, which reflects a blending of Mississippian and Nebraska variant traits, represents a Mississippian site-unit intrusion. Henning argues that while Steed-Kisker manifestations were "obviously influenced by Cahokia or a comparable configuration, the traits exhibited are not sufficiently similar to be suggestive of a site-unit intrusion" (1967:190).

The use of migration models to account for the development of Oneota and Mill Creek has been downplayed in recent years due mainly to the increasing number of radiocarbon dates which indicate that the development of both Oneota and Mill Creek are coeval with the development of Mississippian culture in the Upper Mississippi

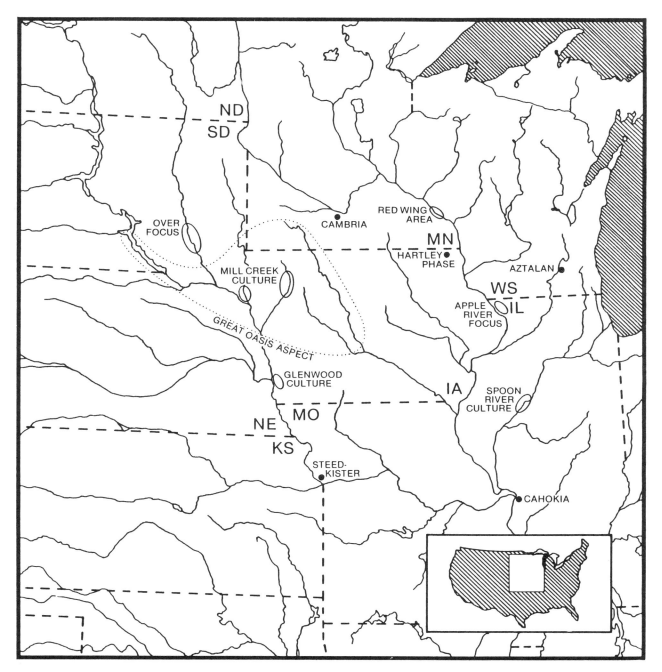

Figure 9.1. Map showing the location of archaeological sites and cultures discussed in this chapter. The distribution of the Great Oasis Aspect is derived from Henning (1971b).

Valley. Henning's (1970) and Gibbon's (1972) earlier statements follow Brown's assessment that:

> Oneota arose as a coherent cultural complex too early to be a "simple" offshoot of more complex Mississippian type cultures. . . , rather than dating after the formation of the classic expression of Cahokian culture sometime around A.D. 1000, Oneota was discovered to be equally old. As a result it is no longer possible to conceive of Oneota as a descendant of a complex Mississippian culture which was transformed through cultural drift at the northern margins of the midwest (1982:107).

Henning has summarized the evidence for in situ development of the Mill Creek culture as follows: "No evidence for the construction of flat-topped pyramidal mounds by Mill Creek peoples or any other local groups has been forthcoming. The ceramic complex does yield evidence for Mississippian influence, but it is definitely not 'pure' Mississippian at the base of the earliest sites. The earliest ceramics indicate the use of indigenously derived ceramic traits" (1967:188).

This viewpoint was also expressed by Eugene Fugle (1957), who noted that despite close similarities in ceramics and projectile points most of the Mississippian traits present were of a generalized nature. A number of Mill Creek items do appear to be similar to those in Mississippian groups. These include "stone pulley type earspools, chunkey stones, profuse amounts of marine shell for ornamentation, stone hoes (rare), triangular shaped retouched drills, double conoidal elbow pipes, large numbers of polished celts, shell columella pendants, the scalloped shell disc gorget and the use of wattle and daub in house construction." He concludes, however, that "there are more differences between Mill Creek . . . and the Middle Mississippi phase than there are similarities" (1957:347).

Thus the early dates for Mill Creek (Tiffany 1981), the lack of a Mississippian component in the earliest Mill Creek sites, and the predominant use of indigenous pottery types throughout the Mill Creek sequence all point to a trait-unit rather than a site-unit intrusion to account for the Mississippian material culture present in Mill Creek sites.

Groups represented by the Great Oasis Aspect are now considered as probable ancestors of the Mill Creek culture (Henning 1971b; Tiffany 1982a, 1983). The Glenwood culture may have developed from resident Late Woodland period cultures in the region, or it may represent peoples with a fully developed Nebraska variant complex who moved into the Glenwood locality for a relatively short period of time (Hotopp 1978; Zimmerman 1977b).

Gibbon (1972) once argued that Oneota developed out of some portion of the Effigy Mound tradition among peoples who adapted to intensive agriculture and diffusing Mississippian ideas. He now notes (1982:86), however, there is no Late Woodland period group in the Upper Mississippi Valley exhibiting Oneota-like traits which could provide the transitional link for the Woodland-Oneota metamorphosis.

Iowa Cultures

MILL CREEK CULTURE

The Mill Creek culture of northwest Iowa dates from A.D. 900 to 1300 (Anderson 1981; Tiffany 1982a). Mill Creek is composed of early and late Little Sioux phases and a Big Sioux phase representing sites in the Little Sioux and Big Sioux valleys. Taxonomically, the Mill Creek culture is considered part of the Initial variant of the Middle Missouri tradition (D. Anderson 1969; Henning 1971b; Henning and Henning 1978; Tiffany 1983), and includes several diagnostic traits (Alex 1971:38–40; Anderson 1987; Tiffany 1983:17–18).

First, some Mill Creek sites, apparently those in the latter part of the sequence, are fortified. The fortifications consist of stockade lines on truncated spurs of land. The Wittrock site (13OB4), however, is fortified with a bastioned stockade, a ditch, and a rampart. Second, the village plans for the Big Sioux and Little Sioux phases as reported from the Chan-ya-ta (13BV1), Wittrock (13OB4), and Kimball (13PM4) sites show small, compact villages with houses laid out in rows (Orr 1963; Tiffany 1982a). Third, Mill Creek houses are semisubterranean, rectangular structures with either internal or external entryways. House size and form, however, are more variable in Mill Creek sites than in other villages of the Initial variant. The superstructure on Mill Creek and Over Focus (Lower James phase) houses appears to be different than commonly reported for Initial variant houses. Wattle-and-daub construction has been suggested as well as earth-lodge type construction and banking the exterior walls with earth (Alex 1973, 1981a; Baerreis and Alex 1974; Tiffany 1982a).

Fourth, the stone, bone, and shell industries of Mill Creek culture sites as described by Anderson (1973), Baerreis (1968), Dallman (1977), Fugle (1957, 1962), and Tiffany (1982a) show that Mill Creek assemblages fall within the range of like assemblages found on Initial variant sites (Lehmer 1971:73–95). Important Mill Creek artifact types in these categories include catlinite elbow pipes, notched and unnotched triangular projectile points—the latter include side- and basal-notched specimens reminiscent of Cahokia points—and discoidals or chunky stones. Stone hoes and pulley-shaped earspools have been reported from Mill Creek sites, but their occurrence is very rare (Fugle 1957:132). A common feature of Mill Creek assemblages is the presence of both marine and fresh water (*Anculosa*) shell beads. Large sections of cut marine shell as well as whole marine shells have been found in the Big Sioux phase sites (Henning 1967:189–90). Recently, two long-nosed god masks were reported from Mill Creek sites (Anderson 1975; Anderson et al. 1979). Fifth, only one small piece of copper from the Wittrock site (13OB4) is known for the Mill Creek culture. Fugle (1957:276) also commented on the scarcity of copper from Mill Creek sites.

Sixth, Mill Creek pottery is most similar to the ceramics from the Over Focus specifically and the Initial variant sites on the main trench of the Missouri Valley generally. Incising (trailing) and tool impressions are the main decorating techniques; decoration is confined to the exterior lip/rim and the upper shoulder of the vessels. Common types include Mitchell Modified Lip, Kimball Modified Lip, and Chamberlain Incised. Cord-impressed decoration on Mill Creek pottery is rare (Ives 1962). While Mill Creek sites may have as much as twenty percent of the ceramic assemblage composed of locally made Mississippian influenced forms, Mississippian trade pottery constitutes less than one percent of any assemblage (Alex 1971: 34; Tiffany 1983); appendages including effigy forms, lugs, and handles are characteristic Mill Creek ceramic traits. The frequency of various types of Mississippian-influenced, locally made pottery and Mississippian vessel forms in Mill Creek sites appears to shift coevally with the Mississippian sequence at Cahokia; Mississippian influence also appears to increase through time in Mill Creek sites (Anderson 1981; Henning 1967:188; Tiffany 1983).

Finally, burial patterns of the Mill Creek culture are poorly known. Primary burials within the villages have been reported (Orr 1963) as have bluff top ossuaries (Anderson et al. 1979). Mound and scaffold burial has been inferred (Alex 1971:39).

Other important features of Mill Creek assemblages include the absence of any evidence for Oneota interaction with Mill Creek (Henning 1967:191–92), the presence of Great Oasis Aspect pottery in very small amounts in some Mill Creek assemblages, and the sporadic evidence for contact with other Late Woodland period groups in western (Anderson 1981) and eastern Iowa (Tiffany 1982b).

HARTLEY PHASE

Mill Creek contact with eastern Iowa is seen in the presence of both Hartley Fort (13AM103) ceramics at the Chan-ya-ta site and with Mill Creek pottery and Mill Creek-influenced Late Woodland period ceramics

in association with Mississippian trade pottery at the Hartley Fort, type site of the Hartley phase, in northeastern Iowa (McKusick 1973; Tiffany 1982b). Other finds of Mill Creek pottery in northeast Iowa include the Waterville Rockshelter (13AM124), the O'Regan Terrace (13AM21), the Sixteen Rockshelter (13AM122), and surface finds of Mill Creek pottery from the confluence of Pleasant Creek with the Mississippi, just west of the Apple River culture sites in Illinois (fig. 9.1). Orr's (1963) excavation notes on the aforementioned rockshelters are unclear, but it appears that the Mill Creek pottery was found in association with Late Woodland components in each site represented by Madison Cord Impressed, Madison Plain, and Lane Farm Cord Impressed pottery. A few Oneota sherds were found in each rockshelter but in both instances appear to represent later components postdating the mixed Late Woodland/Mill Creek units. Additionally, the Waterville Rockshelter produced a fragment of a red-slipped seed jar.

Other eastern Iowa Woodland sites have produced Mississippian artifacts. Items found include a small hooded waterbottle from the Aicher Mound group (13JH1) just north of Iowa City and a circular shell gorget depicting a coiled rattlesnake with a feline head from the Keyes phase (Effigy Mound tradition) component of Hadfields Cave (13JN3) on the Maquoketa River (Benn 1980:117). Stirling phase-equivalent Mississippian pottery has been recovered apparently from the Late Woodland component of the Gast Farm site (13LA12) in the Mississippi Valley in southeast Iowa and a locally made, rolled lip rim has been recovered from 13WS61, a small Late Woodland campsite near the Iowa River in southeast Iowa (Tiffany 1986a:240–45).

With the exception of the Hartley Fort, all of the sites in question have either been largely destroyed or never excavated. The contextual association of the Mississippian and Mill Creek materials, even where excavation records are present, is poor. Even though there is an apparent linkage among Late Woodland groups and Mississippian expansion in the Upper Mississippi Valley (Stoltman 1986), the relationships among Mississippian, Late Woodland period, Mill Creek, and Oneota cultures in northeast and eastern Iowa will remain inferential until other stratified sites are found.

GREAT OASIS ASPECT

Henning (1967:188–90) has cited the presence of *Anculosa* and marine shell beads and Great Oasis pottery from the Eveland Spoon River culture site as evidence of Mississippian–Great Oasis Aspect interaction. The Great Oasis Aspect is a regional Late Woodland period pottery complex that in northwest Iowa was probably ancestral to the Mill Creek culture (Tiffany 1983:20). The affiliation of Great Oasis with Late Woodland period cultures in the Upper Mississippi Valley can be most clearly seen in vessel form and decoration on Great Oasis pottery. Great Oasis vessels are globular in shape with flared rims; the decorative patterns on the exterior of Great Oasis rims are basically trailed versions of the cord-impressed design elements found on the rims of pottery types like Madison Cord Impressed, Minott's Cord Impressed, and Maples Mills pottery (Henning 1971b:8–9; Johnson 1969; Tiffany 1982a). Alex (1981b:40) has noted that the Great Oasis Aspect is not particularly well dated (Henning and Henning 1978; Tiffany 1981). The suggested range of A.D. 850–1100 indicates that the Great Oasis Aspect both pre-dates the Mill Creek culture and is contemporaneous with it and other Initial variant Middle Missouri tradition complexes.

Henning and Henning (1978:14) have used the Great Oasis radiocarbon dates and the similarity in house types and village plan from essentially one Great Oasis site to suggest that the Great Oasis Aspect is part of the Middle Missouri tradition. The site in question, West Broken Kettle (13PM25), is just across a small stream from the Broken Kettle (13PM1) Mill Creek site. Collections from the West Broken Kettle site in the repository of the Office of the State Archaeologist of Iowa contain three Foreman ware rims (a Middle Missouri-tradition pottery type), a bowl, and a shell-tempered Fairmount phase-like rim (Tiffany 1983:19). Generally, Great Oasis pottery has been found on Mill Creek sites, and Great Oasis influence in Mill Creek pottery is readily apparent. Except for what may be mixed components, however, Mill Creek pottery is not found on Great Oasis sites (Henning 1982:282–84, 293). There is also no evidence for Great Oasis–Oneota interaction (Henning 1967:191).

The Great Oasis Aspect is not considered part of the Initial variant of the Middle Missouri tradition as Henning and Henning (1978:14) have argued because: (1) Great Oasis sites are distributed differently than Initial variant sites—Great Oasis sites are found in both riverine and lacustrine locales (Henning 1971a); (2) Great Oasis sites are not fortified; (3) Great Oasis sites generally lack the elaborate bone tool industry associated with Initial variant assemblages; (4) regardless of general similarities in vessel form and decoration, Great Oasis groups did not make Initial variant pottery; and (5) trade goods, artifacts, and decorative styles indicative of Mississippian contact and interaction after A.D. 1000, which are characteristic of eastern Initial variant sites, are virtually absent from Great Oasis sites (Tiffany 1983:21).

Some of the similarity between Great Oasis pottery found within the Mill Creek culture site distribution specifically and Initial variant pottery generally is probably a result of the overlapping distribution of the two com-

plexes and reflects both developmental and possibly later interactive relationships. The broad distribution of Great Oasis sites suggests that more than one group is sharing in a regional ceramic tradition (Henning 1982:284). The limited Mississippian artifacts present in Great Oasis sites indicate that most Great Oasis sites may pre-date the development of Mississippian culture at Cahokia. The presence of Mississippian artifacts in a Great Oasis site, as in the case of West Broken Kettle, has led to the suggestion that "those Great Oasis groups coming under Mississippian influence became Mill Creek/Initial variant cultures and those that did not (or did not accept Mississippian ideas in the same way) continued on with the more conservative Great Oasis lifeway" (Tiffany 1983:22). Alex (1981b:40) has formulated a model based on Great Oasis subsistence and the regional ecology supportive of this viewpoint. Alex proposes that riverine-oriented Great Oasis groups developed a Plains Village lifeway as a result of being in a more optimal area for floodplain agriculture and having better access to northern Plains bison herds and trade or contact with Mississippian groups, whereas lake-oriented Great Oasis groups continued with the older Woodland lifeway because they were in less desirable areas for agriculture and bison hunting.

GLENWOOD CULTURE

The Glenwood culture of southwest Iowa exhibits the subsistence and settlement pattern and material culture traits characteristic of the Nebraska variant of the central Plains tradition (W. Wedel 1959:560–62). Unlike Mississippian community patterns the seasonally utilized, isolated farmsteads of the Glenwood culture are not linked to broader interactive settlements such as towns and ceremonial centers. Although radiocarbon dates from several Glenwood house sites range from A.D. 430 to 1640 (Tiffany 1981:65–67), recent analysis of the radiocarbon dates and computer simulation suggest that the occupation of the Glenwood locality was short and occurred between A.D. 1100 and 1250 (Hotopp 1978:259–60; Zimmerman 1977b:132). The Glenwood culture thus appears to represent a relatively late movement of a fully developed Nebraska variant group into southwest Iowa.

The percentage of shell-tempered pottery is much higher (up to thirty-two percent of the total ceramic assemblage) in some Glenwood culture house sites than reported for the Mill Creek culture (Zimmerman 1977a:74). As Anderson and Anderson (1960:33) note, however, the overwhelming majority of these ceramics are either examples of shell-tempered Glenwood pottery types emulating Oneota pottery or are Oneota vessels.

Unlike Mill Creek, the evidence for Mississippian trade vessels and Mississippian-influenced vessel forms is inconsistent from site to site and rarely constitutes three percent of the total ceramic sample from a house site (Anderson 1961). Mississippian or Mississippian-influenced traits in the Glenwood culture include earspools, red-slipped sherds, effigy lugs and handles, pottery figurines, side- and basal-notched projectile points, discoidals, beakers, bowls, seed jars, one red-slipped high-neck waterbottle, and limited examples of Southern Cult iconography, the latter being the result of findings postdating Henning's (1967) analysis.

Although Glenwood pottery has been reported from Spoon River culture sites (Henning 1967), Mississippian-Glenwood culture contact appears to be an example of trait-unit intrusion; but unlike Mill Creek, Glenwood contact with Mississippian culture is restricted, indirect, and discontinuous. Furthermore, the Mississippian presence in the Glenwood culture need not be from Cahokia given the generalized nature of Mississippian materials from Glenwood culture sites.

ONEOTA

Oneota sites in Iowa have been radiocarbon dated from A.D. 690 to historic times (Tiffany 1981). These sites range from small, compact villages to large, dispersed villages over 120 hectares in extent. Most Iowa Oneota sites are unfortified, multicomponent occupations consisting of diffuse village scatters of less than two hectares in extent (Tiffany 1982c:12). House types, where reported (Harvey 1979; McKusick 1973), consist of bark- or mat-covered ovoid longhouses. Several types of burials are reported from Iowa Oneota sites, including primary interments within villages, cemeteries near villages, and intrusive burials in Woodland stage mounds (M. Wedel 1959; Alex 1971:39).

Evidence for Mississippian-Oneota interaction from Iowa sites is isolated and rare, almost to the point of being nonexistent (Fugle 1957:276; Henning 1970:165).

With respect to shell tempering, Brown (1982:108) has noted that this long-assumed Mississippian trait associated with Oneota ceramics may have nothing to do directly with Mississippian influence but instead with the spread of corn agriculture through the Upper Mississippi Valley (Gibbon 1974:133; Hall 1967a:177–79). In general, other purported Mississippian influences such as small side and basally notched projectile points, globular jars with handles or lugs, and fortified villages may be more reflective of Late Woodland stage cultural development involving the spread of the bow and arrow and intensive agriculture in the upper Midwest. If this is the case, rather than a developmental relationship, Mississippian and non-Mississippian groups like Oneota simply share a number of regional technological developments common to the cultures of the region.

Mississippian contact or influence in Iowa Oneota sites is represented by occasional finds of side and basally notched projectile points, discoidals, bowls, effigy lugs, waterbottles, and marine shell artifacts. Work in catlinite, however, in the form of disc pipes, is a diagnostic Oneota trait, and copper artifacts are found in some but not all Oneota components.

There is no evidence for Oneota interaction with Great Oasis and Mill Creek. The latter part of the Glenwood culture occupation of southwest Iowa is heavily influenced by Oneota (Anderson 1961; Henning 1967:191). In northeast Iowa Oneota burials are intrusive into the Hartley Fort (Tiffany 1982b). The Hartley Fort and the unfortified Grant Oneota site (13AM201) lie within 600 meters of each other. Even though the Hartley Fort certainly predates the Grant site, the radiocarbon assays from both sites overlap (McKusick 1973:10; Tiffany 1981). There is no evidence, however, for contact between the Grant site and the Hartley Fort; and as discussed earlier, the Oneota occupation in northeast Iowa appears to be later than the Hartley Fort/Mill Creek occupation of the region.

Discussion

Based on Willey et al.'s classification (1956), the relationship between Mississippian and the Mill Creek and Glenwood cultures is seen as trait-unit intrusions. Mississippian traits occur in combination with indigenous cultural traits, resulting in a fusion through time dominated by the recipient culture. The nature of the ongoing Mississippian interaction among these cultures was different. Interaction between the Mill Creek culture and Cahokia appears to have been extensive, continuous, and direct. Mississippian interaction with the Glenwood culture was indirect and discontinuous and is represented by

Mississippian traits of such a generalized nature that the source may not have been a major Mississippian center like Cahokia.

Trading is generally cited as the main mechanism for interaction between the Mill Creek culture and Cahokia (Alex 1971; Henning 1967:190). Evidence for contact between Mill Creek and Mississippian centers is abundant on Mill Creek sites but virtually nonexistent on Mississippian sites. With the exception of the northeast Iowa Late Woodland-period sites with Mill Creek pottery, the non-Mississippian archaeological manifestations between Mill

Creek and Cahokia show little if any evidence for either Mill Creek or Mississippian contact. It can be assumed as others have suggested (Gibbon 1974) that Mississippian centers like Cahokia were the dominant partner in trading activities among non-Mississippian cultures of the Upper Mississippi Valley and that the trading contacts made were probably initiated by the Mississippians.

While the nature of Mill Creek/Mississippian exchange appears to be largely one-way, Henning (1967:190; 1982: 288–89) and Alex (1971) argue for the presence of a large-scale trade network between Mill Creek and Cahokia involving marine shell. Henning (1967:190) suggests that some groups of the Great Oasis Aspect served as middlemen for this exchange. The evidence presented supports the alternative proposed by Alex (1971:43–45) and Tiffany (1987) that Mill Creek groups themselves served as intermediaries or gateway communities in a reciprocal exchange network where buffalo hides and other animal products such as dried meat were obtained from northern Plains hunting and gathering groups by Mill Creek traders. These items were exchanged at Mississippian centers like Cahokia for marine shell which in turn was made into beads and other items by Mill Creek villagers for trade with northern Plains cultures. The presence of whole marine shells, large cut pieces of marine shell, and finished marine shell artifacts in Mill Creek sites of the Big Sioux phase attest to the fact that trade in marine shell was probably substantive. Although the evidence for bison hides or other perishable items is based on indirect evidence, there is certainly abundant data from Mill Creek sites that bison were hunted and processed. Such items as bison hides were thus attainable by Mill Creek groups and may have been in demand in the large, agricultural-based Mississippian communities. Recent research has demonstrated the feasibility of large-scale, long-distance trade in foodstuffs between the Mill Creek culture and Mississippian centers like Cahokia (Little 1987; Tiffany 1987).

If such a trade network were operative, either a mutualistic exchange system as described by K. A. Spielmann (1982, 1983) for the late prehistoric-period Pueblo/southern Plains trade or a model derived from the Historic-period trade among Plains village and hunting and gathering groups as detailed by J. Jablow (1950:22, 45–46), A. J. Ray (1974:38–40, 55–57, 75) and W. Raymond Wood (1980) provide well-documented analogies for Mill Creek–Mississippian interaction. Thus, contrary to Anderson's (1987:531) suggestion, Mississippian pottery and artifacts found on Mill Creek sites may reflect a necessary and important social mechanism for establishing and conducting ongoing exchange. These artifacts were used by Mississippians to develop and sustain a more gen-

eral interactive economic system with non-Mississippian groups that was beneficial to all parties.

To summarize, the archaeological record clearly indicates trade took place between Mill Creek and Mississippian groups. Models dealing with the rationale and mechanisms for this exchange can be derived from ethnographic and ethnohistoric data. Archaeological verification of all aspects of Mill Creek/Mississippian trade is unlikely, however (Drennan 1984:35–38; Earle and Erickson 1977:3). Regardless, the presence of heavily Mill Creek-influenced ceramics as well as Mill Creek and Mississippian pottery at the Hartley Fort in northeast Iowa suggests an on-site intrusion by Mill Creek groups into an area where other aspects of a regional Late Woodland-stage society dominated and functioned. The scattered finds of Mill Creek pottery in other locales in northeast Iowa in close proximity to the Apple River culture, the recovery of Mill Creek pottery from formative Spoon River culture sites, and the scattered finds of Mississippian artifacts in Late Woodland-period contexts in eastern Iowa, all suggest the establishment of a trade network among Mill Creek and Stirling phase–equivalent Mississippian communities in the Upper Mississippi Valley.

The assemblages and distribution of sites associated with either Mill Creek or Glenwood appear to represent parts of social entities that were biologically, culturally, and linguistically distinct. Glenwood and Mill Creek are thus seen as representing archaeological manifestations of societies in an anthropological sense. The archaeological record shows Mill Creek and Glenwood interacted with each other sparingly and with Mississippian culture in different ways.

Mississippian–Glenwood culture interaction appears to be less extensive, discontinuous, and more indirect than Mississippian–Mill Creek interaction. As Henning noted, "Contact between Mill Creek and nearly adjacent Nebraska culture groups was minimal. Mississippian traits so characteristic of the Big Sioux Mill Creek sites are very rare on Nebraska culture components" (1967:191).

Categorizing Mississippian-Oneota relationships is much more difficult. Oneota sites in Iowa and northern Missouri have long been thought to be related to historical Chiwere-speaking Siouan groups (Griffin 1937; M. Wedel 1959). The archaeological record shows that Deighan-speaking Siouan groups and possibly some Algonquin-speaking tribes also had an Oneota material culture (Brown 1965; Henning 1970:4). Oneota has been called a "pottery culture" (Henning 1970:13). Given the broad spatial and temporal distribution of sites in the upper Midwest sharing Oneota pottery, it is reasonable to assume that, like the Great Oasis Aspect and unlike Mill

Creek or Glenwood, archaeologists are not dealing with a single sociopolitical entity with Oneota. Instead, at any one time in the archaeological record, Oneota probably represents a number of cultures that are sharing in a generalized ceramic tradition and whose archaeological manifestations, with respect to subsistence, settlement, and items of material culture such as the chipped stone assemblage, catlinite disc pipes, and tablets, appear similar because the groups involved interacted and adopted similar exploitative strategies in adapting to the various ecotones of the Prairie Peninsula.

Interpretive problems with Oneota are compounded by the lack of taxonomically defined, dated components. Concepts such as Orr or Blue Earth are now largely meaningless because they have been redefined to describe assemblages from many sites representing several hundred years in time and which are distributed over an enormous geographic area (cf. Henning 1970 and M. Wedel 1959 on the Orr phase). What is needed, as Gibbon states, is "the breaking down of Oneota assemblages into their constituents in order to explore the complexity of spatial and social relationships that must have existed in the past" (1982:87). It is thus difficult to categorize Mississippian-Oneota interaction because of how researchers have interpreted the Oneota tradition (Gibbon 1982:87).

Looking at the Iowa data, even though radiocarbon dates indicate contemporaneity of Mill Creek, Glenwood, Great Oasis, and western Iowa Oneota (Tiffany 1981), there is no evidence for interaction between Great Oasis and Oneota or Mill Creek and Oneota. The Wittrock Mill Creek site (13OB4) has produced "a few [Oneota] rimsherds" (Henning 1967:189), but no Mill Creek pottery has been found on any Oneota site. The Wittrock specimen apparently consisted of a single Oneota rim sherd found in the stockade (Robert A. Alex, personal communication, 1983). There is no Oneota pottery present in the Wittrock site collections that are housed in the repository of the Office of the State Archaeologist of Iowa.

Oneota-like pottery and locally made pottery with Oneota shoulder designs have been recovered from late Glenwood culture sites (Anderson 1961:67; Henning 1967:191). No Glenwood materials have been reported from western Iowa Oneota sites. Given this fact and the evidence for differential contact of Oneota with coeval cultures in which contemporaneity can be established by the archaeological assemblages independent of radiocarbon dates, a possible explanation would be that groups bearing Oneota material culture did not develop or were not present throughout much of Iowa until A.D. 1150. Support for this explanation comes from those who argue that fortified Mill Creek sites appear late in the Mill Creek sequence and are a response to the Oneota (Alex 1971;

D. Anderson 1969; Anderson 1981:120; Anderson 1987; Tiffany 1982a). Furthermore, Oneota sites lying within the Mill Creek site distribution, such as the Bastion site (13CK28), postdate the Mill Creek occupation (Tiffany 1981).

Although recent radiocarbon research and linguistic studies suggest the contrary (Dobbs 1982; Springer and Witkowski 1982), it is arguable that groups bearing Oneota material culture expanded onto the prairies after A.D. 1150, replacing Plains Village and Woodland groups and disrupting Mississippian interaction. There seems to be little doubt among researchers that Oneota became the dominant archaeological culture on the prairies after A.D. 1350 (Alex 1971:44; Gibbon 1972, 1974). This can be seen in the appearance of Oneota materials in late Spoon River culture sites (Conrad, chap. 6; Harn 1978: 247) and the widespread use of Oneota pottery design elements on the ceramics of indigenous late prehistoric groups in the central and northern Plains, the eastern prairies, and to the south (Brown 1982:108; Grange 1968; Henning 1970; Spaulding 1956).

Oneota material culture has been generally treated as a single, simple entity with respect to Mississippian contact, interaction, and influence. An approach that seeks to organize and define the variability of Oneota assemblages in space and through time would be preferable. Researchers may discover, as Gibbon (1982:87) notes, that "Oneota" can be explained in several ways depending upon what assemblage is being examined. For example, the Orr Focus in the Paleozoic Plateau region of northeast Iowa probably represents the protohistoric Ioway tribe even though the transformation and spread of Oneota material culture in the late prehistoric period as exemplified by ceramics with Orr Focus shoulder designs occurred among non-Chiweran-speaking groups throughout the Prairie Peninsula (Gibbon 1972; Henning 1970).

Much of the evidence researchers cite regarding the origins, development, and interrelationship of Mississippian and non-Mississippian cultures in the western Prairie Peninsula is based on radiocarbon dates from Iowa. For the Oneota, Glenwood, Great Oasis, and Mill Creek sites in question, these dates for the most part were collected piecemeal from secondary contexts from multicomponent sites. These assays may accurately date fragments of charred wood, but they do not necessarily date the prehistoric occupations with which they are associated. It is not necessary, however, to rely upon radiocarbon dating to establish the archaeological relationships among the prehistoric cultures in question. Henning's (1967) study and the data presented in this chapter can be summarized as follows: (1) the Great Oasis Aspect preceded Mill Creek but is contemporaneous with the early part of the Mill Creek sequence; (2) Mill Creek and the Hartley phase were contemporaneous and preceded Oneota; (3) Glenwood culture was contemporaneous with later Mill Creek sites; and (4) since Oneota influence is present in late Glenwood sites and not in Mill Creek or Great Oasis sites, Mill Creek people may have abandoned western Iowa prior to the termination of the Glenwood culture, perhaps as a result of Oneota development in western Iowa.

Summary

This chapter reviewed evidence on the Mississippian presence in Iowa and represents the first such study since Henning's comprehensive 1967 summary. A definition of Mississippian culture was presented that is thought to reflect a consensus of how Middle Mississippian is perceived by researchers in the upper Midwest. Based on this operational definition, various theories on the origins of and interaction among Mississippian-influenced cultures in Iowa were discussed. Using trait lists it was shown that the development of and interaction among Oneota, Mill Creek, and Glenwood with Mississippian cultures are examples of trait-unit rather than site-unit intrusions. In all cases, Mississippian traits were incorporated into indigenous assemblages with local patterns predominating. The nature of Mississippian interaction with non-Mississippian groups in Iowa was also discussed. It was suggested that the Mill Creek culture had a direct, continuous relationship with Cahokia involving a reciprocal exchange system.

Glenwood-Mississippian interaction, on the other hand, was characterized as indirect and discontinuous because of the limited evidence for Mill Creek–Glenwood culture contact and the fact that there is less evidence in Glenwood culture sites generally for Mississippian contact from site to site among both contemporaneous sites and through time. The difficulty in characterizing Oneota-Mississippian interaction was seen as a problem of incorrectly perceiving Oneota "as a mass, composite, unitary phenomenon" (Gibbon 1982:87). It was suggested that Oneota may represent a number of prehistoric societies sharing in a similar material culture which expanded onto the prairies after A.D. 1150, generally replacing Plains Village and Mississippian groups. This expansion may have been a response to a decline in Mississippian influence in the Upper Mississippi Valley brought on or intensified by the Oneota expansion, changing climatic conditions, or some combination of these factors.

ACKNOWLEDGMENTS

I would like to thank Duane Anderson, Stephen Lensink, Robert Burchfield, the volume editors, and the symposium participants for providing comments on this paper. This chapter is *Iowa Quaternary Studies Contribution* no. 13.

10

Ancient Aztalan: The Cultural and Ecological Context of a Late Prehistoric Site in the Midwest

LYNNE G. GOLDSTEIN

JOHN D. RICHARDS

Traditionally, sites on the northern periphery of the Middle Mississippian cultural sphere have been viewed as evidence of Mississippian site-unit intrusion with resultant acculturation of local Woodland and Oneota groups (e.g., Griffin 1946, 1960b). While it is clear that sites such as Aztalan in southeastern Wisconsin and Bryan and Silvernale in southeast Minnesota represent some degree of Mississippian presence, the nature of that presence is not well understood. The interpretive problems surrounding northern Mississippian manifestations can be traced to two major sources. First, few of these sites have been systematically excavated, fully analyzed, and the results published. Comparative data are thus scarce. Second, emphasis on the Mississippian aspects of these sites has directed attention away from the specific cultural and environmental context of each particular site. Sometimes, comparisons between the northern Mississippian sites and the large centers of the heartland are conducted

as though the northern sites existed in a cultural and environmental vacuum. If we are to move beyond speculation to construct meaningful interpretations of northern Mississippian sites, each site must be viewed in terms of its specific regional context.

We suggest that such analyses can be profitably conducted on three separate, but related, levels: (1) intrasite analyses of site structure, artifact distribution, stratigraphy, and chronology; (2) ecological evaluations of site environment and available resource distribution; and (3) reconstructions of local and regional cultural systems.

In this chapter we briefly describe the intrasite context of Aztalan and examine this site's ecological and cultural context. Although a comprehensive analysis is beyond the scope of the present effort, we intend the following discussion to serve as a foundation upon which future, more complete, analyses can be built.

The Aztalan Site

The Aztalan site (47Je1) is situated on the west bank of the Crawfish River, approximately five miles (8.05 kilometers) north of the confluence of the Rock and Crawfish rivers (fig. 10.1) in Jefferson County, Wisconsin. Currently, Aztalan is operated as a state park by the Wisconsin Department of Natural Resources and is managed and maintained by the Town of Aztalan.

Prehistorically, the site consisted of a palisaded mound-and-village complex oriented around a central plaza-like area (figure 10.2 outlines some of the major features of the site). Available radiocarbon dates range from A.D. 750 ± 150 (M-1037) to A.D. 1630 ± 200 (M-642) (Boszhardt 1977). However, the majority of assays suggest a major

occupation ca. A.D. 1100–1300 (Baerreis and Bryson 1965).

Approximately nine hectares of gently sloping land were completely encircled by about 1,340 meters of palisade. At intervals of twenty or twenty-five meters, square bastions protruded outward from the palisade walls (fig. 10.2). The wooden palisade and bastions were of single-post construction and were heavily plastered with a mixture of mud and grass (Baerreis 1958; Barrett 1933).

Flat-topped pyramidal mounds were located in the southwest, northwest, and northeast corners of the enclosure, while a naturally occurring gravel knoll formed a high prominence in the southeast corner (fig. 10.2). A

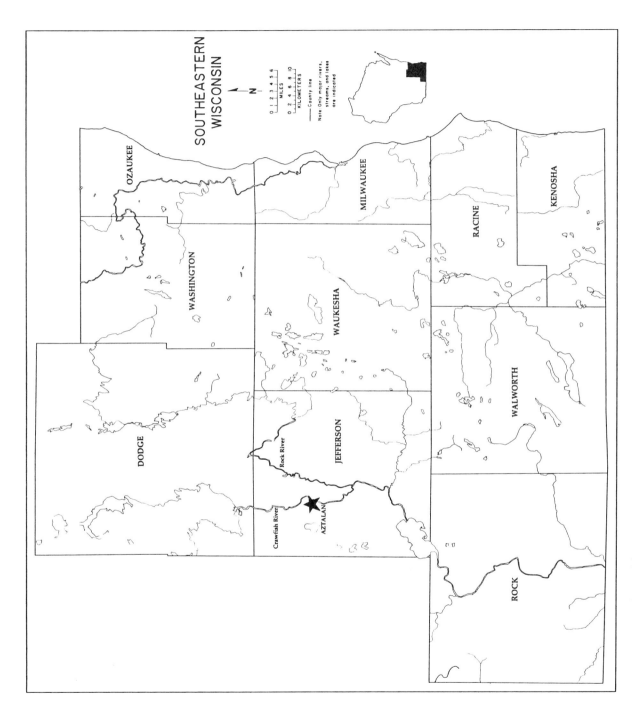

Figure 10.1. The General Geographic Location of the Aztalan Site

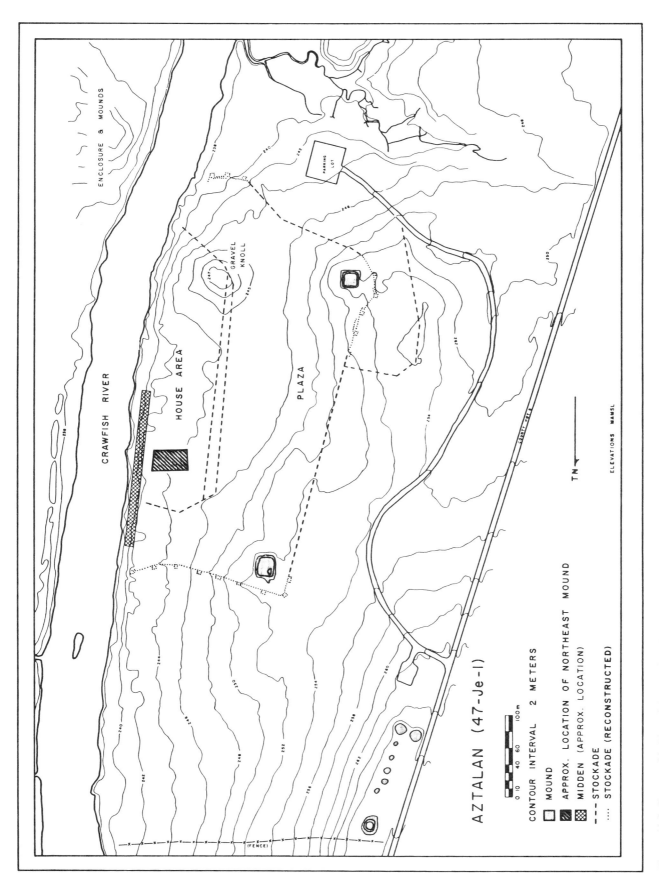

Figure 10.2. Topographic Plan of the Aztalan Site, with Major Areas and Features Indicated

large, roofed structure was situated atop the southwest mound, and a large, open structure occupied the summit of the northeast mound. Evidence is lacking for similar structural features atop the northwest mound, although a burned mortuary structure is reported for the top of the second stage of mound construction (Rowe 1958). The uppermost portions of the northwest mound were destroyed by plowing and erosion.

Although the summit of the gravel knoll was apparently devoid of building construction, portions of the knoll were traversed by an interior, bastioned palisade. Extending north from the gravel knoll, the interior palisade encircled the northeast mound and enclosed approximately 2.5 hectares adjacent to the river bank. Archaeological evidence suggests that the majority of domestic structures, pit features, and hearths were located within the northern one-half of this enclosure (area is generally indicated on figure 10.2).

Approximately three hectares of open, plaza-like area in the central portion of the site were also enclosed by a wooden palisade. This third palisade system appears to lack the bastions characteristic of the other palisade lines at the site. The archaeologically documented palisades at Aztalan may represent a single, coeval system or sequential constructions reflecting expansion or contraction of the settlement.

A number of site-related features were located beyond the outermost palisade. A single domestic structure is reported approximately 150 meters south of the southwest pyramidal mound. Numerous associated pit features suggest an extended occupation and domestic activities (Wittry and Baerreis 1958).

The most striking feature external to the outermost palisade is a series of conical mounds originating 200 meters west of the northwest pyramidal mound (fig. 10.2). Increase A. Lapham (1855) documented at least thirty mounds arranged in a linear fashion and extending northward for almost 400 meters (fig. 10.3). Barrett

(1933) recovered evidence of large, centrally placed posts in five of the remaining mounds.

In addition to the remains on the west bank of the Crawfish River, a mound and earthwork complex is located directly opposite Aztalan on the river's east bank (fig. 10.4). Mapped by Barrett (1933:253), the three-hectare complex includes a low, rectangular earthwork that encloses about one-half hectare. A bear effigy mound and a badly eroded conical mound occupy the interior of the enclosure. South of this feature, a second group includes a lizard effigy and two low, linear ridges. East of these groups are seven conical mounds of varying size. Barrett (1933) suggested that the earthworks on the east bank were not related to the major occupation of the west bank. Additional testing by T.M.N. Lewis in 1929 (published in 1954) and the University of Wisconsin-Milwaukee in 1979 (Goldstein 1979) tends to support Barrett's interpretation of the east bank complex as essentially "non-Aztalan" in nature.

Excavations at Aztalan have produced a large and relatively homogeneous artifact assemblage. Ceramics include shell-tempered and grit-tempered vessels similar to forms typical of Stirling phase assemblages from the American Bottom (Bennett 1952; Peters 1976). A large percentage of the recovered ceramics are, however, grit-tempered, cordmarked or cord-impressed types typical of Late Woodland wares in the Upper Great Lakes region (Baerreis and Freeman 1958). Nonceramic materials include small, triangular, unnotched and notched points; hoes of chert and freshwater mussel shell; chunky stones or discoidals; earspools; sandstone abraders; columella pendants; and copper long-nosed god masks (Barrett 1933).

Floral remains from Aztalan suggest aboriginal use of corn, squash, and nuts (Barrett 1933; Yerkes 1980). Faunal materials include white-tailed deer, elk, and a variety of small mammals. In addition, fish, freshwater mussels, turtles, and birds are present (Parmalee 1960).

Archaeological Interpretations

Aztalan has been the focus of scholarly and popular interest ever since Judge Nathaniel Hyer published the initial description of the site in 1837. However, despite the interest in the site and the extensive excavations of S. A. Barrett (1933), the Wisconsin Archaeological Survey (Baerreis 1958), and the State Historical Society of Wisconsin (Schneider 1964), Aztalan remains an anomaly in midwestern prehistory. A review of site-related literature yields a variety of interpretations of Aztalan's origins and significance.

The earliest interpretation was proposed by Judge Hyer

in 1837. He considered Aztalan the legendary place of origin of the Aztecs. Hyer's interpretation, and his subsequent naming of the site, was apparently based on the writings of Baron von Humboldt (the nineteenth-century German naturalist; von Humboldt 1814), and the notion that the legends of Aztec origins had persisted over hundreds of years among the aboriginal peoples of Wisconsin (Barrett 1933:25; Birong 1979; Hall n.d.; McKern 1942:2).

Baron von Humboldt noted that Aztec chronicles referred to an ancestral homeland called "Aztlan," which

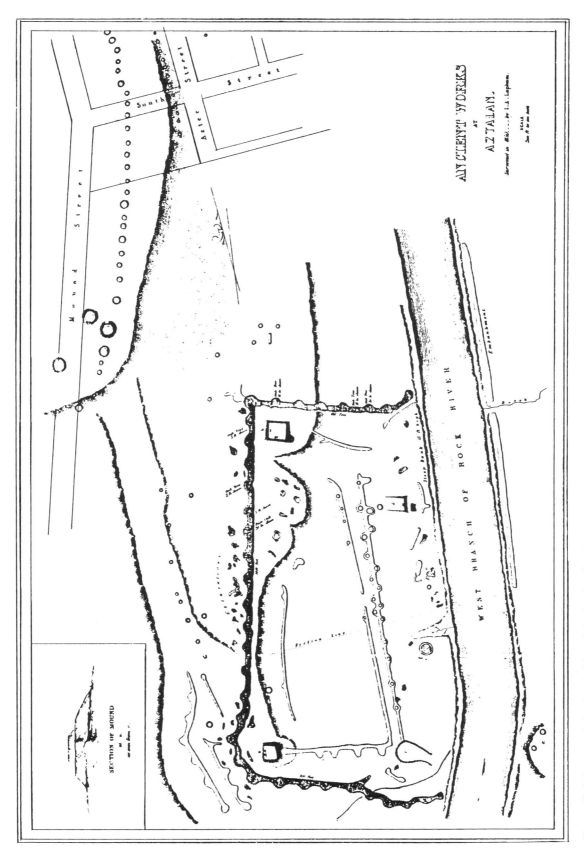

Figure 10.3. Increase A. Lapham's Map of the Aztalan Site (from Lapham 1855: pl. 34)

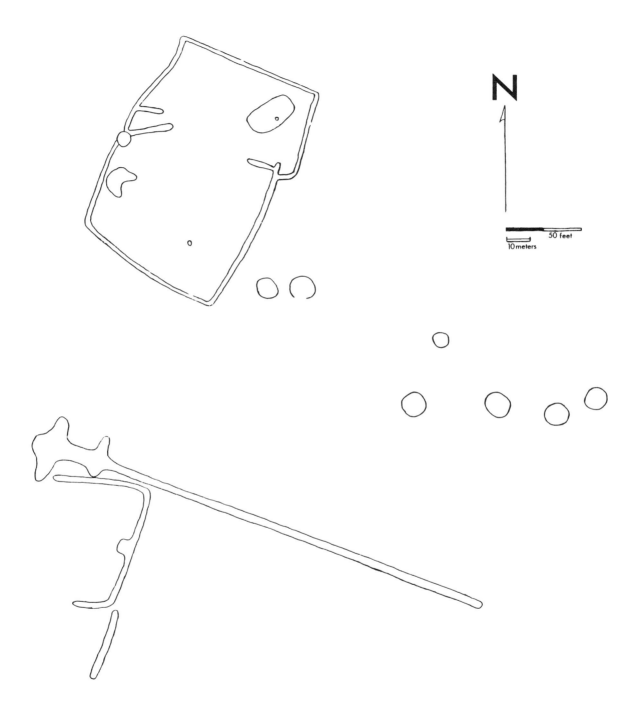

Figure 10.4. Earthworks on the East Bank of the Crawfish River (adapted from Barrett 1933:253, fig. 58)

was said to be located north of the Basin of Mexico. Hall (n.d.) has suggested that Hyer's bestowal of the name Aztalan on the Wisconsin site was the result of a faulty translation of von Humboldt's notoriously difficult French prose.

Another interpretation of Aztalan was provided by Increase A. Lapham in 1855. Lapham's (1855) careful and comprehensive survey of Aztalan (fig. 10.3) provided the first detailed information on the archaeological remains at the site. Based on his observations, Lapham concluded that Aztalan represented the work of a different group than those responsible for Wisconsin's effigy mounds. Accordingly, Lapham suggested that structural similarities between Aztalan and the Mayan site of Tulum argued for Aztalan's use as a ceremonial center erected by a group of Mexican colonists.

Perhaps the most frequently cited interpretations of the Aztalan site relate the occupation to Middle Mississippian sites further south. For example, similarities in material culture between Aztalan and the Cahokia site in southern Illinois have led to a variety of models linking these two sites. Barrett (1933:370–72) placed Aztalan within the Monks Mound aspect of Middle Mississippian and called the site a "southern island" in an otherwise Woodland environment. Fowler (1974), Griffin (1960b), and Hall (1962) have seen Aztalan as a Cahokian outpost. Aztalan has also been regarded as a trading post supplying Cahokia with a variety of goods (Gibbon 1974; Peters 1976; Porter 1969; Stuebe 1976). A third scenario has been suggested by Riley and Apfelstadt (1978), who speculate that Aztalan represents the results of successful proselytization by Middle Mississippian missionaries.

More recently, Fowler and Hall (1978) and Hall (1973) have suggested that Aztalan may not represent direct interaction with Cahokia. Rather, they would derive the site from Mississippianized Woodland peoples in northern Illinois. Hurley (1975) also suggests a generalized Mississippian base for Aztalan and sees the site as a hybrid resulting from interaction between Middle Mississippian and Effigy Mound peoples; other authors have proposed similar ideas (e.g., Stout 1911; Stuebe 1976).

The Intrasite Context of Aztalan

Almost 150 years of archaeological investigations at Aztalan have succeeded in eliminating only the Hyer and Lapham interpretations of the site. Archaeologists' inability to agree on a single interpretation for Aztalan stems from the complexity of the problem and from an interest in getting answers to more basic questions before tackling the larger issues. However, the larger question is difficult to answer for other reasons as well; there must be a comprehensive synthesis of available data and the site must be viewed in terms of its specific cultural and environmental context.

Several specific problems relative to interpretation of Aztalan's intrasite context can be identified. First, a generalized picture of the entire site should include the materials from Barrett's extensive excavations. Much of the research at Aztalan has focused on answering specific questions regarding chronology and typology, especially in terms of pottery. For example, analysis of the Late Woodland pottery at the site has tended to focus on very specific problems, as in Baerreis and Freeman's (1958) analysis of the kinds of collared ware at the site, or Hurley's (1977) comparison of collared to other Late Woodland pottery types. Similarly, published analyses of the shell-tempered pottery have either been very specific (as in Porter's 1966 thin-section study), or limited to collections recovered subsequent to Barrett's major work at the site (e.g., Bleed 1970). Given the problems of fine-grained provenience documentation, researchers have tended to use the data they have collected, rather than include Barrett's data in their analyses (Maher and Baerreis's 1958 analysis of the Aztalan lithic complex is a notable exception).

Second, Aztalan is a very complex site, and a variety of archaeologists have worked there. Because of the site complexity and the number of past efforts, no one has done a complete synthesis of all past excavations. This means that it is difficult to discuss the interrelationships of features, structures, houses, mounds, and other elements at the site.

Third, to get an understanding of the organization of Aztalan requires an explication of the site's spatial structure. Other than an early summary of the house types present at the site (Wittry and Baerreis 1958), there have been no published analyses of the spatial structure of Aztalan.

Fourth, excavations since Barrett have generally been done in response to park development projects. This has meant that work has focused on very specific areas of the site. Although reports of the work in these areas are available, a detailed discussion of the overall site stratigraphy has not been prepared since the publication of Barrett's initial work in 1933.

Finally, the limits of the occupied portion of the site have traditionally been defined as the area bounded by the palisade walls. As a consequence, little attention has been given to the potential existence of related structures or features outside the palisade.

As a result of the current state of synthesis, it is not now possible to discuss confidently Aztalan's intrasite context in detail. This, in turn, prevents meaningful comparisons between Aztalan and other sites or site-complexes in the Midwest. Clearly, what is needed is a comprehensive analysis and synthesis of all of the available data. Once this has been accomplished, a model of site structure and organization can be developed to guide future research and inform comparative studies.

Aztalan's Ecological Context

The geography around Aztalan (fig. 10.5) is a distinctive and unique combination of geologic, physiographic, and vegetation features. The region is studded with drumlins and intervening wetland strips. On the western boundary is a north-pointing wedge of outwash plains, wetlands, and lakes. The center of the region is a Y-shaped pattern of wetlands along the Crawfish and Rock rivers. The southern boundary is the Lake Mills recessional morainic system and the eastern boundary is near the edge of the geologic phenomenon known as the Kettle Moraine.

The region's distinctive vegetation pattern is characterized by oak openings on the west side of the Crawfish River, maple-basswood forest on the east side of the Rock River, and a mixed forest between the two rivers (fig. 10.6; Curtis 1959; Dorney 1980, 1981; Zicker 1955). The region is also noted for its varied wetlands, which are among the most extensive in the state. Included in this category are swamps, tamarack bogs, wet prairies, and sedge meadows (fig. 10.5).

In southeastern Wisconsin, three environmental zones have especially high food potential for humans (Clarke 1976; Goldstein 1987; Whittaker 1975). These zones are the deciduous forest; swamps and marshes; and lakes, rivers, and stream valleys. While archaeologists have long noted the food values in the forest and the lakes-rivers-streams, the swamps and marshes have been largely ignored. However, swamps and marshes are among the richest ecological zones in the world.

The Crawfish River would have been a particularly desirable location for prehistoric settlement for several reasons (Goldstein 1987). First, southeastern Wisconsin has the most suitable soils in the state for wildlife habitats, but the Crawfish area has soils with fewer limitations than does the Rock (Kay 1979). Second, from a location on the Crawfish River, one could easily gain access to all vegetation zones in the region, including the area's most extensive and productive wetlands. Third, the drumlin fields in the region are concentrated to the east of the Rock River, leaving a more level, rolling landscape to the west.

Fourth, local residents indicate that the numerous free-flowing springs that drain into the Crawfish River apparently prevent complete winter freezing of the river. Thus, barring extreme conditions, the river and its resources may have been available year-round.

Fifth, in particular, fall and winter sites should be more likely along the Crawfish, and along the Rock at and below their confluence, because sites on the upper Rock would not have as easy access to the large deer herds in the oak forest and oak forest/wetlands. The confluence area would be particularly appealing because settlements near here would also have easy access to the maple-basswood forest.

Sixth, the Rock River is the major river in southeastern Wisconsin, and could be considered the prime "avenue of communication" (Gibbon 1972) for this region. One would, therefore, expect sites along the Rock. However, it should be noted that if one wanted access to groups or resources to the west and north, the Crawfish River would be more logical. From the Crawfish, one can easily move west and north—continuation along the Rock will not result in as efficient a trade route.

Most of the previous archaeological work in the Crawfish-Rock region (fig. 10.5) focused on Aztalan itself, on mounds within the area, or along the Rock River south of the region near Lake Koshkonong. Charles E. Brown's 1935 Rock River survey and some highway projects constituted the major non-mound or non-Aztalan oriented work. Our knowledge of the greater Aztalan area, therefore, was biased and sketchy. The University of Wisconsin-Milwaukee's (UWM) Crawfish-Rock archaeology project, concentrating on survey and testing, was initiated in 1976. It should be noted that James W. Porter, then of Loyola University, also did survey in the Crawfish Valley in 1975 and 1976 (Stuebe 1976); UWM joined him in 1976 and developed a separate, although complementary, survey strategy. UWM's multiphase survey strategy was designed to be the first step in a long-term regional program.

The primary goals of UWM's Crawfish-Rock project include: (1) an unbiased archaeological survey of the region; (2) an examination of prehistoric land-use patterns as a means of understanding settlement and subsistence adaptations and changes; and (3) an examination of the area for insights into the nature of Aztalan and its relationships to other contemporaneous cultural systems.

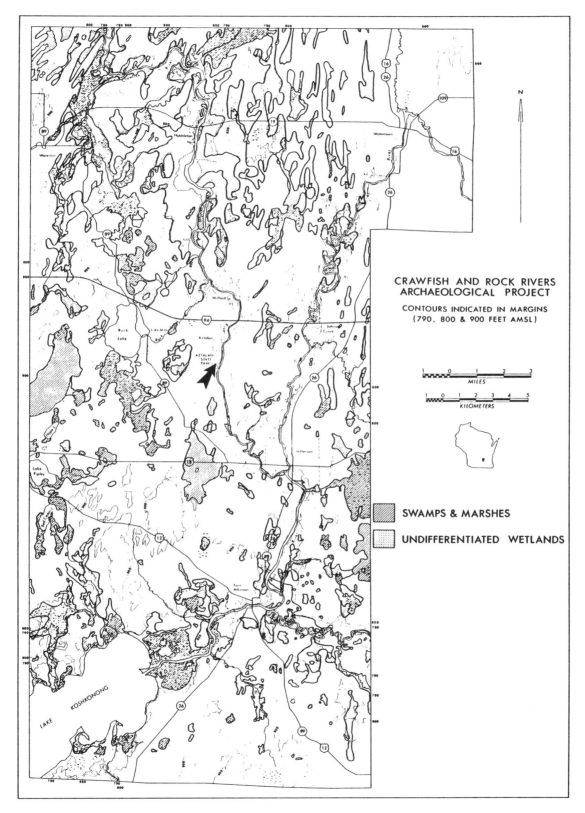

Figure 10.5. The Setting of the Aztalan Site within the Crawfish-Rock Project Area and in Relation to Wetlands

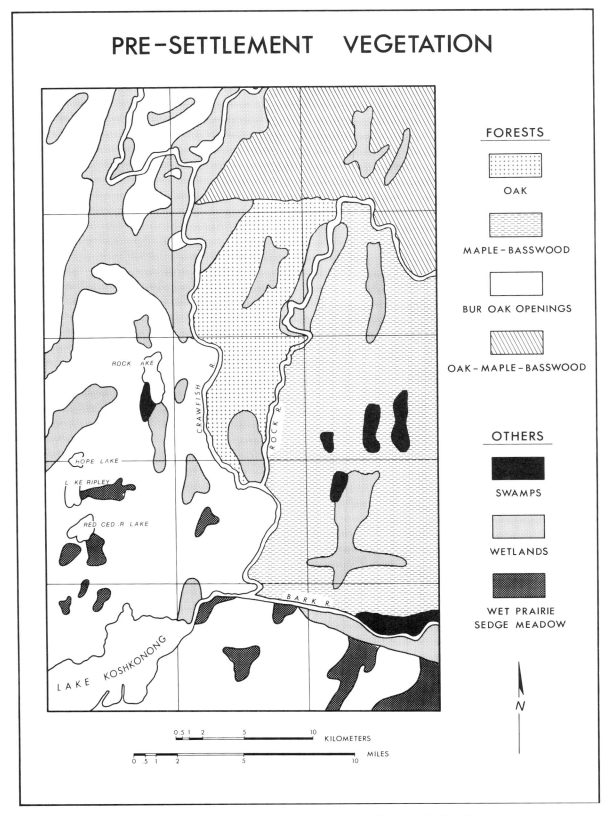

PRE-SETTLEMENT VEGETATION

FORESTS

OAK

MAPLE-BASSWOOD

BUR OAK OPENINGS

OAK-MAPLE-BASSWOOD

OTHERS

SWAMPS

WETLANDS

WET PRAIRIE
SEDGE MEADOW

N

0 .5 1 2   5   10   KILOMETERS

0 .5 1   2   5   10   MILES

Figure 10.6. Pre-European Settlement Vegetation Zones within the Crawfish-Rock Project Area

The archaeological survey has been multiphase in design (Goldstein 1979, 1980a, 1981, 1982, 1987), with each phase reflecting refinements based on the previous phases. The survey design is based on a 15% stratified proportional sample. The strata are based on a combination of landforms and other physiographic variables. Close-interval pedestrian survey and shovel probing techniques were employed in all survey phases, and one or more sites were also test excavated each year. The sampling unit was one quarter of a quarter-section (40 acres; i.e., about 16 hectares). The 15% sample of the approximately seventy square miles (ca. 181 square hectares) has been completed; over 7,000 acres (2,833 hectares) have been surveyed and over 400 new sites have been recorded.

From UWM's surveys, we find that few sites can be even generally classified as Mississippian. Only two sites (other than Aztalan) had shell-tempered pottery, and in each case fewer than three sherds were present. Indeed, all designations of sites as "Mississippian" were based on the presence of small triangular projectile points or shell-tempered pottery. Since both artifacts are also characteristic of Oneota, these sites could as easily be classified as Oneota. Likewise, the sites with small triangular points and no shell-tempered pottery could also be called Late Woodland. In any event, there are few "Mississippian" sites and none are particularly large or extensive. It should be noted that sites of every other time period are found in relative abundance; unless there is something very unusual about Mississippian sites, it is assumed that the lack of sites in some way represents the real prehistoric distribution.

Site survey has demonstrated that the region is rich in archaeological sites, suggesting significant prehistoric utilization of the area, and especially in relationship to rich wetland resources. However, both survey and excavations have shown that even sites that have high debris densities reflect *repeated* occupation *through time*, rather than *extended* occupation *at one time* (Goldstein 1987). Aztalan's apparent continuous occupation would thus appear anomalous. However, if one examines the area in terms of resources *and* the presence of other groups (e.g., Oneota), Aztalan's location might make more sense. If Aztalan represents a Middle Mississippian occupation, at least in part populated from points south, then it might be in the position of competition from surrounding groups. The village would not be established in a location that was clearly claimed by another group (say, around Lake Koshkonong), nor one that would directly interfere with another group's activities. Location on the Crawfish makes sense since the oak openings allow easy farming, and all the aquatic resources are still readily available. From Aztalan's location, the extensive marshes are certainly exploitable. Indeed, Aztalan's more riverine-oriented location would be most similar to environments further south. One could postulate that the people occupying Aztalan were actually here first, and the Oneota distribution is in response to them. Alternately, the few "Mississippian" sites found in the survey may represent seasonal camps for those living at Aztalan.

Aztalan's Cultural Context

Archaeologists have wrestled with the problem of contemporaneity of Late Woodland, Middle Mississippian, and Oneota populations for a long time. Regardless of perspective, however, there seem to be several items on which most archaeologists agree: namely, that there was at least some Middle Mississippian "influence" in the development of Oneota; that Oneota cannot be understood solely in the context of Middle Mississippian societies—that indigenous development from Late Woodland groups must also be taken into account; and that there is ample evidence of contemporaneity between Late Woodland, Middle Mississippian, and Oneota groups in at least some areas (Brown 1982; Gibbon 1972, 1974; Hall 1986; Henning 1970; Overstreet 1978; Tiffany 1981). We agree with Brown (1982) that overconcerns with issues of origin and the necessity to document the same origins for all Mississippian cultures create a series of false problems and dead ends.

In an attempt to define better Aztalan's cultural context, we will examine contemporaneity and development problems by briefly looking at Oneota lifeways and subsistence adaptations; Oneota as represented in southeastern Wisconsin; and Late Woodland and Middle Mississippi as represented in southeastern Wisconsin and at sites that may be similar to Aztalan.

Recent research has indicated that Oneota subsistence encompasses more than the traditional "mixture of corn agriculture and bison hunting" (Brown 1982). Indeed, recent work suggests that Oneota sites are placed to exploit items such as upland game and marsh and stream resources; many sites also cluster around arable land (Brown 1982). Significantly, the importance of wetland resource utilization has been documented in faunal reports from Oneota sites (Brown 1982; Cleland 1966; Savage 1978). Brown (1982) suggests that a mixture of bottomland, upland prairie, and wetlands constitutes the focus of the basic Oneota adaptation. It must be noted that Oneota sites have been found in a variety of habitats—while parameters of adaptation remain the same, the economy was flexible enough to adjust to differing specific situations.

Many researchers have discussed the degree of dependence on agriculture within Oneota economy. Indeed, archaeologists often debate the relative importance of agriculture within all so-called Mississippian cultures, as well as many Late Woodland societies. It is not clear what level of dependence upon maize agriculture existed, or whether this dependence was uniform across a region or regions. It is clear, however, that the environments within which we find Oneota societies are rich in natural food resources.

We commonly think of corn agriculture as providing economic security for populations (e.g. Griffin 1967); while this is true, the reliability of the wetlands in this region must not be overlooked. Wetlands not only tend to be stable resource zones, they regenerate themselves quickly after droughts and other extreme climatic fluctuations. Further, they provide food at a time when it is not readily available elsewhere, and many of the foodstuffs available from wetlands are themselves storable. It could be that heavy dependence on food production was not necessary or desirable; agriculture may have simply been an addition to an already stable subsistence base. Perhaps, as long as the basic set of strategies (upland hunting, wetland harvesting, and corn agriculture) was possible within an area, the specific mixture could assume a variety of ratios (Brown 1982). It is interesting that recent work by Gallagher (Gallagher et al. 1985) has found ridged Oneota agricultural fields in a wetland setting. Since wetlands are organically rich and are warmer in the winter, farming in the wetlands may be a good hedge against a variable and short growing season.

Figure 10.7 indicates the known distribution of Oneota sites in the ten counties of southeastern Wisconsin; the few sites represented are either located around Lake Koshkonong or near Horicon Marsh. Two additional sites have been reported in northern Milwaukee and in southern Ozaukee counties. Upon viewing this "distribution," one's tendency might be to raise questions of survey bias or lack of survey coverage, but the results of long-term systematic surveys in the region suggest that the pattern (or lack of pattern) is valid (Brazeau and Bruhy 1980; Goldstein 1981, 1982, 1987). Further, extensive interviews with collectors have yielded no additional evidence of Oneota materials (Goldstein 1981, 1987; David F. Overstreet, personal communication, 1983). Nonetheless, as Overstreet (1976) has noted, current knowledge of Oneota settlement systems may be inadequate to allow identification of the full range of site types present.

However, assuming a real lack of sites, what does this mean? Extensive Oneota occupations are present to the north, west, and south of the southeastern Wisconsin region, yet this area and adjacent portions of northern Illinois appear not to have been settled by Oneota peoples. It is interesting that the few Oneota sites indicated in figure 10.7 are located along or near the edges of the region. Since research has indicated that the region is rich in resources, including wetlands (Goldstein 1987), one would expect Oneota settlement to be possible. It seems most likely, therefore, that they chose not to settle this area. Roland Rodell's (1983) analysis of Oneota settlement patterns in southeastern Wisconsin suggests that Oneota sites appear to be associated with large, shallow-basin, flow-through (eutrophic) lakes situated along major rivers. If this association is a determinant of settlement location, we would not expect to find substantial Oneota occupations east of the Rock River. Alternatively, Oneota settlements in this region may have been prevented or limited by the presence of Late Woodland groups following an analogous (if not identical) strategy. Examination of this possibility brings us to the third part of "cultural context."

Various Oneota and other so-called Upper Mississippian phases are located just outside the limits of the study area (Goldstein 1987; Fowler and Hall 1978). All of these "manifestations" are characterized by the practice of agriculture to some degree. Within southeastern Wisconsin, we find both Oneota and Middle Mississippi sites along the edges of the study area and Late Woodland occupations throughout the majority of the region. It is now apparent that at least some of these Late Woodland groups also practiced agriculture (Salkin 1987). From presently available data, it would appear that while there are stylistic differences between the various phases, there are more organizational similarities than was generally thought. Indeed, instead of postulating a Cahokian-type organization for these groups, it might be more logical to argue hunting-agriculture-wetlands utilization, with interactions to the south. Perhaps agriculture in this context is better seen as one more addition to the food base, rather than the catalyst for substantive change.

There is little question that there is a Middle Mississippian context for Aztalan. What we have questioned is the nature of the Mississippian relationship and the kind of organization represented by Aztalan. Preliminary inspection of Aztalan ceramics at the Milwaukee Public Museum suggests that much of the shell-tempered pottery is stylistically similar to types characteristic of Stirling phase assemblages in the American Bottom. Bleed's (1970) analysis of the shell-tempered ceramics recovered subsequent to Barrett's work also demonstrates close stylistic similarity to Cahokian wares. In addition, the presence of large pyramidal mounds, extensive palisades, and site structure also argue for some Middle Mississippian

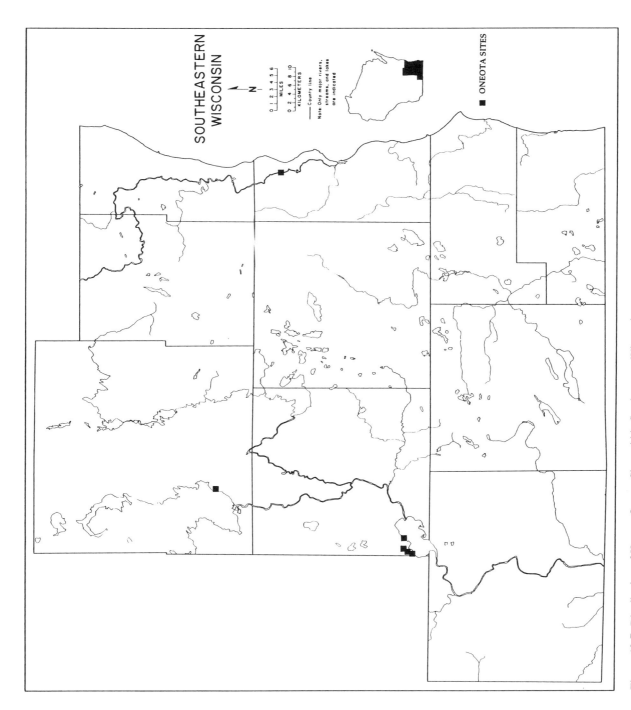

Figure 10.7. Distribution of Known Oneota Sites within Southeastern Wisconsin

relationship. Finally, the riverine location and open setting of Aztalan seem to more logically follow from a subsistence strategy based heavily on food production. Perhaps, as Brown, Bell, and Wycoff have suggested for the Caddoan area, we are seeing "the result of an advanced Mississippian subsistence-settlement system responding to a marginal environment for that system" (1978:195). Given our statements above, however, the significance and extent of this Middle Mississippian/Late Woodland relationship are unclear. While Aztalan still appears locally unique, our understanding of Aztalan's neighbors and cultural context is still incompletely understood and formulated. Clear interpretation of the site will require detailed analyses of all three different types of context discussed.

Conclusions

While this chapter has not been able to explain why people decided to build the Aztalan site *in* southeastern Wisconsin, we have been able to address a number of issues that help us to understand Aztalan's location *within* southeastern Wisconsin. Two specific questions can now be addressed: Why is Aztalan on the Crawfish River, and why is Aztalan at that specific location along the Crawfish? Traditionally, archaeologists have viewed Aztalan's location as unusual; it is farther north than any other Middle Mississippian village, and the Crawfish River does not initally appear a likely location for a Middle Mississippian outpost. In fact, however, the location is quite reasonable in view of the ecological and cultural context. First, the Crawfish River can be used as a means of transportation to locations further north and west, as well as further south and west. For the kinds and routes of trade proposed for Mississippian cultures, Aztalan's location on the Crawfish River would be suitable for participation in that trade or interaction.

Second, the specific location of the site allows relatively easy access to all vegetation and resource zones present in the region.

Third, the wetland resources available from Aztalan's position on the Crawfish River are significantly richer than those available from a comparable position along the Rock River.

Fourth, soils along the west bank of the Crawfish are better drained than those east of the river and are thus more suitable for maize agriculture. In addition, the west bank of the Crawfish is characterized by oak openings or savannas, which are easier to clear for farming.

Fifth, the Crawfish River, although smaller than the Rock River, apparently is not as susceptible to freezing over in the winter because of numerous springs; both the river and its resources might be accessible for greater portions of the year.

Finally, with the posited difference in emphasis or degree of dependence upon agricultural food resources between Middle Mississippian and Oneota people, it is possible that the former would prefer the river bank location with its easier exploitation of the oak openings for intensive agriculture. Given that Lake Koshkonong was probably occupied by Oneota people at the time of Aztalan's development, that occupation is perhaps one more reason to settle at the Aztalan locality.

This chapter has focused on the importance of context. To properly understand Aztalan, it is necessary to examine the structure of the site, its ecology, and its cultural relationships. Barrett's work of over fifty years ago has withstood the test of time, but it is now our responsibility to incorporate all that we have learned since.

11

The Middle Mississippian Presence in Minnesota

GUY E. GIBBON

In Minnesota Middle Mississippian traits are concentrated in very mixed assemblages in two areas, at the confluence of the Cannon and Mississippi rivers near the city of Red Wing and along the trench of the Minnesota River from near the town of Cambria to the Red River of the North (fig. 11.1). Both areas were northern deciduous gallery forest habitats surrounded by extensive prairies before modern agricultural practices changed the environment. Few other Middle Mississippian traits have been found outside these two areas.

This review briefly summarizes the evidence for the Middle Mississippian presence in Minnesota, the dating and distribution of Oneota and other possibly related cultural complexes, and sociocultural processes that may have integrated peoples living in southern Minnesota between about A.D. 1000 and 1300. Some of the problems that remain in understanding the Middle Mississippian presence in the state are discussed in the final section.

The Silvernale Phase

Of the two areas in Minnesota where Middle Mississippian traits are concentrated, the clearest expression occurs in the Red Wing area in a complex of sites on the terraces and bottomlands of the Cannon and Mississippi river valleys. The presence of thousands of earthern mounds and rock cairns in this rough and hilly section of extreme northeastern Goodhue County attracted many of the state's pioneer archaeologists. T. H. Lewis, Jacob V. Brower, and others systematically surveyed these mounds and cairns in the late nineteenth century (Brower 1903; Winchell 1911:150–54; see fig. 11.2). These prominently visible archaeological features remained a focus of archaeological interest until their destruction in the mid-twentieth century (e.g., Schmidt 1941).[1]

The first professional excavations in the Red Wing area were conducted by Moreau S. Maxwell for Beloit College in 1948 and by Lloyd A. Wilford of the University of Minnesota in the 1950s. Maxwell excavated three conical, one panther effigy, and two oval mounds at the Mero (Diamond Bluff) site (47PI02) on the Wisconsin side of the Mississippi River (Maxwell 1950); Wilford excavated portions of the Bryan (21GD4), Silvernale (21GD3), and Bartron (21GD2) village sites, and two conical mounds adjacent to Silvernale on the Minnesota side of the river (Gibbon 1979; McKusick 1953; Stortroen 1957; Wilford 1952, 1956b, 1958, 1985, n.d.e).

Archaeological investigations in the Red Wing area have intensified in the last two decades. Elden Johnson of the University of Minnesota excavated five small conical mounds of the Birch Lake Mound group and portions of the Bartron village site on Prairie Island in the Mississippi River bottoms between 1968 and 1970 (Gibbon 1979; Johnson, Peterson, and Streiff 1969). Still unreported important excavations were conducted in the 1970s at the Silvernale site by Christina Harrison for St. Olaf College, at the Mero site by Robert A. Alex for the University of Wisconsin-Milwaukee, and at Bryan by David Nystuen for the Minnesota Historical Society. Extensive surveys of portions of the area have also been carried out as part of the Minnesota Statewide Archaeological Survey (Harrison n.d.), the Great River Road Project (Penman 1984), the Minnesota Trunk Highway Archaeological Reconnaissance Survey (Nystuen 1971; Yourd 1983), by members of the Institute for Minnesota Archaeology (Birk

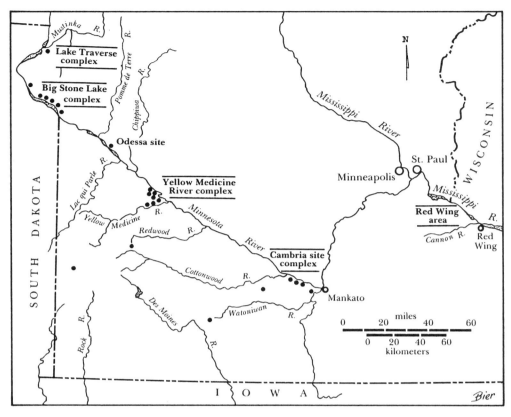

Figure 11.1. Location of Red Wing Area and Selected Cambria Phase Sites

1984; Dobbs 1985a), and for the U.S. Army Corps of Engineers (Overstreet et al. 1983).

The most concerted effort to investigate the archaeological resources of the Red Wing area was initiated in 1983 by Clark A. Dobbs of the Institute for Minnesota Archaeology. Dobbs has excavated portions of the Bryan, Adams (47PI12), and Energy Park (21GD158) sites, conducted extensive surveys, and directed the analysis of artifact samples from the area (e.g., Dobbs 1984, 1985a, 1985b, 1986a, 1986b; Dobbs and Breakey 1987; Grivna 1986; Wendt 1986a, 1986b).

Interpretation of the archaeological resources of the Red Wing area has been hampered by a variety of factors, including large-scale site destruction, unanalyzed or unreported site excavations, the absence until recently of a long-term regional study, and by prior archaeological models. The Bryan site, for instance, has been almost completely destroyed by gravel-removal operations, and the Silvernale and Mero sites are both badly damaged.[2] In addition, only a few of the several thousand mounds and cairns that once dotted the landscape have survived the plow and, more recently, urban and industrial expansion. Yourd has chronicled the history of the destruction of the Bryan site (Yourd 1985).

In spite of these and other problems, an understand-ing of the Middle Mississippian presence in the Red Wing area is beginning to emerge. Middle Mississippian traits in the area include ceramic forms and motifs, flat-topped earthen mounds, tri-notched triangular projectile points, a silver colored "pulley" earspool, and possibly Southeastern Ceremonial Complex items, side-notched triangular projectile points, several figurines, chunky stones, and elements of the settlement-subsistence system. A flat-topped rectangular platform mound on a terrace between Silvernale and Bryan was surveyed by T. H. Lewis in 1885 (Winchell 1911:151–54; see fig. 11.3). At the time the mound was 1.2 meters high and 14.6 by 18.3 meters at the base; the flat top platform was 7.3 by 11 meters on its sides and "the ascent from the base to the top is 12 feet [3.6 meters] wide all around" (1911:154). A flat-topped circular mound was also mapped in a cluster of otherwise conical mounds on the south end of Prairie Island (1911:144 and insert 3 opposite p. 144). A single tri-notched projectile point was found by Wilford at both Silvernale and Bartron, and the silver colored "pulley" earspool was salvaged by an amateur collector from the Bryan site (Gibbon 1979:47). These traits along with ceramic vessel forms and style motifs to be discussed below seem from my northern perspective to be Middle Mississippian.

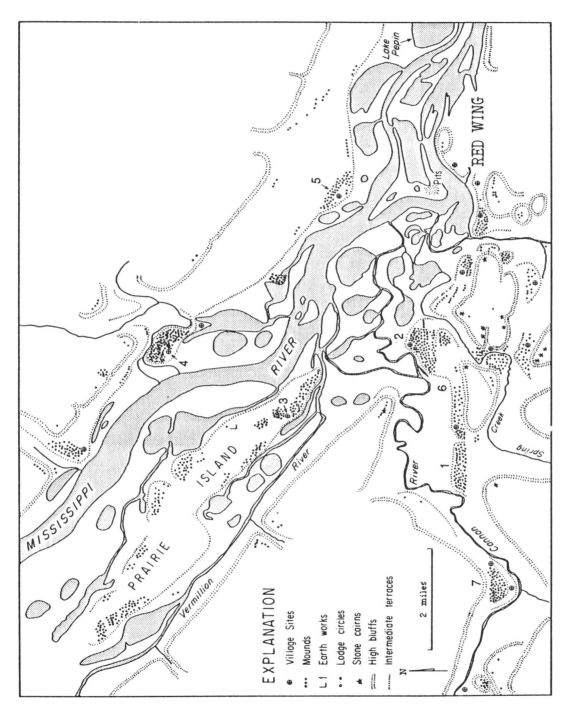

Figure 11.2. Distribution of Sites and Mounds in the Red Wing Area: 1, Bryan complex; 2, Silvernale complex; 3, Bartron; 4, Mero complex; 5, Adams; 6, Energy Park; 7, Belle Creek (map redrafted from an original in Jacob Brower's 1903 report).

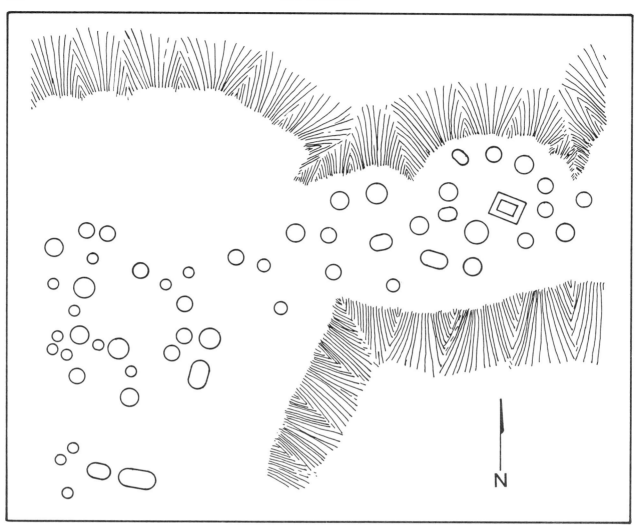

Figure 11.3. Pyramidal Mound Between Bryan and Silvernale

Other possible Middle Mississippian traits found in Red Wing area sites include a small long-nosed god mask (at Mero), small copper maces or batons (at Mero and Bryan), chunky stones (at Adams, Silvernale, and Bartron), a clay insect lug on a ceramic vessel (at Bryan), fragments of two and possibly three clay human figurines (at Bryan and Silvernale), a rock with a "feline" face carved on it (at Bryan), thunderbird motifs on a ceramic vessel (at Bryan), rectangular posthole houses with basin-shaped floors (at Bryan and Mero), and side-notched triangular projectile points (at least at Bryan, Silvernale, and Bartron) (Gibbon 1979; Lawshe 1947; Link 1975, 1979, 1980b; Williams and Goggin 1956:32, 38, 47). Because these traits are unusual for Minnesota and seem to coincide in time with the traits listed above, they are most likely associated in some manner with the Middle Mississippian presence in the state. [3]

The key question, of course, is the context of these traits within the Red Wing complex of sites. For instance, do they occur together as spatially distinct clusters within larger sites? Are they more or less evenly dispersed among other types of artifacts in middens at all sites? Are they primarily special status grave goods? and so on.

Dobbs has suggested that sites within the area can be subdivided within habitation and mound/embankment categories (Dobbs 1985a:51–61). Types of habitation sites include major villages (Bryan, Silvernale, Adams, Bartron, and Mero), smaller secondary villages (Energy Park, Double, and possibly Belle Creek), outlying sites (farmsteads or minor communities), and several different kinds of special-function sites. Whereas Bartron and Adams are Oneota sites with a few Middle Mississippian traits, the sole or dominant component at Bryan, Silvernale, Mero, Energy Park, Double, and (probably) Belle Creek is Silvernale phase. Outlying and special-function sites have, with few exceptions, not been assigned to a cultural complex, for they contain undiagnostic shell-tempered sherds and/or lithics. For this reason, however, the relationship between these habitation site types remains conjectural. In addition, radiocarbon dates are only available for Bryan, Silvernale, Mero, and Bartron. Nonetheless, some idea of the nature of the Middle Mississippian presence in the Red Wing area can be gleaned from examining the contents of a large Silvernale phase village site, of an Oneota village site, and of the excavated mounds.

The most extensively excavated and examined Silvernale phase site is Bryan (Dobbs 1985b, 1986a; Gibbon 1979; Stortroen 1957, 1985; Wilford 1956b, 1985). Bryan is a 6.1–8 hectare multicomponent village site on a terrace overlooking the Cannon River. Both Wilford and Dobbs discovered portions of a palisade on the western side of the site area, house floors, and numerous storage/refuse pits. A small and probably earlier Oneota component is on the northwestern edge of the terrace (Dobbs 1985b). Attempts to isolate distinct Middle Mississippian, Oneota, and Cambria components in the remaining site area have, however, not been successful. Stortroen, for example, could find "no significant stratigraphic differences . . . among either the major pottery types or among the various types of artifacts" (1957:94) in his analysis of material recovered from Wilford's major 1954 excavation. In spite of the presence of several trends in Wilford's excavation units (e.g., Oneota traits are most commonly found in the western part of the site; and grit-tempered sherds [Cambria ware], although always a small minority, are more common proportionately in lower levels than in upper levels), my own attempts to isolate distinctive associations of materials and pits/excavation units using clustering techniques revealed only a wide horizontal distribution of similar materials (Gibbon 1979:60). The spatial association of Middle Mississippian and Oneota-like ceramics illustrates this feature of the component. As a generalization, for instance, the greater the number of rims in a storage/refuse pit, the more likely rolled (Middle Mississippian) and high (Oneota) rim sherds occur together (high and rolled rims occur together in 32% of all pits excavated by Wilford). With the exception of the small Oneota component, Bryan is, then, a single component site containing a mixture of Middle Mississippian, Oneota, and Cambria traits. It is this mixture that comprises a Silvernale phase artifact assemblage.

The nature of the artifact classes within this component can be quickly summarized. Of the 13,818 sherds recovered from Bryan by Wilford, 8% were grit-tempered Cambria sherds and the remaining 92% were shell tempered. For convenience, rim profiles can be divided into rolled (Middle Mississippian), short (transitional or, in some cases perhaps, also Middle Mississippian), and high (Oneota) (fig. 11.4). Although the proportions of these profile categories varied somewhat in Wilford's various excavation samples, high (Oneota) rims only accounted for 10%–27% of the rim assemblage. In Wilford's 1955–57 sample, for instance, 39% of the rims were rolled, 41% short, and 10% high. Of particular interest is the intertwining of Oneota and Middle Mississippian traits (Gibbon 1979:120–45; Gibbon and Dobbs 1987:5–9). Oneota chevrons and Middle Mississippian scrolls, for example, are associated with both high flaring rims and rolled rims. The ceramic assemblage is not, then, just a physical mixture of Middle Mississippian and Oneota (and Cambria) ceramic types, but an amalgam as well in many instances of attributes of form and style.

Although the Bryan ceramic assemblage has a strong Middle Mississippian ("Old Village") cast to it, this presence is confined to jars. Other characteristic Middle Mississippian ceramic artifacts, such as pottery trowels and pans, water bottles, beakers, plates, juice presses, and stumpware, have not been found. Also absent at Bryan are wall-trench structures, tri-notched projectile points, discoidals, and Mississippian hoes, spades, and knives. Other elements of the artifact assemblage have an Oneota cast to them. For example, the chipped stone assemblage with its relatively large numbers of scrapers resembles Oneota village site assemblages more closely than assemblages from Middle Mississippian habitation sites. The stone materials used also seem local to the Upper Mississippi River Valley (e.g., a fine gray chert, oolitic chert, jasper, quartzite, agate).

An additional non–Middle Mississippian characteristic of the Bryan assemblage is the presence of an extensive worked bone-antler-tooth complex. This complex includes deer third phalange projectile points, fishhooks, bison scapula hoes and picks, elk antler picks, bone and antler punches, beaver tooth incisors, bone and antler awls of a variety of types, needles, battens, and shuttles, deer jaw sickles, beamers, bison scapula cleavers, bison(?) hide grainers, bison rib knives, antler tool handles, spatulas, antler gaming counters, tubes, bird bone pins, armlets or pendants, perforated deer phalanges (for the pin-and-cup game?), whistles, and fish teeth beads. Although Wilford's artifact sample from the Silvernale site is quite small, it is consistent with this description of the Silvernale phase assemblage from Bryan (Gibbon 1979:63–90; Gibbon and Dobbs 1987).

A variety of house types has been found at Bryan. Wilford discovered two semisubterranean (probably posthole) houses (Gibbon 1979:13–15). One was rectangular in outline (2.3 by 2.0 meters) with a floor 0.5 meters below the surface of the C horizon of the soil profile. Associated ceramics consisted of rolled rim and short

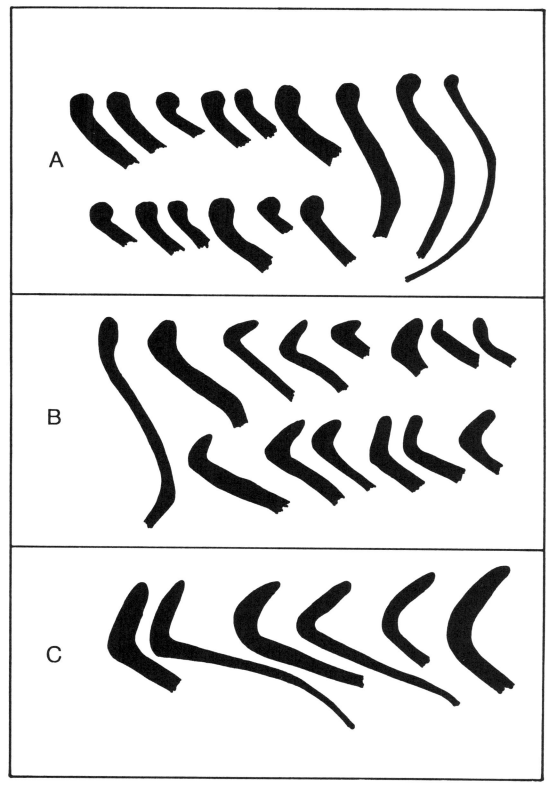

Figure 11.4. Rim Profiles from the Bryan Ceramic Assemblage: A, rolled rims; B, Bryan short rims; C, high rims (not to scale; redrawn from Gibbon 1979).

rim shell-tempered jars and Cambria ware. The other was circular (2.6 meters in diameter) with a floor about 0.7 meters below the surface of the sod. This house was associated with six high rims, one short rim, and a scroll design on a body sherd; the high rims with attached shoulder sections have atypical Oneota decorative elements, such as large external nodes. Two additional house types were discovered by Dobbs during his 1983–84 excavations. One was represented by a square pattern of post molds in an essentially sterile area devoid of features. The other, which appears to have had several construction phases, was represented by a circle of post molds. Still another house was uncovered in the early 1970s during a Minnesota Trunk Highway Archaeological reconnaissance survey (Nystuen 1971; Yourd 1985:17). Although destroyed by vandals shortly after discovery, it seems to have been a long, rectangular posthole structure.

Even though Wilford did not save faunal and floral food debris, a number of crude measures based on relative percentages of artifact classes (e.g., scapula hoes, projectile points) and numbers of pits indicate that the inhabitants of Bryan were probably more involved in the processing of plant foods than inhabitants of Oneota sites (Bartron, Sheffield, Bornick, Walker-Hooper) used for comparison (Gibbon 1979:150–55). The main plant processed was most likely maize, as indicated by the large quantities (more than five liters) of carbonized cobs and kernels recovered by Dobbs from Bryan; a preliminary analysis of this sample by Robert McK. Bird identified four categories of cobs, at least one of which has "8-12 rows with cupule widths ranging from 6.4 to 8.2 mm" (Dobbs 1986a:78 and appendix E).

The context of Middle Mississippian traits in the nearby Blue Earth Oneota Bartron village site is quite different from that of Bryan and Silvernale (Gibbon 1979:91–119). Bartron is a 2.8–4-hectare palisaded village site on a low island in the Mississippi River (fig. 11.2). Radiocarbon determinations indicate it was occupied sometime between A.D. 1050 and 1200 (table 11.1); the distribution and density of features and artifacts suggest occupation was relatively short term (e.g., less than fifty years). With few exceptions, all Middle Mississippian traits were concentrated in the area of a nearly square (9 by 9.5 meters) posthole house with a black "depressed" floor and an Oneota artifact assemblage. These traits consisted of a tri-notched projectile point, some scroll motifs on shell-tempered jars (represented by two vessels with high "Oneota" rims and four body sherds), and a few angular shoulders on jars. The other traits that may be Middle Mississippi-related—a wall-trench structure and a jar with an angular shoulder—were found in other areas of the site. Whether the wall-trench structure is Middle Mississippian-related remains unclear, for the excavated portion consists of a continuous

squared corner (rather than the usual juncture of two walls that do not quite meet) whose wall thickness is almost a meter.

Other descriptive features of Bartron can be quickly summarized: (1) a bone-antler-tooth complex similar to that at Bryan is present; (2) the cult items (e.g., thunderbird motifs, copper batons) and figurines found at Bryan are not present at Bartron; (3) of 221 vessels and rim fragments examined for my 1979 report, only three are grit tempered and all are non-Woodland; (4) of 648 decorated body sherds in this sample, only eleven are grit tempered and all are non-Woodland (three have curved line decoration and the rest straight line and/or punctate decoration); (5) Cambria ware is not definitely present, although some of the grit-tempered sherds could be associated with this ware (but then they could be Oneota, too); (6) of 221 rim profiles examined, three are short and the remainder high Oneota profiles (rolled and pseudo-rolled rims

Table 11.1. Radiocarbon dates from selected sites

| Site | Estimated Age | | Sample No. |
	Date B.P.	Date A.D.	
Bryan	825 ± 150	905–1355	I-781
	760 ± 90	1055–1350	I-782
	500 ± 120	1310–1515	I-783
	740 ± 50	1215–1330	Beta 8840
	870 ± 50	1035–1255	Beta 8841
	920 ± 50	930–965	Beta 8842
		1015–1235	
	780 ± 100	1045–1340	Beta 8843
	840 ± 70	1050–1265	Beta 8844
Silver-nale	740 ± 130	1230 ± 140	GX-7036
	830 ± 125	1180–1150 ± 135	GX-7037
	650 ± 120	1300 ± 130	GX-7038
Bartron	815 ± 125	1180 ± 135	GX-7034
	405 ± 130	1440 ± 140	GX-7035
	890 ± 55	1070 ± 65	WIS-434
	850 ± 55	1120–1090 ± 65	WIS-423
Mero	910 ± 55	1050 ± 65	WIS-841
	890 ± 55	1070 ± 65	WIS-842
	955 ± 55	1020 ± 65	WIS-846
	790 ± 55	1190 ± 65	WIS-849
	755 ± 55	1220–1200 ± 65	WIS-845
Cambria	815 ± 125	1180 ± 135	GX-6778
	775 ± 130	1210 ± 140	GX-6779
Price	845 ± 80	1140–1110 ± 90	I-8881
	885 ± 80	1080 ± 90	I-8882
	1000 ± 80	980 ± 90	I-8883
Great	2980 ± 180	930 B.C.	I-785
Oasis	1050 ± 60	850	WIS-522
(21MU2)	1420 ± 65	975	WIS-532

Sources: Anfinson 1987:14; Dobbs 1982:102–3; Dobbs 1985b:58

are absent); and (7) although there is evidence that maize horticulture was practiced, subsistence seems based on hunting to a greater extent than at Bryan (or even at other Oneota sites such as Walker-Hooper and Bornick).

The relationship of the surrounding mounds to the Silvernale phase and Oneota sites discussed above remains somewhat moot, although Middle Mississippi and/ or Oneota ceramics are present in most of the mounds that have been excavated. Maxwell (1950), for instance, found shell-tempered sherds in the fill of all of the mounds he excavated at Mero that contained cultural material (four of six mounds). Two of these mounds (6 and 38) contained only nondescript shell-tempered sherds, but the other two (4 and 26) contained jars with combinations of Middle Mississippi and Oneota or Woodland traits. One of these jars from Mound 26, a panther effigy, is described as "a jar which in decoration and shape resembled some jars of the Upper Mississippi phase, but which embodied certain design elements which are more characteristic of the Middle Mississippi phase" (Maxwell 1950:441). Another shell-tempered jar with a rolled rim and angular shoulder was found at the edge of a burial pit under the same mound. Woodland sherds or in one case (Mound 26) a Woodland projectile point were also found in the fill of each of the four mounds containing cultural material.

Excavations at other nearby mound groups demonstrate that the association of Mississippian ceramics and earthen mounds may not be an unusual occurrence in the Red Wing area. Elden Johnson recovered a shell-tempered loop handle from one of the five Birch Lake Mound Group mounds he excavated on Prairie Island (Johnson, Peterson, and Streiff 1969), and Dr. W. M. Sweney reported finding sherds containing "pulverized shells" in apparent association with mounds he investigated near the turn of the century (quoted in Brower 1903:62). Although Wilford hesitated in assigning the two mounds he excavated near the Silvernale site to any particular cultural tradition (Wilford 1955:140), he did find a shell-tempered sherd and a side-notched triangular projectile point in the fill of one mound (Mound 36) and both "Silvernale" and "Cambria" sherds in the fill of the other (Mound 45) (Gibbon 1979:70–73).

The Silvernale phase clearly seems an amalgam of Oneota, Middle Mississippi, and Plains Village (Cambria) traits. This particular amalgam raises a host of puzzling questions. For instance: Why is this particular combination of Middle Mississippi traits part of the amalgam (i.e., both "classic" and imitated ceramic jars, tri-notched projectile points, cult items)? What role do Plains Village (Cambria) traits play in this amalgam (besides Cambria ware, these might include side-notched triangular points, semisubterranean house forms, and part of the bone-antler-tooth complex)? Were Oneota villages such as Bartron and Adams occupied at the same time as the larger Silvernale phase villages? Who were the inhabitants of Silvernale phase sites (e.g., southern immigrants, acculturated Oneota folk, a potpourri of Woodland, Cambria, Oneota, and Middle Mississippi entrepreneurs)? Several interpretations of this amalgam are summarized after the Middle Mississippian presence in the Cambria phase is reviewed.

The Cambria Phase

Cambria phase sites have been grouped into four categories by Elden Johnson (1986:1): (1) large village sites on terraces within the Minnesota River Valley, (2) secondary villages near the large sites, (3) small upland prairie-lake and riverine sites, and (4) burial sites (fig. 11.1). Two large village sites—Cambria (21BE2) and Gillingham (21YM3)—and three to four secondary villages—Owen D. Jones (21BE5), Price (21BE36), Gautefald (21YM1), and perhaps Saienga (21CP2)—are known. All of these sites are within the trench of the Minnesota River, except Gautefald, which is twenty kilometers to the southwest at the juncture of Spring Creek and the Yellow Medicine River. Small upland and mound sites are numerous. General reviews of the phase can be found in Anfinson (1987:172–91), Johnson (1986), Ready (1979), and Wilford (1945b, 1955).

Most of the mounds and larger habitation sites that have been associated with the Cambria phase were mapped by T. H. Lewis and other pioneer surveyors in the late nineteenth century and are reported by Winchell (1911). Anfinson (1987:72–76) has provided a review of these and more recent major surveys in southwestern Minnesota. The first extensive professionally sponsored excavations of a Cambria phase habitation site were conducted at Cambria, the type site of the phase, by W. B. Nickerson for the Minnesota Historical Society in 1913 and 1916 (Nickerson 1917). Wilford also excavated at Cambria, and at Owen D. Jones, Gautefald, and Gillingham, in the 1930s and 1940s (Wilford 1941a, 1945a, 1945b, 1946, 1951, 1953). Nickerson's and Wilford's combined sample from Cambria remains the most intensively studied artifact assemblage from a major Cambria phase habitation site (Knudson 1967; Shay 1966; Watrall 1968a, 1968b, 1974). More recent excavations have been conducted by Michael Scullin of Mankato State University in 1974 and 1975 at Price (Scullin 1979), and by myself at Cambria in

1974 to obtain material for radiocarbon dating (O. Shane 1980).

Many earthen burial mounds with probable Cambria phase affliation and small upland prairie-lake and riverine sites with Cambria phase components have also been excavated. Among the mounds are Judson (21BE5), Lewis (21BE6), Schoen #1 (21BS2), Schoen #2 (21BS1), Lindholm (21BS3), Miller (21BS4), Holtz (21BS5), Hartford Beach (39RO4), and Hiawatha Beach (39RO6) (Anfinson 1987:190; Haug 1982; Johnson 1961; Wilford 1955, 1956a, n.d.a, n.d.b, n.d.c, n.d.d). Small numbers of plain grit-tempered sherds with trailed line decoration occur in the upper levels of many of the major lacustrine and riverine habitation sites in southwestern Minnesota and eastern South Dakota, including Fox Lake (21MR2), Mountain Lake (21CO1), Pederson (21LN2), Stielow (21BS14), Artichoke Island (21BS23), Strader (21TR9), and Browns Valley (21TR5) (Streiff 1972; Ready 1979; Anfinson 1987:188).[4] While most of these sites are situated south of the Minnesota River Valley, Cambria sherds have also been found north of the valley at a few sites in Otter Tail County in west-central Minnesota (Lucking 1977; Michlovic 1979). As mentioned in the last section, Cambria ceramics have been found in small amounts along with other possible phase traits in the Red Wing area in southeastern Minnesota.

Just what the Cambria phase represents in terms of an ethnographic reality has never been clearly defined. A brief review of the contents of several habitation and burial sites will provide, however, some idea of the nature of the Middle Mississippian presence in this phase. This review will concentrate upon ceramics, lithics, the bone assemblage, mound form and artifact content, and burial mode.

The most detailed study of Cambria phase ceramics remains Ruth Ann Knudson's analysis of Nickerson's and Wilford's combined sample from Cambria (Knudson 1967; Shay 1966). Habitation debris at Cambria covers 3.5 acres (150,000 square feet) of an intermediate terrace of the trench of the Minnesota River some twenty-five kilometers northwest of the town of Mankato (fig. 11.1). The site is generally considered in a defensive position, and Johnson, in his recent review, has suggested that it was probably palisaded (Johnson 1986:4). Cambria ceramics consist, for the most part, of globular jars with grit temper, constricted necks, pronounced shoulders, and smooth surfaces. Knudson divided this sample into five types with varieties. Two of the types have rolled rims (Powell Plain, Ramey Broad Trailed), two have outflaring rims (Linden Everted Rim, Mankato Incised), and one has an S-shaped rim (Judson Composite). Linden Everted Rim is most similar to Initial Middle Missouri Chamberlain ceramics, while Judson Composite resembles Over

Focus and Missouri River S-shaped rims; both types contain vessels with Middle Mississippian traits, such as angular shoulder profiles, chevron or curvilinear designs, and polished shoulder areas (Johnson 1986:4; Knudson 1967:263–67; Shay 1966).

Knudson's conclusion from a distributional study that these five types are associated together in one assemblage (that is, that Cambria is a single-component site) reveals an even more variant ceramic assemblage, from a Middle Mississippian perspective, than do Silvernale phase ceramic assemblages. For instance, her Powell Plain and Ramey Broad Trailed types account for only 15% of all vessels, are nearly always grit-tempered (only 13% of the Ramey Broad Trailed vessels and 1.3% of all sherds have shell temper), and occasionally display cordmarking on the exterior surface (5% of all Ramey Broad Trailed rims have some cordmarking). Middle Mississippian traits are not confined to these two types, however, for Linden Everted Rim vessels have short to medium rims, some curvilinear design motifs, and occasional shell tempering (1% of the vessels in the type), and some Judson Composite vessels combine S-shaped rims, angular shoulders, and chevron or curvilinear designs. These latter "transitional" vessels may occupy the same ceramic niche that Silvernale short rim vessels do in the Red Wing area. Still, the assemblage as a whole has stronger stylistic relationships with Woodland, Mill Creek, Great Oasis, and Oneota assemblages, and with assemblages in South Dakota from the Brandon, Mitchell, and Swanson sites. On the basis of these latter relationships, the phase has been assigned to the Initial variant of the Middle Missouri tradition (Knudson 1967; Tiffany 1983). The two (uncalibrated) radiocarbon dates for the site are A.D. 1135 ± 125 (GX-6778) and A.D. 1175 ± 130 (O. Shane 1980; table 11.1).

The percentage breakdown of Knudson's five types at Cambria is 15% Powell Plain–Ramey Broad Trailed, 64% Linden Everted Rim, 12.3% Mankato Incised, and 8.7% Judson Composite. These percentages vary widely, however, in ceramic assemblages in other Cambria components. The breakdown at Price is 20% Powell Plain–Ramey Broad Trailed, 58% Linden Everted Rim, 22% Mankato Incised, and 2% Judson Composite. Rolled rim types are apparently completely absent, however, in all other Cambria phase assemblages, except for the Lewis mounds to be described below. For instance, the Owen D. Jones site near Cambria contained only Linden Everted Rim vessels (Wilford 1946), and rims at Gillingham were either everted (63%) or S-shaped (37%) (Wilford 1951). Cambria ceramics at small special-activity components in the uplands outside the trench of the Minnesota River are primarily varieties of Linden Everted Rim (Johnson 1986:7). While Cambria ceramics do exhibit a Middle

Mississippian presence, then, this presence seems confined to two habitation sites and a mound group situated near one another on the easternmost edge of Cambria phase site distribution.

Charles Watrall (1968a, 1968b) has described many of the bone, shell, and stone artifacts from Cambria sites. A conclusion of his study is that some of the notched triangular projectile points, bone awls, ground celts, bone beamers, and bone cylinders can probably be considered Middle Mississippian traits within the Cambria artifact assemblage (Watrall 1968a:93). Whether or not these are all actual Middle Mississippian traits, they still constitute only a very small portion of the artifact assemblage at a few sites such as Cambria. For instance, of 141 relatively complete triangular projectile points in Nickerson's and Wilford's sample from Cambria, only three are trinotched "Cahokia points" and only one has double side notches. The remaining points have a single set of side notches (n = 46) or are unnotched (n = 91). Cahokia hoes are absent at Cambria, as are other characteristic Middle Mississippi lithics, with the possible exception of ground celts (which, however, are a characteristic feature of other contemporary artifact complexes, such as Blue Earth Oneota). In fact the percentage breakdown of chipped-stone tools by category (25% projectile points, 56% scrapers, 14% blades, and 5% perforators/drills/gravers) and the large amounts of worked bone (203 pieces made up of awls, punches, quill flatteners, beamers, projectile points, fishhooks, scapula hoes, picks, sickles, and decorated objects) seem more typical of other contemporary regional assemblages (Oneota, Silvernale, Middle Missouri) than of Middle Mississippi assemblages to the south. This conclusion is also supported by the ground-stone assemblage from Cambria, which at present is made up of nine grooved stone mauls, seven celts, thirty-three hammerstones, eleven pitted hammerstones, nine grinding stones, and thirty-six sandstone abraders.

The nonceramic assemblage from Price resembles that at Cambria, except for a much smaller number of worked bone objects and a lower number of scrapers (n = 47) compared to projectile points (n = 49). The projectile points from Price are mainly side-notched triangular varieties. Little is known of other Cambria phase nonceramic assemblages, largely because of the problem of mixing in multicomponent sites (Gillingham, for example, contains a major Woodland component).

Another probable Middle Mississippian trait associated with the Cambria phase is the flat-topped earthen mound (Johnson 1961, 1986). T. H. Lewis mapped at least four flat-topped pyramidal mounds within the trench of the Minnesota River Valley and on a bluff overlooking Lake Traverse in the late nineteenth century (Johnson 1961: 76–77; Winchell 1911; fig. 11.1). An example is the Odessa site, which is situated on a twenty-meter terrace on the northeast side of the river. When mapped, the "diamond-shaped" pyramidal structure measured 16.4 by 12.8 meters at the base and had a flat top measuring 6.1 by 8.5 meters; no elevation seems to have been recorded. An associated long embankment was 220 meters long, 6.1 meters wide, and 0.4–0.6 meters in height (fig. 11.5).

A little-known archaeological phenomenon is the presence in Minnesota of about eighty circular, flat-topped mounds, most of which were also mapped during the T. H. Lewis survey (Johnson 1961). One has already been mentioned as part of a cluster of regular conical mounds near the Bartron site, and two are in western Hennepin County near present-day Minneapolis. The rest are situated along the Upper Minnesota and Des Moines rivers, and around lakes Big Stone and Traverse, in the western half of the state. This distribution coincides with the known distribution of Cambria phase sites (Johnson 1961: 72; Johnson 1986:6). It is tempting to see these mounds as evidence of a Middle Mississippi presence in Minnesota too, but only the Schoen mounds have been professionally excavated. The mounds did contain, however, some Cambria sherds and semiflexed primary burials (Wilford n.d.a, n.d.b; Wilford 1955:139).

Small conical burial mounds are also associated with each of the Minnesota River Valley Cambria phase habitation sites. The Lewis mound group located on a high terrace three kilometers southeast of the Cambria site is the only other Cambria phase site presently known besides Cambria and Price to contain Middle Mississippi-like ceramics with rolled rims (Wilford 1956a). Mound 1 contained shell-tempered sherds and five extended primary burials in a shallow subsoil pit; several rolled rims were in the fill of Mound 2. Other mounds apparently associated with the phase, such as Schoen Mound #1 (21BS2), the Miller mound (21BS4), the Lindholm mound (21BS3), Schoen Mound #2 (21BS1), the Judson mound (21BE5), the Hartford Beach Mound (39RO4), and the Hiawatha Beach mound (39RO6), contained flexed primary burials, which further separates the Cambria site cluster from other sites in the phase and enhances its "Mississippian" character.

The four categories of Cambria phase sites are assumed to be integrated together in a seasonal settlement-subsistence pattern that involved maize horticulture at village sites, bison hunting on the prairies, and the exploitation in the trench of the Minnesota of a wide variety of plant and animal resources (e.g., Anfinson 1982; Anfinson 1987:183–86; Johnson 1986; Watrall 1974). However, the data base necessary to fill in the details of this "bare bones" pattern is still unavailable. Although Nickerson's excavations at Cambria did recover several liters of charred maize (Eastern eight-row or Northern

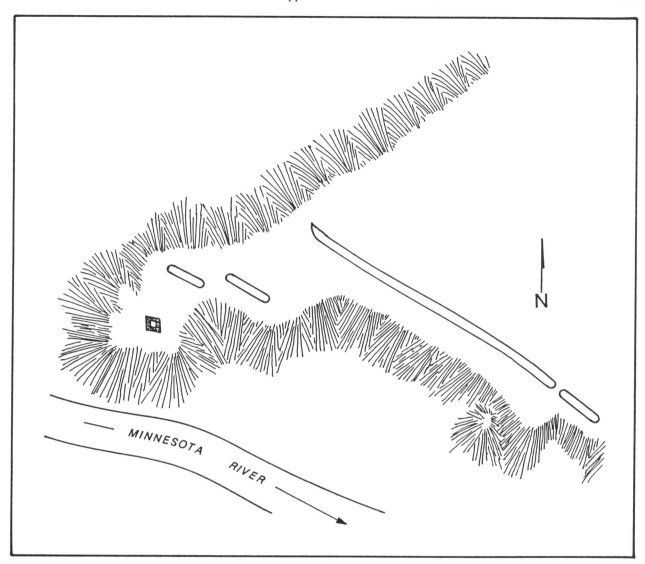

Figure 11.5. Diamond-shaped Pyramidal Mound at Odessa

Flint) from a storage pit, both his and Wilford's excavations were carried out before fine-scale screening and water flotation became a common practice. As a result, their samples are biased toward large or easily observable floral and faunal remains.

The large quantity of animal bone in Nickerson's and Wilford's combined sample from Cambria has been analyzed by Lukens (1963) and Watrall (1968a, 1974). Their results demonstrate the exploitation of a varied assemblage of upland and wetland fauna. This conclusion is supported by my own excavations at Cambria and by Scullin's excavations at Price. An analysis of flotation debris from Price by Linda Shane (1980) demonstrated the presence of both cultigens (maize kernels, cucurbits,

sunflower) and wild plants (chenopodium, walnut, rose, *Prunus* sp., *Polygonum* sp.).

Cambria remains the most poorly known phase within the Initial Middle Missouri tradition. The broad outlines as sketched above suggest a settlement-subsistence pattern in which larger agricultural villages were situated within the trench of the Minnesota and smaller, probably warm weather, hunting and gathering sites along smaller rivers and around lakes in the adjoining prairies. The Middle Mississippi presence in this setting seems confined to the Cambria site cluster (Cambria, Price, Lewis) and to a series of more widely distributed flat-topped earthen mounds. Several models that account for this presence are reviewed below.

Temporal Placement of Other "Mississippian" Complexes in Minnesota

Lloyd Wilford, who identified and named the cultural complexes in southern Minnesota discussed in this review (1941b), was also the first person to propose a model of the relationships of these complexes (Wilford 1955:138–42). On the basis of possible artifact trends at Bryan and Silvernale, and then current theory, Wilford suggested a continuum in time and developmental stage from Cambria, Silvernale, and Bryan through Blue Earth phase sites such as Bartron to the Orr phase. This suggestion was in part an expression of the popular Middle Mississippi–Oneota transformation model in which Oneota culture devolved from an intrusive Middle Mississippian base sometime after A.D. 1300. The explanation for the appearance of the simpler Oneota lifeway was the gradual adjustment of the more intensely horticultural Middle Mississippi subsistence pattern to the rigors of more stressful fringe environments, such as the northern deciduous forest zone and the prairies of the Dakotas, Iowa, and Minnesota. Possible stratigraphic trends at Bryan and Silvernale, and the mixture and blend of ceramic forms and style motifs at these sites, were interpreted as evidence supporting this hypothesized sequence.

Wilford's own observations and an increasing array of radiocarbon dates have cast doubt on the validity of this developmental sequence. Wilford, for instance, did accept the stratigraphic association in one site or another of ceramics from all of these phases except Orr (e.g.,

Wilford 1955:138, 140). It was suggested earlier in this review that the Silvernale phase dates somewhere between A.D. 1000 and 1300 and the Cambria phase between A.D. 900 and 1300 (Tiffany 1983:92; Johnson 1986:2; table 11.1). Mean dates from Oneota (probably Blue Earth phase) components in the Red Wing area stretch from A.D. 950 to 1300. Dates for other Blue Earth components indicate that the phase probably stretched from the middle of the tenth century to the historic period (Dobbs 1982:98; Dobbs 1985b:58; Henning 1970). A similar time span now seems reasonable for the Orr phase (Dobbs 1982). The Great Oasis phase in southwestern Minnesota and adjoining states, also regarded like Cambria as a phase of an eastern division of the Initial Variant of the Middle Missouri tradition, is dated to "A.D. 900-1100 and probably later" (Henning and Henning 1978:12; also see Tiffany 1983:96; Tiffany, chap. 9).

However these radiocarbon dates are interpreted, it seems apparent that there was considerable overlap between the Oneota, Silvernale, Cambria, and Great Oasis phases. This overlap seems to invalidate the traditional Middle Mississippi–Oneota transformation model in Minnesota, although its recognition does not necessarily bring us any closer to understanding the origins of these complexes or the nature of their interrelationship (e.g., Gibbon 1982).

Interpreting the Middle Mississippian Presence in Minnesota

If the processes of migration and adjustment to a horticulturally marginal northern deciduous forest–prairie environment no longer adequately explain the presence of Middle Mississippian traits in Minnesota, what processes do? An interpretation of the internal and external relationships of the Bryan, Silvernale, and Bartron sites based on data presented in Gibbon (1979) and on data from other midwestern sites was constructed in an attempt to present an alternative model for consideration (Gibbon 1974). The purpose of this alternative hypothetical construction is to provide a set of research expectations that can be used to structure excavation strategies that will, in turn, challenge the usefulness of the hypothetical construct.

Although space does not allow an extended discussion of this alternative model, its main propositions can be listed and their implications for understanding the Middle Mississippian presence in the state briefly discussed. The following propositions are adapted from Gibbon (1974):

1. Cahokia was the focus of a complex social organization having a chiefdom or theocratic state-level of integration;

2. A symbiotic-extractive network centered on the Cahokia core area was expanded to its greatest areal extent after this level of integration was attained in the core zone;

3. The widespread appearance between A.D. 1050 and 1300 of large, relatively permanent, defended villages in the Prairie Peninsula and the northern deciduous forest zone that contain some Middle Mississippian traits is directly related in many instances to the expansion of this Cahokia-centered exchange network;

4. The exchange network was extractive and operated under the umbrella of magico-religious sanctions and guarantees;

5. Exchange "nodes" in the hinterland, here the Red Wing area, were inhabited by a predominantly hinterland population, although Cahokians may have been involved in the functioning of these exchange/extractive centers;

6. Major demographic, stylistic, and organizational

changes apparent throughout the northern hinterland zone by A.D. 1250 or 1300 are directly related to the collapse/demise of the Cahokia-centered exchange network with climatic change a possible exacerbating factor.

The extension of the Cahokia-centered symbiotic-extractive network into a variety of ecological niches by A.D. 1100 can be traced by the distribution of a complex of traits generally regarded in the north as Middle Mississippian (see Kelly, chap. 4; Hall, chap. 1; Emerson, chap. 12 for extended discussion). This complex includes such items as shell-tempered Ramey Incised and Powell Plain pottery, flat-topped pyramidal mounds, ear plugs, discoidals, and elements of the "Southeastern Ceremonial Complex," such as copper pendants, forked-eye motifs, and long-nosed god pendants. These traits seem to occur at strategic or "nodal" points around the northern periphery of the Middle Mississippian core zone, a periphery already inhabited by Emergent Oneota and other groups (such as Mill Creek) that shared traits that had diffused widely throughout the upper Midwest a century or two earlier.

Radiocarbon dates support the view that the small Oneota components at Bryan and Bartron (at least in part) pre-date the emergence of the Silvernale phase cultural complex (table 11.1); that the area may already have been experiencing some "Mississippianization" is indicated by the presence of the few concentrated Middle Mississippian traits at Bartron, by the contents of the mounds excavated by Maxwell and others, and by the

presence near Bartron of a flat-topped circular mound (a confused imitation or a symbolic blending of indigenous and foreign traits?). In this interpretation Silvernale phase villages represent Oneota occupations altered sufficiently by Middle Mississippian material and adaptive traits to warrent a new phase designation. It was the occupants of these large villages who acted as "nodal" intermediaries in the extraction of goods from central and western Minnesota for the Cahokia core area downriver. As Elden Johnson (1986:11–12) has recently argued, the Cambria site itself may have been a central extractive center for the processing of meat and hides, and the manufacture of quill decorated robes and bison scapula hoes, for shipment through the Red Wing node. The presence of some rolled rim vessels and a partial wall-trench structure in the Mille Lacs Lake area of central Minnesota suggests that this area had some connection with the southern network too, but investigation of the nature of this connection has just recently begun.

Following the apparent collapse/demise of the far-flung Cahokia-centered exchange network around A.D. 1250 or 1300, Bryan, Silvernale, Cambria, and many other archaeological complexes in the hinterland zone, in particular "intermediaries" and "nodes," disappeared or were severely altered. Continuities in Minnesota are represented by Blue Earth phase sites, such as Sheffield on the St. Croix River and Vosburg and Humphrey along the Blue Earth River, and probably later by Orr phase sites in the southeastern corner of the state.

Problems and Alternative Interpretations

The model briefly sketched above was first presented at a regional archaeological conference in 1972. It still seems a plausible reconstruction of events and processes in prehistoric Minnesota. Nonetheless, it remains plausible perhaps only because of our continued ignorance, for gaps in our knowledge (and a certain theoretical opaqueness) still hinder our understanding of the Middle Mississippian presence in the state.

A significant number of these problems are external. For instance: What traits are specific to the Middle Mississippian cultural complex? Do these traits generally occur together or in differing combinations? What are their histories? Was Cahokia the center of a chiefdom or a theocratic state (and what implications does the answer have for the generation of processual models for the northern periphery)? Were Middle Mississippian-related villages in the upper Midwest tightly integrated in an exchange/extractive network or not? and so on. It is not clear to me, at least, which traits can legitimately be considered

Middle Mississippian and which have a more diffuse context. For example, do side-notched triangular points ("Cahokia points") have too diffuse a context in the upper Midwest to be considered Middle Mississippian? Is the same true for many cult items, such as thunderbird motifs? Do "short" rim forms on Silvernale phase ceramic jars (Bryan Short Rim) represent a true intermediate form between Middle Mississippi rolled rims and Oneota high rims, or Middle Mississippian rim forms that are not recognized as such by Minnesota archaeologists?

Our in-state problems are just as basic. For example: Are there still unrecognized developmental sequences at Bryan, Silvernale, and Cambria? Are all types of sites in the categories proposed for the Silvernale and Cambria phases contemporaneous or are some middle-range sites (Price and Energy Park, for example) earlier? Are the Middle Mississippian traits at Bartron contemporaneous with their presence at Bryan and Silvernale or earlier as argued above? If there was an exchange network, what was the actual process of social interaction? These and many other questions remain unanswerable given our existing data base. Extensive new excavations, such as are now occurring in the Red Wing area, are a clear priority.

Alternative interpretations of the distribution and nature of the Middle Mississippian presence in the state are not difficult to construct. Middle Mississippian traits could, for instance, be the product of incidental exchange of ideas and goods up the Mississippi and Minnesota rivers. Instead of being tightly integrated in an exchange network, interaction between groups in this model would have been more casual and even, perhaps, hostile (e.g., Emerson, chap. 12). The lack of tight integration would explain such odd features as flat-topped conical and diamond-shaped pyramidal mounds and grit-tempered and cordmarked Ramey ceramics. Ideas recently advanced by Tiffany (1986b; chap. 9) and Anderson (1987) for Mill Creek are worth exploring too. Whatever other characteristics these alternative interpretations might possess, they should be processual and lead to clear research expectations concerning the dating of specific components, the composition of tool kits, the spatial distribution of components, and so on. Research efforts that finally conclude that one component is not Blue Earth Oneota because mean rim height on jars is six millimeters less than the mean of rims in a component several hundreds of kilometers away seem archaic at best.

Summary

The Middle Mississippian cultural sphere had its greatest impact in Minnesota sometime between A.D. 1050 and 1300. At present, there is no evidence of a site-unit intrusion of any kind. Instead only selected Middle Mississippi traits occur in what I interpret as culture contact situations involving a largely local population base. Such traits are most abundant in Silvernale phase sites in the Red Wing area at the juncture of the Mississippi and Cannon rivers. These include "Ramey Incised" and "Powell Plain" ceramics, cult objects, flat-topped mounds, a significant emphasis on horticultural activities, tri-notched triangular projectile points, and possibly other traits, such as roughly square semisubterranean posthole house forms. The general assemblage of Silvernale phase sites is dominated, however, by Oneota and what may be Oneota–Middle Mississippi "blended" artifacts and structures. Middle Mississippian-related traits also appear in a few Cambria phase sites along the Minnesota River in a still more diluted form. Examples include grit-tempered Powell and Ramey ceramic jars, tri-notched triangular projectile points, and probably flat-topped circular and pyramidal mounds.

The presence of these traits and the distinctive nature of Silvernale and Cambria assemblages have been tentatively explained by the expansion of a Cahokia-centered extractive-exchange network into southern Minnesota between A.D. 1050 and 1100. The collapse of this network within a century or two resulted in extensive new exchange alliances. These new alliances led in turn to the termination of both phases as recognizable archaeological entities. Although greatly oversimplified and certainly not the only model that could be used to interpret the Middle Mississippian presence in Minnesota, the Cahokia-centered extractive-exchange model does explain our data as they are presently known. Given the quality of these data, however, the proliferation of alternative interpretations with specific test implications has been encouraged as a spur to fresh excavation and the analysis/reanalysis of extant collections.

NOTES

1. The exact number of mounds and cairns in the area has been variously reported. Schmidt (1941:71) claims that there may have been as many as 4,000 at one time, while an actual count of mapped mounds by Clark A. Dobbs indicates that the number may have been closer to 2,000.

2. Amateur archaeologists in the state were instrumental in saving much valuable information from Bryan as it was being destroyed (e.g., Blessing 1967; Link 1975, 1980b).

3. Chunky stones are an exception, for they are found on Oneota sites in the state after the demise of the Silvernale phase. Their introduction into the state, however, seems to coincide with the influx of other Middle Mississippian traits.

4. As Anfinson notes, however, in Minnesota sherds that are non-Great Oasis and that "are smooth surfaced, grit-tempered, and from globular vessels" have been traditionally defined as Cambria phase (1987:187). Since a few scattered sherds of this general description in a multicomponent site could actually be associated with other cultural complexes, such as Mill Creek and the Over Focus, it seems best to exercise caution in their taxonomic assignment (Michlovic 1979:30).

12

Some Perspectives on Cahokia and the Northern Mississippian Expansion

THOMAS E. EMERSON

The purpose of this book is to bring together researchers concerned with Cahokia and the development of Mississippian culture in the Upper Mississippi River Valley. This goal has been achieved and a wealth of information, ideas, and models presented. These papers have illuminated major advances in our understanding of the emergence, florescence, and decline of Mississippian societies in the American Bottom and Upper Mississippi River Valley. In this chapter, I build on previous research, note the data gaps, and propose a new model for Cahokia and the northern Mississippian expansion.

Midwest Mississippian

The rich cultures of the late prehistoric peoples in the Upper Mississippi Valley did not long escape the notice of the first European settlers. Easily located by their large platform mounds, rich cemeteries, and artifact-laden villages, they were early subjects of collector and antiquarian interest. When scientific investigations began in the region in the late 1920s and early 1930s, these same sites were among the first to attract archaeological attention. This period saw early excavations by Warren K. Moorehead and A. R. Kelly at Cahokia, Fay-Cooper Cole and Thorne Deuel were working with Spoon River sites in the Central Illinois Valley, the University of Chicago crews were surveying and testing Apple River sites in Jo Daviess County, and Samuel A. Barrett was completing his monumental excavations at Aztalan.

All of these early excavators were impressed by how different these late prehistoric sites, now known as Middle Mississippian, were from the other known regional cultures and by their strong resemblance to the late cultures of the southeastern United States. The continued emphasis on this southern connection led researchers to argue that such sites represented a northern intrusion by migrants possessing a basically southern culture. The point of origin of this intrusion was seen as the massive Cahokia site. Central and northern Illinois, southern Wisconsin, and Minnesota sites were easily accounted for by postulating migrations out of Cahokia.

Through the intervening years investigators have become increasingly sophisticated in modeling the roles of such factors as trade, religion, warfare, migration, and diffusion in the spread of Mississippian culture throughout the Upper Mississippi Valley. Yet despite half a century of research, we are still faced with many of the same basic questions that plagued those earlier midwestern archaeologists. In large part the understanding of Cahokia-hinterland interaction was hampered by a lack of both basic archaeological information and appropriate models to assist in comprehending what data were available.

The first attempt to provide an integrative overview of the Middle Mississippian phenomena in the Midwest was provided by James B. Griffin (1960b) in his now classic paper "A Hypothesis for the Prehistory of the Winnebago." In it he synthesized, for the first time, the necessary evidence to make a convincing argument for the northward movement of Stirling phase peoples out of Cahokia and their subsequent spread throughout much of the Midwest. In addition, shortly thereafter, Griffin (1961) also provided a climatic explanation for this spread. To a significant degree, this model still dominates much of the regional literature.

In the three decades since Griffin proposed his "hypothesis," numerous new excavations have taken place in Mississippian components at Cahokia, the American Bottom, and the Midwest. Extensive research has also been conducted at related Oneota sites. While numerous authors have dealt with the question of secondary Mississippian influences, that is, Oneota and Upper Mississippian cultural development, few (the exceptions being Gibbon 1974 and Hall, chap. 1 and numerous papers) have attempted to repeat Griffin's feat of integrating this information to provide a new regional perspective of Middle Mississippian cultural development.

To a large extent the questions that interested earlier archaeologists are still of concern today (i.e., integrating the Cahokia information and understanding the relationship of Cahokia to the regional manifestations). What distinguished recent research efforts was the concentration on the internal development of the separate regional Mississippian cultures and less concern with the interaction between such cultures. The emphasis of this volume has been on clearly delineating the local sequences, addressing the uniformity and diversity between regional Mississippian groups, and only then assessing the role of Cahokia in this process.

The question has been raised by some researchers, especially those whose perspective is more southeastern in orientation, whether the northern societies discussed in this volume can be defined as Mississippian. Jon Muller and Jeanette Stephens (chap. 17) are strong advocates of this position, arguing, for example, that the Spoon River culture of Central Illinois is not Mississippian. Their argument is based on the premise that differences in environmental setting have provoked organizational responses that distinguish these northern groups from the true Mississippian groups to the south. This position is contested by long-time Central Illinois Valley researchers Alan D. Harn (chap. 7) and Lawrence A. Conrad (chap. 6).

Outside of the Midwest, vigorous debates have been conducted to provide an answer to the question "what is Mississippian?" James Griffin (1985) has extensively documented the changing concepts of archaeologists from the early ceramic definiton of William H. Holmes (1903)

to the more ecologically oriented definition proposed by Bruce D. Smith (1978, 1984b; also Muller and Stephens, chap. 17). Griffin (1985:62–63) concludes his discussion with an attempt to portray Mississippian in a new light —one that is not tied to specific artifact types, construction techniques, arbitrary categories of cultural evolution, specific habitats, or even geographic regions.

To paraphrase Griffin (1985:63), Mississippian societies can be identified as those that (1) participated in a series of new cultural innovations between A.D. 700 and 900; (2) incorporated those disparate innovations into their culture thorough contacts with other groups; (3) constructed planned permanent ceremonial centers, towns, and associated settlement hierarchy; (4) possessed various forms of a hierarchical social, political, and religious system; (5) participated in a religious system emphasizing the interaction of spirit world and humans with a rich iconography expressed in marine shell, copper, ceramics, and stone; (6) participated in extensive trade networks; and (7) reached a cultural "crest" between A.D. 1200 and 1500.

Muller and Stephens, in chapter 17, focus attention on this very important question of variation, as do many of the chapters by Upper Mississippi Valley archaeologists in this volume. Half a century of regional research has been dominated by that very issue. From Griffin's seminal paper (1960b) to the present, researchers have sought to identify and interpret this cultural variation. That there is obvious variation between the northern Mississippian groups and the Cahokian area is beyond question. But what is the significance of this variation? As Harn has noted (chap. 7), increasing research in the Cahokia sphere has demonstrated that the range of variation even within this core area is much greater than previously suspected. The critical question is whether these differences are of such a magnitude that we must develop some other cultural construct to describe them. Virtually all of the papers dealing with such cultures in this book seem to conclude that they are not. The detailed descriptions presented in this volume and elsewhere demonstrate that in every important aspect described by Griffin the Spoon River, Apple River, and very likely the Red Wing and Aztalan manifestations can be subsumed under the rubric of Mississippian societies.

Cahokia

Models of Cahokian origins have been summarized by Hall (chap. 1) and discussed by various authors in this volume and elsewhere (especially see Kelly 1982). As noted, these fall into two categories: "the evolutionary in situ"

and the "contact-migration" models. With the extensive excavations and publications of the FAI-270 Project in the American Bottom on Late Woodland (Kelly, Finney et al. 1984) and Emergent Mississippian sites (Kelly, Ozuk et al. 1984), there can no longer be any serious consideration of large population movements of Mississippian peoples into the area as the stimulus for local Mississippian development. The origins of Cahokia are tied to the wider development of complex societies throughout the Mississippi River Valley and the Southeast at this time and the processes are reflected in the Emergent Mississippian cultures and their eventual transformation into fully Mississippian groups. In general, the factors that can be linked to the emergence of Cahokia are increased population growth/density stimulated by intensive maize agriculture within a environmentally diverse area supporting the development of social and economic complexity. In modeling beyond this point the conjectures of the various authors become just that—conjectures.

Few have been concerned with the actual operation of the local Cahokian Mississippian system. Perhaps one of the least explored topics is the articulation and internal development of the American Bottom Mississippian groups. Only Fowler (1974) has addressed the organizational structure of the American Bottom with his hierarchical classification of first-, second-, third-, and fourth-line communities. James W. Porter (1974) at Mitchell and Michael L. Gregg (1975b) at Horseshoe Lake provide some thoughts on the relationships between these sites and Cahokia. George R. Milner and I (Emerson

and Milner 1981, 1982, 1988; Emerson 1988) have presented some initial concepts on the organization of small disperse villages. Little other information is available.

The decline of Cahokia has been of increasing interest of late and has been addressed by a number of researchers. Such explanations range from Porter's (1969, 1974) version of a "peasant revolution" to Hall's "Shmoo Effect" or cultural de-evolution (Hall 1980, chap. 1). It is apparent that a number of factors have been identified that may have contributed to the declining importance of Cahokia. These include increasing population density with concomitant pressure on resources, perhaps leading to local environmental deterioration. This is followed by an end to the "agricultural circumscription" (cf. Carneiro 1970) that characterized earlier times, probably because of the introduction of northern adapted corn as Hall suggests, and an actual population outflow from the American Bottom beginning in the early to mid-thirteenth century. The details of this general scenario are provided by a number of authors in this volume. The primary facts now seem to indicate that Cahokia was a very short-lived entity that climaxed for a moment in the eleventh and twelfth centuries and then faded from the picture by the end of the thirteenth century. Cahokia did not go out with a bang but rather a fizzle.

Cahokia and American Bottom Research

Over half a century of research at the Cahokia site and adjacent regions has produced numerous collections. Such collections are of varying quality, often dispersed, and seldom adequately reported or analyzed. The history of these early investigations has been summarized by Fowler (1979, 1989). The organization and centralization of these collections along with their analysis and publication is one of the major goals of the Illinois Historic Preservation Agency that took over management of Cahokia Mounds State Historic Site in 1984.

It is very frustrating when one examines the data that are actually available from the Cahokia site. Large-scale excavations were conducted at such major locations as Merrell Tracts 15A and 15B, Monks Mound, and Mound 72 and yet none of these have been fully described or analyzed. Our understanding of Cahokia has been plagued by theorizing at the expense of more mundane data description, analysis, and publication. We have no shortage of theories, only of "old-fashion" data-oriented archaeology.

There are a number of major research problems that need to be addressed in the central Cahokia site area in addition to the actual description and publication of the

information already recovered. These include the following:

(1) The determination of mound chronologies for the more than 120 mounds reportedly in the site area. We have little information on when most of the mounds were built, utilized, and abandoned. Until this information is gathered, it is very difficult to understand the ceremonial spatial organization and the developmental sequence of the various parts of the Cahokia site.

(2) The determination of site organization through time. This could be approached intially by the systematic investigation of all parts of the site through surface collections and some subsurface testing to gather information on the periods of occupation and area function. This work has been partially done for such areas as Ramey Tract (Vander Leest 1980), the Merrell Tract, the ICT II Tract, the Kunneman Tract, and a few other small areas. Such investigations will also serve to provide us with information on the general site layout and use.

(3) The understanding of the role of site geomorphology in the evaluation of the community plan. It will be very difficult to discuss site layout when we are not even sure what parts of the site were water and which were

dry land. Recent investigations near the new interpretive center revealed a large area that had been the location of a prehistoric "land-fill." While the excavation of large borrow pits had been suggested for Cahokia, we were not aware that large-scale filling may have also taken place.

Site geomorphology also extends to our understanding of the relationship of the various creeks, sloughs, and Mississippi river channel positions at the time of the site occupation. Such information may be critical to our understanding of the "why" of Cahokia's location.

The question of the site and floodplain geomorphology brings us to the broader questions concerning Cahokia's place within the American Bottom. The detailing of available water channels will, perhaps, give us insights into transportation/communication routes available during the Mississippian period in the American Bottom. This combined with the data we are already gathering on the disposition of available subsistence resources and raw material sources will provide us with an understanding of the physical setting of Cahokia.

(4) The cultural context of Cahokia in the American Bottom. We know very little about the nature of the other major Mississippian sites in the American Bottom. There are four known major multimound centers that may have been contemporaneous with Cahokia—Pulcher, East St. Louis, St. Louis, and Mitchell. Only Mitchell (Porter 1974) and Pulcher (Griffin and Jones 1977) have even been partially explored. In addition, there are a plethora of smaller mound centers such as Lohmann (Esarey with Good 1981) and Horseshoe Lake (Gregg 1975b). We have little knowledge of these sites.

The understanding of American Bottom Mississippian requires that research be performed at the four large multimound and the smaller mound sites. This may be the single most important research effort facing archaeologists in this ever-expanding metropolitan area. The St. Louis site may be totally destroyed by urban construction, although portions may still be intact among the welter of modern-day debris. Urbanism has almost obliterated the East St. Louis site, but a few large mounds may still exist on its eastern fringe. The Mitchell site, although severely damaged by highway construction, still has some potential for research, especially in the important village areas. Pulcher is virtually intact but will rapidly be threatened by new metropolitan expansion. If we are ever to understand how these sites articulated with one another, with the smaller mound centers and with Cahokia, rapid systematic research is urgent.

Cahokia and the Emergent Mississippian Stage

One of the major benefits of recent research in the American Bottom has been the recognition and delineation of an Emergent Mississippian culture (Kelly, Ozuk et al. 1984). Most recently Kelly (1985, 1987) has portrayed the Emergent Mississippian phenomenon as "a stage in which certain socio-economic transformations occurred." These socioeconomic transformations include such earlier innovations as the introduction of the bow and arrow and the appearance of nucleated villages at about A.D. 600 and the later economic dependence on maize agriculture at circa A.D. 800, as well as population increases, changes in ceramic technology, increasing emphasis on hierarchical social organization, and large-scale trade networks. In the American Bottom these diverse traits coalesce during the two centuries between A.D. 800 and 1000 to create the totally new system we recognize as Mississippian.

A poorly understood corollary has been the effect this transformation process had on the surrounding areas. Although the archaeological record clearly shows regional Mississippian economic and cultural influences during the later Stirling phase, virtually nothing is known about the regional effects of the Emergent Mississippian stage. This is primarily due to the absence of a compa-

rable level of investigations in other areas. The lack of regional information is especially frustrating when widespread trade networks are a much-touted attribute of this stage of cultural development.

In the past, the recognition of Mississippian cultural impacts has only been on the basis of those fully developed cultural traits such as diagnostic shell-tempered ceramics, platform mounds, wall-trench structures, evidence of associated religious activities, and so forth. Very often this recognition involved the postulation of actual site-unit intrusions into the outlying regions. Researchers were hampered in searching for earlier contact evidence by the lack of a clearly defined "transitional Late Woodland–Mississippian" artifact assemblage that could be identified on a regional level. To some degree this problem has been ameliorated by the Emergent Mississippian-stage research in the American Bottom.

At this point let us briefly summarize the nature of the late Emergent Mississippian cultural assemblage. The focus here will be on the last two contemporaneous phases, Lindeman and Edelhardt, that fall during the final half of the tenth century A.D. These phases represent the climax of the Emergent Mississippian development and the final transition to a fully Middle Mississippian cultural assemblage. The summary that follows is based on Kelly, Ozuk et al. (1984) and Emerson and Jackson (1984, 1987a) unless otherwise stated.

During this period, settlement forms vary but most known examples suggest a basic household unit consisting of several single-post structures, set in shallow basins, probably utilized by the members of an extended family. Sometimes such households were clustered along a ridge top, in other areas they were organized around central courtyards, and in one instance these courtyard groupings formed a nucleated "community" of almost 100 structures. No platform mound construction has been documented by excavations for this stage with the exception of Monks Mound.

Subsistence patterns continued to involve the predominance of maize agriculture, combined with utilization of the starchy seed complex and wild plants (Johannessen 1984a). A wide-spectrum exploitation of the rich aquatic and terrestrial faunal resources (Kelly and Cross 1984) characterized this period.

In seeking regional evidence of trade in an archaeological context, the cultural attributes that are the most visible are the nonperishable items such as lithics and ceramics. The Emergent Mississippian stone assemblage is amazingly nondistinctive and of little value in tracing contacts. In the case of lithic raw material it is possible to study the distribution of such American Bottom types as Crescent Hills chert to understand regional trade patterns. Insights into such patterns could also be gained by examining the northern distribution of Mill Creek and Kaolin cherts. It is very likely that these southern cherts would have moved through Cahokian middlemen on their trip upriver.

Late Emergent Mississippian ceramic assemblages do not lend themselves very well to the establishment of diagnostic types. Research suggests that local diversity and rapid change most characterize these ceramics. Ceramic transitions include the change from cordmarked to plain surfaces, a marked increase in the use of red slip, an increase in the use of shell tempering, vessel shape modifications that eventually typify those of early Mississippian assemblages, and the introduction of new forms such as pans and hooded water bottles. Perhaps the key forms that may be useful for seeing regional contacts would be the new shell-tempered Mississippian-like sharp-shouldered, flared-rim vessels. These are virtually identical to the later Powell Plain type but appear in the American Bottom by the middle of the tenth century.

The American Bottom evidence for external contacts is plentiful (Kelly, chap. 4; Hall, chap. 1). The extent of these contacts can be best illustrated by reference to extralocal materials that appear at even the small household sites such as BBB Motor (Emerson and Jackson 1984) or Marcus (Emerson and Jackson 1987b). Tradeware vessels include examples or copies of Coles Creek Incised, Kersey Incised, Varney Red Filmed, and Larto Red Filmed from the Central and Lower Mississippi Valley; Yankeetown vessels from southern Indiana; and "collared" forms from northern and southern Illinois. Chert hoes of Mill Creek were commonly imported from the southern Illinois quarries. Exotic minerals such as galena and hematite also found their way into the American Bottom. This sampling of trade items is not exhaustive but illustrates the range and variety of the Emergent Mississippian networks. Given this background it would be useful to reexamine the information from the outlying areas of the Midwest for evidence of regional American Bottom Emergent Mississippian interaction.

Emergent Mississippian Regional Interactions

The earliest possible Mississippian intrusion into the Northern Mississippi River Valley that can be documented at present appears associated with the flat-topped mounds located in Trempealeau County, Wisconsin (Stevenson, Green, and Speth 1983). Three rectangular platform mounds were observed and briefly investigated by George Squier, a local archaeologist, in the early 1900s. Over the years Squier collected a number of sherds from the site. Although the collections have not yet been relocated, Squier's careful notes and some rim profiles have been reexamined by Stevenson and her colleagues. They suggest that some of the ceramics may represent such early Central Mississippi River Valley forms as Varney Red Filmed, Kersey Incised, and Coles Creek Incised.

Overall the Trempealeau assemblage is dominated by a large proportion of shell-tempered, red-slipped, and polished sherds. These authors suggest that such an assemblage may represent a pre–A.D. 1050 intrusion either directly from the Central Mississippi River Valley or after having been processed through possible middlemen in the Cahokia region.

The authors quite justifiably advise caution in interpreting this assemblage since at present it has not been possible to examine the specimens firsthand. Despite the data limitations a number of facts do seem apparent: (1) flat-topped mounds were constructed at Trempealeau, (2) the ceramic assemblage, on the basis of detailed early notes, appears to be purely Middle Mississippian with no Woodland or Oneota components present, (3) the authors' interpretation of these ceramics as chronologically early is in line with our information from the American Bottom sites, and (4) the site is unusual in having platform mounds located on a narrow jutting ridge crest with apparently no associated village area.

The Central Illinois River Valley may also have seen the presence of pre-A.D. 1050 Mississippian groups and/or influences (McConaughy, Jackson, and King 1985). While Conrad (chap. 6) demonstrates that the major influx of Mississippian peoples occurred at circa A.D. 1050-1100, as evidenced by the ceremonial complex at the Eveland site, recent excavations document that many Mississippian material traits were in the valley by A.D. 1000. McConaughy's investigations at the Rench site in Peoria County revealed two structures, one of wall-trench construction and one characterized as a wigwam form. The presence of early Mississippian ceramic forms in association with a predominate Late Woodland pottery assemblage and radiocarbon dates of A.D. 950, 1020, and 1010 lead him to argue for substantial interaction between this area and the Emergent Mississippian groups in the American Bottom during the tenth century A.D. (McConaughy, Jackson, and King 1985).

The evidence for tenth-century interaction between the Central Illinois River Valley populations and those of the American Bottom gives new importance to the question of the nature of the Mississippian presence in the Lower Illinois River Valley. Lynne Goldstein's (1980b) earlier studies of Mississippian mortuary sites in the lower valley had demonstrated the existence of at least one regional Stirling phase mortuary center, yet no major temple towns were known. A more recent examination of surface collections from all known Mississippian sites in the Lower Illinois River Valley performed by Michael D. Conner (1985) located a number of Stirling phase farmstead occupations, but no earlier Mississippian materials were found. However, recent excavations at the Pere Marquette Lodge site by Kenneth B. Farnsworth (personal communication, 1986) did reveal a wall-trench structure containing Mississippian and Late Woodland ceramics. Although the radiocarbon dates of A.D. 970 and 1100 are ambiguous and the Mississippian ceramic assemblage may be as late as Lohmann, this site is currently the best candidate for an Emergent or early Mississippian intrusion into the Lower Illinois River Valley.

A review of papers dealing with the remaining portions of the Upper Mississippi River Valley illustrates that there is little or no evidence to substantiate Emergent Mississippian contact or trade in the Red Wing area (Gibbon 1979, chap. 11), southern Wisconsin (Goldstein and Richards, chap. 10), Apple River (Emerson, chap. 8), or eastern Iowa (Tiffany 1986, chap. 9). In virtually all these loca-

tions Mississippian interaction cannot be verified until Stirling times, when it is widespread (also see Stoltman 1986; Kelly, chap. 4). While there can be no delusion that the Upper Mississippi River Valley contact suddenly sprang into full bloom at A.D. 1050, the earlier extent and intensity of this contact is difficult to substantiate.

The absence of early contact evidence may be attributed to a number of factors:

(1) The lack of well-documented Late Woodland sequences and extensive site excavations from the period between A.D. 700 and 1100. To a large degree the failure to find evidence of Emergent Mississippian contact is a direct result of archaeologists' failure to find and excavate contemporaneous sites in the Upper Mississippi River Valley. For example, in the lower and central Illinois River valleys, where there is a high probability that such early contacts occurred there has been very little work with the Late Woodland Sepo, Maples Mills, and Jersey Bluff village sites.

(2) The lack of clearly recognizable diagnostic Emergent Mississippian ceramic types. The Stirling horizon is clearly marked in the Midwest because of its distinctive ceramic types, Ramey Incised and Powell Plain. The late Emergent Mississippian has fewer such diagnostic ceramics and, more importantly, many of the ceramic forms of this time continue into the later Mississippian culture. It is possible that many of the Emergent Mississippian contact sites may be masked by subsequent Mississippian components. This is probably especially true in the Illinois River Valley, northwest Illinois, and the Red Wing area.

(3) Differential movement, intensity, and composition of trade materials. It is interesting to note that virtually all of the early trade items in Emergent Mississippian sites in the American Bottom are of southern derivation, for instance, lower and central Mississippi River Valley ceramic forms, southern Illinois cherts, or Missouri galena. Clearly trade from the south into the American Bottom contained large numbers of nonperishable goods, and was at a fairly high level of intensity and of some duration. As indicated previously, the northern trade is less visible. A number of researchers have suggested that the transportation of perishables such as dried meat or hides or small-volume exotics such as copper and galena may have played an important role in this trade network. It is possible that these factors may account for the discrepancy of northern versus southern items that we see in the archaeological record.

From the above review, it becomes clear that there was frequent and continuing interaction between the Emergent Mississippian peoples of the American Bottom area and those Late Woodland populations to the north. The most convincing and best-documented example is the work of

McConaughy, Jackson, and King (1985) at the Rench site near Peoria. Not only do we see the presence of shell-tempered Emergent Mississippian ceramics, but also the intriguing possibility that architectural styles, settlement patterns, and even associated life-styles are being introduced. Unfortunately, it will not be possible to fully understand the impact of tenth-century American Bottom peoples on the lower and central Illinois River Valley until we better understand the basic Late Woodland cultural pattern in these areas.

Potentially the most exciting tenth-century intrusion into the Upper Mississippi River Valley may be that suggested at Trempealeau. Here we have what appears to be a fully Mississippian ceremonial mound complex situated far north of any similar sites. The possibility that this may even represent a Central Mississippi River Valley site-unit intrusion is fascinating but unsubstantiated at this time.

It is certainly not an original idea that the Mississippianization of the Upper Mississippi River Valley began well before the much-heralded Stirling phase expansion. Today, however, we are in a position to begin to document the process at sites such as Rench and Trempealeau. Such research is potentially one of the most rewarding for understanding both culture change and the subsequent rapid acceptance of Mississippian and Oneota lifeways in the region.

The Classic Mississippian Expansion

With the recognition that there was interaction throughout the tenth and eleventh centuries between the populations of the American Bottom and the upper valley, the appearance of fully Mississippian groups in the upper valley by the second half of the eleventh century should come as no surprise. The presence of such groups was recognized early in midwestern archaeological studies, in fact, sites such as Aztalan (Barrett 1933) were essential to the initial definition of the Mississippian culture and "Old Village" at Cahokia. There has been little agreement, however, among scholars as to the dating, cause, effect, or even the basic nature of this phenomena. What has become clear through recent research is that the movement of Mississippian cultural traits into the upper valley is due to many differing factors, and unicausal explanations such as trade or migration are no longer viable.

One of the reasons that we have a better perspective on the Mississippian presence in the upper valley is due to our increased understanding of the cultural and chronological sequence in the American Bottom area (fig. 12.1). The delineation of the Emergent Mississippian culture (Kelly, Ozuk et al. 1984) has demonstrated the gradual transformation of the local Late Woodland peoples into the "classic" (i.e., in the sense of easily recognized "Old Village" assemblage) Mississippian culture that is so readily associated with Cahokia and the expansion to the north. This work has also been instrumental in isolating the Lohmann phase at A.D. 1000 as the initial Mississippian culture around Cahokia (Milner et al. 1984), which precedes the more classic Stirling phase horizon that has been confirmed to date to the mid-eleventh century. It is this Stirling horizon that has been traditionally used to mark the first recognizable Mississippian presence in the upper valley.

James B. Stoltman (1986) has recently summarized the evidence for the appearance of this horizon in the north- ern part of the upper valley outside of the Illinois Valley. His compilation of forty-one radiocarbon dates from these sites substantiates the placement of this horizon between A.D. 1000 and 1200. Four contact "situations" are summarized by Stoltman: (1) contact demonstrated by Ramey-Powell vessels in a Late Woodland context; (2) contact demonstrated by Ramey-Powell vessels combined with Mississippian site organization (Aztalan is the only known example) in a Late Woodland context; (3) Mississippian site-unit intrusions; and (4) subsequent Mississippian-like developments that relate to early Oneota groups.

Only the first three of Stoltman's contact situations are relevant at this point in our discussion of the Stirling phase horizon in the upper valley. The presence of Stirling phase vessels in a Late Woodland–Plains Village context characterizes the Mississippian presence in Iowa (Tiffany 1986b, chap. 9). In the case of the Hartley phase of northwest Iowa, only a minor amount of Mississippian material is present. Mill Creek sites also contain minor amounts of Mississippian materials; however, in this context such items have been interpreted as a significant part of the culture. To explain the presence of such items, Tiffany (1986b) has recently suggested a model involving the movement of buffalo hides and meat into Cahokia and the corresponding movement of marine shells and vessels up the Missouri and the Mississippi tributaries in Iowa to the Mill Creek sites. This is not a completely convincing scenario, but Tiffany's effort marks the first attempt to produce a testable model with quantifiable parameters.

Stoltman's second contact situation, involving essentially Late Woodland peoples with Mississippian ceramics and site structure, is most clearly seen at the often-studied site of Aztalan. He (1986) suggests that this may represent an acculturated Late Woodland group possibly with a resident Mississippian elite. This would closely

Figure 12.1. Chronology of Middle Mississippian Cultures in the Upper Mississippi Valley

	900	950	1000	1050	1100	1150	1200	1250	1300	1350	1400	1450	1500
Cahokia													
Fairmount	********************												
Stirling				**************									
Moorehead							**************						
Sand Prairie									**************************************				
FAI-270													
Lohmann			**********										
Stirling				**************									
Moorehead							**************						
Sand Prairie									*********************				
LIRV Variant													
Jersey Bluff	********************************????????????????												
Stirling Horizon				**************									
Pearl						*********************							
Spoon River Variant													
Eveland				**************									
Orendorf						**************							
Larson							********						
Marbletown Complex								************??????					
LaMoine River Variant													
Gillette				**************									
Orendorf/Larson Horizon						**********************							
Crabtree									**********				
Crable										**************			
Apple River Variant													
Bennett				*********************									
Mills							*********?						
Red Wing Locality													
Silverdale				*********************************									
Cambria				**************									
Blue Earth	**												
Orr	**												
Aztalan Locality													
Aztalan						**************************							
Iowa Locality													
Mill Creek			**										
Great Oasis		*************************											
Glenwood						**********************							
Oneota	**												

Note: All dates are approximate and individual articles should be seen for discussion of their accuracy, reliability, and comparability.

resemble the model that Conrad (chap. 6 and elsewhere) has previously proposed for the Eveland phase intrusion into the Central Illinois Valley.

Some understanding of the variation that might exist in this process can be gained by examining the well-documented Mississippian acculturated Late Woodland peoples who were resident at the Collins site. This site is located in far northeastern Illinois on the Middle Fork of the Vermilion River, which is the major tributary of the Wabash. Extensive work by Douglas (1976) at Collins demonstrated that it was utilized by an essentially Late Woodland population that had adopted certain aspects of Mississippian religious practices including platform mounds and astronomical markers. Subsequent testing by Riley and Apfelstadt (1978) noted, however, that the adoption of such public-oriented Mississippian religious practices had not effected the Collins population's burial practices, which continued to follow the older Late Woodland pattern.

The final contact situation and the most spectacular involves the movement of resident populations of Mississippian peoples into the upper valley. There are only three locations where this can be postulated on the basis of our present information: the Illinois River Valley, the Apple River Valley, and the Red Wing area. The most completely studied example comes from the Central Illinois Valley, where the work of Conrad and Harn through the years has compiled an impressive data base for the Spoon River Mississippian culture. Conrad (chap. 6) discusses at great length the evidence for the actual movement of Mississippian peoples into the valley and there is no need to belabor the point. While there is not comparable evidence from the Lower Illinois River Valley, it is likely that its earliest Mississippian population is derived from the adjacent northern American Bottom.

The next area of Mississippian settlement to the north is in the Apple River Valley of northwest Illinois. Recent research (Emerson, chap. 8) has demonstrated the presence of a Lohmann or Stirling phase intrusion marked by Mississippian ceramics, architecture, platform mounds, and site organization.

The most northern of the site-unit intrusions is that which occurred in the Red Wing area of Minnesota. Although Gibbon (chap. 11) and a number of other researchers view the Silvernale phase as a mixture of Oneota and Mississippian traits, in my opinion this mixture is more reflective of archaeological methodology than cultural reality. The recovery of wall-trench architecture, platform mounds, and traditional Lohmann and Stirling phase ceramics from the Red Wing locality (Gibbon 1979) strongly indicates an early Mississippian site-unit intrusion. Its lack of visibility in the archaeological record is partly due to the utilization of the same sites by later

Mississippian peoples that has often badly mixed the components and partly to the lack of familiarity of many researchers with traditional Middle Mississippian utilitarian ceramics.

In examining the information presented by the various authors on the appearance of Stirling-related materials in their respective area, a number of observations can be made:

(1) For the most part Mississippian influences in the upper valley are best explained as the result of intermittent contacts such as produced through trading networks.

(2) There are a number of geographical gaps in Mississippian site distribution in the upper valley that require investigation. Perhaps the most critical of these gaps is the Mississippi River trench between the northern American Bottom and the Apple River. Present information (or lack thereof) suggests little Mississippian utilization/occupation of the trench despite what appears to have been favorable environmental situations. The valley north of the Apple River also requires investigation since it is only adequately surveyed in restricted localities of the Diamond Bluff and Red Wing areas.

While the Mississippi Valley is critical to our understanding of the northern expansion, almost all of northern and northeastern Illinois could be usefully reexamined for a Mississippian presence. Many of the early surveys in this region operated on the basis of a one-to-one correlation between Mississippian and temple mounds— smaller, less conspicuous nonmound sites were seldom recognized. It is likely that the Mississippian use of the Illinois River Valley north of Peoria, the Rock, the Fox, and the Wisconsin rivers was more common than now thought.

(3) Only in three locations (ignoring Aztalan for the moment) is there reliable evidence for an actual Mississippian population intrusion: the Illinois Valley, the Apple River Valley, and the Red Wing area. Such occupations are associated with floodplain meander environments. In each instance, the Stirling intrusion at circa A.D. 1000–1050 is the culmination of perhaps fifty to one hundred years of interaction with the American Bottom groups.

(4) The initial population intrusions were by relatively small groups but included the full panoply of Mississippian hierarchical and religious trappings. In the Central Illinois Valley, for example, the early Eveland site contained an unusually large number of specialized structures associated with religious and political functions. The initial occupation at the Mills site on the Apple River seems to have initiated the formal plaza arrangement and platform mounds. While the nature of the first Mississippian occupation in the Red Wing area is not known, the presence of platforms mounds, Ramey and Powell ceramics, and other high status/religious objects suggests that they

were introduced fairly early. The Aztalan data is still ambiguous but it may represent a similar situation.

(5) There appear to be strong ties between these various northern areas, often stronger than the relationship that can be seen between each area and Cahokia. The best known at present is the Apple River–Central Illinois connection with contact reflected in strong ceramic simi-larities (e.g., the Dickson Trailed series), the movement of galena into the Central Illinois River Valley, and the almost identical pattern of cultural development of the two areas. Similar ties can be suggested between Red Wing–Apple River–Aztalan. These relationships need to be more fully investigated.

Mississippian Diversification

By the beginning of the thirteenth century the short-lived uniformity that had characterized the classic Stirling phase expansion was completely gone. The spread of this horizon had correlated with the advent of the Stirling phase (A.D. 1050–1150) at Cahokia. Mississippian American Bottom development appears to have maintained the status quo or began declining during the subsequent Moorehead phase. With the coming of the Sand Prairie phase (A.D. 1250–1400) the nucleation that had earlier characterized the American Bottom disappeared and the population seems to have dispersed over the floodplain and into the surrounding uplands. This marks the appearance of single and multimound centers in the northern American Bottom uplands and the Lower Illinois River Valley's secondary drainages (Woods and Holley, chap. 3; Farnsworth, Emerson, and Glenn, chap. 5; Pauketat and Koldehoff 1983).

Interestingly enough, the diversification of Mississippian cultures in the upper valley seems to have preceded the decentralization at Cahokia. By A.D. 1150 the ceramic tradition of the Mississippian populations in the Lower Valley was recognizably differentiated from that of their American Bottom neighbors (Farnsworth, Emerson, and Glenn, chap. 5). Similarly, Conrad (chap. 6) sees this differentiation as occurring in the Central Illinois Valley by A.D. 1100–1150; Emerson (chap. 8) suggests A.D. 1100–1150 for the Apple River Valley; and, perhaps, by A.D. 1150 in the Silvernale phase at Red Wing.

What becomes clear in examining the upper valley classic horizon is its extreme brevity. Within two to three generations each Mississippian area has become sufficiently distinctive that it is best understood in terms of its own internal developmental history. Contact with Cahokia, in terms of traceable stylistic patterns, seems to have stopped almost immediately after the groups arrived in their respective valleys. In fact it is interesting to note that after about A.D. 1100–1150 there may be more similarities between such areas as the Central Illinois River Valley and the Apple River than there are between these areas and Cahokia.

What causes this diversification process? To some ex-tent it seems to be the result of geographical isolation, independent political and cultural evolution, and perhaps the decreasing effectiveness of the subsistence base. When the initial intrusion of Mississippian populations occurs, it specifically targets those areas with a similar environmental diversity (i.e., floodplains with extensive oxbow lakes, sloughs, and rich agricultural land) to that of the American Bottom. The introduction of Mississippian agricultural techniques into such areas may have given that first migrant population a "competitive edge" over the local Late Woodland populations. Within a few generations the competitive advantage of this southern-adapted maize in these marginal northern areas may have dramatically decreased. Such an event can have devastating effects on a culture whose subsistence, religious, and social hierarchy was agriculturally based. What takes place is a de-evolution (Hall's Shmoo Effect) of the Mississippian system in these northern climes. This decline may be hastened by a shifting of the competitive advantage to the surrounding Late Woodland groups.

What is interesting to note is that the "decline" of the northern Mississippian groups clearly pre-dates that of Cahokia. It also pre-dates the introduction of northern-adapted maize into the upper valley. The failure of the Mississippian intrusion seems most likely tied to the poor adaptation of their major agricultural crop to this northern area. It is remarkable that within a generation or two of this decline the Oneota peoples of Wisconsin and Minnesota expand throughout the northern area with virtually an identical agricultural system with one important exception, northern-adapted maize (Cutler and Blake 1976; Blake 1986).

By the beginning of the fourteenth century, the Middle Mississippian utilization/occupation/colonization of the upper valley had drawn to a close. In evaluating the Apple River sequence I am inclined to bring it to a close by circa A.D. 1300–1350. In the northern Central Illinois River Valley this tradition is transformed at some point between about A.D. 1275–1350 with the movement of northern Oneota Bold Counselor phase peoples into the valley (Duane Esarey, personal communication, 1986;

Lawrence A. Conrad, personal communication, 1986). The Mississippian groups in the southern Central Illinois Valley, however, appear to continue unaffected for at least a century (Conrad, personal communication, 1987).

If the above discussion concerning the adaptive advantage of the northern strain of maize is correct, the Central Illinois Valley may represent the southern boundary of this advantage. While Oneota people dominate the upper valley and the northern fringes of the Central Illinois River Valley, their presence in the southern Central Illinois Valley, the Lower Illinois Valley, and the American Bottom was limited to small temporary intrusions. In these areas the strength of the Mississippian adaptive pattern continued well into the thirteenth and fourteenth centuries, forming an effective barrier to Oneota southern expansion.

One of the most rewarding aspects of recent research in the local sequences has been the demonstration of just how compressed the Middle Mississippian interlude in the northern Mississippi Valley really was. In two short centuries it appeared, flourished, and was transformed or vanished. In the following centuries the prehistory of the upper valley saw little influence from the south. By the thirteenth-fourteenth centuries these northern groups are more often the exporters of cultural influences than the recipients.

The Mississippianization of the Upper Valley

To a large extent Mississippian archaeology in the Upper Mississippi River Valley has been dominated by a single question: What is the relationship of these outlying sites to Cahokia? Depending on the scholar's preferences we might see this as direct as the establishment of "colonies of warrior-traders" or as vague as the general diffusion of traits. One thing is very clear however: between A.D. 950 and A.D. 1200 the people of the American Bottom were an important cultural force in the upper valley. No resident of the valley or its fringes could have been totally ignorant of the existence of Cahokian Mississippian culture. The various authors in this book have extensively documented the nature of the Mississippian materials in each research area. Earlier in this chapter I summarized the evidence for the Emergent and classic Mississippian presence in the upper valley. The mechanisms involved are more clearly delineated in this section. Richard Krause (1985, drawing on Rouse 1958) has outlined the factors that need to be identified archaeologically to demonstrate the mechanisms that may have been critical in the introduction of Mississippian into the upper valley. To confirm *immigration* one must (1) identify the parent population, (2) determine reasons for such migrations, (3) demonstrate the presence of "site-unit intrusions," and (4) show that resident populations were displaced. To prove the existence of *diffusion-induced transformation* one should be able to (1) identify compatible local populations, (2) isolate trajectories in that local population's economic and manufacturing practices conducive to the new life-style, and (3) locate the presence of "trait-unit intrusions" that could stimulate the Mississippianization process. The final mechanism represents a blend of the others in that it includes *limited immigration and immigrant-resident fusion*. In this case one must identify (1) the presence of Mississippian peoples in the area and (2) the fusion of the Woodland resident culture with that of the migrants to create new cultural patterns.

In Krause's terminology *Mississippianization* appears confined to the process in which Woodland peoples were transformed to a Mississippian life-style through the introduction of new ideas and practices (Krause 1985:28–29). In this book the term has been used with broader connotations to indicate the introduction of Mississippian culture into the upper valley regardless of the specific mechanism (i.e., from site-unit to trait-unit intrusions). Regardless of the slight differences in terminology, Krause's trio of mechanisms are useful in examining and categorizing the upper valley data.

During the Emergent Mississippian stage in the American Bottom, an examination of the upper valley shows that there is only one possible example representing immigration, Trempealeau Mounds. At present there is insufficient information to evaluate the validity or possible impact of this site. Every other situation on which we have information (Pere Marquette, Rench) indicates that contact during the Emergent Mississippian time period can best be seen as representing diffusion-induced transformations.

Even during the period of classic Mississippian "expansion," the majority of contact situations between Late Woodland and Mississippian peoples are peripheral and perhaps limited to such activities as seasonal trading. Diffusion-induced transformation is dramatically documented at the Collins site and suggested by Robert Hall for the immediate ancestors of the first inhabitants of Aztalan. The immigration of Mississippian populations into the upper valley can be demonstrated for the Red Wing, Apple River, and Central Illinois Valley areas. In central Illinois this initial intrusion rapidly is transformed by a fusion of immigrants and residents to form the Spoon River culture. In the Apple River and the Red Wing localities the Mississippian populations seem to maintain their integrity for a longer time period.

Although Krause argues that one must have evidence of population displacement in order to demonstrate immigration, little such evidence has been forthcoming in the upper valley with the exception of the central Illinois physical anthropology (Blakely 1971, 1973; Conrad, chap. 6). Based on our current knowledge of Late Woodland archaeology in the upper valley, the most plausible explanation seems to be that population density was extremely low in the areas that the Mississippians moved into, thus causing little local disruption. Subsequently, in such areas the carrying capacity may have been enchanced by the introduction of Mississippian crops and agricultural methods (Lawrence A. Conrad, personal communication, 1987). Mississippian northward migration was extremely selective and appears to have sought such low population areas. In the Lower Illinois River Valley, in fact, it appears that the high Jersey Bluff population density was an effective barrier to Mississippian immigration (Emerson 1973; Conrad 1973; Farnsworth, Emerson, and Glenn, chap. 5). Such a selection pattern argues against interpreting the Mississippian intrusions as "conquest-oriented" or even as operating from the position of power.

During the final dispersion of Mississippians during the thirteenth-century Sand Prairie phase, actual outmigration seems to be the most economical explanation. This population movement, however, is limited to the uplands surrounding the American Bottom and perhaps to the Lower Illinois River Valley. The major movement of peoples at this time may be the southward migration of the northern Oneota populations into the central and lower Illinois River valleys and the American Bottom.

The nature and processes involved in the Mississippianization of the Upper Mississippi River Valley is a major question in the late prehistory of the area. During the discussion sessions and paper presentations at the symposium that led to this book, questions concerning this process were consistently raised. To a limited extent some of these questions could be answered by our current data but many of them still linger for future researchers and are presented below:

(1) How uniform is this process of Mississippianization? As demonstrated in a number of chapters, this is one of those questions that we can partially answer. It would appear that at least the results of the process are not uniform. Clearly, the variation between the Lower Illinois Valley populations, those of Collins, or Aztalan demonstrate the possible variations in response. However, we have very little understanding of how much variation there was in the stimuli that produced such results. Part of the answer to this question, of course, lies in one's

view of Cahokia. Is Cahokia a powerful military and economic force that establishes such places as Aztalan and Mills to control the northern resources? Or must we look to less dramatic factors such as diffuse trading patterns or gradual population movements to account for these sites?

(2) Although we stress the uniqueness of the northern valley sites we often find ourselves forced to note the strong similarities in cultural development. At the same time we see real divergence from the American Bottom pattern. What causes this? Having worked with American Bottom, Central Illinois Valley, and Apple River Mississippian materials, I am struck by the very strong relationship that seems to exist between the Apple River and central Illinois. In fact, this relationship is much stronger than anything I can envision between either of these areas and Cahokia. Do these northern sites, perhaps, form a cultural unit? I suggest that it would be worth our while to look more closely at the developmental histories and relationships between these northern Mississippian groups and less at the Cahokia connection.

(3) Much of late prehistoric archaeology in essence can be reduced to ceramics. In the upper valley the questions of shell-tempered ceramics can be approached from two perspectives: technology and chronology. Recent strides have been made in understanding shell-tempered ceramic technology and these will no doubt be of eventual use in understanding the upper valley adoption and distribution of such wares. Of more interest to me is the problem of the usefulness of the Mississippian rim form changes as chronological markers on a regional basis (e.g., Griffin 1960b). The correlations of rim form and time have been well documented for Cahokia, substantiated in the Central Illinois Valley, and suggested for much of the rest of the upper valley. If this correlation holds true for the upper valley as a whole, we will have an invaluable tool with which to control time. One of the areas that will be critical in answering this question will be the dating of pure early components in the Red Wing area, perhaps from such new excavations as Silvernale and Bryan.

(4) What are the key factors controlling the spatial distribution of Mississippian sites across the upper valley? How important is the local environmental setting, and if this is the controlling factor, then why do we seem to have so many "ideal environments" with no Mississippian inhabitants? Is Late Woodland population density an important negative or positive factor in the location of Mississippian sites? Much has been made concerning the location of some sites at critical points to control trade; does this really stand up?

(5) What do we know about Mississippian subsistence outside of the American Bottom? Even in instances where we have a fair amount of information, there are differences of opinion concerning the nature of the central Illi-

nois subsistence pattern. There is little recent subsistence information from any of the other northern Mississippian sites. Is there really a major difference between Cahokia subsistence patterns and those to the north? There has been some suggestion that these northerners had an increased emphasis on hunting, fishing, and collecting and depended less on farming than the American Bottom peoples did. Is there any truth to this picture (e.g., Bender, Baerreis, and Steventon 1981)? Conversely, are there significance differences between the various northern areas?

(6) What was the role of religion in the spread of Mississippian culture into northern areas (cf. Gibbon 1974)? Collins has been suggested to be the work of "missionaries." Sites such as Eveland and Aztalan could certainly be interpreted in a similar fashion. We know that Mississippian symbolism was present among Late Woodland populations in the Upper Mississippi Valley (Salzer 1987). Presumably, religion and economics were inti-

mately blended in the Mississippian trading networks and it would be very difficult to evaluate the impact of each separately. However, researchers may well find it enlightening to put more emphasis on the role of "religion" and less on "economics" in interpreting some of the upper valley events.

(7) Critical to understanding the relationships within and between the northern Mississippian manifestations will be investigations of the political and hierarchical nature of these entities. We have little data at present. Presumably the existence of substructure mounds, status differentiation in burials, human sacrifice, and formal village organization bespeak a hierachical social organization in the Central Illinois Valley Spoon River culture (cf. Conrad 1984, 1989). While there is extensive information on the Spoon River settlement pattern (Harn 1975c, 1978; Conrad, chap. 6) how the system operated is still being debated. Only bits and pieces of comparable information exist for the Apple River and Red Wing areas.

Cahokia Remodeled

The focus of this paper has been an examination of the relationship between the late prehistoric peoples of Cahokia and the Upper Mississippi River Valley. In a number of instances the actual movement of Mississippians into the upper valley seems likely. In other cases we have seen the movement of ideas and materials—sometimes dramatically transforming the receiving cultures, more often only adding a few exotic items to their cultural inventory. It has generally been easier to isolate the results of this interaction than to delineate the causes.

For many researchers the interpretation of the upper valley late prehistoric cultures has been premised on their perception of Cahokia. Unfortunately, most interpretations of Cahokia have not progressed beyond the "Mexican analogy" stage. Fowler (1989), Kelly (1982), and Hall (chap. 1) have all outlined to various degrees the history of research and a summary of theories concerning Cahokia. Only a little over fifty years ago archaeologists were desperately trying to convince the experts that Cahokia and its largest monument, Monks Mound, were "real." Once confirmed, however, Monks Mound has dominated the public perception of Cahokia and that of the archaeologists as well. Virtually no statement on Cahokia fails to include an ode to the greatest earthen mound north of Mexico.

It may be a carryover from the early struggle to convince the general public of Cahokia's greatness; or simply the overwhelming magnitude of Monks Mound; or more likely because of a historical quirk that early investigators at Cahokia were steeped in a mesoamerican or South

American background, but since the inception of scientific research in the 1960s, Cahokia has been held captive by the "Mexican theorists." (For example, see the writings of Fowler 1968, 1974, and elsewhere; Porter 1969, 1974; Lathrap and Porter 1985; O'Brien 1972, 1983; and others). The strongest advocate for the Mexican connection has been Donald Lathrap (cited in Hall, chap. 1) of the University of Illinois. Few would state the case as strongly as Lathrap, but his views seemed to have influenced many whether they are believers in the Mexican/Mississippian "migrations," the applicability of the Mexican analogies, or perhaps even urged some to accept the Cahokian "state."

Yet one thing is clear from all the research conducted at Cahokia and the surrounding American Bottom: at least as long ago as the Late Archaic (Emerson 1980, 1986) this area was culturally part of the larger region referred to as the Southeast (cf. Smith 1986; Steponaitis 1986). As noted by various authors, this affiliation was especially strong during the Emergent Mississippian period. At the beginning of this period the Central Mississippi Valley saw the appearance of "Planned communities, the demarcation of public space and public structures, the possible control of agricultural surplus, and evidence for organized communal labor projects [which] all point to the likely presence of community-level positions of sociopolitical control and marked differential status" (Smith 1986:56).

In the American Bottom there is extensive evidence for the Emergent Mississippian period cultural transformations (Kelly, Ozuk et al. 1984; Kelly 1987; Emerson and Jackson 1987). One very important missing piece of information, however, is when the development of civic-ceremonial mound centers began. There is evidence from a few of the centers to suggest that their origins may have been in the Emergent Mississippian period. Griffin (Griffin and Jones 1977) argues for the pre-Fairmount (i.e., pre-A.D. 900) construction of at least some of the six major mounds at the Pulcher site. Excavations at the single mound centers of Horseshoe Lake (Gregg 1975b) and Lohmann (Esarey with Good 1981) demonstrate pre-Mississippian utilization and occupation. Even the large Mitchell site (Porter 1974) with its eleven mounds may have had substantial use as a mound center before its heyday in Stirling times.

Recent work at Monks Mound (William Woods, personal communication, 1986) confirms that the major portions of the mound were in place by A.D. 1000–1100, while radiocarbon dates indicate a post-A.D. 850–900 date for the beginning of construction. Construction of this mound was underway during the latter portion of the Emergent Mississippian period. Although data are virtually absent for the East St. Louis Metro group of forty-five mounds and the St. Louis group of twenty-six mounds, it is difficult not to believe that both of these sites owe their origins to the Emergent Mississippian period.

By ca. A.D. 900 the American Bottom may have been the setting for a minimum of a half-dozen civic-ceremonial centers supporting simple chiefdoms. Although there is no supporting evidence at present, several of these centers (Pulcher, Cahokia, or East St. Louis) may have already incorporated some of their smaller neighbors to form small-scale complex chiefdoms. There is some evidence that parts of the uplands (cf. Emerald Mounds, Pauketat and Koldehoff 1983) may have been involved in this process. The emergence of chiefdoms, once begun in the area, would tend to have a snowball effect (Carneiro 1981) because of the adaptive advantage of this organizational pattern in dealing with other such groups.

Little discussion has taken place in the American Bottom regarding the role of models of chiefdom-level sociopolitical development to assist archaeologists in understanding this complex situation. Nor have such models been suggested for understanding the northern Mississippian expansion. Given the widespread successful application of such studies in the Southeast, this absence is perplexing.

Chiefdoms have been the subject of extensive ethnographic and ethnohistoric research (e.g., Fried 1967; Goldman 1970; Sahlins 1958; Service 1962) and archaeological studies (e.g., Cordy 1981; DePratter 1983; Helms 1979; Peebles and Kus 1977; Steponaitis 1983). There is

little doubt that chiefdom-level societies existed throughout the Southeast during the Mississippian period (DePratter 1983; Hudson 1976; Swanton 1946). Smith has characterized the sociopolitical pattern of this time as "being loosely woven and consisting of small shifting networks of conflict and alliance. . . . Through time, each of these shifting networks and their constituent polities traced a unique developmental trajectory along a possibility bounded on one end by minimal organization (fragmented segmentary tribes) and on the other by maximum sociopolitical complexity (large complex or regional-level chiefdoms)" (1986:58).

David Anderson (1986:i) has outlined a number of factors that are critical in promoting stability or change in chiefdoms. These include (1) strength of ideologies sanctifying chiefly authority; (2) effectiveness of social mechanisms for dealing with chiefly successions, population growth, territorial maintenance, or expansion; (3) ability of chiefly organizational structures to maintain stability in the face of stress; (4) degree of control over status goods and the position of individual polities in elite goods exchange networks; and (5) impacts from other surrounding societies. It is these factors that must be taken into account when modeling Mississippian sociopolitical development in the American Bottom.

It is an axiom of chiefdoms that they are often unstable and subject to "cycling" behavior. This behavior results in patterns of emergence, expansion, collapse, and reconstitution (Anderson 1986). The concept of chiefly cycling is critical to understanding Mississippian cultural development. If one envisions the tenth-century American Bottom as occupied by at least several competing chiefdoms—some rising in power, some declining—it at least places the "mystery and uniqueness" of Cahokia's eventual rise in a reasonable context.

The middle to late tenth century in the American Bottom was marked by extreme cultural variation between localities, perhaps encouraged by local and regional trading and interaction. By the end of this period Cahokia had become the dominant civic-ceremonial center in the Bottom. This rise to dominance is reflected in the increasing homogeniety of the cultural assemblages during the Lohmann phase and climaxes in the Stirling phase. The period from about A.D. 1000 to 1100 reflects a time of internal and external consolidation for the leading elite at Cahokia. This century also marks the first appearance of large-scale defensive palisades with bastions at Cahokia (Anderson 1969; William Iseminger, personal communication, 1987). In addition, it represents the time for the fullest expression of the fertility iconography (Emerson 1982, 1984a, 1989) that was central to legitimizing and symbolizing the dominant religious and chiefly classes.

What are the implications of this pattern for interpreting

the northern Mississippian expansion? It provides major insights into the question of the relationship of Cahokia and the northern sites. Primary concerns of chiefdoms are the issues of succession, leadership changes, and internal challenges to authority. Leadership challenges from rival factions and subordinates represent a central threat to the stability of such an organizational structure. If we can accept southeastern analogies, chiefly power may have been maintained through a series of elite marriages that cemented alliances with other groups. In other instances rival groups may simply have been subdued through warfare. Neither marriage nor victory can be relied upon to provide permanent solutions to the maintenance of the ruling elite.

I tend to see the late tenth- and early eleventh-century Mississippian political situation in the American Bottom as potentially unstable as various elite groups vied for power as Cahokia gained control. This political and social instability is reflected in the construction of the massive bastioned palisades around Cahokia. Given this scenario the northern expansion might be seen as the exodus of losing or disgruntled elite groups removing themselves from the area controlled by Cahokia. Such conflicts might also be aggravated by increasing environmental degradation (Lopinot and Woods 1988) and population densities (Milner 1986b). If one considers these northern settlements from this perspective, a number of previously nagging questions become less bothersome.

Many reasons have been suggested to explain the location of the Apple River, central Illinois, Aztalan, and Red Wing Mississippian settlements. The primary explanation has been focused on the control of resources and trade for Cahokia, although no one has really addressed the question of why such control suddenly became necessary. What resources were being controlled has seldom been investigated beyond the hypothesis stage. In cases such as Apple River, where it was argued that these sites controlled galena for Cahokia, it must have been discouraging for proponents of the economic approach when Walthall's (1981) study demonstrated that Cahokia received the majority of its galena from Missouri.

It is incumbent on those who see the northern expansion as an economic empire of Cahokia to explain why other areas that are rich in resources do not have Cahokia settlements. It is reasonable to believe that Cahokia was actively engaged in trade both with the Plains and southern Missouri; why no "trading posts" on the Missouri River or in southern Missouri?

I do not find the argument of trade to be a compelling one in explaining the establishment of Mississippian settlements in the upper valley. If one does not accept trade as the primary explanatory device in the placement of these sites, what causes can be invoked? One fact that should be kept in mind is the tremendous distances involved; even on the main channels, it is over 110 river miles to central Illinois, 365 river miles to the Apple River, and 615 river miles to the Red Wing area from Cahokia.

It is clear that the great distances moved up the Mississippi Valley are not because of the lack of suitable environments between Cahokia and the Apple River. It seems that distance from Cahokia was a desirable trait to these migrants, almost the further the better. In this instance the maintenance of a clear buffer zone in the Lower Illinois Valley between the American Bottom populations and those of central Illinois is instructive. Such an attitude would be in keeping with elite groups intent on remaining outside of Cahokia's sphere of control.

I suggest that a more economical solution to this problem can be derived on the basis of our knowledge of the sociopolitics of chiefdoms and American Bottom archaeology. As noted, the eleventh century marked the appearance of cultural homogenity in the Bottom, suggesting the cultural and probably political dominance of a single elite group, likely operating out of Cahokia (this is the time of the first construction of the palisades at Cahokia). Such a dominace could not be achieved without opposition from established elites at other centers. These groups had several options: destruction, incorporation into the Cahokia sphere, or immigration. I believe that the outflowing of Stirling phase Mississippians was a result of the disruptions caused by the consolidation of power that took place at this time because of Cahokian achievement of economic, political, or religious domination in the American Bottom.

If we accept these northern migrants as "refugees" rather than as colonial outposts of Cahokia, a number of facts and subsequent events make more sense. In each case these settlements are located on the rich floodplain environments that were so necessary for Mississippian subsistence practices. These same locations seem to be characterized by a very low density of Late Woodland occupants. In each case it appears that the Mississippian migrants were probably familiar with the area because of the earlier trade contacts that the American Bottom peoples enjoyed in the upper valley. These locations were not simply choosen blindly but rather specifically for those attributes conducive to self-substaining settlements rather than as trading centers.

Characteristically, the northern settlements quickly ceased contact with the American Bottom and began their own independent cultural development. This behavior seems more appropriate for exiles than for colonists or traders sent by Cahokia. The external contacts of these groups most frequently appear to have been with one another, especially between the Apple River and central Illinois peoples, rather than with Cahokia. Given the difficulties of overland contact between the two groups and the relative ease of contact with Cahokia, one must suspect that these people had specific reasons for not communicating with Cahokia.

What does this all do to our picture of Cahokia? Hopefully, it introduces some contextual reality. There is good reason to believe that between A.D. 900 and 1300 there were a number of competing chiefdoms in the American Bottom area, sometimes splintered and warring, occasionally consolidated into a powerful complex chiefdom. Between about A.D. 1000 and 1200 there may have been a period of consolidation when the ruling elite at such a center as Cahokia held sway over much of the American Bottom. This consolidation was a short-term affair and disintegrated by the middle 1100s and was gone forever by 1200. The northern expansion, beginning at about A.D. 1000, is seen as an outgrowth of local conflicts, environmental deterioration, and population pressure in the American Bottom. In this model, Cahokia is returned to its cultural context and heritage in the Southeast and archaeologists can begin to concentrate on exploring the data rather than the "myth" of the archaeological record of this most important site.

PART THREE

The Southern Hinterlands

13

Mississippian in the Upper Kaskaskia Valley: New Data from Lake Shelbyville and New Interpretations

CHARLES R. MOFFAT

The initial late prehistoric chronology of the Kaskaskia River Valley was worked out in the 1960s. At that time the late prehistoric sites in the area were classified within the Middle Mississippi tradition and were regarded as part of the prehistoric cultural system centered around the site of Cahokia. A number of other organizational and systemic properties were attributed to these sites in the light of these culture historical constructs, often without detailed and critical examination of the relevant archaeological evidence. The result was a fairly comprehensive model of prehistoric Mississippian culture in the Kaskaskia Valley that agreed well with what other researchers thought had happened elsewhere in the Midwest in late prehistoric times. This model has been included in some recent syntheses of Midwest prehistory, particularly the one presented by Fowler and Hall (1978).

Archaeological data recovered in the course of recent research in the Shelbyville Reservoir area (fig. 13.1) conflict on so many points with the Cahokia-centered model of Kaskaskia Valley Mississippian cultural development that it has been necessary to reassess many of our assumptions concerning the Mississippian occupation of the area. A new chronology has been developed from analyses of the upper valley data which may be applicable, in part, to the middle valley. A new culture classification scheme has also been devised that distinguishes two Mississippian complexes, one centered in the upper valley and the other in the lower valley. Both complexes appear distinct from Cahokia. This chapter reviews the previous model of late prehistoric Kaskaskia Valley culture history, describes the evidence and the logical processes used in developing the new model, and discusses its significance for the region and for midwestern prehistory.

Natural Setting

The Kaskaskia River has the second largest watershed of all of the Mississippi River tributaries in Illinois (fig. 13.1). The river's headwaters are in the prairie lands of Champaign County in east-central Illinois, and it flows over a 480-kilometer course ultimately emptying into the Mississippi River in Randolph County, Illinois, about sixty-five kilometers south of St. Louis, Missouri (Pickels 1937).

The Kaskaskia Valley has been divided into upper, middle, and lower sections on the basis of topography and geology (Illinois State Planning Commission 1938). The upper valley is north of the Shelbyville Moraine, which marks the maximum extent of Wisconsin glacial advance in central Illinois. The uplands are covered by substantial deposits of glacial drift dating to the Woodfordian substage of the Wisconsin glaciation (Willman and Frye 1970). In its extreme upper course the Kaskaskia River occupies a narrow channel only slightly lower than the adjacent uplands. About fifty kilometers upstream from the Shelbyville Moraine, the river begins to entrench itself in a distinct valley, which widens and deepens downstream as it approaches the moraine. The Kaskaskia River is joined by a major tributary, the West Okaw River, about thirty kilometers south and west of the head of its valley and the combined rivers cut through the Shelbyville Moraine just east of the town of Shelbyville. The Shelbyville Reservoir, a U.S. Army Corps of Engineers project, is the focus of this study. It lies in the upper valley just

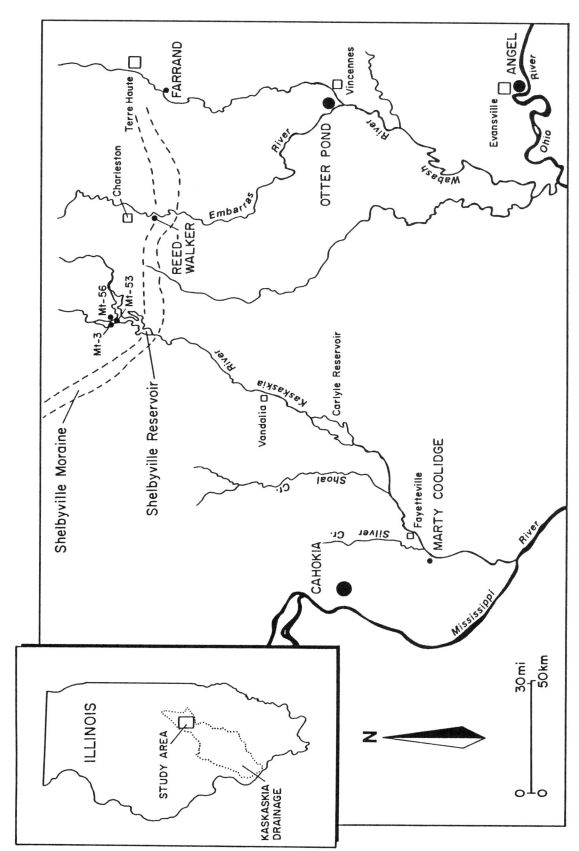

Figure 13.1. Location of the Study Area and Archaeological Sites in Central Illinois

north of the Shelbyville Moraine. The dam that forms the reservoir was built across the moraine itself and the reservoir's flood pool extends some fifty kilometers upstream, nearly to the head of the valley (fig. 13.1).

The Kaskaskia River floodplain above the Shelbyville Moraine is not well developed. It tends to occur as a narrow zone along the river channel, with broader pockets developing behind large meander loops and around the mouths of tributary streams. Typical floodplain physiographic features, such as natural levees, oxbow lakes, and back swamps, are small when they occur at all. A substantial part of the valley floor is covered by a series of terraces that are composed primarily of interbedded gravels and sands. Several isolated upland remnant knolls also occur on the valley floor. Bluff slopes and tops form the edge of the valley. Much of this bluff zone is steeply sloping and dissected by gullies and tributary stream courses. The bluffs are substantially higher in the southern part of the study area near Shelbyville than at its extreme northeastern end. The river valley does not exceed 0.8 kilometers in width upstream from Shelbyville. The uplands surrounding the upper valley are gently undulating and, in some areas, poorly drained.

South of the Shelbyville Moraine the river flows through a region covered by Illinoian glacial drift mantled by deposits of loess that increase in thickness near the Mississippi Valley (Eckblaw 1937; Willman and Frye 1970). The Kaskaskia Valley widens substantially south of Shelbyville, reaching a maximum width of about five kilometers between Vandalia and Fayetteville, Illinois (fig. 13.1). Typical floodplain topographic features are better developed in this part of the drainage, known as the middle valley. A second Army Corps of Engineers project, the Carlyle Reservoir, occupies part of the middle valley. Downstream from Fayetteville the valley narrows again to less than one kilometer in an area where the glacial drift thins and upper Mississippian system shales and sandstones outcrop (Eckblaw 1937). The section of river valley between New Athens and the confluence with the Mississippi River is the lower valley (Kuttruff 1969).

Research History

With the exception of a few small-scale excavations undertaken by the University of Chicago in the 1930s and 1940s in what later became the Carlyle Reservoir, systematic archaeological research was initiated in the Kaskaskia Valley in the late 1950s. It has consisted largely of site surveys and salvage excavations carried out in connection with three U.S. Army Corps of Engineers projects: the Shelbyville Reservoir in the upper valley, the Carlyle Reservoir in the middle valley, and a canalization project in the lower valley. Most of the reports describing this work are either unpublished or are published in limited-distribution series. Those parts of the Kaskaskia Valley that were not affected by these three projects are still largely unknown archaeologically.

The Lower Kaskaskia Canalization Project affected a ninety-six kilometer stretch of river between Fayetteville and the confluence of the Kaskaskia and Mississippi rivers. Survey in this area was begun by Lawrence A. Conrad (1966) for Southern Illinois University and was completed five years later by William B. Iseminger and Michael J. McNerney (1973). Conrad recorded a total of forty-one sites, only two of which had Mississippian occupations. Iseminger and McNerney located another 183 sites, six of which they assigned to the Mississippian period. Five additional Mississippian sites were later located in the New Athens area by L. Carl Kuttruff (1974). Kuttruff (1969, 1972) directed three field seasons of excavation at the multicomponent Marty Coolidge site, which had an extensive Mississippian component.

Seventeen Mississippian structures and twenty-eight pit features, representing three occupations, were identified and excavated. Kuttruff (1972:75) suggested that the Mississippian component at the Marty Coolidge site represented a community that was larger than a simple farming hamlet. Two additional Mississippian sites in the New Athens area, the Lehman site and the Enge site, were also tested by Kuttruff (1974). These sites were apparently both small hamlets.

Archaeological research in the central Kaskaskia Valley has been concentrated within the flood pool of the Carlyle Reservoir (fig. 13.1). The initial survey of the Carlyle Reservoir was carried out by Howard Winters for Southern Illinois University and reported by Melvin L. Fowler (1959). The following year a series of one-meter-square test pits were dug in thirty-seven of those sites (Fowler 1960). As a result of this work, a total of eighty-four sites were recorded and twenty-six sites were shown to have Mississippian components. More extensive excavations were later undertaken at eight of those Mississippian sites: Kerwin (11-Ct-40) and Orrell (11-Ct-34) (Salzer 1963); Toothsome (11-Ct-73), Sandy Tip (11-Ct-61), Hatchery West (11-Ct-10), and the Galley Pond Mound (11-Ct-49) (Binford 1964; Binford et al. 1970); Texas (11-Ct-23) (Morrell 1965); and Boulder (11-Ct-1) (Rackerby 1966, 1968). With the exception of the Galley Pond Mound, all of these sites were small habitation sites, farmsteads, or hamlets. Possible Mississippian agricultural fields were identified at the Texas site (Morrell 1965; Fowler 1969b).

A resurvey of about one-fourth of the Carlyle Reservoir shoreline was undertaken by Sidney G. Denny (1979) and nine Mississippian sites, three of which had been reported in the 1960s, were located. Exposed features, including wall trenches, postmolds, and pits, were discovered at two of the nine Mississippian sites. More recently, the Center for American Archeology surveyed the west shore of Carlyle Lake, revisited four previously recorded sites, and reported forty-six additional sites. Mississippian components were identified at nine sites, including three of the previously recorded sites (Hassen, Schroeder, and Morgan 1984). Excavations were also carried out at the Grey Day site (11-Ct-36), where Late Woodland and Mississippian structures, pit features, and burials had been exposed by erosion (Hassen, McGimsey et al. 1984). The American Resources Group subsequently tested five sites at Rend Lake, including the previously investigated Orrell Site (Sirico 1986). All of the sites recorded during these recent investigations were apparently also farmsteads or hamlets.

The Shelbyville Reservoir flood pool was surveyed by William W. Chmurny (1961), Bernard Golden (1962), and William M. Gardner (1963) prior to the construction of the reservoir. A total of ten Mississippian sites were located. Extensive excavations were subsequently carried out at two multicomponent sites, Jasper Newman (11-Mt-3) and Sweat Bee (11-Mt-18/19), and more limited test excavations were made at two additional sites, Leonard Bolin (11-Mt-12; formerly 11-Mt-1) and Jesse Clayton (11-Mt-22). Gardner (1969a) reported on the Middle Woodland components of the Jasper Newman and Sweat Bee sites in his doctoral dissertation on the Havana occupation of the upper Kaskaskia Valley. However, both of these sites also have substantial Mississippian components.

The most extensive preinundation salvage excavations were carried out at the Jasper Newman site. It was located on a broad terrace in the West Okaw Valley about one and one-half kilometers north of the confluence of that stream with the Kaskaskia River (fig. 13.2). This site was determined to have two Mississippian occupations. Component A, the most extensive of these occupations, consisted of two mounds, a plaza area, two residential areas, and a stockade (Gardner 1969b). The two mounds were thought to have been platform mounds, although their shapes had been altered by many years of plowing. The westernmost mound, the largest of the two mounds, had also been damaged by road construction. Gardner excavated the remaining portion of this mound and uncovered a wall-trench structure with an interior hearth at the base of the mound. The mound fill contained a considerable amount of midden material and indications of basket loading were noted during the excavations. Gardner

(1969b:59) believed that only one construction phase was present. The second mound was only partially excavated. Its fill was more uniform than that of the first mound and a midden layer containing Middle and Late Woodland artifacts was found at its base. One intact stone-box grave containing an incomplete burial of an adult male was discovered during the excavations in this mound. Associated with the burial were a marine shell and a bipointed knife of Mill Creek chert (Gardner 1969b). Amateurs had reportedly found additional Mississippian burials in this mound.

Test excavations made immediately to the south of the mounds indicated an absence of habitation debris there. Gardner (1969b) interpreted this area as a plaza. Two habitation areas were located to the east and west of the mounds. The eastern habitation area contained a wall-trench structure, eight storage pits, thirty-four earth ovens, and five corn cob-filled smudge pits. Excavations in the western habitation area were more limited in extent than those in the eastern area. Two superimposed wall-trench structures were uncovered there and at least twelve stains, which were thought to represent additional structures, were observed on aerial photographs of this area. Finally, a stockade line was discovered running along the entire eastern side of the site. The excavations did not determine whether the northern, southern, and western sides of the site were also enclosed by the stockade (Gardner 1969b).

Four radiocarbon determinations were obtained on wood charcoal samples from three Component A features (table 13.1). Two dates (M-1786 and I-1788) were obtained for House 1 in the western habitation area. One date (M-1787) was obtained for Feature 6, a pit feature in the eastern habitation area, and one date (M-2578) was obtained for the submound structure (Gardner 1969b). The uncorrected ages of these dates cluster in the fourteenth century A.D. and are consistent with Gardner's view that the features assigned to Component A at the Jasper Newman site formed an integral unit.

A second Mississippian component, Component B, was defined near the southeastern end of the terrace (Gardner 1969b). Five structures and three pits (two earth ovens and one possible storage pit) were assigned to this component. The structures were post structures set in roughly circular excavated basins. One of the Component B structures was bisected by the stockade associated with Component A and most of the remaining Component B features were located outside of the area enclosed by the stockade. No radiocarbon dates were obtained for any of the Component B features, but Gardner (1969b) suggested that, in view of this instance of superposition, Component B was earlier than Component A and dated to before A.D. 1300.

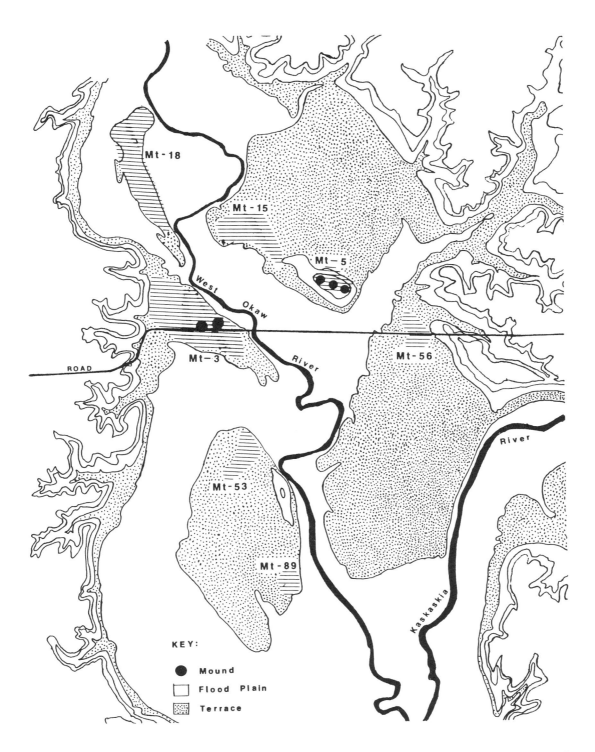

Figure 13.2. Mississippian Sites in the Kaskaskia River/West Okaw River Confluence Area, Shelbyville Reservoir

Table 13.1. Mississippian-Period Radiocarbon Dates for Shelbyville Reservoir Sites

Sample No.	Material	Uncorrected Date (in years B.P.)	Converted to 5730 yr. H/L	MASCA Correction**	Provenience
M-1786[1]	Charcoal	620 ± 110	639 ± 110	A.D. 1320 ± 120	Jasper Newman s. House 1 (F1)
M-1787[1]	Charcoal	520 ± 100	536 ± 100	A.D. 1390 ± 110	Jasper Newman s. Feat. 6
M-1788[1]	Charcoal	570 ± 110	587 ± 110	A.D. 1360 ± 120	Jasper Newman s. House 1 (F1)
I-2578[1]	Uncharred wood	570 ± 85	587 ± 85	A.D. 1360 ± 95	Jasper Newman s. Mound 1 struct.
GX-830[1]	Charcoal and corn	815 ± 105	840 ± 105	A.D. 1180 ± 115	Sweat Bee Feat. 7 (23)
GX-831[1]	Charred wood	370 ± 95	381 ± 95	A.D. 1500–1460 ± 105	Sweat Bee House 1
ISGS-592[2]	Charred wood	715 ± 75	737 ± 75	A.D. 1240 ± 85	Doctor's Island Feat. 3
ISGS-773[2]	Charred wood	860 ± 75*	886 ± 75	A.D. 1170–1110 ± 85	Doctor's Island Feat. 11
Beta-4029[2]	Charred wood	770 ± 70*	793 ± 70	A.D. 1220–1200 ± 80	Doctor's Island Feat. 25a
Beta-4030[2]	Charred wood	360 ± 60*	371 ± 60	A.D. 1500–1460 ± 70	Doctor's Island Feat. 28
ISGS-766[2]	Charred wood	880 ± 75	906 ± 75	A.D. 1080 ± 85	Stop Sign Feat. 3
Beta-4031[2]	Charred wood	950 ± 60*	979 ± 60	A.D. 1020 ± 70	Stop Sign Feat. 6a
Beta-4032[2]	Charred wood	680 ± 50*	700 ± 50	A.D. 1290–1260 ± 85	Stop Sign Feat. 7a
ISGS-591[2]	Charred wood	680 ± 75	700 ± 75	A.D. 1290–1260 ± 85	11-Mt-89 Feat. 3
ISGS-606[2]	Charred wood	560 ± 120	577 ± 120	A.D. 1370 ± 130	11-Sy-62 Feat. 1

* Date corrected for isotopic fractionation.
** Corrected for fluctuations of atmospheric C-14 according to Table 1 in E. K. Ralph, H. N. Michael, and M. C. Han, "Radiocarbon Dates and Reality," *MASCA Newsletter* vol. 9, no. 1 (August 1973).
[1] Gardner 1969b:173
[2] Moffat 1985:12

The Sweat Bee site (11-Mt-18) was located on a ridge in the West Okaw River floodplain about 800 meters north of the Jasper Newman site. In the early 1960s it was flanked by the West Okaw River to the east and an old river channel subject to frequent flooding to the west. The Mississippian component at the Sweat Bee site consisted of a habitation area and two stone-box grave cemeteries, one located to the north of the habitation area and the other located to the south of it (Gardner 1963). No mounds were present. The excavation of less than half of the habitation area by machine stripping resulted in the discovery of eight wall-trench structures, most of which showed evidence of rebuilding, one post structure, and more than twenty large storage pits (Gardner 1969b; Springer 1967). Apparently, many more pits were present in the machine-stripped area, but they were not excavated. A trench was excavated through the northern cemetery and a total of eighteen burials, many of them plow disturbed, were found (Springer 1967). Two radiocarbon dates, A.D. 1210 ± 105 years and A.D. 1480 ± 95 years (uncorrected), were obtained on samples recovered from two different wall-trench structures in the habitation area (Gardner 1969b).

Models of Mississippian Culture History in the Kaskaskia Valley

The Cahokia-centered model for the development of Middle Mississippi culture in the Kaskaskia Valley attributed this culture to movements of people into the valley from the Cahokia site near East St. Louis. This model was developed in the 1960s and has continued to be used as an explanatory framework in recent research (e.g., Hargrave et al. 1983; Hassen, McGimsey et al. 1984; Hassen, Schroeder, and Morgan 1984). It has also found its way into recent syntheses of Illinois prehistory (i.e., Fowler and Hall 1978). It is instructive to examine the historical development of this model and to consider further the assumptions that underlie it.

When the first Mississippian sites were identified in the Carlyle Reservoir basin, they were regarded as temporary camps left by hunters from Cahokia and the American Bottom (Fowler 1959:44). Later, after excavations had been carried out at some of these Carlyle Basin Mississippian sites and wall-trench structures, pits, agricultural fields, and other evidence of a more sedentary way of life were recovered, it was proposed that the sites were agricultural hamlets and farmsteads subordinate to Cahokia and supplying that great center with locally produced foodstuffs (Salzer 1963). The Kaskaskia Valley Mississippian occupation was thought to have resulted from more permanent population movements out of the American Bottom.

The ceramic typology developed for Cahokia by James B. Griffin (1949) and later elaborated by Joseph O. Vogel (1975) and others was used to classify the pottery recovered from the Mississippian sites in the Kaskaskia Valley. The pottery types were then used to cross-date sites in the Kaskaskia Valley with the chronology then in vogue for Cahokia, the Old Village Focus and Trappist Focus scheme. Other relevant chronological data, specifically radiocarbon dates and stratigraphic information, were also obtained in the course of investigations carried out at Mississippian sites in the Kaskaskia Valley in the 1960s, but these data played a distinctly secondary role in chronology building and were not systematically related to the ceramic evidence.

William Gardner, who supervised much of the archaeological research carried out in the Shelbyville Reservoir during the 1960s, was an enthusiastic advocate of the Cahokia-centered model of Mississippian development in the Kaskaskia Valley. In a publication (Gardner 1973a) and two contract reports (Gardner 1969b, n.d.) he proposed the most elaborate and carefully reasoned version of the scheme. Gardner's model of Mississippian development is worth examining closely because he discusses in detail assumptions and hypotheses that are implicit or are only briefly described in other writings that use the Cahokia-centered model. Gardner clearly regards the upper Kaskaskia Valley as an environmentally marginal area for Mississippian occupation. He thinks that the upper Kaskaskia Valley was largely uninhabited in Late Woodland times and that the Mississippian occupation of the area was relatively short-lived (Gardner 1969b, 1973a, 1973b). The Mississippian occupation of the Kaskaskia Valley is thought to have resulted from a mass migration up the Kaskaskia Valley from Cahokia (Gardner 1969b, n.d.). Consequently, Kaskaskia Valley Mississippian settlement and subsistence patterns are believed to have been like those of the Mississippian inhabitants of Cahokia and the Mississippi Valley proper (Gardner 1973a). That is to say, they were agriculturalists who farmed the alluvial soils of the floodplains and exploited the wild resources that were available in the valley bottoms. Gardner thinks that they made relatively little use of resources outside of the main river valley. Furthermore, he assumes that they had a social organization typical of the hierarchically organized Mississippian chiefdoms of the American Bottom.

Gardner (1969b, 1973a) uses this model to organize the Mississippian data recovered during Lake Shelbyville excavations in the 1960s and to explain certain aspects of Mississippian settlement patterning that were apparent at that time. He observes that there was a concentration of Mississippian sites near the confluence of the Kaskaskia River and the West Okaw River, which, he suggests, was due to the relatively greater extent of the floodplain in that locality. He interprets the Jasper Newman site as the local ceremonial center and the residence of the local elite, while the Sweat Bee site and other Mississippian sites in the area are characterized as hamlets or farmsteads occupied by lower-status individuals who supported the elite at the Jasper Newman site with surplus products.

Gardner (1969b, 1973a) argues that the Sweat Bee site and Component A at the Jasper Newman site were contemporaneous. However, the two radiocarbon dates for the Mississippian occupation at the Sweat Bee site diverge greatly from the Jasper Newman site dates and from each other (table 13.1). In order to resolve this difficulty, Gardner (1969b:91) averages the two Sweat Bee site dates and argues that the resulting date of A.D. 1395 is a better estimate of the true age of the Sweat Bee site and is close to the Jasper Newman dates. He then uses this averaged date for the Sweat Bee site to support his hypothesis concerning the contemporaneity of the Jasper Newman site, Component A, and the Sweat Bee site and also his model of upper Kaskaskia Valley social organization and settlement patterning (Gardner 1969b:87–95).

Gardner (1969b:88) observes that there are differences between the ceramic collections from the Jasper Newman site and the Sweat Bee site. Specifically, Jasper Newman has an appreciable percentage of red- or black-filmed and engraved or incised vessels, while filmed or decorated ceramics are nearly absent at the Sweat Bee site. However, Gardner (1969b) argues that these differences in ceramic content need not be viewed as evidence for temporal differences between the two sites. Instead, he suggests that the higher frequency of filmed and decorated ceramics at Jasper Newman reflects the ceremonial importance of that site and the social importance of the people who resided there. Thus ceramic differences between the Jasper Newman site and outlying hamlets, such as the Sweat Bee site, are explained by differences in site function and social status.

Gardner's model of Mississippian culture in the Kaskaskia Valley has a number of interesting implications for the study of Mississippian societies not only in the Shelbyville Reservoir area, but also elsewhere in the Midwest. The issues concerning social status differences that Gardner raises in his interpretation of the ceramic data from the Jasper Newman site and the Sweat Bee site have seldom been considered by midwestern archaeologists. These issues become increasingly important as archaeologists investigate small outlying sites in addition to major ceremonial centers and attempt to use ceramic data from these smaller sites to tighten regional chronologies.

William H. Sears (1973) has previously described striking differences in ceramic content between mounds and domestic midden deposits that occur in certain late prehistoric southeastern complexes. In his discussion of the Jasper Newman and Sweat Bee data, Gardner (1969b: 87–99) proposes that there are similar differences in the ceramic contents of habitation areas occupied by people of high versus low status. Differences of this sort are not unusual in complex societies and might, if they are adequately demonstrated, ultimately prove useful in studying Mississippian social organization at Cahokia and elsewhere in the Midwest. However, in the short run contrasts of this sort may create difficulties in placing outlying hamlets in regional chronologies developed through the seriation of ceramic collections recovered from large ceremonial centers.

Several other implications of the Cahokia-centered model are of significance in evaluating the relationship of the Kaskaskia Valley Mississippian sites to Cahokia. In support of the idea that the Mississippian population of the Kaskaskia Valley originally came from the Cahokia area by means of a mass migration, one expects to find earlier Mississippian sites in the Carlyle Reservoir area and the lower valley than in the Shelbyville Reservoir area. Moreover, the early Mississippian sites should be very similar to sites in the American Bottom of comparable age and position in the settlement system. That is, one expects farming hamlets in the Kaskaskia Valley to be similar to farming hamlets in the American Bottom, both with respect to site layout and artifact content. Small ceremonial centers such as the Jasper Newman site should be similar to secondary ceremonial centers of comparable age in the American Bottom. If regular contacts with Cahokia were maintained after the settlement of the Kaskaskia Valley, as Salzer (1963) implied, similarities between the two areas should persist into the later periods as well. Evidence of regular trade or ceremonial exchanges between the two areas is also expected. If ties between the two areas were broken after the postulated migration, later sites in the Kaskaskia Valley might show divergence from their counterparts in the American Bottom.

Not all archaeologists who worked in the Kaskaskia Valley during the 1960s were convinced that the Mississippian sites in that area were closely related to Cahokia. In his summary of the Carlyle Reservoir investigations, Frank E. Rackerby (1968) observes that there is a scarcity of trade material in that region which is attributable to Cahokia and he suggests that there was, in fact, little interaction between the two areas. He notes Fowler's (1960) and Salzer's (1963) hypotheses that the sites of the Carlyle Reservoir area were either seasonally occupied hunting camps or farming hamlets associated with Cahokia and comments that these hypotheses were "supported by neither site distribution or excavation data" (1968:89). However, Rackerby does not offer an alternative hypothesis to explain the presence of Mississippian sites in the Kaskaskia Valley.

In a contract report and an unpublished paper, Conrad (1966, n.d.) also questions whether the Mississippian occupants of the Kaskaskia Valley were closely related to Cahokia. Conrad does propose an alternative view that "the Mississippian settlers of the Kaskaskia came from the Wabash Valley to the east" (n.d.:23). He argues that whatever resemblances exist between Cahokia and the Kaskaskia Valley Mississippian cultures can be explained by trade or by the imitation of trade goods obtained from Cahokia by the Kaskaskia Valley people. When Conrad wrote this paper, the Mississippian complexes of the Wabash Valley were known only from surface collections obtained during site surveys (Winters 1967). He was, therefore, forced to support his argument with negative evidence—evidence against contact with Cahokia—rather than with positive evidence for contact between the Mississippian occupants of the Kaskaskia Valley and the Wabash Valley. Such arguments are open to question because they do not deal with the possibility of influences from other areas or with the possibility of indigenous development. However, Conrad does provide the framework of a model against which the Cahokia-centric model of Mississippian development in the Kaskaskia Valley may be tested.

Recent Research in the Upper Kaskaskia Valley

During the last few years research by the University of Illinois and other institutions has yielded much new data that can be used to test the hypotheses concerning Mississippian development in the Kaskaskia Valley outlined above. Recent work in the American Bottom in connection with the FAI-270 Project has resulted in a much better idea of what Mississippian farmsteads and hamlets in that region were like (Milner et al. 1984; Milner and Williams 1983, 1984). Excavated data and radiocarbon dates have become available for Wabash Valley Mississippian sites (Pace and Apfelstadt 1974). Additional site surveys and excavations have also yielded new data on the Mississippian occupation of the Lake Shelbyville area. The new data has tended to conflict with the Cahokia-centered model of Mississippian development.

Approximately twenty percent of the Lake Shelbyville shore line was resurveyed by the author in 1978 (Moffat 1979a). Nine new Mississippian sites were located and evidence for Mississippian occupation was obtained at two previously reported sites that had been attributed to other periods. Limited test excavation was carried out at four of the newly discovered sites (11-Mt-89, 11-Mt-104, 11-Sy-62, and 11-Sy-64), but two sites, the Doctor's Island site (11-Mt-53) and the Stop Sign site (11-Mt-56), were the focus of more intensive investigation. Both of these sites are located near the confluence of the Kaskaskia River and the West Okaw River and are less than one kilometer from the Jasper Newman site (fig. 13.2). The Stop Sign site is located on a high terrace directly east of the Jasper Newman site on the opposite side of the West Okaw River. The Doctor's Island site is located on the next terrace south of Jasper Newman on an area of well-drained, level ground flanking a high knoll. This locality is now an island in Lake Shelbyville.

The Doctor's Island site covers an area of about 1.1 hectares. When the site was initially discovered in 1978, considerable erosion was noted along the northern and eastern margins of the site (Moffat 1979a). A number of Mississippian features were exposed in the eroding areas. Excavations were begun in 1978 to salvage some features that were being destroyed (Moffat 1979a). Additional excavation was carried out in 1979 (Moffat 1979b) and 1981 (Moffat 1982). A total of forty features was defined during the three seasons of work at the Doctor's Island site and thirty-seven of these features were excavated. The features included two post and basin structures, two wall-trench structures, twenty-one storage pits, nine earth ovens, four isolated post molds, and two pits whose functions could not be determined.

Using pottery sherd fits and matches, twenty-three of the features excavated at the Doctor's Island site were grouped into two components, designated as the Early Component and the Late Component. The remaining features could not be assigned to a component because of their meager ceramic content. The Early Component consisted of four features, including Feature 11, a storage pit that yielded a charcoal sample radiocarbon dated to A.D. 1090 ± 75 years B.P. (uncorrected) (ISGS-773). Nineteen features were included in the Late Component. Two uncorrected radiocarbon dates of A.D. 1235 ± 75 from Feature 3 (ISGS-592) and A.D. 1180 ± 70 from Feature 25a (Beta-4029) provide an indication of the age of this component.

The Stop Sign site extends over an area of 2.1 hectares and has Archaic, Middle Woodland, and Mississippian

components. The Mississippian component covers about 0.7 hectares at the northern end of the site. Three excavation units covering a total of ninety-nine square meters were excavated in order to investigate the Mississippian occupation area (Moffat 1982). A total of twenty-eight distinguishable features were defined and excavated, including three superimposed wall-trench structures in deep basins, one circular post structure in a shallow basin, one storage pit, eighteen earth ovens, two stone piles, and three large isolated post molds.

Three radiocarbon determinations were obtained from three different features at the Stop Sign site (table 13.1). Two features yielded radiocarbon dates in the eleventh century A.D. An uncorrected assay of A.D. 1070 ± 75 (ISGS-766) was obtained on a charcoal sample collected from Feature 3, an earth oven superimposed on a storage pit. Feature 6a, one of the wall trenches belonging to the second of the three superimposed wall-trench structures, was dated to A.D. 1000 ± 60, uncorrected (Beta-4031). A later uncorrected date, A.D. 1270 ± 50 (Beta-4032) was obtained on a charcoal sample recovered from the post structure, Feature 7. Because of this divergence in radiocarbon dates, during the ceramic analysis Feature 3 and Feature 6 were treated as one component and Feature 7 was treated as a second, separate component.

Recent site surveys recorded thirty-seven previously unreported Late Woodland sites and identified Late Woodland occupations at three previously reported sites at which they had not been recognized earlier (Moffat 1979a; Phillippe and Hodges 1981; McGowan 1984). Stylistic variation in the artifact collections recovered from these sites suggests considerable temporal depth. Recent investigations at the Old Goat Farm site (11-Sy-4) have uncovered an early Late Woodland habitation area containing numerous pits and post molds (McGowan 1985; Lopinot et al. 1986). Four uncorrected radiocarbon assays reported for the Old Goat Farm site are: A.D. 310 ± 70 (Beta-15881), A.D. 370 ± 90 (Beta-15880), A.D. 490 ± 90 (Beta-15883), and A.D. 670 ± 90 (Beta-15882) (Lopinot et al. 1986:100). Consequently, there is now no reason to think that the upper Kaskaskia Valley was abandoned for any great length of time during the Late Woodland period as was once suggested (Gardner 1973b: 222).

The radiocarbon dates for the Stop Sign site and the Doctor's Island site are also not readily reconcilable with Gardner's model of Mississippian development. Both sites were clearly settled villages, but yielded substantially earlier radiocarbon dates than the Jasper Newman site. It is not mathematically possible to reconcile the dates for these sites with the Jasper Newman site dates by adopting the averaging procedures Gardner (1969b) applied to the Sweat Bee site dates. The new dates indicate that all of the Mississippian sites in the upper Kaskaskia Valley cannot be compressed into the narrow time frame that Gardner envisioned for the Mississippian occupation of the region.

Further problems are encountered when the ceramics from the Stop Sign site and the Doctor's Island site are considered. The potsherd collections from the two sites, when contrasted, duplicate the sorts of differences noted by Gardner (1969b) when he compared the collections from the Jasper Newman site and the Sweat Bee site. Like Sweat Bee, the Stop Sign site yielded very few filmed, incised, or engraved vessels, while nearly twenty percent of the ceramic vessels recovered from the Doctor's Island site display these attributes. Filmed, incised, or engraved vessels are nearly as common at Doctor's Island as at the Jasper Newman site. However, both the Stop Sign site and the Doctor's Island site lack mounds. The sherds recovered during the excavations at these sites were derived from feature fills; no special ceremonial structures were noted during the excavations. These observations raise questions about Gardner's explanation of the ceramic differences between the Jasper Newman and Sweat Bee sites. It appears possible that the differences in the ceramic collections from those two sites might reflect temporal variation after all.

The results of recent work in the American Bottom do not lend support to the hypothesis that Mississippian farming hamlets typically lack filmed, incised, or engraved ceramics. Several recently investigated hamlets in the American Bottom, the Stirling phase occupation at the Range site (Mehrer 1982), the Mississippian occupation at the Julien site (Milner and Williams 1984), and the Mississippian components at the Turner and DeMange sites (Milner and Williams 1983) actually have higher frequencies of these sorts of ceramics than were observed at the Jasper Newman site. Clearly, Mississippian site differentiation in the American Bottom is not reflected in the gross differences between the frequencies of decorated and undecorated ceramics that Gardner (1969b) was examining. Apparently, the archaeological correlates of Mississippian social status differences are more subtle and, perhaps, are indicated more clearly by other kinds of data. While Gardner's (1969b) efforts at investigating Mississippian social status in the Kaskaskia Valley have now been shown to be unsuccessful, his research raises problems that have not been resolved and that will require further investigations.

Ceramic Chronology

In view of the differing interpretations concerning the origin of the Kaskaskia Valley Mississippian social groups, a new regional chronology has been developed that is based on radiocarbon dates and stratigraphic data recovered from Mississippian sites in the Lake Shelbyville area. Ceramic cross-dates with the Cahokia sequence or other previously established Mississippian sequences of the Midwest were not used to establish the local chronology. This chronology construction procedure should provide the basis for an unbiased test of the importance of the various influences postulated by Gardner (1969b, 1973a) and by Conrad (1966, n.d.).

The ceramics from three components were analyzed in an effort to discover attribute differences that could be used to indicate trends in ceramic change over time. The ceramic data were drawn from Feature 3 and Feature 6 at the Stop Sign site, the Late Component features at the Doctor's Island site, and Component A at the Jasper Newman site. These three components were the most reliably dated and have yielded the largest samples of ceramics available for the region. Collections from other sites that are not as well dated or not as large were compared with the three major components. An attribute analysis of the Mississippian ceramics from Lake Shelbyville has been described in detail elsewhere (Moffat 1985). Here I will merely summarize the most salient features of the data.

The ceramic collections from all components in the Lake Shelbyville area share certain characteristics that serve to differentiate them from other midwestern Mississippian complexes. Vessel forms consist primarily of jars, bowls, plates, and miniature vessels. Jars make up the major part of all ceramic collections, comprising at least seventy percent of the vessels recovered from every component. Bottles and beakers are very rare. Only four bottles have been recovered from Lake Shelbyville area Mississippian sites: two are from Jasper Newman and the other two were found at the Doctor's Island site. Only two beakers have been found, both in Late Component features at the Doctor's Island site. Several other common Mississippian ceramic forms, notably salt pans and juice presses, are absent in the Lake Shelbyville ceramic collections. Jars are about equally divided between plain-surfaced and cordmarked forms in all collections, regardless of age. The cordmarked jars (fig. 13.3) were equated with the ceramic type Cahokia Cordmarked by previous investigators (Gardner n.d.; Salzer 1963; Morrell 1965), but these Kaskaskia Valley vessels often deviate from Cahokia Cordmarked as Griffin (1949) defines the type.

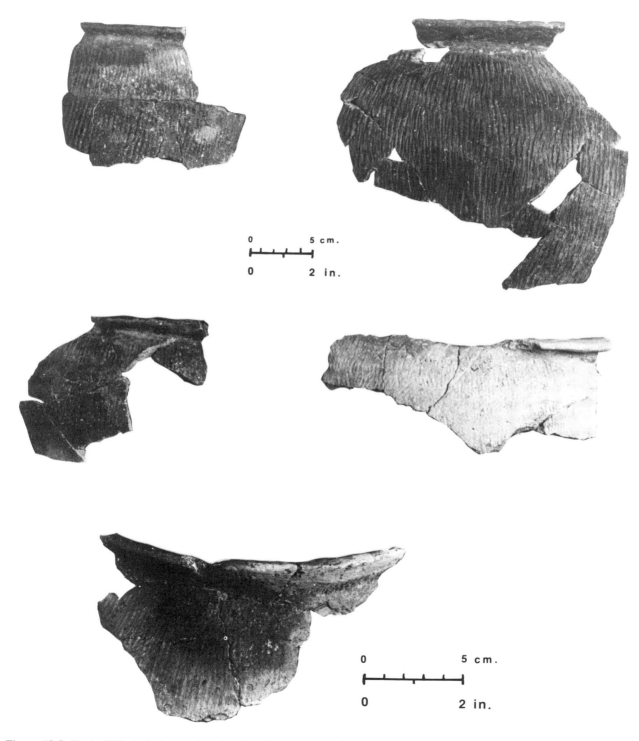

Figure 13.3. Typical Mississippian Cordmarked Jars from the Doctor's Island Site, Late Component

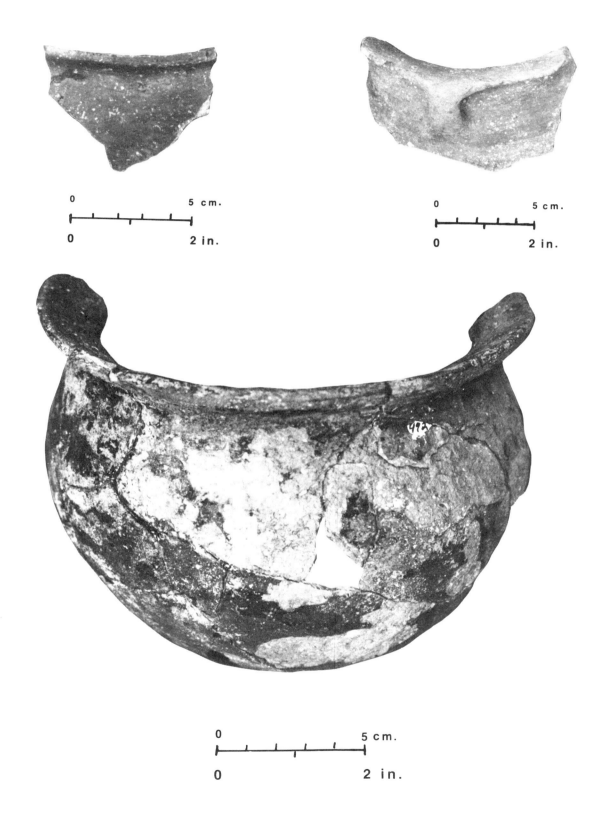

Figure 13.4. Black-filmed and Red-filmed Jars from the Doctor's Island Site, Late Component and from 11-Mt-89

Filmed jars are rare, but a few black-filmed specimens do occur in several collections (fig. 13.4). These vessels were usually classified as Powell Plain by previous investigators, but the upper Kaskaskia Valley specimens almost always lack sharply angled shoulders and rolled rims, two key attributes of this ceramic type as defined by Griffin (1949). Finally, in the upper Kaskaskia Valley prehistoric potters commonly mixed different kinds of tempers. Grog and shell combinations are common and many vessels are tempered with mixtures of shell and sand or sometimes shell, sand, and grog. This tendency to use mixtures of shell and other materials creates problems in using ceramic classification schemes that emphasize one type of temper as a key attribute.

Some differences between the ceramics from the Stop Sign site, the Late Component at the Doctor's Island site, and Component A at the Jasper Newman site appear to reflect temporal trends. First, the use of sand and grit as tempering agents declined over time in favor of the shell/grog mixture or pure shell temper. This is a statistical trend and is noticeable in all vessel forms. Second, there were changes in the rim form of jars over time (fig. 13.5). The jars from the early radiocarbon-dated features at the Stop Sign site tend to display a broad angle of eversion between the rim section and the upper shoulder of the vessel. Jars from the Doctor's Island site and other later components tend to have substantially sharper angles of rim eversion. This trend occurs on both plain-surfaced and cordmarked jars. Jar rim height as defined by Vogel (1975), (i.e., the distance between the lip and the point of eversion at the base of the rim), is not a useful temporal marker in the upper Kaskaskia Valley. High rim jars are common in the ceramic collections from early as well as from late components.

Perhaps the most easily recognized attribute shifts in the upper Kaskaskia Valley concern the use of interior and exterior hematite-base films. Griffin (1949), in his type description for Cahokia Cordmarked jars, observes that more than half of the specimens from Cahokia that he used to define this type had red-filmed interiors. High frequencies of interior red-filming on Cahokia Cordmarked jars from Mississippian sites in the American Bottom have been more recently reported by Vogel (1975) and by Milner and Williams (1984). Interior red-filming of cordmarked jars is much less common in the Lake Shelbyville area. None of the cordmarked jars recovered from the Stop Sign site displayed interior red-filming. The earliest radiocarbon-dated occurrence of this attribute in the upper Kaskaskia Valley is at the Doctor's Island site. Both the Early Component and the Late Component ceramic collections from this site include cordmarked jars with red-filmed interiors. Examples of cordmarked jars with red-filmed interiors are also present at the Jasper

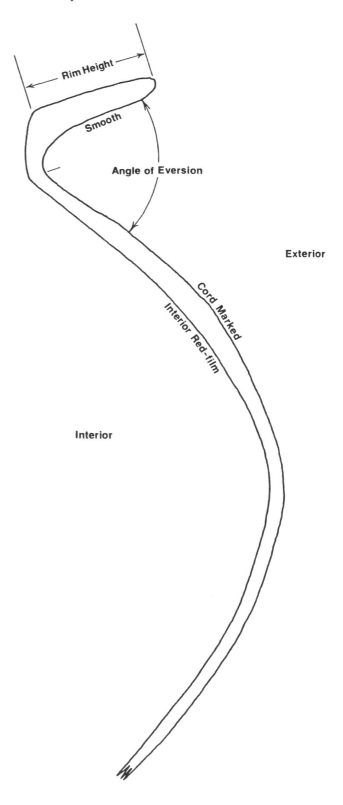

Figure 13.5. Some Temporally Diagnostic Ceramic Attributes Observed on Mississippian Jars

Newman site (Gardner 1969b). However, at none of these sites do more than ten percent of the cordmarked jars have red-filmed interiors and frequencies of two percent to five percent are more usual.

The frequency of exterior red and black films on bowls and plates also increases substantially at later Mississippian sites in the upper Kaskaskia Valley. All of the plates and most of the bowls recovered at the Stop Sign site are plain surfaced. However, at both the Doctor's Island site and the Jasper Newman site more than twenty percent of the bowls are red or black filmed. Some of the

exterior-filmed bowls at the latter site are also decorated by engraving or incising. All of the plates recovered from the Late Component features at the Doctor's Island site are red or black filmed. The majority of the plates from Jasper Newman are either red filmed or black filmed and polished. A number of the plates from Jasper Newman and Doctor's Island are also incised or engraved. These specimens are similar to Wells Incised at Cahokia (Vogel 1975) or to variants of O'Byam Incised in the Cairo Lowlands area of southeastern Missouri (Phillips 1970: 144).

Mississippian Phases in the Upper Kaskaskia Valley

The shifts in ceramic attributes noted above have been used to group the Mississippian components in the Shelbyville Reservoir into three phases described below (table 13.2).

SHELBYVILLE I

The earliest Mississippian phase in upper Kaskaskia Valley dates to approximately A.D. 1000 to 1150. It is largely coeval with the Stirling phase at Cahokia (Fowler and Hall 1975). Wall-trench structures in deep basins are definitely present, but none of the platform mounds reported in the Lake Shelbyville area can be shown to date to this phase. All of the early Mississippian sites identified in the region to date appear to be small hamlets. Evidence for maize agriculture is present at these sites.

Vessel forms during this phase consist primarily of jars

Table 13.2. Mississippian Phases and the Relative Chronology of Radiocarbon-Dated Sites in the Upper Kaskaskia Valley

Calendar Age	Phase	Component
A.D. 1500		
	Shelbyville III	Sweat Bee site (Late Occ.)
A.D. 1400		
		Jasper Newman site (Comp. A)
A.D. 1300		11-Mt-89
	Shelbyville II	Jasper Newman site (Comp. B)
A.D. 1200		Doctor's Island site (L.C.)
		Doctor's Island site (E.C.)
A.D. 1100		Sweat Bee site (Early Occ.)
	Shelbyville I	
		Stop Sign site
A.D. 1000		
A.D. 900	Late Woodland	

with broadly everted rims, simple bowls, undecorated plates, and miniature vessels. Virtually all vessels are either plain surfaced or cordmarked. Vessel temper combinations that include sand are much more common than pure shell or shell and grog tempers. Filmed or incised vessels are very rare and the few examples recovered are probably trade vessels. A significant number of jars display combinations of Woodland and Mississippian traits. The specific combinations seem to be quite variable, but include the following: jars with typical Mississippian everted rim forms that are tempered with coarsely crushed grit; jars with typical Woodland conoidal shapes that are shell and grog tempered; and shell and grog tempered, angled rim jars with stick- or cord-impressed lips.

The Shelbyville I phase is best represented, at present, by the Stop Sign site. In addition, many of the features excavated at the Sweat Bee site seem to date to this phase. The feature (Feature 7) that yielded the earlier of the two Sweat Bee site dates (A.D. 1135 ± 105) probably belongs to the Shelbyville I phase occupation (Moffat 1985: 422–28). However, the sample from which this date was obtained contained corn and cannot be corrected for isotopic fractionation because the C13/C12 ratio was not determined. Correction, if possible, would make the date earlier (Hall 1967d). One other site, 11-Mt-90, which was surveyed in 1978 but not excavated (Moffat 1979a), yielded a characteristic Shelbyville I ceramic assemblage.

SHELBYVILLE II

This upper Kaskaskia Valley phase corresponds most closely to fully developed Mississippian culture as Gardner (1969b, 1973a) conceived of it. Tentative dates for the Shelbyville II phase are A.D. 1150 to 1400. This phase was coeval with the Moorehead phase and part of the Sand Prairie phase at Cahokia (Fowler and Hall 1975). Platform mounds were definitely present at some sites.

The Late Component at the Doctor's Island site represents the early part of this phase. The Early Component at Doctor's Island seems to be transitional between Shelbyville I and Shelbyville II. Despite its late radiocarbon date, 11-Sy-62, an upland campsite, also seems to be very early Shelbyville II. This date has an unusually large standard deviation and may have been contaminated by carbon from a historic Euroamerican occupation at the site. Component B at the Jasper Newman site is also probably early Shelbyville II, whereas Component A at the Jasper Newman site dates to the latter part of this phase. Also included in this phase are 11-Mt-89, a valley-bottom village site tested in 1978 (Moffat 1979a) and again in 1984 (McGowan 1985), as well as two recently investigated sites, the Fultz site (11-Mt-14) and a mound group/village complex, 11-Mt-5/11-Mt-15 (McGowan 1985).

By the beginning of Shelbyville II, the use of pure shell and shell and grog mixtures for tempering increases substantially and, together, they outnumber temper mixtures that include sand. The frequency of shell and shell/grog tempering continues to increase throughout the Shelbyville II period. The practice of red-filming the interiors of cordmarked jars was introduced at the beginning of this phase. Red- and black-filmed exteriors become more common, especially on bowls and plates.

Fine-line incising and engraving also appears on bowls and plates during the Shelbyville II phase and these decorative techniques frequently occur with filmed surfaces. The engraved or incised motifs consist of triangular patterns resembling those found on Wells Incised plates

at Cahokia (Vogel 1975) or O'Byam Incised vessels in southeast Missouri (Phillips 1970). In late Shelbyville II components, such as Component A at the Jasper Newman site, the majority of bowls and plates were filmed, polished, or decorated by engraving or incising. Rare examples of bottles and beakers appear at some Shelbyville II phase sites. Appendages such as loop handles, lip lugs, and effigy heads, are occasionally added to vessels during this phase.

SHELBYVILLE III

The final Mississippian phase in the upper Kaskaskia Valley is the most poorly documented. Tentative dates for this phase are A.D. 1400 to 1550. Apparently, cordmarked and plainware jars continue to be the most common ceramic vessel types during this phase. Occasional examples of broad-trailed Oneota-like vessels also occur. It seems that exterior-filmed, engraved, and incised vessels decline in frequency during Shelbyville III times.

Two components possibly date to this phase. One is at the Sweat Bee site and may include the structure that yielded the late radiocarbon date. The other component is at 11-Mt-63, an extensive site found during the 1978 survey (Moffat 1979a). Recent limited test excavations at this site identified a Shelbyville II occupation, but did not recover any additional late Mississippian ceramics (Lopinot et al. 1986).

External Relationships Reconsidered

The chronological scheme presented above provides a new framework for examining the external cultural relationships of the upper Kaskaskia Valley Mississippian people. It permits consideration of artifactual similarities in a temporal/spatial framework; one may use it to investigate the dates at which analogous forms occur in different complexes in each region. It is also possible to consider how external influences may have affected the trajectory of Mississippian cultural development in the Kaskaskia Valley.

Because previous investigators have emphasized relationships between Kaskaskia Valley Mississippian groups and Cahokia, this problem will be considered first. The earliest Mississippian phase in the upper Kaskaskia Valley, Shelbyville I, dates to the same time interval as the Stirling phase at Cahokia. However, there is little correspondence in ceramic content between these two phases. A number of characteristic Stirling phase ceramic types, particularly Ramey Incised jars and the various red- or black-filmed jar forms, are poorly represented or entirely

absent in the upper Kaskaskia Valley. Conversely, cordmarked and plain-surfaced jars with high rims and broad rim to body angles seem to be rare at Cahokia and its environs in Stirling phase contexts. Shell-tempered, cordmarked jars were reportedly recovered in Fairmont phase contexts at the Horseshoe Lake site (Gregg 1975b:197). The rim forms of jars are similar to the Shelbyville I cordmarked jars, but they diverge from the latter vessels in tempering. They seem to be a quantitatively minor element in the Fairmont phase assemblage.

In Shelbyville II a larger number of ceramic forms with close analogues at Cahokia appear. Included among these ceramics are the beakers, which resemble the Tippets Bean Pot type, and the incised and engraved plates, which are similar to Wells Incised plates. All of these forms are characteristic of the Moorehead and Sand Prairie phases at Cahokia. Cordmarked jars, classified as Cahokia Cordmarked, become common at Cahokia during these phases. Interaction with Cahokia, then, seems to increase around A.D. 1200, well after the initial development of Mississippian culture in the upper Kaskaskia Valley.

These comparisons do not support the migration models proposed by Gardner 1969b, 1973a, n.d.) and Salzer (1963). There is little close similarity to Cahokia ceramics in the asssemblages found at the earliest Mississippian components in the Kaskaskia Valley. Many more similarities would be expected at this time if mass migrations from Cahokia into the Kaskaskia Valley had actually taken place. Instead, the data seem to indicate a gradual increase in the frequency of similarities over time. Recognizable Cahokia influences on ceramics appear only after the evolution of Mississippian culture in the upper Kaskaskia Valley was well under way. Therefore, the original impetus for this development does not seem to have come from Cahokia.

Winters (1967:71–83) described the Vincennes culture, a Mississippian entity occupying the lower Wabash Valley and the lower part of the Embarras River drainage to the east of the upper Kaskaskia Valley. The Otter Pond site, a ceremonial center located near the confluence of the Embarras and Wabash rivers, covering 24–40 hectares and containing twelve large platform mounds is the largest known Vincennes culture site. Several smaller villages, containing one or no platform mounds, are located nearby.

The material culture of the Vincennes area sites is known only from surface collections. According to Winters (1967:82–83), the pottery consists primarily of plainware jars, cordmarked jars, undecorated plates, and simple bowls. Many other typical Mississippian ceramic forms, such as bottles and salt pans, are completely absent. Plain pottery is more common than cordmarked pottery, but the relative proportions of the two vary considerably from site to site. Plain pottery attains its highest relative frequency at the Otter Pond site, but the proportions of plainware and cordmarked pottery are more nearly equal at the outlying villages. Decorated sherds are very rare: Winters's (1967:72) survey recovered only five red-filmed sherds, one incised sherd, one engraved sherd, and two effigy heads. No handles, lugs, or negative painted sherds were found. Winters suggests that the Vincennes culture plainware is derived from Kincaid Plain, the cordmarked pottery is derived from Cahokia Cordmarked, and that the whole complex could be regarded as a "hybridization of ceramic traditions typical of the Cahokia area and the Kincaid area" (1967:83). He also thinks that the Vincennes culture is "a very late Mississippian manifestation."

Recently, excavations at several peripheral Vincennes culture hamlets have yielded additional data that appear to show that the Vincennes culture has much greater time depth than was originally supposed (Barth 1983,

chap. 14). A number of pit features containing Vincennes culture ceramics were excavated at the Farrand site, located in the Wabash Valley near Terre Haute, Indiana (Pace and Apfelstadt 1974; personal communications, 1980). Three uncorrected radiocarbon dates—A.D. 1085 ± 75 (U.Ga. 659), A.D. 1105 ± 100 (U.Ga. 657), and A.D. 1140 ± 75 (U.Ga. 656)—were obtained for three different features associated with the Vincennes component at this site. These dates indicate that this occupation falls within the time range of the Shelbyville I phase in the upper Kaskaskia Valley.

The Farrand site ceramic collection contains the same kinds of vessels that are present in the collections from Shelbyville I phase Mississippian sites in the upper Kaskaskia Valley. Plainware jars, cordmarked jars, plain-surfaced bowls, and plain-surfaced plates constitute the bulk of both assemblages. Other similar characteristics include the presence of mixed shell and sand tempering, large rim heights of both plainware and cordmarked jars, and broad rim to body angles. Shelbyville I ceramics seem to be more similar to early Vincennes culture ceramics than to the ceramics of the coeval Cahokia phase or to any other Mississippian complex yet defined. Thus there appears to be good reason to postulate a close relationship between the two areas in early Mississippian times. Whether these similarities indicate actual population movements from the Wabash Valley into the upper Kaskaskia Valley, as Conrad (n.d.) hypothesized, is unclear at present, but such migrations remain a possibility. An alternative explanation might involve in situ development of Mississippian culture in both the central Wabash Valley and the upper Kaskaskia Valley with considerable interaction between the two regions.

Thus far, comparisons between the upper Kaskaskia Valley Mississippian complex, Cahokia, and the Vincennes culture have emphasized ceramics, but the distribution of certain lithic artifact types is also significant for tracing cultural relationships. Cahokia points, side or basally notched triangular forms, are very rare in the upper Kaskaskia Valley. One hundred twenty-two Mississippian projectile points were recovered during the investigations at the Stop Sign site and the Doctor's Island site. Only two of these points are notched; the remainder are unnotched Madison points.

Several other typical Cahokia chipped-stone artifacts —Ramey knives, chipped stone hoes, and microdrills— are also rare or absent in the Shelbyville Reservoir area. Conversely, some chipped-stone artifact forms are common in Mississippian contexts in the Shelbyville Reservoir area but are rare at Cahokia. These artifact types include end scrapers, triangular knives, and hump-backed knives. The latter artifact type occurs in Upper Mississippi contexts in northern Illinois (Munson and Munson

1972) and has also been found at some Vincennes culture sites (Barth 1975). Vincennes culture projectile points are typically Madison points rather than Cahokia points. The distribution of chipped-stone artifacts, then, provides further support for a close relationship between the upper Kaskaskia Valley Mississippian complex and the Vincennes culture of the Wabash Valley.

The application of the chronology outlined above for the upper Kaskaskia Valley to Mississippian sites in the central and lower Kaskaskia Valley is somewhat problematic. Several Mississippian sites in the Carlyle Reservoir seem to be related to the upper Kaskaskia complex. For example, the Texas site, which was interpreted as a single-occupation hamlet or farmstead, yielded a total of 1,912 shell-tempered sherds (Morrell 1965). Of these, 66% were plain surfaced, 33.4% were cordmarked, and only 0.6% were red filmed, black filmed, or polished. Two radiocarbon dates on corn cobs were obtained for the site (Morrell 1965). These dates (uncorrected) are A.D. 1030 ± 85 (GX-0364) and A.D. 1090 ± 100 (GX-0365), indicating that the occupation at this site was coeval or slightly earlier than the Shelbyville I phase in the upper valley and the Stirling phase at Cahokia.

Mississippian occupations also are reported at the Kerwin site and the Orrell site that consist primarily of plain-surfaced and cordmarked vessels, with very low frequencies of filmed or decorated sherds (Salzer 1963). These components were equated with the Cahokia "Trappist Focus," although at both sites they were stratigraphically below components equated with the Cahokia "Old Village Focus" (Salzer 1963:33). The latter were characterized by low frequencies of cordmarked jars and much higher frequencies of black-filmed and red-filmed vessels than the stratigraphically earlier occupations. Both of the so-called Trappist Focus components appear to be similar to the Shelbyville I components in the upper Kaskaskia Valley.

The situation in the Carlyle Reservoir and the lower Kaskaskia Valley is complicated by the presence of a second Mississippian complex that is clearly distinct from the entity present in the upper Kaskaskia Valley and much more closely related to Cahokia. However, the ceramics associated with this group of sites have certain features that appear to differentiate them from Cahokia and the American Bottom proper. Elsewhere I have proposed the name "Silver Creek complex" for this second Mississippian entity in the lower Kaskaskia Valley (Moffat 1985).

The best reported Silver Creek complex site is Marty Coolidge (Kuttruff 1969, 1972). This site contains a series of at least three occupations ranging in age from the tenth century A.D. to the fifteenth century A.D. Several other Mississippian sites in the Silver Creek drainage, including the Emerald site (Benchley 1974) and the Knoebel site (Bareis 1976), apparently are closely related to Marty Coolidge. Some components in the Carlyle Reservoir, such as the so-called Old Village Focus occupations at the Kerwin and Orrell sites, also belong to this complex. The recently reported Bridges site (Hargrave et al. 1983) in the Crooked Creek drainage south of the Carlyle Reservoir appears to be yet another example of a Silver Creek complex site.

The ceramic assemblages from the Marty Coolidge site and the Silver Creek complex occupations at the Kerwin and Orrell sites include very high frequencies of plain-surfaced vessels, low frequencies of cordmarked jars, and much higher frequencies of filmed, especially red-filmed, vessels, as well as polished vessels. In some of these collections, filmed sherds outnumber cordmarked sherds by a substantial margin. Angled shoulders and rolled rims often occur on jars. Occasional examples of incised jars identified as Ramey Incised occur at these sites. At present, the details of internal chronological variation within this complex are unclear.

Conclusions

The new upper Kaskaskia Valley data indicate that a much more complex situation existed there in late prehistoric times than had previously been supposed. The Kaskaskia Valley was occupied by two distinct Mississippian complexes, both of which had long histories of development in their respective regions. The Silver Creek complex in the lower valley appears to have been a typical Middle Mississippi chiefdom and it seems to have enjoyed a fairly close relationship with Cahokia. The upper Kaskaskia Valley Mississippian complex appears to have had a different, more egalitarian form of social organization, at least in its early phase of development. In its ceramic

and lithic assemblages it combined Woodland, Upper Mississippi, and more typical Middle Mississippi traits. Although the late prehistoric occupation of the upper Kaskaskia Valley was originally assigned to the Middle Mississippi tradition, there now seems to be grounds for questioning that designation.

Previous investigators emphasized migrations from Cahokia as an explanation for late prehistoric developments in the Kaskaskia Valley. It now appears that there was considerable continuity with previous Woodland occupations, at least in the upper valley. Important influences from the Wabash Valley to the east and the upper

Mississippi complexes of the prairies of northern Illinois are also apparent. The development of Mississippian culture in the upper Kaskaskia Valley seems to have occurred slowly as the result of diffusion from more than one external Mississippian center. However, the exact mechanisms by which these changes occurred are not clear. Recognizable Cahokia influence occurs well after the development of Mississippian culture was under way in the upper Kaskaskia Valley.

Various models of Mississippian cultural development have been proposed that, on the one hand, postulate the development of Mississippian culture at a single center, such as Cahokia, from which its constituent elements diffused or were carried by means of migrations to other parts of eastern North America (Griffin 1960b, 1967). On the other hand, the development of the Mississippian tradition has been viewed as the product of interactions between several centers that evolved simultaneously and continually influenced and stimulated one another (Phillips, Ford, and Griffin 1951:451). The new data from the Kaskaskia Valley seem to be more consistent with the second model than the first. It is becoming clear that the lower Wabash Valley was the site of a regional Mississippian tradition that exerted strong influence over much of eastern Illinois and may have limited Cahokia's influence in this direction. The role of this Wabash Valley center in the late prehistory of the Midwest deserves to receive careful consideration. Thus much of the Kaskaskia Valley seems to have been a frontier region subject to influences from two different centers of Mississippian cultural development. Study of Mississippian sites in the Kaskaskia Valley promises to enhance our understanding of the processes governing late prehistoric sociocultural integration and culture change in the Midwest.

ACKNOWLEDGMENTS

The fieldwork on which this study is based was funded by the University of Illinois and the St. Louis District, U.S. Army Corps of Engineers. Funding for the radiocarbon dates was provided by the National Science Foundation Grant No. BSN81–19037 and by Illinois Geological Survey. Dr. Robert Pace, Indiana State University, kindly allowed me to examine the Farrand site field notes and artifact collections. James Balsitis and Mark Phillips assisted with preparing the figures. David Minor printed the photographs. Joan Listen assisted with word processing.

14

The Emergence of the Vincennes Culture in the Lower Wabash Drainage

ROBERT J. BARTH

In 1963, Howard D. Winters (1967) defined two Mississippian manifestations, the Vincennes culture and the Etchison complex, on the basis of an archaeological survey of the Illinois side of the Wabash Valley. Winters (1967:83) argued that the Vincennes culture was probably a very late Mississippian culture. Although the reasons for this late temporal placement were not explicitly outlined, it was apparently based on similarities between cordmarked Vincennes ceramics and Cahokia Cordmarked and between plain Vincennes ceramics and those from the Kincaid site. At the time of the original definition of the Vincennes culture, Cahokia Cordmarked ceramics were assigned to the Trappist Focus at the Cahokia site (Griffin 1949:46). The Trappist Focus was believed to date between A.D. 1300 and 1550 (Hall 1966:8). The Kincaid site was thought to be a late Mississippian site, dating between A.D. 1300 and 1650 (Cole et al. 1951; Munson 1966). The suggestion by Winters (1967:83) that the Vincennes culture seemingly represented a hybridization of the ceramic traditions characteristic of the Cahokia and Kincaid regions implied that the Vincennes culture did not appear until after the ceramic traditions in those areas had become established, further supporting a late temporal placement for the Vincennes culture. Based on the available information, the conclusions reached by Winters were reasonable. Indeed, later researchers (Barth 1975; Clouse 1973; Douglas 1970), employing similar ceramic comparisons, continued to assign late dates to sites with Vincennes components.

The other Mississippian manifestation, the Etchison complex, was defined on the basis of ceramics recovered from six sites in Clark County, Illinois (Winters 1967: 83). Although Etchison complex vessel forms were identical to those of the Vincennes culture, Etchison sherds were also characterized by features normally associated with Woodland ceramics in the Wabash Valley (Winters 1967:83). Winters suggested that this complex might represent a localized variant of the Vincennes culture and he assigned it a temporal placement coeval with the Vincennes culture (Winters 1967: table 1).

Although twenty years have passed since the original definition of the Vincennes culture and the Etchison complex, they continue to be among the least understood Mississippian manifestations in the Midwest. While the number of reported sites has increased, few of these locations have been tested or excavated. Sufficient data have been recovered, however, to suggest that the dating and origins of the Vincennes culture and the Etchison complex need reevaluation. The following discussion summarizes the Vincennes culture data and examines the possibility that an Emergent Mississippian period was present in the Wabash Valley during the same time that Mississippian societies were appearing in other areas of the Midwest.

The Vincennes Culture

Vincennes sites within the Wabash Valley extend from Clark County, Illinois, and Vigo County, Indiana, south to Wabash County, Illinois (fig. 14.1). Additional Vincennes sites have been identified along the Embarras River in Coles County, Illinois.

The Vincennes culture settlement pattern is typical of Mississippian societies, consisting of a central religious/political center with nearby hamlets, dispersed farmsteads or specialized activity camps, and a possible fortress cemetery (Winters 1967:71). The Otter Pond site,

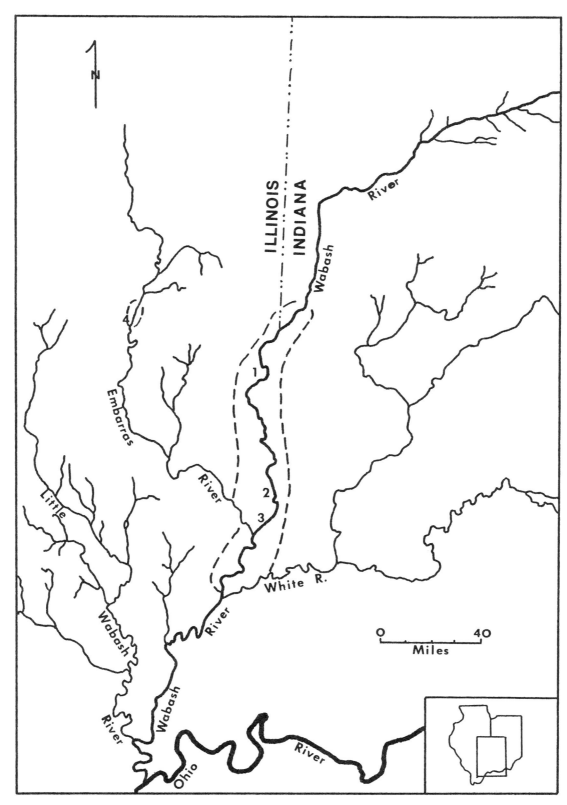

Figure 14.1. Emergent Mississippian Complexes and Sites: (1) Etchison complex; (2) Zaynor site; (3) Lw-7; (4) Johns site. Dashed line marks known distribution of Vincennes culture sites.

the central town, covers 24–40 hectares on the T-1 of the Embarras River and has twelve large platform mounds arranged in a rectangular pattern around a central plaza (Winters 1967:71–72). Hamlets are characterized by a central plaza and a single platform mound. The hamlets described by Winters covered approximately two hectares. The Gray Estate site, which is probably a typical hamlet, consisted of a central plaza with a low mound at the southern end surrounded by a dark midden about fifteen meters in width (Winters 1967:72). Winters estimated that there could not have been more than a single or double row of houses around the plaza. Hamlets were located on both the floodplain and T-1 of the Embarras and Wabash rivers. The Reed-Walker site (Co-18), near Charleston, Illinois, is probably typical of the farmstead/special activity sites. Excavations at this site (Barth 1973, 1975; Douglas 1970) revealed a single wall-trench structure with twenty-eight associated features, including deep storage pits, earth ovens, and refuse pits.

The major distinguishing characteristic of the Vincennes culture is the ceramic assemblage. Most sherds are shell tempered and are either plain or cordmarked. The range of vessel shapes is limited, consisting of plain jars, plates, and bowls and cordmarked jars (Winters 1967:82-83). Jar rims are usually highly everted. Decorations, lugs, and adornos are rare. As noted earlier, cordmarked Vincennes ceramics are very similar to Cahokia Cordmarked. Winters (1967:82) states that the plain Vincennes ware resembles plain ceramics from the Kincaid and Angel sites along the Ohio River. In spite of these similarities, however, the relative simplicity of the Vincennes ceramic assemblage stands in contrast to these sites. The remainder of the Vincennes material culture is similar to that of other Mississippian societies.

Subsistence evidence is available from two sites, Farrand in Vigo County, Indiana, and the Reed-Walker site. Identified floral remains from the Farrand site include maize, beans, pawpaw, hazelnut, groundnut, and wild

Table 14.1. Radiocarbon Dates from Vincennes Components

Site	Laboratory No.	Radiocarbon Age (B.P.)	Uncorrected Date (A.D.)
Farrand			
(12-Vi-122)	UGa-659	865 ± 85	1085
	UGa-657	845 ± 100	1105
	UGa-656	810 ± 70	1140
Reed-Walker			
(11-Co-18)	ISGS-404	520 ± 70	1430

cherry (Apfelstadt 1975:4-5). Vincennes culture pit features at the Reed-Walker site contained charred nutshell, whitetail deer, box turtle, bird, and mussel shells. Winters (1967:72) also reports heavy concentrations of animal bone and mussel shell at the Gray Estate site. The artifact assemblage also includes shell, scapula, and M. Creek chert hoes (Apfelstadt 1975:5; Winters 1967: table 5). This evidence indicates an economy based upon horticulture supplemented by hunting and gathering, an economy identical to that of other Mississippian societies. The fact that hamlets are located on both the floodplain and the T-1 suggests that Vincennes social groups may have followed a divided risk horticultural strategy similar to that suggested by Chmurny (1973) for the Cahokia region.

Four radiocarbon dates are available for Vincennes culture contexts (table 14.1). These dates indicate that, although the Vincennes culture did persist until relatively late in the Mississippian period, it was present in the Wabash Valley earlier than has been previously assumed. It should be further noted that these dates pertain to what may be called "developed" Vincennes culture, indicating that its origins lie even farther back in time. The next section outlines the evidence suggesting the presence of an Emergent Mississippian period, preceding the appearance of the Vincennes culture in the Wabash Valley.

The Emergent Mississippian Period

Ceramics constitute the most important evidence of the presence of an Emergent Mississippian period. Several researchers have reported ceramics that combine Woodland and Mississippian features from Wabash Valley sites. For example, Denzil Stephens (1963:129) reports both sand- and shell-tempered simple stamped sherds from the Zaynor site in Lawrence County, Illinois. Stephens apparently saw no significant differences in the simple stamping on the two pottery types because he interprets them as representing the effects of contacts between Late Woodland and Mississippian groups.

Etchison complex ceramics also combine Woodland and Mississippian features. The Etchison ceramics are predominantly plain, although a few cordmarked sherds also occur. Winters (1967:83) describes the plain black pottery as notable for its crudeness and indifferent smoothing. Woodland characteristics of Etchison ceramics include broad, shallow, notched lips and "piecrust" rims, which occur on forty percent of the examined rims (Winters 1967:83). Although Winters (1967: table 1) believes that the Etchison complex is coeval with the Vincennes culture, both Griffin (1978b:550) and I (1977,

1982) have argued that it may be an earlier variant of Vincennes.

Taken together, these ceramics provide a basis for inferring a Woodland-Mississippian transition in the Wabash Valley. I have suggested elsewhere (1977, 1982) that the Woodland group from which the Vincennes culture ultimately developed was the Allison-LaMotte culture. The Allison-LaMotte culture was originally defined as two separate cultures, Allison and LaMotte, by Winters (1967). At the time, he noted similarities between the two cultures. Pace (1974) presents strong arguments for the inclusion of Allison and LaMotte as earlier and later phases, respectively, of a single cultural entity, the Allison-LaMotte culture. At present it is not possible to draw hard distinctions between the phases.

Most Allison-LaMotte sites are concentrated in the Wabash Valley in a region that extends from Parke County, Indiana, south to Wabash County, Illinois, and Gibson County, Indiana (fig. 14.2). Secondary concentrations of sites extend along the Embarras River northward to Charleston, Illinois, and along the White River at least as far north as Greene County, Indiana (Tomak 1970). There are approximately 100 known Allison-LaMotte sites (Pace and Apfelstadt 1978).

Diagnostic elements of Allison-LaMotte material culture include the Stoner Ceramic Series, the Embarrass Ceramic Series,[1] and the Lowe Flared Base projectile point (Winters 1967:47–48, 52–60). The Allison-LaMotte culture displays many similarities with cultures further to the south. These similarities include: some attributes of the ceramic assemblage (e.g., simple stamping), the presence of winter and summer dwellings, and year-round occupation of sites.

Detailed Allison-LaMotte subsistence evidence is available from two sites, Daugherty-Monroe in Sullivan County, Indiana (Apfelstadt 1975; Pace 1974; Pace and Apfelstadt 1978), and the Lowe Mound in Crawford County, Illinois (Stephens 1974). The evidence from these two sites indicates a broad-based economy utilizing a wide range of nut-bearing trees, spring and summer fruit sources, commensal plant species, and squash horticulture (Apfelstadt 1975:3). Faunal remains indicate an orientation toward riverine resources while maintaining the use of varied animal populations.

Allison-LaMotte villages range in size from one to twenty-four hectares. Wabash Valley sites tend to be larger than those located along the tributaries. Excavations at the Daugherty-Monroe and Reed-Walker sites revealed the presence of two structure types. The first is semisubterranean. The second type is a lighter, single-set post structure. These types are interpreted as winter and summer dwellings, respectively. The presence of both kinds of structures and a wide range of plant remains

at the Daugherty-Monroe site indicates that at least some Allison-LaMotte villages were permanently occupied. This sedentism was permitted by a settlement strategy that put villages in localities that provide ready access to several biotic communities (Barth 1978). Based on a series of radiocarbon dates from the Daugherty-Monroe site, Pace and Apfelstadt (1978:70) suggest that individual Allison-LaMotte villages were occupied, abandoned, and later reoccupied in a cycle that extended over several centuries.

There are eighteen acceptable radiocarbon dates for Allison-LaMotte sites (table 14.2), the majority of which are from the Daugherty-Monroe site. These dates indicate that the Allison-LaMotte culture existed for at least 700 years, from A.D. 55 to 740. It should also be noted that the latest date, A.D. 740 (1210 ± 70 B.P.) from Reed-Walker, does not date the end of the Allison-LaMotte occupation of the site. Therefore, one might reasonably infer that the Allison-LaMotte culture extended even later in time.

Several lines of evidence support the argument that the Vincennes culture developed from the Allison-LaMotte culture. First, all of the Woodland features found on Emergent Mississippian ceramics in the Wabash Valley,

Table 14.2. Radiocarbon Dates From Allison-LaMotte Sites (Modified from Pace and Apfelstadt 1978)

Site	Laboratory No.	Radiocarbon Age (B.P.)	Uncorrected Date (A.D.)
Daugherty-Monroe (12-Su-13)	UGa-1057	1745 ± 80	205
	UGa-1058	1720 ± 95	230
	UGa-655	1715 ± 85	235
	UGa-1056	1595 ± 70	355
	UGa-534	1560 ± 70	390
	UGa-2088	1530 ± 75	420
	UGa-1054	1490 ± 180	460
	UGa-533	1490 ± 105	460
	RL-84	1460 ± 130	490
	UGa-654	1450 ± 95	500
	UGa-2087	1430 ± 100	520
	RL-146	1410 ± 120	540
	RL-145	1380 ± 140	570
Higgenbotham (12-Vi-122)	UGa-1900	1895 ± 110	55
	UGa-2159	1465 ± 125	485
Palestine (11-Cw-4)	Geochron	1830 ± 120	120
Dhom (11-Jp-135)	Geochron	1800 ± 150	150
Reed-Walker (11-Co-18)	ISGS-406	1210 ± 70	740

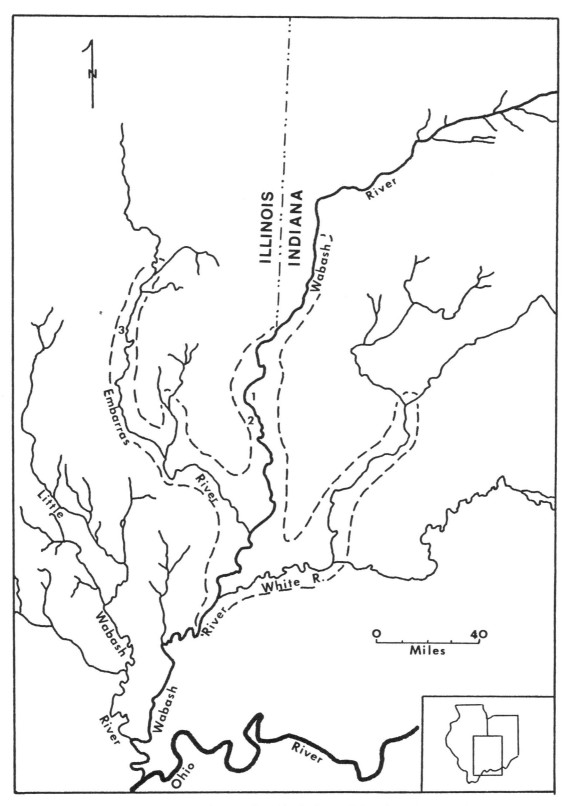

Figure 14.2. Major Allison-LaMotte Sites Mentioned in the Text: (1) Daugherty-Monroe; (2) Lowe Mound; (3) Reed-Walker. Dashed line marks known distribution of Allison-LaMotte culture sites.

which were described above, are also diagnostic features of the Embarrass Ceramic Series of the Allison-LaMotte culture. The Embarrass Ceramic Series is distinct from ceramics found in other regions of the Midwest during the same time period. Charles H. Faulkner (1978) notes similarities between the Embarrass Ceramic Series and ceramics associated with the late Middle Woodland Owl Hollow phase in the Duck River Valley of Tennessee. The Embarrass Series is characterized by three forms of surface treatment: simple stamping, cordmarking, and check stamping. Decoration is rare and sand/grit is the predominant tempering medium. Simple-stamped and check-stamped vessels include elongated jars and constricted orifice bowls. Cordmarked vessels are characterized by a wider range of shapes (Winters 1967:54). Rims on many of the vessels are notched on the lip interior and display a distinctive "pie crust" effect.

Second, there is no evidence of a widespread occupation of the Wabash Valley by any cultural group that would have been intermediate in time between Allison-LaMotte and Vincennes. Thus, if the Vincennes culture did not develop from the Allison-LaMotte culture, the only alternative explanation is the rather implausible possibility that the central Wabash Valley was unoccupied during the two centuries between the latest Allison-LaMotte site and the oldest Vincennes site.

Finally, additional evidence is provided by the results of test excavations at the Johns site (Co-17; fig. 14.1) near Charleston, Illinois (Douglas 1970). Johns is located on the innermost of three depositional point bars within a large meander loop of the Embarras River. Although surface scatter covers an area of approximately three acres, the heaviest concentration of material is confined to an area of 4,000 square meters near the northern end of the point bar. Artifacts representing several periods are present, but most of the surface-collected material can be associated with the Allison-LaMotte and Vincennes components. Testing of sixty-seven square meters of the site by Douglas (1970:16–22) revealed ten features, eight of which were fully exposed and excavated.

Of seven Johns site pit features, two contained no ceramics, three contained Embarrass Series ceramics and two contained both Embarrass Series and Vincennes sherds. No pit feature contained only Vincennes ceramics. The other excavated feature, Feature 7, was a rectangular wall-trench structure with interior dimensions of 2.4 by 3.3 meters. Additional wall trenches that were adjacent to or crossed Feature 7 may represent renovation of the existing structure or later construction. Of interest to the present discussion is the fact that an Embarrass Simple Stamped rimsherd was found on the floor of the structure. In addition, the western wall trench of the structure was cut by a later feature, Feature 8. This pit contained only Embarrass Series ceramics. The combined evidence suggests that this component represents an Allison-LaMotte group in the process of acculturation to a Mississippian way of life. Unfortunately, no radiocarbon dates were obtained for the site. Douglas (1970: 20) suggested a date of A.D. 900–1100 for the component represented by these features. It is suggested here that this occupation is probably closer to A.D. 900–1000.

The evidence outlined above, although limited, supports the hypothesis of an Emergent Mississippian period in the Wabash Valley. Although no radiocarbon dates are available for this period, it should fall between A.D. 800 and 1000. This interval spans the latest end of the radiocarbon date range from the Reed-Walker Allison-LaMotte occupation and the earliest end of the date range for the Vincennes component at the Farrand site. The interval also corresponds to the period when Mississippian societies were developing in other areas of the Midwest.

Elsewhere (Barth 1982) I have presented a model to explain the processes involved in the transformation of Allison-LaMotte into Vincennes. The model views demographic stress as an important element in this transformation. The number of sites increased during the LaMotte phase, and if Pace and Apfelstadt (1978) are correct in their hypothesis of cyclical occupation of Allison-LaMotte village sites, not all of these would have been occupied at the same time. Nonetheless, the overall increase in the number of sites is taken as an indication of an increase in population. Initially, this increase was handled by the fissioning off of small groups to found new settlements. This process is evidenced along the Wabash tributaries. The Allison-LaMotte expansion into the middle Embarras Valley near Charleston, Illinois, appears to have been relatively late, as indicated by the late radiocarbon date from the Reed-Walker site and the absence of any material that can be associated with Allison. Similarly, Tomak (1970) believes that the Allison-LaMotte occupation of the White River in Greene County, Indiana, dates from the LaMotte phase.

Establishment of new settlements may also have taken place within the Wabash Valley as well. This response, however, was only a temporary solution as only a finite amount of new territory was available. This can be seen along the Embarras River. Allison-LaMotte settlement does not extend north of the Cerro Gordo Moraine. North of the moraine, the river narrows to a small stream and the number of vegetation communities decreases. This region would not support the broad-based Allison-LaMotte economy and it effectively halted upstream expansion. Similar environmental or other cultural factors may have halted Allison-LaMotte expansion in other regions. There is also a possibility, presently undocumented, that Allison-LaMotte groups responded to increasing population by expanding their range of utilized resources.

Eventually, Allison-LaMotte groups, having filled the available territory and utilizing almost the entire range of possible resources, were forced to change their subsistence strategy by expanding the horticultural segment of their economy through the addition of maize. This subsistence change had an impact on other cultural patterns as well, including a change in settlement system and an increase in political complexity in a manner suggested by Richard I. Ford (1977). The result of these changes was the transformation of the Allison-LaMotte culture into the Vincennes culture. While not denying the importance of outside influences, the emergence of the Vincennes culture is viewed here as a largely in situ development rather than as the result of an influx of Mississippian people from some other part of the Midwest.

Summary and Conclusions

The data presented here strongly suggest the existence of an Emergent Mississippian period preceding the appearance of the Vincennes culture in the Wabash Valley. This period is marked by the development of the Vincennes culture from the earlier Allison-LaMotte culture, as indicated by ceramic evidence and excavation data from the Johns site. It is argued that Vincennes can no longer be considered either a very late Mississippian manifestation or the result of influences from Cahokia and the Ohio Valley centers. The processes responsible for its development must be sought, instead, in the general Mississippianization of Late Woodland groups over a broad area of the Midwest at approximately the same time period.

NOTE

1. The river is spelled "Embarras," but the ceramic series is spelled "Embarrass" as defined by Winters (1967).

15

Kincaid Revisited:
The Mississippian Sequence in the Lower
Ohio Valley

BRIAN M. BUTLER

The lower Ohio Valley has long been noted as one of the areas of classic Mississippian cultural development, yet refined chronological control is still lacking and there are some significant differences of opinion regarding portions of the local sequence. A critical element in the chronology problem has always been the Kincaid site, the regional-class mound center located on the Ohio near its confluence with the Tennessee and the Cumberland rivers. Although the largest Mississippian site complex in the area and the object of intensive archaeological activity in earlier decades, Kincaid still has not yielded detailed and reliable chronological information. [1]

The uncertain chronology of the site has, in turn, contributed to different views on the nature of the development of Mississippian societies in the area and Kincaid's role in those developments. The purpose of this chapter is to review the Mississippian chronological framework for the region in view of previously existing and newly acquired data from Kincaid and other sites. Although the lower Ohio Valley can be construed as a significantly larger area (see Muller 1986a:ix), for present purposes the area is defined as that portion of the river valley from the confluence with the Mississippi River at Cairo to the confluence with the Wabash, including the lower portions of the Tennessee and Cumberland drainages.

Background

Although a substantial amount of work has been done on Mississippian sites in the lower Ohio region, the investigations have been largely confined to specific locales. The excavations on the Tennessee and Cumberland have been better distributed, but they are virtually all above the Kentucky and Barkely dams. Along the Ohio, from Cairo to the mouth of the Wabash, the only large and usable sets of excavation data, until the last few years, have come from Kincaid and the Black Bottom area. Much of the older archaeological work has never been adequately described or published; and the investigations at several of the key sites were done before the advent of carbon dating. Because of the age and diversity of the investigations, no standardized ceramic typology has been developed for the area. What presently suffices are extensions of the major decorated types defined in adjacent areas of the Mississippi Valley (see Phillips, Ford, and Griffin 1951;

Clay 1963) and most recently the type-variety system of Phillips (1970).

Differing goals of research efforts have also had an impact on the development of a chronological scheme. In the 1970s work by Southern Illinois University in the Black Bottom was concentrated on small sites of farmstead and hamlet sizes. These sites have the advantage of relatively short occupations, but they yield comparatively small collections of ceramics that contain few diagnostics, particularly the decorated types thought to be chronologically sensitive. Thus while these sites have been adequately carbon dated, their ceramics are difficult to compare with materials from large and complex sites such as Kincaid.

The present knowledge of the local Mississippian sequence derives primarily from four sources: the University of Chicago Kincaid project, various efforts by the University of Kentucky in the lower Tennessee and Cumberland drainages, work by Southern Illinois University in the immediate area around the Kincaid site, and most recently, efforts by the University of Illinois along the western border of Kentucky.

From 1934 until 1944 the University of Chicago sponsored an intensive program of archaeological work in the Black Bottom, with most of the effort directed specifically at Kincaid. The results of this work are summarized in the well-known volume *Kincaid, A Prehistoric Illinois Metropolis* (Cole et al. 1951). Two portions of the Chicago research are relevant here. Kenneth G. Orr analyzed the ceramics from Kincaid. The results of this study are incorporated within a broader study of material culture entitled "Change at Kincaid: A Study of Cultural Dynamics" (Orr 1951). The ceramics study was based on collections from proveniences selected to minimize problems with mixed and intrusive material. Unfortunately, Orr's assumptions in selecting and grouping the materials for study resulted, in some cases, in materials being grouped together that were probably not contemporaneous. Thus while Orr's study successfully identifies the general style trends in the Mississippian ceramic sequence, the details are fuzzy and there is little information on specific contexts. Orr ultimately divided the occupational sequence into three segments—Early, Middle, and Late—but these units must be viewed with considerable caution. The early and middle units, in particular, suffer badly from chronologically mixed lots of material.

In another segment of the Chicago project, Robert Bell (1951) attempted to date Kincaid using dendrochronology. Working with red cedar, he developed a master sequence for the region and ultimately succeeded in matching eight archaeological samples with the master chart. The dates he derived, mostly in the sixteenth century, have been the subject of considerable skepticism and controversy over the years and are discussed in greater detail in this chapter.

Data from the lower Tennessee and Cumberland drainages derive from several periods of work by the University of Kentucky. As a part of the W.P.A. program, William S. Webb conducted excavations on a number of sites in the region but most notably at Jonathan Creek on the Tennessee River (Webb 1952). Beginning in the late 1950s, excavations took place on a number of sites on the lower Cumberland as part of the salvage program preceding the impoundment of Lake Barkely. For present purposes, the most important of these was the Tinsley Hill site. Data from these sites and from Webb's earlier work formed the basis of Berle Clay's first presentation of a ceramic and chronological sequence for the area (Clay 1963). Clay's subsequent paper (1979) is a updated and modified version of this 1963 scheme.

In 1967 Southern Illinois University (SIU) conducted some emergency salvage excavations at the Kincaid site (Weigand and Muller n.d.). This activity rekindled research interest in the Kincaid site and the Black Bottom. Muller subsequently developed a long-term effort directed at examining the nature of Mississippian settlement in and around the Black Bottom (Muller 1986a). The SIU efforts explicitly avoided work on the Kincaid site and concentrated on intensive survey and small-scale test excavations on selected sites. The long-term results have provided a detailed characterization not only of the distribution but also of the basic character of the small supporting settlements around Kincaid (Muller 1978a, 1986a; Butler 1977; Riordan 1975; Davy 1982).

Beginning in 1983 R. Barry Lewis and his students at the University of Illinois began a long-term research effort in the western margins of the Jackson Purchase of Kentucky, with particular emphasis on the Mississippian occupation of the area. The Western Kentucky Research Project began with investigations of a group of long-neglected Mississippian mound centers along the Kentucky side of the Mississippi River (Lewis 1986) but has subsequently included survey in some interior drainages and examination of a variety of smaller sites (Sussenbach and Lewis 1987). Most recently, the work has moved into the mouth of the Ohio Valley with work at the large Twin Mounds site, opposite the mouth of the Cache River.

The Chronological Sequence

The sequence proposed here for the lower Ohio region is a modified version of Clay's (1979) scheme with two additional phases. The core of the chronological sequence consists of the Jonathan Creek, Angelly, and Tinsley Hill phases (Clay 1979). In earlier writings on the lower Tennessee-Cumberland area, Clay (1963, 1976) defined only two units, the Jonathan Creek and Tinsley Hill phases. In the more recent paper, however, he recognized that there was a significant chronological gap between these two and has inserted the Angelly phase, defined by Riordan (1975) on the basis of Black Bottom sites. At present, these "phases" should be considered more as subperiods rather than as phases in the classic Willey and Phillips (1958) sense. The sequence may be briefly characterized as follows.

DOUGLAS PHASE (A.D. 850–1000)

The Douglas phase was not originally a part of the Clay sequence, which began only at A.D. 1000. Muller (1986a: 159–62) defined the phase as a terminal Lewis (Late Woodland) unit that bridges the transition to the fully developed Mississippian stage. Chronologically, it is more-or-less equivalent to the Dillinger phase in the Mississippi Valley portion of southern Illinois (Maxwell 1951; Muller 1986a; Webb, Hargrave, and Cobb 1986) and the Duffy/ Yankeetown phase in the lower Wabash and adjacent portions of the Ohio Valley (Muller 1986a; Redmond 1986).

The history of this unit goes back to the early University of Chicago work. At Mx°7, one of the two platform mounds at Kincaid to be extensively investigated, the first mound stage was associated with a late Lewis ceramic complex consisting of clay-tempered cordmarked sherds and plain, slipped, and polished sherds tempered with a mixture of clay and shell. The sample of sherds was small (about 150) but Richard S. MacNeish proposed a Douglas horizon on the basis of it (MacNeish n.d.). In the end, however, MacNeish's arguments were not accepted and no mention of the Douglas horizon appears in the published Kincaid volume (see comments in Muller 1986a: 160). The decorated ceramics in question were explained as trade materials.

Although still not well defined, the Douglas phase is supported by data from survey collections in the Kincaid locality and by some additional excavation data. SIU excavations at Mx-109 located on the terrace adjacent to the Black Bottom have yielded plain clay-tempered ceramics with an associated carbon date of A.D. 1003[2] (1040 ± 90 B.P., DIC-394) (Muller 1986a: table 6.1).

JONATHAN CREEK PHASE (ca. A.D. 1000–1100)

There is little controversy about the Jonathan Creek phase. The type site (Jonathan Creek) was excavated by William S. Webb in the late 1930s and early 1940s; it consisted of a platform mound and a substantial village covering approximately eleven hectares (Webb 1952). The lack of clear stratigraphy in the midden and Webb's excavation technique have combined to leave us no stratigraphic information on the collections. A later Mississippian component is present on the site and the collections are, to some extent, chronologically mixed. Small amounts of similar ceramic material were recovered in stratigraphic context at the Tinsley Hill site on the Cumberland (Clay 1963). Similar materials were recovered from the Dedmon site on the Tennessee River with two associated carbon dates of A.D. 1090 (905 ± 75 and 905 ± 85 B.P., UGa-251 and 247) (Allen 1976). Clay characterized the ceramic complex as one of extreme simplicity, consisting almost entirely of plain ware (Mississippi and Bell Plain) with some fabric-impressed pans (Kimmswick Fabric Impressed) and small amounts of cordmarking (McKee Island Cordmarked) and red filming (Old Town Red). Other than the red filming, there is a total absence of decoration in the form of incising, engraving, punctuation, or painting. The major vessel form is a small globular jar with loop handles.

The one reservation that might be expressed about the Jonathan Creek ceramic complex is that it is probably more elaborate than presently described. The sherd samples used to define the phase are quite small—the analytical sample from Jonathan Creek is around 3,000 sherds and the material from Tinsley Hill is about 350 sherds. One suspects that the present samples do not contain the full representation of vessel forms and decorative treatments (see Wolforth 1987). This is especially clear when one compares Jonathan Creek to the early material from Mound Bottom, a large predominantly early Mississippian mound center in the middle Cumberland drainage (O'Brien 1977).

ANGELLY PHASE (A.D. 1200–1300)

The Angelly phase was defined by Riordan (1975) on the basis of his study of the ceramics from the Black Bottom sites. The ceramics used in his study derived primarily from three sites—two small farmsteads and the Angelly site, a hamlet of slightly over one hectare in area. These sites are securely carbon dated in the period of A.D. 1200–1300. The full range of major vessel forms is present. Strap and loop handles occur on jars in approximately equal numbers. Neither the large loop handles nor the wide strap handles occur. Red-slipped vessels are present. Decorated types include negative painting in both the red-on-black and brown-on-white varieties (Nashville Negative Painted var. Angel), O'Byam Incised, and one or more varieties of Matthews Incised (var. Manley and probably others). Hooded bottles and bean-pot vessels have also been identified. The definition of the phase in terms of its associated ceramics is not entirely satisfactory. The definition is based on small collections from small sites where decorated types are poorly represented; thus a greater range of decorated types and varieties is probably associated with this phase.

Although Riordan originally suggested dates of A.D. 1100–1300 for this phase, all of the diagnostic ceramics are from contexts dated in the thirteenth century. The one small site that pre-dated A.D. 1200 produced no temporally diagnostic materials. Thus the chronological dimensions of this phase are more properly viewed, for the present at least, as A.D. 1200–1300. These dimensions leave a gap in the sequence from A.D. 1100 to 1200.

It is not presently clear if another phase unit is needed or whether the gap should merely be subsumed by the existing phases.

TINSLEY HILL PHASE (A.D. 1300–1450)

The Tinsley Hill phase was defined on the basis of the Tinsley Hill site and a series of other sites in the lower Tennessee-Cumberland drainage. The type site is a two-acre complex consisting of a platform mound and stone-box-grave cemetery near Eddyville, Kentucky. The Tinsley Hill ceramic complex is typical of what is generally recognized as Late Mississippian. The full range of vessel forms is present, and wide strap handles predominate on jars. Decorated types include Matthews Incised *var. Matthews, Beckwith,* and *Manley*; O'Byam Incised *var. Stewart*; and Nashville Negative Painted *var. Nashville*. No one would question that the Tinsley Hill phase is Late Mississippian in the general sense of the term, but there is substantial disagreement about its proper chronological dimensions. Clay (1979) has argued that the phase should last until ca. A.D. 1600, but the position taken here is that Tinsley Hill is more appropriately dated at ca. A.D. 1300–1450. While the difference may seem minor, it has considerable significance in terms of integrating Kincaid into the regional sequence. Tinsley Hill-like materials occur in quantity at Kincaid and are readily identified in drawings and photographs. Typologically, it appears to equate with Orr's division of both Middle and Late Kincaid, an equivalence I find acceptable with the alternative dating proposed here.

In this regard, the recently published Chambers site (Pollack and Railey 1987) is quite instructive. A Mississippian village located on a tributary of the Clarks River in Marshall County, Kentucky, Chambers is well dated with a suite of thirteen radiocarbon dates whose corrected ages indicate a span of occupation from ca. A.D. 1250 to 1350. Partly because of the dates and partly because of their lack of detailed familiarity with the Black Bottom materials, the investigators are reluctant to place it in either the Angelly or Tinsley Hill phase (Pollack and Railey 1987:33). The ceramics do, in fact, fit comfortably in the Angelly phase, although the site probably spans the transition and is in general illustrative of the difficulty in determining a sharp temporal boundary between the two phases.

CABORN-WELBORN PHASE (A.D. 1450–1600)

The Caborn-Welborn phase (Green and Munson 1978) is presently the only Mississippian construct in the lower Ohio Valley that can be clearly shown to extend into protohistoric times. It is defined, however, only for a restricted area that includes the lower portions of the Wabash Valley and adjacent areas along the Ohio River down to the vicinity of Shawneetown, Illinois, and the mouth of the Saline River. Fortunately, Caborn-Welborn assemblages do exhibit some definite, albeit somewhat rare, stylistic and typological forms that make them identifiable (see also Williams 1980). The origins of this complex are still not understood and its chronological dimensions are likewise hazy, but it is hoped that research currently under way will help clarify the situation.

In his volume on the lower Ohio Valley, Muller (1986a: 185) offers, very tentatively, a modified phase sequence for the Kincaid locality:

Caborn-Welborn	A.D. 1450–1600?
Tinsley Hill	A.D. 1250–1400
Kincaid	A.D. 1100–1250
Jonathan Creek	A.D. 1000–1100
Douglas	A.D. 850–1000

The main difference here is substitution of the Kincaid phase for the Angelly phase and the modification of its temporal boundaries to include the as-yet poorly represented A.D. 1000–1100 interval, similar to what was originally proposed by Riordan. In part this is an attempt to rehabilitate the old Kincaid focus (phase) set forth by the University of Chicago investigators (Cole et al. 1951: 229), which because it referred to the entire site sequence was a temporal construct of little value (see Muller 1986a: 179). In developmental terms, the indicated span certainly encompasses the emergence and peak of Kincaid as a major center. Despite the historical attractiveness of the term, there are not yet sufficient data to judge whether the "Kincaid phase" is really useful or appropriate, especially since the ceramic definition of it must still rely heavily on the Angelly materials. The more-limited Angelly phase should be retained, at least until more work is done at the Kincaid site. Also note that Muller favors a slightly earlier ending date for the Tinsley Hill phase than is suggested here.

THE KINCAID DENDROCHRONOLOGY

One of the most persistent problems both in unraveling the occupational sequence at Kincaid and in developing a regional chronological framework has been the continuing argument over the reliability of the dendrochronology dates obtained from the site by Robert E. Bell during the Chicago work in the area (Bell 1951). Working from an earlier study by Florence Hawley (1941), Bell developed a local cedar master chart extending back to about A.D. 1430 with a few ring sequences dating earlier. He regarded his master chart as highly tentative beyond A.D. 1450. Of the numerous archaeologi-

Table 15.1. Kincaid dendrochronology dates

Sample	Range of Cross-Correlated Rings	Estimated Bark Date
Mx^{v}1C 70 L2, DD4.1	A.D. 1483–1588	A.D. 1598–1613
Mx^{o}4 Floor 2	A.D. 1511–1575	no estimate
1		
Mx^{o}4 633B (Floor 2)	A.D. 1522–1573	no estimate
Mx^{o}4 993 (Floor 3)	A.D. 1453–1555	A.D. 1565–1585
Mx^{o}4 No. 1, 70R8, L10	A.D. 1458–1513	A.D. 1523–1538
Mx^{o}4 No. 2, 70R8, L10	A.D. 1431–1499	(Nos. 1–3 form composite estimate above)
Mx^{o}4 No. 3, 70R8, L10	A.D. 1444–1513	
Mx^{o}4 1050 (Floor 6)	A.D. 1426–1514	A.D. 1524–1539

Source: Bell 1951

cal wood samples taken from the Chicago excavations, only eight proved suitable for assigning true annual dates (table 15.1). Seven of the samples were from the badly damaged mound Mx^{o}4 and one was from the village area Mx^{v}1C. True annual dates of from A.D. 1523 to 1613 were assigned to the samples. These dates were correlated with Orr's ceramic periods in the following manner:

Late Kincaid	1598–1613
Middle Kincaid	1525–1598
Early Kincaid	Pre-1523

The dated levels from Mx^{o}4 were considered to be Middle Kincaid so that none of the dates applied specifically to the early period. The general conclusion was that the Mississippian occupation of Kincaid was limited to the period of roughly A.D. 1450–1650.

At the time, the dates seemed plausible in light of current ideas on chronology. With the advent of radiocarbon dating and the accumulation of many Mississippian dates that were significantly older, the accuracy of the Kincaid dates was brought into serious question. Later, however, the Kincaid dates acquired a new-found respectability in some quarters with the dissemination of some late carbon dates from Mississippian sites in the lower Cumberland area (Clay 1963).

Munson's (1966) article was one of the few supporting arguments for the tree-ring dates to appear in print. He reports some successful but limited dendrochronology work done in central Illinois using red cedar. Using the central Illinois results and the late carbon dates from the lower Cumberland, Munson argued for the validity of the Kincaid dates, supported by the association of supposedly late ceramic materials. The gist of the argument is that Mx^{o}4 represents a late addition to the mound group and the terminal occupation on the site. This is essentially the position taken by Clay in subsequent writing. As I

have indicated elsewhere (Butler 1977:186–89), the association of alleged very late ceramics in portions of Mx^{o}4 is no longer a tenable argument. The supposedly protohistoric ceramics (Fort Ancient and Natchesan types, if they have been correctly identified) are now known to have much greater time depth than once thought.

More important, it is possible to mount a very strong case of circumstantial evidence against the reliability of the dates based on a detailed examination of the proveniences of the dated samples. The tree-ring sequence is derived almost entirely from Mx^{o}4. The most recent date on the mound, A.D. 1598, was obtained from what the investigators called Floor 2. There was another floor above this one, and at one time there were at least two other mound levels above that. In fact, Cole suggests that the original mound may have been six feet higher than at the time of the Chicago excavations (Cole et al. 1951:73). Given the date from Floor 2, the later stages would argue for mound-building activity still taking place around A.D. 1650 or later. The tree-ring date from Mx^{v}1C further increases the chronological difficulty. The specimen, with an assigned cutting date of A.D. 1613, was taken from a burned structure at the bottom of a three-foot-deep midden. This heavy concentration of superimposed house floors and refuse deposits did not accumulate in just a few years' time so, if the date is correct, there must be significant occupation on the site into the late seventeenth century. Munson's argument ignores the problem of the missing mound levels and the provenience of the one nonmound sample.

A date of A.D. 1650 or later is hardly believable in terms of the historical documents of the period. French accounts indicate that only a few bands of displaced Shawnee were in the lower Ohio area shortly after 1650 (Temple 1966:173–75). There is some mention of several small groups of uncertain affiliation, chiefly the Kaskinampo, but these are described as living up the Tennessee and Cumberland rivers (see Swanton 1930; Bauxar 1957:286–300). There is no indication in any of the accounts of a major site, especially one capable of supporting mound building, still functioning in the area (see Muller 1986a:262–64). Still, Clay (1979) protested the dismissal of the dendrochronology as "premature."

Clearly, new and direct evidence had to be obtained to finally settle the issue. Short of reexcavating the mound Mx^{o}4, the only direct way to settle the question was to date the wood and charcoal samples from which Bell derived his archaeological dates. The bulk of the samples, notes, and related materials from Bell's dendrochronology project are now in the possession of the Dendrochronology Laboratory at the University of Arizona. Dr. William Robinson examined the Bell Collection and verified that all eight dated archaeological samples were still in the collection. The specific object of the search was the composite sample from the oldest dated level within Mx°4—three pieces attributed to level 10 of square 7OR8 (Bell 1951:269–75). The samples are described as being three large sections of solid cedar wood representing post fragments from the same structure. Two of the pieces were thought definitely to be portions of the same tree (the original log was quartered) and the third was thought probably to represent the same tree. The Bell report also states that these samples were not treated with any preservative and thus would be excellent candidates for radiocarbon dating. Dr. Robinson kindly cut cross-section samples from all three pieces and made them available to SIU. The samples were then submitted for dating.

The samples in question were obtained in 1944 by R. S. MacNeish in a special excavation intended to locate samples suitable for dendrodating. There is still some question about the precise vertical provenience of those samples; critical field records are missing and correspondence with both MacNeish and Bell does not fully resolve the problem. The samples are from either level 5 of zone E or level 4, Floor 5, of zone F. (The latter is favored here.) For present purposes, the difference is minor—the samples (regardless of true provenience) derived from one of the submound habitation levels and the original stratigraphic sequence of the Mx°4 samples is not violated. For this composite sample, Bell derives a date range of A.D. 1431 to 1513 (rings actually present) with a probable bark date of 1523 to 1539.

The carbon dates (table 15.2) form an overlapping cluster with a composite average, tree ring corrected, of about A.D. 1120. Note that the two samples definitely thought to represent the same tree date to within forty radiocarbon years and thirteen calendar years of one another. The dates were obtained from sections of wood cut from the outer ten to twenty rings of the cross sections, although it was not possible to tell in each case if the lobe selected represented the outermost (latest) portion of the cross section.

Table 15.2. Carbon dates from Kincaid dendro samples

Site	Sample	C-14 Years B.P.	Calendar Date A.D. Corrected Range[1]	Calendar Date A.D. Corrected Midpoint[1]
UGa-3455	Mx°4, No. 2 7OR$_8$, L10	850 ± 65	1045–1260	1153
UGa-3456	Mx°4, No. 3 7OR$_8$, L10	890 ± 65	1030–1250	1140
UGa-3457	Mx°4, No. 1 7OR$_8$, L10	950 ± 70	915–1225	1070

[1] Dates tree ring corrected after Klein et al. (1982).

This date is quite reasonable especially since the ceramics associated with the excavation levels in question were described by the Chicago workers as early Middle Kincaid. The lack of precise information on the context of the sample limits interpretation. Unfortunately the ceramics cannot presently be reassembled as a group for study. The important point for present purposes is that the composite sample is almost 400 years older than determined by Bell. The carbon dates directly discredit only the one wood sample, but since the whole dendro sequence consists of supposedly crossmatched and overlapping samples, the elimination of one of the samples calls the whole sequence in question. The evidence is more than ample to conclude that Kincaid dendrochronology dates are incorrect, as has long been suspected. Clearly, the attempt to extend the modern and historic master sequence into prehistoric times resulted in some erroneous matches. The results also suggest that the eight archaeological dendro samples may not even be a reliable relative sequence. Bell's work was an important pioneering effort in dedrochronology, but the state-of-the-art was simply too primitive to ensure reliable results with such a complacent species as red cedar.

The Kincaid Radiocarbon Dates

There are now seven radiocarbon dates from the Kincaid site, all derived in one way or another from samples collected by University of Chicago work (table 15.3). The three dates recently obtained to check the accuracy of the dendro samples have been discussed in the previous section. Those dates relate to a single provenience and are of limited value in interpretation beyond the validity of the dendro dates. The four previously obtained dates will be discussed here.

The first is a date of A.D. 1313 (M-888) (Crane and Griffin 1960:35). This date was obtained from the burial mound, Pp°2, and it supposedly represents a carbon sample from one of the log tombs in the first phase of the mound. The sample was obtained by Joseph Caldwell in 1958, some fourteen years after the Chicago excavations. He visited the site with the specific intent of collecting material for radiocarbon dating (Riordan 1975:69). Caldwell had supervised some of the original work and was

Table 15.3. Summary of Radiocarbon dates from Kincaid
(see also Muller 1986: Table 6.1)

Site	Sample	C-14 Years B.P.	Calendar Date A.D. Corrected Range [1]	Calendar Date A.D. Corrected Midpoint [1]
M-888	Pp°2, burial mound	675 ± 75	1215–1410	1313
DIC-393	Mx[v]1A-41 Base of midden	630 ± 65	1260–1405	1333
DIC-903	Mx°4 Premound level	1110 ± 65	785–1035	910
DIC-904	Mx°10 Last construction phase	660 ± 55	1250–1395	1323
UGa-3455	Mx°4 Premound level	850 ± 65	1045–1260	1153
UGa-3456	"	890 ± 65	1030–1250	1140
UGa-3457	"	950 ± 70	915–1225	1070

[1] Dates tree ring corrected after Klein et al. (1982).

familiar with the mound, but it might have been difficult to return fourteen years later and with a small pit accurately establish the provenience of the carbon sample. The reason for questioning the provenience of Caldwell's sample is because the original report states that charred logs were associated not only with the tomb burials of the first phase but also with the upper surface of the second mound phase (Cole et al. 1951:110).

Assuming that the stated provenience is correct, interpretation is still unclear, because the burials in the first two mound phases produced no artifacts useful for chronological placement. Some stone-box graves occurred in the third construction phase, and these contained ceramics described by Orr as representing both Middle and Late forms (Cole et al. 1951:112). Around the periphery of the third stage were a large number of non–stone box interments with associated Late Kincaid ceramics. The Chicago investigators basically assumed that the first two mound phases were Early Kincaid. The mound fill of the first two phases did contain some Early Kincaid pottery, but this is not surprising because the mound is adjacent to an Early Kincaid habitation area. The carbon date seems reasonable but the lack of associated diagnostics limits its usefulness.

The other three dates were obtained by SIU personnel from charcoal samples found in the University of Chicago collections, now at the Center for Archaeological Investigations, SIU. These three samples had been treated with a gasoline and paraffin preservative mixture at the time of excavation. Radiocarbon laboratories claim that these potential contaminants can be removed by chemical treat-

ment and should pose no inherent problem in obtaining reliable dates. Still, the increased risk of contamination is a factor to consider in evaluating the dates.

The second date was obtained from a section of charred timber from the 1941 Chicago excavations. The sample came from a burned structure in the lowest level of Mx[v]1A-41 Section 70, Square 51, level 5. The date obtained was A.D. 1333 (DIC-393). This date is likewise difficult to evaluate because of questions about its context and the associated ceramics. Mx[v]1A-41 was an area of deep deposits, up to two meters in some cases, which evidenced considerable time depth. The situation is unclear because these units may involve a low substructure mound. Orr classified the lower occupation levels as Early Kincaid. The dated sample derives from the basal level of the midden but an A.D. 1313 date is simply not acceptable for an early component. The date would be acceptable if it were associated with levels Orr would describe as Middle or Late Kincaid. The date will remain problematical until associated materials can be reanalyzed.

A third date was obtained from a burial structure in Mx°4, the platform mound that yielded most of Bell's dendro samples. The date of A.D. 910 (DIC-903) was obtained from House 1 (Feature 7) from occupation level 4, Floor 5 (Cole et al. 1951:66–68). This is a premound occupation level, but not the earliest one in this portion of the site. This is probably the same level that produced the composite dendro sample carbon dated to around A.D. 1135. The A.D. 910 date is clearly too early for the given context.

The most informative date was obtained from charred remains of a house associated with the uppermost level of Mx°10, the large platform mound with the conical addition. The sample is associated with Feature 8, a structure that extended up to the modern sod and that, in the opinion of the excavators, represented the last building phase on Mx°10 (Cole et al. 1951:100–101). The date obtained was A.D. 1323 (DIC-904). The date seems good in terms of the associated ceramics and indicates that construction of Mx°10 ceased around A.D. 1300 or slightly thereafter. Since this is one of the four principal mounds of the main group, the date may also indicate a general cessation of mound construction around this time.

In sum, the acceptable carbon dates from Kincaid range from around A.D. 1000 to slightly after 1300. With the exception of the Mx°10 date, however, the samples were not selected to deal with latter portions of the occupation. Because of the questions about the context and the difficulty in reassembling the associated ceramics, the dates are only of general utility. Although the Mx°10 date may suggest a cessation of mound building around A.D. 1300, it does not necessarily date the latest occupations on the site.

The View from Kincaid

First of all, I should point out that the chronological scheme presented here should be viewed as a working construct, and one should not be wedded to it. Considerable revision is likely to occur as better data become available. In particular, the separations between Jonathan Creek, Angelly, and Tinsley Hill are poorly defined. The chronological boundaries may shift somewhat, and new units may need to be added. Obviously, the present constructs are very gross, and the type-variety ceramic typology is probably not capable of the temporal precision needed to resolve questions of process. Ultimately, future work will need to develop finer-scaled typologies.

The major disagreements concern the later portions of the sequence, specifically, the status of occupations after A.D. 1400 both at Kincaid and in the region at large. The view here is that by A.D. 1400–1450, Kincaid has ceased to function as a mound center and that a dramatic reduction and/or redistribution of population has taken place. On the other hand, if one accepts a sixteenth-century terminus of the Tinsley Hill phase, then Kincaid must be interpreted as existing as a major center into protohistoric times. Such a situation runs counter to what is presently known about other mound centers in the region, where there appears to be significant decline in activity after A.D. 1300. It seems highly unlikely that Kincaid would be such a signal exception to a broad regional pattern.

Data presently available for Kincaid and the Black Bottom suggest a position of Kincaid vis-à-vis the local sequence rather different than the one required by the Clay scenario. First, it is clear that Mississippian culture is present in the Kincaid area at very early time levels and that Kincaid emerges as a major site then. No unmixed lots of ceramics equivalent to Jonathan Creek have been identified, although it is obvious from Orr's report that the early ceramic forms are present. The earliest mound building at Kincaid occurs around or slightly before A.D. 1000 in association with Douglas phase ceramics. There is presently little information on sites and events in the period from ca. A.D. 1100 to A.D. 1200, although clearly Mississippian settlement is well established and Kincaid is developing as a mound center. This period constitutes a gap in the present chronological sequence. One small site in the Black Bottom, BBMx-213, has been carbon dated in the twelfth century, but test excavations did not provide a useful ceramic sample.

Intensive survey of the Black Bottom has delineated very extensive Mississippian habitation of the agricultur-

ally viable portions of floodplain. The settlement pattern is one of clusters of small one- and two-structure "farmsteads" aggregated around "hamlet" class sites of about a hectare in size (see Butler 1977; Davy 1982). The unexpected result of testing a series of these sites was that a majority of these sites date to a relatively narrow time frame, the thirteenth century. To date, none has dated significantly after A.D. 1300. These sites and associated ceramics provide the basis for the Angelly phase. This time period is thought to be the time of maximum mound construction activity at Kincaid and probably represents the peak of secular power and sociopolitical integration. The palisade construction at Kincaid cannot be accurately dated, but evidence from the Chicago excavations at Mx^{r}36 along the bank of Avery Lake indicate that the palisade probably dates to this middle period (Cole et al. 1951:57–58).

There are substantial amounts of later ceramic materials (Tinsley Hill phase) at Kincaid, particularly in the Mx^{v}1C area and in the upper construction levels of several of the major mounds. Mound construction is taking place but much less than previously, and the Mx°10 date suggests that this may have ceased early in the fourteenth century.

A major change in settlement pattern is associated with this period in that there appear to be few small supporting sites in the surrounding area. Habitation area does not increase markedly at Kincaid during the late occupations, so the situation is not explained by a simple concentration of the outlying population into the mound center. Of the small sites investigated to date in the Black Bottom, none has dated significantly after A.D. 1300. Although sampling error is possibly a factor, the current sample does seem large enough for us to conclude that the later habitations are few in number. Test excavations at a small hamlet on the Kentucky side of the Ohio River below Paducah have produced two late carbon dates of A.D. 1418 (490 ± 85 B.P., UGa-3574) and A.D. 1373 (550 ± 65 B.P., UGa-3575) (Butler, Penny, and Robison 1981). The dates appear to be about a century too recent as both the diagnostic ceramics (Angelly phase) and the maize remains from the site suggest a late thirteenth- or early fourteenth-century placement. Also, a third sample from a nearby habitation or activity area produced totally unacceptable means of A.D. 1590 and 1775 (235 ± 70 B.P., UGa-3573).

Terminal Mississippian in the Lower Ohio Valley

There is substantial disagreement and, at present, few clear answers about the terminal Mississippian period in the lower Ohio Valley. As indicated earlier, the Caborn-Welborn phase is presently the only manifestation in the lower Ohio that clearly extends into protohistoric times. Clay (1979) and others have argued that the Tinsley Hill phase should extend into the 1500s and perhaps as late as A.D. 1600. The case for the late duration of the Tinsley Hill phase originally rested on two lines of argument: the Kincaid dendrochronology and a group of late carbon dates obtained from a series of sites in western Kentucky. With the data presented in this paper, the Kincaid dendrochronology can be finally and irrevocably set aside. The dating of late Mississippian complexes in the area must unfortunately still rely on radiocarbon dates and the careful use of cross-dating.

The radiocarbon dates in question (table 15.4) are a group of six age determinations, five from Isotopes Incorporated and one from the University of Michigan, all reported in 1963. In their uncorrected form, these dates were so late as to incite immediate suspicion, but the advent of tree-ring calibration tables has modified the situation somewhat. Calibration makes the calendar dates slightly earlier to the point where two of these, the Roach site (I-479) and the "early" component of the Morris site (I-480), are at least plausible. There are, however, two good reasons for regarding the entire suite of Isotopes dates as suspect, that is, of being too recent. First, with the exception of the Tinsley Hill cemetery date, these

dates were obtained in a consecutive series of age determinations by one commercial laboratory in the early days of commercial dating when sample preparation techniques and basic technology were relatively primitive. It is rather improbable that samples taken from a variety of sites, including one site excavated in the 1930s (Morris), should all prove to be uniformly so late. It is also suspicious that the one sample processed by a different laboratory (University of Michigan), admittedly one from an anomalous context (see Clay 1979:119), is significantly earlier.

Second, it has also been possible to reassess the Tinsley Hill village date by obtaining another date from the same provenience. The I-478 date (A.D. 1548) was obtained from the charred base of one of four support posts associated with a house floor (Feature 23). Associated ceramics include Neeley's Ferry Plain, Bell Plain, Kimmswick Fabric Impressed, and Matthews Incised (Berle Clay, personal communication, 1981). Portions of another of the charred posts were retained in the collections of the Museum of Anthropology, University of Kentucky. The specimen had not been treated with preservative and had been well curated. Outer portions of this post were submitted for dating. The sample yielded a corrected date of A.D. 1380 (520 ± 40 B.P., Beta- 3921) with a range of A.D. 1330 to 1430. Uncorrected, the two dates do not overlap at one standard deviation. Corrected, their 95% confidence intervals just barely overlap, and it is highly improbable that the two dates represent statistical variation around the same true age. On technical grounds alone, the Beta date is considered more reliable, and the date is fully in accord with the chronological arguments presented here.

The issue of the terminal portion of the lower Ohio sequence broaches the larger question of the decline of mound centers and what some see as a dramatic redistribution or reduction of population in certain portions of the central Mississippi Valley, northern extremities of the lower Mississippi Valley, and portions of the Ohio, Tennessee, and Cumberland drainages. This phenomenon has been noted by various observers, but has been most clearly expressed by Stephen Williams in his "Vacant Quarter Hypothesis" (1977). In effect, the view expressed here is that the Kincaid locality and the lower Ohio region in general does fit, to some extent, the "Vacant Quarter" scenario. This view is by no means unanimous. Barry Lewis (Lewis and Mackin 1984; Lewis 1989a, 1989b) does not accept the "Vacant Quarter Hypothesis" for the Ohio-Mississippi rivers confluence region and argues specifically that the abandonment scenario described by Dan F. Morse and Phyllis A. Morse (1983) results from

Table 15.4. Mississippian Carbon Dates
from Western Kentucky

Site	Sample	C-14 Years B.P.	Calendar Date A.D. Corrected Range [2]	Calendar Date A.D. Corrected Midpoint [2]
Roach	I-479	410 ± 85	1345–1650	1498
Goheen	I-477	350 ± 85	1405–1665	1535
Tinsley Hill Village	I-478	300 ± 80	1415–1675	1545
			1710–1805	–
			1925–1950	–
Tinsley Hill Cemetery	M-1150	570 ± 150 [1]	1260–1475	1368
Morris (Early)	I-480	475 ± 90	1320–1535	1428
			1565–1605	1585
Morris (Late)	I-481	270 ± 80	1420–1815	1618
			1840–1885	–
			1915–1950	–

[1] Two standard deviations.
[2] Dates tree ring corrected after Klein et al. (1982).
Sources: Trautman 1963; Crane and Griffin 1963

erroneous cross-dating of ceramic materials and from factors that limit the visibility of late occupations. In Lewis's view Mississippian occupations in the Cairo Lowland, as well as the lower Ohio and Tennessee and Cumberland valleys, persisted at least until the time of the de Soto entradas if not later.

Working in the Cairo Lowland, Lewis (1982) developed a chronological sequence to replace Williams's (1954) Cairo Lowlands phase. The same sequence has been used in his subsequent work along the western Kentucky border and into the mouth of the Ohio Valley (Lewis 1986). The sequence consists of the James Bayou, Dorena, Medley, and Jackson phases, each of 200 years' duration beginning with the James Bayou phase at A.D. 900 and ending with the Jackson phase at A.D. 1700. Some confusion has resulted from the fact that Lewis's phases depart from customary usage in that they represent arbitrary 200-year temporal segments; the temporal boundaries are fixed while the cultural content may be continually revised (Lewis 1989a, 1989b).

Lewis views Tinsley Hill as the lower Tennessee-Cumberland equivalent of both the Medley and Jackson phases. I have no problem with the Medley phase equivalence but remain skeptical that the Jackson phase (A.D. 1500–1700) is "real" in the sense that there is acutally a widespread, identifiable cultural complex in that time interval. As indicated earlier, the evidence for the late extension of Tinsley Hill is not solid. Although investigations have been conducted at a variety of Mississippian sites in the Cairo Lowland and the western Kentucky border area, so far only one site, Hess in the Cairo Lowland (Lewis 1982), has produced post–A.D. 1500 carbon dates, two dates with corrected values of ca. A.D. 1530 (355 ± 75 B.P., UGa-147 and 350 ± 90 B.P., Gak-1309) (see also Lewis 1989a, 1989b). The existence of Jackson phase occupations at other sites is inferred from stratigraphic considerations and the presence of certain artifacts thought to characterize only very late horizons, such as deer astragali dice.

The archaeological visibility of very late Mississippian occupations is clearly an issue. Problems include the mixing or loss of upper levels of midden deposits due to plowing and erosion as well as the limited number of clear-cut temporal markers for the very latest materials (Williams 1980). Also, if population density is declining late in the sequence, as some believe, then at some point such occupations would drop below a threshold of archaeological visibility, that is, the components would be sufficiently rare that archaeologists would have great difficulty in finding them.

While there may have been some protohistoric population along the Ohio River between the mouth of the Saline and the Mississippi rivers or in the lower Tennessee-Cumberland, it is likely to have been small, scattered, and difficult to identify. With the exception of the Caborn-Welborn phase, the status of post–A.D. 1450 occupations in the lower portions of the Ohio, Tennessee, and Cumberland valleys remains problematical.

A final point is that it is not necessary to assume that the effective end of Mississippian occupation was synchronous over a large region. Judging from the disposition and movement of aboriginal populations in the Southeast in later times (seventeenth and early eighteenth centuries), one would expect the abandonment of large areas to be a "patchy" uneven process, and it may well be that Mississippian occupation lasts longer in some of these areas than in others, in which case both arguments could be essentially correct. In other words, there might be protohistoric occupations in portions of the Cairo Lowland or Kentucky border but not in the lower Ohio or Tennessee and Cumberland valleys. Clearly, the issue is far from resolved and only continued work will answer the questions posed here.

The investigation of Mississippian-period organization, settlement, and demography remains a major research focus in eastern Woodlands prehistory, and the lower Ohio, Tennessee, and Cumberland river valleys have great potential to address these questions as research progresses. Ultimately, questions of phase definition and temporal limits, while necessary, are lesser issues; the really important task is to understand the how and why of these developments.

NOTES

1. This chapter is a substantially modified version of a paper originally prepared for the 1983 Midwest Archaeological Conference. It is that version that is cited in Muller's (1986a:184) volume on the Ohio Valley. The paper was subsequently revised in 1985 for inclusion in this volume, but with the passage of an additional three years and the publication of new data, additional revisions were necessary.

2. Radiocarbon dates discussed in this chapter are presented in three forms. Uncorrected radiocarbon ages are given as years B.P. Calendar dates have been dendrochronologically corrected using Klein et al. (1982). Several different calibration tables are now available and they generally produce comparable results. The Klein et al. (1982) tables provide date ranges that represent a 95% confidence interval for the corrected mean, and this range is used here for many of the dates. The midpoint of that range is used here as the corrected calendar date, although as Klein et al. (1982) note, the midpoint is in some cases slightly different from the true mean. The difference is so small as to be negligible, however, and for convenience the midpoint can be taken as the mean. The more precise Stuiver and Pearson (1986) calibration is not used as its values assume prior correction for isotopic fractionation. None of the carbon dates discussed here were corrected for fractionation.

16

The Early Mississippi Period in the Confluence Region and Its Northern Relationships

R. BARRY LEWIS

It is my purpose to summarize the understanding of Mississippian cultural developments in the Ohio-Mississippi rivers confluence region with emphasis on the early Mississippi period and on connections with the American Bottom and the Lower Ohio Valley. The objective is a timely one because important research has recently taken place in this region and the results of those studies have yet to reach a large audience, being for the most part contained in unpublished grant and contract reports.

The Ohio-Mississippi rivers confluence region (also called the confluence region below) is a small part of the northern Lower Mississippi Valley that comprises the Mississippi Valley border of Kentucky, including Ballard, Carlisle, Hickman, and Fulton counties, and all of the Cairo Lowland, most of which is contained in Mississippi County, Missouri (fig. 16.1). The Kentucky portion of the study region is mostly uplands, and the Cairo Lowland lies entirely in the Mississippi River floodplain. A detailed presettlement environmental reconstruction of the region is given in Lewis (1974).

This chapter emphasizes the early Mississippi period archaeology of the study region since the late Mississippi period archaeology has been recently treated elsewhere (Lewis 1989a). A balanced examination of the entire period, at least as it is manifested in Kentucky, is given in Lewis (1989b).

THE MISSISSIPPI PERIOD

I find it useful to view the Mississippi period as a fundamentally temporal unit that spans the interval between A.D. 900 and 1700, and the concept of "Mississippian" as a unit of cultural similarity largely divorced from strong temporal connotations. This practice differs from common usage, in which Mississippian is both a period and

a cultural tradition, and is therefore saddled with stage-like characteristics that incorporate both time and cultural similarity as dominant aspects. Keeping the temporal and cultural dimensions apart helps one to minimize the difficulty of investigating cultural changes when viewed in period-type frameworks that, by design, emphasize cultural stasis.

The Mississippi period, as the concept is applied here, is a unit of archaeological time. Its temporal limits are not assumed to be inherent in the data, but are defined by the archaeologist. It is also clear that the Mississippian cultural tradition was an indigenous, gradual development in the southern Midwest and the Southeast. Therefore, it is unnecessary to search the archaeological record to discover the moment in prehistory that Late Woodland culture ended and Mississippian began. To do so would require treating a process as an event, the process being the gradual development of agriculture-based chiefdoms across much of the prehistoric East (Lewis 1989a). I find it far more productive to simply set A.D. 900 as the beginning of the Mississippi period, the unit of time, and to acknowledge that there exists unequivocal evidence of the gradual, indigenous development of the major features of Mississippian, the unit of cultural similarity, during the Late Woodland period.

PREVIOUS ARCHAEOLOGICAL RESEARCH

The infrastructure of the present regional sequence was constructed between 1950 and 1975 in the Cairo Lowland. It was based principally on the analysis of surface collections and excavated data from two fortified towns: Beckwith's Fort (23Mi2; Cottier and Southard 1977; Southard and Cottier 1973) and Crosno (23Mi1; Williams 1954); and several smaller villages and ham-

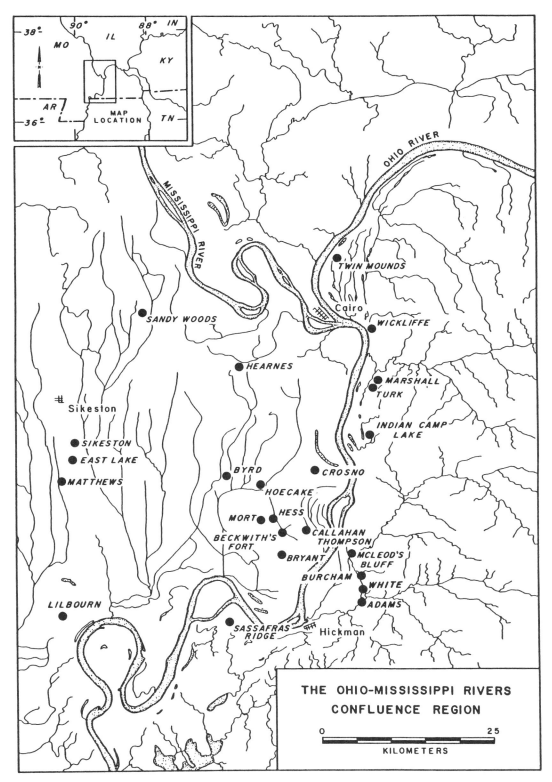

Figure 16.1. The Ohio-Mississippi Rivers Confluence Region Showing Sites Mentioned in the Text (from Sussenbach and Lewis 1987:2)

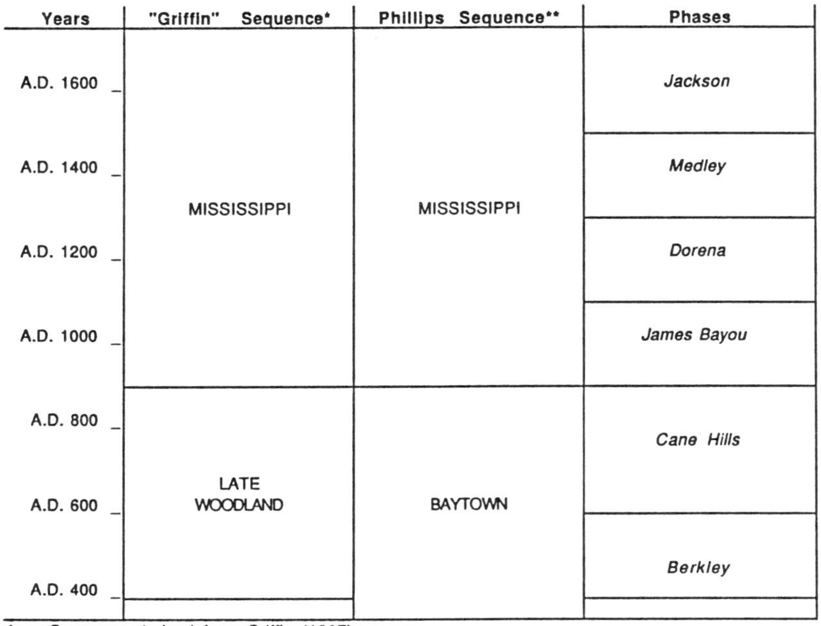

Years	"Griffin" Sequence*	Phillips Sequence**	Phases
A.D. 1600 _			Jackson
A.D. 1400 _	MISSISSIPPI	MISSISSIPPI	Medley
A.D. 1200 _			Dorena
A.D. 1000 _			James Bayou
A.D. 800 _			Cane Hills
A.D. 600 _	LATE WOODLAND	BAYTOWN	
A.D. 400 _			Berkley

*   Sequence derived from Griffin (1967).
** Phillips (1970) sequence adapted to the study region.

Figure 16.2. The Late Prehistoric Sequence in the Confluence Region (adapted from Lewis 1989c)

lets including: Bryant (23Mi59; Williams 1967), Byrd (23Mi53; Williams 1968), Callahan-Thompson (23Mi71; Lewis 1974, 1982), Hess (23Mi55; Lewis 1974, 1982), Hearnes (23Mi7; Klippel 1969), Hoecake (23Mi8; Williams 1974), and Mort (23Mi69; Williams 1968).

In the early 1980s the main focus of archaeological fieldwork and further development of the regional sequence shifted across the Mississippi River to western Kentucky where two research programs began almost simultaneously. First, Murray State University took over the Wickliffe site, a Mississippi period town, and established the Wickliffe Mounds Research Center there (Wesler 1985; Wesler and Neusius 1987).

Second, University of Illinois researchers working under my direction in a program called the Western Kentucky Research (WKY) Project, began a long-range study of the archaeology of this region. The scope of the WKY Project encompasses the entire archaeological record of the confluence region, but emphasizes the study of Mississippian communities. To date, WKY Project excavations have been undertaken at the Adams

(15Fu4), Sassafras Ridge (15Fu3), Turk (15Ce6), and Wickliffe (15Ba4) town sites (Allen 1984; Dunavan 1985; Edging 1985; Lewis 1986; Lewis and Mackin 1984; Stout 1984a, 1984b, 1985, 1987), and at the Burcham (15Hi15), Marshall (15Ce27), Rice (15Fu18), Running Slough (15Fu67), Twin Mounds (15Ba2), and White (15Fu24) village or hamlet sites (Kreisa 1988; Sussenbach and Lewis 1987; Wolforth 1989). Major site survey projects include the extensive examination of four large, western Kentucky sample areas (Sussenbach and Lewis 1987), Kreisa's (1988) survey and mapping of Mississippian "second-order communities," and Kreisa's (1989) Big Bottoms survey.

The phase sequence is based principally on the existing Cairo Lowland sequence through the Middle Woodland period and on the above-referenced western Kentucky research from the beginning of the Late Woodland period to the end of the native American occupation of the region. Figure 16.2 lists the phase names for the portion of the regional sequence that is relevant to the present discussion.

Setting the Chronological Stage

In Kentucky, the Cane Hills phase brackets the A.D. 600-900 interval. This phase was defined by Sussenbach and

Lewis (1987) on the basis of site surveys and the results of excavations at the Marshall site (15Ce27). Additional data on the phase come from Kreisa's (1988, 1989) recent Big Bottoms site survey and from his excavations at the Rice site.

Most Cane Hills villages are small and show sparse midden development. A few, however, are large and possibly contain mounds and public spaces (Kreisa 1988; Sussenbach and Lewis 1987:110). This settlement pattern marks the beginning of a shift toward a site hierarchy that achieved its greatest development in the region after about A.D. 1000.

THE RICE SITE

The Rice site (15Fu18) exemplifies the cultural changes that took place during the Cane Hills phase. According to Kreisa (1988), who recently conducted test excavations there, Rice is the largest (about fifteen hectares) Late Woodland village in the Big Bottoms south of the town of Hickman in Fulton County (fig. 16.1). It differs in several ways from smaller, contemporary sites in that locality. First, Rice may have contained three mounds and possible public spaces (Kreisa 1988:125). Second, the assemblage is more diverse than that of surrounding Late Woodland sites (Kreisa 1988:138–39). The Rice site pottery is dominated by coarse- and fine-paste varieties of Mulberry Creek Cordmarked and Baytown Plain. Red-filmed sherds are rare, and all but a few specimens from this site are tempered with a clay grog (Kreisa 1988:138). Faunal and botanical remains were relatively sparse in the excavated units. Whitetail deer (*Odocoileus virginianus*) and several kinds of nuts dominate the organic remains; one maize (*Zea mays*) cupule was also found in the fill of a pit.

In its size and assemblage diversity alone, Rice shows that there was an emerging differentiation of habitation site types during the Cane Hills phase. This differentiation manifested itself in the apparent concentration of community-based rituals at one or a few villages like Rice, where the necessary spaces, buildings, and other corporate facilities that were fundamental to those rituals were constructed and maintained. The extent to which the differentiation of habitation site functions during this phase was matched by a developing complexity of social and political relations is as yet unknown (Kreisa 1988).

THE LATE WOODLAND COMPONENT AT THE HOECAKE SITE

Across the river in Missouri, the understanding of the Late Woodland, or late Baytown, period archaeology is complicated by the general lack of agreement on the relative ordering and content of the numerous Baytown phases that have been proposed for that region (e. g., Cot-

tier 1977; Hopgood 1969; Lewis 1972; Marshall 1965; Phillips 1970; Williams 1974; Williams 1954). This situation has existed for nearly twenty years and consensus on this part of the regional sequence does not appear to be forthcoming.

The Hoecake site (23Mi8; fig. 16.1) has been the centerpiece of most interpretations of "late" Late Woodland culture in the Cairo Lowland. Hoecake is a large habitation and mound site situated on the outside bank of the old oxbow that defines the Pinhook Ridge locality in Mississippi County (fig. 16.3). It contains Late Archaic through early Mississippi period components, was once dotted with numerous mounds, and covers about eighty hectares. It is considerably larger than the Rice site, but like the latter it is the largest Late Woodland habitation site in its locality.

Most of the published data are from J. Raymond Williams's 1974 excavations in four widely separated portions (Areas I-IV) of the site, and from three log tombs that were uncovered in Story Mound I (Marshall and Hopgood 1964; Williams 1974). Only the Story Mound I is considered here to be Late Woodland. The areas excavated by Williams are clearly part of an extensive early Mississippi period village at Hoecake and are so treated in discussions below.

Of the many mounds that once existed at Hoecake, there are published data for excavations in only two of them, the Story Mound I and the Brock Mound (Marshall 1987; Marshall and Hopgood 1964; Williams 1974). The mound excavations are of interest here because they figure in several recent Emergent Mississippian scenarios (e.g., Marshall 1987; Morse and Morse 1983:215–17). In the Story Mound I excavation, which is the most completely reported of the two mound excavations, three log-lined tombs yielded five potsherds from tomb fill and four potsherds from mound fill (Marshall [1969], cited in Williams [1974:83]). Four of the tomb fill sherds are shell tempered, and the remaining sherds are tempered with clay grog. All of the material is from plain or cord-marked utility wares. A combined sample of wood charcoal that was scraped together from the remains of two of the tombs yielded an estimated age of 1310 ± 130 B.P. (calibrated age of A.D. 677, range of A.D. 620–880; table 16.1).

The Morses (1983:201, 216) offer Story Mound I at Hoecake as one element of support for the beginning of the Mississippian period, as they define it, between A.D. 700 and 800. Marshall, arguing for a somewhat similar interpretation of Story Mound I as the Morses, reports that in this mound, "a red filmed, recurved rim of shell-tempered pottery was found directly associated with typically Woodland tradition log-tomb burials dated at 730 A.D." (1987:160). Marshall's interpretation con-

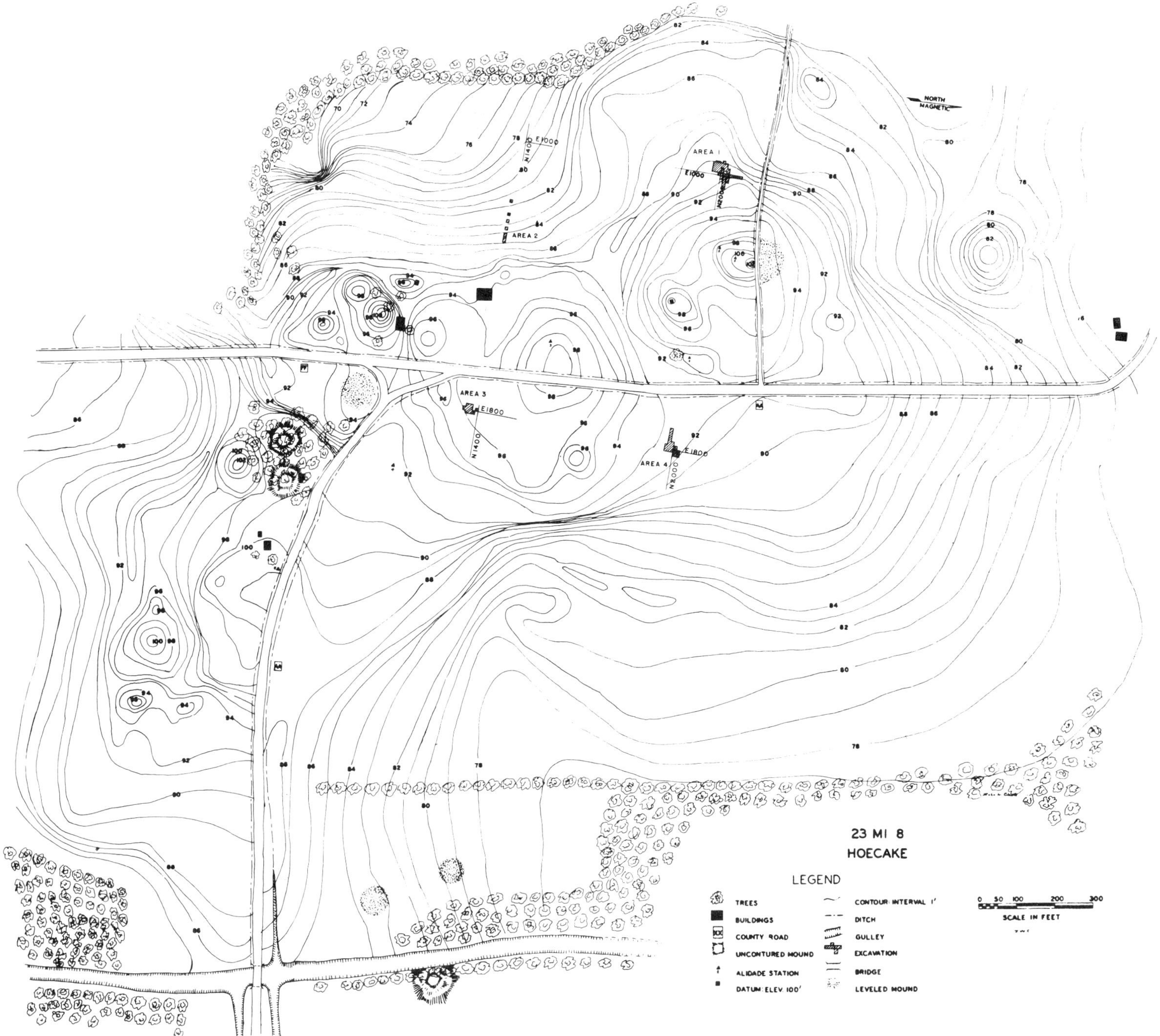
23 MI 8
HOECAKE
LEGEND
TREES
BUILDINGS
COUNTY ROAD
UNCONTURED MOUND
ALIDADE STATION
DATUM ELEV 100'
CONTOUR INTERVAL 1'
DITCH
GULLEY
EXCAVATION
BRIDGE
LEVELED MOUND
0 50 100 200 300
SCALE IN FEET
NORTH
MAGNETIC
AREA 1
AREA 2
AREA 3
AREA 4
E1000
N1400
E1800
N2000

Figure 16.3. The Hoecake Site in Mississippi County, Missouri (from Williams 1974:56)

Table 16.1. Ohio-Mississippi Rivers Confluence Region Early Mississippi-Period Radiocarbon Dates

Sample No.	Context	Dated Material	DCA	ADC	Laboratory Estimate (Yrs BP)	Calibrated Age Range (A.D.)			Reference
						Minimum	Cal. Age	Maximum	
KENTUCKY									
Turk (15Ce6)									
ISGS-1288	Midden	CW	C	C	710 ± 90	1244	(1277)	1379	Edging 1985:15
ISGS-1289	Midden	CW	C	C	700 ± 70	1262	(1279)	1375	Edging 1985:15
ISGS-1323	Midden	CW	C	C	910 ± 70	1024	(1058, 1125, 1156)	1217	Edging 1985:15
ISGS-1324	Midden	CW	C	C	710 ± 70	1259	(1277)	1295	Edging 1985:18
Marshall (15Ce27)									
ISGS-1435	Smudge pit	CW/MC	B	B	910 ± 80	1021	(1058, 1125, 1156)	1221	Sussenbach & Lewis 1987
ISGS-1504	Refuse pit	CW	C	C	1160 ± 70	780	(886)	969	Sussenbach & Lewis 1987
ISGS-1505	House basin	CW	C	C	900 ± 70	1027	(1160)	1221	Sussenbach & Lewis 1987
ISGS-1507	Wall Trench	CW	C	C	790 ± 70	1182	(1252)	1275	Sussenbach & Lewis 1987
Twin Mounds (15Ba2)									
ISGS-1706	Structure	CW	B	B	630 ± 70	1279	(1300, 1365, 1374)	1401	Kreisa 1988
ISGS-1707	Midden	CW	C	C	770 ± 70	1216	(1262)	1279	Kreisa 1988
ISGS-1728	Midden	CW	C	C	1100 ± 130	780	(960)	1030	Kreisa 1988
Wickliffe (15Ba4)									
ISGS-1143	Md. A structure	CW	B	C	830 ± 70	1159	(1221)	1265	Lewis 1986:156
ISGS-1152	Md. A structure	CW	B	C	760 ± 70	1221	(1265)	1281	Lewis 1986:156
ISGS-1171	Midden	CW	C	C	720 ± 70	1252	(1275)	1290	Lewis 1986:156
Beta-12529	Md. A, ref. pit	CW	C	C	520 ± 70	1322	(1414)	1440	Wesler 1985:12
MISSOURI									
Beckwith's Fort (23Mi2)									
UGa-244	Stockade A	CW	A	C	675 ± 70	1268	(1284)	1386	Southard & Cottier 1973:11
N-1250	Stockade A	CW	A	C	835 ± 85	1047	(1219)	1267	Southard & Cottier 1973:11
N-1251	Stockade A	CW	A	C	1090 ± 85	882	(968)	1017	Southard & Cottier 1973:11
N-1253	Stockade A	CW	A	C	1240 ± 145	650	(777)	960	Southard & Cottier 1973:11
N-1252	Stockade B	CW	A	C	995 ± 100	960	(1020)	1160	Southard & Cottier 1973:11
GaK-1681	Structure	CW	E	C	1670 ± 110	240	(391)	530	Williams 1972:200
M-2088	Structure	CW	B	C	420 ± 100	1410	(1448)	1630	Crane and Griffin 1972:
Hoecake (23Mi8)									
GaK-1307	Ref. pit 8	CW	D	C	1530 ± 80	424	(544)	610	Williams 1968:188
GaK-1308	Ref. pit 32	CW	E	C	765 ± 90	1190	(1264)	1284	Williams 1968:188
M-2212/13	Tombs A & B	CW	D	C	1310 ± 130	620	(677)	880	Crane and Griffin 1972:201
Byrd (23Mi53)									
GaK-1683	Structure	CW	C	C	1040 ± 80	897	(999)	1031	Williams 1972:200

Table 16.1. (continued)

Sample No.	Context	Dated Material	DCA	ADC	Laboratory Estimate (Yrs BP)	Calibrated Age Range (A.D.)			Reference
						Minimum	Cal. Age	Maximum	
Hess (23Mi55)									
UGa-147	Refuse pit	CW	C	C	355 ± 75	1445	(1489)	1642	Lewis 1982:53
GaK-1309	Structure	CW	A	C	350 ± 90	1442	(1506)	1648	Williams 1968:167
Bryant (23Mi59)									
GaK-1310	Mound fill	CW	C	C	610 ± 80	1281	(1312, 1353, 1384)	1410	Williams 1968:189
Callahan-Thompson (23Mi71)									
UGa-145	Structure	CW	A	C	480 ± 65	1405	(1431)	1450	Lewis 1982:10
UGa-148	Structure	CW	C	C	570 ± 90	1287	(1398)	1431	Lewis 1982:10

Dated Material	DCA (Degree of Certainty of Association)	ADC (Possible Age Differential Class)
CW – Carbonized Wood	A – Full Certainty	A – Less than 20 years
MC – Maize, cobs & grains	B – High Probability	B – About 20 years to 100 years
	C – Probable	C – More than 100 years
	D – Reasonable Possibility	D – Unknown; Not reported
	E – Unknown; Not reported	

The radiocarbon age estimates were calibrated by the CALIB (Version 2.0) program using the ATM20.14C bidecadal data set (Stuiver and Reimer 1986). CALIB implements the calibration of Stuiver and Pearson (1986). No laboratory error multiplier was included in the calibration. The calibrated age(s) are given in parentheses for each estimate and are bracketed by the minimum and maximum of the 1 sigma range.

flicts directly with the contextual information that was published with the Story Mound I date in the journal *Radiocarbon*: "No direct assoc. with burials in tomb, but some unintentional debris was found in tomb. Assoc. with Mulberry Creek Cord-Marked, Baytown Plain, clay- and shell-tempered sherds, and a shell-tempered loop handle. . . . Samples combined; M-2212 from Tomb A and M-2213 from Tomb B" (Crane and Griffin 1972: 173). Marshall's date of A.D. 730 for this sample comes from inadvertently misreading the *Radiocarbon* entry.

Interesting though the Story Mound I tombs may be, it is doubtful that one radiocarbon date based on a sample from unknown contexts in two different features has much interpretive value. Similarly, there is as yet no basis for asserting that the four shell-tempered sherds found within the tombs were in primary context. It is far more likely that the few sherds in the tombs were redeposited from more recent components at Hoecake, either when the tomb roofs collapsed, as Williams (1974:83) suggests, or through some other noncultural process. Regardless, this mound appears to be a Late Woodland period construction. It does not offer direct evidence of the beginning of the Mississippian cultural tradition in this region beyond that of additional support for the inference of site type differentiation and possible social differentiation during the Cane Hills phase.

This brief review of the Late Woodland evidence makes several points. First, basic cultural changes that are collectively characterized as Mississippian (Griffin 1985), were present in the study region by the end of the Late Woodland period. The incipient development of new village functions is a particularly noticeable change, viewed archaeologically. However, unlike Rice and Hoecake, most large Late Woodland villages that assumed new settlement system roles continued to be important settlement loci throughout the Mississippi period, and their remains are found beneath the middens of most Mississippian towns in the region. Second, the excavated Hoecake mounds for which there are published reports appear to be Late Woodland features, but the excavated habitation areas are part of an early Mississippi period component. With these points in mind, we now turn to a description of the earliest Mississippian phases.

Communities in Transition (A.D. 900–1100)

Around A.D. 900, cultural changes were occurring in the basic fabric of societies in the southern Midwest and the Mid-South. Those changes are reflected markedly in food remains, site plans, domestic architecture, and pottery assemblages. Presumably wishing to highlight these important culture shifts, some researchers (e.g., Bareis and Porter 1984; Kelly 1985; Marshall 1987) treat the time interval between roughly A.D. 800 and 1000 as the Emergent Mississippian period. This concept is not adopted here because it only serves to solidify further certain stage-like qualities of the chronological framework.

Elsewhere I have argued that large, fortified towns with mound and plaza complexes emerged in the study region during the James Bayou phase and had strong roots in local Late Woodland cultural developments (Lewis 1983, 1986; Sussenbach and Lewis 1987). After undertaking an extensive investigation of selected "second-order communities" (Kreisa 1988), my interpretation of these data has necessarily changed somewhat. Although it is clear that planned communities, which often incorporated mounds and public spaces into their design, were present in the region as long ago as the terminal Late Woodland period, those communities appear to have differed qualitatively from towns in the sense that this term is used below. They are more appropriately called "villages with mounds" (Kreisa 1988). Available data suggest that prehistoric towns did not develop in the region until after approximately A.D. 1000, or the late James Bayou phase.

THE MARSHALL SITE

The Marshall site (15Ce27), a village site of about eight hectares on the Mississippi Valley bluffs in northwestern Carlisle County (fig. 16.4), offers the best available excavated information on early Mississippi period components on the Kentucky side of the Mississippi Valley (Sussenbach and Lewis 1987). Test excavations have demonstrated that the major occupations span the James Bayou and Dorena phases (roughly A.D. 900–1300). There is evidence of mounds, other earthworks, and possibly a plaza (Sussenbach and Lewis 1987), but the nature and age of those features are largely unknown. Wall-trench structures and buildings with individually set wall posts, both types of which were constructed in shallow basins, have been excavated, but none have been completely exposed. Here, as elsewhere in the region during the Mississippi period, there is a stratigraphically delineable, but gradual change in domestic architecture from walls comprised of individually set posts to walls formed by posts set in narrow trenches or footings. There is con-

siderable temporal overlap of both wall styles during the Mississippi period.

The economic base of the James Bayou phase community at Marshall was maize horticulture, hunting, and gathering. Faunal preservation at the site is relatively poor, and few animals other than whitetail deer, fish, and turtles have been identified in the collection (Kreisa 1987). Maize cupules, kernels, and glumes were found in nearly all of the flotation samples, and the economic importance of this cultigen is demonstrated by its archaeological abundance in diverse contexts. Gathered plant foods included hickory nuts, pigweed, smartweed, and the American lotus (Woodard 1987).

The material remains are of interest because few early Mississippian sites comparable in age to Marshall have been excavated in this or adjacent regions. The ceramic assemblage is dominated by plain and cordmarked utility wares in jar and bowl forms (Sussenbach and Lewis 1987). The types include Mississippi Plain, Baytown Plain *var. Mayfield*, Mulberry Creek Cordmarked *var. Sandy Branch*, Old Town Red, Kimmswick Fabric Impressed, Bell Plain, Crosno Cordmarked, and Wickliffe Thick, in that order of frequency. The pastes of the utility wares range from a relatively fine-tempered grog (Baytown Plain *var. Mayfield* and Mulberry Creek Cordmarked *var. Sandy Branch*) to the coarse shell of Mississippi Plain. Most of the Baytown paste sherds are unusually hard to sort because they exhibit attributes of both Mississippi Plain and Baytown Plain as those types have been traditionally defined (e.g., Phillips 1970). The sorting difficulty is felt to reflect the changes that ceramic technology was undergoing throughout the Lower Mississippi Valley and adjacent regions during the early Mississippi period (Sussenbach and Lewis 1987).

Artifacts other than potsherds are often sparse on Mississippian sites, and Marshall is no exception. The chipped-stone assemblage is dominated by hoe fragments and bit resharpening flakes. Projectile points, bifaces, scrapers, gravers, picks, and other tools occur, but at relatively sparse densities.

Comparable ceramics, tools, structures, and other features that may date to the James Bayou phase have been found in early Mississippian context at many of the late prehistoric town sites of this region (Lewis 1986). It appears that large villages, which served diverse social and economic functions, were a basic component of the early Mississippi period settlement system. The roots of those communities lie ultimately in Late Woodland villages at the same site loci, which are most closely approximated today by sites such as Hoecake and Rice.

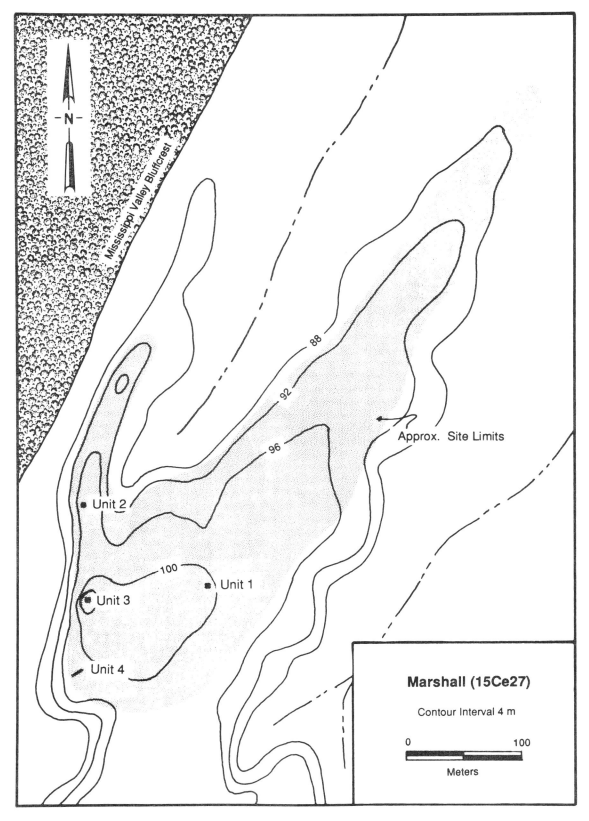

Figure 16.4. The Marshall Site in Carlisle County, Kentucky (from Sussenbach and Lewis 1987:42)

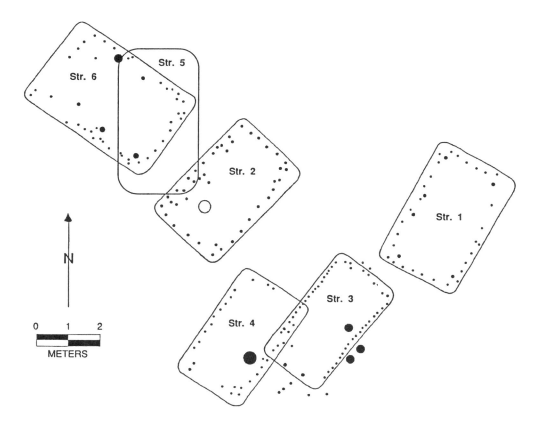

Figure 16.5. Early Mississippi Period Structures at the Hoecake Site (approximate reconstruction based on Williams 1974:60–63)

THE MISSISSIPPIAN COMPONENTS
AT THE HOECAKE SITE

Across the river in the Cairo Lowland, most of the available information on the early Mississippi period comes from the Hoecake site. It is reasonable to assume that at least some of the Hoecake mounds were constructed during the Mississippi period occupation, but as remarked in the preceding section, the two mounds for which we have published excavation reports do not appear to be early Mississippi period earthworks.

The Hoecake village spans James Bayou and at least part of the Dorena phase, or roughly A.D. 900–1200. Williams (1974:82–88) excavated ten houses, two burials, and numerous other features in four separate areas covered by those components. All of the structures are rectangular, single set post houses that were built in shallow basins (fig. 16.5). Each building also has the same essential floor plan and associated features. Few of the house floors have interior hearths or pits, a pattern that is shared with the excavated structure segments at the Marshall site. Partial superpositioning of the house floors occurs, but one does not find the development of a thick

midden comparable to that of Marshall. Given the absence of wall-trench structures, it is tempting to infer that the excavated portions of the Hoecake village, except possibly for Area III, were not occupied as late as the Marshall site. This speculation cannot be assessed without additional excavations at Hoecake.

The economic focus of this large village appears to have been comparable to that of Marshall. The faunal remains include the same species that are common in Mississippian sites throughout the study region (Williams 1974:81). Little information is available about the botanical remains. Williams notes "a small amount of maize was identified as having ten and 12 rows. Persimmons, acorns, pecans, wild grapes, and unidentifiable tubers were also recovered" (1974:81). I suspect that the evidence for maize and many other small macro-remains would be much greater had flotation sampling been in widespread use when Williams worked at Hoecake.

The ceramic assemblage is dominated by Mulberry Creek Cordmarked, Baytown Plain, Larto Red Filmed, and Mississippi Plain. Varney Red, Wickliffe Thick, and Crosno Cordmarked are important minor types (Williams 1974:76–78). Williams does not comment on the extent to which the Hoecake sherds were hard to sort into existing types, but some measure of the frustration that he may have felt can be seen in the relatively large number of sherds that are treated in separate descriptive categories (Williams 1974:76–78). As Sussenbach and Lewis learned in their analysis of the Marshall site assemblage, the "transitional" characteristics of much of the early Mississippi period pottery in this region are often felt most acutely when one attempts to sort the material into existing historical types.

Other fired clay artifacts from the early Mississippi period component include disks, trowels, "marbles," and the stopper-like clay lumps known as "Kersey Clay Objects" (Williams 1974:79). The stone tools include projectile points, scrapers, abraders, adzes, manos, debitage, and a hoe fragment (Williams 1974:81).

Marshall and Hoecake are among the few large communities occupied between A.D. 900 and 1000 for which there are excavated data. They were sedentary agricultural villages in which there appears to have been little status differentiation. Unlike most other major contemporary settlements, which were continuously occupied throughout much of the Mississippi period, the primary settlement locus of the Marshall site community apparently shifted a few hundred meters south to the next bluff spur (i.e., to the Turk site, 15Ce6) during the Dorena phase. As a result, the large, thick James Bayou midden at Marshall was not greatly disturbed or eroded by centuries of subsequent occupation at the same site locus. Hoecake, too, was preserved basically because the focus of settlement shifted elsewhere, perhaps to the south along Pinhook Ridge or east to the Crosno locality near Belmont Landing.

Mississippian Towns and Other Trends (A.D. 1100–1300)

By A.D. 1100 there is unequivocal evidence for the development of towns in the study region. In this context the term *town* refers to a large, planned community, usually greater than three hectares, in which platform and other mounds flank an open public space or plaza and which, in turn, are surrounded by dense midden accumulations that mark the habitation areas. Towns are usually situated in commanding locations along the Mississippi Valley bluffs and terraces and on prominent extinct natural levees of the Mississippi and Ohio rivers. Regardless of their setting, these sites often show archaeological evidence of defensive palisades and earthworks. There is also extensive evidence of differential social statuses and roles, including the existence of an elite sector of society, which appears to have had the dominant political voice in the community, preferential access to choice living areas, and other perquisites (Kreisa 1988). Most other aspects of the settlement system and economic organization of Dorena phase (A.D. 1100–1300) communities are comparable to those of the James Bayou phase.

Dorena phase ceramic assemblages generally show low frequencies of Mulberry Creek Cordmarked, Baytown Plain, and Kimmswick Fabric Impressed relative to older components and low frequencies of the Mississippian incised types (e.g., Matthews Incised, O'Byam Incised) relative to younger components. Among the few incised sherds that one finds in Dorena components, the combination of modes recognized as O'Byam Incised *var. Adams*, particularly on flanged rim bowls, appears to be temporally diagnostic. Sherd frequencies of Bell Plain, a fine-paste ware, show a gradual increase from the James Bayou phase to the end of the aboriginal occupation of this region. Plates are rare in Dorena components. Vessel form diversity may increase slightly during the Dorena phase, but this generalization suffers from our currently inadequate understanding of temporal patterning in Mississippian vessel assemblages.

Excavated components include Marshall (Sussenbach and Lewis 1987), Turk (Edging 1985), several of the Mound A construction episodes and at least part of the village area at Wickliffe (Lewis 1986; Wesler and Neusius 1987), portions of Twin Mounds (Kreisa 1988), Adams (Lewis 1986; Lewis and Mackin 1984), Beckwith's Fort (Southard and Cottier 1973; Wilkie 1988), Crosno (Williams 1954), Hearnes (Klippel 1969), and possibly Area III at Hoecake (Williams 1974). These components are all towns or large villages. There are few available excavation data for Dorena phase hamlets, but this will soon change with the completion of Lynne Wolforth's (1989) report on the Running Slough (15Fu67) test excavations.

THE TURK SITE

Turk (fig. 16.6) is a good example of a Mississippian town that was occupied throughout the Dorena phase. It covers about two and one-half hectares of the dissected Mississippi Valley bluffcrest in northeastern Carlisle County (Edging 1985; Loughridge 1888). It is a compact site relative to other towns in the region. Its small size appears to be simply a function of available building room on the ridge upon which it was constructed rather than early Mississippi period cultural preferences for small towns. The site's center is dominated by the mound-and-plaza

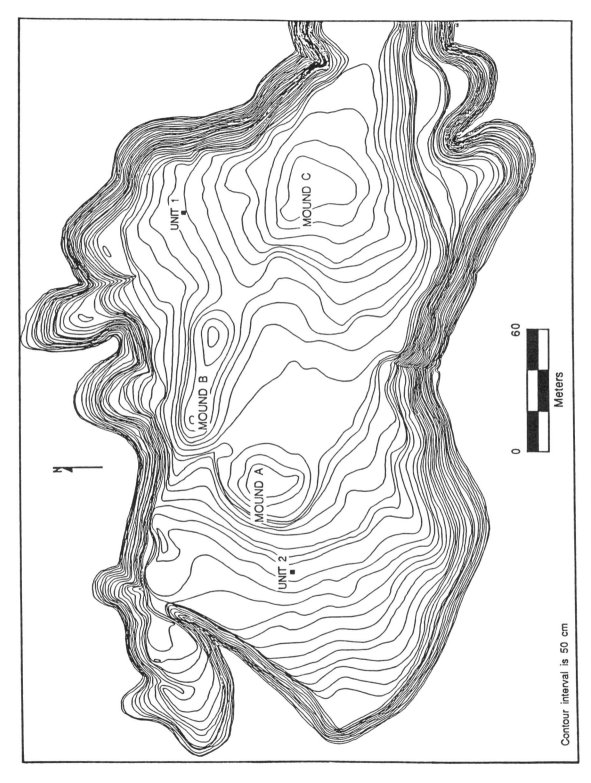

Figure 16.6. The Turk Site in Carlisle County, Kentucky (from Edging 1985:9)

arrangement of public space that is so typically associated with the concept of Mississippian. In the late 1800s several smaller mounds could be identified outside of the area bordering the plaza (fig. 16.7), but they have long since been destroyed. It is not known whether Turk was fortified by stockades; regardless, the topographic characteristics of the ridge spur provided natural defensive advantages.

Test excavations have revealed that the major site occupation began during the Dorena phase and continued into the early Medley phase. All of the site excavations, except for Clarence B. Moore's (1916:506–7) pit in Mound C, have been limited to domestic contexts near the plaza. The midden ranges from one-half to one meter deep and contains a complex stratigraphic record of wall-trench house construction episodes, refuse-filled pits, and fire basins. Excavations at Turk have been too limited in their horizontal extent to permit the investigation of spatial patterning.

Throughout its existence, the economic base of the community was maize horticulture, hunting, and gathering. Staple animal food species included the whitetail deer, raccoon, and wild turkey (Kruger 1985). As at the neighboring Marshall site, maize is ubiquitous in the midden and it was clearly of great economic importance to the community's stability. Gathered plant foods included hickory nuts, goosefoot, marsh elder, and persimmons (Edging 1985).

The ceramic assemblage is dominated by Mississippi Plain and, to a much lesser extent, Bell Plain. Wickliffe Thick, Kimmswick Fabric Impressed, Old Town Red, and O'Byam Incised *var. Adams* also occur in Dorena contexts. Most Matthews Incised and O'Byam Incised *var. O'Byam* sherds at the Turk site have been found in the upper half of the midden and therefore appear to be associated most strongly with the Medley phase component. Baytown Plain and Mulberry Creek Cordmarked compose only one-tenth of one percent of the 1984 collection. Given the low frequencies of the latter types, it is inferred, first, that the Dorena phase occupation represents the oldest major archaeological component on this ridge spur, and second, that the early Mississippi component at Turk marks a settlement shift from the nearby Marshall site (fig. 16.1), which appears to have been abandoned by the early Dorena phase.

Most of the nonceramic artifacts at Turk are hoe fragments and bit resharpening flakes. Adz fragments, abraders, projectile points, and flake tools dominate the rest of the assemblage (Stelle 1985).

THE BECKWITH'S FORT SITE

Across the river in the Pinhook Ridge locality of the Cairo Lowland, investigations at Beckwith's Fort, or the Towo-

sahgy State Historic Site as it is now called (fig. 16.1), have yielded a great deal of information on this important Mississippi period town. The site has been under sporadic development by the Missouri Division of Parks, Recreation, and Historic Preservation for more than twenty years, and most of the archaeological investigations have been guided by this agency's desire to enhance the interpretive potential of this well-preserved town site in the event that it is opened to public visits.

Beckwith's Fort (fig. 16.8) is situated on the natural levee of a long-abandoned Mississippi River channel. It consists of extensive village debris, mounds, and associated plaza and was once almost entirely enclosed by a low earthwork and stockades. The fortified part of the site covers about eight hectares, but the village debris, including the remains of houses, pits, burials, and midden deposits, extends well beyond those limits (Cottier and Southard 1977:237–42; Wilkie 1988:18–46).

As described by Thomas, although somewhat inaccurately, the earthwork that surrounded the town core (fig. 16.9) was "nearly a semicircle in form, with the open base facing the swamp or bayou. . . . The height and width of the wall vary at different points, in some places being as low as 2 feet, while at others it is fully 8 feet high; in some places it is not more than 15 feet wide, while at others it is 30 or more. . . . Running close along the outside of the wall is a ditch varying in width from 20 to 40 feet, and in depth from 4 to 8 feet" (1894:186–88). Little obvious evidence of the earthwork and associated ditch exists today, beyond vegetation marks that stand out in some aerial photographs of the site (Cottier and Southard 1977:244–45). Parts of the southern fortification lines, however, have been traced archaeologically (Cottier and Southard 1977). It is also possible that the "pottery pavement" recently delineated by Wilkie (1988:60–78) outside of the fortification line zone on the south side of the site is part of the ditch, long since filled in, that was noted by Thomas (1894) nearly a century ago.

The Mississippian town at Beckwith's Fort developed out of a Late Woodland (late Baytown) village at this location (Cottier and Southard 1977:265; Healan 1972; Wilkie 1988:47–59). Thus settlement appears to have been continuous from the Late Woodland throughout much of the Mississippi period. The Dorena phase occupation appears to have been a major component. However, Wilkie's (1988:60–78) recent investigation of the "pottery pavement" feature demonstrates that a Mississippian occupation continued into the Medley phase (A.D. 1300–1500). Excavations of the "pottery pavement" yielded a Mississippian ceramic assemblage that includes O'Byam Incised *var. O'Byam*, varieties of Matthews Incised, two painted sherds, and other decorated material typical of post–A.D. 1300 assemblages in this region.

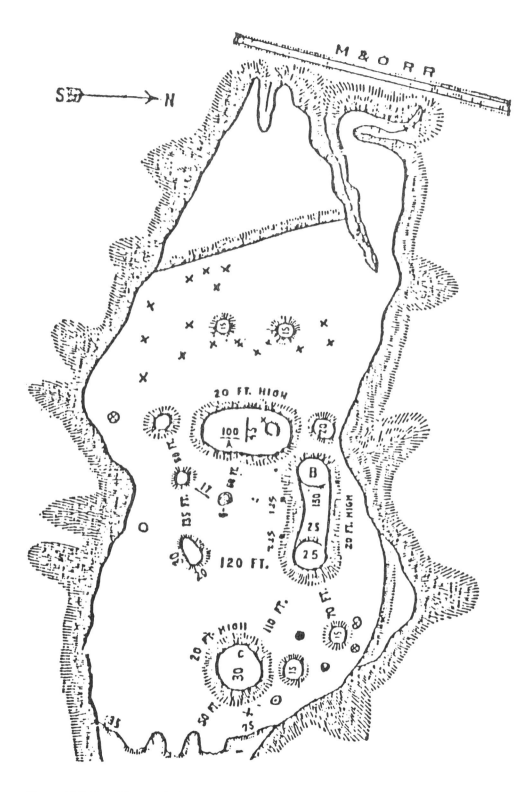

Figure 16.7. Late Nineteenth-Century Sketch Map of the Turk Site (from Loughridge 1888:182)

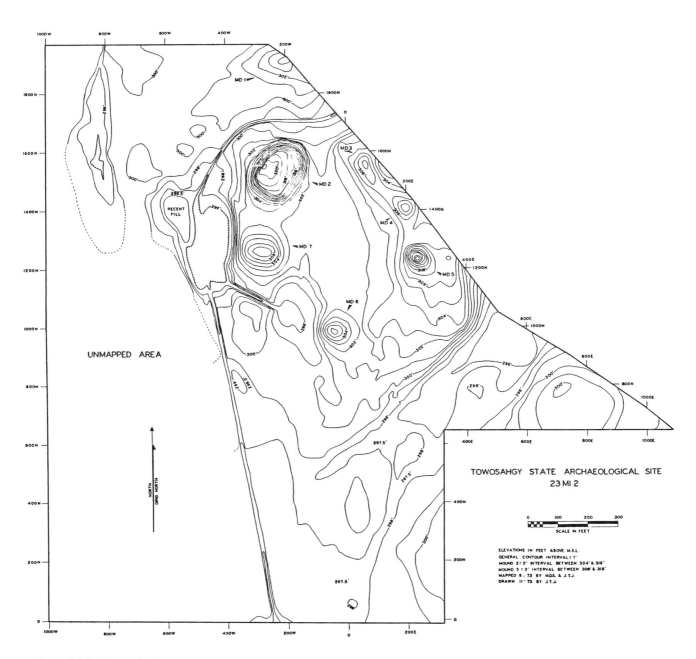

Figure 16.8. The Beckwith's Fort Site in Mississippi County, Missouri (Used with the permission of the Missouri Department of Natural Resources, Division of Parks, Recreation, and Historic Preservation)

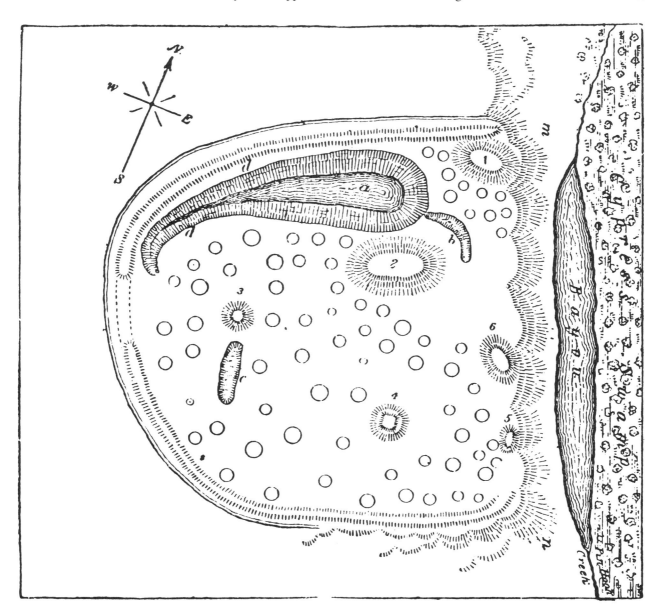

Figure 16.9. Late Nineteenth-Century Sketch Map of the Beckwith's Fort Site (from Thomas 1894:185)

With one exception the excavated structures, inside as well as outside of the fortification lines, are wall-trench houses set in shallow basins (Cottier and Southard 1977: 237–42, 252–62; Wilkie 1988:18–46; Williams 1968: 84–85). The exception is a small, single set post structure that measures about 2.4 meters on a side and is contained within the fortification (Cottier and Southard 1977:260). A wall-trench structure recently excavated by Wilkie (1988:32) included Mississippi Plain, Mulberry Creek Cordmarked, Kimmswick Fabric Impressed, Wickliffe Thick, and Bell Plain sherds in the basin fill; Wilkie interprets the structure as an Emergent Mississip-

pian building. The published data for the other excavated structures are too general to warrant classifying them to a given Mississippi period phase.

The subsistence economy of the Beckwith's Fort inhabitants was comparable to that of the Turk site inhabitants. Little can be added to this general statement because food remains continue to be among the least studied aspects of the archaeology of this town (cf. Lewis 1974). Faunal data are particularly sparse. The early Mississippi period house basin excavated by Wilkie (1988: 123–26) contained maize kernels and cupules in each of the processed samples; small quantities of hickory and walnut nut shells, and a few seeds of persimmon, grape, passionflower, goosefoot, and maygrass also occur. Many of these plants are also mentioned by Southard and Cottier (1973:13-22) in the description of later Mississippi period features at Beckwith's Fort.

In summary, the archaeological perspective of the early Mississippi period from A.D. 1100 to 1300 is currently biased for towns, the most archaeologically visible part of the Dorena phase settlement pattern. There is no evidence that the settlement pattern was strongly nucleated relative to other Mississippi period phases. Dorena phase villages and hamlets are known, but except for Running Slough

and a few other sites they have not yet been investigated.

Town economies were based on maize agriculture, supplemented by the cultivation of other plants, hunting, and gathering. Social ranking existed, but there are as yet few details about the political organization of these chiefdoms (Kreisa 1988). Warfare, or perhaps more accurately the perceived threat of war, was common, if one is to judge from the time and energy that was invested in stockade construction, the erection of earthworks, and the modification of the natural defensive characteristics that had figured in the siting of each town.

The Late Mississippi Period (A.D. 1300–1700)

The remaining centuries of prehistory span an era during which the inhabitants of the study region reached their greatest achievements, as judged by modern archaeologists. It was a time during which towns and major villages grew to their greatest extent, both in the size and complexity of their public precincts and in the size of the associated habitation areas. These centuries also marked the greatest social complexity of Mississippian groups in the region. I have examined the archaeology of these centuries in detail elsewhere (Lewis 1989a, 1989b).

Most of the final Mississippian cultural developments occurred during the Medley phase (A.D. 1300–1500). Components are well represented at towns, including Adams (Lewis 1986), Sassafras Ridge (Lewis 1986), and Beckwith's Fort (Wilkie 1988); major villages, among which are White (Sussenbach and Lewis 1987) and Twin Mounds (Kreisa 1988); and hamlets, including Running Slough (Wolforth 1989) and Burcham (Kreisa 1988).

The archaeological record for the subsequent Jackson phase (A.D. 1500–1700) is sparse. A few components have been identified, for example, Callahan-Thompson and Hess in the Cairo Lowland (Lewis 1974, 1982) and

the large Story Mound village (23Mi510) at Wolf Island (Williams 1968; it is not the same site as the Story Mound I at Hoecake that was excavated by Richard Marshall and James Hopgood). The existence of other components has been inferred at Adams and Sassafras Ridge (Lewis 1986), but additional fieldwork is necessary to test those inferences.

The working hypothesis to explain the relative scarcity of Jackson phase archaeological evidence is that the region was decimated by the primary and secondary effects of introduced European diseases, probably during the sixteenth century (Lewis 1989a). Those effects are of such magnitude that for much of the Jackson phase there does not appear to be an identifiable archaeological record in the study region. It is inferred that the catastrophic events associated with the initial contacts of native Americans with Europeans or their diseases spelled the death knell of most Mississippi period communities in the Ohio-Mississippi rivers confluence region (Lewis 1989a) and effectively truncated the archaeological record until the early eighteenth century.

Regional Comparisons

Given the study region's location at the confluence of two major river systems, its position at the northern end of North America's greatest valley, and its place as the first major expanse of floodplain downstream from the American Bottom, one might reasonably expect it to have been a major force in prehistoric cultural developments throughout much of the midcontinent. Many archaeologists have looked at this region in that light, but inherent in most of those interpretations is an underlying tentativeness that reflects our uncertain grasp on the archaeology of this region.

Several factors have contributed to this situation. First, most excavations have been test pits or have been very limited in scope, and the available data reflect this bias —there is fairly good stratigraphic control on portions of the regional sequence and quite a bit of research time and effort has been invested in culture historical problems. There are few data on site layout, the functional organization of space within communities, mounds and their use histories, and other information of a primarily spatial nature that can come only from the extensive, horizontal exposure of sites. There have also been some excellent spatial studies based on the analysis of surface collected data (e.g., Healan 1972; Stout 1985, 1987), but those projects necessarily yield more general results than excavations. Second, despite the archaeological visibility of the region, alluded to above, relatively few research projects were undertaken in this region until recently. Third, a disturbingly large proportion of these archaeology projects did not reach the publication stage. Fourth, the financial infrastructure of research funding largely created, and certainly perpetuates, these biases. Put into terms more directly relevant to this chapter's scope, there is a rich history of research in this region, but our understanding of its archaeology is still rudimentary in most areas.

With these caveats in mind, let us now turn to comparisons of cultural similarities and differences between the Ohio-Mississippi confluence region and the American Bottom of west-central Illinois and the Ohio Valley from its mouth upstream to southern Indiana.

THE AMERICAN BOTTOM

Late Woodland communities of the Cane Hills phase and the Patrick phase and early Emergent Mississippian phases in the American Bottom appear to have shared a common settlement pattern shift to larger habitation sites than was typical of older sites, and to the incorporation of public spaces into community layouts. Platform, or substructure, mounds may have also been a part of Cane Hills phase villages (e.g., the Rice site [Kreisa 1988]), but the spatial and functional relationships between the mounds and the public spaces have yet to be examined; it cannot be assumed a priori that these relationships were the same as those of the Mississippi period groups. Kreisa (1988:138) also notes general similarities between some of the vessel form and lip decoration modes of the Rice site ceramics and those of the essentially contemporaneous Patrick phase (Kelly, Finney et al. 1984:119-25) sites in the American Bottom.

Interregional similarities are more marked and detailed for the interval A.D. 900–1100, which is called the James Bayou phase in the study region and is split up over several late Emergent Mississippian phases, the Lohmann phase, and part of the Stirling phase in the American Bottom. As demonstrated by excavations at Marshall and Hoecake and several of the FAI-270 Project excavations (Mehrer 1988), domestic architecture trends in the two regions follow one another closely. American Bottom Emergent Mississippian structures are described as "relatively small rectangular structures with posthole foundations and clearly definable patterns of floor plan. Interiors tended to be free of isolated postholes and small pits" (Mehrer 1988:93). This also describes most Hoecake

structures (Williams 1974) and the stratigraphically oldest structures at Marshall (Sussenbach and Lewis 1987). The general absence of large storage pits from the floors of domestic structures older than roughly A.D. 1000, a pattern delineated in the American Bottom by Mehrer (1988: 131), is also shared between the two regions.

One American Bottom archaeological trend that emerged from the results of the massive FAI-270 Project (Bareis and Porter 1984; Mehrer 1988), but is not reported from the Ohio-Mississippi rivers confluence region, is the Emergent Mississippian village arrangement of houses around courtyards. As I noted in the introduction to this section, given the scale of past research projects, large phenomena such as village plans are not yet available from the study region. Nevertheless, I will be surprised if future research there does not show a village/hamlet layout pattern comparable to that of the American Bottom.

Material culture similarities are less striking than those related to settlement patterns and the use of space. During the Late Woodland and part of the Mississippi period, the ceramic assemblages of the study region probably shared more attributes with pottery from the Tennessee-Cumberland region and the Lower Mississippi Valley than with American Bottom region pottery. Although the level of interaction does not appear to have been intense, the flow of ideas, styles, and technological changes in pottery making between the American Bottom and the study region were continuous and sustained. This interaction seems to be particularly evident in mortuary context. For example, two of the shell-tempered jars interred with Burial 2 in Area III at Hoecake, which is probably the most recent of the delineated components, have inflected contour outlines (Williams 1974:75); one specimen also appears to have a rolled rim. These attributes are common to Lohmann and Stirling phase vessels (Milner et al. 1984). A similar specimen was found in association with a hooded bottle in a late James Bayou/early Dorena phase burial mound, called the Effigy Rabbit site (40Ob6), in the Reelfoot Lake region of the northwesternmost corner of Tennessee (Schock 1986:45-48).

Given consideration of the differences in local environments, the general pattern of early Mississippi period subsistence trends were the same in the two regions.

Both regions also experienced the development of social and political complexity during the Mississippi period. The latter developments manifested themselves in archaeological patterns that are often readily interpreted, such as mortuary treatment differences, domestic architecture, and the location of elite dwellings with respect to public spaces. Research has also begun to delineate more subtle effects of those developments. For example, Mehrer (1988:135) suggests that the increased frequency of storage facilities placed inside structures during the Stirling phase may reflect larger changes in the fabric of social relations and statuses in Mississippian society; a comparable change in the location of storage facilities can be traced in the study region.

The developmental trajectories of the two regions appear to have diverged significantly after A.D. 1300. This is not to say that there ceases to be identifiable evidence of interregional interaction (e.g., the obvious stylistic similarities between O'Byam Incised *var. O'Byam* in the study region and Wells Incised in the American Bottom), but the nature of this interaction must have changed. Mississippian settlements appear to have reached a maximum of architectural development in the study region between A.D. 1300 and the early 1500s. At this same time in the American Bottom, Cahokia declined in regional importance and the settlement pattern apparently experienced major changes (Milner et al. 1984:186).

In summary, there is abundant evidence of relatively close interregional interaction between the communities of the American Bottom and the study region during the Late Woodland period and much of the Mississippi period. The intensity of this interaction is essentially that which one might expect given the characteristics of each region's location and the intervening distance. The American Bottom does not appear to have been the source of a strong unidirectional flow of political, religious, or economic influence into the Ohio-Mississippi rivers confluence region. Conversely, the study region does not appear to have provided strong external influences on the prehistoric cultures of the American Bottom.

THE OHIO VALLEY

The Ohio Valley provided the other major northern, or at least midwestern, influence on cultural developments in the Ohio-Mississippi rivers confluence region. Detailed Ohio Valley comparative data are available from two regions, the Black Bottom in southern Illinois and southwestern Indiana. Brian Butler provides an excellent overview of the Black Bottom sequence in chapter 15 and I cannot pretend to improve on his examination of those data. My comments are limited to points directly related to early Mississippi period interregional comparisons.

The Mississippi period sequence for the Black Bottom stems from Southern Illinois University's archaeological field school research at small Mississippi period sites and the University of Chicago's research at the Kincaid site, a major Mississippi town. The basic sequence is described by Butler (chap. 15), Cole et al. (1951), Muller (1978a, 1986a), and Riordan (1975).

There are unmistakable similarities between the James Bayou phase and the Douglas phase that was recently outlined by Muller (1986a:159-62; see also Butler, chap. 15) and tentatively dated at A.D. 850–1000 (Muller 1986a: 185). The latter phase has not yet been the focus of detailed investigations, but Butler's (chap. 15) and Muller's (1986a) reviews suggest that there may be evidence in the Black Bottom of the construction of Douglas phase platform mounds, changes in ceramics that are comparable to that described above for James Bayou, and other examples of a shared developmental trajectory.

The succeeding Jonathan Creek phase (A.D. 1000–1100) was defined to encompass much of the lower Tennessee-Cumberland valleys and part of the lower Ohio Valley, including the Black Bottom region (Butler, chap. 15; Clay 1979; Muller 1986a). Its content is also largely equivalent to that of the James Bayou phase in the Mississippi Valley (Lewis 1989b). Planned towns, some of which were permanent communities that were occupied for decades, if not centuries, appear to have formed one aspect of the settlement pattern. The economic base of those communities was agriculture, supplemented by hunting and gathering. The ceramic assemblage at the Jonathan Creek site (15Ml4), which provided the basis for the original definition of the phase (Clay 1963:113–20; Clay 1979:119–20), is dominated by Mississippi Plain, Kimmswick Fabric Impressed, and Bell Plain. Later incised types, such as O'Byam Incised and Matthews Incised, were absent in the sample used by Clay as a basis for defining the phase. Other Jonathan Creek components also contain small quantities of McKee Island Cordmarked, which is comparable to the type Crosno Cordmarked in the Mississippi Valley, and Old Town Red (Allen 1976; Clay 1979:118).

The Angelly phase, which is dated to A.D. 1100–1300 (Riordan 1975:174) or A.D. 1200–1300 (Butler, chap. 15), appears to be the Black Bottom region counterpart of the Dorena phase and shares many of the same characteristics. Nevertheless, it is difficult to be more than tentative here since, as with the Douglas phase, there are few published data concerning the content of the Angelly phase. Viewed from the perspective of the confluence region sequence, the ceramics associated with the three small components mentioned briefly by Butler (in chap. 15) tend to support his thirteenth-century placement of those sites (i.e., late Dorena phase in the confluence region).

To move farther upstream to southern Indiana, the Mississippi period portion of the regional sequence is currently dominated by the Angel phase (Green and Munson 1978; Honerkamp 1975; Power 1976), which brackets most of the period from A.D. 1050 to 1450. The origins of the Angel phase and its relationships with the preceding Yankeetown phase are incompletely known. This is mostly a function of what little is known about Yankeetown (Blasingham 1953; Redmond 1986). The Angel phase's most visible component is the Angel site itself, a town and ceremonial center, but the major dimensions of the settlement pattern have been delineated (Green 1977; Green and Munson 1978; Munson 1983). The Angel settlement pattern contrasts with that of the Caborn-Welborn phase, a protohistoric temporal unit that slightly overlaps it in time and space, by having a single major community, the Angel site, located more or less at the hub of a region comprised of small villages, hamlets, and farmsteads (Green and Munson 1978:294). This contrasts with the Ohio-Mississippi rivers confluence region in which hamlets, villages, and towns formed the basic habitation site types by the late James Bayou phase.

The extensive Angel site excavations demonstrated that the typical domestic structure was a wall-trench house with a hip roof (Black 1967:497–98). Some of the houses were constructed in shallow basins, but this architectural feature does not appear to have been as common in this part of the Ohio Valley as it was in the Mississippi Valley.

The Angel phase ceramic assemblage consists predominately of undecorated, shell-tempered utilitarian wares. Red filming and negative painting are the principle decorative techniques (15,207 sherds), but are present on less than one percent of 1.8 million sherds from the Angel site (Kellar 1967:472–73). Fabric-impressed salt pan sherds are slightly less common than the painted and filmed material. Shell-tempered cordmarked sherds, which would be classified as Crosno Cordmarked in the Ohio-Mississippi rivers confluence region, are a minor ware at Angel. As in the James Bayou and Dorena phases in the Mississippi Valley, incised vessels are rare (Kellar 1967:468) and offer a strong contrast to the ceramic assemblages of the Medley and Jackson phases in the study region in which incised decoration may occur on roughly three to five percent of the sherds in a collection.

The economy of Angel phase communities was, as in other Mississippian communities throughout the Mid-South, based largely on maize agriculture, hunting, and gathering. The few published data on faunal and botanical remains from Angel phase sites demonstrate that whitetail deer, squirrels, raccoons, and wild turkeys were common food animals, and that maize, beans, pumpkins, and possible other plants were cultivated (Kellar 1967: 481–83).

In summary, there appears to have been cultural interactions between the study region and the Mississippian cultures of the lower Ohio Valley that were of the same nature and intensity as those described earlier for the study region and the American Bottom. Similarities with the Black Bottom were quite close throughout the Mississippi period. It would be surprising were this not true for two reasons. First, the regions lie in close proximity to one another. Second, the Black Bottom is located at the mouths of the Tennessee and Cumberland rivers, and close cultural ties existed between the study region and the Tennessee- Cumberland valleys during late prehistory. Similarities with the Ohio Valley sites in southern Indiana appear to be far more generalized during the Mississippi period, but this impression may be partly a function of the temporally flattened perspective that is currently forced on the southern Indiana data by the "monolithic" Angel phase.

Conclusions

The early Mississippi period in the Ohio-Mississippi rivers confluence region was a time of sweeping cultural changes, the magnitude of which was overshadowed later only by the catastrophic cultural changes of the sixteenth century. One of the many roots of these changes was the emergence of maize agriculture as a significant component of aboriginal economies. This change appears abruptly when viewed from an archaeological perspective; there is little evidence of the exploitation of this plant in Cane Hills phase sites, and it is ubiquitous in the middens of sites that are only one hundred or two hundred years younger. It was probably a far more gentle change when viewed in the context of individual lifetimes.

Interacting with the economic changes were shifts in the nature of habitation sites, their functions, and their organization. Viewed over time, early Mississippi period domestic architecture shows the same general trends in the study region and in the American Bottom; the domain of those changes may have encompassed even more regions of the Midwest and Mid-South. New habitation site types developed, some of which, the towns and villages with mounds in particular, show evidence of intensive occupation for centuries if not for most of the period.

An elite sector of society developed. The impact of this fundamental change in the fabric of society manifested itself in many of the material aspects of Mississippian society, aspects as different as the design of the mound and plaza complexes of towns and the selection of household locations for bulk storage.

There were strong ties to the American Bottom region, which are identifiable in Late Woodland communities, and which continued until about A.D. 1300. During subsequent centuries, the strength of those ties diminished significantly, but they did not cease. Likewise, there exists

solid evidence of sustained interaction with the major
Mississippian communities of the lower Ohio Valley. The
latter ties were maintained with less deterioration after
A.D. 1300 than those with the American Bottom; this is
particularly true of an enduring cultural relationship that
existed between the Ohio-Mississippi rivers confluence
region and the Tennessee-Cumberland region.

ACKNOWLEDGMENTS

This chapter is based partly on a paper presented at the Forty-
eighth Annual Meeting of the Society for American Archaeology, Pittsburgh, and on an overview of the Mississippi period
in Kentucky that I prepared for inclusion in the state preservation plan. I thank Thomas E. Emerson, Paul P. Kreisa,
Susan M. Lewis, Charles B. Stout, and Lynne M. Wolforth for
their helpful comments and criticism.

PART FOUR

Observations

17

Mississippian Sociocultural Adaptation

JON MULLER
JEANETTE E. STEPHENS

Mississippian studies continue to suffer from the use of concepts that are no longer consistent with redefined archaeological goals. The term *Mississippian* itself is a classic example of some of these difficulties. Originally defined as a ceramic complex (Holmes 1903), it has come to be used by some as a descriptive term for nearly all of the Late Prehistoric societies of the Eastern Woodlands while others have attempted to restrict the concept to only a few of these societies. The main goal of this paper is to reaffirm an adaptive approach to the societies of the Eastern Woodlands. If *Mississippian* is to have conceptual utility, we must identify the adaptive features that may be considered to be Mississippian and reassess the terminology applied to those societies of the Late Prehistoric period.

Most of the Late Prehistoric societies of the East shared similar features: (1) local population densities were increasing in relation to available resources; (2) production was predominantly domestic and each coresident group was largely responsible for its own maintenance; and (3) the environments that had the greatest population densities were also those with the greatest degree of economic (and social) risk. Although many societies with these features adapted to their environments in similar

fashion, considerable diversity in responses still existed. Certain societies, often referred to as "core" Mississippian (e.g., Griffin 1978a), shared common features; but treating these features in a trait-list fashion confuses the problem of the "peripheral" societies that did not have quite the same features.

Much of the confusion is the result of assuming a priori that Mississippian was a widespread "culture," in the anthropological sense. In such an argument, identification of Mississippian features and discussion of its development becomes a matter of comparison of similarities and differences among societies that are already assumed to be connected historically. The implicit expectation is that Mississippian had a unitary origin and a single developmental history that can be "discovered." The problem here is to suggest a strategy for approaching the development of Late Prehistoric societies without simply assuming the culture-historical unity of the area. The sections that follow discuss the roots of the terminological problem, present some suggestions for critical adaptive features of Mississippian societies in the Lower Ohio and Central Mississippi valleys, and apply these adaptive concepts to some brief examples.

Concepts of Mississippian

HISTORICAL BACKGROUND

Bruce Smith has discussed the history of this approach in his "Mississippian expansion" paper (1984b) so that detailed discussion of the historical development of the Mississippian concept is not necessary here. However, a brief summary can restate the critical issues. Smith has

documented the implicit assumption of a Mississippian "heartland" and migration from such a supposed center of development. In addition, a few scholars defined the area of origin more broadly, seeing Mississippian in a areal view as part of an area cotradition, in effect (Smith 1984b).

The term *Mississippian* was first used for a ceramic tradition and the presence of shell tempering, globular vessels, and other ceramic features still looms large in assigning complexes to a Mississippian or non-Mississippian status. In the 1930s, Thorne Deuel and his co-workers defined a Mississippi pattern in the Midwestern Taxonomic System that added a number of additional traits to the list of defining criteria for Mississippian (Deuel 1935; Cole and Deuel 1937:35–38, 207–23; McKern 1939; see also Griffin 1943). These traits included rectangular houses, substructure mounds, triangular projectile points, and discoidals, to name only a few.

The difficulties in the core area concept, however, became increasingly apparent as time passed: "The chief difficulty, perhaps, has been our inability to nucleate the culture geographically" (Willey and Phillips 1958:164). Although this difficulty was, perhaps, seen as the result of insufficient archaeological research, the real problem was the fallacious assumption of a single origin and the behavioral unity of cultures sharing the Mississippian traits (e.g., Smith 1984b). As archaeologists moved away from the implicitly culture-historical Midwestern Taxonomic System, however, the assumptions of unity and origin that were embedded in the concept of the Mississippi pattern continued to be accepted implicitly. Because these concepts were not challenged, discussion of Mississippian tended to be channeled into debates on shared traits. Archaeological complexes continued to be assigned to taxonomic categories on the basis of presence of key traits (such as shell-tempered pottery), with little attention given to their organizational and adaptive features. By the late 1970s, new ways of describing Mississippian were developed, but before these are considered, it is important to assess the utility of the traits that have formed the basis of so much Mississippian research.

MATERIAL TRAITS

Traits such as shell-tempered pottery and mound building do not form a fixed assemblage of functional or adaptive connection. As Goldstein and Richards (chap. 10) point out, they are inadequate per se to define a society as Mississippian or not. It should be clear that the supposed Mississippian traits are portions of highly diverse and even distinct cultural systems that need not be related for historical reasons. The technology of shell-tempered pottery has been studied at length (e.g., Morse and Million 1980; Steponaitis 1983). Vessel forms are clearly related to function and technology (e.g., Braun 1983). Decoration reflects self expression and social coding (e.g., Wobst 1977; Braun and Plog 1982) The specific reasons for the adoption of shell tempering and these other features by a particular group of potters can be seen to relate to the materials used and the uses of the pots. With the

possible exception of ritual wares, the attractiveness of this Mississippian ceramic technology and the timing of its acceptance can be seen to be related to cultural circumstances that may have had little or nothing to do with key political and social developments.

There is no reason to believe that any of these regions during late prehistory was socially isolated from other regions. Generalized exchange relationships that had been established during the Late Archaic persisted even through the supposed decline of Late Woodland times. Moreover, the making of utilitarian pottery was quintessentially domestic. Accordingly, it becomes very difficult to see how the acceptance of shell tempering and certain vessel forms in utilitarian pottery can be seen as implying massive influence from other areas or dramatic sociocultural reorganization. Domestic pottery styles and technological traditions can be assumed initially only to relate sociologically to the groups of domestic pottery producers. Arguments that these stylistic groupings have broader sociological significance must be supported by some kind of justification for that claim. The same point applies to each of the technical or stylistic features that have been used to define not only local archaeological phases, but to erect the whole superstructure of a Mississippian "culture." Technological similarities across an area may reflect not only influence, but a whole panoply of sustained, intermittent, direct, or indirect contact; exchange of objects; actual population movements; and simple, common generalized technical knowledge. The time has come to insist that those who postulate "influence" of one locality upon another on the basis of a few sherds out of thousands go further and test specific models of these relationships against the total cultural context.

Because individual traits are themselves parts of adapting cultural systems, their presence or absence in a location is not merely a matter of historical accident or connection. It seems likely that most potters in the Southeast were "aware" of shell tempering by A.D. 1000; most people also probably knew about the possibility of substructure mound construction. Yet only some societies actually adopted these so-called traits. Explanations of Mississippian development that are couched in terms of contact and influence remain untested largely because of the failure to provide bridging argumentation to show how and why these material traits are connected with social and cultural change. The articulations of ceramics and other artifact classes with entire social systems are not intuitively obvious or necessary. Nor are these traits sufficient to define units of study. Reliance on these criteria in the traditional manner results in an inductive and particularistic approach that limits us to consideration of cultural historical types. If we fail to treat so-called traits as the "tools" they were and we fail to understand their use, we are condemned to fruitless quibbling over categories. If the specific tools that we have used as index fossils for Mississippian were not important as components in an adaptation to social and natural environments, can we justify using them to define large-scale cultural entities?

MISSISSIPPIAN ADAPTIVE NICHE

Smith (1978) presents a broader basis for the definition of Mississippian in his model of the "Mississippian adaptive niche." This ecological approach attempts to define the systematic basis for Mississippian developments. Smith proposes

> that the term "Mississippian" be used to refer to those prehistoric human populations existing in the eastern deciduous woodlands during the time period A.D. 800–1500 that had a ranked form of social organization, and had developed a specific complex adaptation to linear, environmentally circumscribed floodplain habitat zones. This adaptation involved maize horticulture and selective utilization of a limited number of wild plants and animals that represented dependable, seasonally abundant energy resources that could be exploited at a relatively low level of energy expenditure. In addition, these societies depended significantly upon an even more limited number of externally powered energy sources (1978:486).

While this model certainly touches upon the main characteristics of a Mississippian adaptation, it is weakened by taking a traditional view of which societies are "Mississippian" and then attempting to find common factors to explain the similarities and variations among diverse, supposedly related groups. As Griffin comments in his foreword to the volume (1978a:xv), a number of the societies included in Smith's *Mississippian Settlement Patterns* (ed. 1978) "by his definition, are not Mississippian cultural complexes." Even so, we generally agree with Smith (1978:480) that "Mississippian" should be reserved for a "set of boundary conditions," defined as "a cultural adaptation to a specific habitat situation, and as a particular level of sociocultural adaptation" (1978:480). We would second Griffin, however, by noting the implication that some of the traditional Mississippian complexes do not meet these and other adaptive criteria for Mississippian status. These issues are expanded below.

In addition, some tendency exists to view Mississippian in a rather optimistic light, stressing low energy expenditures and dependable resources. We wish to emphasize that this apparent low cost and dependability are relative assessments. Mississippian and other Late Prehistoric adaptations involved trade-offs that were not entirely positive. In order to receive the benefits of living in a

Mississippian society, individuals and households had to accommodate a number of external controls and interferences. Any explanation of Mississippian adaptation and development has to identify reasons why individual productive units would sacrifice their autonomy to central control (see Chayanov [1966] for a much misunderstood, but still critical assessment of the relationships of domestic producers to central authority).

MISSISSIPPIAN ORGANIZATIONAL MODELS

Models that focus on Mississippian as an organizational system provide additional useful concepts for the definition and explanation of Mississippian. Christopher Peebles and Susan Kus (1977), through a Moundville example, present a model of Mississippian as a system of organization. This approach emphasizes the information processing and regulating functions of societal organization. It goes hand-in-hand with ecological symbiosis and energy flow as basic systemic processes in the functioning of human societies. Peebles and Kus (1977:434) define Mississippian as having a system of hierarchical organization. They argue that Mississippian had a ranked form of sociopolitical organization in which "chiefs" processed information at a supralocal level and transferred it through ritual programs. This is an extremely useful extension of the Mississippian concept. Peebles and Kus argue, in part, for this function of Mississippian organization by rejecting economic redistribution (à la mode Service 1975). This follows, in part, from a discussion of the likely potential for domestic economic autonomy, similar to Smith's assessment of cost and dependability. However, Service-like models of redistribution are not the only possibility for elite functioning in adaptation (cf. Brumfiel and Earle 1987:20; Isbell 1978; Halstead and O'Shea 1982; and Muller 1978a). Peebles and Kus offer well-constructed correlates to test for social ranking at Moundville. Vincas Steponaitis has further developed this approach (e.g., 1978).

Other organizational models emphasize interregional exchange systems, as in John Kelly's concept of Cahokia as a "gateway center" (chap. 4) and in Guy Gibbon's discussion of Cahokia as a "theocratic state" with an extensive "extractive-symbiotic exchange network" (1974, chap. 11). Both of these models suggest external exchange (or "trade") as a mechanism for establishing and maintaining social complexity at Cahokia and also for the Mississippianization of outlying societies through their participation in the Cahokia exchange network. Gibbon (chap. 11) proposes that ceremonial overlays were used to maintain the exchange relationships among the "Ramey state" and its exchange partners. Leaving aside the question of whether Cahokia was a "state," a usage we be-

lieve to be ill-founded (cf. Sears 1968), the Kelly and
Gibbon models offer only partial explanations of a systemic whole. In addition, there seems to be a component
of post hoc attempts to explain the presence of certain
artifact classes (such as shell-tempered pottery or pyramidal mounds) in "peripheral Mississippian" areas. Not
only are such artifact classes weak evidence of influence,
much less domination, but the exchange system that is
given such prominence is itself treated in isolation from
its cultural matrix. Why and how did exchange come to
be so significant a factor in these societies? Like any other
kind of "tool," exchange is a behavior that has to be examined in terms of its overall adaptive role within each
participating society.

In general, ideological systems, as important as they
may be, are superficial overlays of more "deep-structure"
organization of energy and information flow. It seems un-
satisfying intellectually to suppose that societies simply
"took on" a Mississippian lifeway; that Mississippian
spread by budding; or that expansion of Mississippian
was by domination of local populations, without explaining how and why these events occurred. The supposed

superiority of Mississippian needs to be made explicit in
each case. The irregular timing and variation in results of
Mississippianization throughout the Southeast does not
support the core and periphery models implicit in the
Age-Area hypothesis (see Smith 1984b). Rather, some
individual societies in the area made a combination of
adaptational responses to local and areal ecological challenges and developed systems that archaeologists have
come to call Mississippian. As natural and social circumstances varied over the area, we may expect to find
corresponding gradations in the responses that individual
societies made to these conditions. Although it should be
obvious, it bears repeating that differences and similarities can result from other than culture-historical relationships. As reemphasized in ethnoarchaeological studies,
material assemblage similarities and differences can result
from independent solutions to specific adaptive problems
according to the kinds of information available to the
actors (e.g., Binford 1978, 1981). In this light, the variability seen in late prehistory can be assessed in terms of
the organization and adaptation of these societies rather
than in terms of culture-historical types.

Mississippian Sociocultural Adaptation

Mississippian was primarily an adaptive response to
floodplain environments based on a combination of particular natural and sociocultural conditions. These conditions included sedentism, relatively high population
density in critical floodplain environments, a degree of
social and environmental circumscription, a localized
mode of production, and the development of hierarchical sociopolitical organization. These criteria should
not be conceived of as a trait list, but as adaptive processes by which some societies produced systems that
may be called Mississippian. Each of these conditions
is discussed in this section. Social systems that faced
different social and natural circumstances diverged from
Mississippian to the degree of those differences.

ECONOMIC BASE

Late Prehistoric economies were based on systems of
local food production. The productive base involved the
extraction of floodplain and riverine plant and animal resources (e.g., Larson 1970; Muller 1978b; Peebles 1971;
Smith 1978). Neither the environments nor the specific
production systems, per se, were markedly different from
those of Terminal Late Woodland groups in the same
localities. Nonetheless, Mississippian (and other Late
Prehistoric) organizations arose out of the difficulties that
terminal Late Woodland lifeways had in dealing with

their new production systems (see also Muller 1988). The
floodplain environments involved in these developments
were those with warm habitat species such as cypress,
tupelo, and cane.

Many economically important resources were available
locally in sloughs, backwater areas, and on bottomland
ridges (as at Kincaid: Cole et al. 1951; Muller 1978a,
1986a; Davy 1982). Wild resources were important, first
in attracting intensive human settlement, and then in
providing more-or-less stable food resources so long as
population density remained relatively low. As discussed
below, however, these wild resources are subject to natural fluctuations in yield, and the environments in which
they occur are very prone to perturbations. Under these
circumstances, maize horticulture provided a *resource of
advantage*. A resource of advantage is one that provides
critical adaptive advantage, but it need not necessarily
be one that was the primary item of production. For
example, a product may be essential to survival in the
annual schedule, even though its use may extend over
only a short period, and it may make up only a small
percentage of the total resources exploited in that year.

Maize stands as a fair candidate for status as a resource
of advantage because of its *relative* reliability of yield
compared to native resources, and because it is capable
of efficient production intensification. Increased labor investment in maize production was much more likely to

result in an increase in yield than was a corresponding labor increase in hunting or gathering. Greater work investment in wild foods and native domesticates seems unlikely to have been rewarded to the same degree as a similar investment in maize field labor. If a farmer worried about dangers of too low production of maize under worse-case projections, he or she could undertake to increase yields by increasing acreage. In many regions, maize was capable of being double cropped (although in separate fields, see Hudson 1976:305). Maize production was generally augmented with squash and later beans; but wild foods, especially nuts, remained important.

The percentages of total diet contributed by different production strategies are difficult to determine from archaeological evidence, but Late Prehistoric subsistence in the Southeast and Midwest depended upon a broad spectrum of resources. Even so, the total number of species exploited may have been less than in earlier times. Potential maximum yields of resources are not as important as their reliability is. Variation in yields, resistance to unfavorable environmental conditions, and other such factors are more important in determining the extent to which a given resource gave an advantage to those exploiting it.

Economic production at the *domestic* level was largely similar in technology across the East during the Late Prehistoric period and was predominantly based on the homestead/farmstead residential unit. Diverse and rich resources were *potentially* available to a substantial degree in each farmstead's immediate environment. Each household farming unit produced its own horticultural crops and gathered a wide range of wild resources. This pattern of production has been described in a number of different localities (e.g., Muller 1978a; Peebles and Kus 1977; Smith 1978). To some extent, however, the apparent economic autonomy of the domestic production unit and the rich resources potentially available directly to it may be true only of the best years. This local productive base was not necessarily a positive force that eased subsistence stress for the society as a whole. Local or regional cooperation is not likely to emerge directly from domestic production units in the absence of some compelling pressures (see Chayanov 1966). Other cultural and natural circumstances such as population growth or imposition of controls from outside the domestic level seem necessary to explain the undisputed involvement of these small, domestic producers in larger political and economic systems. In the development of pristine hierarchical systems such as those of Mississippian, external assertion of control is implausible, and some form of internal pressures seems to be required to explain the surrender of local autonomy. Intensification of production systems produces its own contradictions by restricting

alternative economic options at the same time that selective pressures encourage cooperation among producers. The very advantage given by a localized and increased-scale production system also allows survival of larger populations. However, the more persons that depend on a horticultural system, the more difficult it is to switch to alternative food sources in the event of crop failure. The number and kinds of alternative strategies in any given social and natural dimension are restricted under such circumstances. The limits set by local "autonomous" production may require integration and thus restrict autonomy on the society-wide level.

POPULATION AND SETTLEMENT

Mississippian was one of several possible organizational responses to the opportunities and problems of restricted floodplain settings. One of the key conditions promoting a distinctive "Mississippian" response was probably population density, although it was certainly not the only important factor. Muller (1978a, 1986a, 1987), however, has argued for very low populations for major Mississippian sites. Absolute population size should not be confused with the question of population density. The determination of population density and "pressure" is essentially a measure of mobility, circumscription, and productive technology, not of absolute size. For example, hunter-gatherer populations at one person per square kilometer may be severely crowded, depending upon the resources available to them *at their level of technology*. An area that may fail to support 5,000 persons using hoe horticulture may easily support 30,000 persons with animal-drawn plows.

Up to Late Woodland times in the Eastern Woodlands, it seems likely that most production groups had a number of seasonal alternatives provided by low population and mobility. If one resource failed, movement to alternative resources was possible. By Terminal Late Woodland (Emergent Mississippian) times, these alternatives seem to have been choked off by the relatively permanent settlement of critically important river bottom areas. This seems to have occurred as a result of restrictions in mobility through population growth. With more people competing for the same resources, competition shifted from a "scramble" to an "interference" mode (McNaughton and Wolf 1973:293; Muller 1987): "As the predictability of the resource increases, there will be selection for interference if energy spent on reducing the probability of use of the resource by other individuals enhances the reproductive output of the genotype. . . . There may also be natural selection for interference if the resource is superabundant, but resource quality differs" (McNaughton and Wolf 1973:294). Thus interference competition, either on a community or individual level, would be expected to encourage territorial behavior (McNaughton and Wolf 1973:294).

Of course, Terminal Late Woodland populations were small, even by Mississippian standards, but they were still large enough to have established relatively sedentary settlements in the lowland resource localities. Sedentism in these localities would give such settlers advantages in competition with other communities but would also restrict their ability to exploit resources outside the bottomland. Sedentism, population growth, and the establishment of a more predictable resource base are all major factors in the formation of Mississippian systems. Sedentary life encourages the use of resources within a small area around the base settlement, while domesticated plants encourage sedentary settlement in a feedback loop that is difficult to escape, once entered. A trade-off occurs in obtaining a more controllable and predictable resource base. Sedentary horticulturists such as Mississippian groups are tied to specific localities. Vested interests are established in specific parcels of land due to the energy invested in crop production and the monitoring necessary to achieve dependable yields. In addition, individual productive units (such as farmstead households) are circumscribed by other groups using nearby locations in a similar manner. As population increases, range and mobility in general are restricted. Also, sedentism itself, in addition to more fruitful production systems, seems to encourage population growth. Thus sedentary societies may find themselves continually pressured to intensify production to feed growing numbers of people. As an aside, it is worth noting that sedentism, *coupled with population growth*, in earlier periods did produce results in some regions (e.g., Poverty Point, Adena, even Hopewell itself). The key to understanding particular developments, or lack thereof, is in the combination of sedentism, population density, and production technology rather than in any of these factors alone.

Maize, one of the major eastern resources of advantage, itself encourages residence in fixed locations. This is especially true if two maize crops are grown annually. Under these circumstances, pressure on wild resources in the region can be substantially increased, creating dependence on cultivated crops or on distant resources controlled by others. Within such a system, coordination of effort is needed to even out inequalities in yields in areas controlled by individual economic units. Cooperation among units also enhances the safety of crops and access to more localized resources. Where land is available, such a system may grow by spreading out over the landscape, and only a fairly low level of management is needed to coordinate socioeconomic activities. As Carneiro (1970) has stressed, however, limitations

on productive territories can severely limit horizontal growth. Faced with a growing population, such a system is propelled into either increasing its production through improved (or intensified) technology or into increased organizational development (i.e., hierarchical growth) in order to maintain itself. Again, circumscription alone is not the only factor; social organization and technological capabilities affect the response of a particular society to problems of this sort.

In some geographical regions of the East, however, the resources of advantage that provided the adaptive margin may well not have been resources that favored sedentism. In climates that were marginal for aboriginal horticulture, such as the northern Midwest, crops would provide less reliable (and potentially less "intensifiable") resources for large populations. Environmental vagaries would favor greater flexibility in subsistence adaptation and less dependence on one particular resource mode. This would favor greater flexibility in group size, mobility, and settlement organization. Hierarchical sociopolitical organization would be less advantageous than more egalitarian systems that would allow fissioning of social groups in times of stress. Although hierarchical systems would be of as much utility in such areas as elsewhere in terms of controlling information flow, the lack of potential for production intensification would not favor their development as systems of domination. Partly sedentary societies are simply not as amenable to control as are more fixed communities. Mobile groups regularly change their size, affiliation, and location in response to shifts in local conditions, and this makes them politically unstable and difficult to control. Even today, virtually the first step taken by any central authority in dealing with high-mobility peoples is to attempt to settle them.

The term *Mississippian* seems to have its greatest utility in describing societies that developed in environmental zones that favored high degrees of sedentism for maize horticulturists. In environments that were more risky or in which alternative resources were easily available, the benefits of mobility would have outweighed the benefits of centralized coordination and control. In these circumstances, "core" Mississippian societies grade into other forms. Any particular society might show many specific Mississippian traits without integrating these into a system that is meaningfully a Mississippian adaptation.

RESOURCE DISTRIBUTION

All societies employ distribution strategies as a means of managing "commodity" flow. In some societies, these distribution systems evolve into centralized, hierarchical systems that can be characterized as redistributive. Early discussions of redistribution emphasized controlled exchange of different kinds of specialized local production (Service 1975; Peebles and Kus 1977). However, distribution systems of this supposed classic form are rare, if they occur at all in prestate societies (Earle 1977; Muller 1984, 1987). In more developed chiefdoms, at least, chiefs seem to use their power to mobilize resources for their own support (Earle 1977, 1978, 1986). In other, often less-developed, societies, it seems that such systems function primarily as means of reducing inequalities at the level of production (Engels 1878; Ford 1974; Isbell 1978; Muller 1978a, 1987). In order to test for models of redistribution as a means of economic coordination, three important questions must be addressed: (1) did significant inequalities exist in production; (2) what kind of distribution existed; and (3) what was the relationship between hierarchies and distribution?

(1) INEQUALITIES AND NEED. As shown in many different localities (e.g., Butler 1972; Clay 1976; Lewis 1974; Muller 1976, 1978b, 1986b; Smith 1974), a diverse range of resources was potentially available from the more-or-less immediate environs of a given Mississippian site. Work in the Black Bottom of the Ohio River has shown the high potential quality of the diet available from immediate resources (Blakeman 1974; Davy 1982; Rudolph 1981). On the face of it, the individual Mississippian productive unit seems to have had the potential for a high degree of economic autonomy. Individual communities seem to have had the capability to feed themselves and to have had little need for broader-scale distribution or redistribution. But was this really so?

The basic productive capabilities of known Mississippian societies were not actually as self-sufficient as might be concluded from Peebles and Kus's (1977) discussion nor so abundant as naive readings of Smith's (1978) subsistence lists might suggest. Although the best years must have been very, very good, the fact is that the kinds of resources that Mississippian people depended on are highly risky. Even though horticulture provides opportunities for intensification and more predictability, this economy is best practiced in environmental zones that are subject to unpredictable, but common environmental stresses such as flooding. In addition, as indicated, Mississippian peoples were still making heavy use of wild foods—most notably nuts—which vary in yield from one year to the next and from one locality to the next (see Ford 1974). Perfectly ordinary variations in rainfall, temperature, and other environmental conditions would have thus produced random, but common periods of hardship. The test of any adaptation is not how it operates in good conditions, but how it responds to minimal conditions. If stresses occur often enough, human societies will create and maintain systems of social security even in times of plenty. Even if such systems come into use only every few years, their

origins and development have to be sought in relation to their causes, not in the functioning of such systems in years of plenty. This creates a difficult situation for testing. How frequent must stresses be to maintain social responses? It seems likely that small-scale, nonliterate societies would be most likely to maintain protection systems that respond to events that occurred within decades as opposed to those that occurred only once every generation or two. In addition, the temporal relationships between cause and effect here are bound to show some lag. Even so, the model suggests that hierarchical development should be greatest in areas with continuing stress or pressure resulting from either social or environmental causes. Depending upon the specific responses, developing societies may show either improvement or at least stabilization of conditions, continued population growth, or both.

There have been relatively few biological studies of Late Prehistoric populations, and many of these have been done for localities that are arguably different in adaptation from the "core" Mississippian societies of the lower Ohio or Mississippi valleys. Even so, the evidence suggests that measures of potential reliability and richness of food resources may not reflect accurately the real situation on the producer level. Many Late Prehistoric peoples seem to have been subject to fairly common biological stresses (Blakely 1971; Cook and Buikstra 1979; Milner 1982; Powell 1988). Interpretation of the causes of such stresses is difficult, but dietary problems seem likely to have played either a direct or indirect role in the problems. The model presented here suggests a pattern in developing Mississippian societies of irregular, but not infrequent stress markers by comparison with Late Woodland societies of ca. A.D. 600. With the development of a system of more effective distribution, production, or both, some amelioration through central risk management might occur. However, persistence of population growth could easily continue the pattern of stress and social response, leading to still greater centralization. In localities with either a greater natural margin or a greater technological edge, individual physical conditions should improve and political development would be expected to stabilize.

(2) KINDS OF MISSISSIPPIAN DISTRIBUTION. Service's (1975) classic model of redistribution postulated local production of localized resources followed by centralized control of distribution. As noted, this model has not seemed to be very useful in assessing chiefdom-level distribution of goods (Earle 1977, 1978, 1986). The model has been applied, inappropriately, to Mississippian contexts. Long before the publication of *Mississippian Settlement Patterns* (Smith, ed. 1978), Lewis H. Larson, Jr. (1970) and Christopher Peebles (1971) had noted that

the locations of major Mississippian centers were often in ecotonal locations (cf. Davy 1982:78). At first, many took this to be an indication that Mississippian societies functioned as Service had suggested in his model: "Sedentary chiefdoms normally inhabit areas of variegated natural resources with numerous ecological niches requiring local and regional symbiosis" (1975:75).

It now seems more likely that the location of pristine chiefdoms in regions of high diversity reflects the basically domestic and unspecialized nature of production in these societies, rather than diverse production specialization requiring "symbiosis." Specialization is much more likely to be a result of already existing economic and social control than it is to be the cause of it (see Muller 1984, 1986b, 1987). Nonetheless, settlement classifications based on a presumed "specialist" production system have outlasted the theory that gave birth to them. Sites have repeatedly been classified as supposed specialized, extractive stations merely because they happen to be located near some resource (Muller 1979, 1984, 1986b). On closer examination, most such sites turn out to be ordinary Mississippian farmsteads. In a few cases, specialized sites exist at localized resources such as salt springs or chert outcrops, but without necessarily implying producer specialization (Muller 1984).

As Peebles and Kus (1977) argue in rejecting classical redistribution, elites distribute information through regulation and exchange. As they point out, such features as ranking, hierarchical settlement organization, production organization, and other features serve to mark the "chiefly" organization of Moundville society. Peebles and Kus (1977:441–42) further argue that Mississippian localities were autonomous in production. They find no evidence of Service's kind of redistribution in material goods, so they rule out goods redistribution as a factor in the organization of Moundville chiefdoms. They resolve the seeming paradox of clear political nonautonomy and economic autonomy by falling back on a sort of data-redistribution model. Although they may have been premature in abandoning all economic explanations of the interdependence of Moundville producers, there can be no doubt of the value of recognizing that control of different kinds of cultural information can be as important as control of the goods themselves. It would be a mistake, even so, to suggest that the degree of difference in information control between different ranks in these Mississippian societies would have been substantially greater than the corresponding differences in access to basic materials. Such differences would probably not have been as great nor as important as in more complex societies.

In general, a model of redistribution, under the coordination of elites, based on goods sharing in times of scarcity as well as ongoing maintenance of these relationships by information sharing may be proposed for simple ranked societies like Mississippian. Actual survival-critical exchanges of goods may not have taken place frequently, but if they were needed even once in a decade or so, the social costs of maintaining such a system could be justified to those participating in the system. Even under conditions of generalized reciprocity, it might also be expected that those who were more often donors than receivers of goods would achieve higher rank than others. As Muller has proposed elsewhere (1987), the statuses and activities that are likely candidates for "promotion" are the developing institutions of sharing and cooperation to be found in Late Woodland societies. Such features as donor-sponsored festivals could easily become ritual events under the control of elites. As elites developed, the forms of more egalitarian social organization persisted and were transformed.

One major role of elites is their responsibility for sponsorship of major festivals and other ritual activities (see Peebles and Kus 1977; Seeman 1979a for archaeological discussions). Such festivals often have been interpreted as stimulating social solidarity, but it is clear that substantial amounts of goods may be redistributed, in the general sense, through these events (e.g., Seeman 1979b). Although many ritual events commonly occur in times of greatest abundance, as Veletta Canouts (1971, 1986) and John Walthall have argued (1985), this is not necessarily an argument against their functioning as social security measures in the averaging out of temporal or spatial fluctuations. We have already seen that it is unlikely that the social security nets were triggered in most years. The redistributive effects of festivals can be overemphasized, but they should not be denied altogether. Public ceremonies establish and facilitate social connections that affect more than just those events. In addition, the privileged access of ritual sponsors to ritually valuable goods also tends to reinforce their elite status. Ceremonies and the social relations in which they are embedded are also a means of transferring information about how to respond to social and environmental risks. The ceremonies themselves often present allegorical or metaphorical justifications for maintaining relationships.

(3) MISSISSIPPIAN ORGANIZATION. Thus it may be suggested, as is implicit in many earlier discussions, that Mississippian was based on a kind of redistribution of goods and information, manifested in a form of hierarchical organization, and characterized by social security or risk management. The actual means of producing food and other goods is not adequate to explain these developments. Across the East, the basic subsistence pattern was similar enough to create difficulties in making the subsistence pattern per se "explain" the differences that existed in social organization. It is important to recog-

nize that many Woodland societies did not share in these developments. However, in considering any "Mississippian mode of production" characterizing the early stages of development of ranked societies in the Eastern Woodlands, analysts have to deal with societies that still had a basically domestic mode of production but, nonetheless, had social ranking with some degree of central coordination (see analogous systems described by Meillassoux 1964, 1981). Organizational aspects are as important as any other features in understanding Mississippian adaptations. The hierarchical structure of these societies is intimately linked with their production and distribution systems and is not mere "superstructure."

The societies that became Mississippian in this sense were those that depended on variable yield resources and occupied high-risk environments like floodplains. Even in these societies, reciprocal exchange of information and goods at the domestic level was probably adequate in most years. But given predominantly local (rather than collective) production, coordination and management at a supralocal level was necessary. This need resulted in the development of elites. Specifically, the growth of elite groups within these societies can be predicted to be related to (1) the density of population in relation to local resources; (2) variability in yields that might favor continuity in cooperation; (3) the degree to which individual households were able to minimize risk through alternative domestic production strategies; and (4) the location of some production units in zones with higher productive capabilities (such as those relatively freer from flooding). To reiterate, elite development should be found (1) in relatively filled areas, (2) with variable yields, (3) with few production alternatives for the household, and (4) in which some groups tended to give more than they got over several generations.

Cultural Adaptations

Not all Late Prehistoric societies had Mississippian adaptive systems. Because a particular society's adaptive response relates strongly to environmental pressures and responsibilities, the likelihood of producing a Mississippian response should be evaluated in reference to broad physiographic settings as a preliminary step. Particular cultural responses and organization should not be treated as environmentally determined because societies have numerous options open to them in any given environment. Nonetheless, the likelihood of finding Mississippian responses in the absence of certain environmental conditions is small. A gradient of levels of organization exists for societies occupying environments that share only some characteristics of those amenable to Mississippian forms. Among the broad climatological conditions affecting the probability of Mississippian responses are such horticulturally critical factors as rainfall, temperature patterns, and length of growing season. Topographic features, such as the presence of flat land accessible for horticulture and habitation, are also important. Fertile soils that encourage certain patterns of food production and collection are necessary in permanently occupied zones such as floodplains. Floodplains with ridge and swale systems are particularly favorable locations because they provide high ground for habitation as well as experience beneficial flood-renewal cycles. These kinds of zones concentrate population in relatively restricted areas while allowing access to the rich resources of lower, wet areas.

The physiographic conditions most favorable to a Mississippian adaptive response were those of the Mississippi Alluvial Valley Section of the (northern) Gulf Coastal Plain Province (Hunt 1967). These areas have a warm, humid climate, broad alluvial floodplains with rich soils, relatively long growing seasons, and generally southern vegetation communities. Extensions of this kind of environment extend up tributary drainages into portions of the Interior Low Plateau and Central Lowland Provinces. In some of these areas, conditions were sufficiently similar to those of the northern Gulf Coastal Plain to have encouraged the development of Mississippian-like systems.

Mississippian adaptive characteristics are articulated directly with the environments of the northern Gulf Coastal Plain. This is the area described historically as "core" Mississippian and is where many elements of Mississippian culture were first defined by archaeologists. The correspondence between the northern Gulf Coastal Plain and Mississippian is not one-to-one, but it is strong. Many societies, such as that of the Angel site, were located just outside the northern Gulf Coastal Plain proper, in zones that are transitional to adjacent physiographic regions. Responses that were appropriate in the northern Gulf Coastal Plain faced stressful limits in these areas. It is not surprising that Mississippian societies are often very highly organized in precisely those areas where their domestic economy was most challenged by environmental conditions. Late Prehistoric societies displaying greater or lesser organization in marginal conditions and possessing the political economy already described include Cahokia, Kincaid, Angel, and Moundville, to name some of the most important sites on the margins of this adaptive zone.

Cahokia is probably the most complex example of Mississippian organization (Fowler 1978). This site and its satellites are located in the huge American Bottom at the confluence of the Mississippi, Missouri, and Illinois rivers. The American Bottom is also at the junction of four major physiographic provinces (Leighton, Ekblaw, and Horberg 1948; Hunt 1967) at the northern border of the Lower Mississippi alluvial forest zone (Braun 1950:180). Peak Mississippian population in the American Bottom was undoubtedly large, perhaps as many as 10,000 people (see Milner 1986b), and was fairly evenly dispersed across the best soils (as shown in recent work; Kelly, Linder, and Cartmell 1979; Bareis and Porter 1981). A hierarchy of settlements occurred, ranging from the large mound center at Cahokia proper to individual farmsteads (Fowler 1978). Earlier misconceptions of the supposed urban character of Cahokia have been largely corrected, and most of the population probably lived in scattered, small-scale settlements (see Emerson and Milner 1981, 1982; Milner 1982, 1986b; Milner and Williams 1983). Even at Cahokia itself, settlement may have been composed of clusters of smaller units as at other Mississippian sites. Such a pattern of settlement would be consistent with that observed at smaller Mississippian centers (e.g., Muller 1978a, 1986a). American Bottom Mississippian subsistence was based on a combination of locally available floodplain and riverine wild plant and animal resources, nuts, and maize-based horticulture that provided the adaptive margin for the system (Chmurny 1973; Johannessen 1981b; Kelly, Linder, and Cartmell 1979; Kelly 1979). The system was fully sedentary. Groups living at dispersed settlements along floodplain ridges would have each had access to a broad range of resources in their immediate vicinities. These small communities each seem to have produced essentially the same kinds of goods, consistent with the model of risk-sharing (re)distribution outlined above. Inequalities in local production and the large number of people at risk in the broad floodplain encouraged the development of supralocal authorities to mediate competing claims and demands. This same organization also would have coordinated the flow of information among residential groups, given the potential in so circumscribed an environment for each group's activities to have affected the whole society.

Cahokia society was a large and relatively stable system for the Eastern Woodlands, although it did experience fluctuations in organizational intensity. It had a hierarchical structure with ranked sociopolitical units (see Fowler 1969a, 1978; Fowler and Hall 1975; Porter 1969). The relative domination of certain social segments is demonstrated most graphically in the Mound 72 "retainer" burials (Fowler 1969a, 1974). The scale and character of organization and the level of population density were not comparable to more highly organized, stratified state-level societies, however. Continuity in sociopolitical structure is indicated by the quantity, uniformity, and persistence of mound construction at Cahokia and other sites. However, changes did occur in the intensity and extent of such land use through time (see Bareis and Porter 1984). The elite managed resource equity and information coordination at a high level without cutting off direct economic and information flow at lower levels. In addition, the elite may have coordinated extralocal exchange systems. Although production of sumptuary goods for such exchange seems to have remained at a household level (Muller 1984, 1986b, 1987), access to exotic, "high-value" goods may have been easier, at least for the elite. Exchange of such goods was probably also accompanied by more mundane products (Fowler 1969a, 1978; Fowler and Hall 1975; Kelly 1982). The enduring nature of these exchanges within the region, and to a lesser degree within the Eastern Woodlands, also suggests the stability of the economic and political system. The hierarchical settlement pattern also lent itself to efficient internal and external exchange (Fowler 1978; Kelly 1982; Stephens 1981). In these terms, the Cahokia system can be seen to represent a development of the Mississippian adaptive pattern already described, but one that had a higher than average development of ranking.

Kincaid, another north Gulf Coastal Plain society, had similar conditions of population density (although on a smaller absolute scale; Butler, chap. 15 and 1977; Muller 1978b; Muller et al. 1975), land use (Butler 1977; Davy 1982), subsistence (Blakeman 1974), economic organization (Lafferty 1977; Muller 1984), and hierarchical organization (Lafferty 1977; Muller and Rackerby 1971; Riordan 1975; Santeford 1982). The Kincaid site and its sister site, Angel, were certainly smaller than the societies of the American Bottom. Although all of these Mississippian societies manifest similar sociocultural forms, they are not simply variants of some hypothetical core pattern. Each society had its own adaptive system and must be explained in its own environmental and cultural terms.

Even within the northern Gulf Coastal Plain, upland Mississippian-like settlement may have had very different characteristics than was the case in the lowlands. Mississippian-like societies in interior upland areas may have employed patterns of shifting cultivation, and their settlements seem to show a pattern of relative impermanence (see Canouts et al. 1984; Hargrave et al. 1983; Muller, Stephens, and Powell 1981). Evidence of mound construction, centralized control, and elites is substantially less than at main-valley Mississippian sites. The dependency of these upland societies on lowland centers has too often merely been assumed. More effort should be given to test for actual differences and relationships in order to explain them in terms of their own, local adaptive systems, as well as in terms of any possible dependency on river valley Mississippian societies.

Regions outside the northern Gulf Coastal Plain have environmental conditions that promoted sociocultural adaptations that were to a greater or lesser degree different from the pattern already described. Different physiographic and climatic conditions affected the success of a Mississippian lifeway—the West is drier, the North is colder and drier, the East is more rugged and horticulturally less productive, and the southern Gulf Coastal Plain is also less productive for this kind of technology (Hunt 1967). Thus societies in the Central Lowlands, for example, would have had to adapt to more northern climatic conditions than those living in the Lower Mississippi Valley. A shorter growing season precluded a pattern of double (more accurately, overlap) cropping. Plant communities were tall-grass prairie and northern deciduous forest species different from those of the St. Louis, Paducah, or Memphis localities (Braun 1950; Hunt 1967). Cultural adaptations similar to Mississippian occurred where local cultural conditions (such as population pressure, sedentism, maize horticulture, and circumscription) and local environmental conditions (such as swamplands and broad floodplains) created circumstances like those in the northern Gulf Coastal Plain. The degree to which these developments were like Mississippian depended on local conditions. Archaeological complexes with adaptations similar in many respects to the Mississippian societies already discussed include Spoon River, Caddoan, Plaquemine, Lamar, and Fort Walton. Each of these complexes deserves more careful attention in terms of its own conditions and development. Calling Kincaid and Cahokia both Mississippian creates little difficulty, despite the substantial differences in detail. However, using the term *Mississippian* for all of the Late Prehistoric societies of the East obscures differences in adaptation that are far more significant than those distinguishing the American Bottom from the Black Bottom.

Spoon River may be discussed briefly as an example of the adaptive variation found in Late Prehistoric societies farther removed from optimal Mississippian conditions. It is discussed in its own terms elsewhere in this volume. Spoon River was one of the key components in the definition of the Middle Mississippian phase in the Midwestern Taxonomic System (Cole and Deuel 1937), so that traditionalists may be disturbed by any suggestion that it is not true Mississippian. Certainly, Spoon River societies of the central Illinois River Valley were similar to Mississippian societies in many respects, but other adaptive features suggest key differences in the particular underlying sociocultural systems (Harn 1978; Muller and Stephens

1983). Spoon River material traits are usually very like those of Mississippian societies (Conrad and Harn 1972). Such traits include shell-tempered ceramics in various vessel forms, pyramidal mounds, wall-trench structures, marine shell and copper ornaments, and settlement hierarchies (so-called towns, hamlets, and farmsteads). However, such traits relate to very different aspects of the sociocultural system and must be evaluated collectively in the broader context of the system's adaptation. In addition to its similarities to Mississippian, Spoon River societies also had affinities with contemporaneous societies to the north and west (Caldwell 1967a; Conrad and Harn 1976; Hall 1967a; Harn 1971b, 1975b, 1978; Stephens 1979). The adaptational similarities to these latter societies must also be explained and not merely dismissed as of less importance than Spoon River's possession of Mississippian material traits.

Despite the obvious similarities, Spoon River sociocultural systems differed from so-called core Mississippian in significant ways. Spoon River developed in a more temperate climate than that optimal for the usual Mississippian adaptation. The central Illinois River Valley lies well within the Central Lowlands (Hunt 1967) and is broadly surrounded by the Prairie Peninsula (Geis and Boggess 1968). The drier, colder climate produces a shorter growing season than in areas to the south. The Illinois River is a sluggish waterway with a broad, flat floodplain and low-lying backwater lakes and sloughs rather than a developed ridge and swale system (Schwegman 1973). The floodplain is a resource-rich environment that provided some subsistence options similar to portions of the Ohio and Mississippi valley lowlands. But, specific bottomland habitats are dominated by northern species including varieties of maple, elm, ash, and even prairie grasses in some localities, rather than southern species of cypress, tupelo, cane, etc. (Schwegman 1973).

In important ways, Spoon River societies were not as focused on the floodplain as were Mississippian societies. Some three-fourths of known Spoon River settlements, including four of the seven main centers, were located on bluff-tops about thirty meters above the floodplain (Harn 1978: fig. 9.1). While high population density occurred, it was not concentrated in the bottomlands where it would be subject to "Mississippian" adaptive pressures. Hamlets and isolated homesteads with potential nearby horticultural areas flanked the main centers along the bluff-edge (Harn, chap. 7, 1975c; Harn 1978: fig. 9.3). Other small sites occur on the bottomland terraces and on the bluffs overlooking secondary streams (Harn 1978: 244). Thus, as a system, Spoon River involved an upland adaptation as significantly as a bottomland one (Muller and Stephens 1983). This land-use pattern has important implications for understanding Spoon River economic and political organization. The bluff-edge site locations would have allowed access to both bottomland and upland resources far more directly than for many Mississippian societies. Bottomland resources were definitely important aspects of the Spoon River subsistence system (Harn 1971b, 1978; Paloumpis 1981; Speth 1981), but access to such resources could not be controlled as exclusively as in a system of fixed-location bottomland habitation. Individual production units (households) would not have been as dependent on localized resources nor, therefore, on a redistributive system to balance out the vagaries of local production. Rather, more flexible production strategies seem likely (Harn, chap. 7).

Spoon River horticultural production appears to have been concentrated at blufftop locations. Productive strategies would thus necessarily differ from those of flood-renewed lowlands. Although the loess soils of the Illinois Valley uplands are relatively fertile, soil depletion may have been a problem. In addition, the growing season is shorter than to the south (particularly after the post– A.D. 1300 climatic shifts, Baerreis and Bryson 1965). This would have made double-cropping more difficult. Upland gardening would have avoided flood risk, but yields would have been less, with further diminishing returns over time at any given field location. It is not surprising to find Spoon River exploitation of upland forests, valley margins, and possibly prairie resources, as well as of the bottomland resources that dominate central Mississippi Valley subsistence (Emerson 1981; Harn 1978; Paloumpis 1981; Speth 1981). In addition, Harn (chap. 7, 1978) suggests that the Larson center and related settlements were occupied seasonally. This relative mobility and flexibility contrasts strongly with that found at Cahokia or Kincaid. This aspect of the Spoon River system would also have made redistribution to reduce production inequalities less effective. Instead, segmentation into smaller, mobile groups may have been a more workable response to social and environmental stress. Such a system would have had less need for sharing and, concomitantly, for hierarchical sociopolitical organization.

Spoon River settlement patterns suggest that some degree of structured sociopolitical organization was present, but again the patterns seem to be local adaptational responses to potential political instability and mobility for economic reasons rather than a formally imposed hierarchical system (Muller and Stephens 1983). Nucleated centers developed sequentially at a series of different locations up and down the valley. Generally, only one or two of them existed at a given time (Harn 1978). Most of these settlements were situated on relatively defensible upland locations. They were generally surrounded by bastioned palisades and seem to have burned fairly often, suggesting willful destruction. For example, sixty percent of the ninety-nine structures exposed within the palisades of Settlement D at the Orendorf site had been burned (Stephens 1979). Size of centers alone does not automatically indicate sociopolitical complexity. Numerous societies (e.g., Mandan, Iroquois, Kaskaskia) were able to function in large residential communities without concomitant hierarchical organization. Nucleation may as reasonably be an adaptive response to political stress.

Other features of Spoon River societies do support a conclusion of some hierarchical control. The Spoon River centers generally were formally laid out, with central plazas and one or more, relatively small pyramidal mounds. Sociocultural interpretations of these have sometimes inflated the complexity required to explain them, however. Plazas should be recognized as centralized communal-use areas and not presumed to "mean" hierarchical organization. Centralized open spaces are common in sedentary settlements (e.g., Wood 1967) and do not necessarily imply organizational complexity. Similarly, the large buildings present on the plaza edges at Orendorf suggest communal organization and function, but not automatically hierarchical sociopolitical control. The presence of the pyramidal mounds indicates labor coordination by some groups. However, mound construction was generally on a smaller scale and sometimes in different spatial contexts than in more complex Late Prehistoric systems (Harn 1978). For example, the primary stage of the Orendorf pyramidal mound was only one meter high, and the mound was situated outside the major settlement areas, among a group of burial mounds on the bluff margin. Within the Illinois Valley societies, some individuals apparently had differential access to "valued," exotic goods. Importantly, however, ascribed status appears to have been absent within the society as a whole (Harn 1971b, 1980b; Rothschild 1979). Individuals rather than formal segments of society exhibited differential (achieved) status. Even many of the suggested "Mississippian" motifs present on Spoon River artifacts, which may have served as symbols to help legitimize authority, are stylistically "marginal" in execution, suggesting less direct participation by their makers in systems using those motifs (Stephens 1979).

Settlement size hierarchy is present in the form of main villages, hamlets, and farmsteads (Harn 1978; Stephens 1979), although these site size classes may represent varying kinds of seasonal habitations rather than formally subordinate settlements (Harn, chap. 7, 1978). In addition, the larger sites seem to have been relatively unstable spatial entities, frequently changing size and orientation within their immediate confines. For example, the Orendorf site was formally relocated three times (Orendorf

Settlements B/C, C, and D) within a ten-hectare area between approximately A.D. 1150 and 1250, as well as sustaining growth and organizational change within each of those individual settlements (Santure 1981; Stephens 1976, 1979).

The local redefinition of centers and their differential relocation within the valley may well reflect the waxing and waning of political entities as well as economic pressures (such as soil depletion). These patterns suggest political competition within the region and a lack of sustained ability to defend political boundaries. The presence of a violently opposed Oneota occupation, literally in the middle of the region and sequence, also strongly suggests substantial political instability. In addition, segments of individual communities may well have moved in and out of a locality fairly regularly. Thus even though the Spoon River population was large, its organization may have been fairly flexible. Mobile groups are difficult to control politically, as they fission in response to adaptive needs. Thus while the material assemblage of Spoon River looks strongly Mississippian, the societies differ in some fundamental adaptive responses. Rather than trying to hammer Spoon River into some idealized Mississippian mold, either as part of the Mississippian "core" (see Griffin 1978a:xvi) or as Mississippian "variant," it deserves to be investigated in its own terms, as indeed is done on the practical level. Spoon River was a dynamic sociocultural system adapted to its own local environmental and cultural conditions, and its interpretation is harmed, not helped, by emphasizing its "Mississippianness" at the expense of its other characteristics. The point is that we should not expect typologically significant boundaries so much as a gradient of degrees of similarity to "core" Mississippian.

Other late prehistoric societies in regions with greater environmental differences are even more divergent from Mississippian forms as defined here. These societies have sometimes been designated as "peripheral" Mississippian systems and include such different manifestations as Oneota, Apple River, Red Wing, Steed-Kisker, and Fort Ancient. Wisconsin Oneota, for example, has long been recognized typologically as a distinctive Upper Mississippi unit, and for that reason less concern has been expressed in claiming or defining its Mississippianness. Oneota possessed many outwardly Mississippian traits (such as shell-tempered pottery and wall-trench houses), but as an adaptive system, Oneota employed a divided-risk subsistence strategy (Muller and Stephens 1983). This pattern was one of exploiting local bottomland plant and animal resources near rivers and lakes, as well as hunting large game on the prairies (Cleland 1966; Gibbon 1972; Gallagher and Stevenson 1983; Overstreet 1978, 1981). The pattern has been suggested to have involved seasonal population movements, with winter dispersal for hunting and summer convergence at the large settlements for horticulture (Cleland 1966; Gibbon 1972, 1974; Hurley 1978). Thus Oneota groups were not dependent on constricted parcels of land to assure adequate subsistence. Any effects of population size could be mediated by seasonal out-migration, precluding the need for intensified social control mechanisms for reducing production inequalities. Mobility also reduced the ability to control behavior on a society-wide basis and decreased the ability of certain groups to acquire and maintain disproportionate access to goods and services. As in all cases discussed here, the key element is to try to understand the nature of Oneota adaptation, not to classify it.

Conclusions

The Mississippian pattern can best be understood in terms of the special environmental and social circumstances of the northern Gulf Coastal Plain and the extensions of its conditions into surrounding areas. Mississippian, to the extent that it exists at all, is seen as the historical response to a series of pressures that resulted from sedentary life in environmentally circumscribed floodplains. Additional features leading to the development of elites were population pressure, the need for coordination and intensification of production, the need to reduce inequalities in production, the control of internal and external exchange, and the need for general management of social and ecological information. The model suggests that small-scale producers dispersed across relatively similar high-risk

environments will require social insurance in the form of centrally sponsored events that stimulate internal exchange of goods and information and mobilize production efforts. In the case of Mississippian, these pressures were strong enough to stimulate the development of ranking and descent mechanisms that may be roughly characterized as being at a chiefdom level. In other geographical regions, or in greatly different environments even within the same regions, alternative strategies that did not lead to the formation of elites may have been used to mitigate hard times. Among these potential kinds of alternative systems are patterns of shifting cultivation, reduction of stress by depending less on floodplain resources, lower dependence on maize horticulture, maintenance of low population density, or retention of mobility through the development of alternative subsistence systems. The development of Mississippian should not be seen as the inevitable result of cultural elaboration in the East, but merely as one of many different adaptive, organizational responses to particular combinations of social and enviromental problems.

References

Adams, Robert McC.
1941 *Archaeological Investigations in Jefferson County, Missouri, 1939–1940*. Transactions of the Academy of Science of St. Louis vol. 30(5).
1974 Anthropological Perspectives on Trade. *Current Anthropology* 15(3):239–58.

Ahler, Stephen R.
1984 *Archaic Settlement Strategies in the Modoc Locality, Southwest Illinois*. Ph.D. diss., Department of Anthropology, University of Wisconsin-Milwaukee.

Alex, Robert A.
1971 Upper and Plains Mississippian. Ms. on file, Office of the State Archaeologist of Iowa, Iowa City.
1973 Architectural Features of Houses at the Mitchell Site (39DV2), Eastern South Dakota. *Plains Anthropologist* 18:149–58.
1981a *The Village Cultures of the Lower James River Valley, South Dakota*. Ph.D. diss., Department of Anthropology, University of Wisconsin, Madison.
1981b Villages Off the Missouri River. In *The Future of South Dakota's Past*, ed. L. J. Zimmerman and L. C. Stewart, pp. 39–46. Special Publication no. 2, South Dakota Archaeological Society.

Allen, Mark W.
1984 Preliminary Report on Human Skeletal Remains from the Adams Site (15Fu4). In *Late Prehistoric Research in Kentucky*, ed. David Pollack, Charles Hockensmith, and Thomas Sanders, pp. 181–86. Kentucky Heritage Council, Frankfort.

Allen, Roger C.
1976 Archaeological Investigations at Two Sites in the U.S. Interstate Highway 24 Right-of-Way in Marshall County, Kentucky. Report submitted by the University of Kentucky. Ms. on file at the Office of the State Archaeologist, Lexington.

Anderson, Adrian D.
1961 The Glenwood Sequence: A Local Sequence for a Series of Archaeological Manifestations in Mills County, Iowa. *Journal of the Iowa Archeological Society* 10:3.

Anderson, Adrian D., and B. Anderson
1960 Pottery Types of the Glenwood Foci. *Journal of the Iowa Archeological Society* 9(4):12–39.

Anderson, David
1986 Stability and Change in Chiefdom-level Societies: An Examination of Mississippian Political Evolution on the South Atlantic Slope. Paper presented at the Forty-third Annual Meeting of the Southeastern Archaeological Conference, Nashville.

Anderson, Duane C.
1969 Mill Creek Culture: A Review. *Plains Anthropologist* 14:134–43.
1973 *Brewster Site (13CK15); Lithic Analysis*. Journal of the Iowa Archeological Society vol. 20.
1975 A Long-Nosed God Mask from Northwest Iowa. *American Antiquity* 40:326–29.
1980 Long Nosed God Masks and Other Items. *Iowa Archeological Society Newsletter* 97:16–17.
1981 *Mill Creek Ceramics: The Complex from the Brewster Site*. Report no. 14, Office of the State Archaeologist, University of Iowa, Iowa City.
1987 Toward a Processual Understanding of the Initial Variant of the Middle Missouri Tradition: The Case of the Mill Creek Culture of Iowa. *American Antiquity* 52:522–32.

Anderson, Duane C., Joseph A. Tiffany, Michael Fokken, and Patricia M. Williams
1979 The Siouxland Sand and Gravel Site (13WD402): State Law Protecting Ancient Cemeteries. *Journal of the Iowa Archeological Society* 26:119–46.

Anderson, James
1969 A Cahokia Palisade Sequence. In *Explorations into Cahokia Archaeology*, ed. Melvin L. Fowler, pp. 89–99. Illinois Archaeological Survey Bulletin no. 7, Urbana.

Anfinson, Scott F.
1979 *A Handbook of Minnesota Prehistoric Ceramics*. Occasional Publications in Minnesota Anthropology, no. 5. Minnesota Archaeological Society, Fort Snelling.
1982 Faunal Remains from the Big Slough Site (21MU1) and Woodland Cultural Stability in Southwestern Minnesota. *Minnesota Archaeologist* 41:53–71.
1987 *The Prehistory of the Prairie Lake Region in the Northeastern Plains*. Ph.D. diss., University of Minnesota, Minneapolis.

Anonymous
1923   State Parks and Beauty Spots in Illinois. In *Blue Book of the State of Illinois for 1923–1924*, pp. 486–93. Springfield.
1948   Relics Show Dinner Bell Popular in Illinois in 1347. *Journal of the Illinois State Archaeological Society* 5(3): 20–21.
1983   Photographs of Large Mill Creek Chert Blade and Three Small Annular Gorgets from Illinois Valley. *Central States Archaeological Journal* 30:140–41.

Apfelstadt, Gary A.
1975   Cultigens in Wabash Valley Prehistory. Paper presented at the Twentieth Midwest Archaeological Conference, Ann Arbor.

Arzigian, Constance
1987   The Emergence of Horticultural Economies in Southwestern Wisconsin. In *Emergent Horticultural Economies of the Eastern Woodlands*, ed. William F. Keegan, pp. 217–42. Southern Illinois University at Carbondale, Center for Archaeological Investigations, Occasional Paper no. 7.

Asch, David L., and Nancy B. Asch
1977   Chenopod as Cultigen: A Re-evaluation of Some Prehistoric Collections from Eastern North America. *Midcontinental Journal of Archaeology* 2:3–45.
1978   The Economic Potential of *Iva annua* and its Prehistoric Importance in the Lower Illinois Valley. In *The Nature and Status of Ethnobotany*, ed. Richard I. Ford, pp. 301–41. University of Michigan, Museum of Anthropology, Anthropological Papers, no. 67. Ann Arbor.
1985   Prehistoric Plant Cultivation in West-central Illinois. In *Prehistoric Food Production in North America*, ed. Richard I. Ford, pp. 149–203. University of Michigan, Museum of Anthropology, Anthropological Papers, no. 75. Ann Arbor.

Asch, David L., Kenneth B. Farnsworth, and Nancy B. Asch
1979   Woodland Subsistence and Settlement in West-central Illinois. In *Hopewell Archaeology: The Chillicothe Conference*, ed. David S. Brose and N'omi Greber, pp. 80–85. Kent State University Press, Kent, Ohio.

Asch, David L., Kenneth B. Farnsworth, H. Carl Udesen, and Ann L. Koski
1978   *Development of Preliminary Predictive Models of Regional Prehistoric Settlement in the Lower Illinois and Adjacent Mississippi River Drainages (IDOC Regions III and IV), Illinois.* Center for American Archeology, Contract Archeology Program, Report of Investigations no. 45, Kampsville, Illinois. Submitted to Illinois Department of Conservation, Springfield.
1981   Upper Mississippi River and Lower Illinois River Units (III-South and IV). In *Predictive Models in Illinois Archaeology: Report Summaries*, ed. Margaret K. Brown, pp. 55–72. Illinois Department of Conservation, Division of Historic Sites, Springfield.

Baerreis, David A.
1958   Aztalan Revisited: An Introduction. *Wisconsin Archeologist* 39(1):2–5.
1968   Artifact Descriptions: Bone, Stone and Shell. In *Climatic Change and the Mill Creek Culture of Iowa*, ed. Dale R. Henning. Journal of the Iowa Archeological Society vol. 15.

Baerreis, David A., and R. A. Alex
1974   An Interpretation of Midden Formation—the Mill Creek Example. *Minnesota Prehistoric Archaeology Series* 11:143–48. Minnesota Historical Society, St. Paul.

Baerreis, David A., and Reid A. Bryson
1965   Climatic Episodes and the Dating of the Mississippian Cultures. *Wisconsin Archeologist* 46:203–20.
1968   Introduction and Project Summary. In *Climatic Change and the Mill Creek Culture of Iowa*, ed. David A. Baerreis and Reid A. Bryson, pp. 1–34. Journal of the Iowa Archaeological Society vol. 15.

Baerreis, David A., Reid A. Bryson, and John E. Kutzbach
1976   Climate and Culture in the Western Great Lakes Region. *Midcontinental Journal of Archaeology* 1:39–57.

Baerreis, David A., and Joan E. Freeman
1958   Late Woodland Pottery as Seen from Aztalan. *Wisconsin Archeologist* 39:35–61.

Baker, Frank C.
1941   A Study in Ethnozoology of the Prehistoric Indians of Illinois. In *Contributions to the Archaeology of the Illinois River Valley*, ed. James B. Griffin and Richard G. Morgan, 51–71. Transactions of the American Philosophical Society n.s., vol. 32(1). Philadelphia.

Bareis, Charles J.
1964   Meander Loops and the Cahokia Site. *American Antiquity* 30:89–91.
1969   *Final Report on Salvage Work Undertaken at the Knoebel Site (S-71) on FAI 64, St. Clair County, Illinois.* Report by the Department of Anthropology, University of Illinois at Urbana-Champaign, submitted to the Illinois Division of Highways, Springfield.
1972   *Reports on Preliminary Site Examinations Undertaken at the Holliday No. 2 Site (S-68) and the Lienesch Site (S-67) on FAI 64, St. Clair County, Illinois.* Report by the Department of Anthropology, University of Illinois at Urbana-Champaign, submitted to the Illinois Division of Highways, Springfield.
1976   *The Knoebel Site, St. Clair County, Illinois.* Illinois Archaeological Survey, Circular no. 1. Urbana.

Bareis, Charles J., and William M. Gardner
1968   Three Long-Nosed God Masks from Western Illinois. *American Antiquity* 35:495–98.

Bareis, Charles J., and James W. Porter
1965   Megascopic and Petrographic Analyses of a Foreign Pottery Vessel from the Cahokia Site. *American Antiquity* 31:95–101.

Bareis, Charles J., and James W. Porter (editors)
1981   *Archaeology in the American Bottom: Progress Report on the Illinois FAI-270 Archaeological Mitigation Project.* University of Illinois at Urbana-Champaign, Department of Anthropology, Research Report, no. 6.
1984   *American Bottom Archaeology.* University of Illinois Press, Urbana.

Barrett, S.
1933   *Ancient Aztalan.* Bulletin of the Public Museum of the City of Milwaukee vol. 13. Milwaukee.

Barth, Robert J.
1973   *Archaeological Excavations at the Reed-Walker Site.* Report by the Department of Anthropology, University of Illinois at Urbana-Champaign, submitted to the National Park Service, Northeast Region, Philadelphia.
1975   *Archaeological Excavations at the Reed-Walker Site, 1973 and 1974.* Report by the Department of Anthropology, University of Illinois at Urbana-Champaign,

submitted to the National Park Service, Northeast Region, Philadelphia.

1977 The LaMotte Culture in the Middle Embarras Valley: A Systems Perspective. Paper presented at the Fifty-third Annual Meeting of the Central States Anthropological Society, Cincinnati.

1978 Allison-LaMotte Settlement Pattern and Settlement Strategy. Paper presented at the Fifty-fourth Annual Meeting of the Central States Anthropological Society, South Bend.

1982 *The Allison-LaMotte and Vincennes Cultures: Cultural Evolution in the Wabash Valley.* Ph.D. diss., Department of Anthropology, University of Illinois at Urbana-Champaign. University Microfilms, Ann Arbor.

1983 The Emergence of the Vincennes Culture in the Lower Wabash Drainage. Paper presented at the Society for American Archaeology Meetings, Pittsburgh.

Bastian, Edson S.
1931 *The Fluorspar Deposits of Hardin and Pope Counties, Illinois.* Illinois State Geological Survey Bulletin no. 58. Springfield.

Batura, James M., and Kenneth B. Farnsworth
1981 *Archeological Survey at Beaver Dam State Park, Macoupin County, Illinois.* Center for American Archeology, Contract Archeology Program, Report of Investigations no. 117, Kampsville, Illinois. Submitted to Illinois Department of Conservation, Springfield.

Bauxar, J. Joseph
1957 Yuchi Ethnoarchaeology. *Ethnohistory* 4:279–301, 369–464.

Beadle, Bernard V.
1942 A Recent Find of Carved Shell Effigies. *Minnesota Archaeologist* 8:169.

Beaubien, Paul L.
1957 Notes on the Archeology of Pipestone National Monument. *Minnesota Archaeologist* 21:1–19.

Bell, Robert E.
1951 Dendrochronology at the Kincaid site. In *Kincaid, a Prehistoric Illinois Metropolis*, by Fay-Cooper Cole et al., pp. 233–92. University of Chicago Press, Chicago.

1958 *Guide to the Identification of Certain American Indian Projectile Points.* Oklahoma Anthropological Society, Special Bulletin no. 1. Norman.

1960 *Guide to the Identification of Certain American Indian Projectile Points.* Oklahoma Anthropological Society, Special Bulletin no. 2. Norman.

1972 *The Harlan Site, Ck-6, A Prehistoric Mound Center in Cherokee County, Eastern Oklahoma.* Oklahoma Anthropoogical Society Memoir no. 2. Norman.

Benchley, Elizabeth
1974 *Mississippian Secondary Mound Loci: A Comparative Functional Analysis in a Time-Space Perspective.* Ph.D. diss., Department of Anthropology, University of Wisconsin-Milwaukee. University Microfilms, Ann Arbor.

1976 *An Overview of the Prehistoric Resources of the Metropolitan St. Louis Area.* Cultural Resource Management Studies, U.S. Department of the Interior, National Park Service, Washington, D.C.

Bender, Margaret M., David A. Baerreis, and R. Steventon
1981 Further Light on Carbon Isotopes and Hopewell Agriculture. *American Antiquity* 48:346–53.

Bender, Margaret M., Reid A. Bryson, and David A. Baerreis
1975 University of Wisconsin Radiocarbon Dates XII. *Radiocarbon* 17:121–34.

Bender, Marilyn J., and Paul A. Webb
1983 *Archaeological Investigations at the Roos Site, St. Clair County, Illinois.* Southern Illinois University at Carbondale, Center for Archaeological Investigations, Research Paper no. 43.

Benn, David W.
1980 *Hadfields Cave: A Perspective on Late Woodland Culture in Northeastern Iowa.* Report no. 13, Office of the State Archaeologist, University of Iowa, Iowa City.

Bennett, Gwen Patrice
1984 *A Bibliography of Illinois Archaeology.* Illinois State Museum Scientific Papers, vol. 21. Springfield.

Bennett, John W.
1945 *Archaeological Explorations in Jo Daviess County, Illinois.* University of Chicago Press, Chicago.

1952 The Prehistory of the Northern Mississippi Valley. In *Archaeology of Eastern United States*, ed. James B. Griffin, pp. 108–23. University of Chicago Press, Chicago.

Bielwaski, Ellen
n.d. Helton Mound 22. Ms. on file, Bioanthropology Laboratory, University of Chicago.

Binford, Lewis R.
1964 *Archaeological Investigations in the Carlyle Reservoir, Clinton County, Illinois, 1962.* Southern Illinois University Museum, Archaeological Salvage Report no. 17. Carbondale.

1971 Mortuary Practices: Their Study and Their Potential. In *Approaches to the Social Dimensions of Mortuary Practices*, ed. James A. Brown, pp. 6–29. Society for American Archaeology Memoir no. 25.

1978 *Nunamiut Ethnoarchaeology.* Academic Press, New York.

1981 *Bones: Ancient Men and Modern Myths.* Academic Press, New York.

Binford, Lewis R., Sally R. Binford, Robert C. Whallon, and Margaret Ann Hardin
1970 *Archaeology at Hatchery West.* Memoirs of the Society for American Archaeology no. 24.

Birk, D. A.
1984 Prairie Island Survey. In *Institute for Minnesota Archaeology Summary Report 1982–1984*, p. 11. Institute for Minnesota Archaeology, Minneapolis.

Birong, Marcia
1979 Aztalan-Interpretive Models. Ms. on file, Department of Anthropology, University of Wisconsin-Milwaukee.

Black, Glenn A.
1967 *Angel Site: An Archaeological, Historical, and Ethnological Study.* 2 vols. Indiana Historical Society, Indianapolis.

Blake, Leonard
1986 Corn and Other Plants from Prehistory into History in Eastern United States. In *The Protohistoric Period in the Mid-South: 1500–1700*, ed. D. Dye and R. Brister, pp. 3–13. Mississippi Department of Archives and History, Jackson.

n.d. Notes on ongoing analysis of Orendorf seeds. Western Illinois University Archaeological Research Laboratory, Macomb.

Blake, Leonard W., and Rosalind M. Dean
1963   Corn from Plum Island. In *Reports on Illinois Pre-
            history: 1*, ed. Elaine A. Bluhm, pp. 92–94. Illinois
            Archaeological Survey Bulletin no. 4. Urbana.

Blakely, Robert L.
1971   Comparison of the Mortality Profiles of Archaic, Mid-
            dle Woodland, and Middle Mississippian Skeletal
            Populations. *American Journal of Physical Anthro-
            pology* 34:43–54.
1973   *Biological Variation among and between Two Prehis-
            toric Populations at Dickson Mounds*. Ph.D. diss.,
            Department of Anthropology, Indiana University,
            Bloomington. University Microfilms, Ann Arbor.

Blakeman, Crawford
1974   *The Late Prehistoric Paleoethnobotany of the Black
            Bottom, Pope and Massac Counties, Illinois*. Ph.D.
            diss., Department of Anthropology, Southern Illinois
            University at Carbondale. University Microfilms, Ann
            Arbor.

Blakeslee, Donald
1975   The Plains Interband Trade System: An Ethnohis-
            toric and Archaeological Investigation. Ph.D. diss.,
            Department of Anthropology, University of Wisconsin-
            Milwaukee.
1978   Assessing the Central Plains Tradition in Eastern Ne-
            braska: Content and Outcome. In *The Central Plains
            Tradition: Internal Development and External Rela-
            tionships*, ed. Donald Blakeslee, pp. 134–43. Report
            no. 11, Office of the State Archaeologist, The Univer-
            sity of Iowa, Iowa City.
1981   The Origin and Spread of the Calumet Ceremony.
            American Antiquity 46:759–68.
1983   Kinks in the Calibration Curve: Reassessing Radiocar-
            bon Dates. In *Man and the Changing Environments in
            the Great Plains*, ed. Warren W. Caldwell, C. Bertrand
            Schultz, and T. Mylan Stout, pp. 29–35. Transactions
            of the Nebraska Academy of Sciences, vol. 11. Lin-
            coln.

Blasingham, Emily J.
1953   Temporal and Spatial Distribution of the Yankeetown
            Cultural Manifestation. M.A. thesis, Department of
            Anthropology, Indiana University, Bloomington.

Bleed, Peter
1970   Notes on Aztalan Shell-Tempered Pottery. *Wisconsin
            Archeologist* 51:1–20.

Blessing, F. K.
1967   Salvage work at the Bryan site. *Minnesota Archaeolo-
            gist* 29:57–65.

Boszhardt, Robert
1977   Wisconsin Radiocarbon Chronology—1976, A Second
            Compilation. *Wisconsin Archeologist* 58:87–143.

Bowman, Isaiah
1907   Water Resources of the East St. Louis District. In *Illi-
            nois State Geological Survey Bulletin* 5:1–18. University
            of Illinois, Urbana-Champaign.

Braun, David P.
1983   Pots as Tools. In *Archaeological Hammers and Theo-
            ries*, ed. J. A. Moore and A. S. Keene, pp. 107–34.
            Academic Press, New York.

Braun, David P., James B. Griffin, and Paul F. Titterington
1982   *The Snyders Mounds and Five Other Mound Groups
            in Calhoun County, Illinois*. University of Michigan,
            Museum of Anthropology, Technical Report no. 13.
            Ann Arbor.

Braun, David P., and S. Plog
1982   Evolution of "Tribal" Social Networks: Theory and
            Prehistoric North American Evidence. *American
            Antiquity* 47:504–25.

Braun, E. Lucy
1950   *Deciduous Forests of Eastern North America*. Blakiston
            Company, Philadelphia.

Brazeau, Linda, and Patricia Bruhy
1980   *Archaeological Survey and Test Excavations in the Fox
            River Drainage . . . Waukesha, Racine and Walworth
            Counties. Vol. 1, Survey Results*. GLARC, Inc. Report
            of Investigations no. 90. Waukesha, Wisconsin.

Bronson, Bennet
1977   The Earliest Farming: Demography as Cause and Con-
            sequence. In *Origins of Agriculture*, ed. Charles A.
            Reed, pp. 23–48. Mouton, The Hague.

Brower, Jacob V.
1903   *Memoirs of Explorations in the Basin of the Mississippi,
            vol. 6: Minnesota*. H. L. Collins, St. Paul.

Brown, Alan J., James M. Collins, Bonnie L. Gums, George R.
Holley, Mikels Skele, Christy L. Wells, and William I. Woods
1986   Recent Archaeological Investigations by Southern Illi-
            nois University at Edwardsville (May 1985-May 1986).
            Illinois Archaeological Survey Newsletter 1(1–2):2–7.

Brown, Alan J., George R. Holley, Neal H. Lopinot,
and William I. Woods
1988   Cultural and Natural Explanations for Buried Late Pre-
            historic Sites in the American Bottom. Paper presented
            at the Fifty-third Annual Meeting of the Society for
            American Archaeology, Phoenix.

Brown, James A.
1965   *The Prairie Peninsula: An Interaction Area in the
            Eastern United States*. Ph.D. diss., Department of
            Anthropology, University of Chicago.
1971   *Spiro Studies: Pottery Vessels*. Vol. 3, First Part of the
            Third Annual Report of Caddoan Archaeology. Spiro
            Focus Research, Norman.
1976   *Spiro Studies: The Artifacts*. Vol. 4, Second Part of the
            Third Annual Report of Caddoan Archaeology. Spiro
            Focus Research, Norman.
1982   What Kind of Economy Did the Oneota Have? In
            Oneota Studies, ed. Guy E. Gibbon, pp. 107–12.
            Publications in Anthropology no. 1. University of
            Minnesota, Minneapolis.

Brown, James A. (editor)
1961   *The Zimmerman Site: A Report on Excavations at the
            Grand Village of Kaskaskia, LaSalle County, Illinois*.
            Illinois State Museum Reports of Investigations, no. 9.
            Springfield.
1975   *Perspectives in Cahokia Archaeology*. Illinois Archaeo-
            logical Survey Bulletin no. 10. Urbana.

Brown, James A., Robert E. Bell, and D. G. Wyckoff
1978   Caddoan Settlement Patterns in the Arkansas River
            Drainage. In *Mississippian Settlement Patterns*, ed.
            Bruce D. Smith, pp. 169–200. Academic Press, New
            York.

Brown, James A., Roger W. Willis, Mary A. Barth,
and Georg K. Neumann
1967   *The Gentleman Farm Site, LaSalle County, Illinois*. Illi-
            nois State Museum, Reports of Investigations no. 12.
            Springfield.

Brumfiel, E. M., and T. K. Earle
1987   Specialization, Exchange, and Complex Societies: An
            Introduction. In *Specialization, Exchange, and Complex*

Societies, ed. E. M. Brumfiel and T. K. Earle, pp. 1–9. Cambridge University Press, Cambridge.

Bryson, Reid A., D. A. Baerreis, and W. M. Wendland
1970   The Character of Late-glacial and Post-glacial Climatic Changes. In *Pleistocene and Recent Environments of the Central Great Plains*, ed. W. Dort and J. K. Jones. Department of Geology, University of Kansas Special Publication no 3. Lawrence.

Bryson, Reid A., and W. M. Wendland
1967   Tentative Climatic Patterns for Some Late Glacial and Postglacial Episodes in Central North America. In *Life, Land and Water*, ed. W. J. Mayer-Oakes, pp. 271–98. University of Manitoba Press, Winnepeg.

Buikstra, Jane E.
1975   Cultural and Biological Variability: A Comparison of Models. Paper presented at the annual meeting of the American Association of Physical Anthropologists, Denver.
1977   Biocultural Dimensions in Archaeological Study: A Regional Prespective. In *Biocultural Adaptation in Prehistoric America*, ed. Robert L. Blakely, pp. 67–84. Southern Anthropological Association Proceedings no. 11. University of Georgia Press, Athens.
1989   Carbon Isotope Perspective on Dietary Variation in Late Prehistoric Western Illinois. Paper presented at the Thirty-fourth annual Midwest Archaeological Conference, Iowa City.

Burghardt, A. F.
1971   A Hypothesis about Gateway Cities. *Annals of the Association of American Geographers* 61:269–85.

Bushnell, David I., Jr.
1904   The Cahokia and Surrounding Mound Groups. *Papers of the Peabody Museum of American Archaeology and Ethnology* 3(1):3–20. Harvard University, Cambridge, Massachusetts.
1922   Archaeological Reconnaissance of the Cahokia and Related Mound Groups. Explorations and Field Work of the Smithsonian Institution in 1921. *Smithsonian Miscellaneous Collections* 72(15):92–105. Washington, D.C.

Butler, Brian
1972   Early Vegetation of the Kincaid Area. Ms. on file, Center for Archaeological Investigations, Southern Illinois University at Carbondale.
1977   *Mississippian Settlement in the Black Bottom, Pope and Massac Counties, Illinois*. Ph.D. diss., Department of Anthropology, Southern Illinois University at Carbondale. University Microfilms, Ann Arbor.

Butler, Brian M., Jo-Anne M. Penny, and Cathy A. Robison
1981   *Archaeological Survey and Evaluation for the Shawnee 200 M.W. A.F.B.C. Plant, McCracken County, Kentucky* Southern Illinois University at Carbondale, Center for Archaeological Investigations, Research Paper no. 21.

Cadillac, Lamothe
1947   The Memoir of Lamothe Cadillac. In *The Western Country in the 17th Century*, ed. M. Quaife, pp. 1–83. Lakeside Press, Chicago.

Caldwell, Joseph R.
1958   *Trend and Tradition in the Prehistory of the Eastern United States*. American Anthropological Association Memoir no. 88.
1961   Untitled paper presented at the annual meeting of the

Central States Anthropological Society in Bloomington, Indiana.
1964   Interaction Spheres in Prehistory. In *Hopewellian Studies*, ed. Joseph R. Caldwell and Robert L. Hall, pp. 133–43. Illinois State Museum, Scientific Papers no. 12. Springfield.
1967a   The House That "X" Built. *The Living Museum* 28: 92–93.
1967b   New Discoveries at Dickson Mounds. *The Living Museum* 29:139–42.
n.d.   Untitled draft manuscript on the Eveland site. Ms on file, Illinois State Museum, Springfield.

Canouts, Veletta
1971   *Towards a Reconstruction of Creek and Pre-Creek Cultural Ecology*. M.A. thesis, Department of Anthropology, University of North Carolina, Chapel Hill.
1986   *The Effects of Boundary Conditions on the Archaeological Record: A Stylistic Analysis of Havana Hopewell and Marksville Pottery*. Ph.D. diss., Department of Anthropology, Southern Illinois University at Carbondale.

Canouts, Veletta, Ernest E. May, Neal H. Lopinot, and Jon Muller
1984   *Cultural Frontiers in the Upper Cache Valley, Illinois*. Southern Illinois University at Carbondale, Center for Archaeological Investigations, Research Paper no. 16.

Carneiro, Robert L.
1970   A Theory of the Origin of the State. *Science* 169: 733–38.
1974   A Reappraisal of the Roles of Technology and Organization in the Origin of Civilization. *American Antiquity* 39:179–86.
1981   The Chiefdom: Precursor of the State. In *The Transiton to Statehood in the New World*, ed. G. Jones and R. Kautz, pp. 39–79. Cambridge University Press, Cambridge.

Caso, Alfonso
1958   *The Aztecs: People of the Sun*. University of Oklahoma Press, Norman.

Catlin, George
1973   *North American Indians*. 2 vols. Dover Publications, New York.

Chapman, Carl H.
1980   *The Archaeology of Missouri, II*. University of Missouri Press, Columbia.

Chapman, Carl H., and Eleanor F. Chapman
1964   *Indians and Archaeology of Missouri*. Missouri Handbook no. 6. University of Missouri Press, Columbia.

Chapman, Charles C., and Co.
1879   *History of Fulton County, Illinois*. C. C. Champan and Co., Peoria.

Chapman, Jefferson, and Andrea Brewer Shea
1981   The Archaeobotanical Record: Early Archaic to Contact in the Lower Little Tennessee River Valley. *Tennessee Anthropologist* 6:64–84.

Chayanov, A. V.
1966   *The Theory of Peasant Economy*, ed. D. Thorner, B. Kerblay, and R.E.F Smith. The Economic Association, Homewood, Illinois.

Cheverud, James E.
n.d.   Helton Mound 20. Ms. on file, Bioanthropology Laboratory, University of Chicago.

Chmurny, William W.
1961   *Preliminary Appraisal of the Archaeological Resources*

of the Shelbyville Reservoir. Contract report submitted to the U.S. Department of the Interior, National Park Service, Northeast Region.

1973   *The Ecology of the Middle Mississippian Occupation of the American Bottom.* Ph.D. diss., Department of Anthropology, University of Illinois at Urbana-Champaign. University Microfilms, Ann Arbor.

Clarke, David L.
1976   Mesolithic Europe: The Economic Basis. In *Problems in Economic and Social Archaeology*, ed. G. de G. Sieveking, I. H. Longworth, and K. E. Wison, pp. 449–81. Duckworth, London.

Clay, R. Berle
1963   *Ceramic Complexes of the Tennessee-Cumberland Region in Western Kentucky.* M.A. thesis. Department of Anthropology, University of Kentucky, Lexington.
1976   Tactics, Strategy, and Operations: The Mississippian System Responds to Its Environment. *Midcontinental Journal of Archaeology* 1:137–62.
1979   A Mississippian Ceramic Sequence from Western Kentucky. *Tennessee Anthropologist* 4:111–28.

Cleland, Charles E.
1966   *The Prehistoric Animal Ecology and Ethnozoology of the Upper Great Lakes Region.* University of Michigan, Museum of Anthroplogy, Anthropological Papers no. 29. Ann Arbor.

Clouse, Robert A.
1973   *Archaeological Survey in the Lower Wabash Valley, Illinois: Cross Wabash Valley Waterway.* Report by the Department of Anthropology, University of Illinois at Urbana-Champaign, submitted to the National Park Service, Northeast Region, Philadelphia.

Colburn, Mona
1990   Mississippian Faunal Remains from the Lundy Site (11JD140), Jo Daviess County, Illinois. *Illinois Archaeology* 1 (1):5–38.

Cole, Fay-Cooper, Robert Bell, John Bennett, Joseph Caldwell, Norman Emerson, Richard MacNeish, Kenneth Orr, and Roger Willis
1951   *Kincaid, A Prehistoric Illinois Metropolis.* University of Chicago Press, Chicago.

Cole, Fay-Cooper, and Thorne Deuel
1937   *Rediscovering Illinois: Archaeological Explorations in and around Fulton County.* University of Chicago Press, Chicago.

Conard, Nicholas, David L. Asch, Nancy B. Asch, David Elmore, Harry E. Gove, Meyer Rubin, James A. Brown, Michael D. Wiant, Kenneth B. Farnsworth, and Thomas G. Cook.
1984   Accelerator Radiocarbon Dating of Evidence for Prehistoric Horticulture in Illinois. *Nature* 308:443–46.

Conner, Michael D.
1984   *Population Structure and Biological Variation in the Late Woodland of Westcentral Illinois.* Ph.D. diss., Department of Anthropology, University of Chicago.

Conner, Michael D. (editor)
1985   *The Hill Creek Homestead and Late Mississippian Settlement in the Lower Illinois Valley.* Center for American Archeology, Kampsville Archeological Center, Research Series, vol. 1. Kampsville, Illinois.

Conrad, Lawrence A.
1966   *An Archaeological Survey of the Lower Kaskaskia Canalization Project.* Southern Illinois University Museum, Archaeological Salvage Report no. 26.

Carbondale. Submitted to the National Park Service, Northeast Region
1967   1966 Excavations at the Dickson Mounds. Report of field work on file, Dickson Mounds Museum, Lewiston, Illinois.
1970   The Berry Site: A Multicomponent Site in the Central Illinois River Valley. Ms. on file, Western Illinois University Archaeological Research Laboratory, Macomb.
1971   Hungry Wolf Site field notes. Ms. on file, Western Illinois University, Macomb.
1972   *1966 Excavations at the Dickson Mound: A Sepo-Spoon River Burial Mound in Fulton County, Illinois.* M.A. thesis, Department of Anthropology, University of Wisconsin, Madison.
1973   The Nature of the Relationship Between Cahokia and the Central Illinois River Valley. Paper presented at the annual meeting of the Central States Anthropological Society, St. Louis.
1981   *An Introduction to the Archaeology of Upland West Central Illinois: A Preliminary Archaeological Survey of the Canton to Quincy Corridor for the Proposed FAP 407 Highway Project.* Western Illinois University Archaeological Research Laboratory, Reports of Investigations, no. 2. Macomb. Submitted to the Illinois Department of Transportation, Springfield.
1984   The Southeastern Ceremonial Complex on the Northern Middle Mississippian Frontier: Late Prehistoric Politico-Religious Systems in the Central Illinois River Valley. Paper presented at the Conference on the Southern Ceremonial Complex. Conference held at the Cottonlandia Museum, Greenwood, Mississippi.
1988   The Liverpool Lake Site: A Substantial Maple Mills Habitation Site in the Central Illinois River Valley. Paper presented at the Thirty-third annual Midwest Archaeological Conference, Urbana, Illinois.
1989   The Southeastern Ceremonial Complex on the Northern Middle Mississippian Frontier: Late Prehistoric Politico-Religious Systems in the Central Illinois River Valley. In *The Southern Ceremonial Complex: Artifacts and Analysis: The Cottonlandia Conference*, ed. Patricia Galloway, pp. 93–113. University of Nebraska, Lincoln.
n.d.   Cahokia as a Pre-Industrial City. Manuscript in possession of the author.

Conrad, Lawrence A., and Duane Esarey
1983   Oneota in West Central Illinois. Paper delivered at the Twenty-eighth Midwest Archaeological Conference, Iowa City.

Conrad, Lawrence A., Susan L. Gardener, and J. Joseph Alford
1984   An Archaeological Survey of the Lima Lake Area of Adams County, Illinois. Paper presented at the Thirtieth annual Midwest Archaeological Conference, Evanston, Illinois.

Conrad, Lawrence A., Timothy Good, and Susan Jelly
1981   Analysis of Cordmarked Ceramics from Settlement C. In *The Orendorf Site Preliminary Working Papers 1981*, comp. Duane Esarey and Lawrence A. Conrad, vol. 1, pp. 117–59. Western Illinois University Archaeological Research Laboratory, Macomb.

Conrad, Lawrence A., and Alan D. Harn
1972   The Spoon River Culture in the Central Illinois River Valley. Ms. on file, Dickson Mounds Museum, Lewistown, Illinois.

1976   Evidence for Contact Between the Spoon River Area and the Plains: Some Observations. Paper presented at the Twenty-first Midwest Archaeological Conference, Minneapolis.

Cook, Della C., and Jane E. Buikstra
1979   Health and Differential Survival in Prehistoric Populations: Prenatal Dental Effects. *American Journal of Physical Anthropology* 51: 649–64.

Cook, Thomas G.
1982   The Audrey Site: A Summary of Research Through 1981. Center for American Archeology, Special Report for Audrey Alumni (12 pp). Kampsville, Illinois.
1983a   The Audrey Site: A Summary of Research Through 1982. Center for American Archeology, Special Report for Audrey Alumni no. 2 (20 pp). Kampsville, Illinois.
1983b   Mississippianization of the Lower Illinois Valley: The Audrey North Village, Greene County, Illinois. Paper presented at the Twenty-eighth Midwest Archaeological Conference, Iowa City.

Cordy, Ross
1981   *A Study of Prehistoric Social Change: The Development of Complex Societies in the Hawaiian Islands.* Academic Press, New York.

Cottier, John W.
1977   An Area Archaeological Construction. *Missouri Archaeologist* 38:49–69.

Cottier, John W., and Michael D. Southard
1977   An Introduction to the Archaeology of Towosahgy State Archaeological Site. *Missouri Archaeologist* 38: 230–71.

Cowan, C. Wesley
1978   The Prehistoric Use and Distribution of Maygrass in Eastern North America: Cultural and Phytogeographic Implications. In *The Nature and Status of Ethnobotany*, ed. Richard I. Ford, pp. 263–88. University of Michigan, Museum of Anthropology, Anthropological Papers, no. 67. Ann Arbor.

Cowan, C. Wesley, H. Edwin Jackson, Katherine Moore, Andrew Nicklehoff, and Tristine Smart
1981   The Cloudsplitter Rockshelter, Menifee County, Kentucky: A Preliminary Report. *Southeastern Archaeological Conference Bulletin* 24:60–76.

Cox, Stephen D.
1985   *Art and Artisians of Prehistoric Middle Tennessee: The Gates P. Thruston Collection at Vanderbilt University Held in Trust by the Tennessee State Museum.* Tennessee State Museum, Nashville.

Crane, H. R., and James B. Griffin
1960   University of Michigan Radiocarbon Dates V. *Radiocarbon* 2:31–48.
1963   University of Michigan Radiocarbon Dates VIII. *Radiocarbon* 5:228–53.
1972   University of Michigan Radiocarbon Dates XIV. *Radiocarbon* 14:155–94.

Crawford, Gary
1982   Late Archaic Plant Remains from West-central Kentucky: A Summary. *Midcontinental Journal of Archaeology* 7:205–24.

Crites, Gary D.
1978   Plant Food Utilization Patterns During the Middle Woodland Owl Hollow Phase in Tennessee: A Preliminary Report. *Tennessee Anthropologist* 3:79–92.

Crook, A. R.
1916   The Composition and Origin of Monks Mound. *Trans-*

actions of the Illinois State Academy of Science 9: 82–84. Springfield.
1922   *The Origin of the Cahokia Mounds.* Bulletin of the Illinois State Museum (May). Springfield.

Curry, Hilda J.
1950   *Negative Painted Pottery of Angel Mounds Site and Its Distribution in the New World.* Indiana University Publications in Anthropology and Linguistics, Memoir no. 5. Supplement to the International Journal of American Linguistics, vol. 16 (4). Baltimore.

Curtis, John T.
1959   *The Vegetation of Wisconsin.* University of Wisconsin Press, Madison.

Cutler, Hugh C.
1958   *Corn Cob from Shelter, Van Buren County, Arkansas.* Missouri Archaeological Society Newsletter no. 119. Columbia.

Cutler Hugh C., and Leonard W. Blake
1969   Corn from Cahokia sites. In *Explorations into Cahokia Archaeology*, ed. Melvin L. Fowler, pp. 122–36. Illinois Archaeological Survey Bulletin no. 7. Urbana.
1973   *Plants from Archaeological Sites East of the Rockies.* Missouri Botanical Garden, St. Louis.
1976   *Plants from Archaeological Sites East of the Rockies.* University of Missouri-Columbia, American Archaeology Division, Reports no. 1. Microfiche.
1977   Corn from Cahokia Sites. In *Explorations into Cahokia Archaeology*, 2d ed., ed. Melvin L. Fowler, pp. 122–36. Illinois Archaeological Survey Bulletin no. 7. Urbana.

Dallman, J. E.
1977   *Dietary Evaluation of Two Mill Creek Sites: The Matt Brewster and the Phipps Sites, in Northeast Iowa.* Ph.D. diss., Department of Anthropology, University of Wisconsin, Madison.

Davis, Hester A.
1969   The "Non-Nosed" God Mask. *Arkansas Archaeologist* 10:63.

Davis, Hester, Don G. Wyckoff, and Mary A. Holmes (editors)
1971   *Proceedings of the Eighth Caddo Conference.* Oklahoma Archaeological Survey, Occasional Publication no. 2. Norman.

Davis, Leslie B., and Charles D. Zeier
1978   Multi-Phase Late Period Bison Procurement at the Antonsen Site, Southwestern Montana. In *Bison Procurement and Utilization: A Symposium*, ed. Leslie B. Davis and Michael Wilson, pp. 222–35. Plains Anthropologist, Memoir no. 14.

Davy, Douglas M.
1982   *Proximity and Human Behavior: Settlement Locational Pattern Change in Prehistoric Illinois.* Ph.D. diss., Department of Anthropology, Southern Illinois University at Carbondale. University Microfilms, Ann Arbor.

De La Ronde, John T.
1876   Personal Narrative. *Wisconsin Historical Collections* 7:345–65. State Historical Society of Wisconsin, Madison.

Dennell, R. W.
1976   The Economic Importance of Plant Resources Represented on Archaeological Sites. *Journal of Archaeological Science* 3:229–47.

Denny, Sidney G.
1974   Recent Archaeological Excavations at the Olin Site. Paper presented at the Forty-sixth Annual Midwest Archaeological Conference, East Lansing.

1976 *A Report of Archaeological Inventory Reconnaissance for the Proposed Richland Creek Flood Abatement Project in the Vicinity of Belleville, Illinois*. Report submitted to the Illinois Department of Transportation, Springfield.

1979 *Archaeological Survey of Selected Portions of Carlyle Lake, Clinton County, Illinois*. Reports in Contract Archaeology no. 8. Southern Illinois University, Edwardsville.

Denny, Sidney G., and James P. Anderson

1974 An Archaeological Survey of the Upland Areas Adjacent to the American Bottoms Region. In *Preliminary Report of 1973 Historic Sites Survey, Archaeological Reconnaissance of Selected Areas in the State of Illinois: Part I, Summary*, pp. 144–51. Illinois Archaeological Survey, Urbana.

1975 An Archaeological Survey of the Upland Areas Adjacent to the American Bottoms Region. In *Preliminary Report of 1974 Historic Sites Survey, Archaeological Reconnaissance of Selected Areas in the State of Illinois: Part I, Summary*, pp. 136–45. Illinois Archaeological Survey, Urbana.

Denny, Sidney G., William I. Woods, and Brad Koldehoff

1983 Upland Mississippian Settlement/Subsistence Systems in the Cahokia Region. Paper presented at the Forty-eighth Annual Meeting of the Society for American Archaeology, Pittsburgh.

DePratter, Chester

1983 *Late Prehistoric and Early Historic Chiefdoms in the Southeastern United States*. Ph.D. diss., Department of Anthropology, University of Georgia.

Deuel, Thorne

1935 Basic Cultures of the Mississippi Valley. *American Anthropologist* 37:429–45.

Diener, Paul

1968 The Demographic Dilemma of Food-Producing Revolutions: Hopewell. Paper presented at the annual meeting of the Central States Anthropological Society.

Dillehay, Tom D.

1974 Late Quaternary Bison Population Changes on the Southern Plains. *Plains Anthropologist* 19(65):180–96.

Dobbs, Clark A.

1982 Oneota Origins and Development: The Radiocarbon Evidence. In *Oneota Studies*, ed. Guy E. Gibbon, pp. 91–106. Publications in Anthropology no. 1. University of Minnesota, Minneapolis.

1984 *Oneota Settlement Patterns in the Blue Earth River Valley, Minnesota*. Ph.D. diss., University of Minnesota, Minneapolis.

1985a *An Archaeological Survey of the City of Red Wing, Minnesota*. Reports of Investigations no. 2. Institute for Minnesota Archaeology, Minneapolis.

1985b Excavations at the Bryan Site: 1983–1984. *Minnesota Archaeolgist* 43:49–58.

1986a *Archaeological Investigations at the Bryan Site (21GD4), Goodhue County, Minnesota: 1983–1984*. Reports of Investigations no. 8. Institute for Minnesota Archaeology, Minneapolis.

1986b *A Preliminary Report on Investigations at the Energy Park Site (21GD158)*. Reports of Investigations no. 16. Institute for Minnesota Archaeology, Minneapolis.

Dobbs, Clark A., and Kim Breakey

1987 A Preliminary Report on Investigations at the Energy Park Site (21GD158): A Silvernale Phase Village at the Lake Pepin Locality. Paper presented at the Midwest Archaeological Conference, Milwaukee.

Dorney, John R.

1980 *Presettlement Vegetation of Southeastern Wisconsin: Edaphic Relationships and Disturbance*. M.A. thesis, Department of Botany, University of Wisconsin-Milwaukee.

1981 The Impact of Native Americans on Presettlement Vegetation in Southeastern Wisconsin. Paper presented at the annual meeting of the Wisconsin Academy of Sciences.

Dorothy, Lawrence G.

1980 The Ceramics of the Sand Point Site (20BG14), Baraga County, Michigan: A Preliminary Description. *Michigan Archaeologist* 26 (3–4): 39–71.

Douglas, John G.

1970 *Archaeological Testing in the Middle Embarras Valley, Illinois: Lincoln Reservoir*. Report submitted to the National Park Service, Northeast Region, Philadelphia.

1976 *Collins: A Late Woodland Ceremonial Complex in the Woodfordian Northeast*. Ph.D. diss., Department of Anthropology, University of Illinois at Urbana-Champaign. University Microfilms, Ann Arbor.

Dowling, John

1983 The Goodfellows vs. the Dalton Gang: The Assumptions of Economic Anthropology. *Journal of Anthropological Research* 35:292–308.

Drennan, Robert D.

1984 Long-Distance Movement of Goods in the Mesoamerican Formative and Classic. *American Antiquity* 49: 27–43.

Droessler, Judith

1981 *Craniometry and Biological Distance: Biocultural Continuity and Change at the Late Woodland-Mississippian Interface*. Center for American Archeology, Research Series, no. 1. Evanston, Illinois.

Dudzik, Mark J.

1974 An Archaeological Survey of the Illinois Side of the Mississippi River Valley from the Mouth of the Des Moines River to the Wisconsin Border. In *Preliminary Report of 1973 Historic Sites Survey, Archaeological Reconnaissance of Selected Areas in the State of Illinois: Part 1, Summary*, pp. 75–84. Illinois Archaeological Survey, Urbana.

Duffield, Lathal Flay

1964 *Engraved Shells from the Craig Mound at Spiro, Le Flore County, Oklahoma*. Oklahoma Anthropological Society Memoir no. 1, Norman.

Dunavan, Sandra L.

1985 *Mississippian Ethnobotany at the Adams Site (15FU4)*. Undergraduate senior honors thesis, Department of Anthropology, University of Illinois at Urbana-Champaign.

Earle, Timothy K.

1977 A Reappraisal of Redistribution: Complex Hawaiian Chiefdoms. In *Exchange Systems in Prehistory*, ed. T. K. Earle and J. E. Ericson, pp. 213–29. Academic Press, New York.

1978 *Economic and Social Organization of a Complex Chiefdom: The Halalea District, Kaua'i, Hawaii*. University of Michigan, Museum of Annthropology, Anthropological Papers, no. 63. Ann Arbor.

1986 Specialization and the Production and Exchange of Wealth: Hawaiian Chiefdoms and the Inca Empire. In *Specialisation, Exchange, and Social Complexity*, ed. E. Brumfiel and T. Earle. Cambridge University Press, Cambridge.

Earle, T. K., and J. E. Ericson (editors)

1977 *Exchange Systems in Prehistory*. Academic Press, New York.

Eckblaw, George E.

1937 Surficial and Subsurface Geology and Structure. In *A Report on Certain Physical, Economic and Social Aspects of the Valley of the Kaskaskia River in the State of Illinois*, pt. 1, pp. 13–20. University of Illinois, Urbana.

Edging, Richard B., Norman Meinholz, and Thomas Berres

1982 Preliminary Report of a Controlled Surface Collection and Exploratory Testing at the Apple River [Lundy] Site, 11-Jd-140, Jo Daviess County, Illinois. Ms. on file, Resource Investigation Program, University of Illinois at Urbana-Champaign.

Edging, Richard (editor)

1985 *Archaeological Investigations at the Turk Site (15Ce6), Carlisle County, Kentucky*. University of Illinois, Department of Anthropology, Western Kentucky Project Report no. 3. Urbana.

Emerson, Thomas E.

1973 The Middle Mississippian Manifestation in the Northern Mississippi River Valley. Ms. in possession of the author.

1981 Ungulate Remains from the Orendorf Village Site. In *The Orendorf Site Preliminary Working Papers 1981*, comp. Duane E. Esarey and Lawrence A. Conrad, vol. 1, pp. 161–79. Western Illinois University Archaeological Research Laboratory, Macomb.

1982 *Mississippian Stone Images in Illinois*. Illinois Archaeological Survey, Circular no. 6. Urbana.

1984a The BBB Motor Site and Its Implications for Understanding Aspects of Middle Mississippian Symbolism at Cahokia. Paper presented at the Southern Ceremonial Complex Conference held at the Cottonlandia Museum, Greenwood, Mississippi.

1984b *The Dyroff (11-S-463) and Levin (11-S-462) Sites*. American Bottom Archaeology FAI-270 Site Reports, vol. 9, pp. 199–362. University of Illinois Press, Urbana.

1984c The Stirling Phase Occupation. In *The BBB Motor Site*, by Thomas E. Emerson and Douglas K. Jackson, pp. 197–321. American Bottom Archaeology FAI-270 Site Reports, vol. 6. University of Illinois Press, Urbana.

1986 Late Archaic Adaptations to the Interior-Riverine environments of southwestern Illinois. Paper presented at a symposium entitled "The Lake Forest Archaic: Papers in Honor of Robert Ritzenthaler" at the Midwestern Archaeological Conference, Columbus.

1988 The Mississippian Disperse Village as a Social and Environmental Adaptive Strategy. Paper presented at the Forty-sixth International Congress of Americanists, Amsterdam.

1989 Water, Serpents, and the Underworld: An Exploration into Cahokian Symbolism. In *Southern Ceremonial Complex: Artifacts and Analysis: The Cottonlandia Conference*, ed. Patricia Galloway, pp. 45–92. University of Nebraska Press, Lincoln.

Emerson, Thomas E., and Douglas K. Jackson

1984 *The BBB Motor Site (11-Ms-595)*. American Bottom Archaeology FAI-270 Site Reports, vol. 6. University of Illinois Press, Urbana.

1985 The Edelhardt and Lineman Phases: Setting the Stage for the Final Transition to Mississippian in the American Bottom. Paper presented at the Mid-South Archaeological Conference, Starkville.

1987a The Edelhardt and Lineman Phases: Setting the Stage for the Final Transition to Mississippian in the American Bottom. In *The Emergent Mississippian: Proceedings of the Sixth Mid-South Archaeological Conference, June 6–9, 1985*, ed. Richard A. Marshall, pp. 172–93. Cobb Institute of Archaeology, Occasional Papers, no. 87–01. Mississippi State University.

1987b *Emergent Mississippian and Early Mississippian Homesteads at the Marcus Site (11-S-631)*, American Bottom Archaeology FAI-270 Site Reports, vol. 17 no. 2. University of Illinois Press, Urbana.

Emerson, Thomas E., and George R. Milner

1981 The Mississippian Occupation of the American Bottom: The Communities. Paper presented at the Midwest Archaeological Conference, Madison.

1982 Community Organization and Settlement Patterns of Peripheral Mississippian Sites in the American Bottom, Illinois. Paper presented at the Forty-seventh Annual Meeting of the Society for American Archaeology, Minneapolis.

1988 Internal Structure, Distribution, and Relationships among Low-Level Mississippian Period Communities in Illinois. Paper presented at Fifty-third Annual Meeting of the Society for American Archaeology, Phoenix.

Emerson, Thomas E., George R. Milner, and Douglas K. Jackson

1983 *The Florence Street Site (11-S-458)*. American Bottom Archaeology FAI-270 Site Reports, vol. 2. University of Illinois Press, Urbana.

Emmons, Merrill, Patrick J. Munson, and Joseph R. Caldwell

1960 A Prehistoric House from Fulton County, Illinois. *The Living Museum* 22(5):516–17.

Engels, Frederick

1878 *Herrn Eugen Dührings Umwälzung der Wissenschaft (Anti-Dühring)*. (Reprint, 1972, International Publishers, New York).

Esarey, Duane

1987 Mississippian Spider Gorgets. Paper presented at the Thirty-second annual Midwest Archaeological Conference, Milwaukee.

1988a *The Liverpool Lake Site: Results of Archaeological Monitoring at 11Mn163, Mason County, Illinois*. Report submitted to U.S. Fish and Wildlife Service, Minneapolis.

1988b Negative Painted Pottery and Mississippian Trade in the Illinois River Valley. Paper presented at the Mid-South Archaeological Conference, Paducah.

Esarey, Duane, and Lawrence A. Conrad (compilers)

1981 *The Orendorf Site Preliminary Working Papers 1981*. Vols. 1–3. Western Illinois University Archaeological Research Laboratory, Macomb.

Esarey, Duane, with Timothy W. Good

1981 *Final Report on FAI-270 and Illinois Route 460 Related Excavations at the Lohmann Site (ll-S-49), St. Clair County, Illinois*. Archaeological Research Laboratory,

Western Illinois University, Reports of Investigations, no. 3, and Department of Anthropology, University of Illinois at Urbana-Champaign, FAI-270 Archaeological Mitigation Project, Report no. 39.

Farnsworth, Kenneth B.
1970 Gracey Mound Group: A Hopewell Mortuary Site from the Macoupin Valley. Manuscript in the possession of the author.
1973 *An Archaeological Survey of the Macoupin Valley.* Illinois State Museum, Reports of Investigations no. 26. Springfield.

Farnsworth, Kenneth B., and David L. Asch
1986 Early Woodland Chronology, Artifact Styles, and Settlement Distribution in the Lower Illinois Valley Region. In *Early Woodland Archeology*, ed. Kenneth B. Farnsworth and Thomas E. Emerson, pp. 326–457. Center for American Archeology, Kampsville Seminars in Archeology no. 2. Kampsville, Illinois.

Farnsworth, Kenneth B., and Thomas E. Emerson
1989 The Macoupin Creek Figure Pipe and Its Archeological Context: Evidence for Late Woodland-Mississippian Interaction Beyond the Northern Border of Cahokian Settlement. *Midcontinental Journal of Archaeology* 14(1):18–37.

Farnsworth, Kenneth B., and Thomas E. Emerson (editors)
1986 *Early Woodland Archeology.* Kampsville Seminars in Archeology, vol. 2. Center for American Archeology Press, Kampsville, Illinois.

Farnsworth, Kenneth B., and Phillip D. Neusius
1978 *The Archeology of Pere Marquette State Park: 1878–1978.* Center for American Archeology, Contract Archeology Program, Report of Investigations no. 46, Kampsville, Illinois. Submitted to Illinois Department of Conservation, Springfield.

Faulkner, Charles H.
1972 *The Late Prehistoric Occupation of Northwestern Indiana, A Study of the Upper Mississippi Cultures of the Kankakee Valley.* Prehistory Research Series vol. 5(1). Indiana Historical Society, Indianapolis.
1978 Ceramics of the Owl Hollow Phase in South-Central Tennessee: A Preliminary Report. *Tennessee Anthropologist* 3:187–202.

Fehrenbacher, J. B., G. O. Walker, and H. L. Washer
1967 *Soils of Illinois.* Bulletin no. 725, University of Illinois College of Agriculture Experiment Station in cooperation with the Soil Conservation Service, U.S. Department of Agriculture, Washington, D.C.

Fenneman, N. M.
1911 *Geology and Mineral Resources of the St. Louis Quadrangle—Missouri-Illinois.* U.S. Geological Survey Bulletin no. 438. Washington, D.C.

Fenner, Gloria J.
1963 The Plum Island Site, LaSalle County, Illinois. In *Reports on Illinois Prehistory: I.* ed. Elaine Bluhm, pp. 1–106. Illinois Archaeological Survey Bulletin no. 4. Urbana.

Fiedel, Stuart J.
1987 *Prehistory of the Americas.* Cambridge University Press, Cambridge.

Finney, Fred A.
1985 The Carbon Dioxide Site (11-Mo-594). In *The Carbon Dioxide Site (11-Mo-594)* by Fred A. Finney, and *The Robert Schneider Site (11-Ms-1177)*, by Andrew C. Fortier, pp. 1–167. American Bottom Archaeology

FAI-270 Site Reports, vol. 11. University of Illinois Press, Urbana.

Finney, Fred A., and James B. Stoltman
1986 The Fred Edwards Site: A Case of Stirling Phase Culture Contact in Southwest Wisconsin. Paper presented at the Fifty-first Annual Meeting of the Society for American Archaeology, New Orleans.

Fletcher, Alice C., and James Murie
1904 *The Hako, A Pawnee Ceremony.* Twenty-second Annual Report of the Bureau of American Ethnology, pt. 2. Washington, D.C.

Ford, James A.
1969 *A Comparison of Formative Cultures in the Americas.* Smithsonian Contributions to Anthropology vol. 2. Smithsonian Institution Press, Washington, D.C.

Ford, James A., and Gordon R. Willey
1941 An Interpretation of the Prehistory of the Eastern United States. *American Anthropologist* 43:325–63.

Ford, Richard I.
1974 Northeastern Archeology: Past and Future Directions. *Annual Review of Anthropology* 3:385–413.
1977 Evolutionary Ecology and the Evolution of Human Ecosystems: A Case Study from the Midwestern U.S.A. In *Explanation of Prehistoric Change*, ed. James N. Hill, pp. 153–84. University of New Mexico Press, Albuquerque.
1981 Gardening and Farming Before A.D. 1000: Patterns of Prehistoric Cultivation North of Mexico. *Journal of Ethnobiology* 1:6–27.

Fowke, Gerard
1896 Stone Art. *Thirteenth Annual Report of the Bureau of American Ethnology*, pp. 57–184. Washington, D.C.
1910 *Antiquities of Central and Southeastern Missouri.* Bureau of American Ethnology, Bulletin no. 37. Smithsonian Institutuion, Washington, D.C.

Fowler, Melvin L.
1952 The Clear Lake Site: Hopewellian Occupation. In *Hopewellian Communities in Illinois*, ed. Thorne Deuel, pp. 131–74. Illinois State Museum Scientific Papers no. 5. Springfield.
1959 *An Archaeological Site Survey of the Carlyle Reservoir.* Contract report submitted to the U.S. Department of the Interior, National Park Service.
1960 *Test Excavations of Selected Archaeological Sites in the Carlyle Reservoir.* Contract report submitted to the U.S. Department of the Interior, National Park Service.
1962 Radiocarbon Assays. In *First Annual Report: American Bottoms Archaeology, July 1, 1961–June 30, 1962*, ed. Melvin L. Fowler, pp. 49–57. Illinois Archaeological Survey, Urbana.
1963 Radiocarbon Assays. In *Second Annual Report: American Bottoms Archaeology, July 1, 1962–June 30, 1963*, ed. Melvin L. Fowler, pp. 46–52. Illinois Archaeological Survey, Urbana.
1968 The Temple Town Community: Cahokia and Amulucan Compared. In *The Rise and Fall of Civilizations*, ed. J. Sabloff and C. Lamberg-Karlovsky, pp. 209–16. University of New Mexico Press, Albuquerque.
1969a The Cahokia Site. In *Explorations into Cahokia Archaeology*, ed. Melvin L. Fowler, pp. 1–30. Illinois Archaeological Survey Bulletin no. 7. Urbana.
1969b Middle Mississippian Agricultural Fields. *American Antiquity* 34:365–75.
1971 Agriculture and Village Settlement in the North Ameri-

can East: The Central Mississippi Valley Area, A Case History. In *Prehistoric Agriculture*, ed. Stuart Struever, pp. 391–403. Natural History Press, Garden City, New York. (Originally published in 1966, *36th Congreso International de Americanistas* 1:229–40.)

1973   Midwestern Prehistory, Cognitive Dissonance and Conspicuous Assumptions: An Essay. *Missouri Archaeologist* 35:45–54.

1974   Cahokia, Ancient Capital of the Midwest. *Addison-Wesley Module in Anthropology* no. 48:3–38.

1975   A Precolumbian Urban Center on the Mississippi. *Scientific American* 233(2):92–101.

1977   The Cahokia Site. In *Explorations into Cahokia Archaeology,* 2d ed., ed. Melvin L. Fowler, pp. 1–30. Illinois Archaeological Survey Bulletin no. 7. Urbana.

1978   Cahokia and the American Bottom: Settlement Archaeology. In *Mississippian Settlement Patterns*, ed. Bruce D. Smith, pp. 455–78. Academic Press, New York.

1979   A History of Investigations at the Cahokia Mounds Historic Site and an Atlas of Mounds and Other Aboriginal Features. Ms. on file, Illinois Historic Preservation Agency, Springfield.

1989   *The Cahokia Atlas: A Historical Atlas of Cahokia Archaeology*. Studies in Illinois Archaeology no. 6. Illinois Historic Preservation Agency, Springfield.

Fowler, Melvin L. (editor)

1962   *First Annual Report: American Bottoms Archaeology July 1, 1961–June 30, 1962*. Illinois Archaeological Survey, Urbana.

1963   *Second Annual Report: American Bottoms Archaeology July 1, 1962–June 30, 1963*. Illinois Archaeological Survey, Urbana.

1964   *Third Annual Report: American Bottoms Archaeology July 1, 1963–June 30, 1964*. Illinois Archaeological Survey, Urbana.

1969   *Explorations into Cahokia Archaeology*. Illinois Archaeological Survey Bulletin no. 7. Urbana.

1975   *Cahokia Archaeology: Field Reports*. Illinois State Museum Research Series, Papers in Anthropology, no. 3. Springfield.

Fowler, Melvin L., and Robert L. Hall

1972   *Archaeological Phases at Cahokia*. Illinois State Museum Research Series, Papers in Anthropology, no. 1. Springfield.

1975   Archaeological Phases at Cahokia. In *Perspectives in Cahokia Archaeology,* ed. James A. Brown, pp. 1–14. Illinois Archaeological Survey Bulletin no. 10. Urbana.

1978   Late Prehistory of the Illinois Area. In *Northeast,* ed. Bruce G. Trigger, pp. 560–68. Handbook of North American Indians, vol. 15, William G. Sturtevant, general editor. Smithsonian Institution, Washington, D.C.

Frankforter, W. D.

1969   Faunal Study of Large Ruminants from Mill Creek Culture Sites in Nowthwest Iowa. *Journal of the Iowa Archeological Society* 15:286–301.

Freimuth, Glen A.

1974   *The Lunsford-Pulcher Site: An Examination of Selected Traits and Their Social Implications in American Bottom Prehistory*. M.A. thesis, Department of Anthropology, University of Illinois at Urbana-Champaign.

Fried, Morton

1967   *The Evolution of Political Society*. Random House, New York.

Fritz, Gayle J.

1984   Identification of Cultigen Amaranth and Chenopod from Rockshelter Sites in Northwest Arkansas. *American Antiquity* 49:558–72.

1986   *Prehistoric Ozark Agriculture*. Ph.D. diss., Department of Anthropology, University of North Carolina, Chapel Hill.

Fugle, Eugene

1957   *Introduction to the Artifact Assemblages of the Big Sioux and Little Sioux Foci*. M.A. thesis, Department of Sociology and Anthropology, University of Iowa, Iowa City.

1962   Mill Creek Culture and Technology. *Journal of the Iowa Archeological Society* 11:4.

Gallagher, James P., Robert F. Boszhardt, Robert F. Sasso, and Katherine Stevenson

1985   Oneota Ridged Field Agriculture in Southwestern Wisconsin. *American Antiquity* 50:605–12.

Gallagher, James P., and Katherine Stevenson

1983   Oneota Subsistence and Settlement in Southwestern Wisconsin. In *Oneota Studies*, ed. Guy E. Gibbon, pp. 15–27. Publications in Anthropology no. 1, University of Minnesota, Minneapolis.

Gardner, William M.

1963   *Progress Report on the Shelbyville Reservoir*. Contract report submitted to the U.S. Department of the Interior, National Park Service.

1969a   *The Havana Cultural Tradition Occupation in the Upper Kaskaskia River Valley, Illinois*. Ph.D. diss., Department of Anthropology, University of Illinois at Urbana-Champaign. University Microfilms, Ann Arbor.

1969b   *The Mississippian Occupation in the Kaskaskia and Okaw Drainage*. Contract report submitted to the U.S. Department of the Interior, National Park Service, Northeast Region.

1973a   Ecological or Historical Determinants in Cultural Patterning Among the Prehistoric Occupants of the Upper Kaskaskia River Valley, Illinois. In *Variation in Anthropology*, edited by Donald W. Lathrap and John Douglas, pp. 189–97. Illinois Archaeological Survey, Special Papers no. 1, Urbana.

1973b   The Vandalia Complex: A Late Woodland Complex in the Central Kaskaskia River Drainage. In *Late Woodland Site Archaeology in Illinois I: Investigations in South-central Illinois,* ed. James A. Brown, pp. 214–27. Illinois Archaeological Survey Bulletin no. 9. Urbana.

n.d.   *Final Report on the Shelbyville Reservoir, 1964–1965*. Contract report submitted to the U.S. Department of the Interior, National Park Service.

Gates, Richard I.

1966   *Historical Geography of Salt in the Old Northwest*. M.A. thesis, Department of Geography, University of Wisconsin, Madison.

Geis, James W., and William R. Boggess

1968   The Prairie Peninsula: Its Origin and Significance in the Vegetational History of Central Illinois. In *The Quaternary of Illinois,* ed. R. E. Bergstrom, pp. 89–95. University of Illinois, College of Agriculture, Special Publication no. 14.

Gibbon, Guy E.

1972   Cultural Dynamics and the Development of the Oneota
         Life-Way in Wisconsin. *American Antiquity* 37:166–85.

1973   *The Sheffield Site: An Oneota Site on the St. Croix
         River*. Minnesota Prehistoric Archaeology Series
         no. 10. Minnesota Historical Society, St. Paul.

1974   A Model of Mississippian Development and its Im-
         plication for the Red Wing Area. In *Aspects of Upper
         Great Lakes Anthropology*, ed. Elden Johnson, pp.
         129–37. Minnesota Prehistoric Archaeology Series
         no. 11. Minnesota Historical Society, St. Paul.

1979   *The Mississippian Occupation of the Red Wing Area*.
         Minnesota Prehistoric Archaeology Series, no. 13.
         Minnesota Historical Society, St. Paul.

1982   Oneota Origins Revisited. In *Oneota Studies*, ed.
         Guy E. Gibbon, pp. 85–89. University of Minnesota
         Publications in Anthropology, no. 1. Minneapolis.

1983   The Blue Earth Phase of Southern Minnesota. *Journal
         of the Iowa Archeological Society* 30:1–84.

Gibbon, Guy E., and Clark A. Dobbs

1987   The Middle Mississippian Presence in the Red Wing
         Area. Revised version of a paper delivered at the Fifty-
         first Annual Meeting of the Society for American
         Archaeology, New Orleans, 1986.

Gleason, Henry A., and Arthur Cronquist

1963   *Manual of Vascular Plants of Northeastern United States
         and Adjacent Canada*. D. Van Nostrand, New York.

Goddard, T. M. and Larry R. Sabata

1986   *Soil Survey of Madison County, Illinois*. Illinois Agri-
         cultural Experiment Station Soil Report no. 120.
         U.S.D.A. Soil Conservation Service, Urbana.

Goggin, John M.

1952   *Space and Time Perspective in Northern St. Johns
         Archaeology, Florida*. Yale University Publications in
         Anthropology no. 47. New Haven, Connecticut.

Golden, Bernard

1962   *Report on the 1961 Site Survey of the Shelbyville
         Reservoir Area*. Contract report submitted to the U.S.
         Department of the Interior, National Park Service.

Goldman, I.

1970   *Ancient Polynesian Society*. University of Chicago
         Press, Chicago.

Goldstein, Lynne G.

1973   Soil Types and Mississippian Site Distribution. Manu-
         script on file, Center for American Archeology,
         Kampsville Archeological Center, Kampsville, Illinois.

1979   *An Archaeological Survey of Portions of the Craw-
         fish and Rock River Valleys near Their Confluence
         in Jefferson County, Wisconsin*. Report submitted to
         the Historical Preservation Division, State Historical
         Society of Wisconsin. University of Wisconsin- Mil-
         waukee Archaeological Research Laboratory, Report of
         Investigations, no. 32.

1980a   *A Continuing Archaeological Survey of Portions of the
         Crawfish and Rock River Valleys near Their Confluence
         in Jefferson County, Wisconsin*. Report submitted to the
         Historic Preservation Division, State Historical Society
         of Wisconsin. University of Wisconsin-Milwaukee
         Archaeological Research Laboratory, Report of Investi-
         gations, no. 45.

1980b   *Mississippian Mortuary Practices: A Case Study of Two
         Cemeteries in the Lower Illinois Valley*. Northwestern
         University Archaeological Program, Scientific Papers,
         no. 4. Evanston, Illinois.

1981   *A Continuing Survey of Portions of the Rock River
         Drainage in Jefferson County, Wisconsin*. University
         of Wisconsin-Milwaukee Archaeological Research
         Laboratory, Report of Investigations, no. 52.

1982   *Archaeology in the Southeastern Wisconsin Glaciated
         Region: Phase I*. Report to the Historical Preserva-
         tion Division, State Historical Society of Wisconsin.
         University of Wisconsin-Milwaukee Archaeological
         Research Laboratory, Report of Investigations, no. 64.

1987   *The Southeastern Wisconsin Archaeology Project:
         1986–87 and Project Summary*. Report to the Historical
         Preservation Division, State Historical Society of Wis-
         consin. University of Wisconsin-Milwaukee Archaeo-
         logical Research Laboratory, Report of Investigations,
         no. 88.

Grange, R. T.

1968   *Pawnee and Lower Loup Pottery*. Publications in
         Anthropology no. 3. Nebraska Historical Society,
         Lincoln.

Green, Thomas J.

1977   *Economic Relationships Underlying Mississippian Settle-
         ment Patterns in Southwestern Indiana*. Ph.D. diss.,
         Department of Anthropology, Indiana University,
         Bloomington.

Green, Thomas J., and Cheryl A. Munson

1978   Mississippian Settlement Patterns in Southwestern Indi-
         ana. In *Mississippian Settlement Patterns*, ed. Bruce D.
         Smith, pp. 293–330. Academic Press, New York.

Green, William

1976   Preliminary Report on the Bauer Branch Complex, a
         Late Woodland Manifestation in West-central Illinois.
         Wisconsin Archaeologist 57:172–88.

Gregg, Michael L.

1975a   A Population Estimate for Cahokia. In *Perspectives in
         Cahokia Archaeology*, ed. James A. Brown, pp. 126–
         36. Illinois Archaeological Survey Bulletin no. 10.
         Urbana.

1975b   *Settlement Morphology and Production Specializa-
         tion: the Horseshoe Lake Site, a Case Study*. Ph.D.
         diss., Department of Anthropology, University of
         Wisconsin-Milwaukee. University Microfilms, Ann
         Arbor.

Griffin, James B.

1937   The Archaeological Remains of the Chiwere Sioux.
         American Antiquity 2:180–81.

1943   *The Fort Ancient Aspect: Its Cultural and Chronological
         Position in Mississippi Valley Archaeology*. University
         of Michigan Press, Ann Arbor.

1946   Culture Change and Continuity in Eastern United
         States Archaeology. In *Man in Northeastern North
         America*, ed. Frederick Johnson, pp. 37–95. Papers of
         the Robert S. Peabody Foundation for Archaeology.
         Andover, Massachusetts.

1949   The Cahokia Ceramic Complexes. In *Proceedings of
         the Fifth Plains Conference for Archeology*, assem.
         John L. Champe, pp. 44–58. Laboratory of Anthro-
         pology, Notebook no. 1. University of Nebraska,
         Lincoln.

1952a   Culture Periods in Eastern United States Archeology. In
         Archeology of Eastern United States, ed. J. B. Griffin,
         pp. 352–64. University of Chicago Press, Chicago.

1952b   A Preview of the Ceramic Relationships of the Synders
         Sites, Calhoun County, Illinois. In *The Synders Site,*

Calhoun County, Illinois, pp. 14–21. Greater St. Louis Archaeological Society.

1960a Climatic Change: A Contributory Cause of the Growth and Decline of Northern Hopewellian Culture. *Wisconsin Archeologist* 41:21–33.

1960b A Hypothesis for the Prehistory of the Winnebago. In *Culture in History: Essays in Honor of Paul Radin*, ed. Stanley Diamond, pp. 809–65. Columbia University Press, New York.

1961 Some Correlations of Climatic and Cultural Change in Eastern North America Prehistory. *Annals of the New York Academy of Science* 95(1):710–17.

1966 *The Fort Ancient Aspect: Its Cultural and Chronological Position in Mississippi Valley Archaeology*. Museum of Anthropology, University of Michigan, Anthropological Papers no. 28. Ann Arbor.

1967 Eastern North American Archaeology: A Summary. *Science* 156(3772):175–91.

1970 Introduction. In *The Burial Complexes of the Knight and Norton Mounds in Illinois and Michigan*, by James B. Griffin, Richard E. Flanders, and Paul F. Titterington, pp. 1–10. University of Michigan, Museum of Anthropology, Memoirs no. 2. Ann Arbor.

1978a Foreword. In *Mississippian Settlement Patterns*, ed. Bruce D. Smith, pp. xv-xxii. Academic Press, New York.

1978b Late Prehistory of the Ohio Valley. In *Northeast*, ed. Bruce G. Trigger, pp. 547–59. Handbook of North American Indians, vol. 15, William G. Sturtevant, general editor. Smithsonian Institution, Washington, D.C.

1984 Observations on the FAI-270 Project. In *American Bottom Archaeology*, ed. Charles J. Bareis and James W. Porter, pp. 253–61. University of Illinois Press, Urbana.

1985 Changing Concepts of the Prehistoric Mississippian Cultures of the Eastern United States. In *Alabama and the Borderlands*, ed. R. Badger and L. Clayton, pp. 40–63. University of Alabama Press, University.

Griffin, James B., Richard E. Flanders and Paul F. Titterington
1970 *The Burial Complexes of the Knight and Norton Mounds in Illinois and Michigan*. University of Michigan, Museum of Anthropology, Memoirs no. 2. Ann Arbor.

Griffin, James B., and Volney H. Jones
1977 The University of Michigan Excavations at the Pulcher Site in 1950. *American Antiquity* 42:462–88.

Griffin, James B., and Richard G. Morgan (editors)
1941 *Contributions to the Archeology of the Illinois River Valley*. Transactions of the American Philosophical Society, n.s. vol. 32 (1). Philadelphia.

Griffin, James B., and Dan F. Morse
1961 The Short-Nosed God from the Emmons Site, Illinois. *American Antiquity* 26:560–63.

Griffin, James B., and Albert C. Spaulding
1951 The Central Mississippi Valley Archaeological Survey, Season 1950—A Preliminary Report. *Journal of the Illinois State Archaeological Society* 1:75–81, 84.

Griffin, John W.
1946 *The Upper Mississippi Occupation at the Fisher site, Will County, Illinois*. M.A. thesis, Department of Anthropology, University of Chicago.

Griffin, John W., and Donald E. Wray
1946 Bison in Illinois Archaeology. *Transactions of the Illinois State Academy of Science* 38:21–26. Springfield.

Griffith, William J.
1954 *The Hasinai Indians of East Texas as Seen by Europeans, 1687–1772*. Philological and Documentary Studies vol. 2(3). Middle American Research Institute, Tulane University, New Orleans.

Grimm, R. E. (editor)
1950 *Cahokia Brought to Life*. Greater St. Louis Archaeological Society, St. Louis.

Grivna, Walt
1986 *Analysis of Feature 363 from the Bryan Site (21GD4)*. Reports of Investigation no. 11. Institute for Minnesota Archaeology, Minneapolis.

Gums, Bonnie L., and Alan J. Brown
1986 *Archaeological Investigations at the William Pfeffer #2 Site (11-S-204), St. Clair County, Illinois*. Report submitted to the Illinois Historic Preservation Agency, Springfield.

Hall, Robert L.
1962 *The Archeology of Carcajou Point*. 2 vols. University of Wisconsin Press, Madison.

1963 Report of General Activities. In *Second Annual Report: American Bottoms Archaeology July 1, 1962–June 30, 1963*, ed. Melvin L. Fowler, pp. 24–27. Illinois Archaeological Survey, Urbana.

1964 Illinois State Museum Projects. In *Third Annual Report: American Bottoms Archaeology July 1, 1963–June 30, 1964*, ed. Melvin L. Fowler, pp. 11–15. Illinois Archaeological Survey, Urbana.

1965 Current Research: Northern Mississippi Valley. *American Antiquity* 30:535–41.

1966 Cahokia Chronology. Paper presented at the annual meeting of the Central States Anthropological Society, St. Louis.

1967a The Mississippian Heartland and Its Plains Relationships. *Plains Anthropologist* 12:175–83.

1967b More About Corn, Cahokia and Carbon-14. Report presented at the Cahokia Field Conference, Collinsville, Illinois.

1967c Radiocarbon Dates for Early "Non-Ramey" Mississippian Complexes at Cahokia. List distributed at the Thirty-second Annual Meeting of the Society for American Archaeology, Ann Arbor.

1967d Those Late Corn Dates: Isotopic Fractionation as a Source of Error in Carbon-14 Dates. *Michigan Archaeologist* 13(4):171–80.

1968 The Goddard-Ramey Cahokia Flight: A Pioneering Aerial Photographic Survey. *Wisconsin Archeologist* 49:76–80.

1972 Pottery Representing Some Ceramic Periods at Cahokia. Sketches prepared for distribution at the annual meeting of the Society for American Archaeology, Miami.

1973 The Cahokia Presence Outside of the American Bottom. Topics for consideration of participants in the symposium Cultural Interaction on the Northern Mississippian Frontier, organized by Robert L. Hall. Annual meeting of the Central States Anthropological Society, St. Louis.

1974 Review of *A Formal Analysis of Cahokia Ceramics from the Powell Tract*, by Patrica J. O'Brien. *American Anthropologist* 76:956–57.

1975a Chronology and Phases at Cahokia. In *Perspectives in Cahokia Archaeology*, ed. James A. Brown, pp. 15–31. Illinois Archaeological Survey Bulletin no. 10. Urbana.

1975b   Ramey Incised and the Emergence of the Blue Earth Oneota Style. Paper presented at the Midwest Archaeological Conference, Ann Arbor.

1975c   Some Problems of Identity and Process in Cahokia Archaeology. Paper prepared for the proceedings of the advanced seminar Reviewing Mississippian Development held at the School for American Research, Santa Fe.

1976   Spirit Adoption, Mourning, and the Calumet Dance. Manuscript in the possession of the author.

1977   An Anthropocentric Perspective for Eastern United States Prehistory. *American Antiquity* 42:499–518.

1979   In Search of the Ideology of the Adena-Hopewell Climax. In *Hopewell Archaeology: The Chillicothe Conference*, ed. David S. Brose and N'omi Greber, pp. 258–65. Kent State University Press, Kent, Ohio.

1980   An Interpretation of the Two-Climax Model of Illinois Prehistory. In *Early Native Americans*, ed. David L. Browman, pp. 401–62. Mouton, The Hague. (Originally presented in 1973 at the Ninth International Congress of Anthropological and Ethnological Sciences.)

1981   Mississippian Iconography and Symbolism. Lecture presented at the Science Museum of Minnesota, St. Paul, as part of the series Town and Temples.

1982   Calumet Ceremonialism, Xipe Worship, and Mechanisms of Long-Distance Trade. Paper presented at the Eighty-first Annual Meeting of the American Anthropological Association, Washington, D.C.

1983a   The Evolution of the Calumet-Pipe. In *Prairie Archaeology*, ed. Guy E. Gibbon, pp. 37–52. University of Minnesota Publications in Anthropology, no. 3. Minneapolis.

1983b   Long Distance Connections of Some Long-Nosed Gods. Paper presented at the Eighty-second Annual Meeting of the American Anthropological Association, Chicago.

1983c   Some Thoughts on Afterlife and Afterworld. Comments reported in *The Study of Ancient Human Skeletal Remains in Iowa: A Symposium*, ed. Patricia J. Carmack, pp. 14–18, 54–58. Special publication of the Office of the State Archaeologist of Iowa, Iowa City.

1984a   The Cultural Background of Mississippi Symbolism. Manuscript in the possession of the author.

1984b   The Misunderstood Case of the Flayed Princess, or The Honor of the Aztecs Restored? Paper presented at the Seventh Midwest Mesoamerica Conference, Loyola University, Chicago.

1984c   A Plains Indian Perspective on Mexican Cosmovision. Revision of a paper presented at the symposium Arqueoastronomia y Etnoastronomia en Mesoamerica, Mexico City.

1984d   A Reassessment of the Absolute Time Scale of Late Woodland and Mississippian Culture Phases in the American Bottom. Paper presented at the Midwest Archaeological Conference, Evanston, Illinois.

1985a   A Critique of the Time-Frame for the Mississippian Emergence in the Cahokia Area. Paper presented at the Sixth Annual Mid-South Archaeological Conference, Starkville, Mississippi.

1985b   Medicine Wheels, Sun Circles, and the Magic of World Center Shrines. *Plains Anthropologist* 30(109):181–93.

1986   Upper Mississippi and Middle Mississippi Relationships. *Wisconsin Archeologist* 67(3–4): 365–69.

1987   Calumet Ceremonialism, Mourning Ritual, and Mechanisms of Inter-Tribal Trade. In *Mirror and Metaphor: Material and Social Constructions of Reality*, ed. Daniel W. Ingersoll, Jr., and Gordon Bronitsky, pp. 29–43. University Press of America, Lanham, Maryland.

n.d.   The Early Documentary History of Aztalan. Manuscript in possession of author.

Halstead, P., and J. O'Shea

1982   A Friend in Need Is a Friend Indeed: Social Storage and the Origins of Social Ranking. In *Ranking, Resource and Exchange*, ed. C. Renfrew and S. Shennen, pp. 92–99. Cambridge University Press, Cambridge.

Hamilton, Henry W.

1952   *The Spiro Mound*. Missouri Archaeologist, vol. 14.

Hamilton, Henry, Jean Tyree Hamilton, and Eleanor F. Chapman

1974   *Spiro Mound Copper*. Missouri Archaeological Society Memoir no. 11. Columbia.

Hanning, Mary

1979   The Star Bridge Site—A Cooperative Venture. *Illinois Association for the Advancement of Archaeology, Newsletter* 11(1): 1–2.

Hargrave, M. L., G. Oetelaar, N. Lopinot, B. Butler, and D. Billings

1983   *The Bridges Site (11-Mr-11): A Late Prehistoric Settlement in the Central Kaskaskia Valley*. Southern Illinois University at Carbondale, Center for Archaeological Investigations, Research Paper no. 38.

Harlan, Jack R.

1975   *Crops and Man*. American Society of Agronomy and Crop Science Society of America, Madison, Wisconsin.

Harn, Alan D.

1970   Notes on the Mississippian Occupation of the Central Illinois River Valley. Paper presented at the Sixty-ninth Annual Meeting of the American Anthropological Association, San Diego.

1971a   An Archaeological Survey of the American Bottoms in Madison and St. Clair Counties, Illinois. In *Archaeological Surveys of the American Bottoms and Adjacent Bluffs, Illinois*, pp. 19–39. Illinois State Museum, Reports of Investigations, no. 21. Springfield.

1971b   *The Prehistory of Dickson Mounds: A Preliminary Report*. Dickson Mounds Museum Anthropological Studies, no. 1. Illinois State Museum, Springfield.

1972   A Long-Nosed God Mask from Dickson Mounds. *The Living Museum* 34:112–13, 117.

1973   Cahokia and the Mississippian Emergence in the Spoon River Area of Illinois. Paper presented at the annual meeting of the Central States Anthropological Society, St. Louis.

1974   New Excavations at the Myer/Dickson Site. *Illinois Association for Advancement of Archaeology, Newsletter* 6(4):27–32.

1975a   Another Long-Nosed God Mask from Fulton County, Illinois. *Wisconsin Archeologist* 56(1):2–8.

1975b   Cahokia and the Mississippian Emergence in the Spoon River Area of Illinois. *Transactions, Illinois State Academy of Science* 68(4):414–34. Springfield.

1975c   The Larson Community: A Mississippian Settlement System in the Spoon River Area of Illinois. Paper presented at the Twentieth Annual Midwest Archaeological Conference, Ann Arbor.

1978   Mississippian Settlement Patterns in the Central Illinois

River Valley. In *Mississippian Settlement Patterns*, ed. Bruce D. Smith, pp. 233–68. Academic Press, New York.

1980a   Comments on the Spatial Distribution of Late Woodland and Mississippian Ceramics in the General Cahokia Sphere. *Rediscovery* 1:17–26.

1980b   *The Prehistory of Dickson Mounds: The Dickson Excavation*. Rev. ed. Illinois State Museum, Reports of Investigations, no. 35. Springfield.

1983   Subsistence, Seasonality, and Site Function at Upland Camps in the Larson Community: A View from the Other End of the Telescope. Paper presented in the Mississippian Roundtable, Iowa City.

n.d.a   The Archaeology of Dickson Mounds: Cultural Change and Demographic Variation in the Life of a Late Woodland-Middle Mississippian Cemetery. In preparation.

n.d.b   Variation in Mississippian Settlement Pattern: The Larson Community in the Central Illinois River Valley. Ms. on file, Dickson Mounds Museum, Lewistown, Illinois.

Harn, Alan D., and David A. Baerreis (editors)
n.d.   The Larson Site (11F^{V}1109): A Spoon River Variant Town in the Central Illinois River Valley. In preparation.

Harn, Alan D., and William Weedman
1975   Archaeology, Aircraft, and Answers. *The Living Museum* 27(6):348–52.

Harrison, Christina
n.d.   Report on an Archaeological Survey of Dakota and Goodhue Counties for the Minnesota Statewide Archaeological Survey. Ms. on file, Minnesota Historical Society, St. Paul.

Harvey, Amy E.
1979   *Oneota Culture in Northwestern Iowa*. Report no. 12, Office of the State Archaeologist, University of Iowa, Iowa City.

Hassen, Harold, Charles R. McGimsey, Karen Atwell, Marilyn J. Bender, and David T. Morgan
1984   *Archeological Salvage Excavations at the Grey Day Site (11-Ct-36), Clinton County, Illinois*. U.S. Army Corps of Engineers, St. Louis District Cultural Resource Management Report no. 13. Center for American Archeology, Kampsville, Illinois.

Hassen, Harold, Erich Schroeder, and David Morgan
1984   *Archaeological Investigations Along the Kaskaskia River Drainage: Cultural Resource Survey of Selected Portions of the Carlyle Lake Project Area*. U.S. Army Corps of Engineers, St. Louis District Cultural Resource Management Report no. 15. Center for American Archeology, Kampsville, Illinois.

Haug, James K.
1982   *Excavations at the Winter Site and at the Hartford Beach Village, 1980–81*. South Dakota Archaeological Research Center, Ft. Meade.

Hawks, Preston
1985   *Report of Supplemental Phase I Documentation and Survey and Phase II Archaeological Testing at Selected Sites for the Proposed FAP-413 Highway Project, Madison County, Illinois*. Report submitted to the Illinois Department of Transportation, Springfield.

Hawley, Florence
1941   *Tree-ring Analysis and Dating in the Mississippi Drain-*

age. University of Chicago, Publications in Anthropology, Occasional Paper no. 2.

Healan, Dan M.
1972   *Surface Delineation of Functional Areas at a Mississippi Ceremonial Center*. Missouri Archaeological Society, Memoir no. 10. Columbia.

Heiser, Charles B.
1985   Some Botanical Considerations of the Early Domesticated Plants North of Mexico. In *Prehistoric Food Production in North America*, ed. Richard I. Ford, pp. 57–72. University of Michigan, Museum of Anthropology, Anthropological Papers, no. 75. Ann Arbor.

Helms, Mary
1979   *Ancient Panama: Chiefs in Search of Power*. University of Texas Press, Austin.

Hendrickson, Carl F., Theresa J. Cartmell, and John E. Kelly
1977   *The Archaeological Reconnaissance of the Proposed FAP-409 Alignment in St. Clair, Clinton, and Marion Counties, Illinois*. Illinois Department of Transportation, District 8, Fairview Heights.

Henning, Dale R.
1961   *Oneota Ceramics in Iowa*. Journal of the Iowa Archeological Society vol. 11 (2).

1967   Mississippian Influences on the Eastern Plains Border: An Evaluation. *Plains Anthropologist* 12:184–94.

1969   Ceramics from the Mill Creek Sites. *Journal of the Iowa Archaeological Society* 15:192–280.

1970   *Development and Interrelationships of Oneota Culture in the Lower Missouri River Valley*. Missouri Archaeologist no. 32.

1971a   Great Oasis Culture Distributions. In *Prehistoric Investigations*, ed. Marshall McKusick, pp. 125–34. Report no. 3, Office of the State Archaeologist, University of Iowa, Iowa City.

1971b   Origins of Mill Creek. *Journal of the Iowa Archaeological Society* 18:6–13.

1982   *Subsurface Testing Program: Proposed Perry Creek Dam and Reservoir Area, Plymouth County, Iowa*. Technical Report 82–05. Division of Archaeological Research, Department of Anthropology, University of Nebraska, Lincoln.

Henning, Dale R. (editor)
1968   *Climatic Change and the Mill Creek Culture of Iowa, Part 1*. Journal of the Iowa Archaeological Society no. 15.

Henning, Dale R., and E. R. Henning
1978   Great Oasis Ceramics. *Occasional Publications in Minnesota Anthropology* 2:12–26. Minnesota Archaeological Society, St. Paul.

Higgins, S. K.
1987   *Soil Survey of Monroe County, Illinois*. Illinois Agricultural Experiment Station Soil Report no. 126. U.S.D.A. Soil Conservation Service, Urbana.

Hill, A. T., and Waldo R. Wedel
1936   Excavations at the Leary Indian Village and Burial Site, Richardson County, Nebraska. *Nebraska History Magazine* 17:3–73.

Hinkes, Madeline J.
1977   Mortuary Site Archaeology at Helton Mound 21 in West-central Illinois. M.A. thesis, Department of Anthropology, University of Kansas, Lawrence.

Hirth, Kenneth G.
1978   Interregional Trade and the Formation of Prehistoric Gateway Communities. *American Antiquity* 42:35–45.

Hodder, Ian
1982   Toward a Contextual Approach to Prehistoric Ex-
        change. In *Contexts for Prehistoric Exchange*, ed.
        Jonathon E. Ericson and Timothy K. Earle, pp. 199-
        211. Academic Press, New York.

Hodges, Richard
1982   The Evolution of Gateway Communities: Their Socio-
        Economic Implications. In *Ranking, Resource and
        Exchange*, ed. Colin Renfrew and Stephen Shennan,
        pp. 117–23. Cambridge University Press, New York.

Hoffman, Margaret L.
1960   The Irving Thompson Site. In *Indian Mounds and
        Villages in Illinois*, ed. Elaine A. Bluhm, pp. 80–89.
        Illinois Archaeological Survey Bulletin no. 2. Urbana.

Holley, George R.
1989   *The Archaeology of the Cahokia Mounds ICT-II: Cer-
        amics*. Illinois Cultural Resources Study no. 11. Illinois
        Historic Preservation Agency, Springfield.

Holley, George R., and Alan J. Brown
1988   *Archaeological Monitoring of the Proposed Glen Car-
        bon Interceptor Sewer Line, Divisions 3 thru 7, Madison
        County, Illinois*. Archaeology Program Research Re-
        port no. 1. Contract Archaeology Program, Southern
        Illinois University at Edwardsville.

Holmes, William H.
1883a   Art in Shell. *Transactions of the Anthropological
        Society of Washington* 2:106–7.
1883b   Art in Shell of the Ancient Americans. *Second An-
        nual Report of the Bureau of American Ethnology for
        1880–1881*, pp. 179–305. Washington, D.C.
1903   Aboriginal Pottery of the Eastern United States. *Bureau
        of American Ethnology, Annual Report*, pp. 1–237.
        Washington, D.C.

Holstein, Harry, Jerry Fairchild, and Wayne Shields
1975   An Archaeological Survey of the Lower-Central Illi-
        nois and La Moine River Drainages. In *Preliminary
        Report of 1974 Historic Sites Survey, Archaeological
        Reconnaissance of Selected Areas in the State of Illi-
        nois: Part I, Summary, Section A*, pp. 56–65. Illinois
        Archaeological Survey, Urbana.

Honerkamp, Marjory W.
1975   *The Angel Phase: An Analysis of a Middle Missis-
        sippian Occupation in Southwestern Indiana*. Ph.D.
        diss., Department of Anthropology, Indiana University,
        Bloomington.

Hopgood, James F.
1969   *Continuity and Change in the Baytown Pottery Tradition
        of the Cairo Lowland, Southeast Missouri*. M.A. thesis,
        Department of Anthropology, University of Missouri,
        Columbia.

Hotopp, J. A.
1978   *Settlement Patterns, Structures and Temporal Placement
        of the Central Plains Tradition in Iowa*. Ph.D. diss.,
        College of Education, University of Iowa, Iowa City.

Houart, Gail L.
1971   *Koster: A Stratified Archaic Site in the Illinois Val-
        ley*. Illinois State Museum, Reports of Investigations
        no. 22. Springfield.

Howard, James H.
1968   *The Southeastern Ceremonial Complex and its Interpre-
        tation*. Missouri Archaeological Society Memoir no. 6.
        Columbia.

Howland, Henry R.
1877   Recent Archaeological Discoveries in the American

Bottom. *Buffalo Society of Natural Sciences Bulletin*
        3(5):204–11.

Hudson, Charles
1976   *The Southeastern Indians*. University of Tennessee
        Press, Knoxville.

Hunt, Charles B.
1967   *Physiography of the United States*. W. H. Freeman, San
        Francisco.

Hurley, William M.
1970   *The Wisconsin Effigy Mound Tradition*. Ph.D. diss.,
        Department of Anthropology, University of Wisconsin,
        Madison.
1975   *The Analysis of Effigy Mound Complexes in Wisconsin*.
        University of Michigan, Museum of Anthropology,
        Anthropological Papers, no. 59. Ann Arbor.
1977   Aztalan Revisited. *Wisconsin Archeologist* 58:256–94.
1978   The Armstrong Site: A Silvernale Phase Oneota Village
        in Wisconsin. *Wisconsin Archeologist* 59:3–145.

Hurt, Wesley R.
1954   Pottery Types of the Over Focus, South Dakota. In
        Prehistoric Pottery of the Eastern United States, vol. 1–
        54. ed. James B. Griffin. Museum of Anthropology,
        University of Michigan, Ann Arbor.

Hyer, N. F.
1837   Ruins of the Ancient City of Aztalan. *Milwaukee
        Advertiser*, February 26, 1837.

Illinois State Planning Commission
1938   *Report on the Kaskaskia River Basin*. State of Illinois,
        Department of Public Works and Buildings, Division of
        Waterways, Springfield.

Isbell, William H.
1978   Environmental Perturbations and the Origin of the An-
        dean State. In *Social Archaeology: Beyond Subsistence
        and Dating*, ed. Charles L. Redman et al., pp. 303–13.
        Academic Press, New York.

Iseminger, William B., and Michael J. McNerney
1973   *An Archaeological Survey of the Lower Kaskaskia
        Canalization Project: 1970 Season*. Southern Illinois
        University Museum, Archaeological Survey Report
        no. 36. Carbondale.

Ives, John C.
1962   *Mill Creek Pottery*. Journal of the Iowa Archeological
        Society 11(3).

Jablow, J.
1950   *The Cheyenne in Plains Indian Trade Relations, 1795–
        1840*. Monographs of the American Ethnological
        Society no. 19.

Jackson, Douglas K.
1979   *An Archaeological Survey of the Wood River Basin,
        Madison County, Illinois*. Report submitted to the
        Illinois Department of Transportation, Springfield.
1984   *The Determann Borrow Site, Madison County, Illinois*.
        Resource Investigation Program Research Reports
        no. 14. Department of Anthropology, University of
        Illinois at Urbana-Champaign.

Johannessen, Sissel
1981a   Floral Remains from the Lohmann site (11-S-49). In
        *Final Report on FAI-270 and Illinois Route 460 Related
        Excavations at the Lohmann Site (11-S-49), St. Clair
        County, Illinois*, by Duane Esarey with Timothy W.
        Good, pp. 186–97. Archaeological Research Labo-
        ratory, Western Illinois University, Reports of Ines-
        tigations no. 3, and Department of Anthropology,
        University of Illinois at Urbana-Champaign, FAI 270

Archaeological Mitigation Project, Report no. 39.

1981b   Interim Report of Paleoethnobotanical Analysis. In *Archaeology in the American Bottom: Progress Report of the Illinois FAI-270 Archaeological Mitigation Project*, ed. Charles J. Bareis and James W. Porter, pp. 141–58. Report no. 6, Department of Anthropology, University of Illinois at Urbana-Champaign.

1984a   Paleoethnobotany. In *American Bottom Archaeology*, ed. Charles J. Bareis and J. W. Porter, pp. 197–214. University of Illinois Press, Urbana.

1984b   Plant Remains from the Julien Site. In *The Julien Site*, by George R. Milner and Joyce A. Williams, pp. 244–73. American Bottom Archaeology FAI-270 Site Reports, vol. 7. University of Illinos Press, Urbana.

1985   Plant Remains. In *The Carbon Dioxide Site (11-Mo-594)*, by Fred A. Finney, and *The Robert Schneider Site (11-Ms-1177)*, by Andrew C. Fortier, pp. 97–108. American Bottom Archaeology FAI-270 Site Reports, vol. 11. University of Illinois Press, Urbana.

1987   Plant Remains. In *The George Reeves Site*, by Dale L. McElrath and Fred A. Finney, pp. 349–56. American Bottom Archaeology FAI-270 Site Reports, vol. 15. University of Illinois Press, Urbana.

1988   Plant Remains and Culture Change: Are Paleoethnobotanical Data Better Than We Think? In *Current Paleoethnobotany: Analytical Methods and Cultural Interpretations of Archaeological Plant Remains*, ed. Christine A. Hastorf and Virginia S. Popper, pp. 145–166. University of Chicago Press, Chicago.

Johnson, Elden

1961   Cambria Burial Mounds in Big Stone County. *Minnesota Archaeologist* 23:52–81.

1969   Decorative Motifs on Great Oasis Pottery. *Plains Anthropologist* 14:272–76.

1986   Cambria and Cahokia's Northwestern Periphery. Paper presented at the Fifty-first Annual Meeting of the Society for American Archaeology, New Orleans.

Johnson, Elden, Martin Q. Peterson, and Jan E. Streiff

1969   Birch Lake Burial Mound Group. *Minnesota Academy of Science Journal* 36:3–8.

Johnson, Elden, and Philip Taylor

1956   *The Lee Mill Cave*. Spring Lake Archaeology Science Museum Bulletin, no. 3, pt. 2. Science Museum, St. Paul, Minnesota.

Jones, Volney

1936   The Vegetal Remains of Newt Kash Hollow Shelter. In *Rockshelters in Menifee County*, Kentucky, ed. William S. Webb and William D. Funkhouser, pp. 147–65. University of Kentucky Reports in Anthropology and Archaeology vol. 3(4).

Kay, Jeanne

1979   Wisconsin Indian Hunting Patterns, 1634–1836. *Annals of the Association of American Geographers* 69:402–18.

Kellar, James H.

1967   Material Remains. In *Angel Site: An Archaeological, Historical, and Ethnological Study*, by Glenn A. Black, pp. 431–87. Indiana Historical Society, Indianapolis.

Kelly, Arthur R.

1932   Illinois. In Reports of Archaeological Field Work in North America During 1931, ed. Carl E. Guthe. *American Anthropologist* 34:476–509.

1933   Some Problems of Recent Cahokia Archaeology. *Transactions of the Illinois State Academy of Science* 25(4): 101–3. Springfield.

Kelly, Arthur R., and Fay-Cooper Cole

1932   Rediscovering Illinois. *Blue Book of the State of Illinois 1931–1932*, ed. William J. Stratton, pp. 318–41. Springfield.

Kelly, John E.

1982   *Formative Developments at Cahokia and the Adjacent American Bottom: A Merrell Tract Perspective*. 2 vols. Western Illinois University Archaeological Research Laboratory, Macomb. (Originally cited as 1980, Ph.D. diss., Department of Anthropology, University of Wisconsin.)

1984   Wells Incised Plates: Their Context and Affinities with O'Byam Incised. Paper presented at the Paducah Ceramic Conference, Wickliffe, Kentucky.

1985   Emergent Mississippian and the Transition From Late Woodland to Mississippian: The American Bottom Case for a New Concept. Paper presented at the Mid-South Archaeological Conference, Starkville, Mississippi.

1987   Emergent Mississippian and the Transition from Late Woodland to Mississippian: The American Bottom Case for a New Concept. In *The Emergent Mississippian: Proceedings of the Sixth Mid-South Archaeological Conference, June 6–9, 1985*, ed. Richard A. Marshall, pp. 212–26. Cobb Institute of Archaeology, Occasional Papers no. 87–01. Mississippi State University.

Kelly, John E., Fred A. Finney, Dale L. McElrath, and Steven J. Ozuk

1984   Late Woodland Period. In *American Bottom Archaeology*, ed. Charles J. Bareis and James W. Porter, pp. 104–27. University of Illinois Press, Urbana.

Kelly, John E., Jean R. Linder, and Theresa J. Cartmell

1979   *The Archaeological Intensive Survey of the Proposed FAI-270 Alignment in the American Bottom Region of Southern Illinois*. Illinois Transportation Archaeology Scientific Reports, no. 1. Illinois Department of Transportation, Springfield.

Kelly, John E., Steven J. Ozuk, Douglas K. Jackson, Dale L. McElrath, Fred A. Finney, and Duane Esarey

1984   Emergent Mississippian Period. In *American Bottom Archaeology*, ed. Charles J. Bareis and James W. Porter, pp. 128–57. University of Illinois Press, Urbana.

Kelly, Lucretia S.

1979   *Animal Resource Exploitation by Early Cahokia Populations on the Merrell Tract*. Illinois Archaeological Survey Circular no. 4. Urbana.

Kelly, Lucretia S., and Paula G. Cross

1984   Zooarchaeology. In *American Bottom Archaeology*, ed. Charles J. Bareis and James W. Porter, pp. 215–32. University of Illinois Press, Urbana.

Kerber, Richard A.

1982   *Woodland Social Change Reconsidered: Helton Mounds 46 and 47*. M.A. thesis, Department of Anthropology, Northwestern University, Evanston, Illinois.

Keslin, Richard O.

1964   *Archaeological Implications on the Role of Salt as an Element of Cultural Diffusion*. Missouri Archaeologist vol. 26.

King, Frances B.

1980   Plant Remains from Phillips Spring, a Multicomponent Site in the Western Ozark Highland of Missouri. *Plains Anthropologist* 25:217–22.

1985   Early Cultivated Cucurbits in Eastern North America.
            In *Prehistoric Food Production in North America*, ed.
            Richard I. Ford, pp. 73–97. University of Michigan,
            Museum of Anthropology, Anthropological Papers,
            no. 75. Ann Arbor.

Klein, Jeffrey, J. C. Lerman, P. E. Damon, and F. K. Ralph
1982   Calibration of Radiocarbon Dates: Tables Based on the
            Consensus Data of the Workshop on Calibrating the
            Radiocarbon Time Scale. *Radiocarbon* 24:103–50.

Klippel, Walter Emerson
1969   *The Hearnes Site: A Multicomponent Occupation Site
            and Cemetery in the Cairo Lowland Region of Southeast
            Missouri*. Missouri Archaeologist vol. 31.

Knudson, Ruth Ann
1967   Cambria Village Ceramics. *Plains Anthropologist* 12:
            247–99.

Koldehoff, Brad
1982a   A Coles Creek Vessel from Cahokia's Hinterland.
            Illinois Antiquity 14(2–3):20–23.
1982b   An Ecological Approach to the Upland Components of
            the Cahokia-American Bottom Settlement System: A
            View from Up Above. Ms. on file, Center for Archaeo-
            logical Investigations, Southern Illinois University at
            Carbondale.

Koldehoff, Brad, Christy L. Wells, and William I. Woods
1983   *A Cultural Resource Survey of Ten Proposed Dry Re-
            tention Basins in the Harding Ditch Area of St. Clair
            County, Illinois*. Reports in Contract Archaeology
            no. 3. U.S. Army Corps of Engineers, St. Louis
            District.

Konigsberg, Lyle W.
1987   *Population Genetic Models for Interpreting Prehistoric
            Intra-Cemetery Biological Variation*. Ph.D. diss., De-
            partment of Anthropology, Northwestern University,
            Evanston, Illinois.

Kraus, Lyn M.
1980   *Archeological Evaluation of "The Buried Gardens of
            Kampsville" (T.B.GOK), Calhoun County, Illinois*.
            Center for American Archeology, Contract Archeology
            Program, Report of Investigations no. 87, Kampsville,
            Illinois. Submitted to Illinois Environmental Protection
            Agency, Springfield.

Krause, Richard
1985   Trends and Trajectories in American Archaeology:
            Some Questions About the Mississippian Period in
            Southeastern Prehistory. In *Alabama and the Border-
            lands: From Prehistory to Statehood*, ed. R. Badger and
            L. Clayton, pp. 17–39. University of Alabama Press,
            University.

Kreisa, Paul
1987   [Marshall Site] Faunal Remains. In *Archaeological
            Investigations in Carlisle, Hickman, and Fulton Coun-
            ties, Kentucky: Site Survey and Excavations*, by Tom
            Sussenback and R. Barry Lewis, p. 67. University
            of Illinois, Department of Anthropology, Western
            Kentucky Project Report no. 4. Urbana.
1988   *Second-Order Communities in Western Kentucky: Site
            Survey and Excavations at Late Woodland and Missis-
            sippi Period Sites*. University of Illinois, Department of
            Anthropology, Western Kentucky Project Report no. 7.
            Urbana.
1989   *Prehistoric Settlement Patterns on the Big Bottoms,
            Fulton County, Kentucky*. University of Illinois, De-

partment of Anthropology, Western Kentucky Project
            Report no. 8. Urbana.

Kruger, Robert P.
1985   The Faunal Remains. In *The Turk Site: A Mississippian
            Town of the Western Kentucky Border*, ed. Richard
            Edging, pp. 35–51. Department of Anthropology, Uni-
            versity of Illinois, Western Kentucky Project Report
            no. 3.

Kuttruff, L. Carl
1969   *Lower Kaskaskia River Valley Archaeology: 1967
            and 1968 Seasons*. Southern Illinois Studies Series
            '69, no. S1A. University Museum, Southern Illinois
            University at Carbondale.
1972   *The Marty Coolidge Site, Monroe County, Illinois*.
            Southern Illinois Studies no. 10. University Museum,
            Southern Illinois University at Carbondale.
1974   *Late Woodland Settlement and Subsistence in the
            Lower Kaskaskia River Valley*. Ph.D. diss., Depart-
            ment of Anthropology, Southern Illinois University at
            Carbondale. University Microfilms, Ann Arbor.

Lafferty, Robert
1977   *The Evolution of the Mississippian Settlement Pattern
            and Exploitative Technology in the Black Bottom of
            Southern Illinois*. Ph.D. diss., Department of Anthro-
            pology, Southern Illinois University at Carbondale.
            University Microfilms, Ann Arbor.

Langford, George
1927   The Fisher Mound Group: Successive Aboriginal Occu-
            pations near the Mouth of the Illinois River. *American
            Anthropologist* 29:(3)152–205.

Lapham, Increase A.
1855   *The Antiquities of Wisconsin*. Smithsonian Contribu-
            tions to Knowledge, vol. 7. Washington, D.C.

Larson, Lewis H., Jr.
1957   An Unusual Wooden Rattle From the Etowah Site.
            Missouri Archaeologist 19:6–11.
1970   Settlement Distribution during the Mississippian
            Period. *Southeastern Archaeological Conference Bulle-
            tin* 13:18–25.

Lathrap, Donald W., and James W. Porter
1985   Mississippian Farmers and the Dominance of Cahokia.
            In *Illinois Archaeology*, ed. J. W. Porter and D. S.
            Rohn, pp. 70–78. Illinois Archaeological Survey
            Bulletin no. 1 (revised). Urbana.

Lawshe, Fred E.
1947   The Mero Site—Diamond Bluff, Pierce County, Wis-
            consin. *Minnesota Archaeologist* 13:74–95.

Lehmer, D. J.
1971   *An Introduction to Middle Missouri Archaeology*.
            Anthropological Papers no. 1. National Park Service,
            Washington, D.C.

Leighton, Morris M.
1923   The Origin of the Cahokia Mounds. *Transactions of the
            Illinois State Academy of Science* 16:327. Springfield.
1928   The Geological Aspects of Some of the Cahokia (Illi-
            nois) Mounds. *University of Illinois Bulletin* 26, no. 4,
            pt. 2:109–43. Urbana.

Leighton, Morris M., G. E. Eckblaw, and L. Horberg
1948   *Physiographic Divisions of Illinois*. Illinois State Geo-
            logical Survey Report of Investigations no. 129.
            Springfield.

Lewis, R. Barry
1972   *Land Leveling Salvage Archaeology in Portions of Stod-*

dard and Scott Counties, Missouri, 1969. American Archaeology Division, University of Missouri, Columbia. Report submitted to the National Park Service, Midwest Region, Lincoln, Nebraska.

1974   *Mississippian Exploitative Strategies: A Southeast Missouri Example*. Missouri Archaeological Society, Research Series no. 11. Columbia.

1982   *Excavations at Two Mississippian Hamlets in the Cairo Lowland of Southeast Missouri*. Illinois Archaeological Survey, Special Publication no. 2. Urbana.

1983   The Mississippi Period in the Cairo Lowland, Missouri. Paper presented at the annual meeting of the Society for American Archaeology, Pittsburgh.

1989a   The Late Prehistory of the Ohio-Mississippi Rivers Confluence Region. In *Towns and Temples Along the Mississippi: Late Prehistoric and Early Historic Indians in the Memphis Area*, ed. David H. Dye and Cheryl A. Cox. University of Alabama Press, University. In press.

1989b   *The Mississippi Period in Kentucky*. Western Kentucky Project, Department of Anthropology, University of Illinois at Urbana-Champaign. Report submitted to the Kentucky Heritage Council, Frankfort.

1989c   The Archaeology of the Western Kentucky Border and the Cairo Lowland. Paper presented at the Twenty-fourth annual meeting of the Southern Anthropology Society, Memphis, Tennessee.

Lewis, R. Barry (editor)

1986   *Mississippian Towns of the Western Kentucky Border: The Adams, Wickliffe, and Sassafras Ridge Sites*. Kentucky Heritage Council, Frankfort.

Lewis, R. Barry, and Lynne M. Mackin

1984   The Adams Site Ceramic Assemblage in Regional Perspective. In *Late Prehistoric Research in Kentucky*, ed. David Pollack, Charles Hockensmith, and Thomas Sanders, pp. 187–204. Kentucky Heritage Council, Frankfort.

Lewis, T.M.N.

1954   Mound Group Opposite Aztalan. *Wisconsin Archeologist* 35:37–41.

Linder, Jean R., Theresa J. Cartmell, and John E. Kelly

1978   *Preliminary Archaeological Reconnaissance of the Segments Under Study for FAP-413 in Madison County, Illinois*. Illinois Department of Transportation, District 8, Fairview Heights.

Link, Adolph W.

1975   A Bird Motif on a Mississippian Pot. *Minnesota Archaeologist* 34:71–82.

1979   Chunky: The Game and Its Probable Use by Mississippians in Minnesota. *Minnesota Archaeologist* 38: 129–45.

1980a   Discoidals and Problematical Stones from Mississippian Sites in Minnesota. *Plains Anthropologist* 25: 343–52.

1980b   Three Papers on the Archaeology of the Bryan Site (21GD4), Goodhue County, Minnesota. *Minnesota Archaeologist* 39:111–17.

1982   Handles, Lobes and Appendages on Ceramics from the Bryan Site (21 GD 4). *Minnesota Archaeologist* 41: 30–44.

Little, E. A.

1987   Inland Waterways in the Northeast. *Midcontinental Journal of Archaeology* 12:55–76.

Logan, Wilfred D.

1976   *Woodland Complexes in Northeastern Iowa*. U.S.

Department of the Interior, National Park Service Publications in Archaeology no. 15. Washington, D.C.

Lopinot, Neal H., Joseph L. Harl, Patti J. Wright, and Joseph M. Nixon

1986   *Cultural Resource Testing and Assessments: the 1985 Season at Lake Shelbyville, Shelby and Moultrie Counties, Illinois*. U.S. Army Corps of Engineers, St. Louis District Cultural Resource Management Report no. 30. University of Missouri, St. Louis.

Lopinot, Neal H., and William I. Woods

1988   Archaeobotany, Environmental Degradation, and the Collapse of Cahokia. Paper presented at the Fifty-third Annual Meeting of the Society for American Archaeology, Phoenix.

Loughridge, Robert H.

1888   *Report on the Geological and Economic Features of the Jackson Purchase Region*. Kentucky Geological Survey, Lexington.

Lucking, L.

1977   The Prehistoric and Protohistoric Peoples of Otter Tail County. Ms. on file, Otter Tail County Historical Society Museum and Minnesota Historical Society, St. Paul.

Lukens, Paul W., Jr.

1963   *Some Ethnozoological Implications of Mammalian Faunas from Minnesota Archaeological Sites*. Ph.D. diss., University of Minnesota, Minneapolis.

Lynott. M. J., T. W. Boutton, J. E. Price, and D. E. Nelson

1986   Stable Carbon Isotopic Evidence for Maize Agriculture in Southeast Missouri and Northeast Arkansas. *American Antiquity* 51:51–65.

MacCurdy, George Grant

1913   Shell Gorgets from Missouri. *American Anthropologist* 15:395–414.

MacDonald, Edgar S.

1950   The Crable Site, Fulton County, Illinois. *Illinois State Archeological Society Journal* 7:16–18.

MacNeish, Richard S.

1944   *The Establishment of the Lewis Focus*. M.A. thesis, Department of Anthropology, University of Chicago.

n.d.   An Early Middle Mississippi Horizon at the Kincaid site. Ms. on file, University of Chicago Kincaid Project records, Center for Archaeological Investigations, Southern Illinois University at Carbondale.

Maher, Robert F.

1958   The Excavation and Reconstruction of the Southwest Pyramidal Mound at Aztalan. *Wisconsin Archeologist* 39:77–100.

Maher, Robert F., and David A. Baerreis

1958   Aztalan Lithic Complex. *Wisconsin Archeologist* 39: 5–26.

Marshall, Richard A.

1965   *An Archaeological Investigation of Interstate Route 55 through New Madrid and Pemiscot Counties, Missouri*. Highway Archaeology Report no. 1. University of Missouri, Columbia.

1969   The Story Mound Excavation at the Hoecake Site. Ms. on file, Department of Anthropology, University of Columbia, Missouri.

1987   A Brief Comparison of Two Emergent Mississippi Substage Settlement Patterns in Southeast Missouri and Northwest Mississippi. In *The Emergent Mississippian: Proceedings of the Sixth Mid-South Archaeological Conference, June 6–9, 1985*, ed. Richard A. Marshall,

pp. 160–66. Cobb Institute of Archaeology, Occasional
Papers no. 87–01. Mississippi State University.

Marshall, Richard A., and James F. Hopgood
1964   *A Test Excavation at Hoecake, 23Mi8, Mississippi
County, Missouri.* Missouri Archaeological Society
Newsletter vol. 177.

Martin, Alexander C., and William D. Barkley
1961   *Seed Identification Manual.* University of California
Press, Berkeley.

Martin, Lawrence
1965   *The Physical Geography of Wisconsin.* University of
Wisconsin Press, Madison.

Maxwell, Moreau S.
1950   A Change in the Interpretation of Wisconsin's Prehistory. *Wisconsin Magazine of History* 33:427–43.
1951   *Woodland Cultures of Southern Illinois.* Logan Museum
Publications in Anthropology Bulletin no. 7. Beloit,
Wisconsin.
1952   Clay Ear Spools from the Aztalan Site, Wisconsin.
American Antiquity 18:61–63.
1959   The Late Woodland Period. *Illinois Archaeology,*
ed. E. A. Bluhm, pp. 27–32. Illinois Archaeological
Survey, Bulletin no. 1. Urbana.

McAdams, William H.
1881   Ancient Mounds of Illinois. *Proceedings of the American Association for the Advancement of Science,* vol 29,
pp. 710–18.
1882   Antiquities. In *History of Madison County, Illinois,* pp.
58–64. W. R. Brink, Edwardsville, Illinois.
1887   *Records of Ancient Races in the Mississippi Valley.*
C. R. Barns, St. Louis.
1895   Archaeology. *Report of the Illinois Board of World's
Fair Commissioners at the World's Columbian Exposi-
tion,* pp. 227–304. H. W. Rokker, Springfield.

McConaughy, Mark A.
1984   Saving the Past: Highway Salvage Archaeology at the
Rench Site. *The Living Museum* 46:2–5.

McConaughy, Mark A., C. Jackson, and Francis King
1985   Two Early Mississippian Period Structures from the
Rench Site (11P4), Peoria County, Illinois. *Midcontinental Journal of Archaeology* 10:171–94.

McElrath, Dale L.
1983   Mississippian Chert Exploitation: A Case Study from
the American Bottom. Paper presented at the annual
meeting of the Society for American Archaeology,
Pittsburgh.
1986   *The McLean Site (11-S-640).* American Bottom
Archaeology FAI-270 Site Reports, vol. 14. University
of Illinois Press, Urbana.

McElrath, Dale L., and Fred A. Finney
1987   *The George Reeves Site (11-S-650).* American Bottom
Archaeology FAI-270 Site Reports, Vol. 15. University
of Illinois Press, Urbana.

McGimsey, Charles R., Michael D. Wiant, Erich A. Schroeder,
Edwin R. Hajic, Duane Esarey, and Alan D. Harn
1987   Chapter 5: Results. In *Archaeological Reconnaissance
and Testing at Sites 11-F-2713 and 11-F-25, Liverpool
Levee Project, Fulton County, Illinois,* ed. Charles R.
McGimsey, pp. 10–109. Submitted to the U.S. Army
Corps of Engineers, Rock Island District by the Illinois
State Museum Society.

McGowan, Kevin P.
1984   *A Cultural Resource Survey at the Shelbyville Reser-*

voir Shoreline South of the Findlay Bridge. U.S. Army
Corps of Engineers, St. Louis District Cultural Resource Management Report no. 14. University of
Illinois at Urbana-Champaign.
1985   *Cultural Resource Testing and Data Sampling at Thirteen Archaeological Sites in the Lake Shelbyville Project
Area, Illinois.* U.S. Army Corps of Engineers, St.
Louis District Cultural Resource Management Report
no. 27. University of Illinois at Urbana-Champaign.

McKern, William C.
1939   The Midwestern Taxonomic Method as an Aid to
Archaeological Culture Study. *American Antiquity* 4:
301–13.
1942   The Stockaded Village. In *The Story of Aztalan,* pp.
3–8. Lake Mills-Aztalan Historical Society, Lake Mills,
Wisconsin.
1945   Preliminary Report of the Upper Mississippi Phase in
Wisconsin. *Bulletin of the Public Museum of the City of
Milwaukee* 16(3):109–285.
1946   Aztalan. *Wisconsin Archeologist* 27:41–52.

McKusick, Marshall B.
1953   *The Bartron Village Site.* M.A. thesis, University of
Minnesota, Minneapolis.
1973   *The Grant Oneota Village.* Report no. 4, Office of the
State Archaeologist, University of Iowa, Iowa City.

McNaughton, S. J., and L. L. Wolf
1973   *General Ecology.* Holt Rinehart and Winston, New
York.

McPherron, Alan L.
1967   *The Juntunen Site and the Late Woodland Prehistory
of the Upper Great Lakes Area.* University of Michigan, Museum of Anthropology, Anthopological Papers
no. 30. Ann Arbor.

Mehrer, Mark W.
1982   *A Mississippian Community at the Range Site (11-S-47),
St. Clair County, Illinois.* Department of Anthropology,
University of Illinois at Urbana-Champaign, FAI-270
Archaeological Mitigation Project, Report no. 52.
1988   *The Settlement Patterns and Social Power of Cahokia's
Hinterland Households.* Ph.D. diss., University of
Illinois at Urbana-Champaign.

Meillassoux, Claude
1964   *Anthropologie économique des Gouro de Côte d'Ivoire:
De l'économie de subsistance à l'agriculture com-
merciale.* Le Monde d'Outre-mer Passé et Present,
Première Serie, Études vol. 27. Mouton, Paris.
1981   *Maidens, Meal and Money: Capitalism and the Domestic Economy.* Cambridge University Press, Cambridge.

Melby, F. Jerome
1963   *The Kane Burial Mounds.* Southern Illinois University Museum Archaeological Salvage Report no. 15.
Carbondale.

Messinger, John
1808   Field Notes for South Edge of Town 9 North, Range
3 West of Third Principal Meridian, dated Saturday,
January 9th. In *Illinois Land Records, Original Field
Notes* 12:76. Illinois State Archives, Springfield.

Michlovic, Michael G.
1979   *The Dead River Site (21OT51).* Occasional Publications in Minnesota Anthropology no. 6. Minnesota
Archaeological Society, Ft. Snelling.

Miller, David
1958   The Mound Lake Site Spade Cache. *Central States
Archaeological Journal* 4:96–98.

Milner, George R.
1982   *Measuring Prehistoric Levels of Health: A Study of Mississippian Period Skeletal Remains from the American Bottom, Illinois.* Ph.D. diss., Department of Anthropology, Northwestern University. University Microfilms, Ann Arbor.

1983   *The East St. Louis Stone Quarry Site Cemetery.* American Bottom Archaeology FAI-270 Site Reports, vol. 1. University of Illinois Press, Urbana.

1984   Social and Temporal Implications of Variation Among American Bottom Mississippian Cemeteries. *American Antiquity* 49:468–88.

1986a   Mississippian Period Cultural and Demographic Transformations in the American Bottom, Illinois. Paper presented at the Fifty-first Annual Meeting of the Society for American Archaeology, New Orleans.

1986b   Mississippian Period Population Density in a Segment of the Central Mississippi River Valley. *American Antiquity* 51:227–38.

Milner, George R., Thomas E. Emerson, Mark W. Mehrer, Joyce A. Williams, and Duane Esarey
1984   Mississippian and Oneota Period. In *American Bottom Archaeology*, ed. Charles J. Bareis and James W. Porter, pp. 158–86. University of Illinois Press, Urbana.

Milner, George R., and Joyce A. Williams
1983   *The Turner (11-S-50) and DeMange (11-S-447) Sites.* American Bottom Archaeology FAI-270 Site Reports, vol. 4. University of Illinois Press, Urbana.

1984   *The Julien Site (11-S-63).* American Bottom Archaeology FAI-270 Site Reports, vol. 7. University of Illinois Press, Urbana.

Moffat, Charles R.
1979a   *A Final Report of a Cultural Resource Survey of Selected Portions of the Shelbyville Reservoir Shoreline Area.* Contract report submitted to the Department of the Army, Corps of Engineers, St. Louis District.

1979b   *A Final Report of an Emergency Cultural Resource Survey of Selected Portions of Lake Shelbyville.* Contract report submitted to the Department of the Army, Corps of Engineers, St. Louis District.

1982   *A Final Report of Test Excavations at Three Archaeological Sites in the Shelbyville Reservoir, Illinois.* Report submitted to the Research Board, University of Illinois, Urbana, and the Department of the Army, Corps of Engineers, St. Louis District.

1983   Mississippian in the Upper Kaskaskia Valley: New Data from Lake Shelbyville and New Interpretations. Paper presented at the Forty-eighth Annual Meeting of the Society for American Archaeology, Pittsburgh.

1985   *The Mississippian Occupation of the Upper Kaskaskia Valley: Problems in Culture History and Economic Organization.* Ph.D. diss., Department of Anthropology, University of Illinois at Urbana-Champaign.

Montgomery, Frederick H.
1977   *Seeds and Fruits of Plants of Eastern Canada and the Northeastern United States.* University of Toronto Press, Toronto.

Moore, Clarence B.
1894   *Certain Sand Mounds in the St. John's River, Florida* Journal of the Academy of Natural Sciences of Philadelphia, vol. 10.

1916   *Some Aboriginal Sites on Green River, Kentucky; Certain Aboriginal Sites on Lower Ohio River; Addi-*

tional Investigation on Mississippi River. Journal of the Academy of Natural Sciences of Philadelphia vol. 16.

Moorehead, Warren K.
1922   *The Cahokia Mounds: A Preliminary Report.* University of Illinois Bulletin no. 19. Urbana.

1923   *The Cahokia Mounds: Part I, A Report of Progress by Warren K. Moorehead and Part II, Some Geological Aspects by Morris M. Leighton.* University of Illinois Bulletin no. 21(6). Urbana.

1929   The Cahokia Mounds: Part 1, Explorations of 1922, 1923, 1924, and 1927, *University of Illinois Bulletin* 26(4):1–106. Urbana.

Morgan, David T.
1985   Ceramic Assemblage. In *The Hill Creek Homestead and Late Mississippian Settlement in the Lower Illinois Valley*, ed. Michael D. Conner, pp. 18–54. Center for American Archeology, Kampsville Archeological Center, Research Series vol. 1. Kampsville, Illinois.

Morrell, L. Ross
1965   *The Texas Site, Carlyle Reservoir, Clinton County, Illinois.* Archaeological Salvage Report no. 23. Southern Illinois University Museum, Carbondale.

Morse, Dan F.
1960   The Southern Cult: The Crable Site, Fulton County, Illinois. *Central States Archeological Journal* 7:124–35.

1969   The Crable Site. In *Ancient Disease in the Midwest*, by Dan Morse, pp. 63–68. Illinois State Museum Reports of Investigations no. 15. Springfield.

1972   A Pot Full of Beads. *Bulletin of the Arkansas Archeological Society* 13(3–4):67–72.

1975   *Report of Excavations at the Zebree Site, 1969.* Arkansas Archeological Survey Research Report no. 4. Fayetteville.

Morse, Dan F., and Michael G. Million
1980   Biotic and Nonbiotic Resources. In *Zebree Archeological Project*, ed. Dan F. Morse and Phyllis A. Morse, pp. 1–30. Report submitted to the Memphis District Corps of Engineers.

Morse, Dan F., and Phyllis A. Morse
1983   *Archaeology of the Central Mississippi Valley.* Academic Press, New York.

Morse, Dan F., Phyllis Morse, and Merrill Emmons
1961   The Southern Cult: The Emmons Site, Fulton County, Illinois. *Central States Archeological Journal* 8:124–40.

Morse, Dan, George Schoenbeck, and Dan F. Morse
1953   Fiedler Site. *Journal of Illinois State Archaeological Society* 3:34–46.

Muller, Jon
1976   Mississippian Population and Organization: Kincaid Locality Research, 1970–75. Ms. on file, Center for Archaeological Investigations, Southern Illinois University at Carbondale.

1978a   The Kincaid System: Mississippian Settlement in the Environs of a Large Site. In *Mississippian Settlement Patterns*, ed. Bruce D. Smith, pp. 269–92. Academic Press, New York.

1978b   The Southeast. In *Ancient Native Americans*, ed. Jesse D. Jennings, pp. 280–325. W. H. Freeman, San Francisco.

1979   From the Ridiculous to the Sublime: Small Sites in Complex Systems. Paper presented at the Seventy-eighth Annual Meeting of the American Anthropological Association, Cincinnati, Ohio.

1984   Mississippian Specialization and Salt. *American Antiquity* 49:489–507.

1986a   *Archaeology of the Lower Ohio River Valley*. Academic Press, New York.

1986b   Pans and a Grain of Salt: Mississippian Specialization Revisited. *American Antiquity* 51:405–9.

1987   Salt, Chert, and Shell: Mississippian Exchange and Economy. In *Specialization, Exchange, and Complex Societies*, ed. E. Brumfiel and T. K. Earle, pp. 10–21. Cambridge University Press, Cambridge.

1988   Lower Ohio Valley Emergent Horticulture and Mississippian. In *Emergent Horticultural Economies of the Eastern Woodlands*, ed. W. F. Keegan, pp. 243–73. Center for Archaeological Investigations,

Muller, Jon, Robert Lafferty, James Rudolph,
and Crawford Blakeman
1975   Kincaid Environs Archaeology. *Southeastern Archaeological Conference Bulletin* 18:148–57.

Muller, Jon, and F. Rackerby
1971   Kincaid Site and Its Environs. Ms. on file, Center for Archaeological Investigations, Southern Illinois University at Carbondale.

Muller, Jon, and Jeanette E. Stephens
1983   Mississippian and its Frontiers. Paper presented at the Forty-eighth Annual Meeting of the Society for American Archaeology, Pittsburgh.

Muller, Jon, Jeanette E. Stephens, and Terry Powell
1981   Shawnee Unit (X). In *Predictive Models in Illinois Archaeology: Report Summaries*, ed. Margaret K. Brown, pp. 119–32. Illinois Department of Conservation, Springfield.

Munson, Cheryl Ann
1983   Variation in Regional Settlement Organization and Community Behaviors: A Comparison of the Mississippian Angel and Caborn-Welborn Phases. Paper presented at the annual meeting of the Society for American Archaeology, Pittsburgh.

Munson, Patrick J.
1966   Midwestern Dendrochronology and Archaeological Dating. *Transactions of the Illinois State Academy of Science* 59:241–45.

1968   *Report on Preliminary Site Examination Undertaken at the Knoebel Site (S-71) on FAI 64, St. Clair County, Illinois.* Report submitted to the Illinois Division of Highways, Springfield.

1971   An Archaeological Survey of the Wood River Terrace and Adjacent Bottoms and Bluffs in Madison County, Illinois. In *An Archaeological Survey of the American Bottoms and Adjacent Bluffs, Illinois*, pp. 3–17. Illinois State Museum, Reports of Investigations no. 21.

1973   The Origins and Antiquity of Maize-Beans-Squash Agriculture in Eastern North America: Some Linguistic Implications. In *Variation in Anthropology*, ed. Donald W. Lathrap and Jody Douglas, pp. 107–35. Illinois Archaeological Survey, Urbana.

1974   Terraces, Meander Loops, and Archaeology in the American Bottoms, Illinois. *Transactions of the Illinois State Academy of Science* 67:384–92. Springfield.

1986   Hickory Silvaculture: A Subsistence Revolution in the Prehistory of North America. Paper presented at the Conference on Emergent Horticultural Economies of the Eastern Woodlands, Center for Archaeological Investigations, Southern Illinois University at Carbondale.

Munson, Patrick J., and Cheryl Ann Munson
1972   Unfinished Triangular Projectile Points or Humpbacked Knives? *Pennsylvania Archaeologist* 42(3):31–36.

Murie, James R.
1981   *Ceremonies of the Pawnee*. Smithsonian Contributions to Anthropology no. 27, ed. Douglas R. Parks. Washington, D.C.

Nickerson, William Baker
1917   Archaeological Evidence in Minnesota: Explorations of the Minnesota Historical Society in 1913 and 1916 in the Valley of the Minnesota River. Ms. on file, Minnesota Historical Society, St. Paul.

Norris, F. Terry
1978   *Excavations at the Lily Lake Site: 1975 Season*. Reports in Contract Archaeology, no. 4. Southern Illinois University at Edwardsville.

Nystuen, David W.
1971   *The Minnesota Trunk Highway Archaeological Reconnaissance Survey: Annual Report-1970*. Minnesota Department of Highways and the Minnesota Historical Society, St. Paul.

O'Brien, Michael J.
1977   *Intrasite Variability in a Middle Mississippian Community*. Ph.D. diss., Department of Anthropology, University of Texas at Austin. University Microfilms, Ann Arbor.

O'Brien, Patricia J.
1969   The Chronological Position of the Cambered Jar at Cahokia and its Implications. *American Antiquity* 34:411–16.

1972a   *A Formal Analysis of Cahokia Ceramics from the Powell Tract*. Illinois Archaeological Survey Monograph no. 3. Urbana.

1972b   Urbanism, Cahokia, and Middle Mississippian. *Archaeology* 25(3):188–97.

1978a   Steed-Kisker and Mississippian Influences on the Central Plains. In *The Central Plains Tradition: Internal Development and External Relationships*, ed. Donald J. Blakeslee. Report no. 11, Office of the State Archaeologist, University of Iowa, Iowa City.

1978b   Steed-Kisker: A Western Mississippian Settlement System. In *Mississippian Settlement Patterns*, ed. Bruce D. Smith, pp. 1–20. Academic Press, New York.

1983   Cahokia and Cultural Taxonomy. Paper presented at the annual meeting of the Society for American Archaeology, Pittsburgh.

Orr, Ellison
1963   *Iowa Archaeology Reports 1934–1939*. 10 vols. Archives of Archaeology, Society for American Archaeology.

Orr, Kenneth G.
1941   The Eufaula Mound: Contributions to the Spiro Focus. *The Oklahoma Prehistorian* 4(1):2–15.

1951   Change at Kincaid: A Study of Cultural Dynamics. In *Kincaid: A Prehistoric Illinois Metropolis*, by Fay-Cooper Cole et al., pp. 293–359. University of Chicago Press, Chicago.

Orr, Kenneth G. (editor)
1950   *Symposium on Northern Mississippi Valley Archaeology Held in Chicago, Illinois, April 16–17, 1949*. Illinois State Museum, Springfield.

Orthwein, Walter E.
1965   Tests Show Monks Mound Not Wholly Man-Made. *St. Louis Globe-Democrat*, Sept. 28, 1965.

Osborn, Nancy M.
1982   The Clarkson Site (13Wa2), An Oneota Manifestation in the Central Des Moines River Valley. *Journal of the Iowa Archeological Society* 29:ii-102.

Overstreet, David F.
1976   *The Grand River, Lake Koshkonong, Green Bay and Lake Winnebago Phases: Eight Hundred Years of Oneota Prehistory in Eastern Wisconsin.* Ph.D. diss., Department of Anthropology, University of Wisconsin-Milwaukee.
1978   Oneota Settlement Patterns in Eastern Wisconsin: Some Considerations of Time and Space. In *Mississippian Settlement Patterns*, ed. Bruce D. Smith, pp. 21–52, Academic Press, New York.
1981   Investigations at the Pipe Site (47-Fd-10) and Some Perspectives on Eastern Wisconsin Oneota Prehistory. *Wisconsin Archeologist* 64:365–525.

Overstreet, David, Robert P. Fay, Carol I. Mason, and Robert F. Boszhardt
1983   *Cultural Resources Literature Search and Records Review-Upper Mississippi River Basin.* Reports of Investigation no. 116. Great Lakes Archaeological Research Center, Waukasau, Wisconsin.

Pace, Robert E.
1974   *Archaeological Salvage, Daughtery(sic)-Monroe Site: Island Levee Local Protection Project, Sullivan County, Indiana.* Report submitted to the National Park Service, Northeast Region, Philadelphia.

Pace, Robert E., and Gary A. Apfelstadt
1974   Ceramics of the Multicomponent Farrand Site, Vigo County, Indiana. *Proceedings of the Indiana Academy of Science* 83:63.
1978   *Allison-LaMotte Culture of the Daugherty-Monroe Site, Sullivan County, Indiana.* Report submitted to the Office of Archeology and Historic Preservation, Interagency Archaeological Service, Atlanta.

Palkovich, Ann M.
1975   *Point Pattern Analysis and Limited-Activity Sites: an Example from Survey.* M.A. thesis, Department of Anthropology, Northwestern University, Evanston, Illinois.

Paloumpis, Andreas A.
1981   Analysis of Fish Bones from the Orendorf Site. In *The Orendorf Site Preliminary Working Papers 1981*, comp. Duane Esarey and Lawrence A. Conrad, vol. 1, pp. 193–99. Western Illinois University Archaeological Research Laboratory, Macomb.
1983   Analysis of Fish Bones from the Orendorf Site (Revised Version). Ms. on file, Western Illinois University Archaeological Research Laboratory, Macomb.

Panshin, A. J., and Carl de Zeeuw
1970   *Textbook of Wood Technology*, vol. 1. 3d ed. McGraw-Hill, New York.

Parker, Kathryn E.
1987   Plant Remains. In *The Radic Site*, by Dale L. McElrath, Joyce A. Williams, Thomas O. Maher, and Michael Meinkoth, pp. 221–45. American Bottom Archaeology FAI-270 Site Reports vol. 17(1). University of Illinois Press, Urbana.
1988   Plant Use Patterns in the Edelhardt Lake Locality. Paper presented at the Thirty-third annual Midwest Archaeological Conference, Urbana, Illinois.
1989   Archaeobotanical Assemblages. In *The Holding Site: A Hopewell Community in the American Bottom*, by Andrew C. Fortier et al., pp. 429–64. American Bottom Archaeology FAI-270 Site Reports vol. 19. University of Illinois Press, Urbana.

Parmalee, Paul W.
1960   Animal Remains from the Aztalan Site, Jefferson County, Wisconsin. *Wisconsin Archeologist* 41:1–10.
n.d.   Notes on faunal species present in various collections from the Crable site. On file at the Illinois State Museum, Springfield.

Parsons, Jeffrey R.
1971   *Prehistoric Settlement Patterns in the Texcoco Region, Mexico.* University of Michigan, Museum of Anthropology Memoirs no. 3. Ann Arbor.

Pauketat, Timothy R.
1983   A Long-Stemmed Spud from the American Bottom. *Midcontinental Journal of Archaeology* 8:1–15.
1987   Mississippian Domestic Economy and Formation Processes: A Response to Prentice. *Midcontinental Journal of Archaeology* 12:77–88.

Pauketat, Timothy R., and Brad Koldehoff
1983   Emerald Mound and the Mississippian Occupation of the Central Silver Creek Valley. Paper presented at the Twenty-eighth annual Midwest Archaeological Conference, Iowa City.

Pecotte, Michael J.
1972   A String of Shell Beads. *Bulletin of the Arkansas Archeological Society* 13(1–2):77–79.

Peebles, Christopher
1971   Moundville and Surrounding Sites: Some Structural Considerations for Mortuary Practices II. In *Approaches to the Social Dimensions of Mortuary Practices*, ed. James A. Brown, pp. 68–91. Memoirs of the Society for American Archaeology no. 25.
1978   Moundville Phase. In *Mississippian Settlement Patterns*, ed. Bruce D. Smith, pp. 369–416. Academic Press, New York.

Peebles, Christopher, and Susan Kus
1977   Some Archaeological Correlates of Ranked Societies. *American Antiquity* 42:421–48.

Penman, John T.
1984   *Archaeology of the Great River Road: Summary Report.* Wisconsin Department of Transportation Archaeological Report no. 10. Wisconsin Department of Transportation, Madison.
1988   Neo-Boreal Climatic Influences on the Late Prehistoric Agricultural Groups of the Upper Mississippi Valley. *Geoarchaeology* 3:139–45.

Perino, Gregory
1959   Recent Information from Cahokia and Its Satellites. *Central States Archaeological Journal* 6:130–38.
1966   Short History of Some Shell Ornaments. *Central States Archaeological Journal* 13:4–8.
1967   *The Cherry Valley Mounds, Cross County Arkansas, and Banks Mound 3, Crittenden County, Arkansas.* Central States Archaeological Societies, Memoir no. 1.
1968   *Guide to the Identification of Certain American Indian Projectile Points.* Oklahoma Anthropological Society Special Bulletin no. 3. Norman.
1971a   *Guide to the Identification of Certain American Indian Projectile Points.* Oklahoma Anthropological Society Bulletin no. 4. Norman.
1971b   The Mississippian Component at the Schild Site (no.4), Greene County, Illinois. In *Mississippian Site Archaeology in Illinois: I*, ed. James A. Brown, pp. 1–148.

Illinois Archaeological Survey Bulletin no. 8. Urbana.

1971c   The Yokem Site, Pike County, Illinois. In *Mississippian Site Archaeology in Illinois: I,* ed. James A. Brown, pp. 149–86. Illinois Archaeological Survey Bulletin no. 8. Urbana.

1972   The Yokem Site Late Woodland Mounds, Pike County, Illinois. In *Certain Hopewell and Late Woodland Sites in West-Central Illinois,* by Gregory Perino, pp. 308–76. Ms. on file, Center for American Archeology, Kampsville Archeological Center, Kampsville, Illinois.

1973a   The Koster Mounds, Greene County, Illinois. In *Late Woodland Site Archaeology in Illinois: I,* ed. James A. Brown, pp. 141–206. Illinois Archaeological Survey Bulletin no. 9. Urbana.

1973b   Late Woodland Component at the Schild Site, Greene County, Illinois. In *Late Woodland Site Archaeology in Illinois: I,* ed. James A. Brown, pp. 90–140. Illinois Archaeological Survey Bulletin no. 9. Urbana.

1974   A Rare Short-Nosed God Mask. *Central States Archaeological Journal* 21:84–85.

1975   The Hacker Mounds, Jersey County, Illinois. Ms. on file, Center for American Archeology, Kampsville Archeological Center, Kampsville, Illinois.

1985   *Selected Preforms, Points and Knives of the North American Indians.* Vol. 1. Points and Barbs Press, Idabel, Oklahoma.

Perkins, Raymond W.
1965   The Frederick Site. In *Middle Woodland Sites in Illinois,* ed. Elaine Bluhm Herold, pp. 68–95. Illinois Archaeological Survey Bulletin no. 5. Urbana.

Peske, G. Richard
1973   Commentary. In *The Grant Oneota Village,* by Marshall McKusick, pp. 164–66. Report no. 4, Office of the State Archaeologist, University of Iowa, Iowa City.

Peters, Gordon R.
1976   A Reevaluation of Aztalan: Some Temporal and Causal Factors. *Wisconsin Archeologist* 57:2–11.

Phillippe, Joseph S., and Denise Hodges
1981   *A Cultural Resource Survey of Selected Portions of the Shelbyville Reservoir Shoreline.* Contract report submitted to the Department of the Army, Corps of Engineers, St. Louis District.

Phillips, Philip
1970   *Archaeological Survey in the Lower Yazoo Basin, Mississippi, 1949–1955.* Papers of the Peabody Museum of Archaeology and Ethnology no. 60. Harvard University, Cambridge.

Phillips, Philip, and James A. Brown
1975   *Pre-Columbian Shell Engravings from the Craig Mound at Spiro, Oklahoma.* Vols. 1–3. Peabody Museum Press, Harvard University, Cambridge, Massachusetts.

Phillips, Philip, James A. Ford, and James B. Griffin
1951   *Archaeological Survey in the Lower Mississippi Alluvial Valley, 1940–1947.* Papers of the Peabody Museum of American Archaeology and Ethnology no. 25. Harvard University, Cambridge, Massachusetts.

Pickels, G. W.
1937   Land Reclamation and Flood Control. In *A Report on Certain Physical, Economic and Social Aspects of the Valley of the Kaskaskia River in the State of Illinois,* pt. 1, pp. 102–11. University of Illinois, Urbana.

Pickering, Robert B.
n.d.   The Ledders Site. Ms. on file, Bioanthropology Laboratory, University of Chicago.

Piesinger, Constance M.
1972   *The Mansker Site: A Late Prehistoric Village in Southern Illinois.* M.A. thesis, Department of Anthropology, University of Wisconsin, Madison.

Poehls, R. L.
1944   Kingston Lake Site Burials. *Journal of the Illinois State Archaeological Society* 1 (April): 36–38.

Pollack, David, and Jimmy A. Railey
1987   *Chambers (15ML109): An Upland Mississippian Village in Western Kentucky.* Kentucky Heritage Council, Frankfort.

Porter, James W.
1961   Hixton Silicified Sandstone: A Unique Lithic Material Used by Prehistoric Cultures. *Wisconsin Archeologist* 42:78–85.

1963   *Bluff Pottery Analysis—Thin Section Experiment no. 2: Analysis of Bluff Pottery from the Mitchell Site, Madison County, Illinois.* Southern Illinois University Museum Lithic Laboratory, Research Report no. 4. Carbondale.

1966   Thin Section Analysis of Ten Aztalan Sherds. *Wisconsin Archeologist* 47:12–28.

1969   The Mitchell Site and Prehistoric Exchange Systems at Cahokia: A.D. 1000 ± 300. In *Explorations into Cahokia Archaeology,* ed. Melvin L. Fowler, pp. 137–64. Illinois Archaeological Survey Bulletin no. 7. Urbana.

1974   *Cahokia Archaeology as Viewed from the Mitchell Site: A Satellite Community at A.D. 1150–1200.* Ph.D. diss., Department of Anthropology, University of Wisconsin, Madison. University Microfilms, Ann Arbor.

Powell, Mary Lucas
1988   *Status and Health in Prehistory: A Case Study of the Moundville Chiefdom.* Smithsonian Press, Washington, D.C.

Power, Marjory W.
1976   Delineation of the Angel Phase: A Middle Mississippian Occupation in Southwestern Indiana. *Southeastern Archaeological Conference Bulletin* 19:26–30.

Prentice, Guy
1983   Cottage Industries: Concepts and Implications. *Midcontinental Journal of Archaeology* 8:17–48.

Prentice, Guy, and Mark Mehrer
1981   The Lab Woofie Site (11-S-346): An Unplowed Mississippian Site in the American Bottom Region of Illinois. *Midcontinental Journal of Archaeology* 6:33–53.

Price, James E., and Cynthia R. Price
1984   *Phase III Testing of the Shell Lake Site, 2 WE-627, Near Wappapello Dam, Wayne County, Missouri, 1984.* St. Louis District Cultural Resource Management Report no. 11.

Rackerby, Frank E.
1966   *Archaeological Investigations at the Boulder Site: First Season.* Archaeological Salvage Report no. 27. Southern Illinois University Museum, Carbondale.

1968   *Carlyle Reservoir Archaeology: Final Season.* Southern Illinois Studies Series '68, no. S1A. Southern Illinois University Museum, Carbondale.

Radin, Paul
1948   *Winnebago Hero Cycles: A Study in Aboriginal Literature.* Waverly Press, Baltimore.

1970   *The Winnebago Tribe.* University of Nebraska Press, Lincoln.

Ralph, E. K., H. N. Michael, and M. C. Han
1973   *Radiocarbon Dates and Reality.* Museum of Applied Science Center, Archaeology Newsletter 9 (1).

Rau, Charles
1867   Indian Pottery. *Annual Report of the Smithsonian Institution, 1866*, pp. 346–55. Washington, D.C.
1869   Deposit of Agricultural Flint Implements in Southern Illinois. *Annual Report of the Smithsonian Institution, 1868*, pp. 407–7. Washington, D.C.

Rauh, Eric J.
1971   An Archaeological Survey of the Silver Creek Drainage and the Central Kaskaskia Valley. In *Preliminary Report of the 1971 Historic Sites Survey, Archaeological Reconnaissance of Selected Areas in the State of Illinois: Part I, Summary*, pp. 35–43. Illinois Archaeological Survey, Urbana.
1975   An Archaeological Survey of the Silver Creek Drainage and the Central Kaskaskia Valley. In *Preliminary Report of 1974 Historic Sites Survey, Archaeological Reconnaissance of Selected Areas in the State of Illinois: Part I, Summary*, pp. 42–48. Illinois Archaeological Survey, Urbana.

Rauh, Eric J., and Anne W. Wilson
1972   An Archaeological Survey of the Silver Creek Drainage and the Central Kaskaskia Valley. In *Preliminary Report of 1972 Historic Sites Survey, Archaeological Reconnaissance of Selected Areas in the State of Illinois: Part I, Summary*, pp. 34–42. Illinois Archaeological Survey, Urbana.
1974   An Archaeological Survey of the Silver Creek Drainage and the Central Kaskaskia Valley. In *Preliminary Report of 1973 Historic Sites Survey, Archaeological Reconnaissance of Selected Areas in the State of Illinois: Part I, Summary*, pp. 35–43. Illinois Archaeological Survey, Urbana.

Ray, A. J.
1974   *Indians in the Fur Trade: Their Role as Trappers, Hunters, and Middlemen in the Lands Southwest of Hudson Bay*. University of Toronto Press, Toronto.

Ready, Timothy
1979   Cambria Phase. In *A Handbook of Minnesota Prehistoric Ceramics*, ed. Scott F. Anfinson, pp. 51–65. Occasional Publications in Minnesota Anthropology no. 5. Minnesota Archaeological Society, Ft. Snelling.

Redmond, Brian G.
1986   *A Study of Yankeetown Phase Settlement Patterns in the Lower Ohio Valley*. Glenn A. Black Laboratory of Archaeology, Indiana University, Reports of Investigations 86–84. Bloomington.

Reed, Nelson A., John W. Bennett, and James W. Porter
1968   Solid Core Drilling of Monks Mound: Technique and Findings. *American Antiquity* 33:137–48.

Renfrew, Colin
1975   Trade as Action at a Distance: Questions of Integration and Communication. In *Ancient Civilization and Trade*, ed. J. A. Sabloff, and C. C. Lamberg-Karlovsky, pp. 3–59. University of New Mexico Press, Albuquerque.
1977   Alternative Models for Exchange and Spatial Distribution. In *Exchange Systems in Prehistory*, ed. Timothy K. Earle and Jonathan E. Ericson, pp. 71–90. Academic Press, New York.

Riley, Thomas J., and Gary A. Apfelstadt
1978   Prehistoric Missionaries in East Central Illinois. *Field Museum of Natural History, Bulletin* 49(4):16–21.

Rinaldo, John B.
1937   *The Pere Marquette Park Sites*. M.A. thesis, Department of Anthropology, University of Chicago.

Rindos, David
1984   *The Origins of Agriculture: An Evolutionary Perspective*. Academic Press, New York.

Riordan, Robert
1975   *Ceramics and Chronology: Mississippian Settlement in the Black Bottom, Southern Illinois*. Ph.D. diss., Department of Anthropology, Southern Illinois University at Carbondale.

Rodell, Roland
1983   *The Late Prehistory of Eastern Wisconsin: A Survey of the Archaeological Research and Interpretations Pertaining to Oneota Settlement and Subsistence*. M.A. thesis, Department of Anthropology, University of Wisconsin-Milwaukee.

Rolingson, Martha (editor)
1982   *Emerging Patterns of Plum Bayou Culture: Preliminary Investigations of the Toltec Mounds Research Project*. Toltec Papers no. 2. Arkansas Archaeological Survey Research Series vol. 18. Fayetteville.

Rothschild, Nan A.
1979   Mortuary Behavior and Social Organization at Indian Knoll and Dickson Mounds. *American Antiquity* 44: 658–75.

Rouse, Irving
1958   The Inference of Migrations from Anthropological Information. In *Migrations in New World Culture History*, ed. R. Thompson, pp. 63–68. Social Sciences Study no. 27. University of Arizona Press, Tucson.

Rowe, Chandler W.
1958   A Crematorium at Aztalan. *Wisconsin Archeologist* 39: 101–10.

Rudolph, Teresa Perry
1981   *The Distribution of Late Woodland Sites in the Black Bottom Area, Pope and Massac Counties, Illinois*. M.A. thesis, Department of Anthropology, Southern Illinois University at Carbondale.

Rusch, Lynn A.
1985   The Springview Site: A Possible Late-Seventeenth Century Mascouten Village. *The Wisconsin Archeologist* 66:157–75.

Sahlins, Marshall
1958   *Social Stratification in Polynesia*. University of Washington Press, Seattle.
1972   *Stone Age Economics*. Aldine, Chicago.

Salkin, Philip H.
1987   A Reevaluation of the Late Woodland Stage in Southeastern Wisconsin. *Wisconsin Academy Review* 33 (2): 75–79.

Salzer, Robert J.
1963   *The Kerwin and Orrell Sites, Carlyle Reservoir, Clinton County, Illinois*. Southern Illinois University Museum, Archaeological Salvage Report no. 4. Carbondale.
1974   The Wisconsin North Lakes Project: A Preliminary Report. In *Aspects of Upper Great Lakes Anthropology, Papers in Honor of Lloyd A. Wilford*, ed. Elden Johnson, pp. 40–54. Minnesota Prehistoric Archaeology Series no. 11. Minnesota Historical Society, St. Paul.
1987   Preliminary report on the Gottschall site (47Ia80). *Wisconsin Archeologist* 68(4):419–72.

Sampson, Kelvin, and Duane Esarey
1988   Embossed Copper Artifacts from the Illinois River Valley. Paper presented at the Midwest Archaeological Conference, Urbana.

Santeford, Lawrence
1982   *Mississippian Political Organization and Chipped
          Stone Artifacts: A Typological Model for the Study
          of a Prehistoric Society in Southern Illinois.* Ph.D.
          diss., Department of Anthropology, Southern Illinois
          University at Carbondale.
Santure, Sharron K.
1981   The Changing Community Plan of Settlement C. In *The
          Orendorf Site Preliminary Working Papers 1981*, comp.
          Duane E. Esarey and Lawrence A. Conrad, vol. 1,
          pp. 5–81. Western Illinois University Archaeological
          Research Laboratory, Macomb.
Santure, Sharron K., Alan D. Harn, and Duane Esarey
1990   Archaeological Investigations at Morton Village
          (11Fᵛ19) and Norris Farms #36 Cemetery (11F°2167),
          Fulton County, Illinois. Ms. on file, Illinois State
          Museum, Springfield.
Sauer, Carl O.
1969a   *The Early Spanish Main.* University of California Press,
          Berkeley.
1969b   *Seeds, Spades, Hearths, and Herds: The Domestica-
          tion of Animals and Foodstuffs.* 2d ed. The MIT Press,
          Cambridge, Massachusetts.
Savage, Howard
1978   Armstrong: A Faunal Analysis. *Wisconsin Archeologist*
          59:118–45.
Schmidt, E. W.
1941   A Brief Archaeological Survey of the Red Wing Area.
          Minnesota Archaeologist 7:70–80.
Schneider, Kathryn J. (editor)
1964   Aztalan. *Wisconsin Then and Now* 11(2):1–5.
Schock, Jack M.
1986   An Archaeological Excavation of Mounds 1, 2, and 4
          at 40-OB-6 (The Effigy Rabbit Site) in Obion County,
          Tennessee. Report submitted to the ASCS, Nash-
          ville, Tennessee. Arrow Enterprises, Bowling Green,
          Kentucky.
Schwegman, John E.
1973   *Comprehensive Plan for the Illinois Nature Preserves
          System: Part 2, The Natural Divisions of Illinois.* Illinois
          Nature Preserves Commission, Springfield.
Scullin, Michael
1979   Price Site (21BE36): Preliminary Notes on a Previ-
          ously Unidentified Site of the Cambria Focus. Ms.
          on file, Department of Anthropology, Mankato State
          University, Mankato, Minnesota.
Sears, William H.
1968   The State and Settlement Patterns in the New World. In
          Settlement Archaeology, ed. K. C. Chang, pp. 134–53.
          National Press Books, Palo Alto, Calfornia.
1973   The Sacred and Secular in Prehistoric Ceramics. In
          Variations in Anthropology, ed. Donald W. Lathrap
          and Jody Douglas, pp. 31–42. Illinois Archaeological
          Survey, Urbana.
Seeman, Mark F.
1979a   Feasting with the Dead: Ohio Charnal House Ritual as
          a Context for Redistribution. In *Hopewell Archaeology:
          The Chillicothe Conference*, ed. David S. Brose and
          N'omi Greber, pp. 39–46. Kent State University, Kent,
          Ohio.
1979b   *The Hopewell Interaction Sphere: The Evidence for
          Interregional Trade and Structural Complexity.* Indiana
          Historical Society, Prehistoric Research Series vol.
          5(2).

Service, Elman R.
1962   *Primitive Social Oganization.* Random House, New
          York.
1975   *Origins of the State and Civilization: The Process of
          Cultural Evolution.* W. W. Norton, New York.
Shalkop, Robert L.
1949   *The Jersey Bluff Archaeological Focus, Jersey County,
          Illinois.* M.A. thesis, Department of Anthropology,
          University of Chicago.
Shane, Linda
1980   Seed Analysis: Price Site, Blue Earth County, Mn. Ms.
          on file, Department of Anthropology, Mankato State
          University, Mankato, Minnesota.
Shane, Orrin C., III
1980   *Grantees' Reports 1980.* American Philosophical
          Society, Philadelphia.
Shaw, John
1888   Indian Chiefs and Pioneers of the Northwest. *Wiscon-
          sin Historical Collections* 10:213–22. State Historical
          Society of Wisconsin, Madison.
Shay, Ruth Ann Knudson
1966   Cambria Village Ceramics. M.A. thesis, University of
          Minnesota, Minneapolis.
Shelford, Victor E.
1963   *The Ecology of North America.* University of Illinois
          Press, Urbana.
Shields, Wayne F.
1969   Recent Archaeology at Dickson Mounds. *The Living
          Museum* 31:132–35.
Shippee, James M.
1972   *Archaeological Remains in the Kansas City Area: The
          Mississippian Occupation.* Missouri Archaeological
          Society, Research Series no. 9. Columbia.
Shoemaker, Bert, and Louise Shoemaker
1969   *The Shipps Ferry Site.* Arkansas Archaeologist vol.
          1(4).
Simpson, Anson M.
1937   Various Types of Kingston Site Burials. *Transactions
          of the Illinois State Academy of Sciences* 30:95–96.
          Springfield.
1939   *The Kingston Village Site.* Archaeological Section of the
          Peoria Academy of Science, Peoria, Illinois.
1952   The Kingston Village Site. *Journal of the Illinois
          Archaeological Society* 2(2–3):63–77. Springfield.
Sirico, Michael W.
1986   *Phase I and Phase II Archaeological Investigations in
          Conjunction with the Shoreline Erosion Study, D.M.
          no. 14, Carlyle Lake, Illinois.* U.S. Army Corps of
          Engineers, St. Louis District Cultural Resource Man-
          agement Report no. 28. American Resources Group,
          Ltd., Carbondale, Illinois.
Skele, Mikels
1988   *The Great Knob: Interpretations of Monks Mound.*
          Studies in Illinois Archaeology no. 4. Illinois Historic
          Preservation Agency, Springfield.
Skinner, Alanson
1925   Traditions of the Ioway Indians. *Journal of American
          Folk-Lore* 38:425–506.
Skinner, Robert R.
1953   The Oakwood Mound: An Upper Mississippian Com-
          ponent. *Journal of Illinois State Archeological Society*
          3:2–14. Springfield.
Smail, William
1952   Crable Site Mace. *Journal of Illinois State Archaeologi-
          cal Society* 2(2–3):87.

Smith, Bruce D.
1974   Middle Mississippian Exploitation of Animal Popu-
        lations: A Predictive Model. *American Antiquity* 39:
        274–91.
1978   Variation in Mississippian Settlement Patterns. In *Mis-
        sissippian Settlement Patterns*, ed. Bruce D. Smith, pp.
        479–503. Academic Press, New York.
1984a   Chenopodium as a Prehistoric Domesticate in Eastern
        North America: Evidence from Russell Cave, Alabama.
        Science 226:165–67.
1984b   Mississippian Expansion: Tracing the Historical De-
        velopment of an Explanatory Model. *Southeastern
        Archaeology* 3:13–32.
1985a   *Chenopodium berlandieri* ssp. *jonesianum*: Evidence
        for a Hopewellian Domesticate from Ash Cave, Ohio.
        Southeastern Archaeology 4:107–33.
1985b   Mississippian Patterns of Subsistence and Settlement.
        In *Alabama and the Borderlands*, ed. R. Badger and
        L. Clayton, pp. 64–79. University of Alabama Press,
        University.
1985c   The Role of *Chenopodium* as a Domesticate in Pre-
        Maize Garden Systems of the Eastern United States.
        Southeastern Archaeology 4:51–72.
1986   The Archaeology of the Southeastern United States:
        From Dalton to de Soto, 10,500–500 B.P. In *Advances
        in World Archaeology*, ed. F. Wendorf and A. E. Close,
        pp. 1–92. Academic Press, New York.
1987a   The Economic Potential of *Chenopodium berlandieri*
        in Prehistoric Eastern North America. *Journal of
        Ethnobiology* 7:29–54.
1987b   The Independent Domestication of Indigenous Seed-
        Bearing Plants in Eastern North America. In *Emergent
        Horticultural Economies of the Eastern Woodlands*,
        ed. William F. Keegan, pp. 3–47. Southern Illinois
        University at Carbondale, Center for Archaeological
        Investigations, Occasional Paper no. 7.
Smith, Bruce D. (editor)
1978   *Mississippian Settlement Patterns*. Academic Press,
        New York.
Smith, Hale G.
1951   *The Crable Site, Fulton County, Illinois: A Late Pre-
        historic Site in the Central Illinois Valley*. University of
        Michigan, Museum of Anthropology, Anthropological
        Papers no. 7. Ann Arbor.
Smith, Harriet
1969   The Murdock Mound: Cahokia Site. In *Explora-
        tions into Cahokia Archaeology*, pp. 49–88. Illinois
        Archaeological Survey Bulletin no. 7. Urbana.
Smith, R. S., E. E. DeTurk, F. C. Baker, and L. H. Smith
1932   *Fulton County Soils*. Soil Report no. 51, University of
        Illlinois Agriculture Experiment Station, Urbana.
Snyder, John Francis
1877   Deposits of Flint Implements. *Annual Report of the
        Board of Regents of the Smithsonian Institution, Mis-
        cellaneous Document* no. 46:433–41. Government
        Printing Office, Washington, D.C.
1909   Certain Indian Mounds Technically Considered. Part
        Third: Temple or Domiciliary Mounds. *Journal of the
        Illinois State Historical Society* 2:71–92.
1913   *The Prehistoric Mounds of Illinois*. Published by "The
        Monks of Cahokia," Springfield, Illinois.
1914   Prehistoric Illinois—The Great Cahokia Mound. *Illinois
        State Historical Society Journal* 6:506–8.
1917   The Great Cahokia Mound. *Illinois State Historical
        Society Journal* 10:256–59.

1962   Prehistoric Illinois: The Brown County Ossuary. In
        John Francis Snyder: Selected Writings, ed. Clyde C.
        Walton, pp. 216–29. Illinois State Historical Society,
        Springfield.
Southard, Michael O., and John W. Cottier
1973   Beckwith's Fort Site 23Mi2, Renamed Towosahgy
        State Archaeological Site by the Missouri State Park
        Board, 1967. Ms. on file, Department of Anthro-
        pology, University of Illinois at Urbana-Champaign.
Spaulding, Albert C.
1956   *The Arzberger Site, Hughes County, South Dakota*.
        University of Michigan, Museum of Anthropology,
        Occasional Contributions no. 16. Ann Arbor.
Speck, Frank G.
1909   *Ethnology of the Yuchi Indians*. Anthropological Pub-
        lications of the University Museum, University of
        Pennsylvania, vol. 1, no. 1. Philadelphia.
Speth, Janet M.
1981   Bird Bones from the Orendorf Site. In *The Orendorf
        Site Preliminary Working Papers 1981*, comp. Duane
        Esarey and Lawrence A. Conrad, vol. 1, pp. 180–92.
        Western Illinois University Archaeological Research
        Laboratory, Macomb.
Spielmann, K. A.
1982   *Inter-Societal Food Acquisition Among Egalitarian
        Societies: An Ecological Analysis of Plains/Pueblo
        Interaction in the American Southwest*. Ph.D. diss.,
        Department of Anthropology, University of Michigan,
        Ann Arbor.
1983   Late Prehistoric Exchange Between the Southwest and
        Southern Plains. *Plains Anthropologist* 28:257–72.
Springer, James W.
1967   *Preliminary Report on Excavations in the Shelbyville
        Reservoir: Summer 1967*. Contract report submitted
        to the U.S. Department of the Interior, National Park
        Service.
Springer, James W., and Stanley R. Witkowski
1982   Siouan Historical Linguistics and Oneota Archaeology.
        In *Oneota Studies*, ed. Guy E. Gibbon, pp. 69–84.
        Publications in Anthropology, no. 1. University of
        Minnesota, Minneapolis.
Squier, George H.
1905   Certain Archeological Features of Western Wisconsin.
        Wisconsin Archeologist o.s. 4(2):25–38.
Stelle, Len J.
1985   The Lithic Assemblage. In *The Turk Site: A Mississip-
        pian Town of the Western Kentucky Border*, ed. Richard
        Edging, pp. 28–34. Department of Anthropology, Uni-
        versity of Illinois, Western Kentucky Project Report
        no. 3.
Stephens, B. W.
1958   Handled Pottery of the Illinois River Valley. *Central
        States Archeological Journal* 4(3):84–85.
Stephens, Denzil
1963   Simple Stamped Pottery Decoration of the Wabash Val-
        ley. In *Reports on Illinois Prehistory: 1*, ed. Elaine A.
        Bluhm, pp. 126–30. Illinois Archaeological Survey
        Bulletin no. 4. Urbana.
1974   *Excavations at the Stoner and Lowe Sites*. Illinois State
        Museum Research Series Papers in Anthropology,
        no. 2. Springfield.
Stephens, Jeanette E.
1972   An Archaeological Survey of the Coal Region and
        Neighboring Areas of the Illinois River Valley in West-

Central Illinois. In *Preliminary Report of 1972 Historic Sites Survey, Archaeological Reconnaissance of Selected Areas in the State of Illinois, Part I, Summary Section A*, pp. 49–56. Illinois Archaeological Survey, Urbana.

1976   Mississippian Settlement Relocation at the Orendorf Site. Paper presented at the Twenty-first Annual Meeting of the Midwest Archaeological Conference, Minneapolis.

1979   The Orendorf Site: A Nucleated Mississippian Frontier Site. Paper presented at the Thirty-sixth Annual Meeting of the Southeastern Archaeological Conference, Atlanta.

1981   Exchange and the Spatial Structure of Settlement Systems: An Example from Cahokia. Manuscript in possession of the author.

Steponaitis, Vincas

1978   Location Theory and Complex Chiefdoms: A Mississippian Example. In *Mississippian Settlement Patterns*, ed. Bruce D. Smith, pp. 417–53. Academic Press, New York.

1983   *Ceramics, Chronology, and Community Patterns: An Archaeological Study at Moundville*. Academic Press, New York.

1986   Prehistoric Archaeology in the Southeastern United States, 1970–1985. *Annual Review of Anthropology* 15: 363–404.

Stevenson, Katherine, William Green, and Janet Speth

1983   The Middle Mississippian Presence in the Upper Mississippi Valley: The Evidence from Trempealeau, Wisconsin. Paper presented at the Midwest Archaeological Conference, Iowa City, Iowa.

Stoltman, James B.

1978   Temporal Models in Prehistory: An Example from Eastern North America. *Current Anthropology* 19: 703–46.

1983   Ancient Peoples of the Upper Mississippi River Valley. In *Historic Lifestyles in the Upper Mississippi River Valley*, ed. John Wozniak, pp. 197–255. University Press of America, Lanham, Maryland.

1986   The Appearance of the Mississippian Cultural Tradition in the Upper Mississippi Valley. In *Prehistoric Mound Builders of the Mississippi Valley*, ed. James B. Stoltman, pp. 26–34. Putnam Museum, Davenport, Iowa.

Stoner, Louis J.

1972   The Carlin Site: Salvage Archaeology on a Late Woodland Village. *Illinois Association for the Advancement of Archaeology, Newsletter* 4(3):21–22.

Storck, Peter

1972   *The Archaeology of Mayland Cave*. 2 vols. Ph.D. diss., Department of Anthropology, University of Wisconsin, Madison.

Stortroen, Charles E.

1957   *The Bryan Site: A Prehistoric Village in Southern Minnesota*. M.A. thesis, University of Minnesota, Minneapolis.

1985   The Bryan Site: A Prehistoric Village in Southern Minnesota. *Minnesota Archaeologist* 43:37–48.

Stout, A. B.

1911   *Prehistoric Earthworks in Wisconsin*. Ohio Archaeological and Historical Publications, vol. 20(1).

Stout, C. B.

1984a   Gross Spatial Patterning at a Large Mississippian Town and Ceremonial Center. Paper presented at

the Forty-first Annual Meeting of the Southeastern Archaeological Conference, Pensacola, Florida.

1984b   Mississippian Sites in Western Kentucky: Variations on a General Mississippian Theme? In *Late Prehistoric Research in Kentucky*, ed. David Pollack, Charles Hockensmith, and Thomas Sanders, pp. 167–79. Kentucky Heritage Council, Frankfort.

1985   *The Adams Site: A Spatial Analysis—Preliminary Report*. University of Illinois, Department of Anthropology, Western Kentucky Project Report no. 2. Urbana.

1987   *Surface Distribution Patterns at the Adams Site, A Mississippian Town in Fulton County, Kentucky*. University of Illinois, Department of Anthropology, Western Kentucky Project Report no. 6. Urbana.

Straffin, Dean

1971   *The Kingston Oneota Site*. University of Iowa, Iowa City.

Streiff, Jan E. (compiler)

1972   *Roster of Excavated Prehistoric Sites in Minnesota to 1972*. Minnesota Prehistoric Archaeology Series, no. 7. Minnesota Historical Society, St. Paul.

Struever, Stuart

1960   The Kamp Mound Group and a Hopewell Mortuary Complex in the Lower Illinois Valley. M.A. thesis, Department of Anthropology, Northwestern University, Evanston, Illinois.

1968   Flotation Techniques for the Recovery of Small-Scale Archaeological Remains. *American Antiquity* 33: 353–62.

1973   *Report on Preliminary Site Examination Undertaken at the Carlin Site on FAP 38, Calhoun County, Illinois*. Center for American Archeology, Contract Archeology Program, Report of Investigations no. 4, Kampsville, Illinois. Submitted to Illinois Department of Transportation, Springfield.

Struever, Stuart, and Felicia Antonelli Holton

1979   *Koster: Americans in Search of their Prehistoric Past*. Anchor Press/Doubleday, Garden City, New York.

Struever, Stuart, and Gail L. Houart

1972   An Analysis of the Hopewell Interaction Sphere. In *Social Exchange and Interaction*, ed. Edwin N. Wilmsen, pp. 47–79. Museum of Anthropology, University of Michigan, Anthropological Papers no. 46. Ann Arbor.

Stuebe, Fred K.

1976   Site Survey and Test Excavations in the Aztalan Area. *Wisconsin Archeologist* 57:198–259.

Stuiver, Minze

1982   A High-Precision Calibration of the A.D. Radiocarbon Time Scale. *Radiocarbon* 24:1–26.

Stuiver, Minze, and Gordon W. Pearson

1986   High-Precision Calibration of the Radiocarbon Time Scale, A.D. 1950–500 B.C. *Radiocarbon* 28:805–38.

Stuiver, Minze, and P. J. Reimer

1986   A Computer Program for Radiocarbon Age Calibration. *Radiocarbon* 28:1022–30.

Stuiver, Minze, and Hans E. Suess

1968   On the Relationship Between Radiocarbon Dates and True Sample Ages. *Radiocarbon* 8:534–40.

Stuiver, Minze, and Renee Kra (editors)

1986   *Calibration Issue: Proceedings of the Twelfth International Radiocarbon Conference—Trondheim, Norway*. Radiocarbon vol. 28(2B).

Sussenbach, Tom, and R. Barry Lewis
1987   *Archaeological Investigations in Carlisle, Hickman, and Fulton Counties, Kentucky: Site Survey and Excavations.* Department of Anthropology, University of Illinois, Western Kentucky Project Report no. 4. Urbana.

Swanton, John R.
1911   *Indian Tribes of the Lower Mississippi Valley and Adjacent Coast of the Gulf of Mexico.* Bulletin of the Bureau of American Ethnology no. 43. Washington, D.C.

1922   *Early History of the Creek Indians and Their Neighbors.* Bulletin of the Bureau of American Ethnology no. 73. Washington, D.C.

1928   Religious Beliefs and Medical Practices of the Creek Indians. *Annual Report of the Bureau of American Ethnology*, pp. 473–672. Washington, D.C.

1930   The Kaskinampo Indians and Their Neighbors. *American Anthropologist* 32:405–18.

1946   *The Indians of the Southeastern United States.* Bureau of American Ethnology, Bulletin no. 137. Washington, D.C.

Tainter, Joseph A.
1975   *The Archeological Study of Social Change: Woodland Systems in West-Central Illinois.* Ph.D. diss., Department of Anthropology, Northwestern University, Evanston, Illinois.

Telford, Clarence J.
1927   *Third Report on a Forest Survey of Illinois.* Bulletin of the Illinois State Natural History Survey, vol. 16.

Temple, Wayne C.
1966   *Indian Villages of the Illinois Country: Historic Tribes.* Rev. ed. Illinois State Museum Scientific Papers, vol. 2, no. 2. Springfield.

Thomas, Cyrus
1894   Report on the Mound Explorations of the Bureau of Ethnology. *Annual Report of the Bureau of American Ethnology*, pp. 1–742. Washington, D.C.

Thurston, Gates P.
1897   *The Antiquities of Tennessee*, 2d ed. Cincinnati, Ohio.

Tiffany, Joseph A.
1978   Discoidals from Mill Creek Sites. *Iowa Archaeological Society Newsletter* 87:6–12.

1981   A Compendium of Radiocarbon Dates for Iowa Archaeological Sites. *Plains Anthropologist* 26:55–73.

1982a   *Chan-ya-ta: A Mill Creek Village.* Report no. 15, Office of the State Archaeologist, University of Iowa, Iowa City.

1982b   Hartley Fort Ceramics. *Proceedings of the Iowa Academy of Science* 89:133–50.

1982c   Site Catchment Analysis of Southeast Iowa Oneota Sites. In *Oneota Studies*, ed. G. Gibbon, pp. 1–14. Publications in Anthropology no. 1. University of Minnesota, Minneapolis.

1983   An Overview of the Middle Missouri Tradition. In *Prairie Archaeology: Papers in Honor of David A. Baerreis*, ed. Guy E. Gibbon, pp. 87–108. Occasional Publications in Anthropology no. 3. University of Minnesota, Minneapolis.

1986a   Ceramics From the F-518 Project. In *Archaeological Investigations Along the F-518 Corridor*, ed. S. C. Lensink, pp. 227–45. Iowa Quaternary Studies Contribution no. 9. Department of Geology, University of Iowa, Iowa City.

1986b   Modeling Mill Creek-Mississippian Interactions. Paper

presented at the annual meeting of the Society for American Archaeology, New Orleans.

1987   *Modeling Mill Creek-Mississippian Interaction.* Iowa Quaternary Studies Contribution no. 12. Department of Geology, University of Iowa, Iowa City.

Titterington, Paul F.
1935   Certain Bluff Mounds of Western Jersey County, Illinois. *American Antiquity* 1:6–46.

1938   *The Cahokia Mound Group and Its Village Site Materials.* Privately printed, St. Louis.

1943   The Jersey County, Illinois, Bluff Focus. *American Antiquity* 9:240–45.

1947   Four Diorite Spuds. *Journal of the Illinois State Archaeological Society* 4(3):18–20.

n.d.   Certain Bluff Mounds of Western Jersey County, Illinois. Unpublished notebooks (books 1–9) curated at the Illinois State Museum, Springfield.

Tomak, Curtis H.
1970   *Aboriginal Occupations in the Vicinity of Greene County, Indiana.* M.A. thesis, Department of Anthropology, Indiana University, Bloomington.

Transeau, E. N.
1935   The Prairie Peninsula. *Ecology* 16:423–37.

Trigger, Bruce G.
1969   *The Huron: Farmers of the North.* Holt, Rinehart and Winston, New York.

U.S. Department of Interior
1970   *The National Atlas of the United States of America.* Washington, D.C.

Van Hartesveldt, Eric N. (preparer)
1980   Kuhn Station Site (Illinois Archaeological Survey no. Ms-29). National Register of Historic Places Inventory-Nomination Form. Illinois Historic Preservation Agency, Springfield.

Vander Leest, Barbara J.
1980   *The Ramey Field, Cahokia Surface Collections: A Functional Analysis of Spatial Structure.* Ph.D. diss., Department of Anthropology, University of Wisconsin-Milwaukee. University Microfilms, Ann Arbor.

Vogel, Joseph O.
1964   *A Preliminary Report on the Analysis of Ceramics from the Cahokia Area at the Illinois State Museum.* Illinois State Museum, Contract Report. Springfield.

1975   Trends in Cahokia Ceramics: Preliminary Study of the Collections from Tracks 15A and 15B. In *Perspectives in Cahokia Archaeology*, ed. James A. Brown, pp. 32–125. Illinois Archaeological Survey Bulletin no. 10. Urbana.

von Humboldt, Baron Friedrich Meinrich Alexander
1814   *Researches Concerning the Institutions and Monuments of the Ancient Inhabitants of America.* 2 vols. London.

Wadlow, Walter L.
1951   Some Conclusions Regarding Jersey Bluff Cultures. *Greater St. Louis Archaeological Society Bulletin* 6:12–18.

Wagner, Gail E.
1976   IDOT Flotation Procedure Manual. Ms. on file, Illinois Department of Transportation, District 8, and Department of Anthropology, University of Illinois at Urbana-Champaign, FAI-270 Archaeological Mitigation Project.

1982   Testing Flotation Recovery Rates. *American Antiquity* 47:127–32.

Wallace, D. L.
1978   *Soil Survey of St. Clair County, Illinois.* Illinois Agricultural Experiment Station Soil Report no. 104. U.S.D.A. Soil Conservation Service, Urbana.

Walthall, John A.
1981   Galena and Aboriginal Trade in Eastern North America. *Illinois State Museum Scientific Papers*, no. 17. Springfield.
1985   Early Hopewellian Ceremonial Encampments in the South Appalachian Highlands. In *Structure and Process in Southeastern Archaeology*, ed. R. S. Dickens, Jr. and H. T. Ward, pp. 243–62. University of Alabama Press, University.

Walthall, John A., and Elizabeth Benchley
1986   *The River L'Abbe Mission: A French Colonial Church for the Cahokia Illini on Monks Mound.* Studies in Illinois Archaeology no. 2. Illinois Historic Preservation Agency, Springfield.

Walthall, John A., and Stuart Struever
1985   Prehistoric Trade. In *Illinois Archaeology*, ed. J. W. Porter and D. S. Rohn, pp. 101–8. Illinois Archaeological Survey, Bulletin no. 1 (revised). Urbana.

Waring, Antonio J.
1968   The Southern Cult and Muskhogeon Ceremonial. In *The Waring Papers*, ed. Stephen Williams, pp. 30–69. Papers of the Peabody Museum, Harvard University, vol. 58. Cambridge, Massachusetts.

Waring, Antonio J., and P. Holder
1945   A Prehistoric Ceremonial Complex in the Southeastern United States. *American Anthropologist* 47:1–34.

Watrall, Charles R.
1968a   *An Analysis of the Bone, Stone, and Shell Materials from the Cambria Focus.* M.A. thesis, University of Minnesota, Minneapolis.
1968b   Analysis of Unmodified Stone Materials from the Cambria Site. *Minnesota Academy of Science Journal* 35: 4–8.
1974   Subsistence Pattern Change at the Cambria Site: A Review and Hypothesis. In *Aspects of Upper Great Lakes Anthropology, Papers in Honor of Lloyd A. Wilford*, ed. Elden Johnson, pp. 138–42. Minnesota Prehistoric Archaeology Series no. 11. Minnesota Historical Society, St. Paul.

Watson, Virginia Drew
1950   *The Wulfing Plates.* Washington University Studies, Social and Philosophical Sciences, n.s. no. 8. St. Louis.

Watt, Bernice K., and Annabel L. Merrill
1963   *Composition of Foods.* Agricultural Research Service, United States Department of Agriculture, Agriculture Handbook no. 8. Washington, D.C.

Webb, Clarence H., and Monroe Dodd, Jr.
1939   Further Excavation of the Gahagan Mound: Connections with a Florida Culture. *Texas Archaeological and Paleontological Society Bulletin* 11:92–126.

Webb, Paul, Michael Hargrave, and Charles Cobb
1986   The Dillinger Complex of Southern Illinois: Phase, Style Zone, or Adaptation? Paper presented at the Southeastern Archaeological Conference, Nashville.

Webb, William S.
1952   *The Jonathan Creek Village.* Department of Anthropology, University of Kentucky Reports on Anthropology, vol. 18, no. 1. Lexington.

Wedel, Mildred Mott
1959   *Oneota Sites on the Upper Iowa River.* Missouri Archaeologist vol. 21(2–4). Columbia.
1973   The Identity of La Salle's Pana Slave. *Plains Anthropologist* 18(61):203–17.

Wedel, Waldo R.
1940   Cultural Sequence in the Central Great Plains. *Smithsonian Miscellaneous Collections* 100:291–352. Washington, D.C.
1943   *Archeological Investigations in Platte and Clay Counties, Missouri.* United States National Museum Bulletin no. 183. Washington, D.C.
1959   *An Introduction to Kansas Archaeology.* Bureau of American Ethnology, Bulletin no. 174. Washington, D.C.

Weigand, Phil C., and Jon D. Muller
n.d.   Preliminary report on investigations at the Kincaid site. Ms. on file, Center for Archaeological Investigations, Southern Illinois University at Carbondale.

Weltfish, Gene
1977   *The Lost Universe.* University of Nebraska Press, Lincoln.

Wendland, Wayne M.
1978   Holocene Man in North America: The Ecological Setting and Climatic Background. *Plains Anthropologist* 23(82):273–87.

Wendt, Dan
1986a   *An Analysis of Endscrapers from the Bryan Site.* Reports of Investigation no. 9. Institute for Minnesota Archaeology, Minneapolis.
1986b   *An Analysis of Triangular Projectile Points from the Bryan Site.* Reports of Investigation no. 10. Institute for Minnesota Archaeology, Minneapolis.

Wesler, Kit W.
1985   *Archaeological Excavations at Wickliffe Mounds, 15BA4: Mound A, 1984.* Murray State University, Wickliffe Mounds Research Center Report no. 1. Wickliffe, Kentucky.

Wesler, Kit W., and Sarah W. Neusius
1987   *Archaeological Excavations at Wickliffe Mounds, 15BA4: Mound F, Mound A Addendum, and Mitigation for the Great River Road Project, 1985 and 1986.* Murray State University, Wickliffe Mounds Research Center Report no. 2. Wickliffe, Kentucky.

Wettersten, Vernon H.
1983   *A Study of Late Woodland Cultural Change in the Lower Illinois River Valley.* Ph.D. diss., Department of Anthropology, Northwestern University, Evanston, Illinois.

Whalley, Lucy A.
1983a   Plant Remains from a Mississippian Community at the Range Site. Ms. on file, FAI-270 Archaeological Mitigation Project, Department of Anthropology, University of Illinois at Urbana-Champaign.
1983b   Plant Remains from the Turner Site. In *The Turner (11-S-50) and DeMange (11-S-447) Sites*, by George R. Milner and Joyce A. Williams, pp. 213–43. American Bottom Archaeology FAI-270 Site Reports, vol. 4. University of Illinois Press, Urbana.
1984   Plant Remains from the Stirling Phase. In *The BBB Motor Site (11-S-595)*, by Thomas E. Emerson and Douglas K. Jackson, pp. 321–35. American Bottom Archaeology FAI-270 Site Reports, vol. 6. University of Illinois Press, Urbana.

Wheeler, H. A.
1921   Letter of September 17, 1921, from H. A. Wheeler, consulting mining engineer, St. Louis, Missouri, to A. R. Crook, chief, Illinois State Museum. Illinois State Museum correspondence files.

White, Alice C., and Diana L. Seider
1980   Rediscovering Rediscovering Illinois. Paper presented at the Twenty-fifth Annual Midwest Archaeological Conference, Chicago.

White, William P.
1984   Geomorphology. In *American Bottom Archaeology*, ed. Charles J. Bareis and James W. Porter, pp. 15–30. University of Illinois Press, Urbana.

Whittaker, Robert H.
1975   *Communities and Ecosystems*. 2d ed. Macmillan, New York.

Wilford, Lloyd A.
1941a   Report on Cambria Village Excavation, 1941. Ms. on file, Department of Anthropology, University of Minnesota, Minneapolis.
1941b   A Tentative Classification of the Prehistoric Cultures of Minnesota. *American Antiquity* 6:231–49.
1945a   The Cambria Village Site—1938. Ms. on file, Department of Anthropology, University of Minnesota, Minneapolis.
1945b   Three Village Sites of the Mississippi Pattern in Minnesota. *American Antiquity* 11:32–40.
1946   Owen D. Jones Village Site. Ms. on file, Department of Anthropology, University of Minnesota, Minneapolis.
1951   The Gillingham Site. Ms. on file, Department of Anthropology, University of Minnesota, Minneapolis.
1952   The Silvernale Mound and Village Site. Ms. on file, Department of Anthropology, University of Minnesota, Minneapolis.
1953   The Gautefald and Hoff Sites, 1948. Ms. on file, Department of Anthropology, University of Minnesota, Minneapolis.
1955   A Revised Classification of the Prehistoric Cultures of Minnesota. *American Antiquity* 21:130–42.
1956a   The Lewis Mounds. Ms. on file, Department of Anthropology, University of Minnesota, Minneapolis.
1956b   The Ralph Bryan Site (1951–1952). Ms. on file, Department of Anthropology, University of Minnesota, Minneapolis.
1958   The Ralph Bryan Site (1955 and 1957). Ms. on file, Department of Anthropology, University of Minnesota, Minneapolis.
1985   The Ralph Bryan Site, 1951–1952. *Minnesota Archaeologist* 43:21–36.
n.d.a   Schoen Mound Number Two. Ms. on file, Department of Anthropology, University of Minnesota, Minneapolis.
n.d.b   Schoen Mound Number One at Ortonville. Ms. on file, Department of Anthropology, University of Minnesota, Minneapolis.
n.d.c   The Lindholm Mounds. Ms. on file, Department of Anthropology, University of Minnesota, Minneapolis.
n.d.d   Miller Mound on Big Stone Lake. Ms. on file, Department of Anthropology, University of Minnesota, Minneapolis.
n.d.e   The Bartron Site. Ms. on file, Department of Anthropology, University of Minnesota, Minneapolis.

Wilkie, Duncan C.
1988   *Final Report: 1987 Field Work at Towosahgy State Historic Site*. Southeast Missouri State University, Center for Regional History and Cultural Heritage. Cape Girardeau, Missouri.

Willey, Gordon R.
1966   *An Introduction to American Archaeology: Vol. 1, North and Middle America*. Prentice-Hall, Englewood Cliffs, New Jersey.

Willey, Gordon R., and Philip Phillips
1958   *Method and Theory in American Archaeology*. University of Chicago Press, Chicago.

Willey, G. R., C. C. DiPeso, W. A. Ritchie, I. Rouse, J. H. Rowe, and D. W. Lathrap
1956   An Archaeological Classification of Culture Contact Situations. In *Seminars in Archaeology, 1955*, ed. R. Wauchope, pp. 1–30. American Antiquity Memoirs no. 11, pt. 2.

Williams, J. Raymond
1967   Land Leveling Salvage Archaeological Work in Southeast Missouri, 1966. Report submitted to the National Park Service, Midwest Region, Lincoln, Nebraska.
1968   Southeast Missouri Land Leveling Salvage Archaeology: 1967. Report submitted to Region Two, National Park Service, Washington, D.C.
1974   *The Baytown Phases in the Cairo Lowland of Southeast Missouri*. Missouri Archaeologist, vol. 36. Columbia.

Williams, Kenneth, and William I. Woods
1977   An Archaeological Reconnaissance of FAP-410 (Bypass 50 to Pickneyville). Report submitted to the Illinois Department of Transportation, Springfield.

Williams, Stephen
1954   *An Archaeological Study of the Mississippian Culture in Southeast Missouri*. Ph.D. diss., Yale University, New Haven, Connecticut.
1971   Session I: Round Table of Definition of Mississippian. *Newsletter of the Southeastern Archaeological Conference* 10(2):1–19.
1977   Some Ruminations on the Current Strategy of Archaeology in the Southeast. Paper presented at the Southeastern Archaeological Conference, Lafayette, Louisiana.
1979   Some Negative Painted Pottery in the Southeast. Paper presented at the Southeastern Archaeological Conference, Atlanta.
1980   Armorel: a Very Late Phase in the Lower Mississippi Valley. *Southeastern Archaeological Conference Bulletin* 22:105–10.

Williams, Stephen, and Jeffery P. Brain
1983   *Excavations at the Lake George Site, Yazoo County, Mississippi, 1958–1960*. Papers of the Peabody Museum of Archaeology and Ethnology, vol. 74. Harvard University, Cambridge, Massachusetts.

Williams, Stephen, and John M. Goggin
1956   The Long-Nosed God Mask in Eastern United States. *Missouri Archaeologist* 18(3):1–72.

Willman, H. B., and John C. Frye
1970   *Pleistocene Stratigraphy of Illinois*. Illinois State Geological Survey Bulletin no. 94. Urbana.

Wilson, Hugh D.
1981   Domesticated *Chenopodium* of the Ozark Bluff Dwellers. *Economic Botany* 35:233–39.

Winchell, N. H.
1911   *The Aborigines of Minnesota*. Minnesota Historical
            Society, St. Paul.

Winters, Howard D.
1963   *An Archaeological Survey of the Wabash Valley in Illi-
            nois*. Illinois State Museum Reports of Investigations
            no. 10. Springfield.

1967   *An Archaeological Survey of the Wabash Valley in
            Illinois*. Rev. ed. Illinois State Museum Reports of
            Investigations no. 10. Springfield.

1968   Value Systems and Trade Cycles of the Late Archaic in
            the Midwest. In *New Perspectives in Archeology*, ed.
            Sally R. Binford and Lewis R. Binford, pp. 175–221.
            Aldine, Chicago.

1974   Some Unusual Grave Goods from a Mississippian
            Burial Mound. *Indian Notes* 10(2):34–46. Museum of
            the American Indian, New York.

1981   Excavating in Museums: Notes on Mississippian Hoes
            and Middle Woodland Copper Gouges and Celts. In
            *The Research Potential of Anthropological Museum
            Collections*, ed. Anne-Marie E. Cantwell, James B.
            Griffin, and Nan A. Rothschild, pp. 17–34. Annals of
            the New York Academy of Sciences, vol. 376.

Winters, Howard D., and Stuart Struever
1962   The Emerald Mound Group and Village. *The Living
            Museum* 23(11):86–87.

Wittry, Warren L.
1959   The Wakanda Park Mound Group, Dn1, Menomonie,
            Wisconsin. *Wisconsin Archeologist* 40:95–115.

1969   The American Woodhenge. In *Explorations into
            Cahokia Archaeology*, ed. Melvin L. Fowler, pp. 43–
            48. Illinois Archaeological Survey Bulletin no. 7.
            Urbana.

Wittry, Warren L., John C. Arnold, and Charles O. Witty
1982   The Holdener Site (11-S-685 in Borrow Pit #25): An
            Early Late Woodland Mortuary. FAI-270 Archaeologi-
            cal Mitigation Project Report. Ms. on file, Department
            of Anthropology, University of Illinois, Urbana.

Wittry, Warren L., and David A. Baerreis
1958   Domestic Houses at Aztalan. *Wisconsin Archeologist*
            39:62–77.

Witzig-Hofsess, Mary Alyce
1983   Human Osteological Material from the Orendorf
            Mound (11Fu416) Fulton County, Illinois. Ms. on
            file in the Western Illinois University Archaeological
            Research Laboratory, Macomb.

Wobst, H. Martin
1977   Stylistic Behavior and Information Exchange. In *For
            the Director: Research Essays in Honor of James B.
            Griffin*, ed. Charles Cleland, pp. 317–42. University of
            Michigan, Museum of Anthropology, Anthropological
            Papers no. 61. Ann Arbor.

Wolforth, Lynne Mackin
1987   *Jonathan Creek Revisited: The House Basin Structures
            and Their Ceramics*. University of Illinois, Department
            of Anthropology, Western Kentucky Project, Report
            no. 5. Urbana.

1989   *Archaeological Investigations at the Running Slough
            Site, Fulton County, Kentucky*. University of Illinois,
            Department of Anthropology, Western Kentucky
            Project Report no. 9. Urbana.

Wood, W. Raymond
1961   The Pomme de Terre Reservoir in Western Missouri
            Prehistory. *Missouri Archaeologist* 23:1–131.

1967   *An Interpretation of Mandan Culture History*. River
            Basin Surveys Papers no. 39, Bureau of American
            Ethnology, Bulletin no. 198. Washington, D.C.

1980   Plains Trade in Prehistoric and Protohistoric Intertribal
            Relations. In *Anthropology on the Great Plains*, ed.
            W. R. Wood and M. Liberty, pp. 98–109. University of
            Nebraska Press, Lincoln.

Woodard, S. Justine
1987   (Marshall Site) Botanical Remains. In *Archaeological
            Investigations in Carlisle, Hickman, and Fulton Coun-
            ties, Kentucky: Site Survey and Excavations*, by Tom
            Sussenbach and R. Barry Lewis, pp. 67–72. Univer-
            sity of Illinois, Department of Anthropology, Western
            Kentucky Project Report no. 4. Urbana.

Woods, William I.
1986   *Prehistoric Settlement and Subsistence in the Upland
            Cahokia Creek Drainage*. Ph.D. diss., Department of
            Geography, University of Wisconsin-Milwaukee.

1987   Maize and the Late Prehistoric: A Characterization
            of Settlement Location Strategies. In *Emergent Hor-
            ticultural Economies of the Eastern Woodlands*, ed.
            William F. Keegan, pp. 273–92. Center for Archaeo-
            logical Investigations, Southern Illinois University at
            Carbondale, Occasional Paper no. 7.

1988   A Study of Prehistoric Settlement-Subsistence Rela-
            tionships in Southwestern Illinois. Paper presented at
            the Eighty-fourth Annual Meeting of the Association of
            American Geographers, Phoenix.

Woods, William I., and Sidney G. Denny
1982   Mississippian Horticultural Exploitation of Upland
            Alluvial Settings: An Example Study from the Cahokia
            Region. Paper presented at the Fifty-fourth Annual
            Midwest Archaeological Conference, Cleveland.

Woods, William I., and Donald W. Meyer
1988   Soil Selection and Management Criteria for Late Pre-
            historic Midwestern Agriculture. Paper presented at
            the Forty-sixth International Congress of Americanists,
            Amsterdam.

Woods, William I., and Robert D. Mitchell
1978   *A Survey of Aboriginal Chert Sources in the Waterloo,
            Illinois Area*. Submitted to the Illinois Department of
            Transportation, Springfield.

Woolverton, Donald G.
1974   Electron Microprobe Analyses of Native Copper Arti-
            facts. *Missouri Archaeological Survey Memoir* 11:
            207–12.

Worthen, A. H.
1866   *Geology of Illinois*. Illinois Geological Survey, vol. 1.
            Urbana.

Wray, Donald E.
1952   Archeology of the Illinois Valley: 1950. In *Archeology
            of the Eastern United States*, ed. James B. Griffin, pp.
            152–64. University of Chicago Press, Chicago.

n.d.   The Kingston Lake Sequence. Ms. on file, Dickson
            Mounds Museum, Lewistown, Illinois.

Wray, Donald E., and Richard S. MacNeish
1958   The Weaver Site: Twenty Centuries of Illinois Pre-
            history. Ms. on file, Dickson Mounds Museum,
            Lewistown, Illinois.

Wright, Gary A.
1967   Some Aspects of Early and Mid-Seventeenth Cen-
            tury Exchange Networks in the Western Great Lakes.
            Michigan Archaeologist 13:181–97.

Yarnell, Richard A.

1969   Contents of Human Paleofeces. In *The Prehistory of Salts Cave, Kentucky,* by Patty Jo Watson et al., pp. 41–54. Illinois State Museum, Reports of Investigations no. 16. Springfield.

1972   *Iva annua var. macrocarpa*: Extinct American Cultigen? *American Anthropologist* 74:335–41.

1974   Plant Food and Cultivation of the Salts Caves. In *Archeology of the Mammoth Cave Area*, ed. Patty Jo Watson, pp. 113–22. Academic Press, New York.

1978   Domestication of Sunflower and Sumpweed in Eastern North America. In *The Nature and Status of Ethnobotany*, ed. Richard I. Ford, pp. 289–99. University of Michigan, Museum of Anthropology, Anthropological Papers, no. 67. Ann Arbor.

Yerkes, Richard W.

1980   Flotation, Fish Scales, and Seasonal Patterns in the Abundance of Charcoal, Maize, and Nuts at the Site of Aztalan, Jefferson County, Wisconsin. Manuscript in possession of author.

1983   Microwear, Microdrills, and Mississippian Craft Specialization. *American Antiquity* 48:499–518.

Yourd, William J.

1983   *An Archaeological Assessment Study of Proposed MnDOT Project S. P. 2514–71, T. H. 61: Reconnaissance and Limited Excavation at the Bryan Site, Goodhue County, Minnesota.* Minnesota Trunk Highway Archaeological Reconnaissance, Ft. Snelling.

1985   Going . . . Going . . . Gone? Archaeological Observations Amidst the Destruction of the Bryan Site-Complex 1854–1980. *Minnesota Archaeologist* 43: 7–20.

Zicker, Wilma A.

1955   *An Analysis of Jefferson County Vegetation Using Surveyors' Records and Present Data.* M.A. thesis, Department of Botany, University of Wisconsin, Madison.

Zimmerman, L. J.

1977a   The Glenwood Local Sequence: A Re-Examination. *Journal of the Iowa Archeological Society* 24:62–83.

1977b   *Prehistoric Locational Behavior: A Computer Simulation.* Report no. 10. Office of the State Archaeologist, University of Iowa, Iowa City.

Notes on Contributors

Robert J. Barth received his Ph.D. from the University of Illinois at Urbana for research on late prehistoric cultures in the Wabash drainage. He is currently Associate Professor at the University of Wisconsin-Eau Claire where he is engaged in research on the archaeology of central Wisconsin.

Brian M. Butler has been involved in archaeological research in southern Illinois and the mid-South for over twenty years. He obtained his M.A. and Ph.D. in Anthropology from Southern Illinois University at Carbondale for research on Black Bottom Mississippian prehistory. He is currently Associate Director at the Center for Archaeological Investigations, Southern Illinois University at Carbondale.

Lawrence A. Conrad is Associate Professor of Anthropology and Director of the Archaeological Research Lab at Western Illinois University. He received his B.A. from Southern Illinois University at Carbondale and his M.A. from the University of Wisconsin at Madison where he is currently A.B.D. Over the past twenty-five years Conrad has conducted extensive research in central Illinois, most notably as principal investigator of the Orendorf Project. He has also carried out fieldwork in Georgia, Florida, and Egypt.

Thomas E. Emerson is Chief Archaeologist for the Illinois Historic Preservation Agency. He has carried out fieldwork and published on numerous sites in the Midwest, as well as working in the Plains and Norway. Emerson received his M.A. from the University of Wisconsin at Madison, where he is currently A.B.D.

Kenneth B. Farnsworth received his B.A. from Northwestern University and his M.A. from the University of Michigan, where he is currently A.B.D. He was introduced to Lower Illinois Valley archaeology in 1968, and joined the staff of the Center for American Archeology at its Kampsville Archeological Center in 1971. Since 1975, he has directed the KAC's Contract Archeology Program. In addition to cultural resource management activities, his research interests and publications focus on the use of sampling strategies, ceramic typologies, and subsistence and settlement pattern analyses for regional Early and Middle Woodland studies.

Guy E. Gibbon is an Associate Professor in the Department of Anthropology at the University of Minnesota. He received a B.S., M.S., and Ph.D. from the University of Wisconsin at Madison, where he concentrated on the archaeology of the American Midwest. He has written numerous articles, especially in the field of Oneota studies, and is the author of *Anthropological Archaeology* (Columbia University Press, 1984) and *Explanation in Archaeology* (Basil Blackwell, 1989).

Lynne G. Goldstein is an Associate Professor of Anthropology at the University of Wisconsin at Milwaukee. She has focused most of her research efforts on examining the nature of Late Woodland and Mississippian societies. Goldstein has specifically studied and published on mortuary practices and regional settlement patterning in Wisconsin and Illinois.

Robert L. Hall is a Professor of Anthropology at the University of Illinois-Chicago, where he began teaching in 1968 and served as departmental chairman for ten years. Among other jobs, he was previously Curator of Anthropology for Illinois State Museum (1962–67), Director of the Institute of Indian Studies, University of South Dakota (1959–61), and Assistant Curator of Anthropology for the Wisconsin State Historical Museum (1949–52). He received his B.A. and Ph.D. from the University of Wisconsin at Madison. His fieldwork activities have been conducted in Illinois, Wisconsin, Kentucky, South Dakota, North Dakota, and Venezuela.

Alan D. Harn is Associate Curator of Anthropology, Illinois State Museum and Research Coordinator of Anthropology, Dickson Mounds Museum. During the past twenty-six years he has conducted extensive excavations, research, and published numerous articles focused on the archaeology of the Central Illinois River Valley. His primary archaeological interests have concentrated on the Late Woodland and Mississippian cultures of the Midwest.

George R. Holley received his Ph.D. in Anthropology from Southern Illinois University at Carbondale. He is Adjunct Assistant Professor in the Department of Geography and Earth Sciences and Laboratory Director for the Contract Archaeology Program, Southern Illinois University at Edwardsville. His research and twenty-two authored or co-authored publications have centered on complex societies and associated ceramics in Mesoamerica and the eastern United States.

Sissel Johannessen was a paleoethnobotanical analyst for the FAI-270 Archaeological Mitigation Project from 1978 until 1983. During that time she performed extensive research and published numerous articles on the paleoethnobotany of the American Bottom, Illinois. Johannessen received her M.A. and is working toward a Ph.D. in Anthropology from the University of Illinois at Urbana-Champaign where she also taught courses in paleoethnobotanical techniques. She is currently part of a team at the University of Minnesota conducting paleoethnobotanical research in the late prehistory of the Peruvian Andes.

John E. Kelly received his Ph.D. from the University of Wisconsin at Madison. The focus of his dissertation and more recent research has been on the origins of Cahokia. For over a decade, Kelly has conducted excavations and research in the American Bottom area of Illinois. His most recent publication has been on the Late Woodland and Emergent Mississippian components at the Range site (University of Illinois Press, 1989). He is currently employed with the Archaeology Program at Southern Illinois University at Edwardsville.

R. Barry Lewis received his Ph.D. from the University of Illinois at Urbana-Champaign, where he is Associate Professor of Anthropology. His research interests and numerous publications have focused on the investigation of prehistoric cultural adaptations in the northern Lower Mississippi Valley, the Mississippi Gulf Coast, and the Illinois Prairie.

Rebecca Miller Glenn grew up on the Carlinville, Illinois, area, where she received a B.A. from Blackburn College. She is a long-time associate of the Macoupin County Historical Society with interest in recording and evaluating the region's archaeological resources.

Charles R. Moffat was born in Prairie du Chien, Wisconsin, and lived at various times during his childhood in Milwaukee, St. Louis, and Salt Lake City. He received a B.A. from the University of Wisconsin-Milwaukee, an M.A. in Anthropology from the University of Pennsylvania, and a Ph.D. in Anthropology from the University of Illinois at Urbana-Champaign. His dissertation research dealt with the Middle Mississippian occupation of the middle Kaskaskia River Valley. For the past seven years he has been making a living doing cultural resource contract archaeology. He is currently with the Mississippi Valley Archaeology Center at the University of Wisconsin-La Crosse.

Jon Muller is a Professor and current Chair of the Department of Anthropology, Southern Illinois University at Carbondale. He received a Ph.D. in Anthropology from Harvard University and is the author of *Archaeology of the Lower Ohio Valley* (Academic Press, 1983). Some of his research interests include late prehistoric cultures of the Southeast, prehistoric art styles, and specialization.

John D. Richards has done archaeological fieldwork in the midwestern United States and Mexico. Currently a doctoral candidate at the University of Wisconsin-Milwaukee, he directed that school's 1984 excavations at the Aztalan site. His thesis focuses on Aztalan's cultural and political relationships during the Late Prehistoric period in the Midwest.

David Rindos received his joint Ph.D. in Anthropology and Botany from Cornell University. His primary research interests have focused on human-plant relationships and he is the author of *The Origins of Agriculture: An Evolutionary Perspective* (Academic Press, 1984). He is currently associated with the Department of Prehistory, Australian National University, Camberra.

Jeanette E. Stephens received her M.A. from Southern Illinois University at Carbondale and is currently an archaeologist with the Center for Archeological Investigations. She is also Editor for *Illinois Archaeology*, the journal of the Illinois Archaeological Survey.

Joseph A. Tiffany is currently Associate Dean, College of Arts, California State Polytechnic University at Pomona. Tiffany received his B.A. Honors degree from the University of Iowa and his M.A. and Ph.D. in Anthropology from the University of Wisconsin at Madison. He has written many articles on Iowa and midwestern archaeology and formerly was Associate Director of the Office of State Archaeology in Iowa. His research interests include settlement systems, site formation processes, North American archaeology and museum studies.

William I. Woods received his Ph.D. in Geography from the University of Wisconsin-Milwaukee. He is an Associate Professor in the Department of Geography and Earth Science and Coordinator of the Contract Archaeology Program at Southern Illinois University at Edwardsville. Over the past twenty years, he has conducted field investigations in the midwestern United States, Europe, and Latin America. This research has focused on human-land relationships associated with the origins of complex societies and agricultural development, as well as the application of soil chemistry to archaeology, and resulted in seventy-five authored or co-authored publications and reports.

Index

Note: Archaeological sites identified solely by number in the text are listed alphabetically under the entry "Site." All numbers are alphabetized as if spelled out, not in numerical order. Subheadings have been eliminated when their use would have required excessive duplication of page locator references within a single entry.

DUE DATE